Intellectual Property in Australia

Second Edition

For Alistair and Douglas
For Susan and Madeleine

Intellectual Property in Australia

Second Edition

Jill McKeough
BA, LLB (NSW), LLM (Hons) (Syd)
Associate Professor, Faculty of Law
University of New South Wales

Andrew Stewart
BA (Juris), BCL (Oxon)
Professor, School of Law
Flinders University of South Australia

Butterworths
Sydney— Adelaide — Brisbane — Canberra
Melbourne — Perth
1997

AUSTRALIA	BUTTERWORTHS 271-273 Lane Cove Road, North Ryde, NSW 2113
	111 Gawler Place, Adelaide, SA 5000
	Oxley House, 25 Donkin Street, West End, Qld 4101
	53-55 Northbourne Avenue, Canberra, ACT 2601
	461 Bourke Street, Melbourne, Vic 3000
	178 St Georges Terrace, Perth, WA 6000
	On the Internet at: www.butterworths.com.au
CANADA	BUTTERWORTHS CANADA LTD Toronto and Vancouver
FRANCE	EDITIONS DU JURIS-CLASSEUR Paris
HONG KONG	BUTTERWORTHS ASIA
INDIA	BUTTERWORTH & CO (ASIA) PTE LTD New Delhi
IRELAND	BUTTERWORTH (IRELAND) LTD Dublin
ITALY	GIUFFRE Editore SpA
MALAYSIA	MALAYAN LAW JOURNAL SDN BHD Kuala Lumpur
NEW ZEALAND	BUTTERWORTHS OF NEW ZEALAND LTD Wellington and Auckland
POLAND	WYDAWNICTWA PRAWNICZE Warsaw
SINGAPORE	BUTTERWORTHS ASIA Singapore
SOUTH AFRICA	BUTTERWORTH PUBLISHERS (PTY) LTD Durban
SWITZERLAND	VERLAG STAMPFLI & CIE AG
UNITED KINGDOM	BUTTERWORTH & CO (PUBLISHERS) LTD London and Edinburgh
USA	MICHIE Charlottesville, Virginia

National Library of Australia Cataloguing-in-Publication entry

McKeough, Jill.
Intellectual property in Australia.
2nd ed.
Includes index.
ISBN 0 409 30677 0.

1. Intellectual property — Australia. I. Stewart, Andrew
(Andrew John), II. Title.
346.94048

©1997 Reed International Books Australia Pty Limited trading as Butterworths
First edition 1991.

Printed in Australia by Allwest Print Pty Ltd.

Contents

PART II
Confidentiality

PART III
Copyright, Designs and Related Rights

Contents

PART IV
Patents

PART V
Business Reputation

Contents

Preface to the Second Edition

Much has happened in the field of intellectual property since the first edition of this book was written. Apart from the inevitable stream of judicial decisions, there have been two new Trade Marks Acts (one never proclaimed), the Patents Act 1990 has come into operation, and draft amendments to the Copyright Act have presaged (among other things) the introduction into Australian law of the concept of moral rights. There have been major reports on the designs system, the impact on copyright law of new communication technologies, the protection of computer software, the petty patents regime and the enforcement of intellectual property rights in general. At an international level, the conclusion of the TRIPS Agreement and the creation of the World Trade Organisation has significantly advanced the cause of harmonisation of intellectual property laws and enforcement procedures around the world.

In incorporating these and other developments, we have benefitted enormously from the assistance of many people. We would like to thank Andrew's various research assistants, Simon Morris, David Lewis and David Worswick, for all their hard work in digging up material; Anna Crago, Alex Craig and Tiffany Hutton at Indigo Ink for working on the manuscript and putting up with our foibles; Annabel Adair for proofreading; and Margaret McLachlan at Butterworths for her patience and cheerfulness. Andrew would also like to thank Susan for her love and support, not to mention her keen eye for unintelligible subclauses (she bears no responsibility for any that remain). Finally we wish to acknowledge the help and inspiration we have drawn from our colleagues in the Intellectual Property Teachers and Researchers group. Long may we meet, argue and swap war stories!

Jill McKeough

Andrew Stewart   *March 1997*

Abbreviations

Blakeney	M Blakeney, *Legal Aspects of the Transfer of Technology to Developing Countries*, 1989
CCG	Copyright Convergence Group, *Highways to Change: Copyright in the New Communications Environment*, 1994
Computer Software Protection	Copyright Law Review Committee, *Computer Software Protection*, 1995
Cornish	W R Cornish, *Intellectual Property: Patents, Copyright, Trade Marks and Allied Rights*, 2nd ed, 1989
Creighton and Stewart	B Creighton and A Stewart, *Labour Law: An Introduction*, 1990
Dean	R Dean, *Law of Trade Secrets*, 1990
Designs	Australian Law Reform Commission, *Designs*, ALRC No 74, 1995
Drahos	P Drahos, *A Philosophy of Intellectual Property*, 1996
Goff and Jones	Lord Goff of Chieveley and G Jones, *Law of Restitution*, 3rd ed, 1986
Grubb	P W Grubb, *Patents in Chemistry and Biotechnology*, 1986
Gurry	F Gurry, *Breach of Confidence*, 1984
Kerly	T A Blanco White and R Jacob, *Kerly's Law of Trade Marks and Trade Names*, 12th ed, 1986
Lahore, *Copyright*	J Lahore, *Intellectual Property in Australia: Copyright Law*, 1996
Lahore, *Patents*	J Lahore, *Intellectual Property in Australia: Patents, Designs, Trade Marks*, 1996
Mason and Carter	K Mason and J W Carter, *Restitution Law in Australia*, 1995
Meagher, Gummow and Lehane	R P Meagher, W M C Gummow, J R F Lehane, *Equity: Doctrines and Remedies*, 3rd ed, 1992

Murumba	S K Murumba, *Commercial Exploitation of Personality*, 1986
Phillips and Firth	J Phillips and A Firth, *Introduction to Intellectual Property Law*, 3rd ed, 1995
Ricketson	S Ricketson, *Law of Intellectual Property*, 1984
Ricketson (1994)	S Ricketson, *Intellectual Property: Cases, Materials and Commentary*, 1994
Shanahan	D R Shanahan, *Australian Trade Mark Law and Practice*, 1982
Simpson	S Simpson, Review of Australian Collecting Societies, Report to the Minister for Communications and the Arts and Minister for Justice, 1995
Spry	I C F Spry, *Principles of Equitable Remedies*, 4th ed, 1990
Straus	J Straus, *Industrial Property Protection of Biotechnological Inventions*, 1985
Tilbury	M J Tilbury, *Civil Remedies: Vol 1 — Principles of Civil Remedies*, 1990
WIPO Background Reading	World Intellectual Property Organisation, *Background Reading Material on Intellectual Property*, 1988

Table of Cases

Ocean Pacific Sunwear Ltd v Ocean Pacific Enterprises Pty Ltd (1990) ...... [16.8]

Ocean Routes (Australia) Pty Ltd v M C Lamond [1984] .... [7.3]

Oertli AG v Bowman (London) Ltd [1959] .... [16.8]

Office Cleaning Services Ltd v Westminster Window & General Cleaners Ltd (1946) .... [17.4], [18.9]

Ogden Industries Pty Ltd v Kis (Australia) Pty Ltd [1982] .... [10.14]

Olin Corp v Pacemaker Pool Supplies (1984) .... [19.45]

—v Super Cartridge Co Pty Ltd (1977)... [14.7]

Ormonoid Roofing and Asphalts Ltd v Bitumenoids Ltd (1930) .... [3.7], [4.14], [4.27], [4.35]

Orton v Melman [1981] .... [4.36]

Otto v Linford (1862) .... [12.5]

Ownit Homes Pty Ltd v D & F Manusco Investments Pty Ltd [1987] ...... [6.31]

Oxford v Moss (1978) .... [3.15]

Oxford University Press v Registrar of Trade Marks (1989) .... [19.30]

—v—(1990) ....[19.22], [19.23], [19.30]

Ozi-Soft Pty Ltd v Wong (1988) ....[8.21], [9.13]

Pacific & Southern Co Inc v Duncan (1984) .... [8.28]

Pacific Dunlop Ltd v Hogan (1989) .... [16.15], [16.28], [16.29], [18.11], [18.16], [18.17]

Pacific Film Laboratories Pty Ltd v Federal Commissioner of Taxation (1970) .... [6.2]

Panayiotou v Sony Music Entertainment (UK) Ltd [1994] .... [5.10], [7.14]

Pancontinental Mining Ltd v Commissioner of Stamp Duties [1989] ...[3.19]

Paracidal Pty Ltd v Herctum Pty Ltd (1983) .... [16.28]

Paragon Shoes Pty Ltd v Paragini Distributors (NSW) Pty Ltd (1988) .... [16.35], [17.7], [19.51]

Parison Fabric Ltd's Application (1949) .... [19.25]

Parkdale Custom Built Furniture Pty Ltd v Puxu Pty Ltd (1982) ..... [16.32], [17.7], [17.8], [18.2], [18.6], [18.10], [18.11], [18.14]

Parker-Knoll Ltd v Knoll International Ltd [1962] .... [17.6]

Parks-Cramer Co v G W Thornton & Sons Ltd [1966] .... [12.24]

Parry-Jones v Law Society [1969] ... [4.3]

Paterson Zochonis Ltd v Merfarken Packaging Ltd [1983] .... [2.7]

Pavey & Matthews Pty Ltd v Paul (1987) .... [3.17]

Pearce v Paul Kingston Pty Ltd (1992).... [14.11]

Pearson v Morris Wilkinson & Co (1906) .... [10.5]

Pepsico Australia Pty Ltd v Kettle Chip Co Pty Ltd (1996)..................... [20.3]

Performing Right Society Ltd v London Theatre of Varieties Ltd [1924]... [2.4]

Perpetual Development Corp v Versi Pty Ltd (1987) .... [18.16]

Peter Isaacson Publications Pty Ltd v Nationwide News Pty Ltd (1984) .... [16.41], [17.4], [18.9]

Peter Pan Manufacturing Corp v Corsets Silhouette Ltd [1963] .... [2.16], [4.3], [4.7], [4.8], [4.28], [4.29]

Peters Foods Australia Pty Ltd v Tip Top Ice Cream Co Ltd (1996) .... [19.52]

Petersville Sleigh Ltd v Sugerman (1987) ....[16.15], [17.19]

Pfizer Corporation v Minister for Health [1965]........................... [7.24]

Pharmacy Guild of Australia (Qld Branch), Re (1983) .... [22.39]

Philip Morris Inc v Adam P Brown Male Fashions Pty Ltd (1981) .... [2.21]

Philippart v William Whiteley Ltd [1908] .... [19.26]

Philips Gloeilampenfabrieken NV v Mirabella International Pty Ltd (1993) .... [11.7]

—v—(1995)......................[12.2], [12.9]

Phillips v Harbro Rubber Co (1920) ..... [10.19]

Phonographic Performance Co of Australia Ltd, Re [1991] .... [22.37]

Photocrom Co Ltd v H & W Nelson Ltd [1923–28] .... [7.9]

Pianotist Co's Application (1906) [20.5]

Pioneer Concrete Services Ltd v Galli [1985] .... [4.36]

Pioneer Kabushiki Kaisha v Registrar of Trade Marks (1977) ...[19.11], [20.4], [20.14]

Pizza Pizza Ltd v Registrar of Trade Marks (1989) .... [19.48]

Playboy Enterprises Inv v Frena (1993) ... [9.29]

Table of Statutes

Chapter 1

An Overview

1. WHAT IS INTELLECTUAL PROPERTY?

[1.1] Introduction. Intellectual property is one of those concepts whose content is largely familiar but which is exceedingly difficult to define. The uninitiated have a tendency to greet the term itself with a blank stare. Any confusion is at least partly dispelled when it is explained that intellectual property is about 'copyright, patents — you know, that sort of thing'. However, while this will usually suffice to divert any further questioning, the problem remains of finding a more comprehensive answer. Even the most seasoned of intellectual property lawyers will struggle to go beyond a 'that sort of thing' definition which lists rather than justifies. Broadly speaking, we can say that intellectual property is a generic term for the various rights or bundles of rights which the law accords for the protection of creative effort — or, more especially, for the protection of economic investment in creative effort. As a generalisation this is acceptable, but only barely so. Apart from the fact that some forms of creative endeavour (or investment therein) are not protected at all, some rights which are now described as forms of intellectual property have only a tenuous connection with the creative process, particularly those such as trade marks which are associated with business reputation and competitive relations. Moreover the nature and scope of the rights accorded can and do vary greatly.

[1.2] Historical foundations. The principal reason why it is so difficult to define intellectual property lies in the history of the subject. As with the law of tort(s), the tale is that of a group of established actions or heads of protection coming to be treated under a common rubric. The basic concepts underlying the systems created to protect copyright, patents, trade marks and so on had mostly been worked out by the time it became fashionable to group them together. Not only had each system developed independently of the others, evolving its own solutions to the problems of how best to recognise the type of effort with which it was concerned, but that

1

system had also been shaped by different forces from country to country. Thus the law of copyright which evolved in England after the development of the printing press in the fifteenth century differed in significant respects to that which had emerged in Europe, while having little impact on the nascent system for rewarding inventors with letters patent granting them exclusive rights over the exploitation of their inventions. Even when the link was made between the systems, as it certainly was from the middle of the nineteenth century onwards, it was common to use two terms rather than one: *intellectual property* for the 'higher' forms of literary and artistic endeavour recognised by copyright, and *industrial property* for the less prosaic world of commerce in which patents and trade marks operated. Given especially the modern scope of copyright, not to mention the addition of other heads of protection which cannot easily be categorised in this way, these terms are now virtually interchangeable.[1] The former is in greater use as an all-encompassing description and is accordingly preferred in this work. Nevertheless despite the emergence of the subject as a popular field of study and the appearance of treatises spanning the individual regimes (notably, in an Anglo-Australian context, those of Cornish and Ricketson), intellectual property remains more a collection of similar rights than a single theory of protection. This is not to say that general observations may not be offered, for that is indeed the objective of much of this and the following chapter. But until the various regimes are uprooted and replaced by some general right or principle, a prospect discussed below, intellectual property must still be treated as something whose parts are greater than its sum.

[1.3] The WIPO and TRIPS 'definitions'. This point is perfectly emphasised by the 1967 Convention Establishing the World Intellectual Property Organisation (WIPO), a body whose significance is explained later on. Article 2(viii) of the Convention defines 'intellectual property' to

include the rights relating to:

(1) literary, artistic and scientific works;
(2) performances of performing artists, phonograms and broadcasts;
(3) inventions in all fields of human endeavour;
(4) scientific discoveries;
(5) industrial designs;
(6) trademarks, service marks, and commercial names and designations;
(7) protection against unfair competition;

and all other rights resulting from intellectual activity in the industrial, scientific, literary or artistic fields.

Note the lack of any internal logic in this list, other than that provided by the broad term 'intellectual activity'. In reality, this is not so much a definition as an ambit claim, enumerating all those matters which might conceivably fall within the concept of intellectual property, or perhaps ought ideally to do so. The extent to which protection is actually given varies from country to country. Some nations, Australia among them, have failed to provide any protection at all where some items on the list have been concerned.

---

1.   Though the division lives on in terms of administrative responsibilities within the federal government: see [1.10].

The same point can be made about what is now the most important international convention in the field, the Trade Related Aspects of Intellectual Property Rights (TRIPS) Agreement. This instrument contains no definition at all of 'intellectual property', other than to indicate (in Art 1.2) that the term refers to the seven categories of rights or subject matter which are dealt with in the Agreement: copyright and related rights, trade marks, geographical indications, industrial designs, patents, layout designs of integrated circuits, and undisclosed information. As will be explained later in the chapter, TRIPS has the potential to act as a powerful force for the standardisation of intellectual property laws around the world.

2. CURRENT FORMS OF REGULATION

[1.4] Development of Australian laws. The modern law of intellectual property in this country is still to an extent dictated by our former ties to the United Kingdom. The first laws on the subject in force in the Australian colonies, as they then were, emanated from the British parliament; although as the nineteenth century wore on imperial legislation in relation to copyright, patents and trade marks came to be supplemented by local statutes of similar content.[2] After federation, legislative responsibility passed to the Commonwealth, whose statutory regimes today dominate the field. Many of the early federal statutes were little more than re-enactments of their British counterparts. Indeed the Copyright Act 1912 simply declared the Copyright Act 1911 (UK) to be in force throughout Australia, a state of affairs which continued until 1969, 13 years after the 1911 Act had ceased to apply in Britain![3] Nevertheless, over the course of this century Australian legislative policy in the 'core' areas of copyright, patents, designs and trade marks has gradually diverged, in some instances quite considerably. This trend has become particularly evident over the past decade, with major changes to Australian copyright and patents law occurring at a time when Britain has revamped much of its legislation.[4] The approaches taken by the two countries in these areas are still essentially predicated on common values and assumptions, and there is little question that there are more resemblances than dissimilarities. Nonetheless the regulatory detail is increasingly different.

[1.5] Constitutional power. The Commonwealth's legislative power in relation to intellectual property stems primarily from s 51(xviii) of the Constitution, permitting it to make laws with respect to 'copyrights, patents of inventions and designs, and trade marks'. This formula has the disadvantage of being limited to those forms of protection which were familiar at the turn of the century, perhaps preventing expansions in the traditional areas, certainly precluding the adoption of entirely new regimes. There has been only one notable instance of legislation being struck down by the High Court for exceeding the limits of s 51(xviii), that being the *Union*

---

2.   New South Wales, for example, enacted the Inventions Registration Act 1852, Trade Marks Act 1865 and Copyright Act 1879.
3.   See [5.6].
4.   Compare especially the changes made by the Copyright Amendment Act 1989 (Cth) and Patents Act 1990 (Cth) with the Copyright, Designs and Patents Act 1988 (UK).

Label case[5] dealing with workers' marks. Nevertheless, the provision for many years cast a pall over attempts to deal with new issues.[6] Fortunately the High Court's expansive view of the scope of the 'external affairs' power in s 51(xxix) has come to the rescue. It is now clear that the Commonwealth may use this power to implement protective regimes which are the subject of an international treaty or agreement to which Australia is a party,[7] even if they would not fall within the terms of s 51(xviii). Since the subject of intellectual property is marked by a relativelsy high degree of international cooperation and comity, as we will see, the external affairs power has proved to be a valuable option in recent years.[8] Nevertheless it remains unsatisfactory that the Commonwealth lacks clear and comprehensive power over intellectual property, a view shared by the Constitutional Commission after its review of the Constitution.[9] Shying away from the term 'intellectual property' itself, on the understandable basis that it might be too narrowly interpreted, the Commission recommended that s 51(xviii) be amended so as to read 'copyrights, patents of inventions and designs, trade marks and other like protection for the products of intellectual activity in industry, science, literature and the arts'. Given the abysmal track record of constitutional reform in this country at the critical stage of winning approval from the populace,[10] it is doubtful that this sensible proposal will ever see the light of day, though hope springs eternal.

[1.6]   The statutory regimes. So far nothing has been said of the nature of copyright, patents and the other heads of protection. Accordingly it will be helpful at this point to give a brief description of the principal statutory regimes currently in force in Australia:

— *Copyright,* governed by the Copyright Act 1968 (Cth), protects the expression in material form of ideas or information — though it does not protect ideas or information as such. Contrary to popular conception, copyright arises without any formal steps being taken to claim it. It suffices that a person exercises originality (in the sense of some minimal degree of skill and effort) in creating a literary, dramatic, musical or artistic work. The work need not possess aesthetic qualities, so that everything from accounting forms to frisbees are protected: this includes computer software, designated as 'literary works' as a result of 1984 amendments. Besides the category of 'works', copyright also subsists in four forms in which works are commonly exploited: sound recordings, films, television and sound broadcasts, and published editions. Copyright is infringed whenever the work or subject matter is reproduced, published, broadcast, sold, imported, etc without the copyright owner's consent. However, independent creation of the same work or matter will not infringe. As far as works are concerned,

---

5.   *Attorney-General (NSW) v Brewery Employees Union of NSW* (1908) 6 CLR 469 (see [19.5]); though see also *Davis v Commonwealth* (1988) 166 CLR 79.
6.   As was the case, for example, with performers' rights: see [6.21].
7.   *Koowarta v Bjelke-Petersen* (1982) 153 CLR 168; *Commonwealth v Tasmania* (1983) 158 CLR 1; *Victoria v Commonwealth* (1996) 138 ALR 129.
8.   As with the introduction, for example, of legislation dealing with performers' rights (see [6.20] ff) and plant varieties (see [15.20] ff).
9.   *Final Report,* vol 2, 1988, paras 10.140–10.153.
10.   See M Coper, *Encounters with the Australian Constitution,* 1988, ch 9.

copyright generally subsists until the expiration of 50 years after the author's death (or after first publication, if this occurs posthumously).

— *Patents* are granted under the Patents Act 1990 (Cth). A patent, for which an application must be made to the Patent Office, provides the exclusive right to exploit an invention for a limited period, in return for which the patentee must publish details of the invention. A standard patent subsists for 20 years. A petty patent, which is cheaper and quicker to obtain and which is designed for gadgets and appliances with a relatively short life in terms of commercial exploitation, may subsist for up to six years. In order to be patentable, an invention must be a 'manner of new manufacture' (that is, a product or process which has some useful commercial application). It must also be novel, in the sense that its creation has not been anticipated by others, and inventive, in the sense that it is not merely an obvious advance in light of existing knowledge.

— *Designs* are governed by the Designs Act 1906 (Cth), which establishes a system for the registration of new or original designs for the visual presentation of commercial products. The design monopoly may last for up to 16 years. Since designs are typically derived from artistic works, important issues arise as to the interrelationship of design and copyright protection.

— *Trade marks* are signs (including devices, labels, names, etc) which indicate that goods or services originate from a particular trader. When registered under the Trade Marks Act 1995 (Cth), the proprietor is entitled to restrain the use of unregistered marks which are substantially identical or deceptively similar. However, in order to obtain and maintain registration, the mark must normally be used in such a way that it becomes and remains distinctive of the proprietor's business.

— *Performers' rights,* although contained in Pt XIA of the Copyright Act, were in fact introduced in 1989 because live dramatic and musical performances do *not* attract copyright, not being fixed in a material form. The rights in question are more limited than copyright, merely allowing performers to restrain or take action against any unauthorised broadcast or recording of their performance.

— *New plant varieties,* which for one reason or another may not be patentable, are the subject of a specific regime established by the Plant Breeders' Rights Act 1994 (Cth). On registration, breeders obtain exclusive rights over their varieties for a period of 20 or 25 years.

— *Circuit layouts* likewise attract special provision. The Circuit Layouts Act 1989 (Cth) provides copyright-style protection for up to 10 years for the layouts of integrated circuits (computer chips).

[1.7] Why statutory regulation? Legislation has obvious advantages as a method of protecting intellectual property. In theory at least, parliament, aided by advice from specialist bodies and committees, can reach decisions on all the factors involved in the extent and appropriate nature of protection, balancing questions of public access with fairness to the right-owner. It can also provide any administrative back-up necessary and monitor the system to determine whether changes might be required. Given the fast-moving nature of the subject and the constant historical link with government interests (as will be seen in the treatment of copyright, for instance), it is not then surprising to find the law of intellectual property dominated by statutory provisions. Even where protection did not originate in statutes, as was the case with copyright and trade marks, the need for appropriate regulation has forced parliament to introduce new statutory systems or to expand established ones. Although there are considerable differences between the regimes outlined above, with some establishing systems of registration backed by bureaucracy and others operating automatically to confer protection, two points of similarity may be noted. In the first place, each creates a right-owner who has rights precisely and only because the statute says so. Second, each is essentially negative in character: the right-owner is empowered merely to prevent others engaging in unauthorised activities.

[1.8]   **Role of the common law.** Having said all that about legislation, it must not be thought that the common law has no part to play in protecting intellectual property. Besides its historical significance as a precursor to some of the modern statutory systems, notably in relation to copyright, the common law is still an important source of intellectual property rights in a number of respects. In the first place, trade secrets and other confidential information may be protected against use or revelation through the equitable doctrine of breach of confidence. This permits knowledge to be safeguarded solely on the basis that it has not yet moved into the public domain. The same objective may be pursued by enforcing contractual obligations of secrecy. The law of contract indeed plays an important role in relation to all forms of intellectual property. Besides facilitating the assignment and licensing of rights, it may help to determine the initial ownership of those rights. This is particularly true in the employment context, where terms implied by the judiciary have steadfastly supported the notion that employers are entitled to the creative work of their employees.[11] The common law also allows the integrity of the connection between a business and its customers to be protected in a way that backs up and even extends the statutory protection given to trade marks. This is achieved through the tort of passing off, which makes it unlawful for a person to deceive a section of the public into identifying that person's business with that of the plaintiff.

The problem with the common law is that, viewed globally, it cannot claim to be thought out on any coherent basis. The sorts of issues in which the courts have tended to be interested have often had little to do with the delicate balance between competing public interests which, as we shall see, is (or should be) the hallmark of policy-making in this area. The law of confidentiality, for instance, allows a person to sit on an idea, no matter how useful, for as long as they wish to keep it secret — a position arguably at odds with the basic premise underlying the statutory systems that ideas as such ought not to be capable of being locked up or denied to others.[12] Moreover it must be remembered that it is the courts that interpret the statutory provisions. In the English tradition, judges are notorious for their aversion to discovering parliament's actual intent, favouring instead a literal approach which looks only for an unambiguous construction, no matter how absurd that might be. This has had a profound effect on the drafting of the relevant provisions. As Cornish observes:[13]

---

11.   See eg the position in relation to ownership of inventions: [13.2] ff.
12.   See [3.10].
13.   Cornish, p 11.

The tendency to proliferate detail and to make complicated cross-references ... is rooted in the assumption that the judges cannot, will not or should not work out the implications of statutory directives for themselves.

Detailed and complex drafting is of course a response which is doomed to failure, since it merely encourages the courts to be even more technical. Ironically, the result in the field of intellectual property has not necessarily been a proliferation of narrow readings: if anything, the reverse has been true. Literal interpretation of the copyright legislation in particular has gradually seen it expand to the point where it threatens the balance of interests established by the other systems. Thus a popular form of litigation today is for a trader to seek to prevent its competitors copying its products by arguing that they are in breach of the copyright in the plans and models from which the product originated. Courts have been quite happy to allow this sort of action to succeed,[14] only rarely responding to the argument that protection of this magnitude simply could not have been parliament's intent.[15]

[1.9] Trade practices and fair trading legislation. One important set of provisions which has not yet been mentioned, but which impacts heavily upon the field of intellectual property, is that contained in the Trade Practices Act 1974 (Cth). Part IV of the Act, which deals with restrictive practices, prohibits contracts, arrangements and covenants which have an anti-competitive tendency, as well as more specific manifestations such as exclusive dealing arrangements and price-fixing. Many standard provisions in agreements which are designed to license or assign intellectual property have the potential to fall foul of Pt IV, although s 51(3) specifically exempts such agreements to a certain degree. More importantly, the consumer protection provisions in Pt V regularly come into play, especially the prohibition in s 52 on misleading or deceptive conduct in the course of trade or commerce. Similar liabilities are imposed by state fair trading statutes, which cover those situations in which the federal Act is inapplicable for constitutional reasons.[16] These provisions have principally been used to reinforce the tort of passing off, to the point indeed where common law liability for misappropriation of business reputation has virtually been subsumed. However, they may also be used to back up a claim alleging infringement of another intellectual property right, the argument being that the public is being deceived as to the ownership of or entitlement to the relevant matter.[17]

[1.10] Administration and policy-making. Responsibility within the federal government for administration of Australian intellectual property laws is curiously fragmented. The main division is between copyright on the

14. See [8.7].
15. Cf *British Leyland Motor Corp Ltd v Armstrong Patents Co Ltd* [1986] 2 WLR 400: see [8.9].
16. See Fair Trading Act 1987 (NSW); Fair Trading Act 1989 (Qld); Fair Trading Act 1987 (SA); Fair Trading Act 1990 (Tas); Fair Trading Act 1985 (Vic); Fair Trading Act 1987 (WA). See also Fair Trading Act 1992 (ACT); Consumer Affairs and Fair Trading Act 1990 (NT).
17. See eg *Fire Nymph Products Ltd v Jalco Products (WA) Pty Ltd* (1983) 1 IPR 79; *Chris Ford Enterprises Pty Ltd v B H & J R Badenhop Pty Ltd* (1985) 4 IPR 485; *Skedeleski v Underwood* (1990) 17 IPR 161; *Trumpet Software Pty Ltd v OzEmail Pty Ltd* (1996) 34 IPR 481.

one hand, and the 'industrial property' areas of patents, designs and trade marks on the other. The former is chiefly the responsibility of the Attorney-General; although the Minister for Communications and the Arts also has a formal involvement in policy-making, an arrangement introduced by the Keating Government and continued by the Howard Government in recognition of the significance of copyright to the industries concerned. Patents, designs and trade marks fall under the aegis of what is currently the Department of Industry, Science and Tourism. Within that department, though operating more or less autonomously, is the Australian Industrial Property Office (AIPO), which administers the registration systems for each of the three regimes. AIPO was formed in 1992, uniting the previously separate Patents, Designs and Trade Marks Offices, and its head office is located in Canberra. Within AIPO the patents and designs bureaucracies are closely linked, with the same person typically filling the dual roles of Commissioner of Patents and Registrar of Designs (as indeed used to be the case before AIPO's formation). Curiously, AIPO does not administer the plant breeder's rights legislation, despite the fact that it too has a registration system. That regime is instead the responsibility of a different government department, Primary Industries and Energy.

This division of responsibilities has caused no little difficulty in relation to law reform. Not only is intellectual property vitally important to the cultural and economic life of this country, it is also an area in which new issues and challenges are constantly arising.[18] Yet there is no single person or body responsible either for policy-making within the government, or for providing expert advice on appropriate legislative and administrative changes. The problem is highlighted by topics such as the interface between the designs and copyright systems and the protection of computer software, which clearly straddle the copyright/industrial property division. In light of the interconnected nature of many of the issues that need to be considered in relation to the various regimes, it is hard to understand why there should be two entirely separate 'standing' committees, reporting to separate ministers, with a brief to consider intellectual property law reform: the Advisory Council on Industrial Property (ACIP), which has taken over from the Industrial Property Advisory Committee (IPAC) in providing advice on patents, designs and trade marks issues; and the Copyright Law Review Committee (CLRC). It is even harder to understand why it is that not only are these committees poorly resourced (in terms of technical and clerical support), but they are also routinely bypassed in favour of other bodies when it comes to matters that plainly fall within their remit. Hence although IPAC, ACIP and the CLRC have produced reports that have led or are likely to lead to major changes in Australian intellectual property law, so too over recent years have a range of other committees: for example the Australian Law Reform Commission (ALRC) in relation to the designs system, the Prices Surveillance Authority on importation of copyright material, and a number of ad hoc working parties (most notably on the rewriting of the trade marks legislation, but also on issues such as the impact of new technologies on copyright and the introduction of 'moral rights' for authors and artists).

The result, to quote Ricketson, has been a general picture of 'confusion and incoherence' in which reform proposals have been formulated in a

18. See [1.18].

8

'haphazard and inadequate way'.[19] With the backing of the Intellectual Property Committee of the Law Council of Australia and others, Ricketson has waged a hitherto unsuccessful campaign to unite intellectual property administration in a single Office of Intellectual Property, with reform proposals to be considered by an independent Intellectual Property Law Reform Commission. One faintly positive sign was the reference of the whole question of the designs system to the ALRC, a decision said to represent 'a belated recognition by Government that the process of intellectual property reform needs to be undertaken by a body that is properly resourced and staffed'.[20] Unfortunately the ALRC's final report simply underscored the problems of duplication and overlap, with perhaps the key issue being left to separate studies rather than being pursued by the Commission itself.[21]

3.   AREAS OF OMISSION

[1.11]   General. As indicated earlier, some forms of intellectual activity comprehended by the WIPO definition are not protected at all under Australian law, or are given only scant protection. The following paragraphs list some of the significant areas in which the current systems are 'deficient', whether for good reasons or bad.

[1.12]   Moral rights. Many countries, especially in Europe, confer rights on authors and artists which subsist even when they have assigned their copyright to someone else, typically a publisher or other entrepreneur who will seek to exploit the relevant work for profit. These 'moral rights' allow the creator of a work to retain some control over the integrity of that work and their connection to it. Beyond penalising false attribution of ownership, Australia does not presently recognise such rights. However, the position may be about to change. In February 1996 the Labor Government released draft amendments to the Copyright Act which would confer on authors and artists the right to be acknowledged as the creator of a work and the right to object to changes to the work or 'derogatory' uses of it which might harm their reputation. The Coalition Government elected a month later has also made a commitment to recognise these rights of 'attribution' and 'integrity', and legislation is expected in the near future.[22]

[1.13]   Scientific discoveries. Scientific breakthroughs as such are not eligible for protection, except to the extent that their secrecy may be preserved. Once published, anyone may use them. Patents are only granted to those who invent a new product or process; the person whose theoretical work contributes to the state of knowledge against the background of which inventive activity takes place has no claim to the fruits of their effort.[23] The same principle means that (at least in theory) the mere discovery of the existence in nature of a particular organism or chemical

19.   S Ricketson, 'The Future of Australian Intellectual Property Law Reform and Administration' (1992) 3 *AIPJ* 3 at 17, 26.
20.   *The Role of Intellectual Property in Innovation — Vol 2, Perspectives*, Prime Minister's Science and Engineering Council, 1993, pp 67–8.
21.   See [1.15].
22.   See [5.12] ff.
23.   See [12.5]. Cf David Vaver's suggestion of a 'theory patent' in 'Intellectual Property Today: Of Myths and Paradoxes' (1990) 69 *Can Bar Rev* 98 at 118.

substance is not patentable: the organism or substance must be put to some new commercial use, and even then monopoly rights may only be acquired over the particular use, not the organism or substance itself. This has significant implications for the protection and exploitation of breakthroughs in the emerging field of biotechnology, as discussed in Chapter 15.

[1.14] Indigenous art and culture. The present regimes are ill suited for the protection of intangible forms of cultural heritage. This is a particular problem for Aboriginal groups, as their folklore has come under threat from persons ranging from the (sometimes) well-meaning researcher to the commercial enterprise which wants to cash in on the latest craving for Aboriginal art.[24] It has been possible in some instances to use the law of confidentiality to restrain the circulation of hitherto secret material,[25] and the law of copyright to protect relatively recent works of art against unauthorised reproduction.[26] However, neither of these avenues will be available in regard to matter which has not been kept secret and which, especially in the case of 'traditional' designs and songs, struggles to satisfy basic requirements for the subsistence of copyright such as the identification of a particular author and the preservation of the work in a 'material form'. Nor is the present law of copyright able to cope with claims which are essentially collective rather than individual in nature. Many Aboriginal designs and rituals are subject to strict rules within the relevant community as to access, use and disclosure.[27] But those customary laws count for little in the face of the assumption that copyright ownership vests in the individual creator, not the community to which they belong.[28] In some instances, indeed, copyright may be allocated to someone outside the community altogether: for instance, where a researcher who is not merely acting as an agent for the community collates or records stories or ceremonies not previously preserved in material form.

There have been a number of proposals designed to overcome the lack of recognition accorded to the customary laws of indigenous groups in this country. In 1981 a working party set up by the federal government proposed an Aboriginal Folklore Act, which would prohibit any non-traditional use of sacred-secret folklore and establish a Commissioner for Aboriginal Folklore to issue clearances and negotiate payment for approved uses.[29] It has also been suggested that the Aboriginal and Torres Strait Islander Heritage Act 1984 (Cth), which at present applies to areas and relics of

---

24. See generally J McKeough and A Stewart, 'Intellectual Property and the Dreaming' in E Johnston, M Hinton and D Rigney (eds), *Indigenous Australians and the Law,* 1997.
25. See eg *Foster v Mountford* (1976) 14 ALR 71.
26. See eg *Milpurrurru v Indofurn Pty Ltd* (1994) 30 IPR 209; and see also C Golvan, 'Aboriginal Art and Copyright: The Case for Johnny Bulun Bulun' [1989] 10 *EIPR* 346.
27. See eg *Milpurrurru,* ibid at 214–15.
28. See eg *Yumbulul v Reserve Bank of Australia Ltd* (1991) 21 IPR 481 at 490; though cf the flexible approach adopted to the assessment of damages for copyright infringement in the *Milpurrurru* case (see [8.36]). See also C Golvan, 'Aboriginal Art and the Protection of Indigenous Cultural Rights' [1992] 7 *EIPR* 227 at 230, suggesting that Aboriginal communities might be regarded as the 'beneficial' or equitable owners of copyright in works created under the laws of those communities.
29. *Report of the Working Party on the Protection of Aboriginal Folklore,* Department of Home Affairs and the Environment, 1981: see R Bell, 'Protection of Folklore: The Australian Experience' (1985) 19 *Copyright Bull* 4.

cultural significance, be amended to allow Aboriginal communities to pursue unauthorised use of artwork.[30] An alternative possibility is to amend the Copyright Act 1968 itself to incorporate such a right, although there are a number of practical difficulties with the notion of vesting what might be regarded as competing rights in the original creator (as the 'author') on the one hand, and a community on the other.[31] More radical ideas include pursuing community claims under an expanded law of blasphemy;[32] or (perhaps more realistically) under the Native Title Act 1993 (Cth),[33] on the theory that cultural property for indigenous groups is so tied up with their relationship to land that it falls within the concept of native title recognised in the *Mabo* decision.[34] In 1994 the federal government released an issues paper which canvassed some of these suggestions and foreshadowed widespread consultation with indigenous groups and other interested parties as the basis for the development of further policy options.[35] Work is still proceeding on the development of those options, though it is unclear whether any concrete proposals will actually emerge from the process.

Lack of legal control over community heritage is also a concern in relation to a slightly different issue: the attempts of 'bioprospectors', often acting on behalf of drug companies or foreign research institutions, to appropriate genetic material or other useful substances drawn from the environments inhabited by indigenous people — or even from those people themselves. This is taken up later in the chapter, and also in Chapter 15.

[1.15] Product simulation and the 'gap' in designs/patent protection. When a firm puts a new product on the market, it may be able to call on a number of different intellectual property rights to prevent (or at least delay) competitors copying the product and cutting into the firm's profits. If the product itself or the process for making it is sufficiently novel and inventive, a patent may be acquired and used to block any commercial exploitation of the same product or process. If it is the distinctive appearance of the product that has been copied, this may infringe registered design rights. If the copy is marketed in such a way as to deceive consumers into thinking that they are getting the original firm's product, or at least that the maker is somehow connected with the original firm, there may be a remedy in the law of passing off or under trade practices legislation. More controversially (though attempts have been made in recent years to curtail this possibility),[36] the firm may seek to argue that the rival product

---

30. C Golvan, 'Aboriginal Art and the Protection of Indigenous Cultural Rights' [1992] 7 *EIPR* 227 at 231.
31. See D Ellinson, 'Unauthorised Reproduction of Traditional Aboriginal Art' (1994) 17 *UNSWLJ* 327.
32. See D Miller, 'Collective Ownership of Copyright in Spiritually-Sensitive Works: *Milpurrurru v Indofurn Pty Ltd*' (1995) 6 *AIPJ* 185.
33. See K Puri, 'Cultural Ownership and Intellectual Property Rights Post *Mabo*: Putting Ideas into Action' (1995) 9 *IPJ* 295; and see also S Gray, 'Wheeling, Dealing and Deconstruction: Aboriginal Art and the Land Post-Mabo' (1993) 63 *Aboriginal Law Bull* 10.
34. *Mabo v Queensland (No 2)* (1992) 175 CLR 1.
35. *Stopping the Rip-Offs: Intellectual Property Protection for Aboriginal and Torres Strait Islander Peoples*, Attorney-General's Department, 1994.
36. See [8.7]–[8.9], [10.24] ff.

infringes copyright in the drawings or models from which the firm's product was originally made.

In many instances, however, none of these laws are infringed, because the product is not *that* inventive, its functional characteristics rather than appearance have been copied, and the competitor has taken steps to dispel any suggestion of the products coming from the same source. This 'gap' in protection has attracted much adverse comment from manufacturers, especially in relation to products which involve 'low level' or 'incremental' innovation at a functional level. These products may require significant investment to develop and produce, yet be susceptible to rapid and relatively inexpensive copying. Three recent Australian reports have accepted the need for the gap to be filled in some way, though with differing suggestions as to how that might be done. The Bureau of Industry Economics considered that the designs system should be broadened to protect the way products work, not just their visual appearance.[37] The ALRC disagreed, taking the view that any expansion in protection (which it agreed was desirable) should be accommodated elsewhere in the intellectual property framework, with the designs system continuing to focus simply on visual features.[38] Besides recommending that the matter be considered in the course of ACIP's review of the petty patent system, the Commission called for consideration to be given to the introduction of a broad principle of 'unfair copying':[39]

> The Commission considers that the potential advantages of an anti-copying right, particularly in terms of reducing the overly legalistic emphasis and cost of design protection, warrant further review. That review should consider the anti-copying right in the context of Australia's overall innovation policy and legal framework, not just designs. It should assess unfair copying and unfair competition laws as part of the review. The review should be conducted jointly by bodies with expertise in economic policy, such as the Industry Commission, and in legal policy.

As for ACIP, it concluded that the petty patent system had not been successful in providing the kind of protection offered to minor or incremental innovations by 'utility model' laws in other countries. Its solution was to recommend a new 'second tier' of patent protection, in the form of 'innovation patents' lasting for eight years. A significantly lower threshold of inventiveness would be required in comparison to standard patents.[40] The federal government announced in February 1997 that this proposal would be implemented, though doubts have been expressed as to whether 'incessant juggling with innovation thresholds will provide long-term solutions'.[41]

[1.16] Unfair competition. There is at present no general principle in Australian law that competitive conduct which does not infringe one of the specific rights already mentioned should be treated as unlawful merely because it is some sense 'unfair'. However, the subject has been one of perennial discussion in academic circles and the ALRC's call for an inquiry

---

37. *The Economics of Intellectual Property Rights for Designs*, Occasional Paper 27, 1995.
38. *Designs*, ch 3: see [10.3].
39. Ibid, para [3.71].
40. *Review of the Petty Patent System*, 1995: see [11.8].
41. J Lahore, 'Designs and Petty Patents: A Broader Reform Issue' (1996) 7 *AIPJ* 7 at 18.

into the creation of a broad anti-copying right is likely to add further fuel to the debate. The issue is discussed in more detail later in this chapter.

4. THE NATURE OF INTELLECTUAL PROPERTY

[1.17] Property rights. So far one significant point has been glossed over — the description of the rights involved in the subject as a form of property. At one level this should cause little difficulty. It has long been apparent that the concept of 'property' is no more than a reference to the bundle of exclusive rights, whether absolute or limited, that the law is prepared to recognise as governing the relations of persons as to a 'thing', whether tangible or intangible.[42] From this perspective it makes sense to describe those rights accorded in relation to creative endeavour as proprietary rights. Indeed most of the relevant statutes expressly state that the rights they confer are personal property.[43] Nor has the common law had any difficulty in treating business goodwill as a proprietary interest worthy of protection through the law of passing off.[44] The only real point of controversy in recent times has been whether secret information can be regarded as property. Although many judges have denied such a possibility, it is increasingly apparent from the development of the equitable doctrine of breach of confidence that a property analysis is appropriate.[45]

This is not to say that the language of (private) property does not create its own difficulties. One is the temptation to apply principles developed in relation to more traditional forms of property without first determining whether they make sense in the context of intellectual activity. There seems little reason, for instance, to import rigid rules as to the status of third party interests such as the principles governing the position of bona fide purchasers.[46] These concepts are not necessarily appropriate in the intellectual property field and can lead to unnecessary tangles in trying, for example, to determine whether legal or equitable interests are involved.

The principal danger in adopting a proprietary analysis, however, lies in forgetting that the term is merely a conclusory statement and in falling into the trap of assuming that any identifiable 'thing' must belong to someone.[47] In the present context this translates into the erroneous belief that all fruits of intellectual activity have some intrinsic claim to be treated as property.[48] As we will see, such a principle is unacceptably broad, for it ignores the fact that important policy factors must be weighed up before it is decided what rights, if any, should be accorded. This process indeed

---

42. See A S Weinrib, 'Information and Property' (1988) 38 *U Tor LJ* 117 at 120–3 and authorities there cited. See further B Edgeworth, 'Post-Property? A Postmodern Conception of Property' (1988) 11 *UNSWLJ* 87; K Gray, 'Property in Thin Air' [1991] *CLJ* 252.
43. See Copyright Act 1968 s 196(1); Patents Act 1990 s 13(2); Designs Act 1906 s 25C(1); Trade Marks Act 1995 s 106; Plant Breeder's Rights Act 1994 s 11; Circuit Layouts Act 1989 s 45(1).
44. See [16.2].
45. See [3.14]–[3.17].
46. Cf *Wheatley v Bell* [1982] 2 NSWLR 544: see [4.15].
47. See Drahos, ch 7.
48. Cf D F Libling, 'The Concept of Property: Property in Intangibles' (1978) 94 *LQR* 103.

provides an answer to those who go to the other extreme of arguing that a proprietary analysis is fundamentally inappropriate in this area. It has been claimed, for instance, that 'allocating property rights in knowledge makes ideas artificially scarce and their use less frequent'.[49] This goes too far, for it all depends on the extent of the rights granted, a point that is true whether or not those rights are described as proprietary. So long as *some* rights are granted, there is nothing wrong with the ex post facto view that the forms of activity to which those rights are attached are property. Whether the content of those rights is appropriate is another matter altogether.

It has been argued by Drahos that the 'proprietarian creed',[50] assigning property rights a fundamental and entrenched status, tends to 'promote factionalism and dangerous levels of private power',[51] and that the better view is to regard intellectual property as a set of privilege-bearing duties with a strongly articulated conception of the public purpose and role of intellectual property.[52] This 'instrumentalist attitude' would locate intellectual property in the context of some broader moral theory and set of values.[53] Nevertheless, the 'highly flexible concept of personal property' applicable to incorporeal property developed through Roman and English law has provided a useful platform for considering the relationships between information, rights, economic growth and power, even if (as Drahos would argue) a proprietary analysis is incapable of founding a general theory of intellectual property.[54]

5. POLICY ISSUES

(a) Introduction

[1.18] Importance of intellectual property. As an area of law, intellectual property is clearly very important, going back to the first printing presses and the medieval guilds. To the writer or composer or artist, their works may represent their livelihood, while to publishers they represent potential profits. To industry, inventions represent large investments of time and money — and the possible creation of enormous wealth. To businesses generally, their reputation, their name and the appearance of their goods represent their position in the market. Intellectual and industrial stock in trade is just as important as buildings or other tangible investments. Thus the law has come to regard the results of intellectual and industrial endeavour as sufficiently identifiable to be capable of protection.

Moreover this protection has gained in importance as the twentieth century has progressed. This can be ascribed to a combination of factors. An important one has been the way that innovation has passed almost completely from the hands of individuals working on their own account. Nowadays it tends to reside with teams of employees engaged by public or

---

49. D Vaver, 'Intellectual Property Today: Of Myths and Paradoxes' (1990) 69 *Can Bar Rev* 98 at 126.
50. Drahos, p 200.
51. Ibid, p 5.
52. Ibid, p 2.
53. Ibid, p 223.
54. Ibid, ch 9.

private enterprises. With the concurrent move towards ever larger con-glomerations of capital, both domestically and globally, the stakes have dra-matically increased where industrial creativity is concerned. Given the colossal amount of investment in innovation and the inevitably urgent need for profitable returns, it is hardly to be wondered that competition has grown fiercer and that great importance is attached to the marginal improvements which a clever idea may produce. There are indeed entire industries, of which the pharmaceutical industry may be the outstanding example, which are founded on new ideas. Where these enterprises are concerned, any loss of protection means failure. The same is true in the communication and entertainment industries, which are heavily depend-ent on the law of copyright. Some idea of the economic significance of the 'copyright-based' industries can be gained from the estimate that in 1990–91 their total turnover in Australia was nearly $19 billion.[55]

A further factor has been the impact of new technology. The nature and sheer weight of the advances made in this century, and the efforts made to exploit them, have placed great pressure on the law to respond with appro-priate protective regimes. Technology here has been a double-edged sword, because the same advances have occurred in relation to copying tech-niques, making it easier for piracy to take place. Think for instance of the effect photocopiers, cassette recorders, bugging devices and digital scan-ners have had on the ability to control the dissemination or exploitation of knowledge. The very medium of computer data storage lends itself to unauthorised access and copying. Again, developments in communications have greatly increased the speed with which ideas may be spread. In terms of business goodwill, there is also the influence of multinationals to con-sider, with their ability to transport products and create instant reputations through advertising. The result has been that the value attached to intellec-tual property has grown, yet at the same time it has become harder and harder to protect.

[1.19] The 'digital agenda'. The digital information environment has indeed fundamentally altered pre-existing notions of intellectual prop-erty rights, confined as these traditionally are to the physical embodi-ment of ideas in tangible goods. Ease of copying, communications and manipulation of data in digital form poses enormous challenges to con-ventional copyright law in particular. In fact a number of critics have sug-gested that traditional intellectual property protection is neither appropriate nor effective in cyberspace: the world of the Internet, inter-active on-line services and e-mail.[56] Most debate, however, has focused on how to protect material in such an environment, rather than whether copyright should be abandoned. Addressing the 'digital agenda' has been the pre-occupation of various government committees in the US,[57] Japan,[58] Australia[59] and Europe.[60] In December 1996 a WIPO Diplomatic

---

55. H H Guldberg, *Copyright — An Economic Perspective*, Australian Copyright Council, 2nd ed, 1993.
56. See Chapter 9.
57. See [9.2], [9.5].
58. See [9.3].
59. See [9.4] ff.
60. See [9.19], [9.20].

Conference on Copyright attempted to bring copyright into the digital age. The conference aimed to produce protocols updating the Berne and Rome Conventions, which are international agreements concerning the protection of copyright in works, films, sound recordings and performances.[61]

An important aspect of the updating process is to introduce new rights for copyright holders. This goes beyond fitting new modes of technology and transmission into existing concepts (an example of which is categorising computer software as 'literary works' so as to come within the protectable subject matter of copyright) and involves a conceptual shift which takes into account the possibilities of the information age. To this end, an expanded 'right of communication to the public' will now cover non-private digital transmissions, including loading of material onto an on-line service available to the public.[62] New rights of distribution and commercial rental and exclusive rights over reproduction, distribution and on-line access to sound recordings and performances (including the possibility of compulsory licensing of broadcasting of such recordings) are to be introduced. These provisions will not, however, extend to films or videos. One matter left unresolved is the expansion of the existing right of reproduction to cover various forms of digital storage. However, negotiating countries agreed on a statement providing 'guidance' as to how to apply the existing reproduction right. In negotiations, Australia expressed opposition to the introduction of an importation right — a serious matter for a nation which is a net importer of copyright material.

The enforcement of new or existing rights is particularly challenging in the digital environment. The updating process proposed by the new WIPO Copyright Treaty includes introducing obligations concerning technical measures, so that devices and activities to circumvent technological protection such as program locks or encryption of data are to be made illegal. Also prohibited is tampering with electronic identifiers incorporated into material so as to indicate its authorship or ownership. These changes to the international conventions will be introduced into Australian law by amending the Copyright Act. In the future, a new Copyright Act will be introduced, following the completion of a review of the present legislation.[63] This and other issues relevant to the digital agenda are discussed in Chapter 9.

(b) Rationales for Protection

[1.20] Moral arguments. Against that background of technological progress, and given the pressure imposed on legislatures and courts to protect creative effort, it becomes vital to identify the rationale for according such protection. Why should the law intervene at all? To a certain extent it can be said that the intervention is based on moral considerations. From the point of view of the person whose intellectual activity is in question,

---

61. See [21.5], [21.15], [21.19].
62. As to the dangers that such an approach may pose to freedom of communication, see W A van Caenegem, 'Copyright, Communication and New Technologies' (1995) 23 *Fed LR* 322.
63. See [5.16].

they might be seen as having some sort of 'natural right' to what they create, an entitlement recognised by Art 27(2) of the Universal Declaration of Human Rights: 'Everyone has the right to the protection of the moral and material interests resulting from any scientific, literary or artistic production of which he [sic] is the author'. This is often backed up by highlighting the inherent 'unfairness' of appropriating another's effort without consent. As the US Supreme Court put it in the *International News Service* case:[64]

> [The defendant], by its very act, admits that it is taking material that has been acquired by complainant as the result of organization and the expenditure of labor, skill and money ... and is endeavouring to reap where it has not sown.

The harvesting metaphor used here has become a powerful image in establishing the illegitimacy of the 'free rider', the person who 'steals' a reward that justly belongs to the original author or inventor. In fact the notion of a 'natural right of property' in abstract objects discovered or created by individuals as a just reward for their industry has a long history, albeit modified by limitations on the sanctity of property rights arising from notions of the 'intellectual commons'.[65]

[1.21] Economic arguments. From the earliest times of legal protection, however, and as the emphasis on expenditure in the passage just quoted reveals, the main considerations in countries bearing the British influence have been economic rather than moral. It was not by chance, for instance, that copyright was introduced in Britain to protect publishers rather than authors, or that the patents system originated in the demands of those aristocrats and landowners of Elizabethan times who operated a certain measure of risk capital. Protection today is still based on recognising the value of creative endeavour to those who are prepared to develop and exploit it.

At this point, however, is encountered an internal or economic contradiction. As Cooter and Ulen explain:

> The distinguishing economic characteristic of each of [the] methods for establishing property rights in information is that they are *monopoly* rights. This seems paradoxical in that, in general, a monopoly is less efficient than a competitive industry, but information is an unusual commodity ... By giving monopoly power to the creator of an idea, that person is presented with a powerful incentive to discover new ideas. However a monopolist tends to discourage use of a good by overpricing it. Put succinctly, the dilemma is that without a legal monopoly not enough information will be produced but with the legal monopoly too little of the information will be used.[66]

The underlying problem here is that information or knowledge is effectively a 'public good'. It is an unusual commodity precisely because it can be consumed by one person and yet still be available to others, and because the cost of preventing others from appropriating it may be so high that private actors are unlikely to want to produce it in the first place. The conferral of a monopoly is thus a response to a (potential) market failure — the problem that ideas will not be developed for fear that free riders will rob the risktaker of any consequent benefit. To return to the harvesting metaphor:

---

64. *International News Service v Associated Press* (1918) 248 US 215 at 239: see [16.20].
65. See Drahos, ch 3.
66. R Cooter and T Ulen, *Law and Economics*, 1988, p 135. See also Drahos, p 121 ff.

> Laws for the protection of intellectual property provide security for invest-
> ment for innovation ... in the sense that they provide a protective barrier
> against third parties who seek to appropriate the work of the innovator and
> take a free ride on that work. Without this barrier, innovation is like a crop
> in an unfenced field, free to be grazed by competitors who have made no
> contribution to its cultivation.[67]

But as Cooter and Ulen point out, the danger of this monopoly is that the
resulting product may not be delivered to the public at a price which would
encourage consumption. Another consequence is that the development of
certain ideas may be deferred, perhaps indefinitely. This may be because
their owners see some benefit in locking them up, not wanting for example
to give an advantage to competitors who are better placed to exploit them,
or wishing to get more mileage out of existing products before introducing
something which will make those products redundant.

This problem of socially beneficial ideas not being developed arises in its
most acute form where private producers are deterred altogether from
moving to exploit an idea because the potential market for it is so unprofit-
able. The classic example is that of 'orphan drugs', medicines which have
enormous potential to treat or cure diseases, but which do not reach the
public because they will benefit so few people that it is in no producer's
interest to pay the substantial development costs involved.[68]

[1.22] Innovation and incentive. What all this comes down to is
whether sufficient incentives are being provided for the right sort of innovation to take place. Once upon a time this might have meant looking at
whether individual authors or inventors were being suitably rewarded for
their efforts and/or protected against the attempts of others to deprive
them of their spoils (note that these are simply a re-hash of the moral arguments discussed above, though placed now in an economic perspective).
But if this were ever the case, which is doubtful, it certainly no longer holds
given the trends and developments to which reference has already been
made. In the modern world the issue is plainly one of *investment,* the
assumption being that those with private capital or public expenditure at
their disposal will themselves create the necessary incentives for individuals
to be creative.

This is not to say that all intellectual property laws are necessarily the
product of a precise economic calculation, that in other words the creation
of intellectual property rights can in each instance be explained by a desire
at the relevant point in history to create appropriate incentives for investment in ideas and innovation. After all, the copyright and patents systems
originated well before this kind of economic analysis became fashionable.[69]
It should also be borne in mind that there have been many societies in
which economic or technological development has occurred without anything in the nature of intellectual property rights. We may note, for example, the suggestion:

---

67. *The Role of Intellectual Property in Innovation — Vol 2, Perspectives,* Prime Minister's
    Science and Engineering Council, 1993, p 61.
68. See eg L Lasagna, 'Who Will Adopt the Orphan Drugs?' (1979) 3(6) *Regulation* 27.
69. Cf the suggestion that the early patent systems were 'evidently ... based on some
    intuitive understanding by the rulers of the need to provide special incentives for
    innovation and the attraction of skilled tradesmen from abroad': Bureau of
    Industry Economics, *The Economics of Patents,* Occasional Paper 18, 1994, p 6.

that far from being universal, it is the ideas of ownership embedded in modern Western intellectual property that are the historical aberrations, and
that these ideas have achieved the currency they now enjoy internationally as
much because they are backed by great economic might as because of their
appeal to our common sense or their innate conceptual force.[70]

But even accepting that the economic rationale for intellectual property
rights is a thoroughly modern and indeed western construct, this is not to
deny its force today. The fact is that it is generally believed, certainly by
policy-makers at both a national and international level, that intellectual
property can and should be justified by reference to its capacity to act 'as a
stimulant to and incentive for innovation'.[71]

[1.23] Corporatist strategies. There are of course ways of creating
incentives to invest in innovation other than by allocating property rights.
During the last few decades growing emphasis has been placed upon
corporatist strategies, whereby the state intervenes in the market to provide
selective assistance in the form of tax concessions, subsidies, the guarantee
of venture capital, coordination of research, and so on. These strategies are
purposive in nature, being designed to further carefully targeted objectives.
However, in some ways this approach is facing a crisis of legitimacy. As Arup
notes:[72]

> Many of the corporatist characterizations of the law [in the 1970s] were
> based upon experience with the provision of assistance to failing industries
> and depressed regions where government was in a relatively strong position
> to insist upon its own terms. In the high technology industries of the 'eight-
> ies and 'nineties, government is often seeking instead to induce a wealthy
> private sector to choose local innovative and productive activity over its
> other investment options in an international economy. Neither the needs of
> producers for state support, the capacity of the state to co-ordinate the econ-
> omy, nor the political acceptance of the approach, can be assumed.

There is increasing scepticism as to whether the state's ability to 'pick
winners' is any better than the market's. Concern has also been expressed
at the reliance placed on unreviewable administrative discretion in the provision of assistance. Against this background pressure has mounted, particularly from those excluded from state favours, for a 'level playing field'.
This conforms to a preferred model of regulation in which the law

> may supplement or even substitute its policy for that of the market, but does
> so through the prescription of standards cast in the form of rules applied
> evenly and at arms length from the private actors. In such an approach, the
> law's role is a limited one, essentially confined to facilitating the processes of
> resource development, exchange and utilisation by the private sector, in par-
> ticular by overcoming the imperfections of the market itself where they
> present obstacles to efficient economic activity.[73]

[1.24] Striking a balance. In itself the allocation of property rights over
creative activity is a classic instance of regulation in the liberal rather than
corporatist tradition. While corporatism has waxed and (perhaps) waned,

---

70. W P Alford, 'How Theory Does — And Does Not — Matter: American Approaches
     to Intellectual Property Law in East Asia' (1994) 13 *Pacific Basin LJ* 8 at 17.
71. *The Role of Intellectual Property in Innovation — Vol 1, Strategic Overview*, Prime
     Minister's Science and Engineering Council, 1993, p 8.
72. C Arup, 'Innovation, Policy Strategies and Law' (1990) 12 *Law and Policy* 247 at
     256.
73. Ibid at 248–9. See further C Arup, *Innovation, Policy and Law*, 1993.

rule-defined intellectual property rights have remained the traditional
response to the perceived need to provide incentives for innovation. However, the formulation of such rights requires a delicate balance to be struck.
If there is too little protection, investment may not take place: for why
spend time and money developing a new concept or approach if it is more
efficient to behave as a free rider? Too much protection, on the other
hand, may lead to useful matter being locked up or, more probably, becoming the source of monopoly profits. Ideally, the aim is to encourage the initial
decision to invest in new ideas, while thereafter providing an appropriate cli-
mate for the benefit of those ideas to spread. So long as those who are prepared to innovate are not entirely deprived of the incentive to do so and
can glean at least some benefit from their risk-taking, there is nothing
wrong with competitors expending their own effort in engaging in further
development of the ideas or products pioneered by the innovators.

[1.25] The limitations of economic analysis. It is easy enough to identify the fundamental policy issue as being whether the conferral of property
rights will work as an incentive or disincentive to appropriate forms of
investment in creativity. It is quite another matter to answer that question
with any confidence. Here we run into one of the major problems with
modern economics, which is basically concerned with the optimal allocation of resources in a given situation — 'optimal', in the sense of maximising social welfare. Since every individual has a different vision of what
constitutes 'social welfare', a different set of personal perceptions and
objectives, determining what might constitute an optimal allocation is an
immensely difficult task. Put simply, there are many factors which cannot
readily be quantified. Good economists of course will nevertheless attempt
to build these factors into their models, no matter how difficult this might
be. Unfortunately — and this has appeared to be a hallmark of some at
least of the writings from the 'law and economics' school — it is much
easier to deal only with those things which can be expressed in terms of dollars and cents, reducing social and economic policy to the deceptively simple goal of maximising income. Coupled with a tendency to confuse the
positive with the normative, whether wittingly or not, many policies advocated by those with an 'economic' outlook seem to the uninitiated difficult
to reconcile with the world we actually live in. This is not to deride the
value of economic analysis, because it can be useful to estimate even in
crude dollar terms what it costs or would cost society to pursue various
objectives, and even more useful to predict the likely reactions of those subjected to particular forms of regulation. In the case of patents, for instance,
much valuable work has been done in an attempt to assess whether the type
of system currently in place here and in most other countries provides a
cost-efficient way of encouraging inventions.[74] At some point though the
decision on appropriate protection must leave the realm in which careful
economic analysis may be determinative. At this juncture the relevant questions depend, or should depend, on broader issues of social policy. Do we
need innovation at all? If so, what sort of innovation?[75] What cultural or
political factors do we consider relevant, beyond the bare financial

74. See [11.6].
75. See D Vaver, 'Some Agnostic Observations on Intellectual Property' (1991) 6 *IPJ*
125.

equation? Of course it is not always easy for these questions to be addressed in any proper fashion. It is all very well to speculate as to what sort of regulatory system we might put in place if we had the chance to start again, but in reality the opportunities to begin from scratch are likely to be rare. The roots of the established intellectual property regimes go back a long way and it would mean an enormous upheaval to displace them altogether.[76] Quite apart from the administrative problems caused by radical change, it is inevitable that those with vested interests in the existing system will fight hard to retain their advantage. Moreover countries like Australia are increasingly constrained by their international commitments, with the TRIPS Agreement in particular acting as a powerful force for the adoption and retention of certain types of intellectual property protection.

[1.26] Importation of books: a case in point. All this is neatly illustrated by the controversy over the effect of copyright laws on the importation into Australia of books. The details of the problem and of the legislative amendments introduced to resolve it are set out in a later chapter.[77] For present purposes, however, the difficulty stemmed from the fact that as a general principle the Australian owner of copyright in a work may prevent a copy of it being imported without authorisation. Where that copy has been pirated, the ability to restrain importation is unremarkable. Suppose though that the copy has been quite lawfully purchased by the importer overseas, having been published there as part of the international exploitation of the work. If the importer seeks to bring it into the country without being the authorised distributor here, this constitutes 'parallel importation'. The publisher or distributor will obviously want to stop this, since the parallel importer's sales will cut into their own local profits. Significantly, the English-speaking world tends to be divided for book publishing purposes into two markets — North America and everywhere else. The non-American rights are typically held by British publishers, whose subsidiaries dominate the Australian scene. These publishers are able to control the non-American markets, and the common charge is that their traditional ability to restrain parallel importation has led to books published overseas not being freely available here, and more generally to Australian consumers being charged higher prices than production and transportation costs would warrant. The issue, therefore, as it emerged in the late 1980s and early 1990s, was whether the prohibition on parallel importation should be repealed or at least relaxed in order to bring down the prices of imported books.

On the face of it this was a straightforward economic contest between the publishers, who supported the prohibition, and small booksellers, who wished to import cheap American copies and compete with the authorised distributors, with the large booksellers perhaps having a foot in either camp. From an economic point of view, the contest should easily have been

---

76. As it was once put, 'If national patent laws did not exist, it would be difficult to make a conclusive case for introducing them: but the fact they do exist shifts the burden of proof and it is equally difficult to make a really conclusive case for abolishing them': E Penrose, *Economics of the International Patent System*, 1951, p 40, quoted in D Vaver, 'Intellectual Property Today: Of Myths and Paradoxes' (1990) 69 *Can Bar Rev* 98 at 115–16.
77. See [8.21]–[8.22].

resolved. If it could be shown that publishers were indeed combining in some form of loose cartel to use their local monopoly to drive up prices — a point on which there was naturally disagreement — then it should surely be appropriate to relax that monopoly and permit parallel importation. However, at this point another factor came into play — the health of the local publishing industry. It was suggested by many leading Australian authors in particular that any 'deregulation' would destroy the local indus- try, since publishers would not have the incentive to publish works by Australian authors who were not already established. Since such works would not necessarily be successful on the larger overseas markets, so the argument went, the small print run involved would mean prices that would not be competitive with mass-produced books imported and sold cheaply.[78] Now it is easy to be sceptical about the motives of some of those advancing this argument, and it should also be pointed out that there are few genu- inely Australian publishers as it is. Nevertheless it raised a significant point: to what extent should we be prepared to sacrifice lower prices in return for the retention and encouragement of some sort of cultural integrity? This is not a question that can easily be answered and it remains to be seen whether the legislative solution adopted (a partial relaxation of the parallel importation prohibition) will have any lasting effect, especially since noises are being made about the amendments breaching our international obliga- tions. Nonetheless the episode does highlight the role that non-economic factors may play in the formulation of intellectual property policy.[79]

[1.27] Another example: ownership of genetic material. Protection of local culture and consumers using the mechanism of the importation provisions of the Copyright Act is just one example of the fact that eco- nomic analysis cannot be the only determinant of the scope of intellectual property rights. An issue that arouses strong emotions is the question of ownership of 'life'.[80] Should whole organisms, or at the other end of the spectrum, stretches of DNA, be the subject matter of exclusive patent rights? There is strong opposition on moral, ethical and indeed, legal grounds to allowing life or its building blocks (DNA) to be monopolised by corporations with the resources to develop and protect commercial appli- cations of the created world. In particular, searching the earth's biota for new products or chemicals, and isolating (and attempting to patent) the genetic material of indigenous people raise fundamental questions as to the extent to which 'biocolonialism' and commodification of human life should be allowed. The Human Genome Diversity Project (HGDP), also known as the 'Vampire Project', aims to draw blood and tissue samples from as many indigenous groups in the world as possible. In 1995, for instance, a patent application was granted by the US Patent Office over the

---

78. Similar arguments are being heard in relation to the importation of sound recordings, an issue still awaiting legislative resolution at the time of writing: see [8.23].
79. Cf A Fels and J Walker, 'The Market for Books and the Importation Provisions of the Copyright Act 1968' (1990) 17 *Melb ULR* 566 at 579, where the authors seek to rebut the argument 'that literature is too important to be subjected to economic analysis'.
80. See further Chapter 15.

genetic material of a member of the Hagahai people from Papua New Guinea.[81]

Apart from issues of ownership, questions of international relations and environmental concerns are relevant. It has been estimated that 25% of all medicines prescribed in the US have active ingredients extracted or derived from plants.[82] Foreign scientists are accused of claiming exclusive ownership of traditional medicines, pesticides and other products derived from plants that have been used by indigenous communities for centuries.[83] Lacking the legal resources and money to fight claims of exclusive patent rights to traditional medicines, dyes, oils and pesticides, local communities are starting to turn away researchers who come to study the use of local plants and animals.[84] Bioprospecting for useful plants and the commercial value of human DNA from remote populations in the diagnosis and treatment of disease and development of vaccines raise a number of competing concerns. These go far beyond issues of asserting property rights in return for the research and creative effort of modern scientists converting the raw material to a new and useful end suitable for patent protection. The conservation of biodiversity and natural habitats such as tropical rainforests, the needs of developing countries, respect for the culture and knowledge of indigenous populations,[85] and indeed the requirements of the modern world in the development of useful products must all be addressed. While one of the most pressing issues is the protection of rights in the raw materials and end results, and the sharing of these rights between foreign researchers and locals,[86] the ownership of rights must be considered in the wider context of international concerns about biodiversity and human rights.[87]

(c) Determining the Scope of Protection

[1.28] Decisions to be made. It should be apparent from the foregoing that the law must be constantly wary of the extent of the protection that it offers to creative effort; there must be a system of checks and balances. Moreover the range of matters encompassed within the conception of intellectual property breaks down into sub-areas to each of which very different considerations may apply. Just as within the law of property different rules may apply to land and chattels, so there is no automatic reason to treat, for example, literary effort in exactly the same way as business reputation. In

81. J McKeough, 'Biocolonialism: The Patenting of Indigenous Persons, Plants and Animals' (1995) 4(5) *Human Rights Defender* 4; and see further [15.7].
82. M J Huft, 'Indigenous Peoples and Drug Discovery Research: A Question of Intellectual Property Rights' (1995) 89 *Northwestern ULR* 1678 at 1679.
83. A E Agarwal and E Narain, 'Pirates in the Garden of India', *New Scientist*, 26 October 1996, p 14.
84. D Posey, 'Finders Keepers Won't Do Anymore', *New Scientist*, 13 July 1996, p 48.
85. See R Gana, 'Has Creativity Died in the Third World? Some Implications of the Internationalisation of Intellectual Property' (1995) 24 *Denver J of Intl Law and Policy* 109.
86. E Da Casta e Silva, 'The Protection of Intellectual Property for Local and Indigenous Communities' [1995] 11 *EIPR* 546.
87. K W Baer, 'A Theory of Intellectual Property and the Biodiversity Treaty' (1995) 21 *Syracuse J of Intl Law and Commerce* 259; M Bowman and C Redgwell, *International Law and the Conservation of Biological Diversity*, 1996.

introducing legislation, various decisions will need to be made: the subject matter to be protected and how it is to be defined; who is to be accorded the benefit of any protection; the width of that protection; the means of informing the public about the protection; the appropriate sanctions, and so on. This can be illustrated by reference to another important issue, the duration of protection. A business only needs protection for its reputation, for instance, while it is indeed in business. Once trading ceases, its style, names and get-up should be available to others, so long as they do not deceive the public. Thus a trade mark is lost through non-use and it is a prerequisite of passing off that the plaintiff have an existing market reputation. Artists and authors, on the other hand, were traditionally thought to require protection for as long as they and their families needed to eat. When both they and their families are dead, there is no reason why their works should not be fair game: hence the typical copyright duration of the author's or artist's life plus 50 years, an exception in some ways to the tendency of copyright law to be driven by commercial considerations.[88] As for inventors, they merely need an opportunity to obtain a reasonable return on their invention. The standard patent term of 20 years is intended to allow this, providing the invention is marketed with vigour.

[1.29] Who should own the rights? Given that a right is to be allocated, the law must obviously have some mechanism for identifying the person who is to exercise that right and be able to transfer it to others. The question is approached in different ways across the different regimes. Most have a general rule that the initial owner is the person responsible for creating the subject matter of the right: the author or maker of a copyright work, circuit layout or registered design, the inventor of a patented invention, the breeder of a new plant variety, or the trader who builds up a reputation sufficient to found an action in passing off. However, there are exceptions to this pattern. The trade mark system, for instance, awards 'proprietorship' to the person who first *uses* a mark in Australia, irrespective of who has actually developed it or whether the mark has been used overseas.[89] With confidential information, the question is posed in terms of standing to enforce a duty of confidence. That duty essentially arises though possession of secret information, no matter how the information came into existence.[90] Even in relation to the 'creator as owner' regimes, there may be specific qualifications. With copyright and designs, for example, commissioned work may in some instances vest in the commissioner rather than the creator;[91] while copyright in works made 'under the direction or control' of the Commonwealth or a state is taken to belong to the Crown.[92]

More importantly though, each regime has adopted a general qualification that in practice is absolutely crucial to the determination of ownership. This is that where the person who would otherwise be regarded as the right-owner has performed the relevant act (creation of the work, design or

---

88. See further K Puri, 'The Long Term of Copyright versus Modern Technology' (1989) 10 *Qld Lawyer* 95.
89. See [19.12] ff.
90. See [4.1]–[4.2].
91. See [7.2], [10.5].
92. See [7.7].

invention (etc), use of a mark, acquisition of information) in the course of employment under a contract of service,[93] ownership is presumed to be vested in the employer rather than the employee unless there is agreement to the contrary.[94] In most of the statutory regimes this presumption is explicit, though in the case of patents (as with confidential information) it is a product of terms implied by law into the employment relationship.[95] The notion of employer ownership is by no means uncontested, however, especially in two particular cases. Print journalists have long been in a special position in relation to the material they write, benefiting from special statutory provisions to the effect that even if they are employees they may retain copyright in their work for purposes other than reproduction in a newspaper, magazine or periodical. Media proprietors have in recent years pressed for this 'privilege' to be removed or at least reduced in scope, a course of action that is looming as ever more likely under the Howard Government.[96]

The other modern battleground is to be found in the higher education sector.[97] For many years, the only claim made by universities over intellectual property generated by academic staff in the course of research or scholarship involved commercially valuable inventions, usually generated by research teams in science, engineering or medical departments. It was (and is) routine for institutions to take out patents over such inventions, subject to an agreed share of any royalties from successful exploitation being returned to the researchers and their departments.[98] By contrast, no attempt was typically made to assert ownership of copyright in the books, journal articles or other creative works generated by academics, who were free therefore to enter into their own arrangements with publishers.[99] However in recent years the position has changed dramatically, with almost all universities adopting new policies on intellectual property that involve sweeping claims to ownership over the work of academics. Most have still avoided claiming copyright in 'traditional' forms of scholarship (or if they have made such a claim, failed to enforce it), but it has become more common for rights to be asserted over teaching materials (especially those developed for external programs or distance learning), computer software, videos, multimedia packages and the like. In relation to inventions, there has also been an increasing

---

93. As to the distinction between a contract of service and other arrangements whereby work is performed, see Creighton and Stewart, ch 7.

94. See generally A Stewart, 'Ownership of Property in the Context of Employment: Some Recent Developments' (1992) 5 *AJLL* 1. Note, however, that this would *not* be the case under any moral rights regime introduced into the Copyright Act (see [5.12] ff), where by definition the individual creator would have the rights of attribution and integrity alone.

95. See [13.2] ff, [4.33] ff. The problem does not arise so much in relation to trade marks, though ordinary principles of agency would seem sufficient to explain why use of a trade mark on behalf an employer will mean that the employer is the proprietor of the mark.

96. See [7.4].

97. See generally Australian Copyright Council, *Teachers and Academics as Creators: Current Issues,* Bulletin 91, 1995; and see also the various articles in (1993) 36 *Aust Universities Rev.*

98. See [13.8]–[13.10].

99. See [7.3].

emphasis on maintaining the secrecy of the work in question so as not to threaten the chances of gaining a patent,[100] notwithstanding the obvious conflict this creates with principles of academic freedom and dissemination of knowledge.[101]

The change in attitude has been prompted by a number of factors. One is simply a drive to maximise any commercial opportunities arising from innovation on campus, especially given the clear expectation on the part of recent federal governments that income must be privately generated to supplement or indeed replace shrinking public funding. There has also been a great deal of pressure exerted by organisations granting research funds or firms participating as 'industry partners' in joint ventures with universities. These bodies greatly prefer to deal with the university as sole owner of any intellectual property either brought to the project or generated in the course of it and often insist that the institution take whatever steps are necessary to put itself in that position. In some instances universities have clearly gone too far in their enthusiasm for acquiring intellectual property rights. For instance a number of institutions now purport to claim not only staff-generated intellectual property, but any rights arising from the work of students (with the possible exception of copyright in theses). But unless a student is also an employee, a university can make no automatic claim on the student's work: any acquisition of intellectual property rights must therefore result from an agreement struck with the student — which, to be safe from challenges based on the law of unconscionability or restraint of trade,[102] should be carefully worded and even more carefully explained to the student. Unfortunately, there are many university policies which, in this respect and others, are ill-conceived, poorly drafted and (quite possibly) legally ineffective.[103]

[1.30] Nature of protection and degrees of exclusivity. Another important issue that must be addressed is the degree to which the right-owner is given exclusive control over the relevant subject matter. This depends to a large extent on how that subject matter is defined in the first place. In the case of a patent, the owner is given control over the idea behind the patented process or product, at least so far as that idea is disclosed in the patent specifications. The patentee's monopoly is an absolute one, for nobody may use that idea during the term of the patent, even if they arrive at the same idea through independent research. On the other hand, this monopoly lasts for a limited time only and the patentee is required to publish details of the invention so that others will be free to use it when protection expires. With copyright, a different balance is struck. In

---

100. Publication prior to filing a patent application may deprive an invention of 'novelty' and hence preclude the grant of a patent: see [12.13] ff.
101. Cf P Loughlan, 'Of Patents and Professors: Intellectual Property, Research Workers and Universities' [1996] 6 *EIPR* 345.
102. See eg [7.14].
103. Cf the cogent advice offered on the subject by the Australian Vice-Chancellor's Committee in *Ownership of Intellectual Property in Universities*, 1995; and see also *Maximising the Benefits: Joint ARC/HEC Advice on Intellectual Property*, National Board of Employment, Education and Training, 1995. The National Tertiary Education Union has developed its own 'model policy' on intellectual property ownership and control, which has proved quite influential and prompted a more moderate approach at a number of institutions.

theory at least, copyright cannot be used to control an idea, only the particular expression chosen by the author. Nor is it any infringement to produce the same work independently, though it may sometimes be difficult to rebut a charge of plagiarism. As against that, copyright subsists for rather longer than patent protection. Nor need the work be published, so that in some instances copyright may be used as an instrument of censorship.[104] The right conferred over a registered trade mark is different again. The proprietor's right may subsist indefinitely, but is confined to restraining others from confusing the public by using the same or a similar mark.

[1.31] Compulsory licensing. Depending on the scope of the particular right, demands may arise for others to be given the chance to use or exploit the relevant matter, even during the subsistence of that right. In some cases this demand may be reflected by the availability of an outright defence to infringement. The Copyright Act, for instance, contains numerous provisions which allow use to be made of copyright material without penalty.[105] Of greater interest though is the possibility of compulsory licensing, whereby the right owner is compelled to permit others to pay for the privilege of using the relevant matter. This is something the courts can in effect accomplish merely by refusing to enjoin an infringement and instead ordering the payment of compensation or an account of profits, though by and large they have not chosen to do so.[106] In any event most of the statutory schemes provide for compulsory licences. The reasoning behind these provisions may vary. In some instances the purpose to which the 'infringer' wishes to put the protected material may be so evidently worthwhile that the right-owner should not be allowed to refuse access to it or set too high a price. Photocopying and taping of broadcasts by educational institutions fall into this category.[107] Alternatively, the concern may be that the right-owner should not be able to sit on an idea which others are willing to exploit to their own and the public's benefit. This explains the power of a court to grant a licence to exploit a patented invention to any person who can show that the patentee has not been satisfying the reasonable requirements of the public.[108] Again, the difficulty of enforcing a particular right may be such that it is better to tax infringers rather than go through the futile and/or costly business of pursuing them through the courts: this strategy in effect establishes a compulsory licence, though it is designed to serve the interests of the right-owner as much as anyone else. A good example is the (currently stalled) proposal for a blank tape levy scheme, which would allow consumers to tape recordings for their own use without infringing copyright, while having to pay more for the blank tapes they purchase.[109]

104. See eg *Commonwealth v John Fairfax & Sons Ltd* (1980) 147 CLR 39; *Salinger v Random House Inc* (1987) 811 F 2d 90: see [8.28].
105. See [8.24]–[8.31].
106. See [2.13].
107. See [7.19]–[7.20].
108. See [13.19]–[13.20]. The same applies to designs (see [10.23]) and plant varieties (see [15.23]). Cf the refusal of the common law to permit revelation of confidential information on the ground that the public would benefit from its availability: see [4.19]
109. See [6.41]–[6.42].

(d) A General Principle?

[1.32] Filling in the gaps. A dominant theme in the discussion so far has been the emphasis on the disunity of intellectual property. The subject, as stated a number of times already, is comprised of various regimes, each of which deal in different ways with different subject matter. The question arises as to whether it is possible, despite the distinct origins of the systems, to develop some sort of unifying principle to underpin the protection of creative effort. Suggestions have included a notion of 'misappropriation of intangible business values'[110] or of 'unfair copying'.[111] Such a principle could perform two functions. The first and less ambitious function could simply be to fill in gaps left by the existing regimes, catching situations in which there has been an unjustified appropriation of the fruit of a person's creative or commercial effort, yet no established intellectual property right has been infringed. The second and more far-reaching function would not merely be to supplement the individual regimes, but to consolidate and replace at least some of them. A broad principle would, it has been suggested, remove the need for 'hybrid' or 'deviant' protective regimes.[112] These are laws which themselves attempt, albeit in an ad hoc and unsystematic way, to plug gaps between the established systems (or 'paradigms') of copyright and patents in response to the 'jostling queue of claimants to new intellectual property, who assert that their investment in what they produce is large enough to justify legal protection against corner-cutting imitators'.[113] Examples from the last two decades include the *sui generis* statutes dealing with circuit layouts and plant varieties, as well as the cramming of computer software into the copyright regime. Rather than continue to respond in a piecemeal way, so the argument goes, why not simply adopt a general scheme which 'does not focus on the specific objects of protection but rather at the methods of acquiring the information or making the copy that, if permitted, would result in disincentives to create or innovate'.[114] As we have already seen, the impetus for an approach of this sort has received a recent boost with the ALRC's call for an investigation into the adoption of a broad anti-copying right, in order to address concerns that incremental or minor innovations are receiving inadequate protection.[115]

---

110. S Ricketson, '"Reaping Without Sowing": Unfair Competition and Intellectual Property Rights in Anglo-Australian Law' (1984) 7 *UNSWLJ* 1. Cf M Spence, 'Passing Off and the Misappropriation of Valuable Intangibles' (1996) 112 *LQR* 472.
111. See eg C Fellner, *The Future of Legal Protection for Industrial Design*, 1985, pp 199–201; J Lahore, 'Intellectual Property Rights and Unfair Copying: Old Concepts, New Ideas' [1992] 12 *EIPR* 428.
112. See J H Reichman, 'Legal Hybrids Between the Patents and Copyright Paradigms' (1994) 94 *Columbia LR* 2432.
113. W R Cornish, 'The International Relations of Intellectual Property' [1993] *CLJ* 46 at 54.
114. J Lahore, 'Designs and Petty Patents: A Broader Reform Issue' (1996) 7 *AIPJ* 7 at 17, citing D S Karjala, 'Misappropriation as a Third Intellectual Paradigm' (1994) 94 *Columbia LR* 2594. Cf the infringement test proposed in M Pendleton, 'Intellectual Property, Information-Based Society and a New International Economic Order — The Policy Options?' [1985] 2 *EIPR* 31, which is grounded in the notion of taking 'unjust or unacceptable short-cuts'.
115. See [1.15].

[1.33]   The Victoria Park Racing case. There seems little doubt that if
such a right is to be introduced, it will need to be done on a statutory basis.
On the surface at least, the courts in this country have resoundingly
rejected any attempt to generate a common law principle of misappropriation of effort or unfair copying. In *Victoria Park Racing and Recreation
Grounds Co Ltd v Taylor,*[116] the plaintiff company ran the Victoria Park
Racecourse, and objected to the defendants broadcasting information as to
starters, scratchings and winners of races, accompanied by a 'particularly
vivid' commentary provided by another defendant, Angles. Mr Angles
acquired this information by standing on a tower built on land near the
racecourse, thus being able to see into the ground and read the notice-
boards. The majority of the High Court confirmed the dismissal of the
action as disclosing no wrong known to the law. Dixon J pointed out that
the law does not necessarily protect any form of effort, enterprise, organisation and labour which may result in something of value for which others
are prepared to pay (here, the establishment and equipping of a racecourse and doing all that is necessary to conduct race meetings). Rather,
the protection of the law is offered 'because the intangible or incorporeal
right [claimed] falls within a recognised category to which legal or
equitable protection attaches'.[117] This much was

> sufficiently evidenced by the history of the law of copyright and by the fact
> that the exclusive right to invention, trademarks, designs, trade name and
> reputation are dealt with in English law as special heads of protected
> interests and not under a wide generalisation.[118]

Almost 50 years later this view was effectively reconfirmed by the High
Court in *Moorgate Tobacco Co Ltd v Philip Morris Ltd (No 2),*[119] when it
rejected the argument that a tort of 'unfair competition' should be recognised. The implications of this decision, which has attracted a certain
amount of criticism, are considered later in the book.[120] For now it suffices
to say that much of the criticism is misplaced. On closer examination, it is
often difficult to discern a compelling public interest in outlawing conduct
which presently falls outside the existing regimes. How was society harmed,
for instance, by the inability of the plaintiff in *Victoria Park Racing* to prevent its meetings being broadcast?

[1.34]   Has the law gone too far? If anything the problem is the
reverse one of preventing the courts going too far in their enthusiasm to
remedy what they perceive to be blatant instances of misappropriation of a
person's effort and investment. The judicial tendency to stretch the existing systems, or at least to prefer a broader interpretation over a narrower
one, has been apparent at times in relation to the use of copyright to
preclude product simulation.[121] It can also be seen in the law of
confidentiality, which has gradually been extended to confer proprietary
control over information;[122] and in certain aspects of the law of passing off

---

116. (1937) 58 CLR 479.
117. Ibid at 509.
118. Ibid.
119. (1984) 156 CLR 414.
120. See [16.20] ff.
121. See [8.7].
122. See [3.17].

and its statutory equivalents, particularly where the practice of character merchandising is concerned.[123] More generally, concern has been expressed that the current policy mix is entirely wrong and that more protection is given than is warranted by the need to encourage innovation. As one writer has argued:

> Instead of encouraging beneficial innovation ... the effect of the intellectual property laws may be more to aid in the concentration of wealth and raise profits. The firms that benefit can then use their increased power to further prevent competition from outside innovators and thus increase their control over the direction of innovation as a whole.[124]

On this view, the conferral of extensive property rights merely entrenches the position of those who would be dominant anyway by providing further barriers to entry into the relevant market. If this is right, it might be possible to reduce intellectual property rights and yet achieve a more open market in ideas by encouraging smaller players. The task that these players face is already a formidable one, for as Arup points out:[125]

> [P]olicy analysis suggests that successful innovation depends not only upon the appropriation of particular inventions but also, and maybe more importantly, upon the command of less discrete and transferable assets such as technological know-how, processing know-how, individual and institutional cumulative learning, and the control over complementary assets such as factors of production and marketing networks, and organisational ability generally.

Accordingly reform of the intellectual property regimes would merely diminish the substantial advantage already enjoyed by some in the race to capture the benefits of innovation.

[1.35] A recipe for uncertainty? Returning to the suggestion that a broad principle of misappropriation or unfair copying be adopted, the biggest problem is in seeing how such a system could ever be implemented on a cost-efficient basis. The uncertainty that would be generated by having an adjudicator weigh every claim against some necessarily nebulous standard of impermissible conduct (or even 'market failure'), not to mention the unlikelihood of consensus emerging on the ideal policy mix, weighs heavily against abandoning the current regimes. These regimes at least offer a measure of predictability in so far as ascertaining the existence of rights is concerned, particularly where registration is required. Of course this last advantage can be overstated, for in each of the registration systems it is common to find doubtful applications being accepted by the authorities on the basis that any controversy over their validity will be resolved in court. The delays and expense occasioned by such challenges can reduce litigation to a game of bluff and encourage an environment in which rights may be obtained, asserted or denied merely in order to secure a settlement in which the right-owner or the challenger is bought off.[126] It is also true, as

123. See [16.26]–[16.29].
124. M Goldhaber, *Reinventing Technology*, 1986, ch 10, quoted in D Vaver, 'Intellectual Property Today: Of Myths and Paradoxes' (1990) 69 *Can Bar Rev* 98 at 116.
125. 'Innovation, Policy Strategies and Law' (1990) 12 *Law and Policy* 247 at 251, citing K Pavitt, 'Sectoral Patterns of Technical Change: Towards a Taxonomy and a Theory' (1984) 13 *Research Policy* 311.
126. This is particularly true where patents are concerned: see [14.9]–[14.10].

Pendleton points out,[127] that many cases under the existing regimes may be decided, consciously or otherwise, by the judge's perceptions as to whether the defendant has been attempting to 'cash in' on the plaintiff's skill and effort — the very question that a general principle of misappropriation or unfair copying might seek to have answered overtly. Nevertheless there does not seem to be an overwhelming case for the practicability of a broad principle of liability. No doubt the present laws could be usefully improved in many respects, but they ought, and indeed are most likely, to be retained in something close to their current form.

(e) International Dimensions

[1.36] General. International cooperation and coordination came relatively early to intellectual property. It was driven primarily by the obvious advantages in countries securing reciprocal protection for the efforts of their own nationals. A spate of bilateral treaties in the middle of the nineteenth century ultimately led to two major multilateral agreements, the Paris Convention for the Protection of Industrial Property in 1883 and the Berne Convention for the Protection of Literary and Artistic Works in 1886. Today there are numerous conventions and treaties, which are discussed in detail in Chapter 21, along with organisations such as WIPO which are central to their formulation and/or administration. Although reciprocal treatment is still a major theme of these arrangements, other policies too may be identified. One, for instance, is to facilitate the administrative steps needed to secure protection in a range of countries, by ensuring that applications made to an international office will be recognised by participating countries as fulfilling procedural obligations demanded by their domestic systems.

[1.37] Harmonisation of laws: the TRIPS Agreement. Another more ambitious aim is to promote greater uniformity in the content of local laws. Although a perennial objective of WIPO and other agencies, the significance attached to harmonisation of intellectual property regimes has been heightened in recent years by a number of factors. The trend towards global markets and the ever-increasing clout wielded by multi-national enterprises have placed pressure on countries to free up their trading laws by treating domestic and foreign producers equally. To some extent this objective can be and has been pursued by the multi-nationals themselves. Their capacity to choose where to invest is a powerful weapon, particularly where their annual turnover dwarfs the gross domestic product of the countries they are targeting. This is a major source of concern for developing countries in particular, whose difficulties in meeting international standards and yet furthering their own priorities in terms of economic and social progress have been the cause of great tension within the various international forums. It is also common to find a large country going into bat for its own producers where they are world leaders in a particular field. This may translate into a demand that local laws not merely treat foreign nationals equally, but provide protection equivalent to that which the demanding country has instituted: the US strategy over semiconductor chips being a

127. M Pendleton, 'Character Merchandising and the Proper Scope of Intellectual Property' (1990) 1 *IPJ* 242 at 254.

classic example.[128] US trade policy has indeed been very effectively employed, at both bilateral and multilateral levels, to address the problem of what are perceived to be 'impenetrable market barriers' around the world.[129]

A new measure of international agreement has been achieved with the conclusion in late 1993 of the Uruquay Round on multilateral trade negotiations. The World Trade Organisation (WTO) was formed to replace the General Agreement on Trade and Tariffs (GATT) as the body responsible for administering international trade. One hundred and thirty nations are presently WTO members, with more still in the process of applying. Countries wishing to join the WTO and gain the market access thus provided must accept a number of agreements, including the Trade Related Aspects of Intellectual Property Rights Agreement. The TRIPS Agreement, as it is known, sets out minimum standards not only for the protection of intellectual property, but also — something which WIPO has been unable to provide — effective enforcement procedures.[130] Together with continuing US pressure, TRIPS is likely to have a major impact over the next few years in standardising intellectual property regimes around the world. While this impact is likely to be greatest in the developing world (including, for this purpose, the former socialist economies in eastern Europe as well as many of our neighbours in the Asia-Pacific region),[131] more 'advanced' nations such as Australia are also feeling its effect. Australia is a signatory to the Agreement and as such has been compelled to make a number of legislative changes in order to comply with its obligations. The most significant of these changes involved the trade mark system, with a new statute (the Trade Marks Act 1994) being rushed through parliament in order to ensure compliance with TRIPS — only to be replaced before its proclamation by the Trade Marks Act 1995, which is now in force.[132] Changes were also made to the copyright and patents regimes,[133] with perhaps the most significant amendment being the lengthening of the standard patent term from 16 years to 20 years.[134] With further instruments on the agenda for international discussion, and Australia committed to play a part in the process of modernisation and harmonisation of intellectual property laws around the world, we can expect further changes to our domestic regimes over the next few years.

[1.38] The global information economy. One area in which that is especially likely to occur is in relation to digital technology. The distribution of information by means of such technology is revolutionising conditions of international trade and bringing into sharp focus the requirements of protection of intellectual property in a world with no physical

---

128. See [9.26].
129. P C B Liu, 'US Industry's Influence on Intellectual Property Negotiations and Special 301 Actions' (1994) 13 *Pacific Basin LJ* 87 at 92; and see further [21.11].
130. See M Getlan, 'TRIPS and the Future of Section 301: A Comparative Study in Trade Dispute Revolution' (1995) 34 *Columbia J of Transnational Law* 175.
131. See eg M Blakeney, 'The Impact of the TRIPS Agreement in the Asia Pacific Region' [1996] 10 *EIPR* 544.
132. See Chapters 19–20.
133. See Copyright (World Trade Organization Amendments) Act 1994; Patents (World Trade Organization Amendments) Act 1994.
134. See [11.27].

boundaries. National differences in copyright protection are tolerable where physical objects embody the intellectual property. But a film (or other material) loaded onto the Internet will, in the absence of a technical barrier, be available instantly and in full all over the world. Development and regulation of the digital world has become the focus of technically advanced nations. In the US a task force was set up in 1993 to implement the National Information Infrastructure (NII), 'a seamless web of communications networks, computers, databases, and consumer electronics that will put vast amounts of information at users' fingertips'.[135] In 1995 the Clinton administration's National Information Infrastructure Task Force Working Group on Intellectual Property Rights issued a White Paper,[136] setting out its vision for protection of content for material disseminated in digital interactive services such as the Internet. Some of the challenges of digital technology in relation to copyright have been addressed in Australia by the Copyright Convergence Group (CCG), whose proposals for copyright law reform are discussed at various points in Chapters 5–9.

The US White Paper is intended to be a model for the Global Information Infrastructure (GII), the development of which was accelerated by the WIPO Diplomatic Conference on Copyright concluding in Geneva in December 1996. The Conference updated two international treaties on the protection of copyright (the Berne Convention) and the protection of performers and phonogram producers (the Rome Convention).[137] As already discussed, the specific aim of the updating exercise is to address the 'digital agenda' and establish the international legal basis to provide intellectual property protection for new technological applications. International trade in information society services will be shaped by the treaty amendments, which are still to be ratified by a number of participating nations.[138]

6.   SCHEME OF THIS BOOK

[1.39]   An organising principle: the protection and exploitation of ideas. It should already be apparent that the nature of the subject makes it difficult to justify structuring the treatment of the various intellectual property regimes in any particular way. Given the historical development of those regimes and the relatively recent acceptance as to their common ground, it could hardly be otherwise. Most books choose to start either with patents or copyright, depending on which of these two core systems is thought to be more important or instructive. In this book, however, we have elected to follow a different scheme, one which has at least some underlying logic. We cannot claim that this is the only way to proceed, or even that it is particularly original,[139] but it appeals to us nevertheless.

---

135. L A Kurtz, 'Copyright and the National Information Infrastructure in the United States' [1996] 3 *EIPR* 120 at 120, quoting the *National Information Infrastructure: Agenda for Action, Executive Summary*, 15 September 1993.
136. See [9.4].
137. See Chapter 21.
138. See [1.19].
139. The scheme was in fact suggested to us by Simon Palk, to whom we repeat the gratitude expressed in the Preface to the First Edition.

Broadly speaking, the scheme involves following the steps that may be taken to protect and/or exploit an idea. At its inception, an idea is simply a piece of information or knowledge, whose only claim to protection lies in the fact that it has not been put in the public domain. Following an overview of enforcement issues in Chapter 2, therefore, Part II of the book looks at how notions of confidentiality are used to protect the secrecy of information. The next step, in all likelihood, is that the idea will be written down or recorded in some way. This takes us into the realm of copyright, which is explored in Part III along with the system for registering designs and the specific issues raised by computer technology. If the idea is inventive, a patent may result: hence Part IV, which includes a chapter devoted to the questions thrown up by biotechnology, as well as the plant varieties legislation. In any event, the result of any successful exploitation of an idea may be that a distinctive commercial reputation is built up. The common law and statutory mechanisms for protecting such a reputation against misappropriation are the subject of Part V. Finally, Part VI looks at two topics which are relevant to each of the individual regimes: the international dimensions of intellectual property law, and the commercial strategies and transactions employed to exploit the various property rights.

Chapter 2

Enforcement of Rights

1. INTRODUCTION

[2.1] **Litigation and other strategies.** This chapter is devoted to some general observations concerning the steps that may be taken to enforce intellectual property rights. The principal focus is on civil litigation, though in some cases criminal offences may also be involved. Naturally, taking a matter to a civil court is likely to prove a costly and perhaps risky business. Evidence of infringement or of participation in infringing activities may be hard to come by. The defendant may have the resources to drag the matter out through several hearings and appeals, particularly by challenging the validity of the right which the plaintiff claims to possess, in the hope that the plaintiff's resolve and/or bank balance will weaken. Patent litigation in particular tends to be a lengthy and expensive exercise.[1]

Against that background, it is important to be aware that strategies other than litigation may be available for the protection of rights. One approach is for individual owners to put their claims in the hands of a collecting society, or indeed any other body or enterprise with the resources to secure payments from licensees or mount effective action against infringers. Another relates to the contractual arrangements pursuant to which intellectual property is created or exploited. By carefully structuring those arrangements, an owner may retain close supervision over the activities of potential infringers or place the responsibility for pursuing infringements on someone else.[2]

[2.2] **Threats and unjustified actions.** At the end of the day though, the owner may find it unavoidable to investigate the possibility of litigation.[3] The aim will ordinarily be to have the claim acknowledged or settled

---

1. See [14.9].
2. See Chapter 22.
3. Note that the limitation period for the institution of intellectual property proceedings is generally six years: see eg Copyright Act 1968 s 134.

35

without reaching court, and indeed, in many instances, it may simply be enough to rattle the sabre to induce the other party to back down. However, great care needs to be taken. Initiation of a patently unfounded action may conceivably attract tortious liability for abuse of process,[4] and malicious allegations of infringement may constitute injurious falsehood or unlawful interference with the targeted person's business.[5] Even innocent but incorrect assertions that infringement has occurred may constitute misleading or deceptive conduct under trade practices or fair trading legislation.[6] Most importantly, the copyright, patents, trade marks, designs and circuit layouts statutes each provide that any threat to institute infringement proceedings is unlawful, even if it is honestly believed that infringement is taking place.[7] Liability can only be escaped under these provisions by actually establishing infringement (or, where a trade mark is concerned, by instituting proceedings with due diligence); though in each case it is not considered to be a threat merely to inform someone that the relevant right exists.

[2.3] Reform of enforcement procedures. In 1992 the Industrial Property Advisory Committee (IPAC) released a report examining ways in which enforcement procedures could be made more effective and costs reduced.[8] Aside from considering jurisdictional issues, in particular whether a specialist court should be established to deal with intellectual property disputes,[9] the report made a range of proposals on evidentiary and procedural matters. These included greater flexibility in the application of the rules of evidence; greater use of witness statements; the facilitation of expert advice from bodies such as the Patents Office on matters of fact or opinion before the court; use of costs 'penalties' for parties guilty of unreasonably delaying the resolution of disputes; the award of indemnity costs in cases involving a substantial 'public interest'; and the extension of the power to award additional or exemplary damages against 'flagrant' infringers, currently found only (at least explicitly) in the Copyright Act.[10] At a more general level, IPAC recommended both that courts take a more 'managerial' or 'interventionist' approach to the resolution of disputes, and that greater reliance be placed on the settlement of disputes by 'alternative' processes such as mediation. The report in this respect mirrors developments that have been occurring in any event over the past decade in the administration of civil disputes generally.[11]

---

4. See eg *Speed Seal Products Ltd v Paddington* [1986] 1 All ER 91; and see generally *Williams v Spautz* (1992) 174 CLR 509.
5. See eg *Jaybeam Ltd v Abru Aluminium Ltd* [1975] FSR 334. The tort of unlawful interference is discussed below; as to injurious falsehood, see further [16.3].
6. See eg *Wanem Pty Ltd v Tekiela* (1990) 19 IPR 435, where a solicitor's letter making such an assertion on behalf of a commercial client was held to be conduct 'in trade or commerce' (see [16.32]) for the purposes of s 52 of the Trade Practices Act 1974 (Cth).
7. See Copyright Act 1968 s 202 (see [8.37]); Patents Act 1990 ss 128–132 (see [14.12]); Trade Marks Act 1995 s 129 (see [20.10]); Designs Act 1906 ss 32C–32G; Circuit Layouts Act 1989 s 46.
8. *Practice and Procedures for Enforcement of Industrial Property Rights in Australia,* 1992.
9. See [2.18].
10. See [2.15].
11. See B C Cairns, *Australian Civil Procedure,* 4th ed, 1996, ch 2; H Astor and C Chinkin, *Dispute Resolution in Australia,* 1992.

There has been no systematic response from the federal government to the IPAC report, many of whose suggestions can also be found in similar or modified terms in subsequent reports by the Australian Law Reform Commission (ALRC) on the designs system and the Advisory Council on Industrial Property (ACIP) on the petty patent regime.[12] However, following a recommendation in the latter report that a way be found to invest a lower-level tribunal with the power to enforce the new 'innovation patents', the Minister for Science and Technology has now announced that the whole issue of the enforcement of 'industrial property' rights (that is, those regimes falling within the minister's remit)[13] is being referred to ACIP for its consideration, ahead of a 'proposed major review of intellectual property scheduled for 1998–99'.[14] It is unclear why a further review was considered necessary at all, given the wealth of material and recommendations contained in the three reports mentioned.

2. ESTABLISHING CIVIL LIABILITY

[2.4] Standing. The first issue to be considered in relation to civil proceedings alleging the infringement of an intellectual property right is the issue of standing to sue. Leaving aside the common law doctrines, which have developed their own rules,[15] the trade practices and fair trading statutes, which have no standing restrictions at all,[16] and the performers' rights scheme, which allows only the performer to take action,[17] a few comments may be made as to the other regimes. The obvious plaintiff is of course the person designated by the relevant statute at the time of the alleged infringement as the owner of the right in question.[18] This is not necessarily the person to whom that right first belonged, since the current owner may have acquired that status as a result of one or more assignments.[19]

In some instances the right to pursue an infringement may be given to a person other than the owner. While the designs and plant breeder's rights legislation make no provision to this effect, the copyright, circuit layouts, patent and trade mark systems each confer this privilege on some at least of those to whom the relevant right has been licensed. The rationale is that in certain instances it may be the licensee who is most actively exploiting the right and who therefore should be able to take action to protect their investment, even where the owner is unwilling or unable to do so. Although

---

12. See *Designs*, ch 13 (see [10.22]); ACIP, *Review of the Petty Patent System*, 1995, pp 52–60.
13. See [1.10].
14. 'Introduction of the Innovation Patent: The Government Response to the Recommendations of the Advisory Council on Intellectual Property (ACIP) Report *Review of the Patty Patent System*', February 1997.
15. See [4.1]–[4.2] (breach of confidence), [16.8] (passing off).
16. See [16.34], [16.41].
17. See [6.22]. These rights cannot even be assigned: Copyright Act 1968 s 248N.
18. See [1.29]. Note that a person holding an equitable interest in the right, for example under a trust or pursuant to a contract, may seek interlocutory relief, but thereafter must either join the legal owner or take an assignment: *Performing Right Society Ltd v London Theatre of Varieties Ltd* [1924] AC 1.
19. See further [22.5] ff. There is generally no obstacle to the assignment of intellectual property rights, provided the parties observe the requisite formalities (usually that the assignment be in writing and, in the case of registration systems, that the change in ownership be officially notified).

the provisions differ between the four regimes, a common thread is that, other than at an interlocutory stage, the owner must always be joined as a party to the proceedings, if necessary as a defendant; although an owner who is added as a defendant but takes no part in the proceedings will not be liable for costs. The patents legislation is the most restrictive in regard to the right to sue, conferring it only upon the patentee or an 'exclusive licensee'. The latter is narrowly defined as a person who is given the sole right to exploit the invention, even to the exclusion of the patentee.[20] By contrast, the same term is used in the copyright and circuit layouts statutes to mean someone who is given the exclusive right to do any act falling within the relevant right.[21] Since copyright and eligible layout rights are divisible by reference to time, area and type of exploitation,[22] this means that there may be a number of exclusive licences granted by the one copyright owner. Each exclusive licensee may sue to protect their particular interest, although no action may be maintained against the owner (or indeed other licensees) and the owner retains a right to seek relief,[23] though in that instance it is the licensee who must be joined. Provision is specifically made as to how damages are to be assessed or profits apportioned where such concurrent rights exist.[24] Finally, under the trade marks system an 'authorised user' of a mark (that is, a person with permission to use the mark, subject to a certain level of control by the owner) may call on the proprietor to institute infringement proceedings and, if this is not done within two months, do so personally.[25]

Another possibility is that one of the 'economic torts', discussed below, may be pressed into service. These may allow a person or body to take action where the deliberate result of the infringement of an intellectual property right is that economic loss is inflicted upon them, even if they are not the owner or a statute-designated plaintiff.[26]

[2.5]   Infringement and the relevance of intention. What constitutes infringement of an intellectual property right obviously depends on how that right is defined. In the case of the statutory regimes, infringement occurs when a person, acting without consent or authority, does any of the acts in relation to the relevant subject matter which are exclusively reserved to the owner to do or to sanction. Similarly, common law rights are infringed when a person commits a wrong, as defined by the relevant doctrine.

For the most part liability is strict, in that a person committing an infringement may be held responsible whether or not they were aware of the existence of the right or that their conduct was unlawful. But while innocence is generally no defence, there are a number of exceptions. In the first place, the copyright system and some of those regimes related to it distinguish between 'direct' and 'indirect' forms of infringement, strict lia-

---

20.   See [13.16], [14.9].
21.   See [7.12], [9.25].
22.   See eg in relation to copyright [5.9], [7.8].
23.   Except, under the Copyright Act 1968, in the case of an action under s 116 in respect of infringing copies (see [8.34]): here only the exclusive licensee may sue (s 119(b),(c)).
24.   Copyright Act 1968 ss 122–124; Circuit Layouts Act 1989 ss 33–35.
25.   See [20.15].
26.   See eg *Carlin Music Corp v Collins* [1979] FSR 548.

bility only being imposed in the former category. In the case of copyright, indirect infringement principally encompasses commercial dealings (importation, sale, etc) with articles whose production involves a direct infringement of copyright, but also allowing a place of public entertainment to be used for an infringing public performance of a copyright work. In each instance, liability for such indirect infringement hinges on some knowledge of wrongdoing being established.[27] Similarly, infringement of performers' rights falls into two categories: recording, broadcasting or transmitting a performance without authorisation, whether with or without any knowledge of that lack of authorisation; or various other acts, including possessing, copying, selling or importing an unauthorised recording, where it is necessary to establish such knowledge.[28] In the same vein, a person is only liable for the commercial exploitation of integrated circuit layouts in which rights have been conferred by the Circuit Layouts Act 1989 if they were aware or should have been aware that the owner had not authorised the conduct in question.[29]

Another exception is provided by the doctrine of breach of confidence. A person who has come under an obligation of confidence does appear to be strictly liable for any use or disclosure of that information, even if they are completely unaware that they are acting unlawfully (as with subconscious plagiarism of another's secret idea).[30] On the other hand, that obligation will not generally arise in the first place unless the recipient of the information is under some sort of notice that it is confidential: thus the very creation of the right requires some element of actual or constructive knowledge.[31] Again, under the trade marks system some consideration is given to the person who innocently uses a mark which is substantially identical or deceptively similar to a registered mark. Where the former mark is used in good faith, various defences may be available to a charge of infringement, as where for example the mark in question consists of the defendant's own name or place of business, or describes the character or quality of their goods or services.[32] Finally and perhaps most significantly, the innocence of a defendant is often a ground for pecuniary relief being refused to the plaintiff, whether in the court's discretion or as a specific consequence of legislative provision to that effect. This is considered further below.

[2.6] Finding the right defendant. It often happens that the person most directly and obviously responsible for an infringement is not the ideal defendant. It may be difficult and/or expensive to find them, as with individuals who tape broadcasts at home or copy friends' software. Even if they can be brought to book, they may not have the resources to meet any pecuniary judgment. In the case of a company, it may have gone out of business or remain beyond the practical reach of the courts within the jurisdiction. Alternatively, it may simply be a front for the activities of the individuals

27. See [8.1], [8.19]. Cf the position under the designs system, which imposes strict liability even in the case of indirect infringement: see [10.20].
28. Copyright Act 1968 s 248G: see further [6.22].
29. See [9.25].
30. See [4.12].
31. See [4.9]–[4.11], [4.14].
32. See [20.9].

who control it, or of a parent company, lacking the assets to make a suit worthwhile. In all these cases, the plaintiff may wish to sue someone else, either instead of or in addition to the principal infringer(s). In many instances these further defendants will themselves be infringers within the terms of the relevant statute or doctrine. It must not be overlooked that intellectual property rights are often infringed not just by those who originally copy or misuse the protected subject matter, but also by those who trade in the resulting products. Thus, as noted above, a copyright owner may sue not only copiers, but those who 'indirectly infringe' by selling or importing reproductions of the work or products in which such a reproduction is contained. Similarly, a patentee may sue anyone who sells a product made by someone else using the patentee's process;[33] and someone who confides secret information to another may proceed against any third party who acquires the information as a result of the confidant's breach of faith and seeks to make use of it.[34] Moreover there is also the concept of joint tortfeasance or joint infringement to consider, whereby those who act together may be jointly and severally liable for their wrong. Joint infringers are those 'who act in concert with one another pursuant to a common design in the infringement',[35] such as the author and publisher of a manuscript which infringes another's copyright.[36] However, the concept of joint infringement only catches 'participation, rather than mere facilitation';[37] hence it is uncertain whether the supplier of a product is to be regarded as jointly liable with a person who uses that product in such a way as to infringe a patented process.[38]

[2.7] Ancillary forms of liability. Sometimes, however, the person whom the plaintiff wishes to sue has not personally infringed the plaintiff's rights, yet nevertheless is in some way to be held responsible for the actions of the infringer(s). An employer, for example, will be vicariously liable for any wrongs committed by employees in the course of their duties, though not for the acts of independent contractors.[39] This may be the case even though the conduct in question is for the employee's personal benefit rather than their employer's.[40] While vicarious liability may be escaped by clearly notifying workers that they are not to engage in or continue conduct which infringes an intellectual property right, such an instruction must be properly policed or the employer risks being found to be condoning the infringement.[41] Conversely, employees who commit infringing acts cannot claim any 'vicarious immunity' from liability for their actions, although if they have acted innocently and within the terms of their employment they may be entitled to claim an indemnity from their employer in the unlikely event that they are indeed sued.[42]

---

33. See [14.2]. Cf the position with trade marks: see [20.4].
34. See [4.14].
35. *CBS Songs Ltd v Amstrad Consumer Electronics plc* (1988) 11 IPR 1 at 13.
36. See eg *Ravenscroft v Herbert* [1980] RPC 193.
37. *BEST Australia Ltd v Aquagas Marketing Pty Ltd* (1988) 12 IPR 143 at 147.
38. See [14.4].
39. See generally J J Macken, G J McCarry and C Sappideen, *Law of Employment*, 3rd ed, 1990, ch 11; J G Fleming, *Law of Torts*, 8th ed, 1992, ch 19.
40. See eg *Warne v Genex Corp Pty Ltd* (1996) 35 IPR 284; and cf *Coulthard v South Australia* (1995) 63 SASR 531.
41. Cf *Apple Computer Inc v Mackintosh Computers Ltd* (1987) 8 IPR 89.

A further range of possible defendants are those who have in some way facilitated or inspired the infringement. Company directors, for example, will be personally liable if they have 'procured' or 'directed' infringing conduct on the part of the company;[43] though not if they have played no role in the relevant decisions, even if their failure to investigate what was happening constitutes a breach of their duty to the company.[44] However, it is unclear whether, aside from the special case of directors, Australian law recognises any general principle of liability for inciting or procuring an infringement.[45] Even if it does, the House of Lords' decision in *CBS Songs Ltd v Amstrad Consumer Electronics plc*[46] indicates that to be wrongful the incitement must be of an identifiable infringement by a particular individual. In that case, Amstrad escaped liability for marketing twin-deck tape recorders which could obviously be used for home taping which would breach copyright, any 'incitement' being at most to the public at large.[47] Amstrad was also held not to have 'authorised' such breaches. Both the copyright and the circuit layouts statutes specifically confer on the owner the exclusive power to authorise those acts which the right comprises:[48] thus any purported authorisation of infringing conduct is itself an infringement. On a liberal view, 'authorisation' might include conduct whose inevitable or likely effect would be to result in infringements occurring, thus taking the concept beyond incitement to cover mere facilitation. However the rejection of this view in *Amstrad* and other cases suggests that authorisation, like the concept of inciting or procuring, adds little if anything to the notion of joint infringement.[49]

A further possibility is for a plaintiff to rely on one of the 'economic torts', a series of wrongs hinging on the intentional infliction of economic loss.[50] These torts include *contractual interference*, the interference with contractual relations by a direct approach to one of the parties or by the use of an independently unlawful act to hinder or prevent performance;[51] *conspir-*

---

42. See J J Macken, G J McCarry and C Sappideen, *Law of Employment*, 3rd ed, 1990, pp 120, 334–40 and cases there cited. Note that an employee who is incidentally involved in a firm's unlawful conduct does not commit an infringement at all provided 'the conduct is not manifestly unlawful and the employee believes it to be lawful and acts in a purely ministerial capacity rather than exercise any independent judgment': ibid p 337.
43. See eg *Kalamazoo (Aust) Pty Ltd v Compact Business Systems Pty Ltd* (1985) 5 IPR 213; *Martin Engineering Co v Nicaro Holdings Pty Ltd* (1990) 20 IPR 241.
44. *King v Milpurrurru* (1996) 34 IPR 11. Cf *APRA Ltd v Jain* (1990) 18 IPR 663, where a director was held to be liable for 'authorising' a copyright infringement (see below) by allowing a situation to develop and continue where he must have known infringement was likely.
45. See *Walker v Alemite Corp* (1933) 49 CLR 643 at 658; *Firth Industries Ltd v Polyglas Engineering Pty Ltd* (1975) 132 CLR 489 at 497; *CCOM Pty Ltd v Jiejing Pty Ltd* (1993) 27 IPR 577 at 627.
46. (1988) 11 IPR 1.
47. The House also rejected an argument that Amstrad was liable in the tort of negligence, denying that it was under any duty of care to prevent or discourage consumers from using the recorders to breach copyright. See also *Paterson Zochonis Ltd v Merfarken Packaging Ltd* [1983] FSR 273.
48. Copyright Act 1968 ss 36(1), 101(1); Circuit Layouts Act 1989 s 9.
49. See [8.16]–[8.18].
50. See generally *Clerk & Lindsell on Torts*, 17th ed, 1995, ch 23.
51. See *Woolley v Dunford* (1972) 3 SASR 243 at 266–8.

acy to injure, the combination of two or more to inflict economic harm, the predominant motive being to injure the plaintiff rather than further the conspirators' own economic interests (something that is rarely established);[52] *conspiracy by illegal means,* the combination of two or more to inflict loss by reason of an unlawful act;[53] *intimidation,* the infliction of loss through the threat of an unlawful act;[54] and *unlawful interference,* a 'genus' tort amalgamating many of the other actions into the general principle that it is tortious to inflict economic loss deliberately by committing an unlawful act.[55] It is unclear just how practically relevant these torts are in the intellectual property field, even in relation to breach of confidence where they offer a means of securing tort damages for what is otherwise an equitable or contractual wrong.[56] However there are three ways in which they might conceivably be used to establish liability which would not otherwise amount to infringement under the individual regimes. In the first place, a person obstructing the performance of a contract to exploit an intellectual property right (for instance a licence agreement) may be liable in the tort of contractual interference. Second, and more controversially, it may be unlawful to 'interfere' with the exercise of an intellectual property right, whether or not an infringement is incited. Other than where it is a term of a contract to respect the right in question, this would have to depend on the embryo tort of 'interference with rights'.[57] Third, the tort of intimidation may come into play where the infringement of a right is threatened but not ultimately effected.

3. REMEDIES IN CIVIL CASES

[2.8] General. We move now to look at the civil remedies that may be obtained in infringement proceedings. In some instances there are principles or practices which are peculiar to particular regimes; these are addressed in the appropriate part of the text later in the chapter. Nevertheless there is much common ground where the remedies of injunction, damages and account of profits are concerned and the role that these play in intellectual property litigation is discussed below. Before getting on to them, however, something needs to be said about pre-trial orders. While we make no attempt here to deal with the many procedural and evidentiary issues that arise in intellectual property proceedings,[58] it would be absurd not to comment upon two particular forms of pre-trial relief, the Anton Piller order and the interlocutory injunction. The former has become a potent, if controversial, weapon in the fight against commercial piracy,

---

52. See *McKernan v Fraser* (1931) 46 CLR 343; *Dominion Rent A Car Ltd v Budget Rent A Car System (1970) Ltd* (1987) 9 IPR 367.
53. Note that, unlike the tort of conspiracy to injure, the defendants cannot escape liability by being predominantly motivated by self-interest: *Williams v Hursey* (1959) 103 CLR 30; *Lonrho plc v Fayed* [1992] 1 AC 448.
54. See *Rookes v Barnard* [1964] AC 1129; *Latham v Singleton* [1981] 2 NSWLR 843.
55. See *Ansett Industries (Operations) Pty Ltd v Australian Federation of Air Pilots* (1989) 95 ALR 211; *Lonrho plc v Fayed* [1992] 1 AC 448.
56. See [4.16], [4.29].
57. See *Associated British Ports v Transport and General Workers Union* [1989] 1 WLR 939 at 952, 959, 963–4.
58. See generally M I Aronson and J B Hunter, *Litigation: Evidence and Procedure,* 5th ed, 1995.

while the latter's practical importance is merely underlined by the number of cases which start and finish at the interlocutory stage.

[2.9]   Anton Piller orders.[59] It is not always easy to secure evidence to support an action for infringement. Use may of course be made of the standard pre-trial procedures for discovery of documents,[60] and the copyright and trade mark statutes also provide a special procedure whereby customs authorities may be asked to seize infringing goods which are being unlawfully imported.[61] In many instances though, particularly where 'pirate' or 'bootleg' operations are involved, it may be difficult in court to substantiate the connection between the defendant and the illicit copies of books, records, videos or other merchandise which are unquestionably reaching the market. Where the whole nature of a business operation is based on unlawful copying, it is obviously in the interests of those running it to dissemble when asked to respond to interrogatories or orders for discovery. It was to meet the needs of plaintiffs faced with this sort of problem that led the English Court of Appeal in *Anton Piller KC v Manufacturing Processes Ltd*[62] to sanction the form of order now known by the name of that case. Anton Piller orders, which are usually granted on the shortest of notice after an ex parte application, typically require a named person (who may be representative of a class of traders)[63] to permit the plaintiff to enter that person's premises to search for and seize infringing articles, or other evidence relevant to the plaintiff's claim. Such an order is often accompanied by a demand that the defendant reveal information about the documents or goods in question, for example relating to the identities of those engaged in dealings with the defendant. The inspection is usually made in the presence of the plaintiff's solicitor, who as an officer of the court will retain any material not returned to the defendant. Any refusal to allow the inspection is usually treated as a contempt of court. On the other hand, the defendant is entitled to resist any part of an order which would compel them to incriminate themselves by supplying information likely to be used against them in forthcoming criminal proceedings;[64] although this may be avoided by the order specifying that the information in question is not to be used for the purposes of any prosecution.[65]

While it must be conceded that such orders are often necessary if intellectual property and other rights are to be effectively protected,[66] the

---

59.   See generally Tilbury, pp 341–7; Spry, pp 547–53.
60.   See Cornish, pp 50–2.
61.   See [8.38], [20.10].
62.   [1976] Ch 55.
63.   See eg *EMI Ltd v Sarwar & Haidar* [1977] FSR 146; and see also *Tony Blain Pty Ltd v Jamison* (1993) 26 IPR 8.
64.   See *Rank Film Distributors Ltd v Video Information Centre* [1982] AC 380; and see generally S B McNicol, *Law of Privilege*, 1992, ch 3 on the privilege of self-incrimination and its various statutory modifications. Although in *Rank* this principle was said to be limited to cases in which prosecution for a serious offence was involved, that limitation was rejected in *Warman International v Envirotech Australia Pty Ltd* (1986) 6 IPR 578. However, note the narrow view also taken in the same case of the circumstances in which the disclosure of information pursuant to an Anton Piller order would ever pose a threat of self-incrimination.
65.   See eg *Busby v Thorn EMI Video Programmes Ltd* [1984] 1 NZLR 461; *Warman International v Envirotech Australia Pty Ltd* (1986) 6 IPR 578.

threat to civil liberties posed by so drastic a remedy being available ex parte is self-evident. Despite the regularity with which they are granted, there is quite understandably a measure of reluctance on the part of the courts to sanction what in practice look very like search warrants.[67] Accordingly, stringent requirements must be met:

> First, there must be an extremely strong prima facie case. Secondly, the damage, potential or actual, must be very serious for the applicant. Thirdly, there must be clear evidence that the defendants have in their possession incriminating documents or things, and that there is a real possibility that they may destroy such material before any application inter partes can be made.[68]

While this last element will usually be a matter of inference rather than hard fact, it may be particularly important to establish 'fraud or dishonesty or contumacy' on the part of the defendant, or that the defendant's business is 'transitory' in nature.[69] A further safeguard is that the plaintiff must give an undertaking as to damages. The defendant is also at liberty to apply for the order to be discharged, even after it has been executed. This will be done, for example, where it turns out that the plaintiff has acted fraudulently, or failed to disclose all relevant information at the time of obtaining the order.[70]

[2.10] Interlocutory injunctions.[71] As will appear presently, injunctive relief is the dominant form of redress in intellectual property cases. Given the delay typically occasioned between the commencement of proceedings and the action coming on for trial, a period often measured in years rather than months, it is inevitable that many plaintiffs will wish to obtain relief from the effect of the defendant's activities pending determination of the parties' dispute. Indeed the stakes are often high, for it is frequently the case that without such an order the plaintiff's own activities, which may be crucial to their financial security, will be irrevocably damaged. Conversely, the effect of a restraining order on the defendant may be to deny to them what ultimately turns out to be a legitimate course of conduct, again producing irrevocable damage. Moreover, what cannot be ignored is that when the court is asked to decide an application for interlocutory relief, that may be the last the court has to do with the matter. The result at this

---

66. A good example is furnished by the raid carried out by two computer software companies, Lotus and Word Perfect, on the offices of various subsidiaries of Mayne Nickless, the transport giant. The inspection apparently turned up evidence of widespread piracy of computer programs, something that is believed to be common practice in many businesses but is exceptionally difficult to establish. Mayne Nickless undertook not to copy the applicants' programs and the case proceeded to an assessment of damages: see J Porter, 'Mayne won't copy Computer Software' *Sydney Morning Herald*, 29 November 1990, p 27.

67. See eg *Gianitsios v Karagiannis* (1986) 7 IPR 36 at 39 where Young J, while granting the order requested, admitted: 'I have a tremendous sense of unease about this case and I feel that I may be being talked into something by [counsel's] expert advocacy that I will live to regret.' See also *Columbia Picture Industries Ltd v Robinson* [1987] Ch 38; *Universal Thermosensors Ltd v Hibben* [1992] 3 All ER 257; *JC Techforce Pty Ltd v Pearce* (1996) 35 IPR 196.

68. *Anton Piller KC v Manufacturing Processes Ltd* [1976] Ch 55 at 62. See also Federal Court of Australia Practice Note No 10, 8 April 1994.

69. *Busby v Thorn EMI Video Programmes Ltd* [1984] 1 NZLR 461 at 477.

70. See eg *Lock International plc v Beswick* [1989] 3 All ER 373; *Milcap Publishing Group AB v Coranto Corp Pty Ltd* (1995) 32 IPR 34.

71. See generally Tilbury, pp 308–26; Spry, pp 437–95.

stage is often so important in its practical effect that it decides the entire case. A successful plaintiff may have achieved everything they desire simply by putting a temporary stop to the defendant's conduct. The business that can prevent its competitor launching a similar product before it has itself had a good run at a market in which the smallest headstart is crucial, the overseas rock star who stops the sale of unauthorised merchandise (T-shirts, etc) during their Australian tour, the company that forestalls the leaking of sensitive information about a takeover it is in the process of mounting — all these plaintiffs may well decide that they have nothing further to gain from taking the matter to a full trial. The same may be true if they lose, although there is perhaps a greater chance that they will then go on to claim compensation. More often, the result at the interlocutory stage will be sufficient to induce the parties to settle, the winning party naturally having the edge in negotiating an appropriate outcome.

Against that background, it would only be natural for a court faced with an interlocutory application to want to hear as much argument as possible as to the merits of the case. By doing so, a court would be bound to feel more comfortable in making the weighty (and possibly final) decision as to whom to favour pending trial. However, the obvious consequence of such an approach would be to turn interlocutory applications into mini-trials, something the courts have quite properly been loath to do. Although proceedings are conducted inter partes,[72] in order to expedite matters evidence is typically presented in the form of affidavits and the opportunity for cross-examination and legal argument is deliberately cut short. Under those constraints, the opportunities for careful fact-finding and considered legal opinions must of necessity be curtailed. It simply has to be accepted that, other than in the clearest cases, the court must postpone to the trial (if it eventuates) a proper decision on the merits. If then the temptation to create a 'trial before the trial' is to be resisted, the problem remains of how to approach interlocutory applications in a way that accords due weight to the interests of both parties. Specifically, how strong a case must the plaintiff make out to have even a chance of obtaining relief? And in any event, how are the courts to balance the competing arguments for and against 'temporary' protection?

[2.11] The American Cyanamid approach. The answer to the first question is derived these days from the House of Lords' decision in *American Cyanamid Co v Ethicon Ltd.*[73] According to Lord Diplock:[74]

> The court no doubt must be satisfied that the claim is not frivolous or vexatious; in other words, that there is a serious question to be tried ... [U]nless the material available to the court at the hearing of the application for an interlocutory injunction fails to disclose that the plaintiff has any real prospect of succeeding in his [sic] claim for a permanent injunction at the trial, the court should go on to consider whether the balance of convenience lies in favour of granting or refusing the interlocutory relief that is sought.

This constituted a departure from the previously accepted approach, which required the court to determine whether the plaintiff had made out 'a prima facie case, in the sense that if the evidence remains as it is there is a

---

72. Although note the availability ex parte of interim injunctions, which are designed to preserve the plaintiff's rights pending a proper hearing: see Tilbury, pp 326–7; Spry, pp 495–504.
73. [1975] AC 396.
74. Ibid at 407–8.

probability that at the trial of the action the plaintiff will be entitled to relief'.[75] While this approach had been adopted by the High Court in *Beecham Group Ltd v Bristol Laboratories Ltd*,[76] like *American Cyanamid* a patent case, more recent High Court judgments have firmly established the lower standard favoured by the House of Lords.[77] It is questionable whether this change was as radical in practice as it appeared on paper, since it was apparent that even under the old approach many courts took very little convincing that the plaintiff had shown enough to have a 'fair chance' of success at trial; while consideration of the merits is by no means irrelevant under the new approach, as will appear. Nevertheless it did and does constitute an important change of emphasis, liberating the courts at least to some extent from the problems of assessing the strength of a case in such hurried circumstances. So long as there is *something* to the plaintiff's argument, the court will now devote its attention almost exclusively to the key question: in whose favour does the balance of convenience lie?

[2.12] Balance of convenience. Although then it is necessary for the plaintiff to have at least a triable case, that does not of itself guarantee success at the interlocutory stage. In essence, the court must be satisfied that the plaintiff's need for protection outweighs any adverse consequences for the defendant. The most important element in this equation, as indeed Lord Diplock stressed in *American Cyanamid*, is that of the adequacy of the compensation available in the event of the interlocutory decision proving to be at variance with that reached at trial. From the plaintiff's point of view, the question is whether, if no injunction is granted, the loss caused by the defendant's conduct is capable of being recouped if the action is ultimately successful. This does not just require an analysis as to the loss that may flow and the nature of the pecuniary relief available to the plaintiff, but also as to the defendant's likely capacity to pay such compensation. Similarly, from the defendant's perspective, it must be determined whether the undertaking as to damages which the plaintiff is almost invariably asked to provide as a condition of obtaining interlocutory relief will provide a sufficient safeguard against the possibility that the plaintiff's claim is rejected at trial. Put simply, whoever appears to be in a better position to make a subsequent claim for compensation is likely to find themselves on the wrong end of the interlocutory decision.

In assessing the adequacy of damages to either party, and indeed more generally in establishing where the 'balance of the risk of doing an injustice'[78] lies, the courts may have regard to a number of factors.[79] Important ones include the courts' innate preference for maintaining the 'status

---

75. *Beecham Group Ltd v Bristol Laboratories Ltd* (1968) 118 CLR 618 at 622.
76. Ibid.
77. See *Australian Coarse Grain Pool Pty Ltd v Barley Marketing Board of Queensland* (1982) 57 ALJR 425; *Murphy v Lush* (1986) 60 ALJR 523. See also *Epitoma Pty Ltd v Australasian Meat Industry Employees' Union (No 2)* (1984) 54 ALR 730; *Sony Music Australia Ltd v Tansing* (1993) 27 IPR 649.
78. *Cayne v Global Natural Resources plc* [1984] 1 All ER 225 at 237.
79. Apart from those listed below, see also [14.11], discussing a special principle formerly (though perhaps no longer) observed in patent infringement cases whereby an interlocutory injunction would only be granted in the case of a patent that had previously been held valid or at least been unchallenged for some years.

quo';[80] the effect that the decision will have on any business being run by either or both parties, there being a strong tendency to favour an established enterprise over a newly developed one;[81] the conduct of the parties, including especially any acquiescence or 'unclean hands' on the part of the plaintiff; and the defendant's willingness to offer and abide by an undertaking not to engage in the conduct in question.[82] While too the *American Cyanamid* approach is designed to play down the importance of the plaintiff's chances of success at trial, perceptions as to the eventual outcome are bound to be influential to some degree, especially where one side clearly has the stronger case and the factors listed above are otherwise inconclusive. There is also likely to be a heightened emphasis on the merits of the case where the court is aware of the unlikelihood of the matter proceeding to trial;[83] or where the court is invited or feels impelled to reach at least a preliminary conclusion on a novel or difficult point of law, the facts being basically uncontested.[84]

[2.13] Final injunctions. Turning to the remedies ultimately available at trial, there can be little question but that injunctive relief has become the dominant remedy in intellectual property cases. Given the essentially negative character of intellectual property rights, this is hardly surprising. The plaintiff's principal aim is usually to stop the defendant doing something that cannot lawfully be done without the plaintiff's permission. Accordingly the plaintiff will seek a prohibitive injunction,[85] restraining the defendant either from continuing to infringe the plaintiff's right or, where the application is made on a quia timet basis and the plaintiff can show a probability of the defendant committing an infringement,[86] from proceeding to do so. The capacity to grant such an order is specifically conferred by intellectual property statutes,[87] but is in any event within the inherent power of those courts invested with equitable jurisdiction.[88]

Where the plaintiff is able to establish an infringement by the defendant, an injunction will be granted unless there is some reason why the court should exercise its discretion to refuse to do so. According to general principle, the most obvious justification for a court declining to impose a restraining order is the adequacy of any remedy in damages available to the

---

80. Although much depends, of course, on *which* status quo is identified as worth preserving: see Tilbury, pp 321–2.
81. See Cornish, p 40.
82. See Spry, pp 468–72.
83. See eg *Hutchence v South Seas Bubble Co Pty Ltd* (1986) 6 IPR 473; *Lansing Linde Ltd v Kerr* [1991] 1 All ER 418. See generally W Sofronoff, 'Interlocutory Injunctions Having Final Effect' (1987) 61 *ALJ* 341.
84. See eg *Lion Laboratories Ltd v Evans* [1984] 2 All ER 417 (see [4.19]). Cf *CBS Records Australia Ltd v Telmak Teleproducts (Aust) Pty Ltd* (1987) 8 IPR 473.
85. Mandatory injunctions, compelling the defendant to take positive action of some sort, are rare in intellectual property cases. However, they are occasionally used in business reputation cases to compel defendants to change their name, even at an interlocutory stage: see eg *Aerospatiale Societe Nationale Industrielle v Aerospatiale Helicopters Pty Ltd* (1986) 6 IPR 219.
86. See Spry, pp 369–73.
87. See Copyright Act 1968 ss 115(1), (2), 248J(2); Circuit Layouts Act 1989 s 27(2); Designs Act 1906 s 32B(1); Patents Act 1990 s 122(1); Plant Breeder's Rights Act 1994 s 56(3); Trade Marks Act 1995 s 126(a). See also Trade Practices Act 1974 s 80.
88. See generally Meagher, Gummow and Lehane, ch 21; Spry, ch 4.

plaintiff. However, in intellectual property cases it is very rare, with the possible exception of actions for breach of confidence,[89] for this reasoning to be employed. The assumption appears to be that an owner's capacity to control exploitation of the relevant subject matter should be treated as an absolute entitlement, and that others should not be able to secure what in effect would be a compulsory licence by infringing the right and then offering to pay damages. If an injunction is to be refused, it will typically be on other grounds: that the defendant is not likely to continue infringing and that any restraint would thus be unnecessary; that the conduct of the plaintiff has in some way been blameworthy, so that they have not approached equity with 'clean hands'; or that they have been guilty of unreasonable delay in bringing proceedings or have in some other way acquiesced in the defendant's conduct.[90]

[2.14]   Ancillary relief. Besides awarding an injunction, a court may also grant any ancillary relief needed to ensure that the infringing conduct is indeed brought to an end. The principal example is an order for the delivery up for destruction of articles which the defendant has created pursuant to the infringing conduct, such as products manufactured with the use of the plaintiff's confidential information or in infringement of the plaintiff's patent.[91] In the case of a person who has infringed a trade mark, they may similarly be ordered to obliterate the offending mark from their goods.[92] In either instance the defendant is usually given the option of carrying out the destruction or obliteration, though if they are not trusted to do so they will be ordered to deliver the material up to the plaintiff for the order to be carried out. This is taken further by s 116 of the Copyright Act 1968, which permits the plaintiff to sue in conversion or detinue, not merely with respect to infringing copies, but also the 'plates' used to make them.[93] This is one of the rare instances in which proprietary relief is given for the infringement of an intellectual property right, since the plaintiff can assert possession of the offending items rather than being forced to have them destroyed.[94]

[2.15]   Damages. Whether or not an injunction is awarded, a successful plaintiff may seek damages for any loss caused by the defendant's infringement. With the partial exception of breach of confidence, where doubts linger as to the precise jurisdictional basis for their availability, damages are firmly established as the principal form of pecuniary relief in intellectual

---

89. See [4.24].
90. See eg [4.26] in relation to breach of confidence.
91. See [4.27], [14.11]; and see also *Geodesic Constructions Pty Ltd v Gaston* (1976) 16 SASR 453 (articles made in infringement of registered design). Note also Copyright Act 1968 s 248T, specifically empowering a court to make such an order where a person is charged with an offence under the performers' rights provisions, whether or not they are convicted.
92. See eg *Slazenger & Sons v Feltham & Co* (1889) 6 RPC 531.
93. See [8.35]. A 'plate' is broadly defined in s 10(1) to include 'a stereotype, stone, block mould, matrix, transfer, negative or other similar appliance'.
94. It appears that little use has been made of the constructive trust in intellectual property cases. On present authority, the defendant would probably have to be in breach of some fiduciary duty before any trust would be imposed on property created or misused as a result of the infringement: see [4.32]. Note also the possibility that an intellectual property right, if created in breach of a fiduciary duty, might itself be the subject of a constructive trust: see eg [7.3].

property cases. However, unless the infringement in question also amounts to a breach of contract, they will not (at least in theory) be available as of right. In the case of (non-contractual) breach of confidence, this is a function of the equitable basis of the doctrine.[95] The statutory systems specifically provide that a court 'may' make an award;[96] although there are a number of recent authorities in relation to breach of copyright which suggest that despite the clear terms of the legislation a court has no discretion to refuse damages (at least once it has decided that an account of profits is inappropriate, as discussed below).[97] In any event it appears that damages will normally be awarded if they are sought, at least where the defendant has been aware that their conduct was unlawful. Where the defendant has behaved 'innocently', different positions obtain in the various regimes. At one extreme, damages will not be awarded at all for passing off unless the defendant 'persists after notice';[98] whereas innocence seems to be no bar at all to an award of compensation for breach of confidence or an infringement of performers' rights, the consumer protection provisions of the Trade Practices Act or a registered trade mark, though of course it is bound to be a discretionary consideration. The remaining systems each specifically provide for innocence to be a defence to a claim for damages under certain circumstances, but in two distinct ways. Under the copyright and circuit layouts legislation, damages are not to be available where the defendant was not aware, and had no reasonable grounds for suspecting, that their conduct constituted an infringement.[99] By contrast, the designs, patents and plant breeder's rights statutes are less forgiving. They provide that the court *may* refuse to award damages where the defendant did not know, and could not reasonably have known, of the existence of the plaintiff's right.[100] Under these provisions, it would not be enough that the defendant believed their conduct not to be an infringement, so long as they knew or should have known that the right existed.

As to the way in which damages are assessed, the Australian courts in particular have shown a commendable reluctance to be drawn into formulating unnecessarily rigid and technical principles, preferring instead the flexibility of looking at each case on its merits.[101] The overarching princi-

---

95. See [4.29].
96. See Copyright Act 1968 ss 115(2), 248J(2); Circuit Layouts Act 1989 s 27(2); Designs Act 1906 s 32B(1); Patents Act 1990 s 122(1); Plant Breeder's Rights Act 1994 s 56(3); Trade Marks Act 1995 s 126(b). See also Trade Practices Act 1974 s 82. Cf Copyright Act 1968 s 116(1) (plaintiff 'entitled' to remedies in respect of infringing copies and plates).
97. *LED Builders Pty Ltd v Masterton Homes (NSW) Pty Ltd* (1994) 30 IPR 447 at 466–8; *Robert J Zupanovich Pty Ltd v B & N Beale Nominees Pty Ltd* (1995) 32 IPR 339 at 355; *A-One Accessory Imports Pty Ltd v Off Road Imports Pty Ltd (No 2)* (1996) 34 IPR 332.
98. See [16.19].
99. Copyright Act 1968 s 115(3); Circuit Layouts Act 1989 s 27(3). Note however that the innocence defence is rather more restrictively defined where an action under s 116 of the Copyright Act (discussed in the previous paragraph) is concerned: see Ricketson, pp 306–7.
100. Designs Act 1906 s 32B(2); Patents Act 1990 s 123(1); Plant Breeder's Rights Act 1994 s 57(1). Note that under the patents legislation damages will not be awarded where the defendant has obtained a non-infringement declaration: see [14.8].
101. See eg *Interfirm Comparison (Australia) Pty Ltd v Law Society of NSW* (1975) 6 ALR 445. Cf *Seager v Copydex Ltd (No 2)* [1969] 2 All ER 718.

ple is simply that the aim of any damages award is to compensate the plaintiff for whatever loss can reasonably be traced to the defendant's conduct. This leaves open the question of the precise measure of assessment to be adopted, which will depend upon the particular circumstances. In practice, as will become apparent from the treatment of the individual regimes later in the book, two measures predominate. Where both parties are in business and the defendant's activities cut into the plaintiff's profits, that loss of profits will be the basis for assessment. Conversely, where the infringement consists of conduct which the plaintiff would have been prepared to authorise or license, damages will typically consist of the fee which the plaintiff could reasonably have charged. As for non-pecuniary loss, damages for such things as distress or disappointment are rare, though not unknown.[102] There is also the question of whether a court can look beyond the compensatory function and 'punish' the defendant for particularly flagrant or 'contumacious' conduct, especially where the defendant has calculated that the profits to be had will exceed any loss caused to the plaintiff. The common law doctrines do appear to allow for exemplary or punitive damages to be awarded,[103] and the copyright and performers' rights regimes specifically provide for 'additional damages' to meet such a case.[104]

[2.16] Account of profits.[105] Whereas damages are designed to compensate the plaintiff for loss suffered as a result of infringing conduct, an account is a restitutionary remedy which looks to the profits made by the defendant, who is forced to give up their 'ill-gotten gains'.[106] Stripping the defendant of any money made from the infringement may be an attractive option where the defendant, by using superior skill or resources in exploiting the relevant subject matter, has been able to make more than the plaintiff could have done, or in any event more than the plaintiff has lost as a result of the infringement. Since the two measures (loss to the plaintiff and gain to the defendant) are diametrically opposed, it is clear that the plaintiff must in practice choose between damages and an account. This is an established principle at common law,[107] which makes an account available both in relation to breach of confidence and passing off. The need to elect is also reflected in the provisions governing remedies for infringement under most of the statutory regimes,[108] although in the case of copyright it is the court rather than the plaintiff that must make the decision.[109] It is important to remember that, quite apart from the terms of

102. See eg *Milpurrurru v Indofurn Pty Ltd* (1994) 30 IPR 209 (see [8.36]).
103. See [4.30], [16.19]. Cf the position under the Trade Practices Act 1974: see [16.34].
104. Copyright Act ss 115(4) (see [8.34]), 248J(3).
105. See generally F Patfield, 'The Remedy of Account of Profits in Industrial and Intellectual Property Litigation' (1984) 9 *UNSWLJ* 189; P Hastie, 'Restitution and Remedy in Intellectual Property Law' (1996) 14 *Aust Bar Rev* 6; M J Leeming, 'When Should a Plaintiff Take an Account of Profits?' (1996) 7 *AIPJ* 127.
106. *Colbeam Palmer Ltd v Stock Affiliates Pty Ltd* (1968) 122 CLR 25 at 32.
107. See eg *Neilson v Betts* (1871) LR 5 HL 1.
108. See Circuit Layouts Act 1989 s 27(2); Designs Act 1906 s 32B(1); Patents Act 1990 s 122(1); Plant Breeder's Rights Act 1994 s 56(3); Trade Marks Act 1995 s 126(b).
109. Copyright Act 1968 s 115(2). As to how this discretion should be exercised, see *Robert J Zupanovich Pty Ltd v B & N Beale Nominees Pty Ltd* (1995) 32 IPR 339. Note also that no provision at all is made for the remedy by the Copyright Act in relation to performers' rights.

those provisions, an account is a discretionary remedy which may be refused on any of the grounds mentioned earlier in relation to injunctions.[110] Indeed an account is generally accompanied by an injunction, thereby precluding the possibility of the defendant continuing to earn profits, though there is no absolute bar to the remedy being awarded on its own.[111] Most significantly, it appears that no account is to be awarded in relation to any period in which the defendant was not aware of the plaintiff's rights,[112] the remedy only being available for profits which are 'dishonestly made' and which it would be 'unconscionable' for the infringer to retain.[113] This principle is by no means fully reflected in some of the statutory provisions. While the designs, patents and plant breeder's rights statutes recognise that innocence may bar pecuniary relief,[114] 'innocence' in this respect is narrowly defined, as we saw above in relation to damages. Moreover the copyright and circuit layouts provisions actually state that, even where damages cannot be obtained against an innocent defendant, the plaintiff remains 'entitled' to an account of profits.[115] Despite this wording, however, it seems likely that the courts will continue to regard the remedy of account as retaining its traditional discretionary character.

In any event, there are a number of difficulties which greatly diminish the utility of the remedy in practice. At a substantive level, there is the problem of determining with any precision the profits of the defendant to which the plaintiff may lay claim. Unless it can be established that the defendant would not have made a profit at all without the aid of the infringement, which is rare,[116] the court will need to find a way of identifying what proportion of the profit is attributable to the infringement. This will be no easy matter where, for instance, the defendant has used the plaintiff's invention merely as the basis for their own product,[117] or attached the plaintiff's trade mark to goods that would have been sold anyway.[118] The upshot is that a good deal of time is likely to be taken up by the court (or, more usually, a master or some other officer) examining the defendant's business in great detail, followed by extensive arguments as to which part of the defendant's operations have been advantaged by the infringement and as to whether the defendant might have made the same profits by acting lawfully.

These difficulties are illustrated by *Dart Industries Inc v Decor Corp Pty Ltd*,[119] in which the defendants' production of plastic kitchen canisters

---

110. *Warman International Ltd v Dwyer* (1995) 182 CLR 544 at 559. This appears to be so even where there is statutory provision for the remedy: see eg *Robert J Zupanovich Pty Ltd v B & N Beale Nominees Pty Ltd* (1995) 32 IPR 339 at 355; though cf *Masterton Homes Pty Ltd v LED Builders Pty Ltd* (1996) 33 IPR 417, where the Full Court of the Federal Court left the point open.
111. *Colbeam Palmer Ltd v Stock Affiliates Pty Ltd* (1968) 122 CLR 25.
112. Ibid at 34.
113. *Dart Industries Inc v Decor Corp Pty Ltd* (1993) 179 CLR 101 at 111; *Apand Pty Ltd v Kettle Chip Co Pty Ltd* (1994) 30 IPR 337 at 358.
114. Designs Act 1906 s 32B(2); Patents Act 1990 s 123(1); Plant Breeder's Rights Act 1994 s 57(1).
115. Copyright Act 1968 s 115(3); Circuit Layouts Act 1989 s 27(3).
116. Though cf *Peter Pan Manufacturing Corp v Corsets Silhouette Ltd* [1963] 3 All ER 402.
117. See eg *Leplastrier & Co Ltd v Armstrong Holland Ltd* (1926) 26 SR (NSW) 585.
118. See eg *Colbeam Palmer Ltd v Stock Affiliates Pty Ltd* (1968) 122 CLR 25.
119. (1993) 179 CLR 101.

with press button seals had been held to infringe the plaintiff's patent, which related only to the seal. The High Court confirmed that an account should be taken of the profits made on the whole product, not just on the seal, on the basis that the 'whole thing came into existence' by reason of the patent infringement.[120] However, the more difficult issue was whether the defendants should be permitted any allowance for the general over-heads of their business in calculating the profits made from the infringe-ment. The court rejected an 'incremental costing' approach, which would have identified the gross profit from the relevant product and then deducted only the costs *directly* associated with making or selling that prod-uct, including overheads solely to the extent that they would not otherwise have been incurred in relation to other products. Instead they preferred an 'absorption costing' method. This permitted the allocation of whatever portion of general overheads could fairly be attributed to the manufacture or sale of the product, though not any 'opportunity cost' (potential profits forgone from using the same capacity to make or sell something else). The reasoning was that since 'the purpose of an account of profits is not to punish the defendant but to prevent its unjust enrichment',[121] the defend-ants should not be put in a worse position than if they had not infringed. This indeed would be the case if they were denied a deduction not only for the opportunity cost but also for 'the cost of the overheads which sustained the [production] capacity that would have been utilized by an alternative product and that was in fact utilized by the infringing product'.[122] The burden, however, was on the infringer to suggest a reasonably acceptable basis for allocating an appropriate portion of the overheads, something which would necessarily vary from case to case. The problem, as it has subsequently been noted, is that 'the variety of methods commonly used for overhead allocation would seem to provide potential justification for a fairly broad range of acceptable methods',[123] so that there remains consid-erable uncertainty as to how costs are to be apportioned. The High Court's decision indeed does little to dispel the doubts surrounding the practicality of taking an account. As one judge put it more than a century ago:

> Accounts ... very seldom result in anything satisfactory to anybody. The liti-gation is enormous, the expense is great and the time consumed is out of all proportion to the advantage ultimately attained.[124]

Those words still ring true today, and it is hardly surprising that most plaintiffs in practice prefer to forgo their chance at a windfall and claim damages instead.

---

120. See *Colbeam Palmer Ltd v Stock Affiliates Pty Ltd* (1968) 122 CLR 25 at 42–3.
121. (1993) 179 CLR 101 at 114; and see also ibid at 123.
122. Ibid.
123. P Blayney and M Wyburn, 'The Remedy of an Account of Profits in a Patent Infringement Action: The Difficulties in Determining a "True" Product Cost' (1994) 5 *AIPJ* 81 at 93. The authors go on to note the possible view that 'the task is made impossible by the fact that various general overheads interact in such a way that any means of relating individual overhead costs to specific products is arbitrary' and that in fact 'no method of allocation will be verifiable' (ibid).
124. *Siddell v Vickers* (1892) 9 RPC 152 at 162.

4. CRIMINAL LIABILITY

[2.17] **Offences against intellectual property.** Apart from general offences such as conspiracy to defraud, which may come into play where rights are infringed,[125] most of the intellectual property statutes establish a series of special offences relating to their particular regimes.[126] For the most part these are relatively unimportant in practice, relating to matters such as failure to comply with a summons to appear before an administrative body, falsely procuring registration or falsely representing the existence of a right. However, one set of provisions that does result in prosecutions from time to time is that contained in the Copyright Act 1968 and relating to deliberate infringements and dealings in articles known to be infringing copies. Revamped in 1986 to allow commercial piracy to be more effectively combated, some of these offences carry a maximum sentence of five years and fines of up to $250,000 for companies who are repeat offenders.[127] The new offences added to the Act to deal with those who infringe performers' rights carry similar penalties.[128] Also of potential significance are the offences designed to punish the forgery of registered trade marks with an intention to defraud, which again are backed by penal provisions which can lead to up to two years in jail.[129]

5. JURISDICTION OF COURTS

[2.18] **General.** The last 20 years or so have seen important changes in the statutory provisions governing the jurisdiction of courts to hear actions or appeals arising out of the various intellectual property systems. Together with the cross-vesting scheme, introduced in 1988, these changes have had the effect of standardising most of the systems and of ensuring that, while appeals from administrative decisions must go to the Federal Court, other actions may be commenced in either the Federal Court or a state or territory court. At the same time, a great deal of routine work has been removed from the High Court. The court was until 1976 the designated appeals court for many of the statutory systems; today its function is merely the general task of overseeing the various systems by acting as a final court of appeal in cases of particular difficulty or significance.[130] In practice it is the

---

125. See eg *Scott v Metropolitan Police Commissioner* [1975] AC 819. As to criminal conspiracy, see generally B Fisse, *Howard's Criminal Law*, 5th ed, 1990, pp 355–8.
126. Copyright Act 1968 Pt V Div 5, ss 172, 173, 203A–203F, Pt XIA Div 3; Designs Act 1906 ss 36, 42B, 42C, 45; Patents Act 1990 s 152(4), Ch 18, Ch 20 Pt 2; Plant Breeder's Rights Act 1994 ss 74–76; Trade Marks Act 1995 Pt 14.
127. See [8.39].
128. See Copyright Act 1968 Pt XIA Div 3.
129. See generally Lahore, *Patents*, para [60,000] ff.
130. Under s 75 of the Constitution, the High Court does however have original jurisdiction over all matters (i) arising under a treaty; (ii) affecting consuls or other foreign representatives; (iii) in which the Commonwealth or a representative thereof is a party; (iv) between states, or residents of different states, or between a state and a resident of another state; or (v) in which a writ of mandamus or prohibition or an injunction is sought against an officer of the Commonwealth. While ordinarily the court might be expected to remit such a matter to a lower court, there will occasionally be exceptions: see eg *Commonwealth v John Fairfax & Sons Ltd* (1980) 147 CLR 39 (see [4.39]), [8.28]).

Federal Court that now plays the most important role in adjudicating intellectual property cases, offering particular advantages in terms of the relative speed with which it can proceed to deal with a matter, compared to the delays often experienced in state courts.

It has sometimes been suggested that a special court, along the lines of the Patents County Court in the UK or the Federal Patent Court in Germany, be created to deal with intellectual property cases. The idea was rejected both by IPAC in its general review of enforcement procedures and by the ALRC in its report on the designs system on the basis that there was no compelling demand for such a body, especially in light of the current volume of intellectual property litigation in this country.[131] However, the notion of a specialised court or tribunal may yet resurface in ACIP's forthcoming report on enforcement issues.[132] It is notable that in its own review of the petty patent system, ACIP perceived a need to provide a cost-effective avenue for enforcement of the proposed new 'innovation patents' at a level lower than the Federal Court or the state Supreme Courts. Given the likely problems of lack of expertise and workload delays in the existing lower level courts, it considered that the answer might lie in a specialised federal magistracy, or indeed in allowing the Commissioner of Patents and the Commissioner's delegates to deal with infringement actions. Since there are constitutional difficulties with either proposal in terms of investing what appears to be federal judicial power in a body other than a 'court',[133] ACIP's ultimate recommendation was that a further study be made of how to overcome those obstacles.[134] It was this recommendation that prompted the government to ask ACIP to take a broader look at enforcement, as previously explained.

[2.19] Commencement of civil proceedings. The current jurisdictional arrangements for the commencement of civil proceedings vary slightly from system to system, though the end result is much the same:

— *Patents, designs and trade marks.* As a general rule, proceedings under each statute must be commenced in a 'prescribed court', defined to mean the Federal Court or the Supreme Court of a state or territory, or the Supreme Court of Norfolk Island.[135] These proceedings include actions for non-infringement declarations, for the rectification of the designs or trade mark registers, or for the revocation of a patent. Proceedings may be transferred between prescribed courts[136] and their jurisdiction is exercised by a single judge.[137] Infringement proceedings, on the other hand, may be instituted in any court, whether prescribed or not, as may proceedings in respect of unjustified threats.[138] An appeal lies in any of these proceedings to the Full Court of the Federal Court or, by special leave, directly to the High Court.[139]

---

131. IPAC, *Practice and Procedures for Enforcement of Industrial Property Rights in Australia*, 1992, ch 6; *Designs*, paras [13.9]–[13.16].
132. See [2.3].
133. See eg *Brandy v Human Rights and Equal Opportunity Commission* (1995) 183 CLR 245.
134. *Review of the Petty Patent System*, 1995, pp 56–9.
135. Patents Act 1990 Sched 1; Designs Act 1906 s 4(1); Trade Marks Act 1995 s 190.
136. Patents Act 1990 s 157; Designs Act 1906 s 40H; Trade Marks Act 1995 s 194.
137. Patents Act 1990 s 156; Designs Act 1906 s 40G(3); Trade Marks Act 1995 s 193.
138. Patents Act 1990 ss 120, 128(1); Designs Act 1906 ss 31, 32C(1); Trade Marks Act 1995 ss 125, 129(1).

— *Copyright, performers' rights and circuit layouts.* The Federal Court is specifically given jurisdiction over infringement proceedings arising out of these regimes.[140] In addition, however, and despite the absence of any explicit statement to that effect in the statutes concerned, this jurisdiction is concurrently vested in the various state or territory courts.[141] All appeals lie to the Full Court of the Federal Court or, by special leave, direct to the High Court.[142]

— *Other proceedings.* The Federal Court has 'exclusive' jurisdiction in respect of proceedings commenced under the Plant Breeder's Rights Act 1994 (s 56). However, this is subject to the cross-vesting provisions of the Jurisdiction of Courts (Cross-vesting) Act 1987 (Cth), which would allow a state or territory court to exercise such jurisdiction. Similarly, while common law or equitable claims 'belong' in the state courts, the cross-vesting scheme also allows these actions to be brought anywhere, although the scheme does provide a mechanism for cases to be transferred to a more appropriate jurisdiction where that is thought necessary.[143] As for the Trade Practices Act 1974, all civil proceedings brought under the consumer protection provisions (other than by the Minister or the Australian Competition and Consumer Commission) may be commenced either in the Federal Court or in a state or territory court, with provision again being made for the transfer of proceedings in appropriate cases (ss 86, 86A).[144]

[2.20] Associated and accrued jurisdiction of the Federal Court. Prior to the Jurisdiction of Courts (Miscellaneous Amendments) Act 1987, which explicitly conferred jurisdiction upon the Federal Court for the first time in relation to each of the intellectual property statutes, cases could only come before it (other than on appeal) if its 'associated' or 'accrued' jurisdiction could be invoked.[145] Under these concepts, if a claim has been brought before the court under the Trade Practices Act, for example, any

---

139. Patents Act 1990 s 158; Designs Act 1906 s 40I(1), (3); Trade Marks Act 1995 s 195(1), (3).
140. See eg Copyright Act 1968 ss 131C, 248M; Circuit Layouts Act 1989 s 47. Note that under Pt VI of the Copyright Act the Federal Court may also have questions of law referred to it by the Copyright Tribunal (see [7.18]), whose President is in any event a judge of the court.
141. See Judiciary Act 1903 (Cth) s 39(2); Australian Capital Territory Supreme Court Act 1933 (Cth) s 11(a); Supreme Court Act 1979 (NT) s 14(1)(b). The only provisions made by the intellectual property statutes in this respect are that any infringement action commenced in a state or territory Supreme Court is to be heard by a single judge (Copyright Act 1968 ss 131A, 248K; Circuit Layouts Act 1989 s 40); and that nothing in them confers on a court the power to grant equitable relief, where it does not otherwise have that power (Copyright Act 1968 s 203; Circuit Layouts Act 1989 s 43).
142. Copyright Act 1968 ss 131B, 248L; Circuit Layouts Act 1989 s 41; and see *Thompson & Morgan (United Kingdom) Ltd v Erica Vale Australia Pty Ltd* (1995) 31 IPR 335.
143. See eg Jurisdiction of Courts (Cross-vesting) Act 1987 (NSW) ss 4, 5. See generally K Mason and J Crawford, 'The Cross-vesting Scheme' (1988) 62 *ALJ* 328; G J Moloney, 'Cross-Vesting of Jurisdiction — Nationalism versus Robust Individualism' (1994) 3 *J Judic Admin* 229.
144. This does mean, however, that proceedings under the Trade Practices Act excluded from ss 86 and 86A can only be brought in the Federal Court, since the cross-vesting legislation may still apply: *Re Wilcox; ex p Venture Industries Pty Ltd* (1996) 137 ALR 47.
145. See Ricketson, pp 42–6.

other related claims may also be heard by the court, even if they arise at common law or under a statute over which the court has no express jurisdiction. However, the other claims must arise from a 'common substratum of facts' to those expressly within the court's remit.[146] This still allows common law claims (particularly in passing off, but also in breach of confidence) to be brought before the court as being related to another statutory claim, without any need to rely on the cross-vesting legislation.

[2.21] **Decisions of administrative bodies: appeals and review.** Under many of the statutory systems, administrative bodies such as the Commissioner of Patents are empowered to make various decisions as to the creation, subsistence and compulsory licensing of rights, as well as on ancillary matters such as the right to intervene or the extension of time limits. Where appeals are provided from these decisions, they lie to the Federal Court and in turn, with leave, to the Full Court of the Federal Court.[147] The statutes also confer on the Administrative Appeals Tribunal (AAT) power to review certain of the decisions.[148] Alternatively any decision of an administrative character may be reviewed by a judge of the Federal Court under the Administrative Decisions (Judicial Review) Act 1977 (Cth), under one of the grounds for review set out in ss 5–7.[149] Judicial review may also be sought in the same court under s 39B of the Judiciary Act 1903 (Cth).[150] The issue of administrative review procedures, and in particular the tangled relationship between the AAT and the Federal Court, is currently the subject of a review by the Administrative Review Council (ARC) in relation to the patent system.[151]

[2.22] **Criminal proceedings.** As far as prosecutions for the various offences listed earlier are concerned, a curious split emerges between the various statutes. Under the designs, patents and trade marks legislation, prosecutions are specifically prohibited from being commenced in the Federal Court and must therefore be initiated in a state court.[152] By contrast, prosecutions under the copyright or performers' rights regimes may be instituted in either the Federal Court or in any other court,[153] whereas it appears that prosecutions under the plant breeder's rights legislation may only be commenced in the Federal Court.[154]

---

146. *Philip Morris Inc v Adam P Brown Male Fashions Pty Ltd* (1981) 148 CLR 457; *Fencott v Muller* (1983) 152 CLR 570.
147. Designs Act 1906 ss 40G(1A), 40I(2); Patents Act 1990 ss 154(2), 158(2); Trade Marks Act 1995 ss 191(2), 195(2).
148. Designs Act 1906 s 40K; Patents Act 1990 s 224; Plant Breeder's Rights Act 1994 s 77; Trade Marks Act 1995 ss 175, 178, 180, 224, 227. As to the AAT, see further M N Allars, *Introduction to Australian Administrative Law*, 1990, pp 72–7, ch 7.
149. See eg *Lyons v Registrar of Trade Marks* (1983) 1 IPR 416; *Kimberly-Clark Ltd v Commissioner of Patents* (1988) 83 ALR 714. See generally Allars, ibid, chs 5–6.
150. See eg *Wimmera Industrial Minerals Pty Ltd v RGC Mineral Sands Ltd* (1995) 32 IPR 89.
151. See ARC, *Administrative Review and Patents Decisions*, Issues Paper, January 1994. Progress of the review has been put on hold pending completion of a related ARC inquiry into appeals from the AAT to the Federal Court, but a report is expected in the near future. See also IPAC, *Practice and Procedures for Enforcement of Industrial Property Rights in Australia*, 1992, paras 6.22–6.30; *Designs*, ch 12.
152. Designs Act 1906 s 40G(1C); Patents Act 1990 s 154(3); Trade Marks Act 1995 s 191(3).
153. See eg Copyright Act 1968 ss 132(7), 133A(3), 248S(1).
154. Plant Breeder's Rights Act 1994 s 56.

PART II

Confidentiality

Chapter 3

The Concept of Rights in Information

1. INTRODUCTION

[3.1] Information as an asset. No one would seriously doubt that information is a valuable commodity in today's society. It has never been more true that 'knowledge is wealth', a preoccupation reflected by the pro- liferation of industries based entirely on information acquisition and dis- semination. The pressure for legal recognition of the value in information and of the concept of private rights in information is ever increasing. A threshold question, of course, is whether we can meaningfully speak at all of rights in something as ephemeral and subjective as 'information'. Com- mon sense, however, suggests a general acceptance in our society of the notion that information may be sufficiently discrete, identifiable and capa- ble of objective valuation to 'belong' to someone. Common sense would also seem to indicate that a person should not be able to monopolise infor- mation which is in the public domain, or which other people create for themselves.[1] This simplifies the matter considerably: any recognition of rights to or in information must necessarily mean allowing individuals or institutions to protect their *secrets*.

[3.2] Categories of information. The tremendous extent to which information can vary in terms of form, content and significance makes any attempt at categorisation a difficult task. It is useful, nevertheless, to iden- tify three broad categories into which 'valuable' information may be seen to fall: business information or 'trade secrets';[2] personal information; and governmental information. The categories primarily depend on the different contexts in which information can be generated, but also on the

---

1.   Cf A Wells Branscomb, *Who Owns Information?*, 1994.

different interests which secrecy is intended to promote. It is these interests which give information its 'value' to its possessor. Thus business information is valuable to the extent that it promotes commercial gain. Since the thrust of the concept of intellectual property is to recognise the right to profit from effort and ideas, it follows that it is the legal protection of information in this category which is principally of interest in a work of this nature. Nonetheless attention will also be given, albeit more briefly, to personal and governmental information.

[3.3] The case for legal protection of trade secrets. The mere fact that secrecy is a prerequisite of information having any value does not mean that the law is compelled to assist those who possess information to keep it secret. It can be argued, however, that without legal protection there would be insufficient incentive to invest in the development and exploitation of information that might secure long-term benefits to the community as well as short-term financial gain.[3] This is essentially the 'free rider' argument discussed in Chapter 1 — that protection is important for reasons both positive (encouragement and reward of creative effort) and negative (penalising those who 'reap without sowing').

Not everyone is prepared to accept this kind of economic argument without question. A society obviously has an interest in ensuring that useful ideas and information circulate effectively, in part so that they may form the basis for further innovation. The patent system strikes this balance by limiting the period during which the patent holder may exercise monopoly rights, and by requiring disclosure of the invention so that other researchers may learn from it. Likewise the copyright system precludes unauthorised reproduction of the particular expression of ideas and information, but not (at least in theory) the taking or use of the ideas or information as such. Some have suggested that this kind of balance would be disturbed, and creativity stifled, if innovators were permitted to 'lock up' useful ideas merely by keeping them secret.[4]

Nevertheless, a convincing case can be made for the creation of property rights over various kinds of 'trade secrets' which would not otherwise qualify for protection under the established regimes of patents and copyright. These include:

- *ideas in their protean form* — discoveries, plans or suggestions which are held in someone's head but are not yet fully worked out, or

---

2. Note that the term 'trade secrets' can also be used in a narrower sense to refer to a sub-category of business information, being information of a particularly significant or valuable nature in regard to competition with other firms (such as secret formulae, manufacturing processes, etc): see *Ansell Rubber Co Pty Ltd v Allied Rubber Industries Pty Ltd* [1967] VR 37 at 46. This has sometimes led to confusion: see [4.35]. The preferable view is that the term be given a broad meaning, extending to *any* information of a business or commercial nature which is kept relatively secret: see *Lansing Linde Ltd v Kerr* [1991] 1 WLR 251 at 260, 270; *Searle Australia Pty Ltd v Public Interest Advocacy Centre* (1992) 108 ALR 163.

3. See generally S Bok, *Secrets*, 1982, Ch 10, esp pp 147–52; H Glasbeek, 'Limitations on the Action of Breach of Confidence' in D Gibson (ed), *Aspects of Privacy Law*, 1980, p 217 at pp 228–44. For an economic analysis, see D D Friedman, W M Landes and R A Posner, 'Some Economics of Trade Secret Law' (1991) 5 *J Ec Perspectives* 61.

4. See eg R G Hammond, 'Quantum Physics, Econometric Models and Property Rights to Information' (1981) 27 *McGill LR* 47.

which have been reduced to material form but may nonetheless be readily appropriated without breach of copyright;

- *unpatentable or unpatented inventions* — ideas for products or processes which have been fully developed, but which cannot be patented for lack of some characteristic such as novelty (in the sense either of being the first to invent or the first to file), or alternatively which the inventor chooses not to patent;

- *technical know-how* — practical expertise that does not consist of a secret formula or process or design as such, but simply accumulated knowledge (often gathered by trial and error) as to what works and what doesn't;

- *customer information* — information as to the identity and special needs of an organisation's clientele; and

- *organisational information* — managerial techniques, structures or strategies which are distinctive to a particular organisation and which contribute to its market position.

There are of course practical steps which may be taken to guard against misappropriation of such valuable information. Leaving aside the simple (though generally self-defeating) expedient of divulging it to nobody at all, the 'owner' may seek to confine to an absolute minimum the number of people who have access to the information. In order to safeguard the information from others, various precautions may be taken, ranging from the simple (locking up documents in a filing cabinet) to the elaborate (electronic alarms, security guards, etc). But apart from the ever-present risk of breach of trust by those permitted access to the information, especially employees who move on to other firms, owners must today cope with an increasingly sophisticated array of information-gathering techniques. Moreover the cost of effective security measures may be so high as to outweigh any benefit to be derived from the information, or at least result in consumers paying higher prices for a product or service than would be generally desirable.[5]

[3.4] Contractual protection and its limitations. For these reasons it is imperative that owners have access to legal mechanisms that permit them to protect their trade secrets. One obvious possibility, and one that is indeed routinely employed, is to secure contractual commitments of confidentiality from those given access to secret information. So long as effective procedures exist for the enforcement of such contracts, the owner may take action to restrain or seek compensation for any use or disclosure that exceeds the limits permitted by the agreement. Confidentiality provisions are common in employment contracts, binding workers not to make unauthorised use of their employer's information both during their period of engagement and after they have left to work elsewhere. The same is true of joint venture agreements, where in order to pursue a particular project the parties must feel able to share information without fear of later misuse.

---

5.   See eg *E I Du Pont de Nemours & Co Inc v Christopher* (1970) 431 F 2d 1012, in which an American court imposed liability for misappropriation of trade secrets through aerial photography of the plaintiff's part-constructed factory. The court reasoned that it would be unreasonable and economically wasteful for the plaintiff and others in a similar situation to be expected to guard against such surveillance by building a special roof.

And of course it is a standard feature of agreements for the transfer of technology that the licensee, in return for access to the technology itself or any other secret information relating to its operation, covenants not to utilise the know-how outside the specific context of the agreement.

Contractual protection, however, has two crucial limitations. The first is that even where a promise not to use or disclose has been secured, the owner may find that the person against whom they wish to take legal action is not the person who gave the promise, but some third party into whose hands the information has now passed. For example, where an employee or ex-employee breaches an obligation of confidentiality and discloses a trade secret to a competitor of their employer (or former employer), it is that competitor and their capacity to use the trade secret to the employer's disadvantage that will be the principal concern. But contract theory generally does not permit a promise to be enforced against anyone other than the promisor. Hence the third party cannot be held to be in breach of contract, no matter how much they may have contributed to the infringement of the owner's rights and how much they stand to gain from that infringement. This limitation is particularly infuriating when the person who has promised to maintain confidentiality and the third party who is now in possession of the information are closely related: for example, where the third party is a company set up by the wrongdoer, or where the wrongdoer and the third party are both companies which belong to the same group.

A second and more fundamental limitation is that there are many situations where there is no contract at all to which the owner of a trade secret may turn. This may occur even where the misuse arises out of a voluntary communication. For instance, the owner may disclose information to another person in the context of discussing a possible venture. If the owner has not taken the precaution of negotiating a confidentiality agreement *before* any disclosure, something that is often overlooked in the enthusiasm for the project and because the parties are operating on mutual trust, the result will be that if the venture does not proceed the other party is free of any contractual commitment in relation to the information. More importantly, and in contrast to each of the situations which have just been discussed, there may be no voluntary communication at all. The trade secret may simply be 'stolen', whether by theft of documents, unauthorised access to computer files, or intensive surveillance. Where this kind of industrial espionage is concerned, and no employee or joint venturer is implicated in the acquisition, the question of contract is simply irrelevant.

[3.5] Recognition of rights in valuable information. The need to protect trade secrets by offering remedies for misuse, in situations which may or may not also involve breach of contract, has long been recognised in many industrialised countries. In the US, for instance, misappropriation of a trade secret attracts such remedies under the common law of tort; while most of the individual states have now enacted legislation based on the Uniform Trade Secrets Act proposed by the Uniform Law Institute in 1979 to codify and refine the common law. Germany and other European countries have offered similar protection as a specific application of more general laws directed against acts of 'unfair competition'. The Anglo-Australian common law, by contrast, has never explicitly recognised misappropriation of commercially valuable information as a wrong. Nevertheless most if not all kinds of misappropriation have come to be identified as 'breaches of confidence' giving rise to remedies in equity. This has created a position where, in the words of Brennan J (as he then was):[6]

> Prima facie, it is the privilege of any person who possesses information to keep the information confidential. That person may wish not to disclose it at all or may wish to disseminate it or to authorize its dissemination only for a limited purpose or to a limited class of persons.

On the other hand, there have been other nations which have been reluctant to offer any protection at all to trade secrets, beyond the capacity to enter into contracts containing stipulations as to confidentiality. While most of these countries have been developing nations, the most notable example has been Japan. Long after the country became an economic powerhouse, the remedies available under Japanese law in respect of misappropriation of commercial secrets remained very limited.[7] However, in 1990 Japan too amended its Unfair Competition Prevention Law to provide both injunctive relief and damages in respect of various kinds of misappropriation of trade secrets. There are a number of possible explanations for this turnabout. Mobility of labour has increased, meaning that Japanese firms can no longer rely so heavily on the tradition of company loyalty to prevent workers leaving and taking their employer's secrets with them. There is also the cynical view that Japan's decades of rapid economic growth were largely based on copying and enhancing technology imported from more 'advanced' nations, and that effective trade secret laws would have stifled the capacity of many of its more successful industries to obtain necessary know-how. Now that Japan has itself become a major licensor of technology, the suggestion goes, it has more to fear from trade secrets being lost (often to other countries using the very strategies which had previously served Japan so well!).

[3.6] US pressure and the TRIPS Agreement. However, while protection for trade secrets is now more likely to be regarded as serving rather than hindering Japanese interests, the principal reason for the 1990 amendments appears to have been the pressure for reform mounted by the US.[8] The same is true of the Law of Protection Against Unfair Competition adopted in 1993 by the People's Republic of China, Art 10 of which specifically prohibits the misuse of trade secrets.[9] As explained in Chapter 1, the US has aggressively used its economic power to cajole these and other countries into passing laws which would protect US-derived technology from being pirated. The imperative to protect trade secrets also now finds expression in the TRIPS Agreement. Article 39 stipulates that 'in the course of ensuring effective protection against unfair competition as provided in Art 10*bis* of the Paris Convention (1967), Members shall protect undisclosed information'. Paragraph 2 of Art 39 spells out in more detail what is required:

---

6. *Johns v Australian Securities Commission* (1993) 178 CLR 408 at 426.
7. See T Doi, *The Intellectual Property Law of Japan*, 1980, Ch 3; J Dratler, 'Trade Secrets in the United States and Japan: A Comparison and Prognosis' (1989) 14 *Yale J Int'l L* 68; J-A Tarr, 'A Comparative Overview of "Know-How" Protection in Japan and Australia' [1993] *JBL* 596.
8. See H E Svetz, 'Japan's New Trade Secret Law: We Asked For It — Now What Have We Got?' (1992) 26 *G Wash J Int'l L Econ* 413 at 421–5.
9. See Zheng Chengsi, 'The First Unfair Competition Law of the People's Republic of China' [1994] 4 EIPR 181.

Natural and legal persons shall have the possibility of preventing information lawfully within their control from being disclosed to, acquired by, or used by others without their consent in a manner contrary to honest commercial practices so long as such information:

(1) is secret in the sense that it is not, as a body or in the precise configuration and assembly of its components, generally known among or readily accessible to persons within the circles that normally deal with the kind of information in question;

(2) has commercial value because it is secret; and

(3) has been subject to reasonable steps under the circumstances, by the person lawfully in control of the information, to keep it secret.

A footnote explains that for the purposes of this provision:

'a manner contrary to honest commercial practices' shall mean at least practices such as breach of contract, breach of confidence and inducement to breach, and includes the acquisition of undisclosed information by third parties who knew, or were grossly negligent in failing to know, that such practices were involved in the acquisition.

Paragraph 3 goes on to deal with the specific situation of undisclosed information submitted to government bodies to gain approval for 'the marketing of pharmaceutical or of agricultural chemical products which utilise new chemical entities'. This must be protected against 'unfair commercial use'.[10]

As already mentioned, Australia does not have a general law which explicitly prohibits misappropriation of 'undisclosed information', though in fact there are numerous statutory provisions dealing with specific situations in which secrecy must be preserved.[11] Nevertheless, it appears that the equitable doctrine of breach of confidence is broad enough to satisfy the requirements of Art 39, and indeed goes beyond the minimum conditions set out in para 2 in a number of respects.[12] It is to that doctrine, therefore, that we now turn.

2. NATURE OF THE ACTION FOR BREACH OF CONFIDENCE

[3.7] History. The origins of the action for breach of confidence lie somewhere in the more general principles developed by equity with respect to relationships of 'trust and confidence'.[13] That it took some time for a clear jurisdiction to emerge in regard to the keeping of secrets is more or less a matter of historical accident. Until the mid-nineteenth century,

10. Cf *Smith Kline and French Laboratories (Aust) Ltd v Secretary, Department of Community Services and Health* (1991) 20 IPR 643: see [4.12].

11. Leading examples are to be found in the Crimes Act 1914 (Cth) ss 70, 79, dealing with disclosure by Commonwealth officers and misuse of 'official secrets' (see L Tsaknis, 'Commonwealth Secrecy Provisions: Time for Reform?' (1994) 18 *Crim LJ* 254); and in s 232(5) of the Corporations Law, which covers improper use of information acquired by an employee or officer of a corporation in the course of their duties (see H A J Ford and R P Austin, *Principles of Corporations Law*, 7th ed, 1995, pp 328–32). For other examples, see J McGinness, 'Secrecy Provisions in Commonwealth Legislation' (1990) 19 *Fed LR* 49.

12. See A Stewart, 'Protecting Trade Secrets under the TRIPS Agreement: How Useful are the Remedies for Breach of Confidence?' (1996) 9 *Aust IP Law Bull* 8 (Pt 1), 25 (Pt 2). There is, however, some question as to whether the same can be said of para 3: ibid at 26–27.

13. See generally Ricketson, Ch 42; Meagher, Gummow and Lehane, paras 4106–7; R G Hammond, 'The Origins of the Equitable Duty of Confidence' (1979) 8 *Anglo-Am LR* 71.

attention was primarily focused on the protection of the secrecy of unpublished literary works: it was unsurprising, therefore, that the jurisdiction should overlap with and to some extent be subsumed by prevailing notions of common law copyright.[14] In a series of famous cases, however, most memorably involving the private etchings of Queen Victoria and her consort,[15] the courts clearly identified the distinct notion of an obligation of confidence imposed on the conscience of one to whom a secret has been communicated. From this point on, breach of confidence actions became commonplace. The great majority of reported cases over the next century involved employees who had been given access to their employers' trade secrets,[16] though litigation in regard to licensing arrangements or joint ventures was not unknown.[17] These cases tended to involve contractual relationships and to some extent it was unclear whether or not the injunctions typically issued to restrain breaches of confidence were grounded merely in equity's 'auxiliary' jurisdiction.[18] It could be argued, in other words, that the obligations of confidence being enforced were contractual in nature, being implied into a pre-existing agreement between the parties. The argument found some support in cases involving negotiations as to a venture which did not eventuate, the courts being prepared to imply an enforceable agreement to respect the confidentiality of information disclosed.[19]

[3.8] Emergence of the modern doctrine. The breakthrough came in 1948 with the decision of the English Court of Appeal in *Saltman Engineering Co Ltd v Campbell Engineering Co Ltd*.[20] While the leading judgment of Lord Greene MR contains little if anything that cannot be located in previous authorities, it proved to be immensely influential. Rejecting the suggestion that liability for breach of confidence necessitated the finding of a contract between the parties, Lord Greene accepted this broad proposition formulated by counsel:[21]

> If a defendant is proved to have used confidential information, directly or indirectly obtained from a plaintiff, without the consent, express or implied, of the plaintiff, he [sic] will be guilty of an infringement of the plaintiff's rights.

The decision played a major role in galvanising English and then in turn Australian courts into regarding breach of confidence as a separate cause of action based on equitable rather than contractual principles.[22] It thus effectively marks the start of the modern era in this field — an era which

---

14. See [5.4].
15. *Prince Albert v Strange* (1849) 2 De G & Sm 652; 64 ER 293; 1 Mac & G 25, 41 ER 1171.
16. See eg *Robb v Green* [1895] 2 QB 315; *Ormonoid Roofing and Asphalts Ltd v Bitumenoids Ltd* (1930) 31 SR (NSW) 347.
17. See eg *Mechanical and General Inventions Co Ltd v Austin* [1935] AC 346.
18. See generally Meagher, Gummow and Lehane, paras 118–22.
19. See eg *Mechanical and General Inventions Co Ltd v Austin* [1935] AC 346; *Johnson v Heat and Air Systems Ltd* (1941) 58 RPC 229.
20. (1948) 65 RPC 203.
21. Ibid at 213.
22. For acceptance of the principle by the High Court, see eg *Commonwealth v John Fairfax & Sons Ltd* (1980) 147 CLR 39; *O'Brien v Komesaroff* (1982) 150 CLR 310; *Moorgate Tobacco Co Ltd v Philip Morris Ltd* (1984) 156 CLR 414; *Attorney-General (UK) v Heinemann Publishers Australia Pty Ltd* (1988) 165 CLR 30; *Johns v Australian Securities Commission* (1993) 178 CLR 408.

has seen breach of confidence become as popular with litigants as it is with commentators.[23]

[3.9] Range of information covered. One facet of the doctrine that calls for comment is the range of information that it covers. Inevitably, most cases will involve a business enterprise or individual seeking to protect trade secrets against the activities either of a former employee or of another enterprise with whom some form of information transaction has been negotiated. Among other things, obligations of confidentiality have been recognised or imposed in relation to:

- ideas which have not been developed or reduced to material form, such as a suggestion for a specific kind of television program;[24]
- an invention which, although not 'novel', has been kept relatively secret, such as a process for freeze drying mussels so as to produce a remedy for arthritis,[25] or the source code of a computer program;[26]
- other technical information, such as the details as to the design, construction and operation of a particular machine;[27] and
- confidential customer requirements.[28]

The courts have also been willing to recognise and enforce confidentiality in non-commercial situations, where the relevant information is of a personal nature,[29] or is generated for government purposes.[30] Indeed it now seems clear that information in any context is capable of generating obligations of confidentiality, provided it satisfies the requirement of secrecy.[31] It has occasionally been said that 'trivial' information may not be protected,[32] which might be taken as suggesting a need to show that the information for which protection is sought has some 'value'. In most cases, however, trivial information will probably turn out not to be secret at all; where it is, and protection is still refused, this may be better viewed as an exercise of the

23. Of the many commentaries on the Anglo-Australian law of breach of confidence, the most comprehensive are those by Gurry and Dean. See also Meagher, Gummow and Lehane, Ch 41; M Richardson and J Stuckey-Clarke, 'Breach of Confidence' in P Parkinson (ed), *The Principles of Equity*, 1996, p 420.

24. *Talbot v General Television Corp Pty Ltd* [1980] VR 224; *Fraser v Thames Television Ltd* [1983] 2 All ER 101; *Wilson v Broadcasting Corp of New Zealand* (1988) 12 IPR 173. Cf *Mar-Con Corp Pty Ltd v Campbell Capital Ltd* (1989) 16 IPR 153, where it was held that the idea of building a 'motor mall' was too general to be considered confidential; and see also *De Maudsley v Palumbo* [1996] FSR 447 (idea for a nightclub not sufficiently developed to be protectable). See generally W R Cornish, 'Confidence in Ideas' (1990) 1 *IPJ* 3.

25. *Aquaculture Corp v New Zealand Green Mussel Co Ltd* (1985) 5 IPR 353.

26. *Ibcos Computers Ltd v Barclays Mercantile Highland Finance Ltd* [1994] FSR 275.

27. See eg *Ansell Rubber Co Pty Ltd v Allied Rubber Industries Pty Ltd* [1967] VR 37.

28. See eg *Thomas Marshall (Exports) Ltd v Guinle* [1979] Ch 227.

29. See eg *Argyll v Argyll* [1967] Ch 302 (marital secrets); *Foster v Mountford* (1977) 14 ALR 71 (Aboriginal tribal secrets); *G v Day* [1982] 1 NSWLR 24 (identity of informer); *Coulthard v South Australia* (1995) 63 SASR 531 (private opinions expressed in meeting).

30. See [4.37]–[4.41].

31. See [4.6].

32. See eg *Coco v A N Clark (Engineers) Ltd* [1969] RPC 41 at 48; *Attorney-General (UK) v Guardian Newspapers Ltd* (No 2) [1988] 3 WLR 776 at 806; *Coulthard v South Australia* (1995) 63 SASR 531 at 547.

court's discretion in framing a remedy.[33] Finally, it should be noted that, with the exception of certain differences as to the burden of proof in the enforcement of confidences relating to government information,[34] courts in England and Australia have generally treated all information alike for the purposes of the doctrine. Thus where American lawyers speak of the 'law of trade secrets', that becomes merely an undifferentiated part of our law of confidential information.[35] On the other hand, unlike the position in the US, Anglo-Australian courts have not been prepared to recognise a wider right of 'privacy'.[36] Hence at common law a person cannot prevent others from obtaining access to information in ways which do not involve an actionable breach of confidence, unless some other wrong (such as trespass) is committed in the process.[37]

[3.10] Trade secrets and the patent system. In some instances, the doctrine of breach of confidence may be used as an alternative to the patent system. An inventor may choose not to patent an idea for any number of reasons: the time and expense of the application process; the need to disclose the idea as part of that process; the fact that exclusivity of exploitation will be lost on expiry of the term of the patent; or more simply a lack of willingness to do anything with the idea other than to deny it to others. If that choice is made, the inventor may wish to keep the idea secret and rely on the doctrine of breach of confidence for protection. This trait does give some cause for concern, in that the maintenance of secrecy that it promotes arguably disrupts the central aim of the patent system: to provide an incentive for the publication of useful ideas by offering a limited period of exclusive exploitation. To the extent that the availability of information rights can be shown to be causative of any neglect to use the patent system,[38] the view may be advanced that no such rights should be recognised in patentable ideas.[39] The arguments against such a view are strong, however.[40] In the first place, the non-patenting strategy is a risky one, for a

33. See *Stephens v Avery* [1988] 2 WLR 1280 at 1285, where the same view was taken about information concerning 'grossly immoral' conduct.
34. See [4.39].
35. See *Ansell Rubber Co Pty Ltd v Allied Rubber Industries Pty Ltd* [1967] VR 37 at 46; *Secton Pty Ltd v Delawood Pty Ltd* (1991) 21 IPR 136 at 149–50.
36. *Victoria Park Racing and Recreation Grounds Co Ltd v Taylor* (1937) 58 CLR 479; *Kaye v Robertson* [1991] FSR 62; *Cruise v Southdown Press Pty Ltd* (1993) 26 IPR 125; though cf *Helliwell v Chief Constable of Derbyshire* [1995] 1 WLR 804 at 807; *Warne v Genex Corp Pty Ltd* (1996) 35 IPR 284. As to the extent to which the action for breach of confidence can or should be used to protect privacy interests, see W Wilson, 'Privacy, Confidence and Press Freedom: A Study in Judicial Activism' (1990) 53 *MLR* 43; M Richardson, 'Breach of Confidence, Surreptitiously or Accidentally Obtained Information and Privacy: Theory Versus Law' (1994) 19 *Melb ULR* 673; and note the implications of the broad view discussed in [4.11] of liability under the equitable doctrine for 'surreptitious' acquisition of information.
37. See eg *Lincoln Hunt Australia Pty Ltd v Willesee* (1986) 4 NSWLR 457; *Emcorp Pty Ltd v Australian Broadcasting Corp* [1988] 2 Qd R 169; K Koomen, 'Under Surveillance: Fergie, Photographers and Infringements on Freedom' (1993) 17 *UQLJ* 234.
38. Cf Gurry, p 11.
39. See eg R G Hammond, 'Quantum Physics, Econometric Models and Property Rights to Information' (1981) 27 *McGill LR* 47 at 59–60; 'Theft of Information' (1984) 100 *LQR* 252 at 260–3.
40. See *Kewanee Oil Co v Bicron Corp* (1974) 416 US 470.

person who makes the same invention independently will not thereby infringe any information rights and may on the contrary be able and willing to secure a patent of their own. Second, the strategy will not be available at all where, as will commonly be the case, exploitation necessarily involves the relevant information being placed in the public domain (for example through the marketing of a device that can be 'reverse engineered' to discover its secrets). Third, the line between patentable and non-patentable ideas is not always easy to discern with any certainty. And finally, information protection reduces the cost of and pressure on the patent system by alleviating the need for inventors to seek patents for all but the 'basic framework of the technology'.[41] In practice the 'know-how' surrounding the realisation of an idea will be protected by information rights, with only the central invention being patented.[42]

[3.11]   **A statutory basis for the doctrine?** Despite the fact that the doctrine of breach of confidence is now firmly embedded in our jurisprudence, a number of questions remain unanswered. There is particular uncertainty as to the precise extent to which persons other than a confidant may be liable and as to the nature and scope of remedies for breach of confidence. The conceptual instability of the area is such that calls are occasionally made for legislative intervention, the leading example being the English Law Commission's recommendation that the breach of confidence action should be formulated as a statutory tort.[43] However, in 1983 the Australian Law Reform Commission, which had been asked to review the doctrine as part of its consideration of the wider issue of privacy, declined to recommend action.[44] Although the Commission's assertion that 'the law is clear' must be viewed with some scepticism, its conclusion that a legislative restatement would be inappropriate seems to have met with general acceptance. For the foreseeable future, it seems, breach of confidence will remain within the immediate control of the judiciary.

[3.12]   **The great debate.** Many (though by no means all) of the difficulties with the doctrine can be traced to the failure by the courts to identify a commonly accepted and consistent rationale for liability. Whole forests have died in order to accommodate the academic ink spilled on the question of the 'true' basis of the action for breach of confidence. The debate has, alas, been less than conclusive. There are probably only two points on which anything near unanimity is possible. The first, concurring with Lord Greene MR's opinion in *Saltman*,[45] is that the action may arise notwithstanding the lack of a contract between the parties and thus cannot be explained on a contractual basis; the second is that the action is, in

41. E W Kitch, 'The Nature and Function of the Patent System' (1977) 20 *J Law & Econ* 265 at 288.
42. See Cornish, p 265.
43. UK Law Commission Report No 110, Breach of Confidence, Cmnd 8388, 1981. See also A Coleman, 'Reform of Canadian Trade Secrets Law' [1987] 8 *EIPR* 228.
44. *Privacy*, Report No 22, 1983, vol 1, paras 931–6; vol 2, paras 1310–11. See also Legal and Constitutional Committee (Vic), *A Report to Parliament Upon Privacy and Breach of Confidence*, 1990.
45. (1948) 65 RPC 203 at 211.

origin at least, an equitable one. Beyond that, however, consensus is hard to find. The views which have achieved most prominence in recent years are discussed in the following paragraphs: as will quickly become apparent, each has its difficulties.

[3.13] **Confidentiality as good faith.** The first suggestion is that the jurisdiction over breach of confidence is based on a broad equitable principle of good faith.[46] The principal merit of this view is that it can claim considerable judicial authority to support it. Courts have generally couched their decisions in these terms and there is no lack of dicta specifically assigning the basis of the action to such a principle.[47] If any dissension has arisen, it has tended to be on the subsidiary question of whether this duty of good faith should be described as a fiduciary duty.[48]

[3.14] **Secret information as property.** An alternative explanation of the action for breach of confidence is that the courts are protecting a proprietary interest in the secrecy of information.[49] There is nothing inherently improbable about regarding secret information as a form of property. The fact that information can be shared, that rights in it may disappear when it ceases to be secret, that any protection offered may lie in the discretion of a court, that rights may exist only in a limited respect or against a limited range of persons — none of these objections are unique to information. So long then as the law is prepared to recognise that the mere possession of secret information generates certain rights, it is conceptually appropriate to speak of those rights as proprietary in nature.[50] This does not mean, however, that the enforcement of confidentiality is sufficient in itself to warrant adopting a property analysis. If the right not to have express or implied confidences broken is the only protection accorded to a possessor of information, there is no necessity to regard the right as one attaching to the information itself. It is just as plausible, and indeed more accurate historically, to say that the right emanates from the confidential relationship between the parties. As Holmes J put it so memorably:[51]

> The word property as applied to trade-marks and trade secrets is an unanalysed expression of certain secondary consequences of the primary fact that the law makes some rudimentary requirements of good faith. Whether the plaintiffs have any valuable secret or not the defendant knows the facts, whatever they are, through a special confidence that he accepted. The property may be denied but the confidence cannot be. Therefore the starting

46. See G Jones, 'Restitution of Benefits Obtained in Breach of Another's Confidence' (1970) 86 *LQR* 463; J Stuckey, 'The Equitable Action for Breach of Confidence: Is Information Ever Property?' (1981) 9 *Syd LR* 402. See also Dean, Ch 1.
47. See eg *Moorgate Tobacco Co Ltd v Philip Morris Ltd* (1984) 156 CLR 414 at 437–8; *Smith Kline and French Laboratories (Australia) Ltd v Secretary, Department of Community Services and Health* (1991) 20 IPR 643 at 656.
48. See [4.32].
49. See S Ricketson, 'Confidential Information — A New Proprietary Interest?' (1977) 11 *Melb ULR* 223, 289; M Neave and M Weinberg, 'The Nature and Function of Equities (Part II)' (1978) 6 *U Tas LR* 115; A S Weinrib, 'Information and Property' (1988) 38 *U Tor LJ* 117 at 122–36.
50. See A S Weinrib, ibid at 126–8; and see further K Gray, 'Property in Thin Air' [1991] *CLJ* 252.
51. *E I Du Pont de Nemours Powder Co v Masland* (1917) 244 US 100 at 102.

point for the present matter is not property or due process of law, but that the defendant stood in confidential relations with the plaintiffs, or one of them.

[3.15] The orthodox judicial view: rejection of the property analysis.
Buoyed by this reasoning, the orthodox approach taken by the courts is that Australian law does not treat secret information as property.[52] True, many courts use the term 'property' when speaking of confidential information and are prepared to refer to it as an asset.[53] It is conceded that information may be transferred,[54] held on trust,[55] or form part of a bankrupt's estate.[56] Nonetheless the dominant view appears to be that

> it is not information per se, nor any intrinsic qualities of *confidential* information, which the courts are protecting. Rather, it is the intangible notion of a confidence, which is formed by the communication of confidential information for a limited purpose, and which therefore exists *in relation to* information.[57]

The orthodox analysis receives support from a series of authorities to the effect that stealing information does not constitute a criminal offence within the ordinary statutory definition of theft. Even where what is capable of being stolen is defined specifically to include things tangible or intangible,[58] these cases suggest that information is not to be treated as property for that purpose.[59] Although misappropriation of information and other types of conduct in regard to databases (such as 'hacking') are seen as problems which call for a measure of criminal sanctions, this has been accommodated by the creation of new offences specifically addressing various forms of 'computer abuse'.[60]

---

52. *Federal Commissioner of Taxation v United Aircraft Corporation* (1943) 68 CLR 525 at 534; *BEST Australia Ltd v Aquagas Marketing Pty Ltd* (1989) 13 IPR 600 at 603; *Smith Kline and French Laboratories (Australia) Ltd v Secretary, Department of Community Services and Health* (1991) 20 IPR 643 at 656; *Breen v Williams* (1996) 138 ALR 259 at 264–5, 271, 288, 301–2. See also *Smith Kline & French Laboratories (Australia) Ltd v Secretary, Department of Community Services and Health* (1990) 17 IPR 545 at 592–4, where although Gummow J was prepared to regard confidential information as property for the purposes of s 51(xxxi) of the Constitution (allowing the Commonwealth to acquire property on just terms), he insisted that this description was only a *consequence* of equity's intervention to protect against abuses of confidence, not an explanation for that intervention. Cf *Colbeam Palmer Ltd v Stock Affiliates Pty Ltd* (1968) 122 CLR 25 at 34.
53. See eg *Federal Commissioner of Taxation v United Aircraft Corporation* (1943) 68 CLR 525 at 547–8; *Boardman v Phipps* [1967] AC 46 at 107.
54. See eg *Bryson v Whitehead* (1822) 1 Sim & St 74, 57 ER 29 (sale); *Canham v Jones* (1813) 2 V & B 218, 35 ER 302 (bequest).
55. See eg *Boardman v Phipps* [1967] AC 46; *Markwell Bros Pty Ltd v CPN Diesels Queensland Pty Ltd* [1983] 2 Qd R 508.
56. See eg *Re Keene* [1922] 2 Ch 475.
57. F Gurry, 'Breach of Confidence' in P D Finn (ed), *Essays in Equity*, 1985, p 110 at p 116 (emphasis in original).
58. See eg Crimes Act 1958 (Vic), ss 71–72.
59. *Oxford v Moss* (1978) 68 Cr App R 183; *R v Stewart* (1988) 50 DLR (4th) 1; *Grant v Procurator Fiscal* [1988] RPC 41. Cf *Carpenter v United States* (1987) 108 S Ct 316. See generally Dean, pp 528–47; J T Cross, 'Trade Secrets, Confidential Information and the Criminal Law' (1991) 36 *McGill LR* 525.
60. See eg Crimes Act 1914 (Cth) Pt VIA; and see generally G Hughes, *Data Protection in Australia*, 1991, Ch 8.

[3.16] **Criticisms of the orthodox view.** The orthodox view that possession of information does not generate proprietary rights can be criticised on two grounds. The first relates to policy. Why should the law protect
confidentiality but not secrecy? Why, in other words, should a person who
deals with a secret in an unauthorised manner be liable if the information
has been disclosed pursuant to a confidential relationship, but not otherwise? A historical explanation can be offered: that the courts entered the
field of information protection on the basis of the 'simple moral precept'
that 'a person ought to keep a secret if he [sic] has said that he will do
so'.[61] This focus on the relationship between discloser and confidant, coupled with the lack at the time of any sophisticated property analysis, naturally drew attention away from the notion that secret information is an asset
and thus deserving of protection. But that does not explain why it should
be so today. Even if it is appropriate to concentrate on the wrong committed in relation to the information, rather than the value in the information
itself, why is it that confidants alone are to be penalised for unauthorised
use? Accepting that the possessor should have no rights against one who
creates the same information independently, that still leaves a range of persons who may acquire the information without authority and deal with it in
such a way that sanctions are called for.

[3.17] **The trend to a proprietary analysis.** In fact the law *does* do
more than protect confidentiality — and therein lies the second criticism of
the orthodox view. That view is premised on the assumption that the law
protects relationships, not any 'property' in information.[62] But the assumption is not borne out by the authorities. The modern action for breach of
confidence exhibits clear signs that the courts have adopted, consciously or
not, a proprietary analysis that takes the secrecy of information rather than
a confidence as its real starting point. The trend can be identified in three
respects. The first lies in the general observation that the scope of liability
for breach of confidence is determined as much by the nature and value of
the relevant information as by the defendant's 'wrongdoing'. This is particularly true where remedies are concerned. Second, it will be seen that the
courts have imposed strict liability on those who are under an obligation of
confidence.[63] This notion, although in itself explicable within a framework
for protection of relationships, is just as consistent and perhaps more compatible with a proprietary approach. At the very least, it is difficult to reconcile with the relation-oriented emphasis on 'good faith' that is a hallmark of
the courts' rhetoric on confidentiality. Third, however, and most crucially,
is the inability of the orthodox approach to explain how non-confidants
come to be liable for misusing information. To a certain extent the point is
true of the liability of third parties who acquire information as a result of a
breach of confidence,[64] though that can be explained (albeit implausibly
in some cases) as merely involving an extension of a confidant's wrongdoing. More pertinent is the liability imposed upon those who acquire information either deliberately (as in the case of surveillance or espionage) or
accidentally (as in the case of receipt by mistake), but at all events without

---

61. Cornish, p 263.
62. Cf S Wright, 'Confidentiality and the Public/Private Dichotomy' [1993] 7 *EIPR* 237.
63. See [4.12].
64. See [4.14].

any consensual communication from the plaintiff.[65] It is true that this liability has been couched in terms of the defendant coming under an obligation of confidentiality. But there is a clear difference between the recognition of an obligation flowing out of a relationship of confidence between the parties and the *imposition* of such an obligation in order to ground a liability that the court thinks ought to exist. In this type of case the court is in effect creating a 'quasi-confidence', a duty based on a fictional relationship in much the same way as 'quasi-contractual' actions were employed in the law of restitution.[66] This remedial use of confidentiality needs to be recognised for what it is — the invocation of a familiar concept to protect an interest of the plaintiff that the courts (at least in this country and the UK) cannot bring themselves to identify overtly.

[3.18] The sui generis view. Given the failure of the good faith and property theories to be at once fully explanatory of the doctrine and generally accepted by the courts,[67] it is hardly surprising to find a compromise view — that breach of confidence is 'a *sui generis* action which has, in terms of conventional categories, a composite jurisdictional basis'.[68] As far back as 1851 Turner VC noted that:

> Different grounds have indeed been assigned for the exercise of [jurisdiction over breach of confidence]. In some cases it has been referred to property, in others to contract, and in others, again, it has been treated as founded upon trust or confidence, meaning, as I conceive, that the Court fastens the obligation on the conscience of the party ... but, upon whatever grounds the jurisdiction is founded, the authorities leave no doubt as to the exercise of it.[69]

On the surface, the approach has much to recommend it. It takes account of the inconsistencies that so plague the good faith and property theories and avoids the problems of trying to impose a theoretical strait jacket on a doctrine that has developed through a combination of historical accident and case by case accretion rather than rigorous conceptualism. So long as courts continue to take a pragmatic approach to the resolution of specific issues, why bother formulating and reformulating theories to explain every twist and turn the doctrine takes? Two answers may be offered. The first lies in the occasional propensity of judges to depart from the pragmatic model of decision-making and to reason instead from rationale to result.[70] In

---

65. See [4.11]. In *Chih Ling Koo v Tai Hing* (1992) 23 IPR 607 at 632–3, the liability imposed on 'takers' of information led Bokhary J of the Supreme Court of Hong Kong to conclude that there must indeed be 'a proprietary interest in confidential information'; though cf E Loh, 'Intellectual Property: Breach of Confidence?' [1995] 8 *EIPR* 405, discussing the decision on appeal in that case.
66. As to the 'implied contract' fiction, see *Pavey & Matthews Pty Ltd v Paul* (1987) 162 CLR 221; Mason and Carter, pp 17–28.
67. The same can be said of other specific theories which have occasionally been advanced: see eg P M North, 'Breach of Confidence: Is There a New Tort?' (1972) 12 *JSPTL* 149, where it is suggested that liability is tortious in nature; though note the support suggested for this view in *X Ltd v Morgan-Grampian (Publishers) Ltd* [1990] 2 WLR 1000, where Lord Bridge repeatedly uses the language of tort.
68. Gurry, p 58. See also J Kearney, *Action for Breach of Confidence in Australia*, 1985, Ch 3.
69. *Morison v Moat* (1851) 9 Hare 241 at 255; 68 ER 492 at 498.
70. See eg *Wheatley v Bell* [1982] 2 NSWLR 544 (see [4.15]), and see also *Breen v Williams* (1996) 138 ALR 259, where the High Court's acceptance that information is not property was an important element in its decision not to recognise any right for patients to access their medical records.

these cases it obviously does make a difference which theory is adopted. Second, however, and more importantly, the prospect of the doctrine developing in an aimless and ad hoc manner is at least as unappealing as the vision of a dynamic body of law being stunted by rigid adherence to a single narrow theory. It should be evident from the following chapter that the doctrine of breach of confidence is still being worked out by the courts and that many important questions remain unanswered. No theory can hope to explain every nuance of every decision. Nevertheless some understanding of the directions being taken by the courts, consciously or not, seems indispensable both in predicting and prompting the outcomes of the choices that remain to be made.[71]

[3.19] Conclusion. The real problem with the debate as to the true basis of the breach of confidence action has been the apparent inability on the part of many commentators to distinguish between what the courts are actually doing and what they *say* they are doing. The view has been advanced above that the courts have steadily been moving towards some form of proprietary theory of liability: that from a historical starting point of protecting relationships of confidence they have come to protect the possessor of information against both breach of confidence and other conduct incompatible with the possessor's valuable interest in the information. On the other hand, what they *say* they have been doing is to recognise equitable obligations of good faith in order to protect confidentiality, stoutly resisting any talk of information being property in any but the loosest of senses. In that light, it cannot be said that the stage has been reached where Anglo-Australian law has developed or is even close to developing a genuine proprietary approach to information rights. So long indeed as the action for breach of confidence remains the lynchpin for information protection, it is unlikely that it will do so. This is in sharp contrast to the US, where most courts appear to have taken the logical step of recognising rights in information without the need to identify a confidential relationship, actual or fictional.[72] It might of course be argued that it does not matter in practice whether or not secret information is treated as property. The answer to that is twofold. In the first place, concentration on confidentiality (even in a remedial sense) rather than property can conceivably make a difference to liability — as to standing to bring suit, for instance.[73] It certainly matters whether information is 'property' in the context of the law of stamp duties, to take one mundane but practically significant example.[74] But more generally, there is the

71. See UK Law Commission Report No 110, *Breach of Confidence*, Cmnd 8388, 1981, para 5.2.
72. See eg *Ruckelshaus v Monsanto* (1984) 467 US 985. Note the Supreme Court's rejection (at 1004, n 9) of the contention that the judgment of Holmes J in *E I Du Pont de Nemours Powder Co v Masland* (1917) 244 US 100 (quoted in [3.14]) is authority against the recognition of property rights in information.
73. See [4.2].
74. See eg *Pancontinental Mining Ltd v Commissioner of Stamp Duties* [1989] 1 Qd R 310 where it was held that confidential information as to mining prospects, sold as an 'asset' for nearly $4.5 million, did not constitute 'property' for the purpose of calculating stamp duty. For a useful discussion of other issues and consequences that might flow from recognising information as personal property, see N Palmer, 'Information as Property' in L Clarke (ed), *Confidentiality and the Law*, 1990, p 83.

observation that the practice of clinging to an outmoded concept — and confidentiality, as the sole basis for information protection, increasingly appears to be just that — can only be harmful in the long run. If the courts are to fashion remedies to protect information against more than broken confidences and if they are to confront the important policy issues involved, an open acknowledgment of the true basis for those remedies seems indispensable.

Chapter 4

Breach of Confidence

1. PRELIMINARY ISSUES

(a) Identifying the Plaintiff

[4.1] To whom does information 'belong'? The action for breach of confidence assumes that a person can be identified who has 'disclosed' information to another in confidence and to whom an obligation of confidentiality can be said to be owed. Now whether or not a proprietary theory of liability is accepted, it is still necessary for this purpose to determine to whom the relevant information 'belongs'. The mere fact of possession does not suffice: it would be absurd to suppose, for instance, that those who acquire information improperly could bring an action against anyone to whom they themselves subsequently disclose that information. More fundamentally, information may be brought into existence in such a way that it is unclear who 'owns' it.[1] The problem may often be resolved by contract. Thus, for instance, a term will usually be implied into every contract of employment that any information discovered or created by the employee in the course of service will 'belong' to the employer. Absent express agreement to the contrary, it will be the employer, therefore, who has the right to sue for breach of confidence — with the defendant often being the employee who created the information in the first place.[2] Where, however, joint effort has produced the information and no agreement can be discerned on the matter, the position appears to be that each of the parties concerned will be able to enforce confidentiality against others to whom they make disclosures, but not against each other.[3]

---

1. Cf *British Franco Electric Pty Ltd v Dowling Plastics Pty Ltd* [1981] 1 NSWLR 448.
2. See further [4.33]–[4.35].
3. See *International Scientific Communications Inc v Pattison* [1979] FSR 429.

[4.2] **Standing to enforce confidentiality.** The identification of the person to whom a duty of confidence is owed does not necessarily resolve the question of standing, for the law might allow another to enforce that duty. In *Fraser v Evans*,[4] however, the English Court of Appeal rejected that possibility. A consultant employed by the Greek government was held to be unable to restrain the publication of a leaked copy of his report. The court found that any duty of confidence as to the contents of the report was owed to the government and that it alone was competent to sue for breach of that duty, whatever the detrimental effects of publication on the consultant.[5] Although this principle has occasionally been overlooked,[6] it seems to be generally accepted as correct. It illustrates one difference between the 'property' and 'relationship' theories of informational protection. Suppose that A and B jointly develop information which B in turn communicates to C in confidence. If C misuses the information, the *Fraser* principle suggests that A cannot sue, even though the information 'belongs' to A and even though A may suffer loss as a result of C's activities. Under a property analysis, on the other hand, it might well be that A should have a remedy — on the basis that C has committed a wrong in regard to something in which A has a valuable interest, whether or not there is a relationship between them. Similar problems may arise where there is a 'chain' of confidences.[7]

There is one situation in which the *Fraser* principle no longer applies. Section 93 of the Privacy Act 1988 (Cth) has the effect that where a Commonwealth agency comes under an obligation of confidence in respect of personal information relating to a person *other* than the confider, the subject of the information is as much entitled to enforce that obligation of confidence as the confider.

(b) Relationship with Contractual Protection

[4.3] **Confidentiality in a contractual context.** It has already been noted that in many of the early breach of confidence cases a contractual relationship existed between the parties: indeed that is still the case today. Where performance of the contract calls for or necessarily involves the disclosure by one party to the other of secret or sensitive information, the law will have no difficulty in implying a term requiring the confidant to respect the confidentiality of the information.[8] Common examples involve

---

4. [1969] 1 QB 349. See also *Finnane v Australian Consolidated Press* [1978] 2 NSWLR 435.
5. Cf *Bacich v Australian Broadcasting Corp* (1992) 29 NSWLR 1, where the directors and sole shareholders of a small company were held to be so involved in its business affairs that any duty of confidence owed to the company was also owed to (and thus enforceable by) them.
6. See eg *Foster v Mountford* (1976) 29 FLR 233 (Aboriginal council suing on behalf of various communities to suppress publication of tribal secrets given many years earlier to anthropologist by unidentified Aborigines); *Falconer v Australian Broadcasting Corp* (1991) 22 IPR 205 (police officer protecting identity of police informer); *Deputy Commissioner of Taxation v Rettke* (1995) 31 IPR 457 (Tax Commissioner protecting confidentiality of information supplied by taxpayers). In none of these cases was the question of standing argued.
7. See P D Finn, *Fiduciary Obligations*, 1977, pp 152–6.
8. See P Finn, 'Professionals and Confidentiality' (1992) 14 *Syd LR* 317. Cf *Esso Australia Resources Ltd v Plowman* (1995) 183 CLR 10 (no implication of confidentiality in relation to agreement for private arbitration).

disclosures by a client to a lawyer,[9] by customer to banker,[10] by patient to doctor,[11] and by employer to employee.[12] It seems clear that in some situations the contractual obligation may indeed go beyond what the equitable doctrine would otherwise require. The most obvious instance is provided by employment cases, where the employee's implied duty to serve the employer faithfully may impose a disability during (but not after) the term of the contract in relation to information which would not be sufficiently secret to be the subject of the equitable duty.[13] The same may well be true in the other contexts referred to above, where professional ethics might demand silence even on matters which are in the public domain. This is also the best explanation of the English Court of Appeal's controversial decision in *Schering Chemicals Ltd v Falkman*.[14] The defendants were restrained from broadcasting a documentary on the controversy surrounding a drug manufactured by the plaintiff. Their 'breach of confidence' lay in using information obtained by two of them while acting as media consultants for the plaintiff. While this information was not secret, having previously been published in newspaper reports, its inclusion in the documentary, even if fairly handled, would revive the controversy and create bad publicity for the plaintiff, precisely the thing that the plaintiff had looked to avoid in engaging the defendants. What the court did in effect was to imply in the particular circumstances a duty, similar to an employee's duty of fidelity, not to use *any* information to the plaintiff's detriment.

Accepting then that the circumstances of a particular relationship may call for a more stringent duty than would be imposed by equity alone (and conceivably sometimes a lesser duty),[15] does this mean that the equitable duty is entirely supplanted whenever a contract exists between confider and confidant? Despite occasional dicta to the contrary,[16] the answer seems to

---

9.   See eg *Parry-Jones v Law Society* [1969] Ch 1. As to the extent to which this duty may preclude a lawyer from acting for other clients, see eg *Carindale Country Club Estate Pty Ltd v Astill* (1993) 115 ALR 112; and see further L Aitken, ' "Chinese Walls" and Conflicts of Interest' (1992) 18 *Mon ULR* 91; F Costigan, 'Conflict of Interest — Chinese Walls and Bamboo Curtains' in C A G Coady and C J G Sampford, *Business, Ethics and the Law*, 1993, p 113.
10. See eg *Tournier v National Provincial & Union Bank of England* [1924] 1 KB 461; J McI Walter and N Erlich, 'Confidences — Bankers and Customers: Powers of Banks to Maintain Secrecy and Confidentiality' (1989) 63 *ALJ* 404. Cf G Tucker, 'Vale Tournier — Salve Privacy Act' (1993) 21 *ABLR* 290; D Clough, 'Misleading and Deceptive Silence: Section 52, Confidentiality and the General Law' (1994) 2 *TPLJ* 76.
11. See eg *Furniss v Fitchett* [1958] NZLR 396; *Slater v Bissett* (1986) 69 ACTR 25; *W v Egdell* [1990] 2 WLR 471; A Dix, M Errington, K Nicholson and R Powe, *Law for the Medical Profession in Australia*, 2nd ed, 1996, Ch 4; P McFarlane, *Health Law: Commentary and Materials*, 2nd ed, 1995, Ch 5.
12. See [4.33]–[4.35]. For examples of employees suing their employers, see *Slavutych v Baker* (1975) 55 DLR (3d) 224; *Prout v British Gas plc* [1992] FSR 351.
13. See [4.34].
14. [1981] 2 All ER 321. Cf *Attorney-General (UK) v Heinemann Publishers Australia Pty Ltd* (1987) 75 ALR 353 at 432–3.
15. See eg Gurry, pp 146–7 (bank's duty of confidence inapplicable where disclosure of customer information necessary for protection of bank's interests). See also *Barclays Bank plc v Taylor* [1989] 3 All ER 563.
16. See eg *Vokes Ltd v Heather* (1945) 62 RPC 135 at 141–2; *Faccenda Chicken Ltd v Fowler* [1986] 1 All ER 617 at 625.

be that it is not and that the equitable and contractual duties may co-exist.[17] The independent role of the equitable doctrine is evident in two respects. In the first place, confiders in some instances have been awarded equitable relief of a type not typically available for breach of contract.[18] Second, it will be seen that redress may be available against a person, not privy to any contract with the confider, into whose hands information comes as a result of the original confidant's breach of duty. Unless such a third party has committed the tort of contractual interference by procuring the breach,[19] their liability can only be explained in terms of the equitable doctrine.[20]

[4.4] The role of express commitments. Where confidential information is made available pursuant to a contractual arrangement, it is not uncommon for the confider to secure an express commitment that the information will not be utilised for a purpose other than that for which it has been communicated. Such clauses will almost inevitably be found, for instance, in service agreements involving managerial employees, consultancy agreements, agreements to license technology,[21] and arrangements designed to facilitate information disclosure during joint venture negotiations.[22] The advantage that they offer, obviously, is that of enhanced certainty as to the parties' rights and obligations. Curiously, however, the precise legal significance of an express obligation is not totally clear. On ordinary contractual principles, it might be expected that the adoption of an express term would oust any implied obligation on the same matter, or would at least prevail to the extent of any conflict.[23] Thus where a clause stipulates a specific duration for an obligation of confidentiality, this should oust the general rule[24] that an obligation of confidentiality subsists for as long as the relevant information remains secret, and indeed there is some authority to that effect.[25] The balance of the authorities, however, adopt a different approach.[26] Thus it has been held that an obligation of secrecy may be enforced despite the presence of an express obligation which offers only limited protection,[27] or which conversely is unenforceable as being in unreasonable restraint of trade.[28] There does not appear to be any

17. See eg *Titan Group Pty Ltd v Steriline Manufacturing Pty Ltd* (1990) 19 IPR 353 at 388.
18. See eg *Peter Pan Manufacturing Corp v Corsets Silhouette Ltd* [1963] 3 All ER 402 (account of profits); *Ansell Rubber Co Pty Ltd v Allied Rubber Industries Pty Ltd* [1967] VR 37 (delivery up for destruction).
19. See [4.16].
20. See eg *Printers & Finishers Ltd v Holloway* [1964] 3 All ER 731 at 739; and see [4.14].
21. For a discussion of some of the interpretation issues that tend to arise in this particular context, see Gurry, pp 129–37.
22. See *Australian Encyclopaedia of Forms and Precedents*, 3rd ed, 1989, vol 7, Forms 15.205–15.225.
23. See J W Carter and D J Harland, *Contract Law in Australia*, 3rd ed, 1996, pp 209, 212.
24. See [4.7]–[4.8]
25. See *Potters-Ballotini Ltd v Weston-Baker* [1977] RPC 202; *Deta Nominees Pty Ltd v Viscount Plastic Products Pty Ltd* [1979] VR 167.
26. See Gurry, pp 30–5.
27. See eg *British Industrial Plastics Ltd v Ferguson* (1939) 56 RPC 271 at 277 (express clause of limited duration); *Thomas Marshall (Exporters) Ltd v Guinle* [1979] Ch 227 (express clause forbidding only disclosure of information, injunction granted to restrain use).
28. See eg *Wessex Dairies Ltd v Smith* [1935] 2 KB 80; *Triplex Safety Glass Co Ltd v Scorah* (1938) 55 RPC 21.

Australian authority on the point, however, and it may be that the more orthodox position will prevail if the matter arises for decision here.

2.   ESTABLISHING LIABILITY

[4.5]   A general test. In *Coco v A N Clark (Engineers) Ltd*[29] Megarry J stated that:

> In my judgment, three elements are normally required if, apart from contract, a case of breach of confidence is to succeed. First, the information itself, in the words of Lord Greene MR in the *Saltman* case [(1948) 65 RPC 203 at 215], must 'have the necessary quality of confidence about it'. Secondly, that information must have been imparted in circumstances importing an obligation of confidence. Thirdly, there must be an unauthorised use of that information to the detriment of the party communicating it.

This test has been widely cited and applied, not only in the business information context to which it was specifically addressed, but also in cases featuring governmental and personal information.[30] The following sections discuss the three elements identified and then examine the most important issue that the judgment does not address, that of the liability of third parties.

(a) Secrecy

[4.6]   Degree of secrecy required. To attract protection, information must 'have the necessary quality of confidence about it, namely, it must not be something which is public property or public knowledge'.[31] The test is essentially a negative one: so long as the information is not in the public domain, it may be the subject of an obligation of confidence. The problem, of course, is that secrecy is not an absolute concept. Clearly, information may be known to persons other than the confider and confidant without ceasing to be a secret: but at what point is information known to or accessible by enough people to be considered public knowledge?[32] The question is further complicated by the fact that the 'relevant public'[33] for this purpose may themselves be a fairly small group. This is illustrated in *Franchi v Franchi*,[34] where Cross J had to decide whether publication of a secret process in a patent specification filed in Belgium had the effect of destroying secrecy in England. In holding that it did, the judge relied heavily on the fact that British patent agents typically inspected foreign specifications and would thus be expected to have learned the details of this process. The assumption here was evidently that merely making the information accessible destroyed secrecy, given the vigilance of the relevant public. The same

---

29.   [1969] RPC 41 at 47.
30.   See eg *Commonwealth v John Fairfax & Sons Ltd* (1980) 147 CLR 39 at 51; *Coulthard v South Australia* (1995) 63 SASR 531 at 534, 546.
31.   *Saltman Engineering Co Ltd v Campbell Engineering Co Ltd* (1948) 65 RPC 203 at 215; *O'Brien v Komesaroff* (1982) 150 CLR 310 at 326–8; *Johns v Australian Securities Commission* (1993) 178 CLR 408 at 432, 438, 461, 475.
32.   See *Interfirm Comparison (Australia) Pty Ltd v Law Society of NSW* (1975) 5 ALR 527 at 541–3; *Stephens v Avery* [1988] 2 WLR 1280 at 1285 ('information only ceases to be capable of protection as confidential when it is in fact known to a substantial number of people').
33.   See *Attorney-General (UK) v Guardian Newspapers (No 2)* [1988] 2 WLR 805 at 868.
34.   [1967] RPC 149.

reasoning can be seen to underlie the High Court's decision in *Johns v Australian Securities Commission*.[35] There the plaintiff, the former managing director of the Tricontinental group of companies, challenged the ASC's decision to release transcripts of interviews with him to a Victorian Royal Commission inquiring into Tricontinental's affairs. The challenge succeeded on the ground that although the ASC had a statutory power to release the information, the decision to exercise that power was invalid since the plaintiff had not been afforded natural justice in the form of a fair hearing. This meant that the plaintiff's confidentiality had been breached. However, the plaintiff's attempt to prevent media outlets publishing material from the transcripts failed. A majority of the court (Brennan, Dawson and Toohey JJ, with Gaudron and McHugh JJ preferring to remit the matter for further investigation) held that since the material had been tendered in evidence before the Royal Commission during a public hearing, it must be regarded as being in the public domain and thus accessible to all. By the same token, any matter published in open court or appearing in the record of parliamentary debates ought, subject to a suppression order from the court or the parliament in question, be treated as being in the public domain.[36]

Conversely, actual publication to a much larger group may in some cases not have the effect of putting information into the public domain. Thus in *G v Day*[37] the confidentiality of the plaintiff's identity was held not to have been lost by the broadcast of his name on two occasions on a Sydney television news service, since the references were 'transitory and brief' and would mean nothing to anyone who did not already know him.

A particularly common problem arises in regard to circulation of allegedly confidential information within a business enterprise. Some degree of access on the part of employees and even customers is inevitable if the most efficient use is to be made of the information, but at some point that circulation will be so widespread that secrecy disappears. In a number of cases judges have drawn up lists of factors to be considered in this connection. Thus in the *Ansell Rubber* case[38] Gowans J drew on American trade secrets law[39] for the following criteria:

> (1) [T]he extent to which the information is known outside of [the employer's] business; (2) the extent to which it is known by employees and others involved in his [sic] business; (3) the extent of measures taken by him to guard the secrecy of the information; (4) the value of the information to him and his competitors; (5) the amount of effort or money expended by him in developing the information; (6) the ease or difficulty with which the information could be properly acquired or duplicated by others.

This does not mean, of course, that it is either possible or desirable to 'slavishly check off the factors against the information, as if one were counting spots on some strange creature to see if it was indeed the species of leopard

---

35. (1993) 178 CLR 408.
36. Cf *Westpac Banking Corp v John Fairfax Group Pty Ltd* (1991) 19 IPR 513; and see A Stewart and M Chesterman, 'Confidential Material: The Position of the Media' (1992) 14 *Adel LR* 1 at 4–7.
37. [1982] 1 NSWLR 24; see also *Wigginton v Brisbane TV Ltd* (1992) 25 IPR 58. Cf *Commonwealth v John Fairfax & Sons Ltd* (1980) 147 CLR 39.
38. *Ansell Rubber Co Pty Ltd v Allied Rubber Industries Pty Ltd* [1967] VR 37 at 49–50.
39. See Restatement (First) of Torts, Art 757, comment.

illustrated in the picture book'.[40] The test will always be whether, in the particular circumstances, 'relative secrecy'[41] can be identified, a matter simply not susceptible to precise formulation. One point that is clear, however, is that a plaintiff must attempt to specify with some care what is confidential and what is not. A 'global' claim covering a wide range of information will be rejected, no matter how clear it is that some of the information is secret.[42]

[4.7] Loss of secrecy and the duration of obligations of confidence. If secrecy is a prerequisite of the creation of an obligation of confidence, then it might be thought logical to adopt a corollary principle to the effect that the persistence of secrecy is necessary to the continuance of that obligation. In other words, once information moves into the public domain the confidant should be as free as anyone else to exploit it. Unfortunately, the actual position is rather less straightforward. In part at least, it depends on who is responsible for the publication.[43] If the publication is made by or with the consent of the confider it seems clear that, subject to the operation of the 'springboard principle' discussed in the next paragraph, the confidant is thereby released from any obligation.[44] It is not so easy to see what should happen, however, where the information is published by a third party, or indeed by the confidant's own action.

The key to resolving the problem is to draw a clear distinction between two separate issues. The first is whether the confidant has done anything prior to the information reaching the public domain which can be considered a breach of confidence. Now so long as the information has been published by someone else (whether the confider or a third party) *and* so long as the confidant has not previously been using the information in an unauthorised manner that has not involved publication, then (again subject to the springboard principle) there is no sense in placing a continuing disability on the confidant in relation to information which everyone else is free to use.[45] Where no prior breach has been established, therefore, the obligation of confidence should be considered to lapse on publication.[46]

If on the other hand there *has* been a breach, whether in prior use or in the very act of publication, the effect of publication on the confidant's

40. *Deta Nominees Pty Ltd v Viscount Plastic Products Pty Ltd* [1979] VR 167 at 193. Cf *Mense v Milenkovic* [1973] VR 784 at 796–8.
41. *Franchi v Franchi* [1967] RPC 149 at 153.
42. *O'Brien v Komesaroff* (1982) 150 CLR 310 at 328; *Attorney-General (UK) v Heinemann Publishers Australia Pty Ltd* (1987) 75 ALR 353 at 424–30; *American Cyanamid Co v Alcoa of Australia Ltd* (1993) 27 IPR 16; and see also [4.35].
43. Cf *Speed Seal Products Ltd v Paddington* [1986] 1 All ER 91 at 94–5.
44. *O Mustad & Son v S Allcock & Co Ltd* (1928) 3 All ER 416; *Fractionated Cane Technology Ltd v Ruiz-Avila* (1988) 13 IPR 609; *ANI Corp Ltd v Celtite Australia Pty Ltd* (1990) 19 IPR 506; *Secton Pty Ltd v Delawood* (1991) 21 IPR 136; *Johns v Australian Securities Commission* (1993) 178 CLR 408 at 461.
45. See *Peter Pan Manufacturing Corp v Corsets Silhouette Ltd* [1963] 3 All ER 402 at 408.
46. Cf *Schering Chemicals Ltd v Falkman* [1981] 2 All ER 321 at 339, where Shaw LJ commented that '[i]t is not the law that where confidentiality exists it is terminated or eroded by adventitious publicity': see also *David Syme & Co Ltd v General Motors-Holden Ltd* [1984] 2 NSWLR 294 at 299. This comment should be read, however, in the context of a duty that appeared to go beyond preserving secrecy: see [4.3].

liability raises a different issue. In this situation, which will inevitably arise where the confidant is responsible for the publication, though not necessarily where the confider or a third party do so, the only question is as to the scope of the relief to be awarded to the confider for the breach that has already occurred. In a sense it is a matter of semantics whether or not the confidant is 'released' from the obligation. The real issues are remedial: whether injunctive relief against further use by the confidant of the information is warranted, notwithstanding the publication, in order to protect the confider's interests; or whether, if damages or an account of profits are to be awarded, account should be taken of loss sustained or profits made after the date of publication.[47]

[4.8] **The springboard doctrine.** Much of the confusion that has surrounded the issue of the duration of obligations can be traced to misapprehensions as to what has come to be known as the 'springboard doctrine'. Its origin lies in the judgment of Roxburgh J in *Terrapin Ltd v Builders' Supply Co (Hayes) Ltd*:[48]

> As I understand it, the essence of this branch of the law, whatever the origin of it may be, is that a person who has obtained information in confidence is not allowed to use it as a spring-board for activities detrimental to the person who made the confidential communication, and spring-board it remains even when all the features have been published or can be ascertained by actual inspection by any member of the public ... It is, in my view, inherent in the principle upon which the *Saltman* case rests that the possessor of such information must be placed under a special disability in the field of competition in order to ensure that he [sic] does not get an unfair start.

The 'doctrine' enunciated in this passage has two effects, one going to liability and the other to remedies. Its thrust as far as liability is concerned is that what appears to be a 'publication' of information should not and does not necessarily relieve the confidant of the obligation not to use the information. This does not in any way conflict with the proposition that confidentiality lapses when information moves into the public domain. It simply calls for a sophisticated analysis of the precise moment when that lapse occurs. The point made directly in the judgment is that information is not published in the requisite sense at the moment when something is done which would enable that information to be ascertained. Thus in *Terrapin* itself the plaintiffs had marketed a type of prefabricated portable building, together with a brochure describing its features. From that moment it was possible to 'reverse engineer' the product by dismantling it in order to work out how it was constructed. Working solely from these marketed items, however, and without the aid of the plaintiff's unpublished plans, specifications and other technical information, it would take some time before the reverse engineering was complete — and even then there would have to be prototypes constructed, tests made, etc, before the information could be fully utilised. The defendants were accordingly held to be liable for using confidential information about the design, obtained from the plaintiff, to

---

47. See *Attorney-General (UK) v Guardian Newspapers Ltd (No 2)* [1988] 3 WLR 776 at 809–13. See further [4.25], [4.28], [4.30], [4.41].
48. [1967] RPC 375 at 391–2. The judgment was affirmed in the Court of Appeal without specific reference to this point: [1960] RPC 128.

put their own similar product on the market after the plaintiff's launch but before the relevant information had *fully* reached the public domain.[49]

On the other hand, the 'springboard does not last for ever'.[50] If a confidant is prepared to delay any exploitation of the relevant information until the point has been reached at which a person working without the benefit of the confidential communication would have been able to ascertain and utilise it, no liability will ensue.[51] This emphasis on the limited duration of any handicap to be imposed on the confidential recipient of information which subsequently moves into the public domain is also at the heart of the second function of the springboard doctrine, which relates to remedies. Where confidence has been breached, but secrecy is subsequently lost, the reference in the *Terrapin* judgment to placing the transgressor under a 'special disability' to remove any 'unfair start' has been used to generate a principle that relief should be framed in such a way that the defendant is 'deprived of the fruits of [the] wrongdoing' without imposing 'an unfair disadvantage *vis a vis* the rest of mankind'.[52]

(b) Receipt of Information in Confidence

[4.9]   Receipt pursuant to a relationship. Expanding on the second of his three requirements for a successful breach of confidence action, Megarry J stated in *Coco v A N Clark (Engineers) Ltd*[53] that:

> [I]f the circumstances are such that any reasonable man [sic] standing in the shoes of the recipient of the information would have realised that upon reasonable grounds the information was being given to him in confidence, then this should suffice to impose upon him the equitable obligation of confidence.

A person must, in other words, have some understanding at the time of receiving the relevant information that they are obtaining it for a limited purpose before they can be termed a confidant.[54] This requirement can be satisfied in a number of ways. The information may for instance be received pursuant to or as a natural incident of a pre-existing relationship between the parties. If the relationship is inherently 'confidential', whether in terms of personal intimacy or professional ethics, the requisite understanding may readily be inferred.[55] More commercially oriented relationships may

49. See also *Harrison v Project & Design Co (Redcar) Ltd* [1978] FSR 81; *Aquaculture Corp v New Zealand Green Mussel Co Ltd* (1985) 5 IPR 353.
50. *Potters-Ballotini Ltd v Weston-Baker* [1977] RPC 202 at 206–7; *Peter Pan Manufacturing Corp v Corsets Silhouette Ltd* [1963] 3 All ER 402 at 408.
51. See eg *British Franco Electric Pty Ltd v Dowling Plastics Pty Ltd* [1981] 1 NSWLR 448; *Titan Group Pty Ltd v Steriline Manufacturing Pty Ltd* (1990) 19 IPR 353. As to whether a confidant can realistically be expected to exercise this sort of self-restraint, see [4.24].
52. *Aquaculture Corp v New Zealand Green Mussel Co Ltd* (1985) 5 IPR 353 at 384; *British Franco Electric Pty Ltd v Dowling Plastics Pty Ltd*, ibid at 451. See further [4.25].
53. [1969] RPC 41 at 48. Cf *Deta Nominees Pty Ltd v Viscount Plastic Products Pty Ltd* [1979] VR 167 at 191; *Carflow Products (UK) Ltd v Linwood Securities (Birmingham) Ltd* (1996) 36 IPR 205.
54. See Gurry, pp 113–15; *Smith Kline & French Laboratories (Australia) Ltd v Secretary, Department of Community Services and Health* (1990) 17 IPR 545 at 567–9.
55. See eg *Argyll v Argyll* [1967] Ch 302 at 322; *Attorney-General (UK) v Heinemann Publishers Australia Pty Ltd* (1987) 75 ALR 353 at 453. Cf *Stephens v Avery* [1988] 2 WLR 1280 at 1286–7. See further P Finn, 'Professionals and Confidentiality' (1992) 14 *Syd LR* 317.

also generate such inferences, however, particularly where the parties are engaged in some form of joint venture.[56] The same is true of employment relationships.[57] The importance of the existence of a relationship in this context is that it may negate any need to examine the particular circumstances in which the information has been acquired so as to locate an overtly confidential communication. Thus it would be no obstacle to confidentiality arising that the recipient has not given any express commitment to that effect or had the opportunity to reject the information, for consent is effectively implied by the mere fact of entry into the relationship. Nor would it matter that the information has not been explicitly communicated by the plaintiff: as where, for instance, an employee 'creates' information or receives it from an external source.[58] What matters is that, as part of the relationship, the plaintiff has allowed the defendant access to the information. On the other hand, it must still be demonstrated that there was at least an implicit understanding that the information was not to be freely available to the confidant; many of the factors which are relevant in determining whether relative secrecy exists will also be relevant in this context.[59]

[4.10] Other forms of voluntary communication. Absent an inference of confidentiality from a relationship between the parties, attention will be focused on the particular circumstances in which the information is received. The most straightforward situation is provided by an intended communication by the confider. If the communication has been solicited by the recipient, and the information is obviously sensitive, then again it will be easy to infer confidentiality. For example in *Johns v Australian Securities Commission*[60] all but one judge in the High Court decided or assumed that when the plaintiff was compelled by the ASC to attend a private examination and discuss the business affairs of the Tricontinental group, the resulting transcripts were subject to an equitable duty of confidentiality enforceable against third parties (besides any statutory duty cast on the ASC itself). Only Toohey J thought that the plaintiff's failure at the time of the examination to seek an explicit assurance of confidentiality precluded any duty arising.

An unsolicited communication, on the other hand, assuming the absence of some pre-existing relationship between the parties from which consent might be inferred, will pose much greater difficulties. Much will turn on the extent to which the recipient has been afforded an opportunity to accept or reject the confidence. In *Fractionated Cane Technology Ltd v Ruiz-Avila*[61] the plaintiff claimed that trials conducted on the defendants' machinery in the presence of the defendants and other witnesses had produced results that were confidential. Since the plaintiff had not sought a prior commitment of confidentiality and since the results had been totally unexpected, it was held that 'objective circumstances attracting an equity of confidence' had not been established. The defendants had not been given

56.   *Coco v A N Clark (Engineers) Ltd* [1969] RPC 41 at 48. Cf *Mar-Con Corp Pty Ltd v Campbell Capital Ltd* (1989) 16 IPR 153.
57.   See [4.33]–[4.35].
58.   See eg *Cranleigh Precision Engineering Ltd v Bryant* [1964] 3 All ER 289.
59.   See [4.6].
60.   (1993) 178 CLR 408 (see [4.6]).
61.   (1987) 8 IPR 502; (1988) 13 IPR 609.

'the opportunity of rejecting the attempted disclosure or of refusing to conduct the trials'.[62] A confidence cannot, in other words, be forced upon an unwilling recipient. That said, even an unsolicited communication may generate an obligation of confidentiality if further circumstances can be established from which consent can reasonably be inferred. Thus if an inventor insists on explaining over the telephone the details of an idea to an officer of a major corporation without first securing a promise of secrecy, there is plainly no duty. If, on the other hand, those details are sent by mail, it may well be that at some point the corporation, through the decision of someone in its office to read through those details rather than return them instantly, may reasonably be supposed to have accepted an obligation of confidentiality. For this reason many corporations have a policy of refusing even to read unsolicited communications unless the discloser signs a form releasing the corporation from any duty of confidence.[63]

[4.11] Acquisition without consent. The extent to which liability for breach of confidence may be imposed on a person in respect of information which they have acquired other than with the consent of the 'owner' is a matter of some debate.[64] It has been said, for example, that information 'blurted out in public' cannot be protected,[65] and indeed that 'a person who utters confidential information must accept the risk of any unknown overhearing that is inherent in the circumstances of communication'.[66] On the other hand there is authority to the effect that information obtained 'improperly or surreptitiously'[67] may be caught by the equitable doctrine. Thus in *Franklin v Giddins*[68] the defendants stole budwood cuttings from the plaintiffs' orchard and thereby acquired information as to the genetic structure of the budwood, which enabled them to grow nectarines in competition with the plaintiffs. They were held to have infringed the plaintiffs' rights, the judge refusing to accept that 'a thief who steals a trade secret ... is less unconscionable than a traitorous servant'.[69]

In *Franklin* the acquisition was plainly unlawful. But what of deliberate acquisition of secret information by lawful means? In *Malone v Commissioner of Police of the Metropolis (No 2)*[70] it was held that police officers who (lawfully) tapped the plaintiff's telephone came under no duty of confidence in respect of the information which they overheard. According to Megarry V-C, a person who uses a telephone takes 'such risks of being overheard as are inherent in the system', which were considered to include not just crossed

---

62. (1987) 8 IPR 502 at 521.
63. See UK Law Commission Report No 110, *Breach of Confidence*, Cmnd 8388, 1981, pp 87–8, 103–6.
64. See G Wei, 'Surreptitious Takings of Confidential Information' (1992) 12 *Leg St* 302; M Richardson, 'Breach of Confidence, Surreptitiously or Accidentally Obtained Information and Privacy: Theory Versus Law' (1994) 19 *Melb ULR* 673.
65. *Coco v A N Clark (Engineers) Ltd* [1969] RPC 41 at 47–8.
66. *Malone v Commissioner of Police of the Metropolis (No 2)* [1979] 2 All ER 620 at 645–6.
67. *Ashburton v Pape* [1913] 2 Ch 469 at 475; *Commonwealth v John Fairfax & Sons Ltd* (1980) 147 CLR 39 at 50; *Johns v Australian Securities Commission* (1993) 178 CLR 408 at 474.
68. [1978] Qd R 72. See also *Crowder v Hilton* [1902] SALR 82; *Exchange Telegraph Co Ltd v Howard* (1906) 22 TLR 375; *Francome v Mirror Group Newspapers Ltd* [1984] 2 All ER 408.
69. [1978] Qd R 72 at 80. See also *X Ltd v Morgan-Grampian (Publishers) Ltd* [1990] 2 WLR 1000, where the House of Lords certainly seems to have assumed this to be the case.
70. [1979] 2 All ER 620.

lines but deliberate interceptions.[71] However, the alternative ground offered in the judgment seems to provide a much better basis for the decision: that the police were justified in their activities by their reasonable apprehension of the plaintiff's participation in criminal activities and hence could plead the public interest by way of defence.[72] This was the approach adopted in *Hellewell v Chief Constable of Derbyshire*,[73] where Laws J struck out an action against the police to prevent circulation to local traders of a photograph of a known thief as part of a campaign against shoplifting. Significantly, the judge made it clear that use of information derived from photographic surveillance of 'private acts' would, in the absence of any defence of justification, amount to a breach of confidence.[74]

This case suggests a broad view of the circumstances in which an obligation of confidence may be imported, to the point indeed where a person may become a 'confidant' merely by taking a deliberate step to acquire information or to be in a position to do so.[75] This could potentially apply to cases of 'accidental' acquisition, at least where there is a point at which the recipient of information has a realistic opportunity to accept or reject the confidence. For example while someone who casually overhears a nearby conversation has no choice but to acquire the information and cannot therefore reasonably be expected to be bound to secrecy, it is a different story where a person finds or is mistakenly sent material that is marked 'confidential' or otherwise appears to be of a sensitive nature. In such a case the decision to use or disclose the material rather than seek to return it arguably should expose the recipient to liability.[76] There is certainly authority to the effect that where documents prepared for litigation by one party accidentally fall into the hands of the other party, the equitable doctrine may be invoked to restrain that party from using them.[77]

(c) Unauthorised Use or Disclosure

[4.12] Scope of the duty. Where a duty of confidence exists, it is breached by the unauthorised use or disclosure of some or all of the relevant information — though not, it would appear, by a mere refusal to allow the confider access to the information.[78] In cases where the information has been appropriated without consent, any form of use or disclosure will

---

71. Ibid at 646. With respect, however, it is one thing for private citizens to be aware of the dangers of phones being tapped and quite another to say that a 'realistic' person would accept the risk of it actually occurring. Cf *Francome v Mirror Group Newspapers Ltd* [1984] 2 All ER 408, where illegal tapping was held to fall outside any principle established in *Malone*. As to legislation regulating the use of listening devices, see Dean, pp 503–28.
72. See [4.17]–[4.21].
73. [1995] 1 WLR 804.
74. Ibid at 807. See also *E I Du Pont de Nemours & Co Inc v Christopher* (1970) 431 F 2d 1012. Cf *Bernstein v Skyways & General Ltd* [1978] QB 479.
75. Cf the far more vague formulation by Lord Goff in *Attorney-General (UK) v Guardian Newspapers Ltd (No 2)* [1988] 3 WLR 776 at 805.
76. For dicta to this effect, see eg *Attorney-General (UK) v Guardian Newspapers Ltd (No 2)* [1988] 3 WLR 776 at 806; *English & American Insurance Co Ltd v Herbert Smith* [1988] FSR 232 at 238; *Helliwell v Chief Constable of Derbyshire* [1995] 1 WLR 804 at 807.
77. *English & American Insurance Co Ltd v Herbert Smith* [1988] FSR 232; *Shaw v Harris* (1991) 3 Tas R 153.

by definition be unauthorised. However, where the information has been communicated with the confider's consent, it will usually have been envisaged that the information might be put to some proper use or disclosed to an appropriate person (especially within an organisation of any size). Hence there may be some question as to what constitutes an impermissible use. It has been suggested that where information has been disclosed for a limited purpose, 'the confidence crystallises around that limited purpose', so that use or disclosure for any other purpose will amount to a breach of confidence.[79] However, in *Smith Kline and French Laboratories (Aust) Ltd v Secretary, Department of Community Services and Health*[80] the Full Court of the Federal Court, while accepting that this test will produce a proper result in many circumstances, indicated that other factors may need to be taken into account in determining the scope of confidentiality. In particular, 'the test of confider's purpose will not ordinarily be appropriate where each party's interest is quite different, and known to be so'.[81] The case concerned product information supplied by a pharmaceutical company to the Department in support of its application for a patent extension. The court held, emphasising the Department's duty to ensure public safety, that it was entitled to use the information when considering applications by other companies for marketing approval in respect of similar products.[82] It did not matter that this was not a purpose for which the information had been supplied. It was enough that the company might reasonably have expected that 'the information would be kept against the day when it might be needed to serve the government's legitimate interests'.[83] In the end, the true test was whether the confidant had made 'unconscientious use' of the information,[84] something not apparent in this case. The decision can be contrasted with *Marcel v Commissioner of Police of the Metropolis*,[85] where police who had gathered material on the plaintiff for a criminal investigation were restrained from handing it over to a third party for use in civil litigation with the plaintiff. This was held to go beyond the purposes for which the police had been given statutory power to seize and use the material.[86]

If a breach of confidence is established, it will be irrelevant that the confidant may not have intended to breach confidence. Thus liability attaches where the confidant negligently allows others to learn of the information,[87] or discloses it by error,[88] or subconsciously plagiarises the confider's secret

---

78. *Breen v Williams* (1996) 138 ALR 259. Cf *Yasuda Fire and Marine Insurance Co of Europe Ltd v Orion Marine Insurance Underwriting Agency Ltd* [1995] 3 All ER 211.
79. F Gurry, 'Breach of Confidence' in P D Finn (ed), *Essays in Equity*, 1985, p 110 at p 118.
80. (1991) 20 IPR 643.
81. Ibid at 655.
82. Similar actions failed in England and New Zealand: *Re Smith Kline & French Laboratories Ltd* [1989] 2 WLR 397; *Smith Kline & French Laboratories Ltd v Attorney-General (NZ)* [1989] FSR 418.
83. (1991) 20 IPR 643 at 655. See also *Joint Coal Board v Cameron* (1989) 90 ALR 208; but cf *Castrol Australia Pty Ltd v Emtech Associates Pty Ltd* (1980) 33 ALR 31.
84. (1991) 20 IPR 643 at 656.
85. [1991] 1 All ER 845.
86. See also *Johns v Australian Securities Commission* (1993) 178 CLR 408 at 423–4, 436, 467.
87. See eg *Weld-Blundell v Stephens* [1919] 1 KB 520.
88. See eg *Interfirm Comparison (Australia) Pty Ltd v Law Society of NSW* (1975) 5 ALR 527; *English & American Insurance Co Ltd v Herbert Smith* [1988] FSR 232.

idea.[89] Likewise, ignorance of the existence or legal significance of a duty of confidence is no defence.[90]

[4.13] A requirement of detriment? A controversial issue, at least theoretically, is whether it must be established that some detriment has been or will be caused to the plaintiff by the defendant's conduct. It is almost impossible to locate in the authorities a clearly accepted view, though it may be that in practice this is of little moment. Even those courts which have asserted a need to prove detriment have stressed that the requirement may be established merely by the plaintiff's desire to avoid criticism or embarrassment,[91] or indeed the infliction of harm on another person.[92] Many of these statements come very close in substance to the proposition that 'it is in the public interest that confidences should be respected, and the encouragement of such respect may in itself constitute a sufficient ground for recognising and enforcing the obligation of confidence even where the confider can point to no specific detriment to himself [sic]'.[93] Besides, the question of detriment will clearly be an important factor in the court's exercise of discretion with respect to remedies and can perhaps best be considered at that stage rather than in determining liability. That said, there is one context in which detriment of a substantial nature must always be established, that being where governmental information is at issue, as discussed later on.[94]

(d) Liability of Third Parties

[4.14] The reach of the equitable doctrine. More often than not the threat of misuse of confidential information does not come solely or perhaps even primarily from the person who originally acquired it from the plaintiff/confider, but from a third party into whose hands the information has come following the breach of confidence. If confidentiality is to be protected to any meaningful extent it is logical and desirable that, in some cases at least, liability be extended to cover such third parties. This equity has readily done. Most of the cases involve persons or companies who are intimately involved with the confidant in the exploitation of the information,[95] or who are the intended instrument of disclosure to the public.[96] The courts, however, have looked much further than these forms of direct participation in the confidant's wrongdoing, adopting the general principle

---

89. See eg *Seager v Copydex Ltd* [1967] 2 All ER 415; *Talbot v General Television Corp Pty Ltd* [1980] VR 224.
90. *O Mustad & Son v S Allcock & Co Ltd* (1928) 3 All ER 416 at 417; *Seager v Copydex Ltd* [1967] 2 All ER 415 at 418, 419.
91. See eg *Commonwealth v John Fairfax & Sons Ltd* (1980) 147 CLR 39 at 51–2; *Attorney General (UK) v Heinemann Publishers Australia Pty Ltd* (1987) 75 ALR 353 at 454.
92. See eg *Coco v A N Clark (Engineers) Ltd* [1969] RPC 41 at 48; *Attorney-General (UK) v Guardian Newspapers Ltd (No 2)* [1988] 3 WLR 776 at 795.
93. *Attorney-General (UK) v Guardian Newspapers Ltd (No 2)* [1988] 3 WLR 776 at 782. See also *Moorgate Tobacco Co Ltd v Philip Morris Ltd* (1984) 156 CLR 414 at 438, where Deane J refers only to the need for secrecy to be 'of substantial concern to the plaintiff', and *Smith Kline & French Laboratories (Australia) Ltd v Secretary, Department of Community Services and Health* (1990) 17 IPR 545 at 584. Cf *Ashmore v Douglas-Home* [1987] Ch 302.
94. See [4.39].
95. See eg *Ansell Rubber Co Pty Ltd v Allied Rubber Industries Pty Ltd* [1967] VR 37.
96. See eg *Argyll v Argyll* [1967] Ch 302.

that any person who receives information[97] as a result of another's breach of confidence may be restrained from using or disclosing the information once they have actual or constructive notice of the breach.[98] The problem is that little attempt has been made to analyse the consequences of this view. One issue that has been neglected is whether the third party's liability is merely an extension of the original confidant's, or arises independently on the basis that the third party's receipt of the information itself satisfies the requirements of the doctrine. While there are dicta which might possibly be taken to suggest the latter view,[99] the notion of the third party's liability being parasitic on that of the original confidant is more consonant with the language generally adopted by the courts. Presumably then, if the original communication or receipt creates no duty for lack of a reasonable awareness of confidentiality on the part of the recipient, then by definition a third party to whom the information passes in turn will be free to use it even if *they* are quite aware that confidentiality was intended by the confider.

This in turn raises the question of whether a third party is automatically bound by a duty of confidence once it is established that the original confidant was in breach. The answer, to all practical intents and purposes, appears to be in the affirmative. It has often been stressed by the courts that a third party, no matter how innocent the circumstances of their acquisition of the information, comes under a duty as soon as they are given notice of the confidant's breach.[100] So long as the confider is prepared to assert a right to protection and provided a breach is in fact established, the third party will be recognised as coming under a duty at some point, even if it is as late as the commencement of proceedings.[101] The rationale for this position, though it has not been articulated, is presumably that the interest in protecting the confider against the consequences of a proven breach overrides the principle that confidentiality ought not to be imposed on a person who has not reasonably understood at the time of receiving information that it was not their own to do with as they liked. But this can produce somewhat strange results. Suppose that in the course of a conversation in a restaurant, A, talking loudly and without any apparent confidentiality, reveals what is in fact hitherto secret information to B, a dinner companion, and also to C, who casually overhears while sitting at a nearby table. Applying the ordinary test of reasonable apprehension of confidentiality, neither B nor C appears to be bound by any duty to A and may make whatever use

---

97. As to whether a third party may be restrained from dealing with property created as a result of another's breach of confidence, despite not having received the information itself, see *Union Carbide Corp v Naturin Ltd* [1987] FSR 538. See further [4.32].

98. *Fraser v Evans* [1969] 1 QB 349 at 361; *Talbot v General Television Corp Pty Ltd* [1980] VR 224 at 239–40; *Johns v Australian Securities Commission* (1993) 178 CLR 408 at 460, 474. For examples of constructive notice, see *Ormonoid Roofing & Asphalts Ltd v Bitumenoids Ltd* (1930) 31 SR (NSW) 347 at 360; *Ansell Rubber Co Pty Ltd v Allied Rubber Industries Pty Ltd* [1967] VR 37 at 45–6; and cf *National Education Advancement Programs (NEAP) Pty Ltd v Ashton* (1995) 33 IPR 281. See also Privacy Act 1988 (Cth) s 92.

99. See eg *Fraser v Evans* [1969] 1 QB 349 at 361.

100. See eg *Printers & Finishers Ltd v Holloway* [1964] 3 All ER 731 at 738–9; *Malone v Commissioner of Police of the Metropolis (No 2)* [1979] 2 All ER 620 at 634; *G v Day* [1982] 1 NSWLR 24 at 35; *Johns v Australian Securities Commission* (1993) 178 CLR 408 at 460, 474.

101. See eg *Talbot v General Television Corp Pty Ltd* [1980] VR 224. Cf *Fraser v Thames Television Ltd* [1983] 2 All ER 101 at 121.

of the information they wish. If, however, the information in question turns out to belong to A's employer, then B and C, who must now be treated as third parties to A's breach of confidence, may be restrained from using the information from the moment they are given notice of that breach, their innocence at the time of receipt notwithstanding.[102]

[4.15] Mitigating third party liability. Some courts have been aware of the unfairness or injustice that may be caused to third parties and have sought ways to mitigate their liability. The most far-reaching suggestion has been that the acquisition of information for value without notice of any breach provides an absolute defence to liability, though support for this lies only in dicta.[103] In *Wheatley v Bell*[104] Helsham CJ in Eq rejected the idea of any defence of bona fide purchase on the ground that no property rights are at stake where breach of confidence is concerned. A better explanation, it is suggested, is that the mere fact that money has been paid to obtain the information does not necessarily make it unfair to impose liability. A third party really seems to have two legitimate arguments. One is that there be no liability to pay compensation or to account for profits in respect of use of the information prior to having notice of the breach: this indeed appears to be the position. The other is that no liability be imposed where the third party has significantly altered their position to their detriment prior to receiving notice, for example by incurring significant expenditure (which may or may not have included a purchase fee) towards exploitation of the information. While on one view 'change of circumstances' should be regarded as a defence in its own right,[105] it is probably more accurate to say that a court may choose to take it into account in framing appropriate remedies for the confider and in particular in determining whether or not to grant injunctive relief.[106] This indeed ought to be the key to dealing with third parties: that a range of factors, of which innocence and change of position are merely the most compelling, may lead a court to treat such defendants somewhat more leniently than they would the original confidant.[107]

[4.16] Liability in tort. Apart from the equitable doctrine itself, the confider may also be able to rely on the economic torts to establish third party liability. If the third party has set out to procure or incite the confidant's breach of confidence, the confider may have remedies in the tort of contractual interference;[108] or possibly, where there is no contract between the

102. One way to avoid this result would be to adopt Jones' suggestion that a person with no reasonable understanding at the time of receiving information that it is confidential may subsequently become bound if they are apprised of the 'true facts': 'Restitution of Benefits Obtained in Breach of Confidence' (1970) 86 *LQR* 463 at 477. However, this view, which would effectively (and in some ways quite logically) equate confidants with third parties, does not appear to find any support in the authorities.
103. See eg *Morison v Moat* (1851) 9 Hare 241 at 263–4, 68 ER 492 at 501–2; *Goddard v Nationwide Building Society* [1986] 3 WLR 734 at 745; *Attorney-General (UK) v Guardian Newspapers Ltd (No 2)* [1988] 2 WLR 805 at 868.
104. [1982] 2 NSWLR 544.
105. See G Jones, 'Restitution of Benefits Obtained in Breach of Another's Confidence' (1970) 86 *LQR* 463 at 477–81.
106. See eg *Stephenson Jordan & Harrison Ltd v MacDonald & Evans* (1952) 69 RPC 10 at 16.
107. See *Attorney-General (UK) v Guardian Newspapers Ltd (No 2)* [1988] 2 WLR 805 at 846–8, 873; [1988] 3 WLR 776 at 797.
108. See eg *Bents Brewery Co Ltd v Hogan* [1945] 2 All ER 570.

confider and confidant, in the embryo tort of 'interference with rights'.[109] In either case the problem for the confider lies in establishing that the third party did not merely suspect that the confidant would be breaching confidence but knew and intended that that should happen.[110] Another possibility is to allege that the confidant and one or more third parties have wrongfully combined to inflict economic loss on the confider, though as noted in Chapter 2 the tort of conspiracy is notoriously difficult to establish.[111] Given the reach of the equitable doctrine, it is hardly surprising that few confidants nowadays bother to plead these torts.

3. DEFENCES

(a) Justified Disclosure

[4.17] The basic principle. The principle is firmly established that liability for breach of confidence may be avoided where it can be established that the defendant has 'just cause or excuse'[112] for disclosing the information in question. Where the plaintiff's claim is founded on a contractual obligation of secrecy, this may be regarded as an instance of public policy rendering an agreement unenforceable.[113] In other cases, the principle effectively operates as a defence, extending indeed to situations where the defendant is sued, not for breach of confidence, but for breach of copyright,[114] or (necessarily as a third party) for the tort of contractual interference.[115]

Disagreement persists, however, as to the range of circumstances in which justification may be pleaded, or indeed as to the underlying rationale for such a concept. In one sense, the confused state of the law on this subject is readily understandable. Most justification arguments are raised at an interlocutory stage, the issue being whether it is appropriate for publication (either general or limited) to take place pending a full trial. The court is frequently required to give fairly hurried consideration, not to whether publication is justified, but as to whether there is a strong argument to that effect which, on balance, tips the scales against the grant of an injunction.[116] On the other hand, it may be a mistake to ascribe the conflicts in the authorities solely to the vagaries of the interlocutory process. It does seem that two distinct approaches have emerged which, while substantially overlapping, will occasionally dictate different results.[117]

---

109. See [2.7].
110. See eg *British Industrial Plastics Ltd v Ferguson* [1940] 1 All ER 479.
111. Cf *Jarman & Platt Ltd v Barget Ltd* [1977] FSR 260.
112. *Fraser v Evans* [1969] 1 QB 349 at 362.
113. See eg *A v Hayden (No 2)* (1984) 156 CLR 532.
114. See *Commonwealth v John Fairfax & Sons Ltd* (1980) 147 CLR 39 at 56–7.
115. See *Church of Scientology of California v Kaufman (No 2)* [1973] RPC 635 at 648–9.
116. For comments on the difficulties facing a court in this situation, see eg *Westpac Banking Corp v John Fairfax Group Pty Ltd* (1991) 19 IPR 513 at 525–6; and see also J Stuckey-Clarke, 'Freedom of Speech and Publication in the Public Interest' in L Clarke (ed), *Confidentiality and the Law*, 1990, p 141.
117. See further K Koomen, 'Breach of Confidence and the Public Interest Defence: Is it in the Public Interest?' (1994) 10 *QUTLJ* 56; J Pizer, 'The Public Interest Exception to the Breach of Confidence Action: Are the Lights About to Change?' (1994) 20 *Mon ULR* 67.

[4.18] The iniquity rule. The first approach derives from the assertion of Wood V-C in *Gartside v Outram* that 'there is no confidence as to the disclosure of iniquity'.[118] The fact that the Vice-Chancellor went on to say that '[y]ou cannot make me the confidant of a crime or a fraud'[119] might be interpreted as limiting the class of information falling within the principle to those particular types of wrong. At least since the English Court of Appeal decision in *Initial Services Ltd v Putterill*,[120] however, a broader view has prevailed. It now appears that 'iniquity' should be taken to include 'any misconduct of such a nature that it ought in the public interest to be disclosed'.[121] There is some difficulty, however, in ascertaining the limits of the principle. The requirement that disclosure in all instances be 'in the public interest' has an important confining effect, permitting the courts to reject the principle's application to 'trivial' wrongs,[122] or to past misconduct whose repeat is not threatened and which lacks present relevance.[123] On the other hand, its very terms focus attention on situations where information arguably ought to be disclosed, yet which do not appear to involve 'misconduct' in any strict sense. Some courts, for instance, have suggested that information which concerns matters 'medically dangerous' to the public would normally fall within the iniquity principle.[124] In *Commonwealth v John Fairfax & Sons Ltd*,[125] Mason J considered that the principle 'makes legitimate the publication of confidential information or material in which copyright subsists so as to protect the community from destruction, damage or harm'. It seems doubtful that a court faced with such information would restrain its dissemination merely because it could not identify misconduct on anyone's part.

[4.19] Balancing public interests. The obvious and logical extension of the iniquity rule to matters of public danger has led English courts in recent times effectively to dispense with the need to identify misconduct. They have instead adopted the broader proposition that disclosure should not be enjoined whenever the public interest in publication outweighs the public interest in confidentiality. The leading case is *Lion Laboratories Ltd v Evans*,[126] in which a firm failed to have two former employees restrained from disclosing to the press information concerning the Intoximeter, a device manufactured by the firm and used by the British police for breath-testing drivers to determine their level of alcoholic intoxication. The information was to the effect that government tests had revealed the device to be unreliable. In light of the possible danger of motorists being wrongly

---

118. (1856) 26 LJ Ch 113 at 114.
119. Ibid.
120. [1968] 1 QB 396.
121. Ibid at 405; *British Steel Corporation v Granada Television Ltd* [1981] AC 1096 at 1169; *A v Hayden (No 2)* (1984) 156 CLR 532 at 545.
122. *A v Hayden (No 2)* (1984) 156 CLR 532 at 545–6, 574.
123. See eg *Weld-Blundell v Stephens* [1919] 1 KB 520 at 527; *Distillers Co (Biochemicals) Ltd v Times Newspapers Ltd* [1975] 1 All ER 41; *Schering Chemicals Ltd v Falkman Ltd* [1981] 2 All ER 321.
124. See eg *Beloff v Pressdram Ltd* [1973] 1 All ER 241 at 260; *Church of Scientology of California v Kaufman (No 2)* [1973] RPC 635.
125. (1980) 147 CLR 39 at 57.
126. [1984] 2 All ER 417. See also *Attorney-General (UK) v Guardian Newspapers Ltd (No 2)* [1988] 3 WLR 776 at 794, 807; *X v Y* [1988] 2 All ER 648; *W v Egdell* [1990] 2 WLR 471; *Marcel v Commissioner of Police of the Metropolis* [1991] 1 All ER 845.

convicted and of the public controversy over the device aroused by previous media reports, the Court of Appeal considered that the public interest lay in these matters being openly debated.

This approach has garnered some support from Australian judges,[127] although others continue to reject it in favour of the iniquity rule.[128] But in the long term it seems likely to gain acceptance, particularly since it is really only taking the present conception of 'iniquity' (that is, misconduct and/or public danger) to its logical conclusion. Moreover, the notion of balancing interests for and against publication is already well established in two closely related contexts: those of actions to protect government information,[129] and of applications for the discovery of confidential documents for the purpose of litigation.[130] Three points should be noted, however. The first is that a distinction should clearly be drawn between matters that ought to be disclosed in the public interest, and those which are merely *of* public interest in the sense that many people would like to know them.[131] If the latter are to be excluded, then it is difficult to support some English decisions which suggest that secrets relating to the personal affairs of celebrities ought to be disclosed merely in order to 'set the record straight' and to counter impressions created by their publicity machines.[132] Second, it appears that the public interest approach could not be taken so far as to compel the publication of information relating to something of benefit to the public,[133] though it is difficult to see why this should be so.[134] Third, it may be argued that one prerequisite for any approach based on balancing public interests would be a rather more sophisticated analysis of why non-governmental confidences are enforced than has hitherto been the case. For instance, the courts' apparent assumption that society is better off if business secrets are kept takes little account of the arguments against this proposition that were discussed in the previous chapter. The need to weigh the importance of secrecy against that of the free flow of information may well serve to drive some of these arguments out into the open.[135]

[4.20] Disclosure to the proper authorities. Whatever the precise formulation for the defence of justified disclosure, it is now established that the scope of the relevant disclosure is a crucial factor in determining the

---

127. See eg *Attorney-General (UK) v Heinemann Publishers Australia Pty Ltd* (1987) 75 ALR 353 at 434; *Westpac Banking Corp v John Fairfax Group Pty Ltd* (1991) 19 IPR 513 at 525.
128. See eg *Castrol Australia Pty Ltd v Emtech Associates Pty Ltd* (1980) 33 ALR 31 at 56; *Corrs Pavey Whiting & Byrne v Collector of Customs (Vic)* (1987) 74 ALR 428 at 445–50; *Bacich v Australian Broadcasting Corp* (1992) 29 NSWLR 1 at 16.
129. See [4.6].
130. See [4.22].
131. See *British Steel Corporation v Granada Television Ltd* [1981] AC 1096 at 1168; *Lion Laboratories Ltd v Evans* [1984] 2 All ER 417 at 423.
132. See eg *Woodward v Hutchins* [1977] 2 All ER 751; *Khashoggi v Smith* (1980) 124 *Sol Jo* 149. See also *Church of Scientology of California v Kaufman (No 2)* [1973] RPC 635.
133. See *Church of Scientology of California v Kaufman (No 2)* [1973] RPC 635 at 649.
134. What, for instance, of an attempt to disclose the details of a novel process for reducing harmful pollution which is being concealed by a firm in order to avoid major expenditure in cleaning up its own industrial activities? Is there a logical difference between disclosing a harmful or potentially harmful state of affairs and disclosing information which would remove or avoid that state of affairs?
135. See generally P D Finn, 'Confidentiality and the "Public Interest"' (1984) 58 *ALJ* 497 (though rejecting the need for a defence of public interest as such).

success of the defence. As a general rule, disclosure must be to the 'proper authorities'.[136] Who these are will depend on the nature and significance of the information. Prima facie, wrongdoing or matters of public danger should be disclosed to the appropriate official or semi-official bodies: the police in the case of criminal conduct,[137] public health authorities in instances of medical danger,[138] and so on. Occasionally, however, a court may decide that wider disclosure to the general public is appropriate. In *Lion Laboratories*,[139] for instance, the Court of Appeal considered that, given on the one hand the government's unbending public support for the Intoximeter, and on the other the mounting disquiet about its reliability, it was appropriate for the confidants' fears to be aired through the media.[140]

The requirement that any disclosure be no more extensive than the public interest dictates helps to provide an answer to two further questions. The first is whether the defendant must adduce evidence as to the accuracy of information whose truth is contested. It has been said that 'a mere allegation of iniquity is not of itself sufficient to justify disclosure',[141] and that the confidant must make out a 'prima facie case that the allegations have substance'.[142] Where the disclosure is to an authority whose function is to investigate such allegations, however, it would seem that this principle does not and should not apply;[143] though by the same token there must be at least reasonable grounds for suspecting wrongdoing.[144] The point is more obvious still in a situation where an investigating authority itself, harbouring a reasonable suspicion as to the existence or threat of wrongdoing or danger, breaches confidentiality in order to further its inquiries.[145] The second issue is whether the motive of the confidant in seeking disclosure is relevant. Again, although it may be that the defence would be refused to one who sought to publish information 'out of malice or spite' or to 'purvey scandalous information for reward',[146] the worst of motives will be overlooked if disclosure is solely to the proper authorities.[147]

[4.21] Effect of establishing justification. Justification is usually thought of as a 'defence' to an action for breach of confidence, though its precise significance must be a matter for conjecture. One question that remains to be settled is whether a confider, though denied injunctive relief on the ground that disclosure is warranted in the circumstances, may nevertheless proceed to claim pecuniary or proprietary relief in respect of what

---

136. *Initial Services Ltd v Putterill* [1968] 1 QB 396 at 405–6; *Attorney-General (UK) v Heinemann Publishers Australia Pty Ltd* (1987) 8 NSWLR 341 at 380–1. It would seem that the proper recipient must in turn be regarded as coming under a duty not to use the information other than to take proper steps to deal with the situation: *Corrs Pavey Whiting & Byrne v Collector of Customs (Vic)* (1987) 74 ALR 428 at 430.
137. See eg *Francome v Mirror Group Newspapers Ltd* [1984] 2 All ER 408.
138. See eg *Duncan v Medical Practitioners Committee* [1986] 1 NZLR 513.
139. [1984] 2 All ER 417.
140. See further A Stewart and M Chesterman, 'Confidential Material: The Position of the Media' (1992) 14 *Adel LR* 1 at 14–21.
141. *Attorney-General (UK) v Guardian Newspapers Ltd (No 2)* [1988] 3 WLR 776 at 807.
142. Ibid at 787. See also *Butler v Board of Trade* [1971] Ch 680.
143. *A v Hayden (No 2)* (1984) 156 CLR 532; *Re a Company's Application* [1989] 2 All ER 248.
144. *Grofam Pty Ltd v KPMG Peat Marwick* (1993) 27 IPR 215.
145. See eg *Malone v Commissioner of Police of the Metropolis (No 2)* [1979] 2 All ER 620.
146. *Initial Services Ltd v Putterill* [1968] 1 QB 396 at 406.
147. *Re a Company's Application* [1989] 2 All ER 248.

must still be regarded as a breach of duty. On one view, taking a literal interpretation of the statement that 'there is no confidence as to the disclosure of iniquity',[148] no duty of confidence at all arises in relation to information which relates to misconduct:[149] so that presumably there can be no entitlement to further relief. But that simplistic rationale does not explain how an inappropriately wide disclosure of such information may be restrained. A more accurate formulation would be that a duty of confidence is not breached by disclosure of iniquity to the proper authorities.[150] But that still does not resolve the problem of whether general publication constitutes a breach of confidence, even if the public interest at the time militates (or would have militated) against the grant of an injunction. What, too, of a situation where the information does not relate to any misconduct on the confider's part? It is suggested that the correct approach is that taken by a majority of the Full Court of the Federal Court in *Corrs Pavey Whiting & Byrne v Collector of Customs (Vic)*.[151] The case arose in the context of a freedom of information (FOI) claim, which was resisted on the ground that disclosure would have constituted a 'breach of confidence'. The FOI statutes and the questions they raise are considered later on.[152] For now it suffices to note that Jenkinson J, with whom Sweeney J concurred, held that the breach of confidence exemption (as it was then worded) extended to any document

> which contains confidential information received under circumstances importing an obligation of confidence, without regard to those considerations of public policy to which courts have allowed an influence in determining whether to grant or withhold remedies for 'breach of confidence' in exercise of equitable or common law jurisdiction.[153]

Justification, in other words, should be treated as a matter going solely to the discretionary award of remedies. On this basis, pecuniary relief might conceivably be awarded to a confider who failed to obtain an injunction, if it could be shown that the public interest would not thereby be prejudiced: presumably, though, this would be a rare situation.

(b) Disclosure Under Legal Compulsion

[4.22] **Statutory and court-ordered disclosure.** In certain circumstances a person may be obliged to disclose confidential information by a duty which overrides that imposed by contract or equity. Where this is so it would seem that the confidant may plead the compulsion as a defence to any action brought by the confider.[154] Disclosure may be required by statute, as for example where a medical practitioner is obliged to notify authorities that a patient has tested positive for the AIDS

---

148. *Gartside v Outram* (1856) 26 LJ Ch 113 at 114.
149. See eg *Corrs Pavey Whiting & Byrne v Collector of Customs (Vic)* (1987) 74 ALR 428 at 446–9.
150. See eg *Attorney-General (UK) v Guardian Newspapers Ltd (No 2)* [1988] 2 WLR 805 at 851–3.
151. (1987) 74 ALR 428.
152. See [4.38].
153. (1987) 74 ALR 428 at 432.
154. It is hard to find authority directly to this effect, but it is a clear corollary of the existence of the higher duty. The position is sometimes clarified by a statute which requires disclosure: see eg Freedom of Information Act 1982 (Cth) s 91(2)(a).

virus,[155] or a lawyer must cooperate with an investigator appointed by a professional body or complaints authority by providing access to confidential files,[156] or a bank must hand over to the Commissioner of Taxation confidential documents relating to income earned by its customers.[157] In such cases the person or body to whom disclosure is required will themselves come under an obligation to respect the confidentiality of the information.[158]

Disclosure may also be ordered by a court for the purposes of litigation. It is established that the confidentiality of information is not of itself a bar to discovery being ordered. Nevertheless, in weighing up whether the public interest in the effective and fair conduct of proceedings demands that information be available to the parties, the court may treat it as a material consideration.[159] In some instances the preservation of confidentiality will have a particular significance that outweighs the immediate demands of the case before the court. Thus in *D v National Society for the Prevention of Cruelty to Children*,[160] discovery was sought from the Society of documents relating to what was alleged to be an ill-founded complaint against the plaintiff, who was now suing the Society for negligence in its handling of the matter. The order was refused, since disclosure of the complainant's identity would have threatened the Society's ability to use guarantees of anonymity as a means of securing information on the sensitive subject of child abuse. By contrast journalists, who lack official or semi-official status, have had a much harder time in protecting the confidentiality of their sources from discovery orders.[161] As with information compulsorily disclosed under statutory authority, it is a condition of an order for discovery that the party given access to the information impliedly undertakes not to use it for purposes other than the immediate litigation.[162] However, where it would be unrealistic to expect such an undertaking to be obeyed (as for example

155. See eg Public Health Act 1902 (NSW) ss 50H–50L. See generally M Neave, 'AIDS — Confidentiality and the Duty to Warn' (1987) 9 *U Tas LR* 1; J Godwin et al, *Australian HIV/AIDS Legal Guide*, 2nd ed, 1993, Chs 1, 3.

156. See eg *Brayley v Wilton* [1976] 2 NSWLR 495; *Rogerson v Law Society of the Northern Territory* (1993) 88 NTR 1.

157. See eg *Federal Commissioner of Taxation v Australia and New Zealand Banking Group Ltd* (1979) 143 CLR 499.

158. See eg *Smith Kline and French Laboratories (Australia) Ltd v Secretary, Department of Community Services and Health* (1991) 20 IPR 643; *Marcel v Commissioner of Police of the Metropolis* [1991] 1 All ER 845; *Johns v Australian Securities Commission* (1993) 178 CLR 408; and see [4.10], [4.12].

159. See eg *Alfred Crompton Amusement Machines Ltd v Customs & Excise Commissioners (No 2)* [1974] AC 405; *Commonwealth v Northern Land Council* (1993) 176 CLR 604; and see generally J D Heydon, *Cross on Evidence*, 5th Aust ed, 1996, pp 735–63. The 'public interest' exception to discovery is codified in s 130(1) of the Evidence Act 1995 (Cth) and Evidence Act 1995 (NSW): see S Odgers, *Uniform Evidence Law*, 1995, pp 218–23.

160. [1978] AC 171. See also *X v Y* [1988] 2 All ER 648.

161. See eg *McGuinness v Attorney-General (Vic)* (1940) 63 CLR 73; *British Steel Corp v Granada Television Ltd* [1981] AC 1096; *John Fairfax & Sons Ltd v Cojuangco* (1988) 165 CLR 346; S Walker, 'Compelling Journalists to Identify Their Sources: "The Newspaper Rule" and "Necessity"' (1991) 14 *UNSWLJ* 302. Cf the proposals for legislative reform in Senate Standing Committee on Legal and Constitutional Affairs, *Off the Record: Shield Laws for Journalists' Confidential Sources*, 1994.

where a firm is seeking access to commercially sensitive information belonging to a competitor and can hardly be expected to 'forget' about it following the litigation), that in itself may be a reason for refusing discovery.[163]

4. REMEDIES

(a) Interlocutory Relief

[4.23] Relevant factors. Pending the trial of a breach of confidence action the plaintiff may be able to seek one or more of the various forms of interlocutory relief described in Chapter 2.[164] Without repeating the general points already made, it should be noted that actions which are primarily designed to preserve confidentiality may carry a particularly strong claim to be supported by the award of an interlocutory injunction.[165] If the whole point of the plaintiff's claim is to prevent publication, as opposed to precluding or halting a use which does not or will not necessarily have the effect of destroying secrecy, and if the plaintiff can show that pecuniary relief is not likely to be an adequate alternative given the interest sought to be protected, refusal of an interim restraint may run the risk of effectively destroying the plaintiff's rights and making a trial pointless. This was the key to the controversial decision to maintain an injunction against publication by British newspapers of the allegedly confidential contents of the book *Spycatcher*, despite the widespread availability of copies imported from America.[166] Having reached the admittedly peculiar conclusion that an injunction might yet be granted against the newspapers at a final trial,[167] the Court of Appeal and the majority of the House of Lords quite logically determined that preservation of the plaintiff's rights demanded that the interlocutory restraint remain in force. As against that, particular factors which may bring the balance of convenience down against the plaintiff include: the damage that might be suffered by a defendant who has already

---

162. *Biltoft Holdings Pty Ltd v Casselan Pty Ltd* (1991) 4 WAR 14; *Mobil Oil Australia Ltd v Guina Developments Pty Ltd* (1995) 33 IPR 82; *Esso Australia Resources Ltd v Plowman* (1995) 183 CLR 10 at 32–3, 36–7, 46. Cf *Rank Film Distributors Ltd v Video Information Centre* [1981] 2 All ER 76 at 81, 85 (use may be permitted in later criminal proceedings); *Brown v Matthews* [1990] 2 WLR 879 (information given for welfare officer's report to one court may be used with that court's consent in other proceedings).
163. *Mobil Oil Australia Ltd v Guina Developments Pty Ltd* (1995) 33 IPR 82.
164. Anton Piller orders in particular may prove useful where confidential information is concerned: see Dean, pp 449–78.
165. Note that an injunction which is designed to protect confidentiality may cover much more than use or disclosure of the confidential information itself. For instance a defendant may even be restrained from making use of non-confidential material, if that use would have the practical effect of destroying the confidentiality of the plaintiff's information: see eg *Falconer v Australian Broadcasting Corp* (1991) 22 IPR 205.
166. *Attorney-General (UK) v Guardian Newspapers Ltd* [1987] 1 WLR 1248. See also *Attorney General (UK) v Newspaper Publishing plc* [1987] 3 WLR 942 at 950, 962; *Attorney-General (UK) v Turnaround Distribution Ltd* [1989] FSR 169; *Westpac Banking Corp v John Fairfax Group Pty Ltd* (1991) 19 IPR 513.
167. See [4.41].

geared up to exploit the information,[168] especially where the plaintiff is not trading in the same market;[169] the weakness of the plaintiff's case,[170] or the strength of any defence likely to be pleaded;[171] and the fact that the plaintiff's claim is interwoven with a libel action to which the defendant intends to plead justification.[172] The court's perceptions of the balance of convenience may also be affected by its expectations as to how quickly the matter is likely to come on for a full trial.[173] In some instances indeed an interlocutory injunction may deliberately be given a limited duration in order to prompt a speedy trial.[174]

(b) Final Injunctions

[4.24]   Injunction or damages? In so far as the essence of a duty of confidentiality is not to make unconscientious use of the information, it follows that an injunction restraining such use is the primary remedy for breach of confidence.[175] Assuming that an actual or threatened breach of confidence has been established and that the plaintiff is not merely interested in pecuniary relief, the issue will therefore be whether any circumstances exist which militate against granting what would seem to be the obvious remedy. The most sweeping argument is that in certain cases an injunction would be inherently unfair, given the nature of the duty cast on the defendant. The case usually cited in this regard is *Seager v Copydex Ltd*,[176] where the defendants were held to have subconsciously plagiarised an idea communicated to them by the plaintiff inventor in the course of unsuccessful negotiations regarding a previous invention. The Court of Appeal preferred to award damages, though making no explanation as to why an injunction was not considered appropriate.

Although innocence per se does not seem to be an automatic bar to the grant of an injunction,[177] Megarry J in *Coco v A N Clark (Engineers) Ltd*[178] also alluded to the plight of the 'law abiding and conscientious citizen' who has acquired confidential information but then improved on it by using other information which is either in the public domain or their own. The springboard doctrine demands that such a person not be in a better position than if they had only used the non-confidential information: they must not, in other words, gain a head start by breaching

---

168. See eg *Potters-Ballotini Ltd v Weston-Baker* [1977] RPC 202; *Concept Television Productions Pty Ltd v Australian Broadcasting Corporation* (1988) 12 IPR 129.

169. See eg *Coco v A N Clark (Engineers) Ltd* [1969] RPC 41.

170. See eg *ANI Corp Ltd v Celtite Australia Pty Ltd* (1990) 19 IPR 506; *Series 5 Software Ltd v Clarke* [1996] FSR 273.

171. See eg *Lion Laboratories Ltd v Evans* [1984] 2 All ER 417.

172. See eg *Woodward v Hutchins* [1977] 2 All ER 751.

173. See eg *Lawrence David Ltd v Ashton* [1991] 1 All ER 385; *Lansing Linde Ltd v Kerr* [1991] 1 All ER 418; *Interpersonnel Pty Ltd v Reynolds* (1994) 55 IR 357.

174. See eg *Slevin v Associated Insurance Brokers of Australia (Queensland) Pty Ltd* [1996] AILR 9–049.

175. See generally M Gronow, 'Injunctions in Breach of Confidence Proceedings' (1995) 6 *AIPJ* 246.

176. [1967] 2 All ER 415.

177. See eg *Nichrotherm Electrical Co Ltd v Percy* [1956] RPC 272; *National Broach & Machine Co v Churchill Gear Machines Ltd* [1965] RPC 61.

178. [1969] RPC 41 at 48–50.

confidence.[179] But how, Megarry J inquired, was this duty to be fulfilled in practice? The recipient might attempt to guess how long it would have taken to reach the same point without the confidential information, an artificial and uncertain inquiry that would be particularly difficult if the information had turned out to be the vital component in making the project successful. Or the 'honourable course' might be taken of standing out of the field altogether until someone else had put the information in the public domain: but this would mean accepting 'a unique disability. He alone of all men [sic] must for an uncertain time abjure this field of endeavour, however great his interest'.[180] The solution, Megarry J thought, in line with the *Seager* case, might be to allow the recipient to ignore the duty, use the information and then pay a reasonable sum for it by way of damages: no injunction would be imposed. This would effectively recognise that in this sort of case the essence of the duty of confidence is 'that of not using without paying, rather than of not using at all'. In a personal information case, the duty might of course 'exist in the more stringent form', presumably because the confider's interest in secrecy is not adequately protected by the payment of a sum of money.[181] There is a great deal of force in these comments, though it is doubtful that they can or should be used to support a generalisation that courts should be willing to compel the licensing of trade secrets by awarding damages rather than injunctive relief.[182] It may be that a better approach is to look to the extent of the recipient's contribution in improving on the original information and, where it is substantial, to rely on that factor as a reason for not granting an injunction.[183]

[4.25] Effect of publication. One powerful argument that may be used against the grant of an injunction is that the point has been reached at which the relevant information, even allowing for the expiry of any head start calculated under the springboard doctrine, has moved into the public domain. In most cases of this type any existing restraints will be discharged and no further injunction issued.[184] Similarly, if the court believes that the defendant's head start has not yet expired, but is likely to do so in the near future, it may grant an injunction which is limited to the intervening period.[185] There may however be cases where an injunction remains appropriate despite publication. Thus in *Speed Seal Products Ltd v*

---

179. See [4.8].
180. [1969] RPC 41 at 49.
181. Ibid at 50.
182. Cf *Terrapin Ltd v Builders' Supply Co (Hayes) Ltd* [1960] RPC 128 at 135; *AB Consolidated Ltd v Europe Strength Food Co Pty Ltd* [1978] 2 NZLR 515 at 525.
183. See Gurry, pp 403–4.
184. See eg *Fractionated Cane Technology Ltd v Ruiz-Avila* (1987) 8 IPR 502; (1988) 13 IPR 609; *Roger Bullivant Ltd v Ellis* [1987] FSR 172.
185. See eg *Fisher-Karpark Industries Ltd v Nichols* [1982] FSR 351. Cf *AB Consolidated Ltd v Europe Strength Food Co Pty Ltd* [1978] 2 NZLR 515. If the court believes there is some possibility of secrecy being lost, but is not convinced that it will, it may grant a permanent injunction but with explicit provision for a swift hearing for vacation of the order in the event of publication: see eg *G v Day* [1982] 1 NSWLR 24 at 41.

Paddington[186] Fox LJ thought it arguable that the plaintiff might at the full trial of the action receive injunctive relief:

> The purpose of an injunction is protection. Whether a plaintiff, in circumstances such as the present, needs protection might depend on the state of the market. If, for example, the only traders seriously competing in the market are the plaintiff and the defendant ... it may be a matter of continuing importance to the plaintiff that the defendant not get the benefit of the wrongdoing. If, on the other hand, the publication has produced a market with a large number of traders, the elimination of one trader (the defendant) might not be of consequence.

The explanation for the grant of an injunction in the first instance posited by Fox LJ is simple. Although the information is *theoretically* in the public domain, in actuality the only person using the information to compete with the plaintiff is the defendant, who is thus still enjoying the head start provided by the original breach. Publication will not deter the grant of an injunction if the court considers that the plaintiff still merits protection against loss caused by the defendant's activities.[187] Suppose, however, that publication has damaged the plaintiff's interests in such a way that no further loss remains to be suffered. Apart from receiving compensation in respect of the detriment inflicted by the breach, can the plaintiff obtain an injunction to restrain the plaintiff's continuing profitable use of the information, even though the profits are not strictly speaking being made at the plaintiff's expense? So long as the underlying thrust of the doctrine of breach of confidence is to *protect* the confider's interests rather than *punish* confidants, the answer must surely be that injunctive relief should be refused.[188]

[4.26] Other reasons for refusing relief. It has already been noted that the triviality of the information which the plaintiff is seeking to protect may be a ground for refusing injunctive relief, as may the fact that the information relates to immoral conduct.[189] A number of other factors may also be relevant in this regard. Of particular significance is the contention that the plaintiff has come to equity with 'unclean hands'. Although there may be a considerable overlap with the defence of justification, slightly different issues are raised. Rather than focusing on whether the public interest demands circulation of the information in question, the unclean hands objection brings into question the propriety of the plaintiff's personal behaviour.[190] Thus the plaintiff may be denied redress, for instance, for using 'deplorable means' to protect the information,[191] or (possibly) for refusing to respect the defendant's confidentiality in return.[192] It is not

186. [1986] 1 All ER 91 at 95.
187. See also *Aquaculture Corp v New Zealand Green Mussel Co Ltd (No 2)* (1986) 10 IPR 319.
188. See eg *Concept Television Productions Pty Ltd v Australian Broadcasting Corporation* (1988) 12 IPR 129; and see also *McLachlan Consultants Pty Ltd v Boswell* (1988) 30 IR 417. Cf [4.41].
189. See [3.9].
190. Cf *Corrs Pavey Whiting & Byrne v Collector of Customs (Vic)* (1987) 74 ALR 428 at 451.
191. See eg *Hubbard v Vosper* [1972] 2 QB 84 at 101; *Church of Scientology of California v Kaufman* [1973] RPC 635. Cf *Aquaculture Corp v New Zealand Green Mussel Co Ltd* (1985) 5 IPR 353 at 385-6.
192. Cf *Argyll v Argyll* [1967] 1 Ch 302 at 330-2, where the plaintiff's conduct in disclosing details of the defendant's personal and financial affairs was considered to be 'of an altogether different order of perfidy' to the defendant's behaviour in threatening to reveal marital confidences.

enough, however, to establish that the plaintiff has behaved improperly: there must be some relationship between the impropriety and the relief being sought.[193] Relief may also be denied, on ordinary equitable principles, where the plaintiff is guilty of delay or laches in seeking redress.[194]

[4.27] **Ancillary relief.** Where an injunction is granted to restrain a breach of confidence, it is common for the court to make ancillary orders in order to ensure the efficacy of the injunction. If the defendant has appropriated or come into possession of a physical item, such as a document, which belongs to the plaintiff and which embodies the relevant information, the defendant will usually be ordered to deliver it up to the plaintiff.[195] Similarly, copies made by the defendant of such an item may be ordered to be delivered up to the court or to the plaintiff for destruction.[196] In some instances the court may go so far as to decree the destruction of property, such as machinery or manufactured goods, which has been independently created by the defendant in order to exploit the information;[197] though the wastefulness of such an exercise may well militate against such an order being granted.

(c) Pecuniary Remedies

[4.28] **Account of profits.** In seeking pecuniary relief in relation to a breach of confidence, the plaintiff may elect either to strip the defendant of any profits made as a result of the breach, or to seek compensation for any loss suffered thereby.[198] In practice, it will be rare for an account of profits to be sought, because of the difficulties with the remedy referred to in Chapter 2.[199] An account works best where it can be established that the defendant would not have been able to engage in the relevant commercial activity at all, were it not for the breach of confidence: in such a case, the plaintiff is entitled to claim all the profits flowing from that activity.[200] It is a different matter where an account would require the profits made from the breach to be segregated from those which would in any event have been made as a result of the defendant's legitimate activities. For example, in accordance with the views expressed earlier in relation to the effect of publication on liability,[201] it would seem that no account should be taken of profits made after the relevant information has become freely available and any head start under the springboard doctrine has expired. It has indeed been suggested that unless an account would be 'practical or simple', the

193. *Talbot v General Television Corp* [1980] VR 224 at 240–1; *Castrol Australia Pty Ltd v Emtech Associates Pty Ltd* (1980) 33 ALR 31 at 57–8.
194. Cf *Aquaculture Corp v New Zealand Green Mussel Co Ltd* (1985) 5 IPR 353 at 386.
195. See eg *Alperton Rubber Co v Manning* (1917) 86 LJ Ch 377.
196. See eg *Industrial Furnaces Ltd v Reaves* [1970] RPC 605; *Franklin v Giddins* [1978] Qd R 72.
197. See eg *Ormonoids Roofing & Asphalts Ltd v Bitumenoids Ltd* (1930) 31 SR (NSW) 347.
198. See eg *Peter Pan Manufacturing Corp v Corsets Silhouette Ltd* [1963] 3 All ER 402; *Ansell Rubber Co Pty Ltd v Allied Rubber Industries Pty Ltd* [1967] VR 37. See further M Gronow, 'Restitution for Breach of Confidence' (1996) 10 *IPJ* 219 at 219–37.
199. See eg *Saltman Engineering Co Ltd v Campbell Engineering Co Ltd* (1948) 65 RPC 203; *Fortuity Pty Ltd v Barcza* (1995) 32 IPR 517.
200. *Peter Pan Manufacturing Corp v Corsets Silhouette Ltd* [1963] 3 All ER 402; *AB Consolidated Ltd v Europe Strength Food Co Pty Ltd* [1978] 2 NZLR 515.
201. See [4.7]–[4.9], [4.25].

court should exercise its discretion against making the necessary order, even if sought by the plaintiff.[202] Other reasons for refusing an account include delay on the part of the plaintiff;[203] and, it would seem, the innocence of the defendant's conduct.[204] On the other hand these factors, especially the practical difficulties of isolating the relevant profits, are likely to weigh less heavily where an account would be the only form of pecuniary relief available. This will tend to occur particularly in non-commercial cases, where it may be very difficult, as noted below, for a plaintiff to establish that compensable loss has occurred. The desire to ensure that defendants do not benefit from their wrongdoing may well lead courts to order accounts in situations where, were damages a realistic option, they would not otherwise do so.[205]

[4.29]   Damages: availability. Where an account of profits is deemed to be impracticable or inappropriate, whether by the court or by the plaintiff, damages may be sought instead to compensate for any loss suffered by reason of the defendant's breach: indeed, damages may now be described as the main pecuniary remedy for breach of confidence, at least in commercial cases.[206] Where the defendant is a confidant who has breached a contractual obligation of confidence, such damages are available as of right for breach of contract.[207] Similarly, where the defendant is a third party who has induced a breach of confidence, damages may be claimed in tort.[208] In theory, there should be a problem where the cause of action rests entirely in equity. However, the courts have effectively ignored any complications and awarded damages anyway, for the most part making no attempt to explain the precise basis for the remedy. When the issue has been considered, the most common reference has been to the statutory power in each jurisdiction to award damages in addition to or in lieu of an injunction,[209] it being held that breach of confidence constitutes a 'wrong' for the purpose of these provisions.[210] An alternative view, advanced by the diehard opponents to the 'fusion fallacy', is that equitable 'compensation' (but not damages, which is a common law remedy) may be awarded so as to compel

---

202. *Aquaculture Corp v New Zealand Green Mussel Co Ltd (No 2)* (1986) 10 IPR 319 at 332.
203. See eg *International Scientific Communications Inc v Pattison* [1979] FSR 429; *Aquaculture Corp v New Zealand Green Mussel Co Ltd (No 2)* (1986) 10 IPR 319.
204. See [2.16]. The innocence of the defendant is often assumed to be the reason for the refusal to grant an account in *Seager v Copydex Ltd* [1967] 2 All ER 415.
205. See eg *Attorney-General (UK) v Guardian Newspapers Ltd (No 2)* [1988] 3 WLR 776.
206. Ibid at 788. Cf Privacy Act 1988 (Cth) s 93, which makes it clear that damages may be claimed for a breach of confidence by a Commonwealth agency or officer in relation to personal information.
207. See eg *Nichrotherm Electrical Co Ltd v Percy* [1957] RPC 207.
208. See [4.16].
209. See Supreme Court Act 1970 (NSW) s 68; Supreme Court Act 1986 (Vic) s 38; Supreme Court Act 1935 (SA) s 30; Supreme Court Civil Procedure Act 1932 (Tas) s 11(13); Supreme Court Act 1935 (WA) s 25(10). These provisions are based upon 'Lord Cairns' Act': Chancery Amendment Act 1858 (UK) s 2. As to the position in Queensland, see *Conroy v Lowndes* [1958] Qd R 375 at 383–4.
210. See eg *Saltman Engineering Co Ltd v Campbell Engineering Co Ltd* (1948) 65 RPC 203; *Talbot v General Television Corp Pty Ltd* [1980] VR 224; *Attorney-General (UK) v Guardian Newspapers Ltd (No 2)* [1988] 3 WLR 776 at 810; *Johns v Australian Securities Commission* (1993) 178 CLR 408 at 429.

the wrongdoer to restore the status quo.[211] In practical terms, it is difficult to see that much turns on the difference between these two views. On either basis, these damages (or compensation) differ from damages for breach of contract in two important respects. In the first place, compensation may be awarded not only for loss suffered prior to the date of the trial, but also in some instances for prospective losses (thus obviating the need for any injunction).[212] Second, both theories suggest that the award must lie in the court's discretion: though this sits ill with the common assertion that plaintiffs are 'entitled' to damages.[213]

[4.30] Damages: assessment. Fortunately, the controversy as to the proper explanation for the availability of non-contractual damages has not prevented the courts from developing principles as to their assessment.[214] It is now settled that the function of an award is to restore the plaintiff, as far as possible, to the position that would have obtained had the breach of confidence not occurred; and that in seeking to do this, the court will adopt whatever method of measuring the plaintiff's loss is most appropriate to the particular circumstances.[215] As far as trade secrets are concerned, the appropriate method will depend upon the particular value of the information to the plaintiff and the extent to which that value has been diminished by the defendant's actions. Two different situations may be discerned. First, the information may consist of an idea which the plaintiff is looking to sell or license to another person for that other to exploit. Where the defendant goes ahead and exploits the information without permission, the measure of damage will be the price that the plaintiff would have expected to receive for the information, whether in terms of a one-off fee or, where the information is more 'special', a series of royalty payments.[216] Where the information is only partially exploited by the defendant, the plaintiff's loss will be the amount by which the chance of fully exploiting it has been diminished: though allowance must be made for the contingency that the plaintiff would not have successfully exploited it all.[217] Second, the information may be used in furtherance of a business carried on by the plaintiff. The appropriate measure here will usually be the profits which are lost as a result of the information being used by the defendant and/or

211. See *Concept Television Productions Pty Ltd v Australian Broadcasting Corp* (1988) 12 IPR 129; Meagher, Gummow and Lehane, para 4127. Cf *Aquaculture Corp v New Zealand Green Mussel Co Ltd* (1990) 19 IPR 527, where the much more sensible view is adopted that with the effective merging of common law and equity there is no reason to limit the availability of remedies for breach of confidence by reference to the historical origins of those remedies.
212. See eg *Saltman Engineering Co Ltd v Campbell Engineering Co Ltd* (1948) 65 RPC 203.
213. See eg *Peter Pan Manufacturing Corp v Corsets Silhouette Ltd* [1963] 3 All ER 402 at 411.
214. See J Stuckey-Clarke, 'Damages for Breaches of Purely Equitable Rights: The Breach of Confidence Example' in P D Finn (ed), *Essays on Damages*, 1992, p 69; M Gronow, 'Damages for Breach of Confidence' (1994) 5 *AIPJ* 94.
215. *Talbot v General Television Corp Pty Ltd* [1980] VR 224; *Dowson & Mason Ltd v Potter* [1986] 2 All ER 418; *Titan Group Pty Ltd v Steriline Manufacturing Pty Ltd* (1990) 19 IPR 353.
216. See eg *Seager v Copydex Ltd (No 2)* [1969] 2 All ER 718; *Interfirm Comparison (Australia) Pty Ltd v Law Society of NSW* (1975) 5 ALR 527; 6 ALR 445. In *Seager* Lord Denning MR suggested (ibid at 720) that, after paying the damages, the information would, by analogy with an action for conversion, 'belong' to the defendant. However, it is difficult to see how this could be so.
217. See eg *Talbot v General Television Corp Pty Ltd* [1980] VR 224.

becoming available to the plaintiff's competitors.[218] Again, however, such damages should only compensate for loss suffered *as a result of the breach* and not, for instance, for loss sustained through activities of the defendant after expiry of any head start calculated under the springboard doctrine. It is much less clear what damages might be awarded where the information has no financial value as such to the plaintiff. In *W v Egdell*[219] it was said that damages could not be claimed for 'shock and distress' occasioned by a breach of confidence, reference being made to the fact that such loss is not compensable in an action for breach of contract. However, even if it is appropriate to equate the two actions, it may be noted that contractual damages can be claimed for mental distress, at least where the essence of the obligation broken is that the plaintiff will not suffer such distress.[220] On that basis, it might be expected that, in relation to personal information whose disclosure would necessarily cause distress, such loss would be compensable.[221] It should also be noted that there is New Zealand authority to the effect that exemplary damages may be awarded in the case of a 'contumelious disregard' for the plaintiff's rights.[222] It remains to be seen whether this would be accepted by an Australian court, though in principle there seems to be no reason why it should not.

[4.31] Quantum meruit. It has been suggested that a plaintiff may be able to recover the reasonable value of the information misused by the defendant by seeking a quantum meruit award.[223] Although no Australian or English court appears as yet to have made such an award,[224] there seems to be no reason why it should not come into play where the information has financial value, yet the plaintiff has not been in a position to exploit it and thus has suffered no loss.

(d) Proprietary Remedies

[4.32] Constructive trust. Some commentators have suggested that a person who misuses confidential information may be treated as a constructive trustee of any benefits obtained as a result of the breach.[225] However, the matter is far from clear. The most obvious way to explain the imposition

---

218. See eg *Dowson & Mason Ltd v Potter* [1986] 2 All ER 418; *Aquaculture Corp v New Zealand Green Mussel Co Ltd (No 2)* (1986) 10 IPR 319. Cf *Fortuity Pty Ltd v Barcza* (1995) 32 IPR 517.
219. [1989] 1 All ER 1089 at 1108–9.
220. *Baltic Shipping Co v Dillon* (1993) 176 CLR 344.
221. It has been recommended that legislation be introduced to provide for such damages in all breach of confidence cases: Legal and Constitutional Committee (Vic), *A Report to Parliament Upon Privacy and Breach of Confidence*, 1990, p 46.
222. *Aquaculture Corp v New Zealand Green Mussel Co Ltd* (1990) 19 IPR 527.
223. See Goff and Jones, p 692.
224. Although damages have sometimes been assessed in such a way as to make them look very much like a quantum meruit award: see eg *Interfirm Comparison (Australia) Pty Ltd v Law Society of NSW* (1975) 5 ALR 527; 6 ALR 445.
225. See eg Meagher, Gummow and Lehane, para 4127; M Gronow, 'Restitution for Breach of Confidence' (1996) 10 *IPJ* 219 at 237–64; though cf M Cope, *Constructive Trusts*, 1992, p 153; A Burrows, *Law of Restitution*, 1993, pp 415–17. As to the difficulties of determining how far such a trust should extend, see *Hospital Products Ltd v United States Surgical Corp* (1984) 156 CLR 41 at 110–16; *Schindler Lifts Australia Pty Ltd v Debelak* (1989) 15 IPR 129 at 155–6.

of a constructive trust would be to treat duties of confidence as a species of fiduciary obligation.[226] But while some might regard 'fiduciary' as a harmless label which adds nothing to the analysis of the duty of confidence,[227] it can in fact be positively misleading. A 'fiduciary' is more usually taken to refer to a person who is under a strict duty to conserve another's interests pursuant to a pre-existing relationship. While confidentiality is certainly one of the standards required of such a person, it may also be imposed in the absence of so clearly defined a relationship and in situations where there is no such general duty.[228] Arguably then a distinction should be maintained between the specific obligation of confidentiality and the more general obligations of a fiduciary, lest the courts fall into the error of imposing too broad a duty on mere confidants.[229] On the other hand, rejection of a fiduciary analysis does not necessarily preclude the possibility of a constructive trust, as the decision of the Supreme Court of Canada in *LAC Minerals Ltd v International Corona Resources Ltd*[230] reveals. There a trust was imposed over property acquired as a result of a breach of confidence, despite the court's finding that no fiduciary relationship existed. Whether the same approach would be taken in Australia remains to be seen, although Deane J has advanced the broad (and admittedly controversial) proposition that

> a constructive trust may be imposed as the appropriate form of equitable relief in circumstances where a person could not in good conscience retain for himself [sic] a benefit, or the proceeds of a benefit, which he has appropriated to himself in breach of his contractual or other legal or equitable obligations to another.[231]

Similar uncertainty surrounds the possibility that a trust may be imposed on a third party who becomes involved in a breach of confidence. According to the second limb of the *Barnes v Addy*[232] principle, such a person would need to have knowingly assisted in a 'dishonest and fraudulent design'. Whether this latter phrase encompasses all breaches of fiduciary

---

226. See eg *Schering Chemicals Ltd v Falkman Ltd* [1981] 2 All ER 321 at 337; *Surveys & Mining Ltd v Morrison* [1969] Qd R 470 at 473.
227. See Gurry, pp 158–9; *Attorney-General (UK) v Heinemann Publishers Australia Pty Ltd* (1987) 75 ALR 353 at 456.
228. See *Smith Kline & French Laboratories (Australia) Ltd v Secretary, Department of Community Services and Health* (1990) 17 IPR 545 at 559; R P Austin, 'Fiduciary Accountability for Business Opportunities' in P D Finn (ed), *Equity and Commercial Relationships*, 1987, p 141 at pp 142–3.
229. Such an approach would be consistent with the High Court's reluctance to regard commercial relationships as generating fiduciary obligations: see *Hospital Products Ltd v United States Surgical Corp* (1984) 156 CLR 41. See also Creighton and Stewart, para [860], where the indiscriminate use of the term 'fiduciary' in the employment context is criticised. Cf *Timber Engineering Co Pty Ltd v Anderson* [1980] 2 NSWLR 488; *Angus & Coote Pty Ltd v Render* (1989) 16 IPR 387; *Fortuity Pty Ltd v Barcza* (1995) 32 IPR 517.
230. (1989) 16 IPR 27.
231. *Hospital Products Ltd v United States Surgical Corp* (1984) 156 CLR 41 at 125.
232. (1874) LR 9 Ch App 244 at 252; *Consul Development Pty Ltd v DPC Estates Pty Ltd* (1975) 132 CLR 373. Note that the first limb involves the receipt of trust property: as to whether confidential information may be treated as property, see [3.14]–[3.17]. Cf R P Austin, 'Constructive Trusts' in P D Finn (ed), *Essays in Equity*, 1985, p 196 at pp 223–5.

duty,[233] and whether 'mere' breaches of confidence would suffice, are again questions which remain to be answered.

5. SPECIAL CASES

(a) Employees

[4.33] Confidentiality in the employment context. A substantial proportion of breach of confidence litigation concerns actions against employees, past or present, who are seeking to use or disclose trade secrets acquired in the course of their engagement with the plaintiff. However, despite the fact that employees represent the most numerous class of recipients of confidential business information, the principles described in this chapter require some qualification before they can be applied in the employment context. Two complicating factors in particular need to be noted. The first is that *during* the employment relationship the employee is subject to a duty of fidelity which is more stringent than the general equitable duty of confidence. Accordingly a careful distinction must be made between the employee's obligations prior to and after the termination of the employment contract. Second, the courts have stressed that the employer's prima facie entitlement to control and take the benefit of information generated or acquired in the course of employment must be balanced against the

> prima facie right of any person to use and to exploit for the purpose of earning his living all the skill, experience and knowledge which he [sic] has at his disposal, including skill, experience and knowledge which he has acquired in the course of previous periods of employment.[234]

[4.34] Misuse of information during the employment period. All employees are obliged to serve their employer 'faithfully' during the period of their employment.[235] Even in the absence of an express contractual promise, therefore, the employee is bound not to damage the employer's interests by disclosing or using *any* information acquired in the course of employment.[236] This duty of fidelity is a strict one. It precludes not just use or disclosure while the employment relationship subsists, but also any deliberate attempts to acquire or memorise information, even if the employee does not plan to use the information until after the employment has terminated.[237] Some cases suggest that a lower standard of fidelity may be expected of employees who have given their notice and are on the verge of departure; these employees, it would seem, are at least to be allowed to plan for their departure, even if that means using the information they

---

233. Cf *Consul Development Pty Ltd v DPC Estates Pty Ltd* (1975) 132 CLR 373 at 397. Gibbs J spoke in this case of 'moral obtuseness' on the part of the third party: ibid at 398. This seems to suggest that before a trust will be imposed there must be some 'want of probity' in their conduct, beyond their mere participation: see *Carl-Zeiss Stiftung v Herbert Smith & Co (No 2)* [1969] 2 Ch 276 at 300–1.

234. *Faccenda Chicken Ltd v Fowler* [1986] 1 All ER 617 at 619. See also *Riteway Express Pty Ltd v Clayton* (1987) 10 NSWLR 238 at 240.

235. *Blyth Chemicals Ltd v Bushnell* (1933) 49 CLR 66 at 81–2; *Independent Management Resources Pty Ltd v Brown* [1987] VR 605 at 612; *Goodchild Fuel Distributors Pty Ltd v Holman* (1992) 59 SASR 454.

236. Cf *Gooley v Westpac Banking Corp* (1995) 129 ALR 628, where it was held that the disclosure in question was in the employer's interests rather than against them.

have acquired.[238] However, other courts continue to treat any use at all of information prior to leaving as an act of perfidy.[239] The exception, of course, is where the information in question is revealed in the public interest to the proper authorities.[240] But while no injunction will be issued to prevent such disclosure, there may be very little (in the absence of a strong trade union) to prevent the employer retaliating by dismissing the employee or subjecting them to some other form of prejudicial treatment. True, such 'disloyalty' is unlikely to be treated as a ground for summary dismissal,[241] and the employee may well be able to seek reinstatement or compensation for unfair dismissal if they are sacked or pressured into resignation.[242] Nevertheless comparatively little attention has been given to this issue in Australia. Legislation specifically designed to protect 'whistleblowers' is gradually being introduced.[243] But only the South Australian *Whistleblowers Protection Act 1993* applies outside the public sector, and there remain concerns as to how effective these measures are in deterring retaliation, let alone in encouraging employees to come forward with information as to wrongdoing at work.

[4.35] Misuse after the employment period. Once the employment ends, a different set of obligations cuts in. The employee may now use any information without breaching the duty of fidelity, so long as it has been properly acquired. Sales officers or managers, for example, may call on their perfectly natural recollections as to the names and needs of their former employer's customers in order to compete for those customers' business, either in their own right or in the service of another employer.[244] The employer is not, however, bereft of protection during the post-employment period. Employees are bound, on the principles discussed earlier in the chapter, by a duty of confidentiality which is distinct from that of fidelity and which remains binding even after the termination of the employment relationship. Consistently with those principles, however, the duty of

---

237. See eg *Robb v Green* [1895] 2 QB 315; *Credit Reference Association of Australia Ltd v Clark* [1995] AILR 7–005; *SWF Hoists and Industrial Equipment Pty Ltd v Polli* (1996) 67 IR 356; *Slevin v Associated Insurance Brokers of Australia (Queensland) Pty Ltd* [1996] AILR 9–049.

238. See eg *Independent Management Resources Pty Ltd v Brown* [1987] VR 605; *McLachlan Consultants Pty Ltd v Boswell* (1988) 30 IR 417.

239. See eg *Angus & Coote Pty Ltd v Render* (1989) 16 IPR 387; *McPherson's Ltd v Tate* (1993) 35 AILR 225. This attitude has been adopted even in relation to employees on 'garden leave' (that is, excused from performing work during their notice period, but still technically employed): see eg *Mason Gray Strange Ltd v Eisdell* (1989) 31 AILR 271; *O U Norman International Pty Ltd v Baker* (1990) 32 AILR 434.

240. See [4.17]–[4.21].

241. See *Associated Dominion Assurance Society Pty Ltd v Andrew* (1949) 49 SR (NSW) 351 at 353–4, 355.

242. See generally Creighton and Stewart, Ch 9.

243. See the measures described in D Lewis, 'Employment Protection for Whistleblowers: On What Principles Should Australian Legislation Be Based?' (1996) 9 *AJLL* 135; and see also R G Fox, 'Protecting the Whistleblower' (1993) 15 *Adel LR* 137; Senate Select Committee on Public Interest Whistleblowing, *In the Public Interest*, 1994.

244. See eg *Metrans Pty Ltd v Courtney-Smith* (1983) 1 IPR 185; *Faccenda Chicken Ltd v Fowler* [1986] 1 All ER 617. See also *A C Gibbons Pty Ltd v Cooper* (1980) 23 SASR 269; *Broadwater Taxation and Investment Services Pty Ltd v Hendriks* (1993) 51 IR 221.

confidentiality is only breached by the misuse of *secret* information. Where the employer has made no particular effort to prevent the information from freely circulating within or outside the enterprise, a claim against an employee who remembers that information and subsequently uses it will fail.[245] In *Faccenda Chicken Ltd v Fowler*,[246] a decision which has been extremely influential in shaping the law not just in England, but in Australia and other countries, the English Court of Appeal put it like this:

> It is clear that the obligation not to use or disclose information [after the employment ceases] may cover secret processes of manufacture such as chemical formulae ... or designs or special methods of constructions ... and other information which is of a sufficiently high degree of confidentiality as to amount to a trade secret. The obligation does not extend, however, to cover all information which is given to or acquired by the employee while in [their] employment, and in particular may not cover information which is only 'confidential' in the sense that an unauthorised disclosure of such information to a third party while the employment subsisted would be a clear breach of the duty of good faith.

Unfortunately, some judges have misinterpreted the reference in this passage to the term 'trade secret', taking it to mean some special class of valuable commercial information which is 'highly' secret and thus excluding protection for more mundane information which an employer has nevertheless gone to considerable pains to keep confidential.[247] This is at odds with numerous authorities on the scope of the equitable doctrine, from which it is clear that a duty of confidentiality will arise in relation to *any* type of information, provided only that it cannot be said to be in the public domain.[248] It is sufficient for this purpose if 'relative' secrecy is maintained, something which hinges on a range of factors including the number of people to whom the information is known, the steps taken to maintain its security, and the ease or difficulty with which others may be able to acquire or duplicate it.[249] The better view then is that 'trade secret' in this context simply denotes a large subset of the range of information caught by the equitable doctrine, covering any information of a business or commercial nature which has been kept relatively secret.[250]

That said, even where an employer can show that *some* confidential material has been taken, this does not guarantee that a remedy will be forthcoming from a court. In the first place, no injunction will be

---

245. See eg *Faccenda Chicken Ltd v Fowler* [1986] 1 All ER 617; *Riteway Express Pty Ltd v Clayton* (1987) 10 NSWLR 238; *Fisher Enterprises v Wootten* (1987) 29 AILR 457; *Secton Pty Ltd v Delawood* (1991) 21 IPR 136. Cf *Schindler Lifts Australia Pty Ltd v Debelak* (1989) 15 IPR 129.

246. [1986] 1 All ER 617 at 625.

247. See eg *Wright v Gasweld Pty Ltd* (1991) 22 NSWLR 317 at 333–4; and see A Stewart, 'Ownership of Property in the Context of Employment: Some Recent Developments' (1992) 5 *AJLL* 1 at 6–10.

248. See [3.9], [4.6].

249. See eg *Ansell Rubber Co Pty Ltd v Allied Rubber Industries Pty Ltd* [1967] VR 37 at 49–50; *Faccenda Chicken Ltd v Fowler* [1986] 1 All ER 617 at 626–7; *Schindler Lifts Australia Pty Ltd v Debelak* (1989) 15 IPR 129 at 171.

250. See *Ansell Rubber Co Pty Ltd v Allied Rubber Industries Pty Ltd* [1967] VR 37 at 46; *IIR Pty Ltd v Buchman* [1989] ATPR 40–955 at 50,426–8; *Lansing Linde Ltd v Kerr* [1991] 1 WLR 251 at 260, 270; and see also *Lancashire Fires Ltd v S A Lyons & Co Ltd* [1996] FSR 629.

granted to restrain the use of trade secrets by an ex-employee unless the employer can specify the precise material that is to be covered by the order.[251] Moreover, in order to be able to claim damages in respect of the breach, the employer must be able to show that any loss of business it has suffered to a rival firm that now includes the ex-employee is properly attributable to the information that was misused, rather than the personal expertise of the ex-employee or others in the rival business.[252] Finally, a court will resist granting an injunction where it feels it would be impracticable to expect the employee to be able to refrain from using the employer's secrets while continuing legitimately to exploit their own 'know-how' — the stock of knowledge, skill and experience built up by working over a long period.[253] The point has almost been reached where so long as workers merely take away information in their head, having made no special effort to acquire it in the first place, they can virtually claim to 'own' it for future purposes, so limited have the employer's remedies become.

[4.36] The role of restrictive covenants. In light of the difficulties that may be faced in enforcing the duty of post-employment confidentiality (as opposed to the duty of fidelity), the natural course for employers concerned to protect their trade secrets is to have their employees agree to express covenants which restrict their post-employment freedom.[254] This is a strategy which has been overtly encouraged by courts in recent years.[255] Rather than securing a promise not to use confidential information, which may be just as difficult to enforce as the implied duty,[256] employers often obtain better results by securing a commitment not to compete with the employer, or to work for a competitor, for a defined period after the termination of employment.[257] The aim is to prevent the employee from ever

---

251. *Lawrence David Ltd v Ashton* (1988) 20 IPR 244; *Lock International plc v Beswick* [1989] 3 All ER 373; *Secton Pty Ltd v Delawood* (1991) 21 IPR 136.
252. *Universal Thermosensors Ltd v Hibben* [1992] 3 All ER 257. Cf *Roger Bullivant Ltd v Ellis* [1987] FSR 172.
253. *Ormonoid Roofing and Asphalts Ltd v Bitumenoids Ltd* (1930) 31 SR (NSW) 347 at 358–9; *Printers and Finishers Ltd v Holloway* [1964] 3 All ER 731 at 735–6; and see eg *Lock International plc v Beswick* [1989] 3 All ER 373; *ANI Corp Ltd v Celtite Australia Pty Ltd* (1990) 19 IPR 506; *Broadwater Taxation and Investment Services Pty Ltd v Hendriks* (1993) 51 IR 221. See further A Stewart, 'Confidentiality and the Employment Relationship' (1988) 1 *AJLL* 1 at 8–12.
254. See generally A Stewart, 'Drafting and Enforcing Post-Employment Restraints' (1997) 10 *AJLL* (forthcoming).
255. See eg *Printers and Finishers Ltd v Holloway* [1964] 3 All ER 731 at 736; *Balston Ltd v Headline Filters Ltd* [1987] FSR 330 at 351–2; *Metrans Pty Ltd v Courtney-Smith* (1983) 1 IPR 185 at 192; *Faccenda Chicken Ltd v Fowler* [1986] 1 All ER 617 at 626–7; *Rentokil Pty Ltd v Lee* (1995) 183 LSJS 444 at 488. For criticism of the trend towards using such covenants see A Stewart, 'Confidential Information and Departing Employees: The Employer's Options' [1989] 3 *EIPR* 88 at 92–4.
256. See eg *Pioneer Concrete Services Ltd v Galli* [1985] VR 675; *Triangle Corp Pty Ltd v Carnsew* (1994) 29 IPR 69. Cf *Wright v Gasweld Pty Ltd* (1991) 22 NSWLR 317, where Kirby P seems to have got into a muddle on this point. He somehow came to the conclusion that information might be sufficiently confidential to be the subject of an express promise of confidentiality, yet not be so 'highly' confidential as to be subject to the equitable or implied contractual duty.
257. Note that such a commitment may be unenforceable by an employer who has wrongfully terminated the contract of employment: see *Kaufman v McGillicuddy* (1914) 19 CLR 1.

getting into any position from which to threaten the employer with the use of secret information. The employer cannot, however, use such covenants merely to stifle competition as such. Restrictive covenants are subject to the common law doctrine of restraint of trade, which proscribes undue interference with freedom of trade, including the right to sell one's personal labour.[258] In the employment context, a post-employment covenant will be unenforceable unless the employer is seeking to protect trade secrets or other confidential information, or to prevent the solicitation of established customers by an employee who has had personal contact with those customers.[259] The covenant must also be no wider than is reasonably necessary to protect the employer's interests, when judged in terms of the duration and area of its coverage and the activities restrained. As an illustration of these rules, in *Commercial Plastics Ltd v Vincent*[260] the defendant, who was the head of the plaintiff's research and development section, had agreed not to work in the plastics industry for one year after leaving the plaintiff's service. The English Court of Appeal refused the plaintiff's action for an injunction to prevent him going to work for its main competitor, holding the covenant in unreasonable restraint of trade. Although the plaintiff did have trade secrets which it could legitimately seek to protect, and although the duration was reasonable, in other respects the covenant was too wide. A reasonable covenant should have been limited to the UK, where the plaintiff's market lay, and to the particular part of the plastics industry in which the plaintiffs operated. It should also be noted that the court refused to 'read down' the clause and enforce it to a reasonable extent only: even though, had it been more reasonably framed, the defendant could legitimately have been restrained from acting in the fashion he had.[261]

(b) Government Information

[4.37]   Information disclosed to government authorities. In discussing the special position of 'government information', it is important to dis-

---

258. See generally J W Carter and D J Harland, *Contract Law in Australia*, 3rd ed, 1996, pp 544–65; M J Trebilcock, *The Common Law of Restraint of Trade*, 1986; D M Meltz, *The Common Law Doctrine of Restraint of Trade in Australia*, 1995. Note that the restrictive practices provisions in Pt IV of the Trade Practices Act 1974 are specifically excluded from applying to employment contracts: s 51(2)(a), (b).
259. *Herbert Morris Ltd v Saxelby* [1916] AC 688; *Lindner v Murdock's Garage* (1950) 83 CLR 628. For other examples of cases in which employers attempted to justify restrictive covenants by reference to the need to protect confidential information, see *Brightman v Lamson Paragon Ltd* (1914) 18 CLR 331; *Drake Personnel Ltd v Beddison* [1979] VR 13; *A Buckle & Son Pty Ltd v McAllister* (1986) 4 NSWLR 426; *IIR Pty Ltd v Buchman* [1989] ATPR 40–955; *Rentokil Pty Ltd v Lee* (1995) 183 LSJS 444.
260. [1965] 1 QB 623.
261. See also *Lindner v Murdock's Garage* (1950) 83 CLR 628; *J A Mont (UK) Ltd v Mills* [1993] FSR 577. Cf Restraints of Trade Act 1976 (NSW), which confers an express power to read down otherwise invalid restrictive covenants and enforce them to the extent they are reasonable: see *Orton v Melman* [1981] 1 NSWLR 583; *Wright v Gasweld Pty Ltd* (1991) 22 NSWLR 317. Note also the increasingly fantastic drafting (in the form of 'step' clauses) used in other jurisdictions to get around the problem: see eg *JQAT Pty Ltd v Storm* [1987] 2 Qd R 162; *Brendan Pty Ltd v Russell* (1994) 11 WAR 280; though cf *Austra Tanks Pty Ltd v Running* [1982] 2 NSWLR 840 where such a clause was struck down for uncertainty.

tinguish between information *held by* government and information *relating* to government. As far as the former is concerned, it is clear that government authorities to whom information is disclosed, whether voluntarily or pursuant to some statutory obligation, are as much subject to the equitable doctrine of confidence as private individuals or institutions. Accordingly any use or disclosure of such information for purposes other than those for which it was supplied may constitute a breach of confidence. However, while blatant misuse for personal gain will plainly be unlawful, the more difficult situation occurs where an authority seeks to use information for a purpose that is within its remit, yet different to that for which it was communicated.[262]

[4.38] Freedom of information and privacy legislation. A further dimension to the issue of the confidentiality of information held by government is added by the enactment of legislation on the subject. As already seen, the Privacy Act 1988 (Cth) ensures that the disclosure of personal information to a Commonwealth agency confers on the subject of the information an enforceable right to confidentiality.[263] More generally, FOI legislation constitutes an important context in which questions of breach of confidence may be raised.[264] Federal, state and territory laws provide rights of access to documents held by public agencies, subject to specific exemptions. Each statute exempts 'trade secrets' and other commercially valuable information,[265] although it would seem that such documents would fall within the broader category of confidential information which is also stipulated to be exempt. Considerable variation exists in the wording of this broader exemption.

Under the original version of the Commonwealth Act, a document was exempt 'if its disclosure under this Act would constitute a breach of confidence'.[266] The Full Court of the Federal Court held in *Corrs Pavey Whiting & Byrne v Collector of Customs (Vic)*[267] that this wording was not to be interpreted in a broad sense, but referred to a disclosure which satisfied the requirements for mounting an action for breach of confidence. On the other hand the majority judges, as noted earlier,[268] further held that no account should be taken of factors relevant to the discretionary grant of remedies: so that, for instance, a document would remain exempt even if its disclosure could have been justified in the public interest. In 1991 the

---

262. See [4.12].
263. See [4.2]; and see eg *Austen v Civil Aviation Authority* (1994) 33 ALD 429. As to the adequacy of this and other safeguards against misuse of personal and commercial information held by the Commonwealth, see House of Representatives Standing Committee on Legal and Constitutional Affairs, *In Confidence*, 1995.
264. See generally *Laws of Australia*, vol 2, Administrative Law, paras [151]–[160].
265. Freedom of Information Act 1989 (ACT) s 43; Freedom of Information Act 1982 (Cth) s 43; Freedom of Information Act 1989 (NSW) Sch 1 cl 7; Freedom of Information Act 1992 (Qld) s 45; Freedom of Information Act 1991 (SA) Sch 1, cl 7; Freedom of Information Act 1991 (Tas) s 31; Freedom of Information Act 1982 (Vic) s 34; Freedom of Information Act 1992 (WA) Sch 1 cl 4. As to the meaning of 'trade secrets' in this context, see *Searle Australia Pty Ltd v Public Interest Advocacy Centre* (1992) 108 ALR 163.
266. Freedom of Information Act 1982 s 45.
267. (1987) 74 ALR 428.
268. See [4.21].

exemption was modified to refer to information which, if disclosed, 'would found an action, by a person other than the Commonwealth, for breach of confidence'. The current wording confirms that the scope of the exemption is to be ascertained by reference to the common law on breach of confidence.[269] But it can also be read as incorporating consideration of 'remedial' issues such as the public interest defence, and to that extent has narrowed the exemption.[270] Similar wording is to be found in the New South Wales, Queensland, South Australian and Western Australian legislation,[271] while the ACT provision still refers to disclosure which 'would constitute a breach of confidence'.[272] By contrast, the Victorian and Tasmanian statutes refer to information or matter 'communicated in confidence',[273] which seems wide enough to cover situations which might not ground an equitable action for breach of confidence.[274]

[4.39] Information belonging to government authorities: the need to establish public interest in secrecy. It is where information relates to the workings of a government authority itself, or is generated within that authority, that a special approach is called for. In *Attorney-General (UK) v Jonathan Cape Ltd*[275] Lord Widgery CJ confirmed that the British government was entitled to protect its information by means of an action for breach of confidence. However, in order to succeed, it must show that the public interest required a restraint on the publication of the relevant information. On the facts before him, involving the diaries of a minister which recorded Cabinet discussions from some ten years before, the judge refused to grant an injunction on the ground that the information was 'stale'.

This reasoning was adopted by Mason J in *Commonwealth v John Fairfax & Sons Ltd*.[276]

> The equitable principle has been fashioned to protect the personal, private and proprietary interests of the citizen, not to protect the very different interests of the executive government ... This is not to say that equity will not protect information in the hands of the government, but it is to say that when equity protects government information it will look at the matter through different spectacles.

---

269. The Australian Law Reform Commission, while recognising the difficulties that this may pose for agencies in interpreting and applying s 45, has recommended that this approach continue: see *Open Government: A Review of the Federal Freedom of Information Act 1982*, ALRC 77, 1995, para 10.32.
270. Cf *Re Kamminga and Australian National University* (1992) 26 ALD 585. Note also that the exemption is inapplicable to information generated within an agency for internal purposes, unless the information is the subject of a duty of confidence owed to someone outside the government (s 45(2)).
271. Freedom of Information Act 1989 (NSW) Sch 1 cl 13; Freedom of Information Act 1992 (Qld) s 46; Freedom of Information Act 1991 (SA) Sch 1, cl 13; Freedom of Information Act 1992 (WA) Sch 1 cl 8. Some of these statutes also exempt 'information obtained in confidence' whose future supply might be prejudiced by disclosure.
272. Freedom of Information Act 1989 (ACT) s 45.
273. Freedom of Information Act 1991 (Tas) s 33; Freedom of Information Act 1982 (Vic) s 35. Note however that there is a further requirement: either that the information, if generated within the agency, would be exempt, or that disclosure would be against the public interest.
274. See *Ryder v Booth* [1985] VR 869 at 878, 883.
275. [1976] QB 752.
276. (1980) 147 CLR 39 at 51–2.

... [I]t can scarcely be a relevant detriment to the government that publication of material concerning its actions will merely expose it to public discussion and criticism ... Accordingly the court will determine the government's claim to confidentiality by reference to the public interest. Unless disclosure is likely to injure the public interest, it will not be protected.

The court will not prevent the publication of information which merely throws light on the past workings of government, even if it be not public property, so long as it does not prejudice the community in other respects ... If, however it appears that disclosure will be inimical to the public interest because national security, relations with foreign countries or the ordinary business of government will be prejudiced, disclosure will be restrained.

On the facts before him, which concerned an attempt to publish foreign and defence policy documents relating to the 1968–75 period, Mason J was not satisfied that any embarrassment caused to the government in its conduct of foreign relations was sufficient to warrant restraint: though he did grant an injunction on the basis of breach of copyright.

[4.40] Scope of the principle. The *Jonathan Cape/Fairfax* approach has been consistently applied in subsequent cases.[277] However, there are a number of issues yet to be fully resolved. The question of who carries the burden of proof in regard to the public interest may be crucial to the outcome of a case. Suppose, for instance, that information is leaked to the press as to confidential speculations by government ministers on the subject of likely successors to the current leader. It would be unlikely that the government could establish that the public interest lay in restraining publication. On the other hand, if a suit were brought by one journalist against another in respect of the same information, it is equally unlikely that the defendant could establish a defence of public interest.[278] This highlights the importance of determining the extent to which the burden of establishing a public interest in secrecy is to be imposed. Presumably the principle applies to government departments and directly controlled agencies, but does it also apply to semi-autonomous public corporations such as Australia Post or Telstra? In *Esso Australia Resources Ltd v Plowman*[279] Mason CJ was strongly of the opinion that it should, accepting the view that in the public sector 'the need is for compelled openness, not for burgeoning secrecy'.[280]

There is also the question of whether all information 'belonging' to government authorities is caught by the principle. In the course of the *Spycatcher* litigation, Street CJ in the New South Wales Court of Appeal expressed the view that where information of a commercial character is concerned, a government's claim for protection should be decided on ordinary principles, public interest considerations being irrelevant in such a case.[281] Arguably too, where confidential information is supplied to a

---

277. See eg *Director-General of Education v Public Service Association of NSW* (1984) 79 FLR 15; *Attorney-General (UK) v Brandon Book Publishers Ltd* [1989] FSR 37. See also the *Spycatcher* cases discussed in [4.41].
278. Cf *Beloff v Pressdram Ltd* [1973] 1 All ER 240.
279. (1995) 183 CLR 10.
280. Ibid at 32, quoting P D Finn, 'Confidentiality and the "Public Interest"' (1984) 58 *ALJ* 497 at 505. Cf *British Steel Corporation v Granada Television Ltd* [1981] AC 1096.
281. *Attorney-General (UK) v Heinemann Publishers Australia Pty Ltd* (1987) 75 ALR 353 at 364–5. Given his comments in *Esso*, it is not clear that Mason CJ would have agreed with this view.

public authority on a confidential basis, it should not be necessary to establish that the public interest favours confidentiality in order to obtain a remedy against misuse or disclosure. Here the interest sought to be vindicated is that of the person concerned, not the authority. Nevertheless, the *Jonathan Cape/Fairfax* principle has recently been invoked in two such cases: *Coulthard v South Australia*,[282] in which a group of people sued to protect the confidentiality of the opinions they expressed in a meeting with government representatives; and *Deputy Commissioner of Taxation v Rettke*,[283] where the action was to protect taxpayers' confidential details being used by a public servant for his own purposes. By contrast, no mention was made of the need to jump the public interest hurdle in *Johns v Australian Securities Commission*,[284] despite the ready acknowledgment by the High Court that the ASC were under a duty of confidence in relation to information compulsorily obtained from the plaintiff.

[**4.41**] **The Spycatcher litigation and the significance of prior publication.** It is impossible to leave the subject of government information without saying something about the extraordinary attempts by the British government to suppress publication of the memoirs of Peter Wright, a member of that country's security services who had come to live in Tasmania (and had thus escaped the reach of British official secrets legislation). Although attracting considerable media attention and giving a wonderful boost to the worldwide sales of *Spycatcher*, the litigation that proceeded to conclusion in Australia, New Zealand and Britain failed to take the existing law on government information very much further.[285] The Australian action, where Wright and his publisher Heinemann were the defendants, ultimately foundered on the High Court's view that the British government was seeking to enforce a foreign public law: this was considered to be forbidden, a prohibition which could not be lifted by the Australian government's support for the claim.[286] Accordingly in no court was Wright's liability for breach of confidence authoritatively determined, since the various other actions all involved media defendants.

Nevertheless one particularly interesting issue did emerge, that of the effect of prior publication in a case involving government information. At first instance in Australia Powell J, after an exhaustive review of the evidence, concluded that the action must fail on the ground that the material in *Spycatcher* had already been the subject of earlier books and documentaries, many of which had drawn extensively on information

---

282. (1995) 63 SASR 531.
283. (1995) 31 IPR 457: though note that having quoted *Fairfax*, Cooper J rather confusingly went on to place the burden of establishing a public interest defence on the defendant.
284. (1993) 178 CLR 408: see [4.10].
285. Cf G Jones, 'Breach of Confidence — After *Spycatcher*' [1989] *CLP* 49. For a useful summary of the various decisions, see F Patfield, 'Spycatcher Worldwide — An Overview' [1989] 6 *EIPR* 201.
286. *Attorney-General (UK) v Heinemann Publishers Australia Ltd* (1988) 165 CLR 30, criticised by F A Mann, 'Spycatcher in the High Court of Australia' (1988) 104 *LQR* 497. The New Zealand Court of Appeal agreed with the characterisation of the action, but considered that the 'door could be unlocked' by the New Zealand government: *Attorney-General (UK) v Wellington Newspapers Ltd* [1988] 1 NZLR 129.

supplied by Wright and others. Furthermore, the British government had taken no action to stop these leaks, the suspicion being that it was happy to have these controversial issues presented by 'sympathetic' authors. In that light, the government simply had no basis for its claim that irreparable harm would flow from the publication of *Spycatcher*.[287] This finding was endorsed in the New South Wales Court of Appeal by Kirby P, who tellingly observed that the real flaw in the British government's argument was their insistence on the dangers of 'books of this kind'. Had this sort of 'class claim' been dropped in favour of an insistence on vetting the manuscript to excise genuinely sensitive information, the result might have been very different.[288] This of course was the key to the failure of the entire campaign. What ultimately destroyed the various actions, even in Britain, was the publication of *Spycatcher* in the US and the consequent flow of illicit copies into other countries. No action was attempted in the US for the simple reason that it would almost certainly have failed: the First Amendment to the US Constitution has been interpreted to preclude any restraint on the publication of unclassified material relating to the security services.[289]

By contrast, the question of prior publication received a markedly different treatment in the British courts. The extensive publication of *Spycatcher* itself eventually led to the lifting of all injunctions on media reporting on the book's contents and a finding that those newspapers which had published stories on the Australian proceedings were not in breach of confidence.[290] On the other hand, the *Sunday Times* was held to have breached confidence by publishing extracts from the book two days before its publication in the US. Furthermore, the House of Lords indicated its firm view that no matter what the evidence might show as to prior publication or justified disclosure, any attempt to publish the book itself in Britain would be restrained in order to 'impede the unjust enrichment of Wright, or preclude him from benefiting, tangibly or intangibly, from his own wrongdoing'.[291] Wright was said to be under a 'lifelong' duty of confidence, so that the public interest would inevitably weigh against any publication by him or by his successors in title, no matter how innocuous or public the material.[292] This view is very difficult to support, especially given the fact that the court otherwise rejected the government's principal argument, that suppression of publication was necessary to encourage other security service members not to follow suit. The outrageously vindictive references to

---

287. *Attorney-General (UK) v Heinemann Publishers Australia Pty Ltd* (1987) 8 NSWLR 341 at 374–9.
288. *Attorney-General (UK) v Heinemann Publishers Australia Pty Ltd* (1987) 75 ALR 353 at 421–30.
289. *United States v Marchetti* (1972) 466 F 2d 1309. Cf *Snepp v United States* (1980) 444 US 507, where an ex-CIA agent was enjoined, but only from breaching an agreement to submit material for prepublication clearance.
290. *Attorney-General (UK) v Guardian Newspapers Ltd (No 2)* [1988] 3 WLR 776. See also *Attorney-General (UK) v Wellington Newspapers Ltd* [1988] 1 NZLR 129.
291. [1988] 3 WLR 776 at 791. See also ibid at 785–6, 796–7, 817. Lord Goff dissented from this view, but even he considered that Wright could properly have been forced to account for any profits made from his alleged breach of confidence, even after publication: ibid at 812.
292. See also *Lord Advocate v Scotsman Publications Ltd* [1989] 2 All ER 852; P Birks, 'A Lifelong Obligation of Confidence' (1989) 105 *LQR* 501; but cf *Attorney-General (UK) v Blake* [1996] FSR 727.

the 'treacherous' Wright — who was, after all, not represented before the English courts — leave the impression that punishment rather than protection was uppermost in the minds of most of the judges who heard the case.

PART III

Copyright, Designs and Related Rights

Chapter 5

Copyright: Basic Concepts

[5.1] What does copyright protect? The basic principle behind copyright protection is the concept that an author (or artist, musician, playwright or film-maker) should have the right to exploit their work without others being allowed to copy that creative output. How far this concept is taken within each legal system may vary considerably, although recent developments at an international level are leading to a greater degree of similarity within different countries. In Australian law copyright has been seen very much as an economic right, focusing on the protection of commercial activities designed to exploit works for profit. As such, publishers and other commercial enterprises are as much the beneficiaries of the copyright system as the authors themselves — perhaps even more so. The Australian copyright tradition may be contrasted with European systems, which have typically protected not only the economic interests of authors, but also their 'moral rights'. These rights give authors various controls over their work, even against the publishers and others who are responsible for commercially exploiting that work. Moral rights are presently the focus of legislative activity in Australia, with a comprehensive scheme relating to works and films included in an Exposure Draft Bill released in February 1996.[1] More is said of moral rights at the end of this chapter,[2] but for now it may be noted that the failure of Australian law to protect such interests in the past may be traced to the way in which copyright developed in England.[3]

---

1. This Exposure Draft Bill was released by the Labor Government just before the March 1996 federal election. The fate of the proposed amendments, which are referred to frequently throughout this chapter, will depend upon the Howard Government.
2. See also the discussion of protection of indigenous culture under existing copyright law at [1.14].
3. See Ricketson, ch 4; J Feather, 'Authors, Publishers and Politicians: History of Copyright and the Book Trade' [1988] 12 *EIPR* 377.

[5.2] The development of English copyright law: the Stationers' monopoly. The first protection in the nature of copyright in England was the simple right to prevent the copying of books by unauthorised persons. Prior to the Statute of Anne in 1709 the Stationers' Company had secured a monopoly over the printing of books. This guild of illuminators, bookbinders and booksellers had come to control book production following the introduction of the printing press into England in the second half of the fifteenth century. Under successive Tudor and Stuart monarchs, it also came to be licensed to control the importation and printing of books as a censorship measure. The protection against unauthorised reproduction or importation of foreign books suited the Stationers' Company's economic interests, while the monarchy were able to prevent the dissemination of unsuitable material to the populace. Henry VIII was particularly concerned to prevent that 'most damnable of Heretykes' — Martin Luther — from 'Perverting Christes Relygion'. Seeking to control the dissemination of heretical and seditious literature but still profit from the burgeoning printing trade, Tudor monarchs aligned themselves with publishers. In exchange for an agreement to enforce the censorship laws, the government granted the Stationers a monopoly right to print, publish and sell works — a copyright. The copyright was limited to members of the guild, so that only registered members could print books. Once a publisher entered the title of a work, their name and the date of publication into the company register, they obtained a perpetual copyright in it. With what was essentially an economic right designed to protect the investment from competition, the publisher could also trade in rights.

[5.3] The Statute of Anne. In the aftermath of the Glorious Revolution, the Stationers' censorship role diminished considerably. Demand grew for a general measure to protect the interests of authors, though the publishers remained in the forefront of those who sought that protection and stood to benefit from it. It was this identification of the interests of authors with those of publishers which helps to explain how copyright came to be viewed in such rigidly economic terms. The result was the Statute of Anne 1709, which described itself as an 'Act for the Encouragement of Learning and for securing the Property of Copies of Books to the Rightful Owners Thereof'. It provided the author of a published book with a right to prevent unauthorised copying for up to 28 years; significantly, this right could be assigned to a publisher.

[5.4] The demise of common law copyright. Although the Statute thoroughly dented the Stationers' copyright, the Stationers retained copyright for a further 21 years in respect of books already published when the Statute was passed. Moreover, the procedure stipulated by the Statute greatly resembled the former system. Nevertheless the guild, perceiving that it had lost its statutory monopoly, attempted to claim for its members a perpetual copyright at common law, independent of the Act. The issue was resolved in 1774 when the House of Lords decided that if there ever had been a common law copyright, the Statute of Anne now governed the law on that topic, at least after publication of the book.[4] On the other hand, it was assumed that authors had absolute sway over use of their work before

---

4. *Donaldson v Beckett* (1744) 4 Burr 2408; 98 ER 257.

publication, so that the idea of a non-statutory copyright in unpublished work persisted for some time. Gradually, however, this notion became submerged in the general protection given by equity to confidential information.[5] The distinction between published and unpublished works is now no longer relevant except with respect to the period of copyright protection,[6] but the criteria for subsistence of copyright are the same. These days copyright is entirely a creature of statute,[7] with the only exception being copyright which emanates from a prerogative right of the Crown.[8]

[5.5] Expansion of statutory protection. The copyright in books conferred on authors by the Statute of Anne was gradually extended to cover other sorts of material including the artistic, dramatic and musical works recognised by the modern law. The protection conferred on other material was not necessarily as extensive as it is today and was found in up to 15 different statutes. It was not until 1911 that an 'all-embracing'[9] copyright statute was passed in the UK. This was the Copyright Act 1911, which repealed the piecemeal legislation enacted in the 200 years since the Statute of Anne and was designed to take account of the Berne Convention, an international agreement by which reciprocal and reasonably uniform protection is to be afforded to authors who are nationals of any country which is a signatory to the agreement.

[5.6] Australian legislation. The Australian colonies enacted copyright statutes during the second half of the nineteenth century.[10] These were subsumed by the Copyright Act 1905 (Cth), and then by the Copyright Act 1912 (Cth). This latter statute did no more than declare the British Act of 1911 to be in force in this country. Australian copyright law is now governed by the Copyright Act 1968 (Cth): all references in this and the next three chapters are to this legislation, unless the contrary is indicated.[11] The 1968 Act is still derived mainly from the law of the UK, being based upon the recommendations of the 1959 Spicer Report[12] and modelled on the Copyright Act 1956 (UK). Significant differences do exist however,[13] and in 1989 more amendments to the Australian Act were passed in an attempt to take account of new types of subject matter and methods of reproduction, as well as the requirements of libraries and educational institutions.

Significant amendments, and indeed the need for an entirely new Copyright Act, are presently under discussion in response to the unprecedented changes in the broadcasting, telecommunications and computing

---

5. See eg *Prince Albert v Strange* (1849) 2 De G & Sm 652; 64 ER 293; 1 Mac & G 25; 41 ER 1171. See [3.7].
6. See [6.52]–[6.54].
7. See Copyright Act 1968 (Cth) s 8.
8. See ibid, s 8A; Ricketson, pp 330–3; A Monotti, 'Nature and Basis of Crown Copyright in Official Publications' [1992] 9 *EIPR* 305. See eg *Attorney-General (NSW) v Butterworth & Co (Australia) Ltd* (1938) 38 SR (NSW) 195.
9. See Ricketson, p 77.
10. See Ricketson, ibid; Lahore, *Copyright*, para [4155].
11. As to the position of rights arising under the earlier legislation, see Pt XI. See further Lahore, *Copyright*, paras [4200] ff; Ricketson, ibid, pp 145–50.
12. Committee appointed by the Attorney-General of the Commonwealth to consider what alterations are desirable to the Copyright Law of the Commonwealth, *Report*, 1959.
13. Especially since the enactment of the Copyright, Designs and Patents Act 1988 (UK).

industries due to rapid technological development. The blurring of boundaries between broadcasting and telecommunication services has introduced a new term into the language: convergence. As well as convergence of industries and delivery systems, there is also convergence of products. The digital era has ushered in the development of multimedia, which allows voice, data, text, image, sound and vision to be carried on the same media. This is because the information is expressed in one way — binary form — a digital code using 0 and 1. Digitisation allows all the media to 'talk' to each other.

> Convergence, 'broadband services', 'multimedia' and the 'information superhighway' are expressions which refer to this breaking down of traditional boundaries between broadcasting, telecommunications and radio-communications, computing and the entertainment industry.[14]

In 1994 the Copyright Convergence Group (CCG) was established by the Minister for Justice to examine ways of updating the Copyright Act to protect copyright materials which are increasingly channelled into the digital pathways of new communications technology. In August 1994 the CCG Report was produced, with recommendations for changes to copyright law where traditional concepts of categories of copyright protection and accompanying rights are becoming blurred.[15]

[5.7] Works and other subject matter. Under the Copyright Act 1968 as it stands, protection is principally given to the traditional classes of 'works': literary, dramatic, artistic and musical. However, the commercial aspects of copyright protection in Australian law were emphasised by the introduction in 1968 of some new varieties of copyright, which are designed to protect the results of entrepreneurial rather than literary or artistic effort. Part IV of the Copyright Act now protects four classes of 'subject matter other than works': films, sound recordings, television and sound broadcasts, and published editions of works. Before the commencement of the 1968 Act (on 1 May 1969) there was no protection for such subject matter, although certain sound recordings (records, perforated rolls and other contrivances) were first protected under the 1911 Act. Films or 'cinematograph productions' were also protected under the 1911 Act as dramatic works where an 'original character' was imparted to the film by the arrangement, acting form or combination of incidents represented. Under the 1968 Act a film itself has its own copyright, separate from any dramatic work on which it may be based. Material that cannot be described as one of these four types of work or does not fall within Pt IV cannot be protected by copyright. Thus in *Computer Edge Pty Ltd v Apple Computer Inc*[16] the majority of the High Court refused copyright protection to computer programs which could not be classified as any 'work' then protected by copyright law.[17]

Digitisation of material, allowing sound, video and text to be carried in one medium, may make these eight categories of subject matter redundant.

---

14. C Hardy, M McAuslan and J Madden, 'Competition Policy and Communications Convergence' (1994) 17 *UNSWLJ* 157 at 160.
15. See CCG. Details of the CCG amendments are included in the Exposure Draft Bill to amend the Copyright Act, February 1996.
16. (1986) 161 CLR 171: see [6.16], [6.34], [9.9]–[9.11].
17. The Act was hastily amended to bring computer programs within the definition of 'literary work': see [6.17], [9.12].

This question is one issue facing the Copyright Law Review Committee (CLRC) in what has become known as the 'Review and Simplification Reference', a wide-ranging inquiry into the Copyright Act 1968 which is discussed at the end of this chapter.

[5.8] Nature of copyright. The right to multiply or make copies of protected subject matter belongs to the owner of the copyright, who is usually, although by no means always, the author or maker of the subject matter.[18] This right, as the Copyright Act states in s 196(1), is personal property. The copyright owner has the exclusive right to do all or any of a number of things in relation to the subject matter. With respect to a literary, dramatic or musical work, copyright is defined in s 31(1)(a) as the exclusive right:

(i)   to reproduce the work in a material form;
(ii) to publish the work;
(iii) to perform the work;
(iv) to broadcast the work;
(v)   to cause the work to be transmitted to subscribers to a diffusion service;
(vi) to make an adaptation of the work;
(vii) to do, in relation to a work that is an adaptation of the first-mentioned work, any of the acts specified in relation to the first-mentioned work in sub-paragraphs (i) to (v), inclusive.

Copyright in artistic works is slightly narrower, consisting of the exclusive right to do all or any of the following acts (s 31(1)(b)):

(i)   to reproduce the work in a material form;
(ii) to publish the work;
(iii) to include the work in a television broadcast;
(iv) to cause a television program that includes the work to be transmitted to subscribers to a diffusion service.

Section 31(1) was amended by the Copyright (World Trade Organization Amendments) Act 1994 to introduce a commercial rental right for copyright owners in relation to sound recordings and computer programs. These amendments came into force from July 1996, to allow a one year transition period to enable rental operators to adapt to the amendments, since they do not apply to existing stock. The amendments provide that copyright includes the exclusive right to:

(c)   in the case of a literary work (other than a computer program) or a musical or dramatic work, to enter into a commercial rental arrangement in respect of the work reproduced in a sound recording; and

(d)   in the case of a computer program, to enter into a commercial rental arrangement in respect of the program.

A new s 30A was also inserted to define 'commercial rental arrangement' in relation to a work reproduced in a sound recording or a computer program.

The Pt IV copyrights are narrower still, being mainly confined to reproduction of the actual subject matter, whether a film, sound recording, broadcast or published edition. Broadcasting a film, sound recording or broadcast is also within the copyright owner's exclusive domain, as is causing the subject matter to be heard or seen in public, as well as most instances of making a copy of the material. The concepts of 'broadcasting', 'diffusion', and 'publication' were formulated in the pre-computer era. Indeed, the whole notion of 'reproduction' has changed or become

18.   See [7.2]–[7.5].

123

redundant when dealing with multimedia. It may well be that the production techniques allowed by newer technology do not fit within the existing model for copyright law, stemming as it does from the conception of a 'literary work' or other work in a fixed form from which reproduction can occur.[19] These matters will be referred to in greater detail in discussing the various 'subject matters' of copyright material.

[5.9]   Divisibility of copyright. Copyright may be split up in a number of ways and the owner may license or assign any bit of it as suits. The most lucrative exploitation of copyright comes from dealing with the material in a number of different ways. For example, a popular novel will have volume rights (to the book as a book) which may be split up as to paperback and hardcover rights, possibly handled by different publishers. There will be serial rights, to have extracts serialised in newspapers and magazines; translation rights; film rights; and dramatisation rights, to have the novel reproduced as a play, opera, musical or ballet. Splitting up copyright in this way is contemplated in s 196(2), which allows for an assignment of copyright to be 'limited in any way', including as to the class of acts that the owner of the copyright has the exclusive right to do. This may encompass a class of acts that is not separately specified in the Act as being comprised in the copyright, but which falls within a class of acts that is so specified. For example, the Act does not mention 'volume' or 'film' rights specifically. Just as paperback books are basically an invention of the past 60 years, so too other rights secreted within copyright's expanding list of protected methods of exploitation have been realised. For example, although the Act does not give a 'rental right' to the owners of film copyright, industry practice has developed a viable business based on the rental of five million videos per week to Australian viewers.[20] Other possible divisions of copyright include limiting its exercise by time and place: this means that the rights or some part thereof may be exercised only for part of the period of time for which copyright subsists, or may be limited as to a place in or part of Australia.

[5.10]   Future copyright. Section 197 allows for an assignment of future copyright, so that the copyright material not yet in existence may be sold before it is even created. Many authors will have such an arrangement with a publisher, or songwriters with a recording company, rather than face the prospect of hawking their manuscript around once completed. The assignment of future copyright will be subjected to general restraint of trade principles in that an agreement which results in unfairness to an author may be overturned in court. In *O'Sullivan v Management Agency & Music Ltd*[21] a young songwriter, Gilbert O'Sullivan, who had been working as a postal clerk but wrote songs in his spare time, entered into an agreement with a management company which resulted in the songwriter completely losing control of his copyrights for several years. Within a short time O'Sullivan had become enormously successful, but increasingly unhappy about his contractual arrangements. Eventually he sued his former manager and

---

19.   See CCG; K Bowrey, 'Copyright, Photography and Computer Works — The Fiction of an Original Expression' (1995) 18 *UNSWLJ* 278.
20.   M Long, 'SBS: Shuffling the Broad and the Narrow' (1994) 14 *Communications Law Bulletin* 14 at 15.
21.   [1984] 3 WLR 448.

others with whom he had been induced to enter agreements. It was found that his services had been obtained 'on bargain basement terms' and that the contracts were void because they were unduly restrictive and hampered the artist's right to pursue and exploit his creativity.[22] On the other hand, in 1994 the singer George Michael was not allowed to dispense with what he described as his life of 'slavery' under a recording agreement with Sony, entered into at the height of his fame, despite the fact that the length of the exclusive commitment was 15 years. Higher royalties had been given by Sony in return for the length of the tie.[23]

[5.11] How to obtain copyright protection. There are no formal requirements to obtaining copyright protection in the sense that there is no procedure for registering a copyright interest in the way that a patent, trade mark or design has to be registered in order to be protected. The US was one of only two jurisdictions in the world (the other being Japan) where copyright protection was obtained by registration. Under the Trade Related Aspects of Intellectual Rights (TRIPS) negotiations in the Uruguay Round of GATT, the registration requirement for copyright has been phased out in those countries. A common misconception in Australia seems to be that an application must be made for copyright protection, whereas in fact it arises upon the meeting of certain criteria set down by the Copyright Act. The main issues concerning the subsistence of copyright arise in the context of 'work' copyrights, rather than with the Pt IV material. Before a work can be said to be protected by copyright it must be classified as something recognised by the Copyright Act: that is, it must be a literary, dramatic, musical or artistic piece of work.[24] Furthermore, the work must be original and in a material form: mere ideas will not be protected.[25]

If these criteria are fulfilled and the author is a qualified person,[26] then the author (or others) will acquire the rights described above for a certain period of time, which may vary according to how long the author lives and whether or not the work is published.[27] In the US the duration of copyright protection was (until amendments to introduce international parity) 75 years from registration. For example, Irving Berlin, the well-known songwriter, saw his most lucrative work ('Alexander's Ragtime Band') lose copyright protection in 1988. Berlin himself celebrated his 100th birthday that year. In Australia, Berlin's work would have retained copyright protection for 50 years from the end of 1989, the year in which he eventually died. Term of copyright protection is another issue covered by the TRIPS Agreement. With some exceptions, a term of at least 50 years must be granted, whether dated from authorised publication or making of the work, or else the term must be calculated on the basis of the life of the

---

22. The contracts were also found to have been obtained by undue influence. See also *A Schroeder Music Publishing Co Ltd v Macaulay* [1974] 1 WLR 1308; *Clifford Davis Management Ltd v WEA Records Ltd* [1975] 1 WLR 61; *Elton John v James* [1991] 18 FSR 397.
23. *Panayiotou v Sony Music Entertainment (UK) Ltd* [1994] EMLR 229; and see further [7.14].
24. See [6.14]–[6.35].
25. See [6.1]–[6.13].
26. See [6.50]–[6.51].
27. See [6.52].

creator. Harmonisation of European Community copyright law has led to adoption of a common term of 70 years from the death of the author, following the German practice.[28] This came into force from 1 January 1996 and has created problems as some public domain material goes back into copyright.[29] The heirs of creators who died between 1925 and 1945, whose work was out of copyright until 31 December 1995, have received a windfall. Sir Edward Elgar (died 1934), D H Lawrence (died 1930), Rudyard Kipling, Beatrix Potter, Virginia Woolf, James Joyce, Sir Arthur Conan Doyle and many other writers, artists and composers have had copyright extended to the 70 year period after their death. In fact, the music and book publishers who purchased the copyrights are the main beneficiaries and lobbied hard for the change, and are now entitled to charge a 'reasonable fee' to anyone exploiting the newly revived copyrights.[30] For example, the plethora of editions of Beatrix Potter's books, not to mention films, a ballet and other merchandise produced since the expiration of copyright in 1986, has largely taken place in an 'unlicensed' marketplace.

[5.12] Moral rights.[31] In Europe, and indeed in many other countries, the personal rights of authors or creators of material in which copyright subsists have included 'moral rights' centred around the person of the author. These rights are completely independent of the author's economic rights and continue to exist even after the transfer of economic rights. The components of moral rights include paternity, the right of the author to be made known to the public as the creator of the work; integrity, which prevents distortion of the work; and others such as the right to choose whether to publish, to restrain excessive criticism of the work, and, more generally, to prevent violations of the author's personality.[32] An important policy issue is whether the author is allowed to contract away these rights. Unlike many European systems, the recently introduced moral rights provisions in Canada and Britain allow for this to happen. This has been rightly criticised on the ground that the superior bargaining power of most publishers and their control over the content of publishing contracts have the potential to render those rights meaningless in many situations.[33]

In Australia, however, copyright law has been overwhelmingly concerned with the exercise of economic interests arising from the creation of material protected by the regime. 'Copyright is not about the protection of a sacred

28. Some commentators argue that the copyright term should be reduced, rather than extended: see eg K Puri, 'The Long Term of Copyright versus Modern Technology' (1994) 10 *Qld Lawyer* 95; and see also D S Karjala, 'Comment of US Copyright Law Professors on the Copyright Office Term of Protection Study' [1994] 12 *EIPR* 531.
29. See P Parrinder, 'The Dead Hand of European Copyright' [1993] 11 *EIPR* 391.
30. M Field, 'Heir-Shirt', *Sydney Morning Herald*, 2 January 1996, p 24.
31. See generally P Anderson and D Saunders (eds), *Moral Rights Protection in a Copyright System*, 1992; G Dworkin, 'Moral Rights and the Common Law Countries' (1994) 5 *AIPJ* 5.
32. F J Kase, *Copyright Thought in Continental Europe: Its Development, Legal Theories and Philosophy*, 1967, p 2.
33. See eg D Vaver, 'Authors' Moral Rights — Reform Proposals in Canada: Charter or Barter for Rights of Creators?' (1987) 25 *Osgoode Hall LJ* 749. The extension of copyright in the EC referred to above erodes moral rights by providing that a copyright licence is a full licence, including the moral rights and once granted the artist can do nothing to interfere with production.

template but rather the right to multiply.'[34] Once copyright has been assigned away (typically, sold to a publisher), the author is no longer free to exercise any control over the use of the work, unless provision for this is made in the contract between the parties. This lack of moral rights in Australian law, and the concept of copyright as being concerned basically with economic exploitation, is illustrated by the case of *Davidson v CBS Records*.[35] The composer of a song assigned copyright to a recording company, but was distressed when his song was changed by the company so that the recorded version was not what he had intended it to sound like. It was held that, since he had disposed of his rights, this included any rights to the integrity of the original.

[5.13]   The CLRC Report. In July 1988 the majority of the Copyright Law Review Committee recommended against the introduction of moral rights into Australian copyright law, with one limited exception: that a right of attribution exist in cases where works are subject to use under a compulsory licence.[36] This would have complemented the existing provisions (ss 189–195) of the Copyright Act which prohibit false attribution of authorship.[37] The majority of the CLRC were of the view that the existing legal framework provided some protection for 'moral rights' of authors through:

(a)   contractual arrangements between an author and user of the work;

(b)   s 190 of the Copyright Act, which prohibits false claims of authorship; and

(c)   actions in passing off to prevent the misappropriation of reputation, and under s 52 of the Trade Practices Act 1974 to prohibit misleading or deceptive conduct.[38]

Furthermore an action for breach of confidence could prevent unauthorised disclosure of a non-commissioned work; while commissioned works are protected to some extent by s 35(5) of the Copyright Act, which allows an author to prevent the commissioner of a work from exercising any of the rights comprised in the copyright of the work for a purpose other than that for which the work was commissioned.[39] Despite the limitations of these avenues of protection for moral rights of Australian authors, the CLRC considered that there were practical problems associated with the protection of moral rights; that the move would be electorally unpopular and a waste of legislative time in view of the apparent infrequency of violations of moral rights; and that there was insufficient indication of support for their introduction and also a lack of identification of a theoretical basis for moral rights protection in a common law system.[40]

The recommendations, which attracted some criticism,[41] were made despite the fact that the moral rights of authors are recognised in

---

34.   C Robson and A Deamer, 'Ownership of Copyright' in *Symposium: Copyright Law and Practice*, Sydney, September 1983.
35.   [1983] AIPC 90–106.
36.   CLRC, *Report on Moral Rights*, 1988.
37.   See [8.32].
38.   See Chapter 16.
39.   See CLRC, *Report on Moral Rights*, 1988, pp 6–8.
40.   Ibid, pp 10–11.
41.   See D Vaver, 'Authors' Moral Rights and Copyright Law Review Committee's Report: W(h)ither Such Rights Now?' (1988) 14 *Monash ULR* 284. See also 'Moral Rights' (1984) 50 *Bulletin of the Australian Copyright Council* 15.

Article 6*bis* of the Brussels (1948), Stockholm (1967) and Paris (1971) Acts.[42] The minority views in the CLRC Report, that Australia should have legislation conferring at least the right of attribution and integrity on authors, were based on a number of grounds. These included a perceived demand from a sufficiently significant section of the copyright community; that such legislation is fair and equitable and necessary to give effect to Australia's treaty obligations; and that the worldwide trend is towards recognition of such rights.[43] The minority views were supported by arguments based on historical and international perspectives and provide an interesting and thorough discussion of the issues. One further argument not explicitly articulated by the minority is the fact that enhanced moral rights increase the bargaining power and therefore commercial clout of authors of works in which moral rights subsist.

[5.14] Moral rights revived. Despite the CLRC's majority recommendation in 1988, the issue of moral rights did not die away and as part of the 'assiduous cultivation of arts industries'[44] by the Keating Labor Government, moral rights remained on the agenda, leading to the release of a Discussion Paper in June 1994 prepared jointly by the Attorney-General's Department and the Department of Communications and the Arts.[45] The Discussion Paper considered the CLRC's 1988 Report, but unlike the majority on that occasion, went on to propose amendments to the Copyright Act to recognise the rights of attribution and integrity for authors of literary, dramatic or artistic works, composers of musical works and directors and producers of films. The 'right of attribution' proposed in the Discussion Paper consists of the rights to:

(i)   be made known to the public as the creator of the work;

(ii) prevent others from claiming authorship;

(iii) prevent wrongful attribution to an author of works they did not produce;

(iv) prevent unauthorised altered versions of material being attributed to the original author.

The 'right of integrity' consists of the right to object to:

(i)   distortions or mutilations;

(ii) other modifications; and

(iii) other derogatory action in relation to an author's work that will harm the honour or reputation of the author.[46]

Article 6*bis* of the Berne Convention binds Australia to introduce moral rights in conformity with rather general guidelines set out there. Interestingly, the TRIPS Agreement in Art 9 states that 'members shall not have

---

42. These are revisions of the Berne Convention 1886: see [21.15]. See further S Ricketson, 'Is Australia in Breach of its International Obligations with Respect to the Protection of Moral Rights?' (1990) 17 *Melb ULR* 462.

43. CLRC, *Report on Moral Rights,* 1988, pp 35–6.

44. M Cooper, 'The Politics of Culture' (1995) 14 *Communications Law Bull* 1 at 1.

45. *Proposed Moral Rights Legislation for Copyright Creators,* 1994. See M Wyburn, 'The Attorney-General's Department's Moral Rights Discussion Paper: Background and Proposals' (1995) 23 *ABLR* 318.

46. As to the difficulties that may arise in applying these tests where one artist or performer 'interprets' another's work, see D Tan, 'Seeing Red over Stravinsky's Firebird' (1996) 7 *AIPJ* 63.

rights or obligations under this Agreement in respect of the rights or obligations conferred under Article 6*bis* of the (Berne) Convention or the rights derived therefrom'. Despite the lack of compulsion resulting from the TRIPS Agreement, the Keating Government was keen to fulfil obligations imposed by the Berne Convention and also respond to increasing lobbying from authors, artists and film-makers. The capacity for digital manipulation of photographs and films and the ease with which electronic piracy of various types of works can occur highlights the role of moral rights, which under the proposals in the Discussion Paper are separate from the economic rights in the material and are incapable of assignment. They would, however, be able to be waived (in writing) and may only be enforced by the author (or legal representative if the author were dead or mentally ill). The Discussion Paper proposed that the full range of remedies be available for infringement.

In February 1996 an Exposure Draft Bill to amend the Copyright Act was released, containing in Sch 1 a new Pt IX for the Act, to implement the government's decision of August 1995 to introduce comprehensive moral rights for creators. The Exposure Draft Bill follows the Discussion Paper with some modifications. Originally it was proposed that moral rights not apply to authors of computer programs, but they are not to be excluded under the draft legislation. Furthermore, the director and the producer of a film are both to be presumed to exercise the moral rights in the film, unless varied by agreement. The Discussion Paper's recommendation that producers exercise the moral rights in a film is considered to be out of step with the general view that the director bears primary artistic responsibility for a film for cinema release. The extent of waiver provisions is also somewhat reduced in the Exposure Draft Bill, with waiver relating only to specific works or films, not future material, unless produced in the course of employment. The waiver may be conditional or unconditional. It remains to be seen whether the Coalition Government will go ahead with the proposals in the Exposure Draft Bill, although it should be noted that its election manifesto included a commitment to implement a legislative scheme that would recognise the moral rights of authors and artists.

[5.15] Effect of moral rights. One function of moral rights ought to be to shore up the economic potential of protected material by increasing the bargaining power of the creator in negotiating with publishers or employers. It is far from clear whether this would occur in practice, especially under any regime that permitted rights to be waived.

> In theory we should have a neat separation of powers in the arts, in which the managers (producers, publishers, etc) retain control of copyright and the artists retain creative control through protection under moral rights. Unfortunately what we are increasingly seeing are deals in which artists lose ownership or control of copyright *and* are asked to waive their moral rights in both existing and future works.[47]

New multimedia technologies not only challenge the moral rights of creators but also provide more methods of exploiting material. For example, a popular cartoon character may feature in video games, interactive television, or may be featured in various sites on the Internet. All this in addition

---

47. I Collie, 'Multimedia, Moral Rights and Copyright' [1994] *Arts and Ent L Rev* 94 at 96 (emphasis in original).

to books, films and television series, the 'traditional' ways of exploiting a character. Quite apart from the problem of signing away (economic) rights to a character which may become a cult figure featuring in many media, the creator may find that their character undergoes a personality makeover or changes political views in a disturbing manner. Apparently, the co-creators of Superman, having assigned their rights to DC Comics, were disturbed to see the liberal fighter for truth and justice become a reactionary cold war warrior during the 1950s.[48]

Even in situations where a creator does not waive their moral rights, the Discussion Paper and proposed legislative scheme set up a regime in which the rights of attribution may only be asserted if it is 'reasonable in all the circumstances' and the right of integrity will only be protected where the treatment of the work is derogatory. The flexible, if somewhat imprecise tests of 'reasonableness' and 'derogatory' will include 'any industry practice relevant to the work',[49] so presumably if it happens now it can continue to occur. The onus will be on the claimant to establish reasonableness. The efficacy of the scheme proposed by the Discussion Paper and draft amendments has been seriously questioned by those working with authors, musicians and film makers, and the blanket waiver allowed for has been described as 'antithetical to the spirit of the [previous] Federal Government's cultural policy statement'.[50]

[5.16] CLRC review and simplification reference. To complete this introduction to the law of copyright, and before getting into the detailed treatment of the present system, mention must be made of the latest reference to the CLRC. This is a wide-ranging inquiry into the Copyright Act 1968 and requires an examination of threshold questions as to whether copyright law will be appropriate in the light of technological, commercial and social change in the coming decades. The final report was originally due in November 1997, although delays in the CLRC's work and a review of the terms of reference by the Coalition Government have made it likely that the report will be delayed somewhat. Nevertheless, when it eventually concludes its deliberations, the CLRC is expected to recommend at the least the repeal of the 1968 Act and a vastly overhauled copyright regime. In submissions received by the CLRC in response to a paper circulated in June 1995 entitled 'Information for interested parties', a wide range of views were evident. 'Some submissions contend that copyright law has served well and should be maintained with minor amendments ... At the other end of the spectrum, one finds a demand for a fundamental rethinking of copyright issues.'[51] The likely effects of current developments and thinking on copyright law will be referred to in the chapters that follow.

---

48. Ibid.
49. Exposure Draft Bill, proposed ss 195AI(2); 195AJ(2); 195AK(2).
50. I Collie, 'Multimedia, Moral Rights and Copyright' [1994] *Arts and Ent L Rev* 94 at 101.
51. CLRC, *Copyright Reform: A Consideration of Rationales, Interests and Objectives*, 1996.

Chapter 6

Subsistence of Copyright

1. THE IDEA/EXPRESSION SEPARATION

[6.1] No copyright in ideas or information. Before discussing exactly what the Copyright Act protects, it is necessary to appreciate the difference between a piece of information or an idea, and its form of expression. Copyright protection is given for the form in which an idea is clothed, but not for information itself.[1] This condition of copyright protection, that it exists not in the idea itself but in the concrete form in which it is expressed, leaving anyone free to use the basic idea, has been described as 'probably the most difficult concept in the law of copyright'.[2] If one person independently arrives at the same result as another, be it in the form of a book, play, painting, song or other expression of an idea, then there is no breach of copyright. In this way, copyright law is different from patent (or design) protection in that 'no absolute monopoly is given to authors analogous to that conferred on inventors of patents'.[3] As noted in Chapter 1, the principle that information itself is not protected unless incorporated into a special head of protected interest is fundamental to all regimes of protection with which this book deals. The closest our legal system comes to protecting 'pure information' is by way of the action for breach of confidence. Typically, however, courts have been reluctant to protect someone against the sharp practices of another, where the impugned behaviour amounted to taking information not protected in a way recognised by the law, as in

---

1. *Hollinrake v Truswell* [1894] 3 Ch 420 at 427; *Blackie & Sons Ltd v Lothian Book Publishing Co Pty Ltd* (1921) 29 CLR 396 at 400; *Victoria Park Racing & Recreation Grounds Co Ltd v Taylor* (1937) 58 CLR 479 at 498; *Autodesk Inc v Dyason* (1992) 173 CLR 330 at 344–5. The TRIPS Agreement maintains this as a fundamental concept. Article 9 states: 'Copyright protection shall extend to expressions and not to ideas, procedures, methods of operation or mathematical concepts.'
2. *Plix Products Ltd v Frank M Winstone (Merchants) Ltd* (1984) 3 IPR 390 at 418.
3. *Corelli v Gray* (1913) 29 TLR 570 at 570.

the *Victoria Park Racing* case.[4] That said, the idea/expression division has often come under strain. A good example of this can be found in the *Autodesk* litigation,[5] which showed that it may be difficult to maintain the distinction between idea and form when the function of a computer program is replicated without the form of expression being adopted.

[6.2] Copyright as a right over intangible property. So copyright law protects certain material only, not just any idea or information. Before exploring the actual subject matter protected it is also important to highlight a distinction to which Dixon J adverted in *Victoria Park Racing,*[6] between rights over intangible or incorporeal property and rights over goods. This is illustrated by *Pacific Film Laboratories Pty Ltd v Federal Commissioner of Taxation.*[7] The plaintiff, a photograph processing company, objected to paying sales tax on prints processed by it and paid for by customers, arguing that there was no sale of goods (on which tax was payable) as the customers owned the negatives and the plaintiff had no general property in the prints. It was held that a distinction is to be made between copyright in the negative (owned by the customer) and property in the prints (owned by the plaintiff until sold to the customers). Property in a chattel may be in one person and copyright in another, as incorporeal property. The agreement was for the sale of a print or duplicate to the owner of copyright, who had no property in the print viewed as a chattel before delivery to the owner of copyright. The company was obliged to pay sales tax on goods sold. This distinction between the incorporeal property and ownership of an item as such was also brought out in *Barson Computers (NZ) Ltd v John Gilbert & Co Ltd.*[8] The defendant in that case had purchased computer products in the UK and imported them into New Zealand to sell. The plaintiffs, who owned the copyright in New Zealand for these products, objected, saying that this infringed that copyright owned by them. The defendant argued that since the products were purchased legally (from the UK copyright owner) they could be dealt with as the new owner wished. The court held that the title acquired by the purchaser of goods, while entitling that purchaser to make such use of the goods as he or she thinks fit, does not enable that person to use the goods in such a way as to infringe any copyright owned by the vendor or in this case an assignee of those rights. Both the Copyright Act 1962 (NZ) and the Australian Act recognise that (with some limitations on the owner's rights) material subject to copyright protection cannot be taken across an international frontier for the purposes of trade without the consent of the person who owns copyright in the country of importation.[9] The object is to protect the interests of persons owning copyright in the country of importation and this result is a consequence of the separation of the two types of property right: over the physical item itself, and the incorporeal, intangible copyright.[10]

---

4. *Victoria Park Racing and Recreation Grounds Co Ltd v Taylor* (1937) 58 CLR 479: see [1.33].
5. See [9.13]–[9.16].
6. (1937) 38 CLR 479 at 509.
7. (1970) 121 CLR 154.
8. (1984) 4 IPR 533.
9. See [8.20].
10. See *Interstate Parcel Express Co Pty Ltd v Time-Life International (Nederlands) BV* (1977) 138 CLR 534; *Computermate Products (Australia) Pty Ltd v Ozi-Soft Pty Ltd* (1988) 12 IPR 487.

[6.3] **Material form.** So far as copyright is concerned, the law will cast its protection around information sufficiently embodied in a material form, not, as *Victoria Park Racing* shows, around information per se. That material form must, furthermore, be something that is encompassed within the terms literary, dramatic, artistic or musical work. Alternatively the information must be 'made' into a sound recording or film or one of the other Pt IV copyrights. Sound and television broadcasts are the one exception to this requirement of fixation in a material form. Section 10(1) defines 'television broadcast' as visual images broadcast by way of television, together with any sounds broadcast for reception along with those images. 'Sound broadcast' is defined as sounds broadcast other than as part of a television broadcast. This provision, introduced in 1968, would have prevented the defendants in *Victoria Park Racing* from intercepting and relaying a broadcast about events at the race track, but still would not confer any proprietary right in the information or events observed by Mr Angles and his co-defendants. The present definition of 'broadcast' is out of date and the Copyright Convergence Group's report *Highways to Change* discussed recasting the Copyright Act to give effect to the practical realities of satellites and other forms of broadcasting in a 'technology neutral' manner.[11] For the purposes of the present discussion on material form, any amendments to give effect to these recommendations are unlikely to affect this fundamental copyright concept.[12]

It has been argued that the requirement of 'material form' is based on a literary model which is not appropriate for other material, and that 'copyright is very good at fictionalising a tangible, real expression from which a right to reproduce may be determined'.[13] For example, it is a pretence that the 'author' of a photograph creates a work in material form at the moment of taking the photograph: 'rather the material form of the "original" only comes into existence as a reproduction after undergoing a separate process to the taking of the shot'.[14] This 'fictionalising' of the point at which photographs are fixed in material form has been achieved (after some struggling with the concept of 'authorship' of a photograph) and recognised by the courts and the Copyright Act 1968. However, with computer works it is even impossible to fictionalise a moment at which the work appears complete.[15] It is in fact the interaction between user, hardware and program writer which creates the expression, while simultaneously reproducing the work. Nevertheless, 'the reality of copyright is that it is indeed a Very Good Thing'[16] and law has largely developed copyright protection around the notion of a material form being given to the expression of an idea. The purpose of this chapter is to explore the traditional notion of

---

11. See CCG.
12. See [6.46], [8.12]. However, part of the terms of reference of the CLRC to review and simplify the Act generally (see [5.16]) is the brief to determine whether the present division of protectable subject matters into categories based on their form of expression is sensible, in view of the fact that digital technology allows all media to be expressed in the same way (for example, 'converged' onto a CD-ROM).
13. K Bowrey, 'Copyright, Photography and Computer Works — The Fiction of an Original Expression' (1995) 18 *UNSWLJ* 278 at 297.
14. Ibid at 279.
15. Ibid.
16. D Vaver, 'Rejuvenating Copyright' (1996) 75 *Can Bar Rev* 69 at 71.

material form, although attempts to refine the concept in response to the challenge of multimedia and computer technology will be discussed in Chapter 9.

[6.4] Identifying material form. In fleshing out the concept of material form it is inevitable to refer to the concept of a 'work' for copyright purposes. Whereas the definitions of the subject matter of Pt IV copyrights are found in the Copyright Act, the word 'work' itself is not defined, although s 10(1) informs us that a work is a 'literary, dramatic, musical or artistic work'. One thing the Act makes clear, however, is that an idea becomes a work when it is 'first reduced to writing or to some other material form' (s 22(1)). 'Material form' and 'writing' are defined in s 10(1) as follows:

> 'material form', in relation to a work or an adaptation of a work, includes any form (whether visible or not) of storage from which the work or adaptation, or a substantial part of the work or adaptation, can be reproduced; . .[17]

> 'writing' means a mode of representing or reproducing words, figures or symbols in a visible form, and 'written' has a corresponding meaning.

Copyright is to subsist, according to s 32(2), in published works. To have been subject to copyright before publication, the work must have taken a material form within s 22(1). If not, s 29(1)(a) provides that:

> a literary, dramatic, musical or artistic work, or an edition of such a work, shall be deemed to have been published if, but only if, reproductions of the work or edition have been supplied (whether by sale or otherwise) to the public.

It would appear that the publication of a work assumes it to be in a material form. Furthermore, s 31(1) gives the exclusive right of reproduction in a *material form,* and s 29(3) provides that publication does not take place where a work is performed or exhibited, so that ephemeral expression does not amount to 'publication'.

[6.5] Material form and computer programs. The Copyright Law Review Committee (CLRC) in its Draft Report on Computer Software Protection of June 1993 discussed the meaning of 'material form', noted that it is an inclusive, not exhaustive definition,[18] and recommended that no change be made to the definition in s 10. Despite industry concerns over the adequacy of the definition, in its Final Report the CLRC decided to retain the definition[19] which should be 'construed as meaning not only something of corporeal form, composed of matter, but as including those forms of storage where a work or adaptation of a work exists in a form that would not normally be regarded as material, such as electronic and magnetic forms of storage, but which are amenable to reproduction'.[20] The Exposure Draft Bill of 1996 does not include any specific amendments with respect to computer technology; presumably these amendments will be

---

17. This definition was inserted in 1984 in order to protect computer programs in object code when fixed in a ROM, which cannot be seen but only dealt with by a computer which recognises what is merely a series of magnetic polarisations. See further Chapter 9.

18. CLRC, *Computer Software Protection, Draft Report,* 1994, para [6.35].

19. *Computer Software Protection,* paras [2.04], [6.11]. However, the Final Report does recommend removal of the words 'whether visible or not' from the definition on the grounds that they are redundant: para [6.11].

20. Ibid, para [6.87].

made as part of the package when the review and simplification of the Act
is completed and a new Copyright Act introduced after the CLRC reports.

[6.6] Ideas and expression: identifying the author of a work. The
dichotomy between an idea and its expression is not always easy to comprehend, but several cases illustrate the operation of copyright statutes in
refusing to protect work which has not been 'made' into a material form.
In *Donoghue v Allied Newspapers Ltd*[21] the plaintiff agreed to give interviews
about his racing career to a *News of the World* journalist. Several articles were
published, with titles such as 'Enthralling Stories of the King of Sports'.
The journalist subsequently got permission from the newspaper to publish
abridged versions of the interviews in another paper. Donoghue asked for
damages for breach of copyright, assuming that he was the owner of copyright as the stories originated with him. It was held that the journalist was
the author of any material in which copyright subsisted, the plaintiff having
only supplied incidents in his life.[22] Farwell J pointed out that there is no
copyright in ideas:

> A person may have a brilliant idea for a story, or for a picture, or for a play,
> and one which appears to him to be original; but if he communicates that
> idea to an author or artist or a playwright, the production which is the result
> of the communication of the idea to the author or the artist or the play-
> wright is the copyright of the person who has clothed the idea in form ...
> The explanation of that is this, that in which copyright exists is the particular
> form of language by which the information which is to be conveyed is con-
> veyed ... [T]he copyright exists in the particular form of language in which
> ... the information or the idea is conveyed to those who are intended to read
> it or look at it.[23]

Farwell J also pointed out, however, that if an author employs a writer to
take down in shorthand a story which the author is composing, word for
word, then that person is a 'mere amanuensis' and does not become the
owner of the copyright.[24] Since s 22(2) provides that a work in the form of
sounds may be reduced to material form by being embodied in an 'article
or thing', presumably the person owning copyright in the work will be whoever embodies the sounds in a tape or on record or such 'article or thing'.
If the skill involved in recording such material is no more than just pressing
a button, however, then perhaps that person will be regarded as a mere
amanuensis and any copyright will in fact be with the person supplying the
information.

[6.7] Authorship and originality. Any discussion of whether a person
has gone beyond being a mere scribe for the provider of ideas raises the
issue of who supplies the requisite effort to make work 'original', a quality
which is discussed further in the next section. It is the originator or author
of the work who is, prima facie, the first owner of any copyright.[25] It may be
that putting an idea into material form implies the exercise of that degree
of original endeavour required for the subsistence of copyright protection.

---

21. [1938] Ch 106.
22. This meant that copyright was owned by the journalist's employer, as the work was
     performed pursuant to a contract of service: see [7.2]–[7.4].
23. [1938] Ch 106 at 109–10. See also *Tate v Fullbrook* [1908] 1 KB 821; *Tate v Thomas*
     [1921] 1 Ch 503.
24. Ibid.
25. See further [7.2], [7.5].

In *Walter v Lane*[26] the Law Lords disagreed as to whether reporters who took down speeches in shorthand and then transcribed them to be published verbatim were mere scribes or had exercised enough effort to be the authors of copyright works. The majority decided that the latter was the case, although the Court of Appeal had dismissed the action by the newspaper for breach of their copyright, saying the reporters were not the authors.[27]

Cummins v Bond[28] illustrates a situation where the person clothing certain communications in material form was the owner of copyright in the resulting written form, rather than the defendant who claimed he was elemental in producing the document, the plaintiff being at best a co-author with him, or possibly a mere scribe for writings inspired by his presence. The plaintiff engaged in psychic research, acting as a spiritualist and medium at seances during which she practised automatic writing while in a trance state. The defendant was an architect who was interested in recent discoveries at the Abbey of Glastonbury and the automatic writings which related to them. Seances with the defendant in attendance resulted in 'The Chronicle of Cleophas', which the plaintiff wrote in her automatic writing. The nature of the writing was archaic, of the sixteenth and seventeenth centuries. Cleophas is mentioned twice in the New Testament as one of the followers of Christ. A dispute arose as to the ownership of copyright in the 'Chronicle', the defendant claiming that the writings were addressed to him and inspired by his presence, or that they were not susceptible to copyright protection at all, being communicated in substance and form by a psychic agent. Eve J held that although the spirit no doubt spoke mainly Aramaic, in order not to appear of too modern an epoch he selected a medium capable of translating his messages into language appropriate to a period some 16 or 17 centuries after his death. The language in which the communications were written was not so antiquated as not to be understood by excavators and others engaged in these discoveries but not so up to date as to make the spirit appear of too modern an epoch. The communications 'could not have reached us in this form without the active co-operation of some agent competent to translate them from the language in which they were communicated to her into something more intelligible to persons of the present day'.[29] Since the court had no jurisdiction extending to the sphere in which the spirit moves, the inquiry must be confined to individuals alive at the time the work first came into existence. It would seem that authorship rested with the plaintiff, to whose gift of extremely rapid writing, coupled with a peculiar ability to reproduce in archaic English matter communicated to her in some unknown tongue, the production of these documents was owed. She was more than a mere conduit pipe and had exercised skill in reproducing these communications.

---

26.   [1900] AC 539.
27.   It should be noted that *Walter v Lane* was decided under copyright legislation which did not require 'originality' as a separate requirement for the subsistence of copyright. Nevertheless, later courts have still referred to *Walter v Lane* in accepting that 'originality' does not necessarily mean novelty but simply that *some* degree of skill is necessary.
28.   [1927] 1 Ch 167.
29.   Ibid at 173.

Further illustration of the fact that copyright concerns itself with the copying of physical material only and not with the reproduction of ideas is found in a line of cases dealing with machinery parts or items of manufacture, rather than with words and their ultimate expression in literary form. In *Mono Pumps (New Zealand) Ltd v Karinya Industries Ltd*[30] the plaintiffs claimed that they had copyright in drawings of pump components, which had been infringed by the defendants.[31] The pump parts had been the subject of a French patent which had expired. It was held that despite copyright protection for the drawings still subsisting, anyone was free to use the ideas, because of 'the fundamental aspect of copyright law — namely, its concern with the copying of physical material only and not with the reproduction of ideas. The idea can be taken, but the drawings embodying it cannot be copied.'[32]

[6.8] The idea/expression separation in US law. United States copyright law also recognises that 'it is axiomatic that copyright protects only the expression of ideas and not the ideas themselves'.[33] In *Digital Communications Associates Inc v SoftKlone Distribution Corporation*[34] the work in issue was the 'status screen' or 'main menu' of a computer program, Crosstalk XVI, which enabled personal computers to be connected with other computers. The status screen listed the information required from users of Crosstalk XVI before the program could be put into effect. The defendant marketed a program with the same function as Crosstalk XVI, which copied the status screen of the plaintiff's program, but not the underlying code. The defendant argued that the status screen was not the proper subject matter of copyright protection, one of the main points being that the status screen was a necessary expression of its idea, so that the idea and its expression merge, making the status screen nothing more than a 'blank form' designed to record the program user's choices of parameter values.[35] The court rejected this analysis, holding that the 'arrangement of the status screen involves considerable stylistic creativity and authorship above and beyond the ideas embodied in the status screen'.[36] Where an idea has only one possible form of expression, then copyright protection does not extend to the protection of the expression. In this case, it was possible to express the same information in the status screen in a number of ways, and there were a number of features of the plaintiff's status screen which showed stylistic decisions had been made which differentiated the expression from the underlying idea.

[6.9] Ideas and expression inseparable. Although courts in Australia and the UK have accepted the proposition that copyright cannot be claimed in the only possible way of expressing a particular idea, the principle is not

---

30. (1984) 4 IPR 505.
31. The defendants counterclaimed for breach of copyright on the basis that they had obtained an assignment to themselves of copyright in drawings of the pumps.
32. (1984) 4 IPR 505 at 508. It should be noted that in Australia copyright in patent specifications vests in the Crown upon publication of the specification (s 177).
33. *Whelan Associates v Jaslow Dental Laboratory Inc* (1986) 797 F 2d 1222 at 1234.
34. (1988) 10 IPR 1.
35. Ibid at 10. This leaves aside the issue of copyright protection for computer programs per se: see Chapter 9.
36. Ibid at 14.

always easy to apply. An early case where the expression of an idea was too close to the idea itself to gain protection is *Kenrick & Co Ltd v Lawrence & Co*,[37] where the publisher of a card to help illiterate voters sought protection for the sketch of a hand holding a pencil in the act of completing a cross within a square. It was held by Wills J that the copyright protection sought would protect the subject or idea rather than the expression alone, since 'a square *can* only be drawn as a square, a cross *can* only be drawn as a cross, and for such purposes as the plaintiff's drawing was intended to fulfil, there are scarcely more ways than one of drawing a pencil or the hand that holds it'.[38]

2.   ORIGINALITY OF EXPRESSION

[6.10]   The need for an original work. It is apparent that sheer originality of thought is not enough to attract copyright protection: there must be something in appropriate material form. Conversely, however, simply having some document, 'article' or 'thing' in which material is embodied does not automatically attract protection. The Copyright Act states in s 32(1) that copyright subsists in certain 'original' works even if unpublished. Section 32(2) also requires published work to be 'original' in order to acquire or retain protection under the Act.

[6.11]   The meaning of originality. The separate requirement of originality was not included in previous copyright legislation, and the insertion of the word 'original' as an additional criterion for copyright protection has therefore been addressed by the courts in an attempt to ascertain the meaning of the word for the purposes of the legislation. To some extent the question of what amounts to a 'work' within the Act (that is, material possessing the status of a literary, dramatic, musical or artistic work) is intertwined with the issue of originality. The cases illustrate the point that material which is too commonplace to be regarded as original will not be a 'work' within the Act. Some common threads of originality which all works must exhibit can be identified. To begin with, in *University of London Press Ltd v University Tutorial Press Ltd*[39] it was said that examination papers could be original, even if composed from information regarded as a stock of knowledge common to persons in the field (in this case, mathematics). The main requirement of originality was that the work must not be wholly copied from another work, but should originate with the author:

> The word 'original' does not in this connection mean that the work must be the expression of original or inventive thought. Copyright Acts are not concerned with the originality of ideas, but with the expression of thought ...The originality which is required relates to the expression of the thought. But the Act does not require that the expression must be in an original or novel form, but that the work must not be copied from another work — that it should originate from the author.[40]

---

37.   (1890) 25 QBD 99.
38.   Ibid at 104. Other cases on this point include *Kalamazoo (Australia) Pty Ltd v Compact Business Systems Pty Ltd* (1985) 5 IPR 213; *FAI Insurance Ltd v Advance Bank Australia Ltd* (1986) 7 IPR 217; *Tate v Thomas* [1921] 1 Ch 503.
39.   [1916] 2 Ch 607.
40.   Ibid at 608. As to the situation where a work is partially copied from another, see [6.35], [8.2].

Similarly, in *Sands & McDougall Pty Ltd v Robinson*[41] the High Court held that a map was original even if prepared from the common stock of knowledge in Australia, since independent intellectual effort, judgment and discrimination had been applied to produce a map that was new in the requisite sense.[42] The discussion of originality has mainly occurred in the context of cases concerned with literary works, but the application of the *University of London Press* case to other types of works has been approved in many subsequent cases, often to do with home plans[43] or other artistic works such as drawings for articles ranging from frisbees[44] to plastic price labelling tags.[45]

[6.12] Compilations. The issue of originality most frequently arises in the context of compilations, or the putting together of material which is generally available and not original in the sense of having novelty in itself. The copying of such compilations has led to questions of what degree of effort confers originality (and therefore the status of a 'work') so as to attract copyright protection against infringers. In *Macmillan & Co v Cooper*[46] Macmillan owned copyright in a book entitled *Plutarch's Life of Alexander, Sir Thomas North's Translation*, from which Cooper, a publisher in Bombay, had selected passages and published them as a textbook for Indian students, adding some introductory notes to link passages of the text. The primary question was whether there was copyright in the Macmillan compilation of Plutarch's work. The Privy Council held that the selection of passages by Macmillan from North's translation had been made with a view to the requirements of school and university students. Labour, sound judgment and literary skill were all needed to fulfil this objective, and this was enough to attract copyright protection for the selected passages. Thus expenditure of labour, skill and capital to impart to the product some quality of character which the raw material did not possess will result in a compilation having copyright protection.

Although the amount of labour the author must bestow is a question of degree in every case, the requirement of originality is not fulfilled simply by making a list or putting several lists together. In *G A Cramp & Sons Ltd v Frank Smythson Ltd*[47] certain tables of information on the weather, sunrise and sunset, times, tides and so on had been included in a diary. The trial judge, Uthwatt J, with whom the House of Lords unanimously agreed, said that this selection of 'gobbets of information' showed no real exercise of knowledge, labour, judgment or skill and the commonplace selection could not be said to confer originality on the whole.[48] To similar effect is *ITP Pty*

41. (1917) 23 CLR 49.
42. See also *Geographica Ltd v Penguin Books Ltd* [1985] FSR 208.
43. See eg *LED Builders Pty Ltd v Masterton Homes (NSW) Pty Ltd* (1994) 30 IPR 447.
44. *Wham-O Manufacturing Co v Lincoln Industries Ltd* (1984) 3 IPR 115.
45. *Dennison Manufacturing Co v Alfred Holt & Co Ltd* (1987) 10 IPR 612. See also *LB (Plastics) Ltd v Swish Products Ltd* [1979] RPC 551; *Johnson & Associates Ltd v Bucko Enterprises Ltd* [1975] 1 NZLR 311.
46. (1923) 40 TLR 186.
47. [1944] AC 329.
48. This does not mean that calendars or diaries may never attract copyright protection. If there is added to such commonplace material a 'collocation of components', perhaps artwork or a particular arrangement of the information, this may confer 'originality' on the material: *Easyfind (NSW) Pty Ltd v Paterson* (1987) 10 IPR 464. See also *Murray v King* (1984) 3 IPR 525.

Ltd v United Capital Pty Ltd,[49] where a tax manual, designed as a guide to teach persons to fill in tax return forms, was substantially denied copyright protection on the grounds that simply putting the forms together did not demonstrate a sufficient degree of labour, skill and ingenuity in the compilation of the material to make it original for copyright purposes.[50] On the other hand, fixed-odds betting coupons for punters wishing to bet on football games have been held to be original works despite the argument that such coupons are nothing more than lists of football matches.[51] It takes apparently a 'vast amount' of skill, judgment, experience and work to select combinations of matches at the right odds and this confers originality on such forms.[52]

Similarly, a compilation of blank accounting forms was found to constitute an original work in *Kalamazoo (Australia) Pty Ltd v Compact Business Systems Pty Ltd*.[53] The system was adapted to the requirements of doctors, solicitors, real estate agents, payroll systems and others. The documents were arranged so that the writing of a receipt resulted in all the necessary accounting details being simultaneously entered. In discussing the 'conflicting and quite irreconcilable judicial statements as to the degree of originality required',[54] Thomas J reviewed the authorities and decided that the preparation of the forms in question had 'required a degree of concentration, care, analysis, comparison, and a certain facility in using and adapting the altered forms to a composite "one-write" system. In each case, some awareness of contemporary developments and the marketability of such forms played a part in their creation.'[55] The composite whole was original, although if the components were viewed separately, item by item, there was negligible originality in the material.

What of the situation where the compilation consists of valuable information (of commercial significance) put together at great effort and/or expense, such as a telephone book, or any other database where the organising principle is alphabetical listing or some descriptive collection of facts? Since copyright protection requires originality and does not protect ideas or information alone, some courts have denied copyright protection even where hard work has gone into compiling facts. The Supreme Court of the United States in *Feist Publications Inc v Rural Telephone Co Inc*[56] referred to:

> the interaction of two well-established propositions. The first is that the facts are not copyrightable; the other, that compilations of facts generally are. Each of these propositions possesses an impeccable pedigree. That there can be no valid copyright in facts is universally understood. The most fundamental axiom of copyright law is that 'no author may copyright his (sic) ideas or the facts he narrates'.

---

49.   (1985) 5 IPR 315.
50.   Some parts of it *were* held to be original literary works.
51.   *Ladbroke (Football) Ltd v William Hill (Football) Ltd* [1964] 1 WLR 273.
52.   Ibid at 275. See also *Football League Ltd v Littlewoods Pools Ltd* [1959] Ch 637; *Bleiman v News Media* [1994] 2 NZLR 673.
53.   (1985) 5 IPR 213. See also *Baillieu v Australian Electoral Commission* (1996) 33 IPR 494.
54.   Ibid at 223.
55.   Ibid at 237.
56.   (1991) 20 IPR 129 at 132.

In *Feist* the white pages telephone book, an alphabetical listing of all telephone subscribers in a certain area, was held not to reach the required threshold of originality in order to qualify for copyright protection. The court rejected the 'sweat of the brow' or 'industrious collection' doctrine, under which effort and investment in compiling information had been protected in some previous US cases. The question of what is 'unprotectable' data and 'protectable' expression is not easy to answer. In *Feist*, selection and organisation of the raw data was required, over and above a simple alphabetical listing of subscribers' names and addresses. Obviously, collections of factual information are valuable and commercially important, even more so when in the form of electronic databases. The CLRC,[57] looking into the protection of computer software, notes that the standard of originality is 'fairly low' but there is a minimum threshold to be met, and the investment of time, money and effort alone does not make a database worthy of copyright protection, however much entrepreneurial effort has gone into compiling it.[58]

[6.13] Originality for Pt IV copyright. The requirement of originality for Pt IV copyright is implied rather than expressly required, in that the Act refers to the *first* publication of such subject matter in calculating the duration of protection and in establishing whether the subject matter qualifies for protection in Australia.[59]

3. WORKS

(a) Literary Works

[6.14] 'Literary'. The 'root requirement'[60] of originality very much conditions the question of whether or not material can be regarded as a 'work'. Indeed, once it has been ascertained that sufficient effort has been expended, a vast array of expressed ideas may be protected, even if not 'literary, dramatic, musical or artistic' in any colloquial sense. The Copyright Act does not exhaustively define 'literary work', but s 10(1) provides that a literary work includes:

(a)   a written table or compilation; and

(b)   a computer program or compilation of computer programs.[61]

Case law provides the most guidance as to the meaning of 'literary' in this context. As was pointed out earlier, many of the cases concerning originality involved this category of work, including examination papers,[62] betting forms,[63] a compilation of extracts from Plutarch[64] and accounting forms.[65]

---

57.   *Computer Software Protection*, para [14.31].
58.   See [9.20] for further discussion of database protection.
59.   See [6.50]–[6.54].
60.   Cornish, p 319.
61.   Note that under this definition it does not appear that a compilation of artistic works will attract copyright protection: see A Monotti, 'The Extent of Copyright Protection for Compilations of Artistic Works' [1993] 5 *EIPR* 156.
62.   *University of London Press Ltd v University Tutorial Press Ltd* [1916] 2 Ch 601.
63.   *Ladbroke (Football) Ltd v William Hill (Football) Ltd* [1964] 1 WLR 273.
64.   *Macmillan v Cooper* (1923) 40 TLR 186.
65.   *Kalamazoo (Australia) Pty Ltd v Compact Business Systems Pty Ltd* (1985) 5 IPR 213.

The classic statement concerning the concept of a literary work comes from *University of London Press,* the 'exam paper' case. Peterson J there said:[66]

> In my view the words 'literary work' cover work which is expressed in print or writing, irrespective of the question whether the quality or style is high. The word 'literary' seems to be used in a sense somewhat similar to the use of the word 'literature' in political or electioneering literature and refers to written or printed matter.

One commentator has written that copyright is a legitimate instrument of social policy where it allows individuals (and society) to develop and gain economically from the protection of the product of intellectual labour. However, the protection of such a wide variety of material as described above has also 'degraded' this notion.

> The group Victor Hugo drew around him in the 19th century to fight for international copyright was certainly not campaigning to protect lottery tickets, money boxes, belt buckles, routine business correspondence, forms and office memoranda ... items that have since been protected at one time or another under US or Commonwealth laws.[67]

This degradation applies not only to the notion of 'literary' works but also where 'trivial artistic skill' has qualified for protection.

[6.15] Meaning and communication. Since s 22(2) states that a literary, dramatic or musical work can exist in the form of sounds embodied in an article or thing, and s 22(1) refers to such works as existing if in writing or 'some other material form', it is obvious that writing as such does not define the essential aspect of a literary work. The fundamental criterion appears to be that the work conveys information or perhaps instruction and pleasure in the form of literary enjoyment. In *Exxon Corporation v Exxon Insurance Consultants International Ltd*[68] copyright protection was sought for the invented word 'EXXON' as a literary work, but this was denied because the word itself, although possibly new and original, 'has no meaning and suggests nothing in itself. To give it substance and meaning, it must be accompanied by other words or used in a particular context or juxtaposition.'[69]

The requirement that a literary work function in this way has been the main issue of contention in recent years where copyright protection has been claimed for such things as accounting forms or computer programs. There are two aspects to this. The first, which was raised in the *Exxon* case, is the question of the material being *substantial* enough to convey meaning. The other concerns the ability of the material to communicate meaning, not because it lacks content, but because of the *form* in which it is presented: for example if the form the information takes is electronic impulses embodied in a silicon chip. In the *Kalamazoo* case[70] the 'one write' accounting system was not only 'original' but also 'literary' in that the compilation of forms was designed and presented in a way that produced meaningful results for the user and was therefore within the *Exxon* formulation, having its own character and apt to 'tell its own story' to the user. Thomas J took as

---

66. *University of London Press Ltd v University Tutorial Press Ltd* [1916] 2 Ch 601 at 608.
67. D Vaver, 'Rejuvenating Copyright' (1996) 75 *Canadian Bar Review* 69 at 74.
68. [1981] 2 All ER 495.
69. Ibid at 503.
70. *Kalamazoo (Australia) Pty Ltd v Compact Business Systems Pty Ltd* (1985) 5 IPR 213.

a starting point the fact that s 32(2) of the Act included a written table or compilation within the term 'literary work'.

The *Exxon* case suggested that a word alone is not substantial enough to convey meaning, and that the same might be true of titles, slogans, phrases and possibly advertisements,[71] although the decision has 'not been treated as definitive or exhaustive by the members of the Full Court of the Federal Court'.[72] A different approach has been taken by some other courts[73] and commentators,[74] to the effect that a word or phrase may be protected if original enough and of so 'extensive a scale and of so important a character as to be a proper subject of protection against copying'.[75] In *Data Access Corp v Powerflex Services Pty Ltd*[76] single words were each held to be a 'computer program' (a type of literary work) since the applicant's software used a number of words which, when encountered by the computer, caused it to perform a certain function.

[6.16] Computer programs as literary works: the Apple case. Perhaps the best known discussion of 'literary work' in Australia is that which occurred in the *Apple* litigation, where the form of presentation was ultimately a barrier to copyright protection for a computer program in object code.[77] Copyright has been regarded as the area of existing law most apt to protect computer software. In the *Apple* saga, the first attempt in Australia to establish copyright in a computer program, it was held by Beaumont J at trial that computer programs in object code were not literary works within the 1968 Act because they did not afford information, pleasure or instruction but merely drove a machine, that is, controlled the sequence of operations carried out by a computer, without performing those other functions.[78] This was reversed on appeal to the Full Federal Court.[79] The High Court by a majority restored the judgment of the trial judge, on the basis that the programs embodied in the ROMs[80] were not expressed in writing or print or any relevant material form, not being visible or otherwise perceptible and not, and not intended to be, capable by

---

71. In some instances it may be possible to establish that the work in question is an artistic work: see eg *Roland Corp v Lorenzo & Sons Pty Ltd* (1991) 22 IPR 245. In any event, protection for these matters may more aptly be provided by protecting any business reputation attached to them, for example by an action for passing off or under s 52 of the Trade Practices Act 1974 (Cth): see Chapter 16.
72. *Apple Computer Inc v Computer Edge Pty Ltd* (1984) 53 ALR 225 at 234–5, 258–9; *Kalamazoo (Australia) Pty Ltd v Compact Business Systems Pty Ltd* (1985) 5 IPR 213.
73. See *Mirror Newspapers Ltd v Queensland Newspapers Pty Ltd* [1982] Qd R 305; *Ladbroke (Football) Ltd v William Hill (Football) Ltd* [1964] 1 All ER 465.
74. S Bridge, 'Advertisers and Copyright' (1988) 66 *Bull Aust Copyright Council*.
75. *Francis Day & Hunter Ltd v 20th Century Fox Corp Ltd* [1940] AC 112 at 123. See also Ricketson, pp 110–12.
76. (1996) 33 IPR 194.
77. See further [9.9]–[9.11].
78. *Apple Computer Inc v Computer Edge Pty Ltd* (1983) 50 ALR 581.
79. *Apple Computer Inc v Computer Edge Pty Ltd* (1984) 53 ALR 225. See J McKeough, 'Case Note — *Apple Computer Inc v Computer Edge Pty Ltd*' (1984) 7 *UNSWLJ* 161.
80. The program in object code, the object program, consists in the first instance of a sequence of electrical impulses which are often stored first on a magnetic disk or tape, and which may be stored permanently in a ROM ('read only memory'), a silicon chip which contains thousands of connected electrical circuits.

themselves of conveying a meaning which could be understood by human beings:

> Obviously, the patterns of the circuits in the ROMs also did not represent or reproduce any words or figures and were incapable of conveying any meaning ... It seems to me a complete distortion of meaning to describe electrical impulses in a silicon chip, which cannot be perceived by the senses and which do not represent words, letters, figures or symbols, as a literary work; still less can a pattern of circuits be so described.[81]

[6.17] The post-Apple amendments. In response to the trial judge's decision legislative changes in 1984 gave specific protection to programs as literary works within the Copyright Act. 'Literary work' is now specified in s 10(1) to include 'a computer program or compilation of computer programs'. 'Computer program' is defined to mean:

> an expression, in any language, code, or notation, of a set of instructions (whether with or without related information) intended, either directly or after either or both of the following:
>
> (1)   conversion to another language, code or notation;
> (2)   reproduction in a different material form, to cause a device having digital information processing capabilities to perform a particular function.

The CLRC has recommended that this definition be deleted and the following be substituted:[82]

> A 'computer program' is a set of statements or instructions to be used directly or indirectly in a computer in order to bring about a certain result.

Many commentators feel that the question of protection for computer programs has gone beyond the issue of whether source and object codes are 'literary works' or adaptations thereof. The 1984 legislative changes pre-empted for several years any further analysis along traditional copyright lines, marketers of computerware preferring to assume that protection exists and enforce it rather than have the basis of any such protection further tested.[83] The CLRC, aware of the need to resolve this debate, approved the above definition on the grounds that it is reasonably broad, covering programs written in source code, object code, microcode or declarative programming language. It is in fact the definition used in the US Copyright Act and thus has a considerable amount of international currency.

(b) Dramatic Works

[6.18] 'Dramatic'. The categories of works may overlap so that a play, for example, may be a literary as well as a dramatic work, and a map can be a literary work (as a compilation) and also an artistic work (a drawing).[84] The Copyright Act does not define 'dramatic work' but s 10(1) states that it includes:

> (a)   a choreographic show or other dumb show; and
> (b)   a scenario or script for a cinematograph film,
>
> but does not include a cinematograph film as distinct from the scenario or script for a cinematograph film.

---

81.   *Computer Edge Pty Ltd v Apple Computer Inc* (1986) 161 CLR 171 at 183–4.
82.   *Computer Software Protection*, rec 2.04(c).
83.   S Bridge, 'Computers and Copyright' (1986) 57 *Bull Aust Copyright Council* 39. See now the *Autodesk* litigation discussed at [9.13]–[9.16].
84.   *Sands & McDougall Pty Ltd v Robinson* (1917) 23 CLR 49; *Geographica Ltd v Penguin Books Ltd* [1985] FSR 208.

Section 4 of the Copyright Act 1905, by contrast, defined a dramatic work as 'any tragedy, comedy, play, drama, farce, burlesque, libretto of an opera, entertainment or other work of like nature, whether set to music or other scenic or dramatic composition'. It seems that in the modern context the word 'dramatic' has a qualifying effect, suggesting that to be protected within this category the work must essentially be intended to be performed or represented.[85] It should be noted that the Copyright Amendment Act 1989 deleted the words 'described in writing in the form in which the show is to be presented' from the definition of dramatic work. This ensures that choreography will be protected if recorded in some material form other than laborious notation, perhaps on film or video.

[6.19] **Dramatic ideas.** Most litigation concerning dramatic works has centred around the question of when an *idea* for a play (film, etc) becomes protected. In *Tate v Thomas*[86] a dispute arose over the ownership of copyright in a play called *The Lads of the Village*, which the defendant, Peterman, had arranged to have made into a film. The plaintiffs had written music, lyrics and dialogue for the production but Peterman claimed that he had supplied ideas, lines of dialogue, catch phrases and the like. It was fairly clear that his contribution amounted to 'accessorial matters' such as scenic effects, and he supplied nothing substantial enough in material form to be afforded copyright protection. The defendant argued unsuccessfully that he was the creator of the mood and staging of the production and it was appropriate to protect this when dealing with a dramatic work.

Although this argument did not succeed in *Tate v Thomas*, other cases have suggested that there should be copyright in the kind of situations, style and incidents shown on screen or stage. In *Hexagon Pty Ltd v Australian Broadcasting Commission*[87] it was claimed that the basic theme of the 'Alvin Purple' movies should be protected as a dramatic work, independent of any script. The plaintiffs succeeded in preventing the ABC making a series based on the Alvin Purple character, but on passing off principles rather than copyright. An example of a film theme being protected is *Zeccola v Universal City Studios Inc.*[88] The respondent claimed that copyright in the film and novel *Jaws* had been infringed by a film produced by the appellants and titled *La Ultimo Squalo* ('Great White'). The infringement alleged was that of making a film about a killer shark terrorising human beings during the holiday season at a popular seaside resort. The appellant claimed that the respondent sought copyright protection for a general idea, and that this was not within the scope of the Copyright Act, which protects only the expression of ideas. It was held that although in general there is no copyright in the central idea or theme of a story of play, however original it may be, copyright does subsist in the combination of situations, events and scenes which constitute the particular working out or expression of the idea or theme. If these are totally different, the taking of the idea or theme does not constitute an infringement of copyright. In this case, however, the trial judge decided that the combination of the principal situations, singular events and basic characters was sufficient to constitute an original work

85. See Ricketson, pp 112–13.
86. [1921] 1 Ch 503.
87. (1975) 7 ALR 233.
88. (1982) 46 ALR 189.

susceptible of copyright protection. This was decided after viewing the two films and noting the marked degree of similarity between them both, which led to an inescapable inference of copying. It was also important in *Zeccola* that the Copyright Act provided that a work may be infringed by the making of a cinematograph film of it (s 21).

An issue similar to that in *Tate v Thomas* arose in *Green v Broadcasting Corporation of New Zealand*[89] where Hughie Green, the compere of a British television talent show called 'Opportunity Knocks', claimed that his title, show format and a few stock phrases[90] were a literary or dramatic work to be protected by copyright law so as to prevent another person televising a similar program in New Zealand. However, the 'hackneyed expressions' and idea for the program were held not to be protected by copyright.[91]

[6.20] **Performers' rights.** It is apparent that although playwrights, composers, set designers and choreographers acquire copyright protection for their work, the performer does not gain any copyright protection for a performance as such. Even if the performance is recorded, the copyright will belong to the maker of the film or sound recording.[92] Performers who write their own material are in a position to enforce their rights against an unauthorised recording or copying of their work, but until recently any 'performers' rights' were ancillary to the ownership of copyright in the material being performed. Naturally, most performers obtain some protection through a contractual arrangement with the producer or entrepreneur which may provide for payment for the performance, and perhaps also for residuals or royalties for repeat broadcasts and ancillary uses.[93]

[6.21] **Background to the introduction of performers' rights.** The Rome Convention which governs this issue was first drafted in the early 1960s and was intended to protect what has been called a 'neighbouring right' to copyright — something that does not fall within the traditional ambit of copyright but is nevertheless closely related. Agitation for performers' rights had been discussed internationally since 1926 when the issue was raised in the International Labour Organisation. The Rome Convention was established in 1961 and attended by delegates from 43 countries (including Australia). This followed the 1945 revision of the Berne Convention when participants decided that the matter of performing rights should be pursued as a neighbouring right to copyright.[94]

The Spicer Committee regarded any introduction of performers' rights by the Commonwealth as being unconstitutional,[95] but nevertheless

89. (1983) 2 IPR 191.
90. Such as 'For [name of contestant], opportunity knocks'; and 'This is your show, folks, and I do mean you'.
91. Nor in passing off since Green's reputation had not extended to New Zealand: see further [17.11] ff. On appeal, the Privy Council endorsed this finding: *Green v Broadcasting Corporation of New Zealand* (1989) 16 IPR 1.
92. See [7.5].
93. See D Sharpe, *The Performing Artist and the Law*, 1985, p 68; 'Performers' Rights After the Copyright Law Review Committee' (1988) 63 *Bull Aust Copyright Council*.
94. D Sharpe, *The Performing Artist and the Law*, 1985, pp 71–3. See further [21.19].
95. Committee on Alterations to Copyright Law, *Report*, 1959, paras 472–7. The view taken by the Comittee was that s 51(xviii) of the Constitution (see [1.5]) is limited to works and other subject matter which can be reduced to material form. Cf Ricketson, pp 139–40.

recommended that a special tribunal be set up with jurisdiction to settle disputes relating to the performing and broadcasting rights in works and sound recordings. In fact, the machinery to set up such a body was included in the 1968 Copyright Act but never invoked. In 1974 the Labor Government, desirous of acceding to the Rome Convention, drafted legislation to introduce performers' rights, presuming perhaps that the High Court would interpret the Constitution liberally enough to uphold such legislation under s 51(xviii).[96] The legislation was never passed.

[6.22] **The CLRC Report and the 1989 legislation.** In 1987 the CLRC published a report on Performers' Protection and unanimously recommended legislation to provide a remedy against 'bootleg' recording of performances and reproduction of such unauthorised recordings. A majority of the Committee recommended against granting copyright in performances or any rights in relation to the use of authorised fixations, except with regard to a performance on a soundtrack, in respect of which the performer should be entitled to prevent the recording being used for other purposes. The changes described were introduced into Pt XIA of the Copyright Act by virtue of the Copyright Amendment Act 1989.

This amendment introduced a right different from traditional copyright protection, which is obsessed with the protected matter being fixed in a material form, as this chapter has explained. Perhaps the introduction of what is regarded as so nebulous a 'right' explains the conservative approach taken by the legislature. The amendments have been described as 'disappointing',[97] despite having taken many years to be introduced into Australian law. Some commentators have asserted that these 'performers' rights' are minimal, and intended mainly to allow Australia to join the Rome Convention[98] although on an ungenerous interpretation of the new provisions they may not in fact even provide the minimum protection needed for that purpose.

The rights conferred by the 1989 Act, which last for 20 years (or 50 years with respect to unauthorised sound recordings)[99] mean that a performer's consent is required for the broadcast or recording of a live performance. Once given, however, that authorised recording may be used in any way without further consent being obtained, *except* that a sound recording may not be used in the soundtrack of a film without permission. Permission is not required when the recording is for educational, private or domestic use

---

96. See Ricketson, pp 434–5.

97. M West, 'Performers' Protection: A Broadcaster's Viewpoint' (1988) 6(5) *Copyright Reporter,* p 10.

98. See S Bridge and L Baulch, *The Copyright Amendment Bill 1988,* Australian Copyright Council, 1988.

99. The Copyright (World Trade Organization Amendments) Act 1994 introduced s 248CA which gives a general protection period of 20 years from the end of the year in which the performance was given, but extends protection to 50 years where the TRIPS Agreement requires this, ie in relation to sound recordings of performances. No rights exist in relation to performances prior to the commencement of Pt XIA, with the exception that it is now an offence to deal commercially with an unauthorised sound recording of a performance which took place at any time in the previous 50 years (ss 248QA, 248CA(2)). For discussion of the 1994 amendments, see D Gruzouskas, 'Performers' Rights; The Right of Personality and the Possibility of a Proprietary Right' (1995) 6 *AIPJ* 92.

or for scientific research purposes. Performers have some rights over the use of unauthorised recordings if they can show that the person using an unauthorised recording knew it was not authorised. This would appear to place an undue burden on potential beneficiaries of the new rights. The legislation confers unassignable civil rights on performers, but unlike copyright these are *not* property rights.

[6.23] '**Performance**'. The sort of performances protected are those of dramatic, musical and literary works and improvisations, as well as dance, circus and variety acts (s 248A(1)). News and documentary presentations with an informational content are not included, and nor are sporting activities and judicial proceedings (s 248A(2)). The Copyright (World Trade Organization Amendments) Act 1994 removed the requirement that one or more performers (of a group) had to be an Australian citizen or resident. This is not a change required by the TRIPS Agreement but was introduced in response to the sale of bootleg recordings of Michael Jackson concerts, not protected here because the artist is a US citizen and the performance took place in a non-Rome Convention country.[100] Protection is now provided to performers from countries which offer reciprocal protection to Australian performers, including the US (ss 248U, 248V; Copyright (International Protection) Regulations regs 4A, 4B).

There is no definition of performer in the Australian Act, rather a performer is a person doing one of the things itemised in the definition of 'performance'. The term 'performance' is defined according to the characteristics of the activity undertaken rather than according to any judgments as to artistry or quality of the performance. This is in line with normal copyright definitions which do not import critical acclaim as part of the definition of subject matter protected by the Act. In the same vein, the Rome Convention defines performer in Art 3 as (inter alia) an actor, singer, musician, dancer, and other persons who act, sing, deliver, declaim, play in or otherwise perform. The distinction between an actor or singer and others who act or sing is presumably to reinforce the point that quality of performance is irrelevant.

[6.24] **Extending performers' rights.** In May 1995 the Federal Government announced an in-principle agreement to extend performers' rights to correspond to the copyrights given to the creators of sound recordings and films. It remains to be seen whether the Howard Government will put the necessary legislation before parliament. Upgrading the present regime would be consistent with the TRIPS Agreement, which equates the rights of performers with those of producers of sound recordings (phonograms) and broadcasters (Art 14). The improvement of performers' rights (and those of sound recording producers) by way of a protocol to the Berne Convention has also been under discussion by WIPO. It is considered appropriate to regard producers of phonograms and performers together since many issues affect both, such as 'home taping', broadcasting and other communication to the public, rental rights and the manipulation of recorded performances made possible by digital technology. The ability to modify or distort a performance using digital technology also raises issues of moral rights for performers, and the strengthening of these has been

---

100. See *Sony Music Australia Ltd v Tansing* (1993) 27 IPR 649.

supported by the international bureau of WIPO.[101] The CCG also identified performers' rights as one of the subject matters where there will be an increasing variety of forms of exploitation, and expressed concern as to the ability of performers adequately to control unauthorised digital creations and manipulations of their performances.[102] The idea of extending performers' rights is not without critics. The record industry and broadcasters prefer the long established system of contracts and industrial awards involving performers and those for whom they work. Increasing performers' rights will add to the complexity and cost of administering those rights, not to mention a corresponding increase in economic power.[103]

(c) Musical Works

[6.25] **'Musical'.** The term 'musical work' is not defined in the Act, although earlier legislation spoke of 'any combination of melody and harmony, or either of them'.[104] Ricketson points out that certain types of work usually thought of as musical composition may not comprise 'combinations of melody and harmony' as traditionally understood, for example, concrete music, electronic and tape music and synthesiser music.[105] However, the adjective 'musical' in the present Act refers to the method of production, and, as with other works, not to any artistic or aesthetic qualities which the work should possess. The score of a song is a musical work, whether it is an advertising jingle or an operatic aria. The words would be a literary work. These may be owned by separate people as they are two distinct copyrights. If the song is recorded then a distinct copyright in the sound recording also exists, quite apart from the work copyrights in the music and words. An opera or musical thus consists of a combination of musical works (the score) and literary works (the lyrics). The choreographic aspect of a ballet or opera would be a dramatic work.

The requirement of 'material form' applicable to all works means that improvised or traditional music will not attract copyright unless or until written down or otherwise embodied. Whether or not the person who does this becomes the 'author' (and therefore first owner) of any copyright depends upon general principles. Bearing in mind the requirements of 'originality', it is obvious that exercising effort so as to produce an arrangement of an existing musical work may attract its own copyright, although since adapting a work is one of the exclusive rights of a copyright owner this could also infringe the copyright subsisting in the material being arranged.[106]

The protection of musical works and corresponding protection for the sound recordings in which they are embodied[107] supports a contemporary music industry, export earnings from which are estimated as about $206

---

101. 'Questions Concerning a Possible Instrument for the Protection of the Rights of Performers and Producers of Phonograms,' Draft Memorandum of International Bureau of WIPO, 29 April 1994.
102. CCG, para [7.10].
103. Music Industry Advisory Council, *Bulletin* No 5, October 1994.
104. Copyright Act 1905 s 4.
105. Ricketson, pp 114–15.
106. See eg *ZYX Music GmbH v King* (1995) 31 IPR 207; and see further [6.35].
107. See [6.39]–[6.40].

million per year.[108] Australia is the third largest supplier of new English language repertoire to the international market. Furthermore, contemporary music in all its forms is regarded as 'the most popular and accessible form of cultural activity'.[109]

(d) Artistic Works

[6.26] 'Artistic'. This is one category of work where the Copyright Act provides an exhaustive definition, although the further definition of individual terms is not always exhaustive. Section 10(1) defines 'artistic work' to mean:

(1) a painting, sculpture, drawing, engraving or photograph, whether the work is of artistic quality or not;

(2) a building or a model of a building, whether the building or model is of artistic quality or not; or

(3) a work of artistic craftsmanship to which neither of the last two preceding paragraphs applies;

but does not include a circuit layout within the meaning of the Circuit Layouts Act 1989.

Although most artistic works, in common with other works, need not possess aesthetic appeal to be designated 'artistic' for copyright purposes,[110] works of artistic craftsmanship in paragraph (c) of the definition of artistic work do need to possess some aesthetic qualities, as well as exhibiting 'craftsmanship'. As far as the other categories in the definition are concerned there only needs to be a degree of originality and reduction to material form, the basic criteria for copyright protection.

[6.27] Paintings. When Adam Ant, the pop singer, sought to protect his facial makeup as an artistic work, a painting, Lawton LJ said that although there was no statutory definition of 'painting', it is a word in the ordinary usage of the English language and it is a question of fact in any particular case whether the subject matter under discussion is a painting or not. It was held that a painting is not an idea, it is an object, and paint without a surface in permanent form is not fixed: hence the singer's claim failed.[111] There was another problem in this case too, apart from the unsuitability of the human face as a surface for a copyright work, in that the artwork itself would not, in the judge's view, have been substantial enough to warrant copyright protection: 'Two straight lines drawn with grease-paint with another line in between them drawn with some other colouring matter, in my judgment, by itself could not possibly attract copyright.'[112] Another example of copyright protection being denied to material of a changeable nature is *Komesaroff v Mickle*,[113] concerning a 'sand sculpture' which was designed to be moved around so that 'sand landscapes' would form between two sheets of perspex.

---

108. Music Industry Advisory Council, *Bulletin* No 5, October 1994, p 7, quoting from *Creative Nation*, the Keating Government's policy statement on the arts.
109. Ibid.
110. See eg *Amalgamated Mining Services Pty Ltd v Warman International Ltd* (1992) 24 IPR 461 (engineering drawings for slurry pumps).
111. *Merchandising Corp of America Inc v Harpbond Ltd* [1983] FSR 32.
112. Ibid at 35.
113. (1986) 7 IPR 295.

[6.28] Sculptures and engravings. The approach taken to defining the meaning of 'painting' in the *Adam Ant* case has also been used to decide the meaning of the other terms included within the list of artistic works. In short, this is to look to the ordinary usage of the English language. This is to be contrasted with the way that some other terms in the Copyright Act are interpreted without necessarily having regard to colloquial use. In *Wham-O Manufacturing Co v Lincoln Industries Ltd*[114] the New Zealand Court of Appeal held that 'frisbee' toys were protected by copyright. A frisbee is a plastic flying disc produced by a manufacturing process which commences with drawings, then the making of wooden models, moulds and dies, ending with the finished product. The models were held to be sculptures and the moulds and dies engravings. The frisbee itself, the final plastic disc, was a print from an engraving but not a sculpture. However, a different approach has been taken in the Australian Federal Court. In *Greenfield Products Pty Ltd v Rover-Scott Bonnar Ltd*[115] Pincus J refused to follow the *Lincoln Industries* case, preferring to define 'sculpture' in accordance with orthodox principles of construction and 'engraving' in a way that did not amount to 'straining the English language'.[116] The applicant had claimed that a drive mechanism for a ride-on mower was protected by copyright, the mechanism itself as a sculpture and the moulds used in manufacture as engravings.

[6.29] Drawings. In protecting drawings, the Copyright Act covers almost anything which can be produced in a two dimensional form (apart from paintings and photographs which are particularly protected by the Act). The concept of a drawing includes a diagram, map, chart or plan, so that 'many items of a prosaic and factual nature have been protected'.[117] Problems in this area arise from the fact that reproducing an artistic work indirectly, perhaps in another dimension, amounts to infringement of copyright in the work. Thus when a person copies a dress, car exhaust system or laser printer cartridge by 'reverse engineering', the copy itself will, prima facie, infringe copyright in the plans or design for such products. This includes the plans or design for many a mass-produced item, and has created an environment of protection for such items which the Copyright Act and some judges have sought to cut down.[118]

The idea/expression dichotomy must be borne in mind with respect to drawings, as with any other work. In *FAI Insurance Ltd v Advance Bank Australia Ltd*,[119] 'how to vote' and proxy vote forms were held not to be protected by copyright since the limits on the modes of expression suitable for conveying such information meant that the idea and expression of the idea almost entirely overlapped.[120]

---

114. (1984) 3 IPR 115.
115. (1990) 17 IPR 417.
116. Ibid at 427.
117. Ricketson, p 122.
118. See further [8.7]–[8.9], [10.24]–[10.28].
119. (1986) 7 IPR 217.
120. See also *Kenrick & Co v Lawrence & Co* (1890) 25 QB 99; *Beck v Montana Constructions Pty Ltd* [1964–5] NSWR 229. Cf *Baillieu v Australian Electoral Commission* (1996) 33 IPR 494.

151

[6.30] Photographs. A photograph is a product of photography or something similar, but not part of a film (s 10(1)). The 'author' of a photograph is the person who takes it, and there need not be any particular exercise of artistic skill in the taking or composition of the photograph in order to attract copyright. On the other hand the taking of a similar photograph of the same person or place does not infringe that copyright, which would only occur by copying the photograph itself, rather than its source.

[6.31] Buildings and models of buildings. Copyright can subsist in a building or model as well as in plans or drawings. Section 10(1) defines a building as being a 'structure of any kind'. A mini tennis court has been held to be a building for this purpose.[121] Thus it is an infringement of copyright to inspect a project home and build a copy of it. Infringement of copyright in such a building is not easy to establish, however, due to the presence of common elements which make the particular portion belonging to the copyright owner hard to single out.[122] Photographing, drawing, painting or otherwise making a two dimensional representation of a building will not infringe (s 66), so that tourists may take their holiday snaps of the Sydney Opera House or the Eiffel Tower with impunity.

[6.32] Works of artistic craftsmanship. This type of artistic work, although not defined in the Act, consists of anything which is not specifically mentioned in the first two paragraphs of the definition of artistic work. The Gregory Committee[123] decided that the term should not be defined by statute but would include items crafted from silver, pottery, wood and embroidery. The purpose of protecting three dimensional items themselves rather than protecting them as reproductions of an underlying work is to ensure that these items do not lose protection through the operation of s 77 of the Copyright Act, which causes loss of copyright protection for most artistic works which are mass produced in a three dimensional form. [124] Section 77 does not apply to works of artistic craftsmanship (nor to buildings or models of buildings). This provision has recently been the subject of important recommendations by the ALRC, as part of its review of the registered designs system.[125] The ALRC proposed that if s 77 were retained, the exception for works of artistic craftsmanship should also stay. However, it went on to recommend that 'artistic craftsmanship' should be defined in the Copyright Act, and that the Act should make it clear that a work can both be a work of artistic craftsmanship *and* fall within the first two paragraphs of the definition of artistic work in s 10(1).[126]

Returning to the present position, this is one category of work where aesthetic considerations are relevant to the subsistence of copyright.

---

121. *Half Court Tennis Pty Ltd v Seymour* (1980) 53 FLR 240.

122. See eg *Beck v Montana Constructions Pty Ltd* (1963) 80 WN (NSW) 1578; *Ancher, Mortlock, Murray & Woolley Pty Ltd v Hooker Homes Pty Ltd* (1971) 20 FLR 481; *Ownit Homes Pty Ltd v D & F Manusco Investments Pty Ltd* [1987] AIPC para 90–426. See further [8.5].

123. Copyright Committee, *Report,* Cmnd 8662, 1952, para 260.

124. See [10.27].

125. See [10.28].

126. *Designs,* paras [17.22]–[17.25]. The recommendation for a definition was made following strong submissions calling for the need for guidance to craftworkers and competitors. The definition should not require artistic merit but rather be directed to the creative work of craftsmanship.

Furthermore, the craft aspect of the work must have been supplied by the same person who provided the artistic input. In *Burke & Margot Burke Ltd v Spicers Dress Designs*[127] the plaintiff designed a dress and her factory seamstresses made it up according to a pattern drawn by her. Another manufacturer copied the dress, which was denied copyright protection. The dress was held not to be a work of artistic craftsmanship because the people who made it were not 'artistic' craftspersons, but merely following instructions, and the artistic element was not supplied by them. In any event some doubts were cast by Clauson J as to whether the dress was 'artistic', being a garment that was 'a mere item of commerce'.[128]

The authorities on the definition of a work of artistic craftsmanship were reviewed in *Merlet v Mothercare plc*,[129] where copyright protection as a work of artistic craftsmanship was claimed for the prototype of a baby's cape, which strapped the baby to its parent. This 'Raincosy' was copied by the defendant, who sold the product as a 'CarryCape'. Walton J held that this could not be a work of artistic craftsmanship as the object had no artistic appeal in itself. Although when in use it may have presented an attractive picture of a baby carried close to its parent, the article must be judged on its own merits without reference to what might be thought to be its natural place in the order of things, just as the dress in the *Margot Burke* case had to be judged on its own, not with reference to the woman of the figure and colouring which it was designed to suit.[130] 'You judge the decanter without reference to its possible contents; you judge the knives and forks as such, without reference to any possible meal in whose consumption they may possibly assist; and you are to judge a baby cape as a baby cape.'[131]

This approach was endorsed by the 'near unanimous authority of the House of Lords'[132] in *George Hensher Ltd v Restawile Upholstery (Lanes) Ltd.*[133] In that case a clear majority of the Law Lords decided that an essential aspect of an 'artistic' work in this context is that it should come into existence as the product of an author who is consciously concerned to produce a work of art. This was not the plaintiff's intention in *Merlet,* where the author had in mind the utilitarian consideration of protecting her child from the rigours of summer in Highland Scotland, nor in *George Hensher* where the article in question was a prototype for making a range of furniture.[134] This approach (of looking to the creator's subjective intention) avoids the court being called upon to make aesthetic judgments based on artistic merit.

---

127. [1936] Ch 400.
128. Ibid at 409. The *Margot Burke* case also provides an interesting illustration of the effect of the now repealed 'non-expert defence', previously found in s 71 (see [10.25]). Clauson J was unable to recognise the dress as being derived from the underlying artistic work (the sketch design) and so the 'non-expert defence' was made out.
129. (1984) 2 IPR 456.
130. Ibid at 461.
131. Ibid at 463.
132. Ibid at 468.
133. [1975] RPC 31. The decision was described by Walton J in *Merlet* as the leading case on the relevant subsection in the UK legislation.
134. See also *Cuisenaire v Reed* [1963] VR 719.

Another aspect of this type of work is that craftsmanship must also be exhibited. In *Merlet* the Raincosy prototype (according to one expert) exhibited incorrect machining, unattractive stitching, and the material was cut 'off grain', all of which meant it may not have qualified as a work of 'craftsmanship' either. Similarly, in *Cuisenaire v Reed*[135] sawing pieces of wood into different lengths and painting them in different colours (to create rods used as part of a system for teaching mathematics) was said to lack craftsmanship.[136]

(e) Adaptations of Literary, Dramatic and Musical Works

[6.33] The right to make an adaptation. One of the exclusive rights of the owner of copyright in a literary, dramatic or musical work is the right to make an adaptation of that work (s 31(1)). An adaptation will attract its own copyright protection provided sufficient originality has been exercised and the usual criteria for subsistence exist (s 31(1)(a)(vii)). Under the definition of 'adaptation' in s 10(1), literary works in dramatic form may be adapted into non-dramatic form and vice versa; literary works in either form may be translated or conveyed solely or principally by means of pictures; and musical works may be arranged or transcribed.

[6.34] Adaptations of computer programs. The definition of adaptation was amended in 1984 to include a 'version' of a computer program, whether or not in the original language code or notation, and not being a reproduction of the work. This amendment was made in response to judicial pronouncements in the *Apple* case to the effect that object code was not an adaptation of source code since it was not turned into another language ('translated') but rather turned into electrical impulses.[137] Furthermore, the words of s 31(1)(a)(vii) suggested that an adaptation must itself be a 'work', and object programs were not works.[138] Nor could the object programs embodied in the ROMs and EPROM be a 'reproduction' of the source code, since two elements are required, one being the derivation of the reproduction from the original work, and also the vital threshold requirement that 'the infringing work sufficiently resembles the copyright work', something which requires 'a sufficient degree of objective similarity between the two works'. This similarity was held not to exist when comparing written source programs with silicon chips and electrical impulses which may be generated in them.[139] The CLRC has recommended[140] that no change be made to the definition of 'adaptation', but that the definition of 'reproduction' be expanded to include but not be limited to:

(a)   an object code version of the program that has been derived from the program in source code by compilation; and

(b)   a source code version of the program that has been derived from the program in object code by decompilation.

The right to adaptation would thus narrow but the concept of reproduction would be expanded with respect to computer programs.

---

135. [1963] VR 719.
136. And also artistry, since the purpose was educational and commercial, not aesthetic.
137. *Computer Edge Pty Ltd v Apple Computer Inc* (1986) 161 CLR 171 at 185.
138. Ibid at 186.
139. Ibid.
140. *Computer Software Protection*, rec 2.04(e)(ii).

Although the above comments by the High Court were made with respect to computer programs and the Copyright Act was amended to give protection to such programs, there is no reason to suppose that the discussion of 'adaptation' is not entirely applicable to works other than computer programs.

[6.35] Copyright in infringing adaptations. Since an adaptation of a work which is not a slavish imitation of the source is also a 'work' with its own copyright, the question arises as to whether copyright can subsist in a work which infringes another. The answer appears to be that it can, provided sufficient effort is expended in creating the adaptation as to satisfy the requirement of originality.[141] Nor is the adaptor disentitled by their own infringement from suing for breach of copyright if the adaptation itself is the subject of unauthorised copying or use by another person.[142] In any event, care must be taken before jumping to the conclusion that an unauthorised adaptation necessarily infringes copyright. In some instances, what has been copied from the earlier work may simply be the unoriginal portions of it, meaning that the earlier work has not been 'substantially' reproduced.[143] In others it may be determined that what has been taken is simply the idea underlying the earlier work, not the expression of that idea.[144]

4. PART IV COPYRIGHT

(a) Introduction

[6.36] Subject matter other than works. Part IV of the 1968 Act introduced new categories of subject matter upon which copyright protection is conferred in order to protect entrepreneurial investment, rather than authorship or the well recognised expression of creative endeavour inherent in the adjectives literary, dramatic, musical and artistic. The Pt IV copyrights cover sound recordings, cinematograph films, television and sound broadcasts and published editions of works. The CLRC has also recommended the introduction of a new class of subject matter protected under Pt IV, 'computer generated material'.[145]

The material protected at present is defined in s 10(1):

'sound recording' means the aggregate of the sounds embodied in a record;

'cinematograph film' means the aggregate of the visual images embodied in an article or thing so as to be capable by the use of that article or thing —

(1) of being shown as a moving picture; or
(2) of being embodied in another article or thing by the use of which it can be so shown,

and includes the aggregate of the sounds embodied in a sound-track associated with such visual images;

'broadcast' means transmit by wireless telegraphy to the public.

---

141. *Redwood Music Ltd v Chappell & Co Ltd* [1982] RPC 109; *A-One Accessory Imports Pty Ltd v Off Roads Imports Pty Ltd* (1996) 34 IPR 306.
142. *ZYX Music GmbH v King* (1995) 31 IPR 207; *A-One Accessory Imports Pty Ltd v Off Roads Imports Pty Ltd (No 2)* (1996) 34 IPR 332.
143. See eg *Warwick Film Productions Ltd v Eisinger* [1969] Ch 508; and see further [8.2].
144. See eg *Joy Music Ltd v Sunday Pictorial Newspapers Ltd* [1960] 2 QB 60; and see further [8.3].
145. *Computer Software Protection*, rec 2.42; and see further [9.21].

The following terms are also defined:

'record' means a disc, tape, paper or other device in which sounds are embodied;

'sound-track', in relation to visual images forming part of a cinematograph film, means —

(1) the part of any article or thing, being an article or thing in which those visual images are embodied, in which sounds are embodied; or

(2) a disc, tape or other device in which sounds are embodied and which is made available by the maker of the film for use in conjunction with the article or thing in which those visual images are embodied;

'sound broadcast' means sounds broadcast otherwise than as part of a television broadcast;

'television broadcast' means visual images broadcast by way of television, together with any sounds broadcast for reception along with those images.

[6.37] Proposed amendments to broadcasting provisions. Following the CCG Report, a new definition of 'broadcast' has been proposed for insertion into s 10(1) and is included in Sch 5 of the 1996 Exposure Draft Bill:

'Broadcast' means transmit to the public where the sounds or visual images, or the sounds and visual images, transmitted constitute sound programs or television programs, but does not include transmit in connection with:

(1) a service (including a teletext service) that provides no more than data, or no more than text (with or without associated still images); or

(2) a service that makes programs available on demand on a point-to-point basis, including a dial-up service.

This definition is consistent with the definition of 'broadcasting service' in s 6(1) of the Broadcasting Services Act 1992 (Cth). The effect of the proposed amendment would be to incorporate all transmissions of broadcasting services presently regulated under this Act. Other definitions included in the draft copyright amendments include terms such as 'reception', 'equipment', 'subscription broadcast', 'to the public', 'transmit' and 're-transmission'. The proposed amendments are framed so as to allow existing statutory licences to operate with respect to transmissions. It remains to be seen what the Howard Government will do concerning the implementation of these amendments.

[6.38] Multimedia and the convergence of technology. The aim of protecting 'new' technology by copyright law is evident in the introduction of Pt IV. Although some aspects of the 1968 Act can be utilised to give protection to multimedia technology, much of it is simply outside the existing framework.

Multimedia works incorporate information of different types and express them in binary form, allowing information once handled in various forms and embodied in different media to be accessed in an integrated fashion. To put this another way, multimedia allows the transformation of, for example, a novel, songs, artwork, or any other type of recorded information into digital code which can be stored on CD-ROM disks or in a computer. Digitisation allows different media to be accessed in an integrated manner from one point, and modified or copied easily and with no loss of quality.[146] Multimedia products make extensive use of copyright material.

146. Digitisation has been described as 'a type of "technological latin" — it makes all subject matters available to all in a common form': A Christie, 'Towards a New Copyright for the Information Age' (1995) 6 *AIPJ* 145 at 155.

A large number of creators and owners may be involved where film, music, literature, performances thereof, and artwork are involved. The problems of obtaining permission to use this (and arranging for remuneration of the copyright owners) are practical rather than conceptual. What is new and challenging to the basic concepts of copyright law is the merging of broadcasting and communication services, the 'convergence' of technology, which bequeaths regulators and proprietors a different world to control, if control is possible at all. A technology-neutral approach has been sought by the Federal Government, and to that end the CCG reported in June 1994 in *Highways to Change — Copyright in the New Communications Environment*. Meanwhile, the existing Act has been described by the former Minister for Justice, Duncan Kerr, as the 'car, bus and truck' legal regime which awaits amendment to protect the freight being carried on the information superhighway. For example, the existing definition of broadcast is inadequate and 'technology specific': hence the recommended change explained in the previous paragraphs.

(b) Sound Recordings

[6.39] The need for protection. The extension of copyright to the 'new' subject matters was recommended by the Spicer Committee,[147] which in turn was based on the Gregory Committee report in the UK.[148] In 1911 s 19 of the British Copyright Act extended protection to records to overcome problems of piracy unknown before the invention of the gramophone. The extended protection was intended to allow recoupment of the risk taken in producing and marketing such 'industrial' (rather than 'intellectual') property. The Spicer Committee reported that, at least in the case of sound recordings, a great deal of artistic and technical skill may be required.[149] This artistic input is supplied by a sound engineer who, with the record producer, is often independent of the record company which presses, markets and distributes the sound recording.[150] However, the first owner of copyright in the sound recording will be the recording company as the 'maker' (s 22(3)), this being the person who pays for the making of the recording, although this may vary by virtue of contractual arrangements between those involved in making the recording. The wide definition of 'record' in the Act covers not only plastic discs and cassette or reel to reel tapes but also the newer compact laser disc and digital audio tape (DAT), which can be used to make perfect digital copies of compact discs. In fact the definition, formulated long before many of these products were imaginable, has proved to be 'technology neutral' and able to embrace new methods of recording.

[6.40] Separate copyright. The subsistence of copyright in a sound recording (or other Pt IV subject matter) in no way affects the copyright in any work from which the subject matter may be derived (s 113). In *CBS Records Australia Ltd v Telmak Teleproducts (Australia) Pty Ltd*[151] one of the

147. Committee on Alterations to Copyright Law, *Report*, 1959.
148. Copyright Committee, *Report*, Cmnd 8662, 1952.
149. See *Gramophone Co Ltd v Stephen Cawardine & Co* [1934] Ch 450 at 454.
150. See S Simpson and G Stevens, Music: The Business and the Law, 1986, ch 10.
151. (1987) 9 IPR 440.

issues between the parties was whether a 'sound alike' (that is, a later sound recording by other performers which is an imitation of the original) was within the description of a copy of a sound recording which is referred to in s 10(3)(c). The dispute concerned a compilation by Telmak entitled *Chart Sounds 16 Hit Songs No 1* in the form of a record and a cassette. CBS owned the 'sound recording' copyright in various of the re-recorded songs. In finding for the defendant on this point, Bowen CJ reiterated that this copyright only protects the actual embodiment of the very sounds on the original record.[152] This is not to say that 'sound alike' recordings will not infringe the musical and literary work copyrights which subsist in recorded music, but these are typically owned by the original composers or their music publishers.

[6.41] Blank tape royalty scheme. A new development introduced by the Copyright Amendment Act 1989 was a blank tape royalty scheme. Home taping of audio material was to be permitted on blank tapes, the price of which was to include a levy which would provide a royalty to copyright owners. The scheme was successfully challenged in the High Court by the Australian Blank Tape Manufacturers Association, who feared that the actual cost of blank tapes to consumers would rise much more than the royalty amount. The blank tape royalty was regarded by the High Court as a tax which could not be introduced by the Copyright Act, since the Constitution in s 55 provides that laws should not both impose taxes and deal with other matters simultaneously.[153] It is expected that the levy will be reintroduced through taxation legislation and that the scheme will operate much as originally planned. The effect of the scheme would have been to legalise home taping on audio tapes and provide for payment to the relevant copyright owners through the Private Audio Visual Copyright Collecting Society,[154] formed to administer the payments derived from the royalty on blank audio tapes with a normal playing time of more than 30 minutes. The Copyright Tribunal would have set the royalty, expected to be between 20 and 50 cents on a blank 60 minute tape. The royalty was to be distributed in three equal shares to the composer/publisher, record producer and artist (through the recording company) respectively. Fifteen percent of the royalty would be paid to a non-profit company set up by the Federal Government to promote Australian music and musicians. The criteria for distribution of royalties would be airplay and record sales. It was thought that the scheme would garner about $10 million per annum to be distributed to the artists, composers, record companies and producers who are presently affected by the widespread practice of home taping.

A further feature of the scheme was that s 135ZZN would have conferred a statutory right on the public at large to copy sound recordings, but only in private for the private domestic use of the person who made it. This was to avoid rental premises springing up where copies of sound recordings could be supplied to the public at a lower cost than purchasing the tape or

152. Ibid at 444.
153. *Australian Tape Manufacturers Association Ltd v Commonwealth of Australia* (1993) 176 CLR 480. The decision forced the government to re-enact all other provisions of the 1989 Act in order to avoid them being held invalid: see Copyright Amendment (Re-enactment) Act 1993 (Cth).
154. See [22.15].

disc.[155] Confining use of the copy to the person making the copy would also prevent the hire, broadcasting or any other sort of trading: technically speaking, even sharing tapes among members of a family would be outside the statutory right of home taping.

[6.42] Scope of the scheme. The copyrights affected would be those in *published* sound recordings (s 85(a)) and also in underlying works (s 31(1)(a)). The soundtracks of films, being part of the cinematograph film copyright, would not be affected. One of the most controversial aspects of the blank tape royalty scheme was to decide which repertoires would share in generating a distribution of the royalty. The position taken by the music industry organisations is that Australian recordings and compositions should be eligible, but the only foreign repertoires to join in should be from countries with similar schemes. The exclusion of countries which did not operate a blank tape royalty scheme or something similar probably means that Australia would have been in breach of Art 9 of the Berne Convention by not affording national treatment to foreign repertoires while at the same time taking away some of the rights comprised in those copyrights by allowing home taping. Any new scheme will presumably provide for repertoire from any country belonging to the World Trade Organisation (WTO) which was formed as a consequence of the TRIPS negotiations which concluded in December 1994. This is consistent with other developments in Australian copyright law which aim to bring us into line with the new international regime.[156]

Despite the High Court challenge, the music industry was successful in persuading legislators to introduce the blank tape royalty scheme after more than a decade of agitation over the futility of enforcing copyright in the age of home taping. The video/film industry was not represented in the scheme as enacted. In part, this is because the industry had not lobbied to the same extent as the music business; further, any harm from the practice of home taping visual material has yet to be established.[157] The main use of home video cassette recorder copying seems to be for the purpose of 'time shifting', taping something to be viewed later.

There is no question that home taping is illegal and will continue to be until the commencement of the statutory licence in the Copyright Act to accompany the tax legislation introducing the blank tape royalty provisions. A whole generation of home tapers has grown up barely realising that taping music for personal use is illegal.[158] In view of the impossibility of pursuing vast numbers of the general public for copyright infringement, attempts had been made to make the suppliers of blank tapes or copying equipment liable to copyright owners, but these attempts were unsuccessful. In *A & M Records v Audio Magnetics Inc*[159] the suppliers of blank tapes

---

155. Note the introduction of a rental right for copyright owners in respect of sound recordings: see [5.8].
156. For example, the amendments in the Exposure Draft Bill 1996, Sch 3, with respect to parallel importing of sound recordings permits importation under the provisions from all members of the WTO.
157. See J Court, 'The Politics of Copyright and the Hometaping Problem' (1986) 4(7) *Copyright Reporter*, p 11.
158. The same could be said of the copying of computer programs.
159. [1979] FSR 1.

were held not to be 'authorising' copyright infringement, since they lacked sufficient control over use of these tapes. Similarly, in *CBS Songs Ltd v Amstrad Consumer Electronics plc*[160] it was held that selling double cassette decks enabling high speed copying did not amount to 'authorising' infringement of copyright.[161]

[6.43] Digital audio tape. A further threat to the music industry appeared to be digital audio tape (DAT), which makes perfect digital copies of compact discs. Japanese manufacturers have perfected this in recent years. The recording industry in the US and the European Economic Community has tried to insist that DAT machines have spoilers fitted (electronic devices that would scramble the sound every time the machine is used to record a compact disc).[162] Naturally, an expensive DAT machine that cannot copy compact discs has minimal appeal compared with top-rate conventional recorders. In the event, the consumer market for DAT machines has not been developing as quickly as expected and although digital technology allows sound recordings to accompany text, video or other material in multimedia products, the use of music on the 'information superhighway', apart from as an adjunct to games, will not develop in a hurry since 'it is not at all clear which market wants to listen to patently inferior sound and watch blatantly inferior images against the background noise of a PC'.[163]

Most commentators seem to agree that private copying is a fact of life, and it is better to recognise it and deal with it, saving technical solutions to detect and deal with commercial piracy if possible.[164] One such possibility would be to develop a means of 'fingerprinting' digital discs so that DAT copies discovered in circulation could quickly be identified as containing copyright material. The blank tape royalty is a practical scheme for counteracting the damage to copyright property caused by developing technology.

(c) Cinematograph Films

[6.44] Copyright in films and soundtracks. Motion pictures have a separate copyright from any underlying work copyrights in the script, choreography or score. Until 1968 this separate copyright did not exist in Australia. The Act provides in s 10(1) that:

'cinematograph film' means the aggregate of the visual images embodied in an article or thing so as to be capable by the use of that article or thing —

(1) of being shown as a moving picture; or
(2) of being embodied in another article or thing by the use of which it can be so shown, and includes the aggregate of the sounds embodied in a sound-track associated with such visual images.

---

160. (1988) 11 IPR 1.
161. Cf *University of New South Wales v Moorhouse* (1975) 133 CLR 133. See further [8.16]– [8.18].
162. G Davies, 'A Technical Solution to Private Copying: The case of DAT' [1987] 6 *EIPR* 158.
163. B Faust, 'Breakdown on the IT Highway', *The Weekend Australian*, 29–30 October 1994, p 28.
164. See T J Brennan, 'An Economic Look at Taxing Home Audio Taping' (1988) 32 *J Broadcasting & Electronic Media* 89; J Court, 'The Politics of Copyright and the Hometaping Problem' (1986) 7(4) *Copyright Reporter*, p 11; A Tettenborn, 'Recordings, Reproductions and Authorising Infringement Yet Again: Time for a Change?' (1986) 2 *IPJ* 227.

The means by which a 'moving picture' is produced is not relevant in determining whether the end result is a 'film'. Thus in *Sega Enterprises Ltd v Galaxy Electronics Pty Ltd*[165] a computer generated video game was held to be a film. The term 'soundtrack' is further defined as meaning either sounds embodied in the film itself or a separate device in which sounds are embodied and which is made available by the maker of the film for use in conjunction with the film. Thus, unauthorised reproduction of a film soundtrack infringes the 'film' copyright rather than a 'sound' right.

(d) Broadcasts

[6.45] The definition of 'broadcast': 1968 Act. Both sound and television broadcasts were first granted copyright protection under the 1968 Act. Broadcasts first made before that time are not protected by copyright law, but otherwise there is no limitation on the subject matter protected as a broadcast: it does not matter whether the broadcast is based on a work or other subject matter, or simply a live broadcast of a sporting event, or an unscripted interview with a politician in which there is no copyright. The 'broadcast rights', like all Pt IV copyrights, exist independently of any underlying copyright in the material being broadcast, although allowing a work to be broadcast is taken to be licensing further broadcasts of the material, much as a performer who gives permission for a recording of a performance to be broadcast will be taken to have licensed all subsequent broadcasts.

The definition of television broadcast in s 10(1) refers to visual images broadcast by way of television, together with any sounds broadcast for reception along with those images. A sound broadcast means sounds broadcast other than as part of a television broadcast. 'Broadcast' itself involves a transmission by 'wireless telegraphy' and this in turn means 'the emitting or receiving, otherwise than over a path that is provided by a material substance, of electromagnetic energy'. This is to be contrasted with transmission of material via a diffusion service, which means 'over wires, or over other parts provided by a material substance' (s 26(1)). Relaying broadcast material is allowed where the service is only incidental to running a hotel, guest home, hospital or other 'premises' at which persons reside or sleep.

[6.46] Proposed changes. Perhaps the main recommendation of the CCG, now incorporated into draft amendments to the Act, has been the proposal for a new 'technology neutral, broad based right to authorise transmissions to the public'[166] in order to overcome the limitations of the present concept of a broadcast under the Act. The new transmission right will cover existing broadcasting (and diffusion) rights to protect the transmission of copyright material in intangible form to the public by any means or combination of means which is capable of being received or made perceivable by a device. Transmissions are to be protected whether made from within or outside Australia, and the necessary licence obtained from respective owners, whether within Australia or not. Re-transmission will be allowed to enable proper reception of the material in an area where a

165. (1996) 35 IPR 161.
166. CCG, rec 1.

signal is inadequate. The CCG recommended retaining the right to broad-cast as part of the new transmission right, a broadcast being a transmission made by a broadcaster under the Broadcasting Services Act 1992. At present, a broadcast can only be made by bodies specifically mentioned in the Copyright Act (ie holders of relevant licences) rather than by reference to the Broadcasting Services Act.[167] Under the provisions of the Exposure Draft Bill of February 1996, s 91 will be amended to provide that copyright subsists in a television or sound broadcast lawfully made from a place in Australia. The recommendations of the CCG as embodied in the 1996 Exposure Draft Bill were initially supported by the Howard Government, although consideration of the scope of a 're-transmission' right is holding up enactment of legislation on this point. The CCG recommends limiting re-transmissions[168] to within the area of the primary broadcast, to enable reception where the broadcast signal is poor. Under the present provisions commercial television stations have been unable to prevent a pay TV opera-tor from re-broadcasting their signals.[169]

One key aspect of the concept of broadcasting, as defined in s 10(1), is that it is 'to the public'. In *APRA Ltd v Telstra Corp Ltd*[170] the Full Court of the Federal Court held that the 'public' that must be considered here is the 'copyright owner's public'. This might be the public at large, or just a sec-tion of the public: what matters is the character of the audience and the intent of the transmission.[171] In this instance the supply of music to mobile telephones while the users were being kept 'on hold' was held to constitute a transmission to the public, even though at any one time the number of such users might be small. This notion of broadcasting as transmission to the public may be contrasted with 'narrowcasting', or transmitting to speci-fied end-users, such as taxi radios, ship to shore radios and other forms of two-way communication. It could be said that cable television, which is dis-cussed in the next paragraph, involves 'narrowcasting', but it also relies to some extent on broadcasting. Similarly, satellite delivery to hotels and clubs throughout Australia via 'Sky Channel' (featuring mainly sport and light entertainment) is arguably 'narrowcasting', but would also be regarded as being transmission to 'the public' on the view taken in cases such as *APRA v Telstra.*[172] The CCG recommended retaining the present definition of 'the public' and the concept of transmission to 'the public' is to be determined by case law, as at present. The proposed amendments are not intended to include in 'broadcast' on-line demand services, interactive services or com-puter networking of material.

[6.47] Cable television. The 1968 Act, based as it was on the Spicer Report produced some ten years earlier, was in some respects already out of date even before being proclaimed. Cable transmission of television

---

167. At present the Copyright Act does not even refer to the Broadcasting Services Act 1992, but to the Broadcasting Act 1942; cf *Amalgamated Television Services Pty Ltd v Foxtel Digital Cable Television Pty Ltd* (1995) 32 IPR 323; (1996) 34 IPR 274.
168. See ss 199(4), 25(3) of the Copyright Act 1968.
169. *Amalgamated Television Services Pty Ltd v Foxtel Digital Cable Television Pty Ltd* (1996) 34 IPR 274.
170. (1995) 31 IPR 289.
171. The Full Court relied in this respect on authorities on the meaning of 'performance in public': see [8.10].
172. See *APRA Ltd v Canterbury–Bankstown Leagues Club Ltd* (1964) 5 FLR 415.

programs, although existing, was confined to two situations: relaying broadcast material around a school, hotel, prison or other such establishments,[173] and improving reception of broadcasts by providing a community aerial from which the broadcast could be diffused to shadow areas. There is no need to refer to specific statutes or particular broadcasters, but in order to attract copyright protection a broadcast must fit within the regulatory scheme. Provision is also made for transnational transmissions by extending 'the public' to mean 'the public within or outside Australia'.

Among the rights of the copyright owner in relation to a 'work' are a diffusion right (s 31(1)(a)(v)),[174] as well as the right to broadcast the work (s 31(1)(a)(iv)). However, until recently cable television has not been available in Australia, although the US experience indicated the potential for consumer choice and viability of cable TV as a business activity. It is estimated that half the homes with TV in the US have cable services or 'pay TV', with a choice of over 60 channels. Revenues for advertising on American cable channels have increased steadily each year since its inception and the number of people watching free TV is declining, as cable delivers more comprehensive sport, news, and new release films (the main types of program to date). There are also channels devoted entirely to music and pornographic material.

In January 1995 'pay TV' came to Australia.[175] The 1968 Act contains no provision at all for developments in cable television. The Australian Broadcasting Tribunal had earlier been asked by the Minister for Post and Telecommunications to consider cable television. The Tribunal reported in 1982 on matters relating to the introduction of cable and subscription television services.[176] Recommendations were made for access to copyright material, as well as that a licensee of a cable television system should have a copyright in an original transmission which is similar to the copyright a broadcaster has in its broadcasts. Under the CCG's recommendation to introduce the general right of transmission to the public and the draft legislation which appeared in February 1996, the references in the Act to 'transmission to subscribers to a diffusion service' would be redundant and are to be deleted.

[6.48] Satellite broadcasting. Satellite program services are programs distributed via a satellite system to commercial licensees for re-broadcast on their stations. In 1988 the ABC was able greatly to increase broadcasting to country areas of Australia by the launch of Aussat. A report into regulation of the use of satellite program services by broadcasters was completed by the Australian Broadcasting Tribunal in 1984.[177] The 1968 Act makes no reference to broadcasting by satellite. The ultimate reception of a satellite

---

173. This is contemplated in s 26 of the Act and allowed for without inducing copyright infringement: see [8.31].
174. As to what constitutes transmission 'to subscribers to a diffusion service', see *APRA Ltd v Telstra Corp Ltd* (1995) 31 IPR 289.
175. Along with fierce debate about 'anti-siphoning' policies which are intended to ensure that major sporting events remain free to air for at least ten years.
176. *Inquiry by the Australian Broadcasting Tribunal into Cable and Subscription Television Services and Related Matters*, 1982.
177. *Report of the Inquiry into the Regulation of the Use of Satellite Program Services by Broadcasters* (2 vols), 1984.

broadcast by a member of the public takes place after the signal from the satellite (the 'down-link) is transmitted directly to the receiver, or after a cable or wire transmission from an earth station which receives the transmission. The 'up-link' or transmission to the satellite is by means of wire telegraphy,[178] but is not itself intended to be received by the public. These problems of new technology were addressed by the Broadcasting Tribunal in its 1984 report, where it was recommended that 'broadcast' should be defined as a 'radiocommunication intended for reception by the general public'. This recommendation was accepted for the purposes of the Broadcasting and Television Amendment Act 1985 (Cth). Section 22(6) of the Copyright Act states that a satellite broadcast is made when transmitted from the earth. The CCG recommended that this section be reworded to provide that the place from which a satellite broadcast is made is the place from which the signals carrying the broadcast are transmitted. Also, the maker of the broadcast is to be responsible for its content. Under the proposed amendments presently in draft form, transmissions originating from Australia and intended for reception abroad will require a licence to be obtained from the Australian owners of copyright in material being transmitted. Also, the maker of the transmission will have the same rights as other broadcasters, which is not the case now as no copyright subsists in transmissions originating from Australia for public reception overseas. However, once outside Australia, protection will be according to the law of the country where reception occurs.

At the international level recognition of the need to resolve satellite transmission and copyright issues led to the establishment in 1974 of the Brussels Convention Relating to the Distribution of Programme-Carrying Signals Transmitted by Satellite. This convention provides for the 'obligation of each contracting state to take adequate measures to prevent the unauthorised distribution on or from its territory of any programme-carrying signal transmitted by satellite'. The basic aim of the 'Satellite Convention' is to protect broadcasters against piracy, particularly 'pirate' radio stations who might otherwise take the signals of transmissions from point-to-point satellites and broadcast or diffuse them locally. The Convention initially overlooked the interests of those owning copyright in the material transmitted, although some attempt was subsequently made to amalgamate the Satellite Convention with existing authors' rights, as interpreted according to the Berne Convention. Australia, like most members of the Berne Convention, has not yet ratified the Brussels Convention.[179]

(e) Published Editions of Works

[6.49] **Protection for publishers.** The fourth category of 'other' subject matter protects the presentation or typographical arrangement of works in printed form (s 92). This type of protection was only introduced with the 1968 Act, so no protection for a published edition exists in a book published before the commencement of that Act (s 224). As with other Pt IV copyrights the published edition copyright is entirely separate from any

---

178. Although 'telegraphy' may be too narrow to cover this sort of transmission.
179. See P Knight, 'The Australian Copyright Act 1968 and Satellite' (1984) 2(3) *Copyright Reporter,* p 4; WIPO, *Background Reading,* pp 371–5. See further [21.21].

copyright in the underlying works: hence it may be protected even if the work presented is itself in the public domain. For example, an edition of Blackstone's *Commentaries* may be protected under this head, or a beautiful presentation of the score for Handel's *Messiah*. The value of this protection to the publisher, who is the owner of the published edition copyright (s 100), is apparent when considering the plethora of new editions of Beatrix Potter's works which have appeared on the market since 1987, when copyright in her well-known literary and artistic works expired.[180] This sort of protection may be compared with that given to a sound recording or cinematograph film which may be no more than (or not even) a vehicle for the dissemination of a work.[181] The scope of the 'published edition copyright' was discussed in *Nationwide News Pty Ltd v Copyright Agency Ltd,*[182] which concerned the question of entitlement to fees collected under a statutory licence for photocopying of material from newspapers. For the purposes of the action, the journalists who wrote the articles were the owners of copyright in those literary works. The proprietors of the newspapers and magazines, being the employers of the journalists, owned copyright in the works when first published in the periodical, and had previously attempted to claim ownership of the journalists' work when put to further use by a press clipping service (or photocopied for educational use).[183] The publishers claimed, however, that copying an article from a newspaper or magazine infringed their copyright in a 'published edition'. The Full Court of the Federal Court accepted that such copyright subsisted in various aspects of the layout of newspaper editions:

> Published edition copyright protects the presentation embodied in the edition. This form of copyright, as the legislative history shows, protects such matters as typographical layout. However, it also protects other aspects of presentation, such as juxtaposition of text and photographs and use of headlines. In the present case, a considerable volume of evidence was adduced on the importance of layout and presentation to magazines and newspapers. In modern times, the work of typesetters is shared among subeditors, layout artists or designers and production editors. It is clear that layout is often extremely important in attracting readers to read a particular story or magazine. It is also clear that the choice of layout, type size, headings and colour is a skilled operation. Published edition copyright thus protects the product of skill, labour and judgment in presenting material in an edition.[184]

The court went on to hold, however, that the copying of single articles did not constitute reproduction of a 'substantial part' of the edition: hence there was no infringement.[185]

5.   CONNECTING FACTORS

[6.50]   Establishing a connection to Australia. In order to receive copyright protection in Australia, there must be a factor connecting the

---

180. Note that Beatrix Potter's copyright has, since 1 January 1996, revived under the extension of term in protection (from 50 to 70 years from the author's death) in the European Community: see [5.11].
181. See Phillips and Firth, para [12.20].
182. (1996) 34 IPR 53.
183. *De Garis v Neville Jeffress Pidler Pty Ltd* (1990) 18 IPR 292; see [7.4].
184. (1996) 34 IPR 53 at 71.
185. See [8.14].

relevant work or subject matter with this country. In the absence of such a factor, any protection in this country will depend upon the international copyright recognition provisions being satisfied.[186] The relevant connecting factors vary according to the type of work or subject matter involved:

- *unpublished original work*: the author must be a qualified person (see [6.51]) when the work or matter is made or for a substantial part of the period during which it is made (s 32(1));
- *published original work (other than a building or artistic work attached to a building)*: the first publication must take place in Australia, or the author must be a qualified person when it is first published, or (if the author dies before publication) the author must have been a qualified person at the time of his or her death (s 32(2));
- *building or artistic work attached to a building*: the building must be situated in Australia (s 32(3));
- *sound recording or film*: the maker must be a qualified person at the time it is made, or it must be made in Australia, or its first publication must take place in Australia (ss 89, 90);
- *broadcast*: the broadcast must be made from a place in Australia by the ABC, SBS or the holder of a television, radio or transmitter licence (s 91);
- *published edition of works*: the first publication must take place in Australia or the publisher must be a qualified person at the date of first publication (s 92).

[6.51] **'Qualified person'.** Many of the connecting factors hinge on the author, maker or publisher being a 'qualified person'. This term is defined, where original works are concerned, to mean an Australian citizen, an Australian protected person or a person resident in Australia (s 32(4)). The same definition obtains for subject matter other than works, with the added alternative of Australian corporations (s 84).

6. DURATION OF COPYRIGHT

[6.52] **The statutory periods.** As with the connecting factors, the period for which copyright protection subsists depends upon the nature of the work or subject matter:

- *literary, dramatic and musical works*: 50 years, either from the expiration of the year of the author's death or from that of the first year in which the work (or an adaptation) is published, performed in public, broadcast or sold in record form, whichever is the later (s 33(2), (3), (5));
- *artistic works (other than engravings or photographs)*: 50 years from the expiration of the year of the author's death (s 33(2));[187]
- *engravings*: 50 years from the expiration of the year of the author's death or of the year of first publication, whichever is the later (s 33(2), (5));

186. See Copyright (International Protection) Regulations 1969 ss 184–188. See generally Lahore, *Copyright*, paras [14,000] ff; Ricketson, ch 14.
187. An important exception arises to the extent that copyright in an artistic work overlaps with industrial design protection: see [10.24] ff.

- *photographs, recordings and films*: 50 years from the expiration of the year of first publication (ss 33(6), 93, 94);
- *broadcasts*: 50 years from the expiration of the year of broadcast (s 95(1));[188]
- *published editions of works*: 25 years from the expiration of the year of first publication (s 96).

The proposed new subject matter 'computer generated material' is to have a 25 year term of protection from the end of the year in which the material is made.[189]

In the case of joint authors, the relevant death for the above purposes is that of the author who dies last (s 80). Where an author is pseudonymous or anonymous, the relevant duration is 50 years from the expiration of the year of the work's first publication, unless during that period the author's identity becomes generally known or is reasonably ascertainable (s 34). Where one or some but not all joint authors are pseudonymous, the relevant death is that of the last author whose identity is known or is disclosed or is reasonably ascertainable (s 81). Where the Crown owns copyright, the relevant duration is 50 years from the year of first publication: the only exception being artistic works (other than engravings and photographs), where it is 50 years from the year of making (ss 180–181).

7. PUBLICATION

[6.53] Establishing whether publication has occurred. The concept of publication is an important element in the copyright regime. It may be important to know when and where a work or subject matter is first published in order to establish the necessary connection with Australia and/or to calculate the duration of protection. As far as original works or editions are concerned, publication occurs only when reproductions are 'supplied (whether by sale or otherwise) to the public' (s 29(1)(a)).[190] It would appear that a work is 'supplied' when and where it is offered to the public, whether or not a sale or receipt actually results.[191] Similarly, a sound recording is published when a record embodying all or part of the recording is supplied to the public (s 20(1)(b)); and a film when a copy is 'sold, let on hire, or offered or exposed for sale or hire, to the public' (s 29(1)(c)).

[6.54] Acts which do not constitute publication. Certain acts are expressly provided by s 29(3) *not* to constitute publications. These are:
- (a)   the performance of a literary, dramatic or musical work;
- (b)   the supplying to the public of records of a literary, dramatic or musical work;
- (c)   the exhibition of an artistic work;
- (d)   the construction of a building or a model thereof; and

---

188. Note that copyright in a re-broadcast only subsists for as long as the copyright in the original broadcast: s 95(2).
189. *Computer Software Protection*, rec 2.42.
190. See [8.2] for the meaning of 'reproduction'. Note, however, that s 29(2) effectively provides that substantial (but not total) reproduction is not sufficient to constitute publication.
191. See *British Northrop Ltd v Texteam Blackburn Ltd* [1974] RPC 57.

(e)   the supplying to the public of photographs or engravings of a building, of a model thereof, or of a sculpture.

The Act also provides that publications should be disregarded where they are unauthorised (s 29(6), (7)) or where they are 'merely colourable' and 'not intended to satisfy the reasonable requirements of the public' (s 29(4)).[192] Finally, it should be noted that a publication in Australia or another country may be treated as the first publication notwithstanding an earlier publication elsewhere, provided the two publications occurred within 30 days of each other (s 29(5)).

[6.55] 'Publication' in the context of copyright infringement.
Although s 29 sets out in detail circumstances in which publication is deemed to have occurred for the purposes of the Act, the High Court has held that it does not control the meaning of the words 'to publish' in s 31, which lists the acts which a copyright owner is exclusively entitled to do in relation to a work.[193] Publication in that context (and thus for the purpose of determining whether an infringement has occurred) is to be taken to mean 'to make public that which has not previously been made public in the copyright territory'.[194]

---

192. See *Francis Day & Hunter v Feldman & Co* [1914] 2 Ch 728.
193. *Avel Pty Ltd v Multicoin Amusements Pty Ltd* (1990) 171 CLR 88.
194. Ibid at 93.

Chapter 7

Exploitation of Copyright

[7.1] **Introduction.** Methods of using and exploiting copyright material are constantly developing. Live performance of works and remuneration from ticket sales are now supplemented, indeed overtaken, by revenue streams from recording and broadcasting. Television and video returns outstrip income earned from cinema release of films, and with all these methods of disseminating material, multiple copyrights are involved. Furthermore, there is a 'convergence of product lines' which is leading to new business practices.

> In simpler times, publishers produced books, record companies made records and filmmakers made films. These days, some publishers, some record companies and some filmmakers, along with computer software and games companies, are developing the same products — for the most part, CD-ROM.[1]

At this stage, the use of creative material, even in new ways, is still largely regulated by copyright law. The basic issue of how to exploit one's copyright material still begins with threshold questions of ownership — of the underlying works, of the sound recordings, films, broadcasts and performers' rights. Moral rights which are personal to the creator of the material will also influence the use of copyright matter. The fact that individual owners can never hope to monitor and regulate all uses of their work leads to 'convergence of the ways the producers/publishers of media products and services sell them and deal with, and pay, the creators'.[2] Collective administration of copyright (particularly under statutory licensing regimes) is discussed in Chapter 22.

The ever increasing control over copyright material and assertion of ownership has been queried by some commentators.[3] On the other hand,

---

1.   J Given, 'Converging Cultures' (1995) 14 *Communications Law Bulletin* 7 at 7.
2.   Ibid.
3.   See eg C Lind, 'The Idea of Capitalism or the Capitalism of Ideas? A Moral Critique of the Copyright Act' (1991) 7 *IPJ* 65.

copyright has always embraced new technology and exacted payment for new ways of using material.[4] There are some who argue that 'everything we know about intellectual property is wrong'[5] and that in a digital era we should abandon existing notions of property altogether and rely on good-will. At the moment, however, the international intellectual property community seems firmly approving of the idea that private proprietary rights should exist,[6] and this chapter discusses the present regime.

1.   OWNERSHIP

(a) Works

[7.2]   General. The owner of copyright in a literary, artistic, dramatic or musical work and the author or creator of the work are not necessarily the same person, but the basic rule is that the author is the first owner of copyright (s 35(2)). There are exceptions to this basic rule which provide that copyright will first belong to a person other than the author in certain circumstances, although each exception may be excluded or modified by agreement (s 35(3)). In the first place, s 35(4) gives the proprietor of a newspaper, magazine or periodical a limited copyright in works produced by a journalist pursuant to employment under a contract of service or apprenticeship. This copyright covers the rights to publish the work in a newspaper, etc, to broadcast it, or to reproduce it for either purpose. In most respects, however, the journalist owns the copyright. Second, s 35(5) provides that a person who commissions a photograph, portrait[7] or engraving owns the copyright in such a work. Where the purpose for which the work is required is communicated at the time of commission, the author does have the limited right to restrain use of the work for any other purpose. The limitation of s 35(5) to certain artistic works only is apparently based on previous copyright legislation,[8] and has not been removed so as to make the section apply more generally, although this was recommended by the Spicer Committee.[9] Third, and where neither of the above applies, the copyright in any work made by an author 'in pursuance of the terms of his

---

4.   For example, the formation of the Copyright Agency Ltd in Australia during the 1970s to deal with the challenge posed to copyright owners in print material by good quality photocopiers.

5.   J Casimir, 'Battle in Cyberspace', interview with John Perry Barlow, *Sydney Morning Herald*, 29 July 1995, Spectrum 5A.

6.   Indeed, Art 27 of the United Nations Universal Declaration of Human Rights provides that 'everyone has the right to the protection of the moral and material interests resulting from any scientific, literary or artistic production of which he [sic] is the author': see S Olswang, 'Access Right: An Evolutionary Path for Copyright into the Digital Era' [1995] 5 *EIPR* 215.

7.   As to the meaning of 'portrait', see *Attorney-General (NSW) v Trustees of National Art Gallery of NSW* (1944) 62 WN(NSW) 212; *Leah v Two Worlds Publishing Co Ltd* [1951] Ch 353.

8.   Ricketson, p 317. Possibly the exceptions are based on privacy considerations due to the personal nature of the commissions mentioned in the subsection.

9.   Committee appointed by the Attorney-General of the Commonwealth to consider what alterations are desirable to the Copyright Law of the Commonwealth, *Report*, 1965, para 85. The same recommendation has been made more recently by the Law Council of Australia Intellectual Property Committee. See also K Puri, 'Copyright in Commissioned Works in Australia' [1995] 6 *EIPR* 290.

or her employment by another person under a contract of service or apprenticeship' belongs to the employer (s 35(6)). The questions of copyright ownership in the context of employment and the special position of journalists are considered in more detail below.

[7.3] Copyright in the employment context. In the absence of any express or implied agreement between the parties, which may always be used to vary the position that would otherwise obtain under the legislation, questions of ownership of copyright in the employment context usually turn on two key questions. First of all, is the author an employee working under a contract of service? The alternative is that they might be an independent contractor, engaged under a contract for services and thus in business on their own account. General principles of employment law will inform the concept of 'contract of service'.[10]

Assuming that the author is an employee, the second question is whether the work is created 'in pursuance of the terms of [the] employment', so that copyright automatically vests in the employer. This may be a far from easy question to answer, not least because there are relatively few authorities from which to derive guidance. The principal determinant, no doubt, is whether creation of the work falls within the employee's 'normal duties'. In *Antocks, Lairn Ltd v I Bloohn Ltd*,[11] for example, copyright in drawings of furniture made by the managing director of a furniture company did not vest in the company, because the work was outside the scope of the director's usual management duties. By contrast, in *Stephenson Jordan & Harrison Ltd v Macdonald & Evans*[12] it was held that a firm providing managerial services based around various accounting principles was entitled to the copyright in a section of a book written by a former executive on the subject of those principles, the section having been written as part of an assignment for one of the firm's clients. On the other hand it would seem that there will be situations where, although the employee is plainly performing a 'normal' duty, in the sense that creation of the work bears a clear relation to the principal duties of the position and can in no way be regarded as extraordinary, nevertheless copyright does not vest in the employer. This was the case in *Stephenson Jordan & Harrison* in relation to a further section of the book, copyright in which was held to remain with the executive despite the section being based on a series of lectures prepared and delivered during his time with the firm. Although the decision is somewhat difficult to follow, the director's duty to promote the company by giving such lectures was evidently regarded as somehow ancillary to his main work.[13]

In the same case Evershed MR went so far as to suggest that:

> prima facie ... a man [sic], engaged on terms that he is called upon to compose and deliver public lectures or lectures to some specified class of persons, would in the absence of clear terms in the contract of employment to the contrary be entitled to the copyright in those lectures.[14]

---

10. See Creighton and Stewart, ch 7; J Macken, G J McCarry and C Sappideen, *Law of Employment*, 3rd ed, 1990, chs 1–2. See eg *Ocean Routes (Australia) Pty Ltd v M C Lamond* [1984] AIPC 90–134. *Erica Vale Australia Pty Ltd v Thompson & Morgan (Ipswich) Ltd* (1994) 28 IPR 589.
11. [1972] RPC 219. Cf *Kambrook Distributing Pty Ltd v Delaney* (1984) 4 IPR 79.
12. (1952) 69 RPC 10.
13. See also *Noah v Shuba* [1991] FSR 14.
14. (1951) 69 RPC 10 at 18.

While this is no doubt of great comfort to academics jealous of the (modest) royalties accruing from their monographs and textbooks, it may be hard to defend as a matter of principle. On the face of it, universities and other educational institutions would seem to have a legitimate claim to copyright in the work of academic employees — certainly where lecture notes are concerned, and arguably also in the case of publications, given that engaging in research is a term of most academics' employment. It may be that any entitlement that academics have had in the past to the fruits of their work has rested on the basis of a contractual term implied by reason of custom and practice, given the long-standing failure of universities to contest the point.[15] Recent discussion of intellectual property policy in universities indicates that most institutions are prepared to let academics continue to own and negotiate with commercial publishers over book copyright. For one thing, the expense and effort of policing and collecting a 'cut' of the royalties is not considered worthwhile, and disruptive industrial issues are created by assertions of ownership by universities in this context.[16]

Mention must also be made of the extraordinary suggestion by members of the House of Lords, unprompted by counsel, that copyright in the book *Spycatcher*, written by former MI5 operative Peter Wright in assumed breach of his duty of confidence, might vest in the Crown in equity.[17] Although there might be scope for deriving from these comments a general principle that copyright in material created by an employee in breach of an obligation of confidence is to be held on trust for the employer, even where the employer would not otherwise be entitled to that copyright, the comments are better regarded as judicial hyperbole occasioned by extreme disgust at the activities of the 'treacherous' Wright.

[7.4] Journalists. It was mentioned above that s 35(4) places employed journalists in a special position, in that their employer is only entitled to copyright in their work for the purpose of publication in a newspaper, magazine or periodical or broadcasts. This was illustrated in *De Garis v Neville Jeffress Pidler Pty Ltd*,[18] a test case brought to determine whether press clipping services infringe journalists' copyright. These services provide compilations of published information collected from a variety of sources, mainly newspapers and other periodicals. Government departments, large companies and indeed journalists have come to rely on such information gathering sources, which can be requested for almost any topic. It is estimated that such services are immensely profitable, with one 1990 estimate indicating an annual turnover of more than $45 million.[19]

The plaintiffs in this particular case were Brian de Garis, a history academic at the University of Western Australia who occasionally wrote book reviews for *The West Australian,* and Matthew Moore, a journalist on the staff

15. Cf *Noah v Shuba* [1991] FSR 14.
16. See A L Monotti, 'Ownership of Copyright in Traditional Literary Works within Universities' (1994) 22 *Fed L Rev* 340; and see further [1.29].
17. *Attorney-General (UK) v Guardian Newspapers Ltd (No 2)* [1988] 3 WLR 776 at 788, 791, 800–1: see [4.41]. See also *Attorney-General (UK) v Blake* [1996] FSR 727 at 737–8.
18. (1990) 95 ALR 625.
19. See C Warren, 'Copyright is Ours' [1990] 10 *Communications* 1.

of the *Sydney Morning Herald*. Each sued the defendant for breach of copyright in respect of pieces written for their respective newspapers which the defendant had subsequently photocopied and distributed to clients. De Garis' ownership of copyright was not seriously disputed. As an occasional contributor, he was plainly not an employee of the paper's proprietor — although it might have been interesting to see how the court would have dealt with an argument that copyright belonged to the University on the basis outlined above. Moore, on the other hand, was an employee of John Fairfax & Sons and had written the relevant articles pursuant to the terms of his employment.[20] This brought s 35(4) into play, the question then being whether the defendant's activities fell within the scope of the copyright possessed by Fairfax, who were not a party to the proceedings. Beaumont J took the view that:

> the distribution of photocopies of selected newspaper articles does not constitute the publication of a newspaper, magazine or similar periodical for the purposes of s 35(4). The activity of providing press clippings on a commercial basis is different in character from the activity of publishing a newspaper.[21]

He also held, in relation to both actions, that the defendant could not rely on a variety of defences.[22] Accordingly the actions succeeded. The effect of the decision is that in order to avoid breaching copyright any commercial press clipping service will now, at least in theory, need to seek the individual permission of all the writers whose pieces they copy: it will not be enough merely to negotiate a deal with the various newspaper and magazine proprietors. In fact, journalists receive payment for the use of their work by way of distribution of licence fees collected by a collecting society, the Copyright Agency Ltd (CAL). After the *Journalists* case publishers sought payment through CAL for use of their published edition and compilation copyrights, arguing that photocopying articles from newspapers infringed those rights, which did not belong to the journalists. It was held that the reproduction of individual items was not an infringement of these rights, since it had not been established that a substantial part of each edition was being copied.[23]

A moot point not at issue in the *Journalists* case is whether, by virtue of s 35(4), the rights of a newspaper proprietor are limited to first publication only. On its face, the provision would seem to encompass an unlimited right to syndicate material,[24] something which has been done since newspaper production began in Australia in 1803.[25] However, the Australian Journalists' Association has taken a different view, arguing that the contract of employment referable to a particular publication limits the proprietor's right to publish in a different newspaper or magazine.[26]

Another cause of concern to journalists is electronic publishing, which allows articles written on computers by staff and stored in a database to be

---

20. See also *Sun Newspapers Ltd v Whippie* (1928) 28 SR (NSW) 473. Cf *Byrne v Statist Co* [1914] 1 KB 622.
21. (1990) 95 ALR 625 at 639.
22. See further [8.28].
23. *Nationwide News v Copyright Agency Ltd* (1996) 34 IPR 53: see [8.14].
24. See also S Bridge, 'Journalists as Copyright Owners' (1989) 23(3) *Copyright Bulletin* 10.
25. See C Warren, 'Copyright is Ours' [1990] 10 *Communications* 1.
26. Ibid.

disseminated to anyone with a personal computer and modem. The Fairfax newspaper group in fact provides such a service through a system called Ausinet. Since this relies on cable delivery, it is not therefore within the proprietor's broadcast right under s 35(4), although other systems such as Channel Seven's Teletext do rely on broadcasting. Proprietors have so far generally proved recalcitrant in relation to compensating their journalists for what appears to be an infringement of their copyright.[27] The publishers have sought amendments to the Copyright Act to ensure that they retain full control over material published in newspapers and magazines for future electronic distribution, arguing that they should be put into the same position as other electronic proprietors such as broadcasters, who retain full control over employees' work. Amendments to the Act along these lines were agreed to in December 1994, under which publishers would be free to use their employees' work for delivery of their newspapers or magazines via computer networks or pay TV services, and also in computer databases established as part of the business. Employed journalists were to retain their copyright for photocopying, sale of original cartoons, photographs and in separate publication as in book form. These amendments to s 35(4) reflected a high degree of agreement between publishers and journalists. The text of the proposed amendments is contained in Sch 2 of the Exposure Draft Bill of February 1996. A Copyright Law Review Committed (CLRC) report into the issue had originally recommended total repeal of s 35(4), leaving journalists in the same position as other employees, that is, with no rights over material created at work and for work purposes.[28] It seems that these draft amendments will not, in fact, be part of a revised Draft Bill to be introduced by the Howard Government in 1997 and the CLRC's recommendations as to treating journalists much as other employees are under consideration. It is true that the print media journalists are presently (and under the proposed amendments) in a privileged position compared with journalists in television or radio. The convergence of product (eg on-line newspapers) may make the differences in copyright ownership anomalous as traditional distinctions between print and electronic media become blurred.

(b) Part IV Copyrights

[7.5] The maker as owner. The first owner of copyright in other subject matter (recordings, films, broadcasts and published editions) is, subject to contrary agreement and the rights of the Crown, the 'maker' or publisher of the subject matter. As discussed in the previous chapter, this is separate from and additional to any copyright in works which are incorporated in the other subject matter.[29] Australian copyright law makes a basic distinction between 'works' and 'other subject matter', the former category encompassing the conventional scope of matter protected by copyright (books, plays, music and works of art but also including computer software), the latter category bringing entrepreneurial effort, rather than original

---

27. Ibid.
28. *Report on Journalists' Copyright*, 1994. See also J Borland and P L Williams, 'An Economic Analysis of the Division of Copyright between Newspaper Publishers and Journalists' (1993) 16 *UNSWLJ* 351.
29. *WEA Records Pty Ltd v Stereo FM Pty Ltd* (1983) 1 IPR 6 at 10.

authorship, within statutory protection. The owner of copyright in sound recordings, films and broadcasts is the person who makes them (ss 97(2), 98(2), 99). The maker of a recording is the owner of the first record embodying the recording (s 22(3)), usually a recording company; the maker of a film is the person who has arranged for it to be made (s 22(4)), usually the producer; and the maker of a broadcast is the ABC, SBS or relevant licence holder (s 22(5), (6)). The Copyright Convergence Group (CCG) recommended that reference to specific broadcasters be removed from the Copyright Act and provision made that the owner of copyright is the person making the broadcast (assuming them to be licensed to make it).[30] It was further recommended that the 'maker' of a broadcast be defined as the person who is responsible for the content of the broadcast and also makes the arrangements necessary for its transmission. Proposed amendments to s 22 to give effect to the recommendations are set out in the Exposure Draft Bill 1996.

In the case of commissioned recordings or films, the maker is displaced as owner by the commissioning person, though this is subject to agreement to the contrary (ss 97(3), 98(3)). Copyright in published editions is owned by the publisher (s 100).

(c) Joint Ownership

[7.6] The concept of joint ownership. This may arise from joint authorship, by agreement, assignment, will or devolution of law. A work of joint authorship is one that is 'produced by the collaboration of two or more authors and in which the contribution of each author is not separate from the contribution of the other author or the contributions of the joint authors' (s 10(1)). Not all jointly produced works result in joint authorship: for example, separate copyrights exist in the words and music respectively of a song (unless, of course, two or more persons produced them together in such a way as to come within the definition of joint authorship).[31] Someone who supplies ideas but has no input into its material form will not be a joint author,[32] unless there is an agreement to that effect.[33] The owners of a work of joint authorship take as tenants in common, any one of whom may sue in respect of an infringement and obtain an injunction and damages for a moiety without necessarily joining the other authors as plaintiffs.[34]

Copyright may be a partnership asset although it is not always easy to decide who owns copyright material produced by partners. Rather than leave it to be decided in court it may be best specifically to address the issue of ownership of copyrights so that it is not in doubt,[35] and also to determine the property, assets or effects of a business upon sale.[36]

30. Cf *Amalgamated Television Services Pty Ltd v Foxtel Digital Cable Television Pty Ltd* (1996) 34 IPR 274.
31. *Chappell & Co Ltd v Redwood Music Ltd* [1981] RPC 337.
32. *Donoghue v Allied Newspapers Ltd* [1938] Ch 106; *Tate v Thomas* [1921] 1 Ch 503; *Bartos v Scott* (1993) 26 IPR 27.
33. See eg *Prior v Lansdowne Press Pty Ltd* [1977] VR 65.
34. Ibid; *Acorn Computers Ltd v MCS Microcomputer Systems Pty Ltd* (1984) 4 IPR 214; *Dixon Projects Pty Ltd v Masterton Homes Pty Ltd* (1996) 36 IPR 136..
35. See *O'Brien v Komesaroff* (1982) 150 CLR 310.
36. See *Murray v King* (1984) 55 ALR 559.

(d) Crown Ownership of Copyright

[7.7] The special position of the Crown. Special provision is made for the Crown to own copyright in works, recordings or films 'made by or under the direction or control of, the Commonwealth or a State, as the case may be' (s 176(2)).[37] This is an extremely wide concept[38] and contemplates that Crown copyright may arise in material that does not otherwise fulfil the criteria of the Copyright Act as to the subsistence of copyright. Thus the nationality or residence of the author, or place of first publication, may be irrelevant if the subject matter is made 'under the direction or control of the Crown'. Similarly, the existence of an employment relationship may be irrelevant, as the phrase does not seem to be confined to situations where a contract of service exists, though of course copyright may arise in the usual way and belong to the Crown by virtue of s 35(6).[39]

The CLRC has not recommended any real changes to the Act in respect of computer software produced by or used by governments, except that programs should be acquired on the basis of 'normal commercial price' and other usual conditions.[40] The Australian Copyright Council had submitted that unauthorised use of software by government agencies may occur; however the CLRC decided that an overall review of ss 176–178 (concerning Crown copyright) was not appropriate within the particular reference. Computer programs and compilations thereof are excluded from the operation of a new statutory licensing scheme for government use of copyright material detailed in Sch 7 of the Exposure Draft Bill to amend the Copyright Act of February 1996.[41]

2. CONVEYANCE OF INTERESTS IN COPYRIGHT

[7.8] Disposal and divisibility. Since copyright is personal property it can be transmitted 'by assignment, by will and by devolution by operation of law' (s 196(1)). Future copyright[42] can also be assigned (s 197). For example, the authors of this book assigned copyright to the publisher before any part of it was written. Copyright is transmissible either as a whole, or in its different parts (s 196(2)), so that the author of a book may assign (or license) the right to publish a book to one company, and the right to make a film using a script based on the book to another. These rights may be further limited so as to apply to a place in or part of Australia (s 196(2)(c)). Furthermore, the class of acts which a copyright owner may sell or license to others is not limited to the exclusive rights set out in s 31(1): these may all be divided up further according to industry practice. Thus the right to publish a work may be subdivided into 'book rights'

---

37. Note that 'state' for this purpose includes the administration of a territory: s 10(3). See further [7.24] on Crown use of copyright material.
38. Cf *British Broadcasting Corp v Wireless League Gazette Publishing Co* [1926] Ch 433.
39. See *Director General of Education v Public Service Association of New South Wales* (1985) 4 IPR 552.
40. *Computer Software Protection*, rec 2.33.
41. See [7.24].
42. That is, copyright which is 'to come into existence at a future time or upon the happening of a future event' (s 10(1)).

(hardcover and paperback 'rights' may belong to separate companies) and newspaper and magazine rights.

A further example of splitting copyright up into separate components in order to exploit it more effectively is provided by the music industry, which has long recognised 'performing rights'.[43] The term 'performing right' is an industry expression denoting the non-dramatic rights of public performance, broadcasting and diffusion in relation to musical works. Typically, the author or publisher of a musical work (or arrangement or lyrics thereof) assigns these three rights to a collecting society,[44] which exercises these aspects of the copyright on behalf of the author or publisher. The partial assignment of copyright made to the collecting society in this example does not usually include the 'grand' or dramatic performance rights, as the author of music written for a ballet, opera, musical play or long choral work is usually able to control the use of material for such purposes. It is the fleeting and widespread use of musical works on radio, in shopping centres and many other venues which the collecting society can conveniently administer.

[7.9] Assignment of copyright. Assignments of copyright must be in writing, signed by or on behalf of the assignor (s 196(3)), though an informal assignment may be given effect in equity.[45] An assignment may be absolute or partial in nature: s 196(2) permits copyright to be assigned as to a particular place, or for a particular time, or as to some only of the acts which the assignor is entitled by the copyright to do. A person who acquires a limited copyright in this way is treated as the owner of a separate copyright for that particular purpose (s 30).[46] Future copyright may also be assigned, the relevant copyright vesting in the assignee or the assignee's successor on coming into existence, provided at that time no other has a better claim (s 197(1)).[47] Once an assignment takes effect the assignor, absent express provision to the contrary, is divested of any control over the copyright assigned. Thus, unless otherwise specified, the assignor has no greater right to infringe the copyright than any other person[48] and cannot prevent the assignee from further assigning or licensing all or part of the copyright or from altering the work or subject matter in any way. The introduction of moral rights may modify this ability of the 'new' owner to alter copyright material.[49] Part IX of the Act already constitutes an exception to

---

43. This is not to be confused with the performers' rights introduced by the Copyright Amendment Act 1989 (see [6.20]–[6.24]).
44. The Australasian Performing Rights Association, or APRA: see [22.8].
45. See eg *Acorn Computers Ltd v MCS Microcomputer Systems Pty Ltd* (1984) 4 IPR 214; *Robert J Zupanovich Pty Ltd v B & N Beale Nominees Pty Ltd* (1995) 32 IPR 339. For other examples of equitable interests in copyright, see eg *Photocrom Co Ltd v H & W Nelson Ltd* [1923–28] MacG Cop Cas 293; *Antocks, Lairn Ltd v L Bloohn Ltd* [1972] RPC 219; *A-One Accessory Imports Pty Ltd v Off Roads Imports Pty Ltd* (1996) 34 IPR 306.
46. With the exception of an assignee of rights within a part of a country, ss 30 and 196(2) not corresponding in this regard: see Ricketson, p 326.
47. As might be the case where there is a gratuitous assignment of future copyright to A, followed by an assignment for value of the same copyright to B: B, if acting in good faith, would have priority in equity in claiming the copyright when it came into existence.
48. Though cf s 72, which gives some protection to artists who draw on previous works in which they do not or no longer have the copyright: see [8.25].
49. See [5.14]–[5.15].

the existing principle, providing authors with rights in respect of false attribution of authorship. The right of attribution and a corresponding right against false attribution, along with the right of integrity, are the three moral rights to be introduced following the passing of the amendments set out in the Exposure Draft Bill to amend the Copyright Act, released in February 1996.

The author may also have a remedy in respect of defamation or misappropriation of business reputation.[50] It should also be noted that assignment in return for royalties may pose problems for the assignor where the assignee further assigns the copyright. While the original assignee may be liable in damages, the assignor, it would seem, has no rights against the further assignee.[51] Where copyright passes to the original assignee's trustee in bankruptcy, on the other hand, s 138 of the Bankruptcy Act 1966 (Cth) operates to protect the assignor's entitlement to royalties.

[7.10] Other transmissions. Copyright may be disposed of by will or may pass to another by operation of law, in the case for instance of intestacy or bankruptcy.[52] Two provisions should be noted. Under s 197(2), where copyright comes into existence after the death of the person who would otherwise have owned it, it devolves as if that person had owned it immediately before their death. Section 198 also provides that a bequest of an unpublished artistic work or of a manuscript of an unpublished literary, dramatic or musical work shall be presumed, unless a contrary intention appears, to include the copyright therein.[53]

3. VOLUNTARY LICENSING

[7.11] General. Licensing is a means of retaining an ongoing interest in the property which is licensed out, rather than the transfer of ownership and control which occurs when copyright is assigned. A licensee may be one of several authorised to deal with the copyright in the same way, although an exclusive licence is defined in s 10(1) as 'one authorising the licensee to do an act within the copyright to the exclusion of all other persons'.[54] Unlike an assignor of copyright, a licensor is free to limit the licensee's right to alter the licensed material.[55]

[7.12] Express licences. A licence granted by a copyright owner binds both the grantor and the grantor's successors in title, even as against a subsequent assignee (s 196(4)). The same applies to licences of future copyright (s 197(3)). It is not always easy to determine whether a given agreement is intended to be a licence or an assignment: the question is ultimately one of construction,[56] and even express words may not be

---

50. See Ricketson, pp 425–31.
51. See eg *Barker v Stickney* [1919] 1 KB 121.
52. As to partnership property, see *O'Brien v Komesaroff* (1982) 150 CLR 310.
53. Cf *Re Dickens* [1935] Ch 267.
54. Note that an agreement to give the exclusive 'distribution' rights in relation to articles containing copyright material does not, without more, create an exclusive licence in relation to copyright: *Avel Pty Ltd v Multicoin Amusements Pty Ltd* (1990) 171 CLR 88. Cf *Broderbund Software Inc v Computermate Products (Australia) Pty Ltd* (1991) 22 IPR 215.
55. Cf *Davidson v CBS Records* [1983] AIPC 90–106.
56. See eg *Wilson v Weiss Art Pty Ltd* (1995) 31 IPR 423.

determinative.[57] The distinction is important, the courts often being prepared to imply restrictions on a licensee that they would not impose on an assignee. Thus, for instance, a licence is usually construed as personal between the parties, so that its benefit may not be assigned by the licensee;[58] and the licensee may be restrained from altering the work in question.[59] A licence need not be in writing, unless it is an 'exclusive licence' as defined in s 10(1). Where the copyright is infringed, an exclusive licensee is entitled by s 119(a) to initiate proceedings under s 115 for an injunction, damages or an account of profits, except against the owner, as if the licence had been an assignment.[60] Where either the owner or exclusive licensee wish to bring an action under s 115, other than for interlocutory relief, the court's leave must be obtained unless the other is joined as a plaintiff or added as a defendant (s 120).[61] By contrast, only the exclusive licensee may bring an action under s 116 in respect of infringing copies, the owner having no concurrent right (s 119(b), (c)).

[7.13] Implied licences. A licence may also be implied from the circumstances in which the owner deals with the work or subject matter. Common examples relate to the use of architectural plans after the architect's engagement is terminated,[62] and to the repair of articles by purchasers without infringing copyright in the drawings from which they were made.[63] Such a licence will only be implied, however, where 'business efficacy' demands it.[64] It was argued in the *Journalists'* case[65] that publication of an article in a newspaper implies a licence for it to be published as part of material collected by a press clipping service. This was held not to be the case since there were no reasons of business efficacy compelling the implication of such a licence, the press-clipping service being provided by a third party, a commercial enterprise independent of the newspaper proprietor both in identity and activities. When the proprietor of the newspaper provides an electronic 'press clipping' service, however, the argument may have more force. In any event, the proposed amendments to s 35(4)

---

57. See eg *Messager v BBC* [1929] AC 151.
58. *Stevens v Benning* (1855) 1 K & J 168; 69 ER 414. Cf *Taylor v Neville* (1878) 47 LJ QB 254.
59. See *Frisby v BBC* [1967] Ch 932. Note that any adaptation of a work by a licensee may in itself attract copyright as an original work: see eg *Redwood Music Ltd v Chappell & Co Ltd* [1982] RPC 109.
60. Note also s 121, to the effect that any defence that would have been available against the owner may also be pleaded against the licensee. One effect is that the licensee is unable to sue anyone deriving title from the owner, such as another licensee.
61. Note that a party who is added as a defendant in this way but does not enter an appearance or take part in proceedings will not be liable for costs (s 125). See further ss 122–123 as to the assessment of damages and apportionment of profits recovered.
62. See eg *Beck v Montana Constructions Pty Ltd* [1964–5] NSWR 229; *Ng v Clyde Securities Ltd* [1976] 1 NSWLR 443; *Gruzman Pty Ltd v Percy Marks Pty Ltd* (1989) 16 IPR 87. Cf *Makeffy Perl Nagy Pty Ltd v Devefi Pty Ltd* (1992) 23 IPR 505.
63. See eg *Solar Thompson Engineering Co Ltd v Barton* [1977] RPC 537. See also *British Leyland Motor Corp Ltd v Armstrong Patents Co Ltd* [1986] 1 All ER 850; *Weir Pumps Ltd v CML Pumps Ltd* (1983) 2 IPR 129; *Green Cartridge Co (Hong Kong) Ltd v Canon Kabushiki Kaisha* (1996) 34 IPR 614.
64. Cf *Interstate Parcel Express Co Pty Ltd v Time-Life International (Nederlands) BV* (1977) 138 CLR 534 and other cases discussing this issue in the context of parallel importing: see [8.20].
65. *De Garis v Neville Jeffress Pidler Pty Ltd* (1990) 95 ALR 625: see [7.4].

refining the division of copyright as between journalist and proprietor were intended to address this point.[66]

[7.14]   Restraint of trade. Licences or assignments of future copyright may operate to restrict the activities of the creator of works over which no control can be exercised. If a songwriter or author of books gets tied up by one publisher, they may not be able to exploit their creative output in order to earn a living. In *Schroeder Music Publishing Co Ltd v Macaulay*[67] the defendants, music publishers, obtained the exclusive services of a songwriter for a period of at least five and possibly ten years, 'full copyright for the whole world' in anything he wrote being assigned to the publisher. The latter was not obliged to publish any music, although the plaintiff was unable to recover copyright in material which the defendant refused to publish. Similarly, in *O'Sullivan v Management Agency & Music Ltd*[68] Gilbert O'Sullivan, the pop singer and composer, had, as a young performer, entered into agreements with the defendants whereby they were to manage all the details of his musical output for a period of five years with an option to extend the arrangement for two more years if the defendants wished. O'Sullivan subsequently signed agreements with the defendants to extend the arrangements beyond this seven year period. The defendants gave exclusive rights in respect of recordings of O'Sullivan's music to EMI, in return for an advance of $US1.2 million to them. O'Sullivan had become more and more unhappy with his contractual arrangements, which prevented him controlling production of his recordings and exercising his own artistic judgment. He had also thought the effect of the contracts was to give him 50% ownership of his copyrights in a 'joint publishing' arrangement, rather than a total assignment.

In both these cases the agreements were held to be void and unenforceable because they were in restraint of trade, being unreasonably long in duration, thereby sterilising the creative output of both plaintiffs and preventing them exploiting their talents in their best interests. The financial arrangements between the parties were also disadvantageous to the songwriters. As well as being in restraint of trade the agreements were unfair from the plaintiff's point of view, the defendants having used their superior bargaining position to obtain unconscionable contracts. Although O'Sullivan said that no actual pressure had been exerted to make him sign the agreements, undue influence was to be presumed because of the special relationship between O'Sullivan and the defendants. They knew they were dealing with a young and inexperienced man who had relied on them entirely and had no independent legal advice. They knew they would not have been able to tie O'Sullivan so firmly to their organisation and get his services on such bargain basement terms if such advice had been given.[69]

Elton John and his lyricist Bernie Taupin found themselves in a similar situation when they were young and inexperienced and in fact minors. In 1967 they had entered into agreements assigning full copyright throughout

---

66. See [7.4].
67. [1974] 1 WLR 1308.
68. [1984] 3 WLR 448.
69. Although the agreements were struck down, it was held that the defendants should get an allowance for reasonable remuneration, including a profit element for all the work done in promoting O'Sullivan and his compositions.

the world in every musical composition written during the term of the agreement for the full period of the copyright. These agreements were renewed, and tied in with performing and recording contracts. It took some considerable time for the plaintiffs to realise that the agreements may have been unfavourable to them: in fact it was publicity over the *Schroeder* litigation that led them to seek legal advice in the early 1970s. In the meantime, the defendants had begun to erect a framework of subsidiary companies throughout the world, whereby the income stream to the main companies paying royalties to the plaintiffs was reduced, thus reducing their personal income. In this case the agreements themselves were not overturned. Although they constituted an unfair bargain in tying two young men at the beginning of their career to such an all-encompassing control of their work, the plaintiffs had in fact obtained sizeable benefits under the agreements. The unfair depletion of the source of income, however, was held to constitute a breach of fiduciary duty.[70] In 1994 the singer George Michael lost a case against Sony, his record company, in which he alleged that a 15 year exclusive commitment to them amounted to 'slavery' for the whole of his creative life. In fact the agreement had been signed in 1988 when he was at the height of his powers and the length of the contractual tie was within his control. Michael had actually negotiated higher advances and royalties for himself than previously, and had been aware of the terms and implications of the contracts. [71]

[7.15]   Restrictive practices legislation. Part IV of the Trade Practices Act regulates restrictive dealings affecting competition and prices. Various contractual or other arrangements are exempted from the operation of Pt IV, including restraints on employees as to their post-employment work (s 51(2)(a)) and there is an exception applying to licenses and assignments to the extent that provisions in such agreements relate to 'the work or other subject matter in which the copyright subsists' (s 51(3)(v)). This exception does not relate to ss 46 or 48 however, dealing with monopolisation and resale price maintenance. Moreover, controls over the licensing activities of a licensee appear not to be exempted from the operation of Pt IV and, since the exceptions do not cover monopolisation (s 46), some licensing activities may be caught. For example, the assignment of performance and broadcasting rights to a collecting society which negotiates with the users of such aspects of copyright may mean that the collecting society, due to the aggregation of assigned rights, 'has a substantial degree of power in a market' within the terms of s 46 and may well be in a position to deter competitive conduct and exercise significant power over those seeking to perform or broadcast copyright material.[72]

[7.16]   Consumer protection legislation. Licensors or sellers also need to be aware of the operation of Pt V of the Trade Practices Act, which implies terms relating, among other things, to the quality, fitness and suitability of 'goods' and 'services' supplied by a corporation to a 'consumer'.[73]

---

70. *Elton John v James* [1991] FSR 397.
71. *Panayiotou v Sony Music Entertainment (UK) Ltd* [1994] EMLR 229; see A Coulthard, 'George Michael v Sony Music — A Challenge to Artistic Freedom' (1995) 58 *MLR* 731.
72. See [22.30] ff for further discussion of trade practices issues.
73. For a full discussion of these terms, see J Goldring, L Maher and J McKeough, *Consumer Protection Law in Australia*, 4th ed, 1993, paras [217]–[221], [734].

Terms may also be implied into contracts by state legislation, including uniform sale of goods legislation, fair trading legislation, and credit Acts. This legislation is not hampered by the constitutional restrictions of the Trade Practices Act (which relies upon the corporations power in s 51(xx) of the Commonwealth Constitution to regulate the activities of 'corporations' engaged in 'trade or commerce'). Apart from the assignment and licensing of copyrights in works referred to in previous paragraphs, the work most frequently dealt with in a licensing agreement is computer software, the appropriate protection for which is copyright or the Circuit Layouts Act 1989, which is intended to protect the layout of integrated circuits with copyright style protection.[74] Furthermore, it has been held in New South Wales that software is 'goods, despite its inherent intellectual characteristics'.[75]

In many cases the prospective licensee will have sought the supplier's advice on the suitability of the licensed product (typically, software or a computer system) for the licensee's business, and on the general nature and functionality of the licensed product. A licensor or assignor affirming the specifications may be making representations which could bring into play the provisions of the state and federal legislation which implies warranties or conditions into contracts where a seller or licensor's expertise is relied upon. Furthermore, such assurances may amount to misleading, deceptive or even false representations with respect to the goods or services being supplied.

[7.17] Revocation of express and implied licences. Whether a licence can be revoked depends on its nature. Applying the general law relating to licences, it would seem that an exclusive licence, being a licence coupled with the grant of a proprietary interest, is irrevocable except in accordance with the terms expressly set out in the grant;[76] whereas a 'bare' licence is revocable at will.[77] In between these extremes are contractual licences. Although the position is far from clear, it appears that a licensor may be restrained from revoking the licence, or at least required to give reasonable notice, where there is a clear express or implied promise not to revoke.[78]

4. COMPULSORY LICENSING

[7.18] The statutory schemes. The Act in many instances permits acts to be done which would otherwise infringe copyright, on condition that a royalty be paid to the copyright owner. These compulsory licensing schemes relate to the following:

- copying by educational institutions or institutions assisting readers with a print disability or persons with an intellectual disability (ss 135ZJ–135ZM, 135ZP, 135ZS);

---

74. See Chapter 9.
75. *Toby Constructions Products Pty Ltd v Computer Bar Sales Pty Ltd* [1983] 2 NSWLR 48 at 54.
76. See *Chaplin v Leslie Frewin (Publishers) Ltd* [1966] Ch 71 at 94.
77. *Trumpet Software Pty Ltd v OzEmail Pty Ltd* (1996) 34 IPR 481.
78. *Computermate Products (Australia) Pty Ltd v Ozi-Soft Pty Ltd* (1988) 12 IPR 487 at 490. See Ricketson, pp 367–9; Lahore, *Copyright*, para [24,050] ff.

- recording of musical works (ss 54–64);
- broadcasting sound recordings or causing them to be heard in public (ss 108–109);
- recording or filming works for the purpose of ephemeral broadcast by another person, or copying such a recording (ss 47(3), 70(3), 107(3));
- copying of broadcasts by educational institutions or institutions assisting persons with an intellectual disability (ss 135A–135ZA);
- Crown use of copyright material (s 183).

Some of these schemes are considered in more detail below. The blank tape levy introduced by the Copyright Amendment Act 1989, but ruled unconstitutional by the High Court, would also have been regarded as a compulsory licence, which conferred the right of home taping in return for a levy or royalty paid at the point of sale and distributed by the relevant collecting society.[79]

A feature of many of the compulsory licensing schemes is the role played by the Copyright Tribunal. The Tribunal was established under Pt VI of the 1968 Act and its jurisdiction includes the fixing of royalties or equitable remuneration in respect of compulsory licenses and the power to arbitrate disputes in relation to the terms of the licences or proposed licensing schemes. The first time the Tribunal was called into action was late in 1977, to inquire into the royalty payable in respect of compulsory licensing of musical works.

[7.19] Photocopying by educational institutions. The Act was amended in 1980 to allow educational institutions, on payment of a royalty, to make multiple copies of certain works for the teaching purposes of the institution. Section 53B was inserted by the 1980 amendments following the recommendations of the Franki Committee, which investigated the extent of copying by means of reprographic reproduction (photocopying) and recommended, in effect, that if you can't beat them, join them, and ask for royalties.[80] Educational institutions were permitted to make multiple copies of periodical articles or other works for the teaching purposes of the institution, provided a record was kept of the material copied. The royalty paid in return for this copying was collected by the Copyright Agency Ltd (CAL), which was established in anticipation of the introduction of the compulsory licensing scheme set up in s 53B. CAL inspected records made by educational institutions and distributed the royalty to relevant copyright owners. The first such distribution was made early in 1989: CAL had collected $6.5 million after inspecting more than 185 million pages on record. The royalty was set at 2 cents per page copied in *Copyright Agency Ltd v Department of Education*,[81] a cooperative action between CAL and various Departments of Education brought as a test case before the Copyright Tribunal (Sheppard J).

79. See [6.41]–[6.42].
80. Cf *Haines v Copyright Agency Ltd* (1982) 64 FLR 184 (see [8.26]), which involved an attempt to use the fair dealing provisions of the Act to get around the compulsory licensing provisions. As to the role of CAL, see [22.11].
81. (1985) 59 ALR 172.

The record-keeping involved for s 53B photocopying proved to be extremely onerous and expensive both for CAL and the recording institutions. In 1987 CAL and educational bodies began entering into voluntary licences which bypassed the wholesale record-keeping and calculation of an actual royalty in favour of a per capita sum to be paid for each enrolled student, with revenue distributed according to a statistical sampling. The Australian Vice Chancellors Committee (AVCC), representing 38 universities throughout Australia, entered such an agreement with CAL and negotiations were also begun with audio and video copyright owners to reach an agreement in respect of off-air taping and copying of broadcast material. The Copyright Amendment Act 1989 streamlined the existing licences to educational institutions to photocopy works. The cumbersome and expensive scheme under s 53B was replaced by ss 135ZH–135ZM, which facilitate the voluntary arrangements previously negotiated and allow a choice between full record-keeping or per capita payments. If record-keeping is chosen, CAL no longer has to inspect records on site as institutions will be obliged to send them to CAL for assessment. The licensing scheme has worked well on the whole, and from licensing educational copying CAL has extended licensing activities to churches, businesses, motels, law firms and government departments, as well as to 'administrative' copying in universities and schools. 'The ultimate aim of CAL's licensing department is to license all organisations across Australia that copy copyright works.'[82]

At present s 135ZM allows educational institutions to photocopy artwork which illustrates or explains text that is copied for educational purposes under the relevant statutory licence. This provision is being reviewed by the government, along with other special exceptions allowing the use of artistic works without permission.[83] The repeal or amendment of s 135ZM was recommended in the Simpson Report,[84] along with the declaration of a new collecting society, VI$COPY, to administer the rights granted under a suggested new statutory licence for the reproduction by educational institutions of artistic works which accompany text. The sampling in educational institutions of use of artistic works will probably be undertaken by CAL.[85]

Publishers of university textbooks have become alarmed at what they call 'anthologising' of parts of different works into sets of course materials. Although the multiple copying licence allows precisely this (within limits as to how much of a particular work may be copied), CAL sued a university on the basis that these 'anthologies' in the bookshop took the copying outside the licence. It was held that the cost of the materials to the students was based on cost recovery and not for 'a financial profit' within the meaning of s 135ZZH.[86] The fact is that CAL members, the publishers who own the relevant copyrights, are wary of the effects of copying on the sale of books. Of course, the distribution of licence fees collected by CAL is intended to compensate for this loss of sales of the texts.

CAL is currently negotiating with universities to provide for the regulation of 'electronic copying', storing text in digital form in photocopiers

82. CAL Newsletter, 'New Directions for Licensing', March 1994, p 1.
83. See [8.31].
84. Simpson, pp 2–5, 264–270.
85. Ibid, p 269.
86. *Copyright Agency Ltd v Victoria University of Technology* (1995) 30 IPR 140.

which scan printed works for storage before reproduction as printed material. Libraries wishing to supply their 'reserve' collection of material stored in this way and disseminated to another computer in a network will do away with long queues of students lining up for hard copies (which may be printed for them, if required, by the new machines).

[7.20] Audio-visual copying. The 1989 amendments also established a statutory licensing scheme to allow educational institutions or institutions assisting persons with an intellectual disability to make off-air copies of television programs to be shown at a more convenient time, and to be retained for repeated use (ss 135A–135ZA). A payment to copyright owners is made through the Audio Visual Collecting Society (AVCS),[87] which arranges for the disparate copyrights in the script, sound recording, background music, film and broadcast to be licensed for the educational use envisaged by the scheme. As with the photocopying schemes, payment may be by way of an amount per student or handicapped person, or according to actual material copied based on full record-keeping.

[7.21] Proposed amendments: 1996 Exposure Draft Bill. It is worth noting that various amendments relating to the administration of the statutory licences discussed above were put forward prior to the 1996 federal election in the Exposure Draft Bill. For the most part, the proposed amendments are minor and designed to streamline the operation of the licences relating to the copying of works by institutions (Sch 9) and the process of declaring institutions subject to the educational compulsory licence (Sch 12). Schedule 8 of the Exposure Draft Bill contains amendments aimed at clarifying the Act's provisions affecting people with print or intellectual disability. Where the Act presently uses the terms 'intellectually handicapped person' or 'handicapped readers' the language used is to change to 'persons with an intellectual disability' and 'persons with a print disability' respectively. Some of the distinctions between relevant copyright licences are also removed to give somewhat greater access to copyright material for readers with a print disability.

[7.22] Musical works. Another important and widely exercised statutory licence is that in respect of the recording of musical works (ss 54–64). The provisions are detailed and complex, but in practice the system operates under an industry-wide agreement between the Australian Music Publishers Association Ltd (AMPAL) and the Australian Record Industry Association (ARIA). The compulsory licence applies to making records for retail sale but does not extend to the use of music in films. This use of materials is negotiated and licensed by the Australasian Mechanical Copyright Owners' Society (AMCOS). Record making is described as an exercise of the 'mechanical right' in the copyright in musical works. The effect of the compulsory licence is that the mechanical rights may be exercised without the composer's permission, once a musical work has been made or imported into Australia for retail sale. The initial recording of the work does, however, require the copyright owner's licence.[88]

87.　See [22.12].
88.　See S Simpson and G Stevens, *Music: The Business and The Law*, 1986, pp 74–5, 93–9 for a summary of the mechanical rights compulsory licence.

[7.23] Lending rights. Although a writer, illustrator or other owner of copyright in a book can prevent the unauthorised reproduction of their work, copyright protection does not extend to further control of the physical item once a work (or a lawfully made copy of it) has been sold. Thus the Copyright Act gives no control over the lending out of books by libraries (or individuals, for that matter). The organised borrowing system in which libraries engage is of no financial benefit to an author or publisher, apart from revenue generated by the original sale, so that multiple users of a book may benefit without authors or publishers receiving a correlative return. To remedy this, a Public Lending Right Committee was established by s 5 of the Public Lending Council Amendment Act 1976 (Cth). The Public Lending Right Act 1985 (Cth) established a statutory basis for the scheme, administered by the Department of Arts, Heritage and Environment. The present scheme came into effect on 1 July 1987 and is administered by the Public Lending Right Committee, constituted by representatives of authors, publishers and libraries including the National Library of Australia. The Committee determines the eligibility of claimants for payment under the scheme. An eligible claimant may be anyone involved in the 'creation' of a book, including authors, illustrators, translators, editors or others. Publishers may also be eligible. All claimants must be Australian citizens or residents or, in the case of publishers, persons whose business consists mainly of book publishing and who regularly publish in Australia. Not all books are eligible under the scheme: they must have at least 48 pages of printed material, except that a book of poetry, drama or a children's work need have only 24 pages. If there are more than three creators or the book is a serial, magazine or annual book, the publication is not an eligible book for the purposes of the scheme.

The public lending right (PLR) applies only in respect of loans of books from public libraries. An educational lending right (ELR) was to have been introduced (from October 1995) to operate in respect of university and school libraries. However, the number of ELR claimants far exceeded expectations and in August 1996 the Howard Government announced that in light of funding constraints the scheme would be scrapped and no payments made. The government was able to take this decision executively since the ELR scheme had only ever been established on an administrative rather than legislative basis. The government also announced that it intends to amend the PLR scheme to cease payments to descendants of deceased creators and to limit payments to books published in the last 25 years.

Sound recordings are also lent out by libraries, and the renting of films on video has become a boom industry in recent years, particularly as Australia has one of the highest levels of video cassette recorder ownership in the world. The blank tape royalty scheme was introduced to compensate the owners of sound recording copyright for home taping,[89] and may soon be reintroduced by way of a taxing measure. Under the TRIPS Agreement legislation for an exclusive rental right for sound recordings was required and introduced by the Copyright (World Trade Organization Amendments) Act 1994, which inserts a new right of commercial rental arrangement with respect to literary, musical and dramatic works reproduced in a

---

89. This does not, of course, cover the lending out of tapes or records by libraries.

sound recording. Section 85 has also been amended to add paragraph (d) which confers a commercial rental right in respect of sound recordings purchased after the commencement of the amending legislation. The Copyright (World Trade Organization Amendments) Act 1994 also introduced a commercial rental right with respect to computer programs as one of the exclusive rights in s 31 of the Copyright Act (s 31(1)(d)). The amendments ensure in s 31(3) that the copyright owner does not have the right to control rental of a copy of a computer program embodied in a machine or device such as a car or washing machine: in other words the program itself must be the essential object of the rental, not the goods in which the program operates, nor the media normally used for storage of computer programs.

[7.24] Crown use of copyright material. Section 183 provides for Crown use of copyright material, allowing a form of statutory licence for government (Commonwealth, state or territory) use of works and other subject matter in circumstances which would otherwise constitute infringement. The Commonwealth in particular is an extremely large user of copyright materials because of the extensive range of functions discharged by various departments and authorities. Where the use of copyright material is 'for the services of' the Crown it will not infringe copyright in that material (s 183(1)). However, the government must, as soon as possible (unless contrary to the public interest) inform the owner of the copyright of the doing of the act and furnish the owner with information which the owner may reasonably require (s 183(4)). The terms of the doing of the act are to be agreed upon between the Crown and the copyright owner, or, in default of agreement, fixed by the Copyright Tribunal (s 183(5)).

The meaning of the phrase 'for the services of the Crown' is not entirely clear but some guidance has been given in decided cases. In *Allied Mills Industries Pty Ltd v Trade Practices Commission*[90] Sheppard J held that the use by the TPC of documents owned by the plaintiffs in preparation for court proceedings was 'for the services of' the Commonwealth.[91] The phrase has also been considered in the context of the use of patented inventions.[92] In *Pfizer Corporation v Minister for Health*[93] the supply of drugs to patients in National Health Service hospitals in Britain was held to be a use 'for the services of the Crown':

> It appears that the natural meaning of use 'for the services of the Crown' is use by members of such services in the course of their duties. Sometimes, as in the case of the armed services, that use will or is intended to benefit the whole community; sometimes such use will benefit a particular section of the community; and sometimes it will benefit particular individuals. I cannot see any good reason for making a distinction between one such case and another.[94]

---

90. (1981) 34 ALR 105 at 147.
91. Cf *Reference by APRA Ltd; Re Australian Broadcasting Commission* (1982) 45 ALR 153 where it was held that radio and television broadcasts conducted by the ABC were not done 'for the services of the Crown'; the Commission, in any event, was not held to be 'the Commonwealth' for the purposes of s 183.
92. See [13.22].
93. [1965] AC 512.
94. Ibid at 535.

In short, 'for the services of' the Crown covers, at the very least, activities by government employees performed in the ordinary course of their employment. By way of further guidance, it is considered that the following are examples of acts which may be done 'for the services' of the Commonwealth:

- copying of materials by government employees for training purposes or seminars;
- copying of materials for inclusion in Departmental reports, submissions or briefing; and
- copying in response to requests from members of the public for information.

It should also be recognised that an act done 'for the services of' the Commonwealth by a person *authorised* by the Commonwealth will also fall within the statutory licence under s 183. Importantly, that authority may be given *before or after* the doing of the relevant act (s 183(3)), but the copyright owner is to be informed 'as soon as possible' in the prescribed form.[95] If the name or address of the copyright owner is unknown, notification in the *Gazette* is sufficient.

A further obligation imposed on the Crown by s 183 is that, when an act has been done under the section, the 'terms' for the doing of the act are to be agreed between the parties or fixed by the Copyright Tribunal. The word 'term' is not defined by the Act. However, it is clear that it would cover any conditions attached to the use of the relevant material by the Commonwealth. Most importantly, it covers the amount to be paid to the copyright owner by the Commonwealth (if requested) for that use.[96] In practice, a standard fee (depending on the type of material) is offered to copyright owners for the use of their material, and those who object receive a letter pointing out the provisions of the Copyright Act as to the Crown's right to use material. It is frequently the case that technology developed by private companies for Crown use, perhaps in defence,[97] will have applications in industry beyond that classified as 'for the purposes of the Crown'. In such a case the Commonwealth's claims to such manufactured products and information often go beyond what is normally expected in private commercial transactions, because defence clearly has strategic and security interests of central relevance to the purposes of the Commonwealth. Nevertheless it is possible to confine Crown use to these purposes, retaining the right to commercialise the intellectual property and enhancements to it privately.[98]

The CLRC in May 1995, reporting on computer software protection referred to concerns in relation to the operation of s 183 and a submission to the effect that the section not apply to computer programs or compilations of computer programs. The Committee endorsed its draft

95. See Copyright Regulations reg 25.
96. See eg *Re Application by Seven Dimensions Pty Ltd* (1996) 35 IPR 1, which was said (at 18) to be the first case under s 183 in which a decision had to be reached by the Tribunal, previous cases having been settled.
97. Which will probably not be protected by copyright, in fact, but rather patent, design or integrated circuit legislation.
98. See J Gilchrist, 'How to Protect Intellectual Property', *Australian Business*, 3 October 1990, p 56.

recommendation that s 183 be amended to provide that copying for government purposes should be restricted to situations where a copy of the program is not available from an authorised source within a reasonable time and at a reasonable price.[99] The provisions relating to Crown use of copyright material generally have been under review for some time, and federal and state governments have in fact entered into agreements for licensing of copying done by government departments. Released in February 1996, the Exposure Draft Bill to amend the Copyright Act provides in Sch 7 amendments 'to implement the Government's decision of March 1994 to streamline the system for owners of copyright works to be paid for the copying of their works by the Government and the subsequent decision to introduce similar amendments for copyright owners of audio-visual materials'.[100] Computer programs are specifically excluded from the scheme. The proposed amendments are largely based on the statutory licence for educational institutions, and provide for a collecting society to be declared by the Copyright Tribunal to administer the scheme of sampling, collection and distribution of payments, much according to existing practice.

---

99. *Computer Software Protection*, rec 2.33, discussed at paras [10.119]–[10.122].
100. Explanatory memorandum to the Exposure Draft Bill, February 1996, para [152].

Chapter 8

Infringement of Copyright

---

1. ESTABLISHING INFRINGEMENT

[8.1]   Direct and indirect infringement. It is an infringement of copyright for any person other than the copyright owner to do any of the things a copyright owner is exclusively entitled to do in respect of the work or other subject matter, unless permission has been granted to perform such acts (ss 36(1), 101(1)). The bundle of exclusive rights encompassed in copyright are enumerated in s 31(1) with respect to works and in ss 85–88 with respect to other subject matter. Thus copying, publishing, performing, broadcasting or adapting a work may be an infringement,[1] as is also transmitting it by cable. Authorising any of these acts also amounts to infringement. In respect of Pt IV copyrights, copying, performing or broadcasting sound recordings, films or broadcasts constitutes infringement, as also does transmitting films by cable. A published edition of a work is only infringed by a reproduction of the edition being made 'by a means that includes a photographic process' (s 88). The effect of a new right of 'transmission', and the upgrading of moral rights as proposed in the Exposure Draft Bill to amend the Copyright Act of February 1996, are also considered in this chapter.

The doing of an act comprised in the copyright is termed a 'direct' infringement. No intention to infringe need be established: a person is still liable if they act in innocence of the plaintiff's copyright.[2] By contrast, certain other 'indirect' infringements do require actual or constructive knowledge of wrongdoing. These occur when infringing articles are imported

---

1.   Note that copyright in an artistic work is not infringed by a 'performance' or an adaptation thereof.
2.   See eg *Andritz Srout-Bauer Australia Pty Ltd v Rowland Engineering Sales Pty Ltd* (1993) 28 IPR 29. Cf P Hastie, 'The Concept of Subconscious Copying: Substantive Law and an Evidentiary Notion' (1995) 6 *AIPJ* 16.

into Australia for trade purposes (ss 37, 102), or sold or otherwise dealt with by way of trade (ss 38, 103); or when a place of public entertainment is allowed to be used for an infringing public performance of a literary, dramatic or musical work (s 39(1)). In 1992 legislation drafted to repeal the requirement of 'knowledge' in respect of parallel importing was not passed (it lapsed due to the calling of the 1993 federal election), but may be reintroduced in the future.[3]

(a) Direct Infringement of Works

[8.2] Reproduction and substantiality. The term 'reproduction' is not defined in the Act, although s 21 does provide that a reproduction of a literary, dramatic or musical work includes a recording or film thereof, and that an artistic work can be reproduced in another dimension.[4] The question of whether a 'work' copyright has been reproduced requires an assessment of the qualitative aspects of the alleged reproduction. The Act provides that a reference to the doing of an act (other than publication) comprised in a copyright includes a reference to the doing of that act in relation to a substantial part of the material (s 14). Thus it is an infringement to reproduce only part of a work, so long as that part is 'substantial'. The concept of a 'substantial part' has been defined by the courts primarily in reference to the quality of what is taken. Accordingly, infringement will be found when an important part of a work is used even if, in terms of quantity, that part is only small.[5] Similarly, 'if the part taken represents the application of a high degree of skill and labour on the part of the author, it may be regarded as substantial although comparatively slight in quantitative terms'.[6] On the other hand, infringement will not occur if an unoriginal part of a work is taken, even if substantial in terms of quantity.[7]

For most works, a 'reproduction' must be recognisable as a copy of the work; there must be 'objective similarity' between the work and the alleged copy and there must be a causal connection between the two. This causes problems when the work is a computer program and in electronic form. Despite apparent acceptance by some judges that object code can be a

---

3. See Copyright Amendment Bill 1992. Minor amendments relating to imported copies of copyright material are proposed in the Exposure Draft Bill of February 1996, but they are of an administrative nature and do not affect the substance of the provisions.

4. Before the Copyright Amendment Act 1989, s 21 was qualified by s 71 which provided a 'non-expert' defence, so that a reproduction of an artistic work in another dimension would not infringe the work unless a non-expert would be able to see the reproduction as having been derived from the work. The object of the defence was to prevent complicated machinery and the like from gaining copyright protection, even if not qualifying for design registration. This was repealed by the Copyright Amendment Act 1989, but had been rendered fairly innocuous by the High Court before that time: see *S W Hart & Co Pty Ltd v Edwards Hot Water Systems* (1985) 159 CLR 466; and see further [10.25].

5. *Hawkes & Son (London) Ltd v Paramount Film Service Ltd* [1934] 1 Ch 593; *Walt Disney Productions v H John Edwards Publishing Co Pty Ltd* (1954) 71 WN (NSW) 150.

6. Ricketson, p 170. See eg *Blackie & Sons Ltd v Lothian Book Publishing Co Pty Ltd* (1921) 29 CLR 396; *Autodesk Inc v Dyason* (1992) 173 CLR 330; (1993) 176 CLR 300.

7. *Klissers Bakeries v Harvest Bakeries* (1985) 5 IPR 533; *Dixon Investments Pty Ltd v Hall* [1990] AIPC 90–714.

'reproduction' of underlying source code, lingering doubts concerning this, based on the reasoning in the *Apple* case,[8] are to be put to rest by the majority recommendation of the Copyright Law Review Committee (CLRC) in its final report on the protection of software that a definition of 'reproduction' be included in the Copyright Act to clarify the situation. The definition is to be inclusive rather than exhaustive: accordingly, a 'reproduction' is to include the converting of a work from a form legible to humans to electronic form, and the converse.[9]

The question of reproduction of a computer program was discussed at length in *Autodesk Inc v Dyason*.[10] At first instance Northrop J held that a device ('Autokey') which reproduced the function of a program hardware lock (designed to protect a program called AutoCAD) was a reproduction of the lock, having regard to the reference to 'function' in the definition of computer program. The Full Federal Court rejected this approach, on the basis that there was no objective similarity between the devices, the Autokey lock on the one hand and AutoCAD on the other. The High Court reversed the appeal decision, on the basis that there was an infringement of copyright not in the lock itself, but in the look-up table of one component of the AutoCAD program (Widget C) by the reproduction of its 127 bit sequence in an EPROM of the Autokey lock. There has been much criticism of the *Autodesk* decision. On the issue of 'reproduction' the CLRC in its final report indicated that:

> the conclusion that the look-up table was a substantial part of the Widget C program, with the result that copying of the look-up table constituted copying of the program, causes the Committee some concern. Further, the conclusion that the creation of the look-up table in Autokey from observation of the operation of Widget C and the AutoCAD lock was a copying of the look-up table in Widget C, even though the maker of Autokey (Mr Kelly) never saw the table, is also viewed by the Committee as a far-reaching and questionable extension of copyright.[11]

Professor Lahore suggests that:

> To put the argument in a different form, the question is whether it would be an infringement of copyright in a railway timetable to stand on a station and observe and write down the times of train arrivals and departures, assuming that those times were the same as those printed in the timetable. This is in essence what Kelly did in relation to the output from the lock. To assert infringement in such a case is to confer a monopoly in the information.[12]

The proposed solution is to recommend prohibition of the manufacture, importation, dealing with or possession for commercial purposes of devices designed to facilitate the unauthorised circumvention of locks or other devices applied to protect computer programs from unauthorised copying.[13] Furthermore, decompilation to defeat program locks will also be prohibited, ruling out modification of a locked computer program for the purpose of circumventing the lock and copying of such modified programs.[14]

---

8.   See [9.9]–[9.12].
9.   *Computer Software Protection*, para [6.55].
10. (1992) 173 CLR 330; (1993) 176 CLR 300. See further [9.13]–[9.16].
11. *Computer Software Protection*, para [5.25].
12. J Lahore, 'Intellectual Property Rights and Unfair Copying: Old Concepts, New Ideas' [1992] 12 *EIPR* 428 at 432.
13. *Computer Software Protection*, para [2.73].
14. Ibid, para [2.29].

[8.3] Degree of similarity. The degree of similarity required between the copyright material and that which infringes it without being identical requires a subjective assessment by the judge as to whether 'copying' has occurred. In *Zeccola v Universal City Studios Inc*,[15] in deciding whether a film version *(Great White)* of a book or screenplay of the movie *Jaws* infringed copyright, 'His Honour, with some degree of fortitude, viewed both films, one after the other'[16] and decided that the marked degree of similarity led to an inescapable inference of copying. In *Corelli v Gray*[17] the author of a novel alleged her copyright had been infringed by a dramatic sketch. Sargant J looked at the striking aggregate of similarities between the sketch and the novel and decided that this indicated copying by the defendant. Although the events in the novel were not very distinctive or original,

> the combination of these ordinary materials may nevertheless be original, and when such a combination has arrived at a certain degree of complexity it becomes practically impossible that it should have been arrived at independently by a second individual.[18]

One type of case that poses some difficulty in this regard is where the allegedly infringing work is a parody of the plaintiff's work. A parody must of its nature draw heavily on another work; typically indeed, the greater the similarity, the more effective the parody can be. Yet to jump too readily to the conclusion that a parody infringes copyright in the original work would be to stifle what is sometimes (though by no means always) a valuable form of expression, especially where the parody has satirical purposes. The US courts have for the most part been prepared to address this issue in terms of the principle of 'fair use', the US equivalent of the Australian defence of 'fair dealing'.[19] Australian and English judges, by contrast, have denied that there is any special principle applicable to parodies: 'the statute grants no exemption, in terms, in the case of works of parody or burlesque'.[20] There has certainly been a willingness to avoid finding infringement where the defendant has expended considerable effort in creating what is plainly itself an original work,[21] or where the defendant has done no more than 'evoke' or 'conjure up' a recollection of the original.[22] Nevertheless, the issue remains whether a 'substantial part' has been taken, when arguably broader considerations of freedom of expression and moral rights should be determinative.[23]

[8.4] Musical works. Musical works will be assessed aurally in deciding whether an alleged infringement possesses the requisite degree of objective similarity. The impression on the ear is what counts, not a note for note

15. (1982) 46 ALR 189.
16. Ibid at 194. Note that it was the literary copyright in the novel or screenplay of *Jaws* that was infringed here, not the 'film' copyright: see [8.14].
17. (1913) 29 TLR 570.
18. Ibid at 571. See also *Hexagon Pty Ltd v Australian Broadcasting Commission* (1975) 7 ALR 233.
19. See eg *Fisher v Dees* (1986) 794 F 2d 432. As to 'fair dealing', see [8.26], [8.28].
20. *AGL Sydney Ltd v Shortland County Council* (1989) 17 IPR 99 at 105.
21. See eg *Joy Music Ltd v Sunday Pictorial Newspapers (1920) Ltd* [1960] 2 QB 60.
22. See eg *Williamson Music Ltd v Pearson Partnership* [1987] FSR 97. Cf *AGL Sydney Ltd v Shortland County Council* (1989) 17 IPR 99.
23. See M Weir, 'Making Sense of Copyright Law Relating to Parody: A Moral Rights Perspective' (1992) 18 *Monash ULR* 194.

comparison.[24] Popular music is particularly vulnerable to attack on the grounds of copyright infringement due to the adoption of similar styles, drawing from a common musical tradition, and the use of 'common tricks of composition'.[25] The authorities indicate that the similarities in much popular music can be put down to coincidence.[26] That is not true, on the other hand, of digital sampling, a staple effect in modern dance music in particular. Modern recording technology allows musicians and producers to 'sample' portions (ranging from a single note to an entire vocal or instrument track) of an earlier recording, digitally encode the selected portion and then insert it (with or without modifications) into a new recording. Whether such deliberate copying requires authorisation from the holder of the various copyrights in the earlier recording and the work(s) embodied in it depends once again on whether a 'substantial' part has been taken, something which may be far from easy to determine.[27]

[8.5] Artistic works. The test to be applied in deciding infringement of an artistic work is purely visual, the work and alleged infringement 'being compared *oculis subjecta fidelibus'*.[28] The fundamental rule of copyright law is that form is protected but not content.[29] If it is not possible to take the content of a work without also adopting the form then in theory there can be no infringement.[30] Taking ideas is not prohibited by copyright law, only the copying of their expression. Thus, the idea of 'Donald Duck' and three nephews (Huey, Dewey and Louie) involved in adventures with a dog (Goofy) and a donkey (Basil) was not necessarily infringed by a comic featuring 'Superduck', a duckling, dog and donkey engaged in similar escapades, unless the drawings of these characters were actually copied.[31] This approach has often been applied where infringement of architectural plans is alleged: the absorption of an architectural concept and application of ideas to a later plan is not infringement.[32]

[8.6] Establishing a causal link. Apart from similarity of subject matter (however subjectively assessed), there must be a causal link between the defendant's article and the plaintiff's work, since independent creation

24. *Francis Day & Hunter Ltd v Bron* [1963] Ch 587.
25. I Brown, 'Sounds Familiar? The *"Chariots of Fire"* Case' [1987] 8 *EIPR* 224.
26. See *Francis Day & Hunter Ltd v Bron* [1963] Ch 587.
27. See further P Keyzer, 'The Protection of Digital Samples Under Australian Intellectual Property Law' (1993) 4 *AIPJ* 127.
28. *King Features Syndicate Inc v O & M Kleeman Ltd* [1941] AC 417 at 435; *Walt Disney Productions v H John Edwards Publishing Co Pty Ltd* (1954) 71 WN (NSW) 150.
29. See [6.1] ff.
30. *Kenrick & Co Ltd v Lawrence & Co Ltd* (1890) 25 QBD 99; but cf *Independent Television Publications Ltd v Time Out* [1984] FSR 64; *Elanco Products v Mandops Ltd* [1979] FSR 46; *John Fairfax & Sons Ltd v Australian Consolidated Press Ltd* (1959) 60 SR (NSW) 413.
31. *Walt Disney Productions v H John Edwards Publishing Co Pty Ltd* (1954) 71 WN (NSW) 150.
32. *Anchor, Mortlock, Murray & Woolley Pty Ltd v Hooker Homes Pty Ltd* (1971) 20 FLR 481. See also *Beck v Montana Constructions Pty Ltd* (1963) 80 WN (NSW) 1578; *Inala Industries Pty Ltd v Associated Enterprises Pty Ltd* [1960] Qd R 562; *Lend Lease Homes Pty Ltd v Warrigal Homes Pty Ltd* [1970] 3 NSWR 265; *Half Court Tennis Pty Ltd v Seymour* (1980) 53 FLR 240; cf *LED Builders Pty Ltd v Masterton Homes (NSW) Pty Ltd* (1994) 30 IPR 447; (1996) 33 IPR 417; *Robert J Zupanovich Pty Ltd v B & N Beale Nominees Pty Ltd* (1995) 32 IPR 339.

does not infringe copyright.[33] If the works are objectively similar, however, a presumption of copying may arise which the defendant then has to rebut.[34] It should also be noted that copying need not be direct: the infringer may for instance copy something which is itself a copy of the relevant work, even if the intermediate work is in a different dimension to the original. This sort of 'indirect copying' is particularly important where artistic works are concerned. Thus a dress copied from another dress could conceivably infringe copyright in a sketch of the garment, even if the infringer has never seen the artistic work on which the garment was based.[35]

[8.7] Copyright infringement and mass-produced items. Somewhat controversially, the concept of indirect copying has been used to make the 'reverse engineering' of functional items unlawful, even though three-dimensional objects do not possess copyright in their own right unless qualifying as 'works of artistic craftsmanship'.[36] An important provision in this regard is s 21(3), which provides that the production of a three-dimensional version of a two-dimensional artistic work is deemed to be a reproduction of that work (and vice versa, where a two-dimensional version is produced of a three-dimensional work). This means that copyright in drawings or plans may be infringed by the creation of the item shown in those drawings or plans — even if the item in question is not itself an artistic work (as it would not be, unless it were a work of artistic craftsmanship).

The notion of indirect copying was first fully articulated in 1963 in the case of *Dorling v Honnor Marine Ltd*,[37] where it was held that building a boat copied from a model of another boat, the model being a reproduction of the plans for the original boat, infringed artistic copyright in those plans. Many similar cases have followed as manufacturers have sought to protect themselves from clever competitors. Thus reverse engineering a car exhaust system may infringe copyright in the drawings of that system;[38] and reproducing a solar hot water system infringed copyright in the design drawings.[39] A verbal or written communication may also be the medium through which copyright in drawings is infringed by the making of an item according to the instructions given. In *House of Spring Gardens Ltd v Point Blank Ltd*[40] a bullet-proof vest was copied by means of a verbal description being given to a designer (through a third party, who had been told about the vest by the intending infringer, who had himself seen it made up from the copyright drawings). In *Frank M Winstone (Merchants) Ltd v Plix Products Ltd*,[41] the Court of Appeal of New Zealand confirmed that indirect copying can be perpetrated through the medium of a verbal description of a copyright work, in that case plastic trays in which kiwifruit were packed for

33. See eg *CCOM Pty Ltd v Jiejing Pty Ltd* (1993) 27 IPR 577.
34. *Francis Day & Hunter Ltd v Bron* [1963] Ch 587; *Corelli v Gray* (1913) 29 TLR 570.
35. *Burke & Margot Burke Ltd v Spicers Dress Designs* [1936] Ch 400.
36. See [6.32].
37. [1965] Ch 1.
38. *British Leyland Motor Corp Ltd v Armstrong Patents Co Ltd* [1986] 2 WLR 400; but see further [10.24] ff.
39. *S W Hart and Co Pty Ltd v Edwards Hot Water System* (1985) 159 CLR 466.
40. [1985] FSR 327.
41. (1985) 5 IPR 156. See also *LED Builders Pty Ltd v Eagle Homes Pty Ltd* (1996) 35 IPR 215.

export. The Kiwifruit Marketing Authority made it a requirement that exported kiwifruit be packed in these trays. The defendant, wishing to manufacture these green plastic trays, had obtained the specifications from the Authority and instructed a designer to design a tray fitting the specifications. After some 200 hours of work the defendant's tray pack was ready to go into production, but the tray was held to infringe the plaintiff's artistic copyright — their drawings, patterns and moulds. The expression of the idea had been taken, not just the idea itself.

[8.8] Restricting protection for functional items: the link to designs protection. The extension of copyright protection to mass-produced items has been regarded by many as undesirable. The long term of protection conferred by copyright, along with uncertainty as to its subsistence and duration, is thought to make it inappropriate for products for commercial use. The Copyright Act therefore attempts to cut down this sort of protection for such items by providing that artistic works used as designs for mass-produced items lose copyright protection in certain circumstances.[42] Until 1989 there had been an anomaly in this scheme, in that plans, blueprints and construction drawings which did not qualify for registration under the Designs Act 1906 (Cth) (which requires that a design be new or original and have a certain appeal to the eye)[43] had been left fully protected by copyright. However, the Copyright Amendment Act 1989 removed copyright protection for all three-dimensional mass-produced items and the drawings, etc on which they are based, whether or not the latter are registrable under the designs legislation.[44]

More recently, the Australian Law Reform Commission (ALRC) has proposed in the course of its review of the Designs Act that a new approach be adopted.[45] This would involve the repeal of s 21(3) and the enactment of new provisions to ensure that in most instances it would *not* be an infringement of copyright to reproduce a two-dimensional artistic work in three-dimensional form. At the same time, copyright in an artistic work would be extended to include an adaptation right. But this would only cover the making of a three-dimensional version which was *itself* an artistic work, which most functional items are not. Hence 'a sculpture made from a drawing of a sculpture would infringe copyright but a pump made from an engineering drawing would not'.[46] This proposal is discussed further in Chapter 10.

[8.9] The 'spare parts' exception. Similar concerns with the anti-competitive potential of copyright protection have prompted English courts to place restrictions on the reach of the principle of indirect copying. Thus it has been established that reverse engineering of spare parts must be possible to some extent in order to allow 'fair repair' and that this will not constitute copyright or patent infringement.[47] Orthodox authorities state that the line between repair and creating a new article altogether must not be crossed, the latter situation leading to a finding of

---

42. See [10.24] ff.
43. See [10.12].
44. See [10.27].
45. *Designs*, ch 17.
46. Ibid, para [17.9].
47. *Weir Pumps Ltd v CML Pumps Ltd* [1984] FSR 33.

infringement of intellectual property rights.[48] One now famous case where the wholesale manufacture of spare parts was held not to infringe copyright is *British Leyland Motor Corp v Armstrong Patents Co Ltd*.[49] In fact, all the courts from first instance to the House of Lords found that there was infringement in the sense that the exhaust systems in question had been reproduced from the plaintiff's design, albeit by reverse engineering. The House of Lords, however, enunciated the 'spare parts exception', the majority deciding that British Leyland should be barred from invoking the Copyright Act to prevent such reproduction by the defendant, since 'the tentacles of copyright' should not be allowed to reach out too far, thereby protecting monopolies for the sale of functional items and taking copyright protection 'into fields far beyond its main original intent and properly to be covered by other forms of protection if at all'.[50] This case has been described as revealing a 'remarkably unashamed case of judicial legislation'[51] and in New Zealand the *British Leyland* 'spare parts exception' has been roundly rejected as revolving around issues of social policy and legal philosophy peculiar to the UK and not to be allowed: copyright has been enforced to its fullest extent.[52] By contrast the legislative changes wrought in this country by the Copyright Amendment Act 1989, as mentioned in the previous paragraph, reveal an apparent relish for the *British Leyland* policy.

In its review of the designs system, the ALRC has recommended no special provision for the 'spare parts exception' but rather that such items be subject to the standard regime, albeit simplified for easier understanding of the system.[53]

[8.10] Performing works in public. It is an infringement of copyright in a literary, dramatic or musical work to perform it in public without the copyright owner's permission. Performance includes 'any mode of visual or aural representation' (s 27(1)(a)), whether it be radio, film or delivery by lecture, address, speech or sermon (s 27(1)(b)) or, presumably, semaphore.[54] In *APRA Ltd v Tolbush Pty Ltd*[55] a shop selling car radios was said to be performing musical works by turning the radios on to demonstrate them to customers. Since the premises were not licensed by APRA to play music broadcast on radio this was an infringement of copyright.[56] Infringing performances take place 'in public'. This term has been defined in relation to the nature of the audience. A domestic circle or private gathering is contrasted with 'the public'. The purpose for a group coming together may be relevant: whether it is to see a performance or whether the gathering is part of the domestic or home life of the person providing the entertainment.

---

48. Ibid; *Solar Thompson v Barton Engineering* [1977] RPC 537; *Gardner v Sykes* [1981] FSR 281; *British Leyland Motor Corp Ltd v Armstrong Patents Co Ltd* [1982] FSR 481; *LB Plastics Ltd v Swish Products Ltd* [1979] RPC 551; *Green Cartridge Co (Hong Kong) Ltd v Canon Kabushiki Kaisha* (1996) 34 IPR 614.
49. [1986] 2 WLR 400.
50. Ibid at 420.
51. A Hampton, 'Difficult Appeal Cases Make Poor Law', *Financial Times*, 8 May 1986, p 43.
52. *Mono Pumps (New Zealand) Ltd v Karinya Industries Ltd* (1986) 7 IPR 25; *Dennison Manufacturing v Alfred Holt & Co Ltd* (1987) 10 IPR 613.
53. See [10.16].
54. See Phillips and Firth, para [13.22].
55. (1985) 62 ALR 521.
56. This does not infringe a Pt IV copyright, however: s 199.

In *Duck v Bates*[57] a play performed in a room of Guy's Hospital was said to constitute a private or domestic performance, since the author's right to money was not injured and the audience were those employed at the hospital, not people who would otherwise go to a performance licensed by the author as a commercial transaction. On the other hand, a play performed at a meeting of the Duston Women's Institute was held to be a public performance[58] and playing dance music at a Leagues Club constitutes public performance of the works despite restriction of the audience to club members and their guests.[59] These authorities were discussed in *APRA Ltd v Commonwealth Bank of Australia*[60] where Gummow J found that the playing of a training video to 11 employees of a bank constituted a public performance of music added as background to 'enliven what intrinsically is unexciting subject matter',[61] despite the small number of viewers and the short amount of music played:

> Running through the authorities I have discussed is the notion that for the purposes of this performing right a performance will be 'in public' if it is not 'in private', and the perception of an antithesis between performances which are in public and those which are 'domestic' or 'private' in character. In determining whether a performance answers the latter description, the nature of the audience is important. In coming together to form the audience for the performance were the persons concerned bound together by a domestic or private tie or by an aspect of their public life? Their 'public life' would include their presence at their place of employment for the supply of a performance to assist the commercial purposes of their employer.[62]

The concept of use of copyright material 'in public' as determined by the courts will continue to be important, particularly in the light of the recommendation by the Copyright Convergence Group (CCG) of a new right of transmission 'to the public', with 'public' to be defined as at present.[63]

[8.11] Broadcasting and cabling. Broadcasting and cabling material are not 'performances' but separate rights of broadcast and diffusion respectively. Broadcasting and transmitting to subscribers of a diffusion service are exclusive rights in relation to all works and other subject matter (apart from published editions). Satellite transmissions are now commonplace, but satellite transmissions do not fit readily into the existing copyright framework. The Copyright Act has been amended to enable satellite transmissions to be treated as broadcasts (s 22(6)), but anomalies are created because satellite transmission often involves the signal travelling on wired paths on the satellite and to the end user by cable distribution, whereas the essence of 'broadcast' is that it occurs by 'wireless telegraphy'. Further anomalies are created by VAEIS operations (Video and Audio Entertainment Information Services) which transmit programs to subscribers to the service, usually clubs and hotels. The copying of VAEIS transmissions for later viewing, the 'footprint' of a satellite transmission

---

57. (1884) 13 QBD 843.
58. *Jenning v Stephens* [1936] Ch 169.
59. *APRA Ltd v Canterbury-Bankstown Leagues Club Ltd* (1964) 5 FLR 415.
60. (1992) 25 IPR 157.
61. Ibid at 159.
62. Ibid at 171.
63. See [8.12]. The transmission right should also cover transmission 'made for a commercial purpose' even if not in the public sphere: see eg *APRA Ltd v Telstra Corp Ltd* (1995) 31 IPR 289.

(which can be received by unlicensed premises or, indeed, other countries) and the jumble of copyrights involved in delivery of such a service have not been of concern to copyright owners to date since VAEIS operations are limited and their subscribers readily identifiable. The negotiation of 'satellite rights' by VAEIS operators has provided a commercial solution, although like 'performing rights' this is an industry term operating in the interstices of copyright law rather than being derived directly from the Act. Problems will arise more frequently as piracy of VAEIS transmissions becomes possible through wider dissemination of satellite receiving equipment and greater activity by operators of such services.

[8.12] The proposed new transmission right. The incapacity of existing copyright legislation to cope with changing communications technology led to the establishment in late 1993 of the CCG with a brief to report on proposals for amendments to copyright and broadcasting legislation. The basic problem is that digital delivery systems and new information and entertainment services are simply not dealt with by the existing copyright regime. Whereas until 1968 there was no copyright protection for broadcasts, there is presently none for material which falls outside the range of protected subject matter. The obliteration of boundaries between products, industries and forms of delivery of copyright material makes traditional modes of exploitation marginal or, in some cases, irrelevant.

The CCG made its recommendations within the existing copyright framework and did not examine the relevance of existing categories of works. For example, a book or article (literary work) in digital form may be indistinguishable from an illustration (artistic work) or song (musical work) when all are expressed in digital form. Already, content may be independent of the medium in which it is expressed and made available to the public, and 'a system of law conceptually linked to the medium, such as copyright, must inevitably undergo some dramatic rethinking'.[64]

In view of the need to provide a copyright framework for audiovisual enterprise, the CCG moved away from specific definitions presently conferring rights based on the means of delivery used in making a transmission. A new broad-based right to transmit copyright material to the public is recommended, encompassing existing rights to broadcast and transmit to subscribers to a diffusion service. The recommended transmission right provides for transmission of copyright material 'in intangible form to the public by any means of being made perceivable or used by a receiving device'. The existing public performance right is to remain, separate from the transmission right. There will also remain in the Act the right to broadcast, as a part of the new transmission right, but the definition will be linked to the concept of 'broadcasting' in the Broadcasting Services Act and the right to broadcast will belong to providers of services under that Act. Satellite broadcasts will be deemed to be made from Australia and protected here if they are directly and lawfully receivable by the public in Australia.[65]

Two new offences concerning unauthorised reception of transmissions are recommended: fraudulent reception of transmissions; and making,

64.   CCG, p 6.
65.   CCG, rec 9.

importing, selling or letting for hire unauthorised decoding devices. These changes are included in draft legislation in Sch 5 of the Exposure Draft Bill of February 1996.

[8.13] Adaptations. One of the exclusive rights of the copyright owner of a musical, literary or dramatic work is the right to adapt it (s 31(1)(a)(vii)). This may amount to reproducing a work in another way, although s 10(1) defines 'adaptation' to include:

(a)   the dramatisation of a literary work;

(b)   the converting of a dramatic work to non-dramatic form;

(c)   translating a work or producing a pictorial version of it (a comic strip, perhaps); and

(d)   arranging or transcribing a work.

In 1984 a new subparagraph (ba) was added to this definition to make it clear that a computer program is adapted if another version of it is produced, even if in an unintelligible language, code or notation or one that is different to the original expression. This resulted from the finding in the *Apple* case[66] that Apple computer programs were not 'reproduced' or 'adapted' by the Wombat company, although undoubtedly copied. The High Court[67] subsequently discussed 'adaptation' and held that on the existing legislation (ignoring the 1984 amendments) the programs in object code could not be regarded as a 'translation' of those programs in source code, since they were not turned into another language, even another computer language, but were turned into electrical impulses:

> The ROMs did not in any way express or render the source programs; rather, the ROMs were the means of putting into action and making effective the instructions written in the source programs ... The electrical charges in the ROMs effectuate, but do not translate, the instructions in the source program.[68]

No amendment to the definition of 'adaptation' inserted in 1984 was recommended by the CLRC on the basis that the suggested clarification of 'reproduction' (to include both object code compiled from source code and source code decompiled from object code) addresses the concern that the adaptation right does not encompass such activity, which will now amount to 'reproduction'.[69] The CLRC noted that 'it does not consider the High Court's analysis of the relationship between source code and object code to be correct',[70] that the *Autodesk* case removed doubts as to the eligibility for protection of a program in object code,[71] and that industry concerns were somewhat overstated. In any event the recommendation that object code be regarded as reproducing source code (and the converse) removes the necessity to discuss the relationship further.[72]

---

66.   *Apple Computer Inc v Computer Edge Pty Ltd* (1983) 50 ALR 581.
67.   *Computer Edge Pty Ltd v Apple Computer Inc* (1986) 161 CLR 171.
68.   Ibid at 185. See further [6.34].
69.   *Computer Software Protection*, para [6.77]: see [8.2].
70.   Ibid, para [6.40].
71.   Ibid, para [6.68].
72.   This does have the effect of narrowing 'adaptation' in relation to computer programs so as to apply only to certain translations, ie from one source code language to another and new versions of a program obtained after porting or error correction: see [6.67]; [9.52].

(b) Direct Infringement of Pt IV Copyrights

[8.14] General. Where Pt IV copyrights are concerned, direct infringement is a much more restricted concept than in relation to works because reproduction is only achieved by copying in like form. Therefore making a 'sound-alike' version of popular songs does not infringe copyright in the sound recording, although it may in the underlying works (the lyrics and music).[73] Similarly, copying a film in the sense of taking all the ideas and working out of the theme has been held to infringe copyright in the book or screenplay upon which the film is based, but not to infringe any copyright in the film itself.[74] Moreover, even where copying of the exact form of expression has taken place, it must still be determined whether a 'substantial part' has been taken (s 14). In *Nationwide News Pty Ltd v Copyright Agency Ltd*,[75] for example, newspaper publishers sought to argue that the unauthorised copying of individual newspaper articles by or within educational institutions would infringe their published edition copyright. Their claim was rejected, the Full Court of the Federal Court holding that such copying did not constitute the reproduction of a substantial part of the edition (that is, the entire newspaper). In reaching this conclusion, the court did not merely emphasise the fact that the items in question represented only a small part of each edition (in both quantitative and qualitative terms), but also looked at other factors. It was stressed that the interest protected by a published edition copyright lies in the 'presentation and layout of the edition, as distinct from the particular words or images'.[76] Accordingly it was relevant to consider the extent to which the allegedly infringing activities interfered with that interest. Here, any copying was not designed to appropriate or take advantage of the work put into the layout or presentation of the articles, but merely their content.

[8.15] Piracy of Pt IV copyrights. In practice a great deal of copyright infringement occurs in the form of piracy of sound recordings and films, as well as computer software. Piracy is the unauthorised copying of copyright materials for commercial purposes. This is to be contrasted with 'bootlegging', which is unauthorised recording of a live performance. Bootlegging raises different issues, since recording a live performance may infringe work copyrights but not those subsisting in other subject matter. Until 1989 there was no copyright protection for bare performances not fixed in a tangible medium of expression. As discussed in a previous chapter, the Copyright Act now provides for a 'performer's right' which may be infringed by bootleggers, which is to be enhanced by amendments to the Copyright Act.[77] An interesting example of a 'gap' in performers' rights occurred in *Sony Music Australia Ltd v Tansing*,[78] where the respondents, trading as Apple House Music, had introduced onto the Australian market 'unauthorised' recordings of Michael Jackson. As Jackson was a US citizen and the recordings were 'bootlegged', there was no relevant protection for them

73. *CBS Records Australia Ltd v Telmak Teleproducts (Australia) Pty Ltd* (1987) 9 IPR 440.
74. *Zeccola v Universal City Studios Inc* (1982) 46 ALR 189.
75. (1996) 34 IPR 53.
76. Ibid at 72.
77. See [6.20]–[6.24].
78. (1993) 27 IPR 649.

here as the US was not a signatory to the relevant international agreement which would have conferred reciprocal protection of the performer.[79]

Along with the means of communicating and disseminating material through sound recordings, films and computer software have come significant advances in the means of reproducing such material. The invention of magnetic tape and digital audio tape, the development of higher quality and cheaper cassette recorders and the introduction of video recorders enables pirates to reproduce audiovisual material of saleable quality cheaply. Unlike the original producers of the subject matter, pirates do not have any investment to recoup and usually offer copies at a reduced price, thereby undermining the author's and investor's return for their work and investment.[80] The advent of high quality photocopying and the ease with which computer programs may be copied has led to similar problems for owners of literary copyrights in these forms. Some of the issues raised by such copying are taken up below.[81]

(c) Authorisation of Infringement

[8.16]   General. Authorising the doing of any act comprised in the copyright of a work or other subject matter, without the licence of the owner, amounts to a direct infringement of the copyright (ss 36(1), 101(1)), since authorising others to do an act in relation to a copyright in a work is one of the owner's exclusive rights (s 13(2)). The courts have held that to 'authorise' an infringement is to 'sanction', 'approve' or 'countenance' it.[82] This can include a situation where a person in authority in an organisation allows a situation to develop in that organisation in which copyright infringements may occur.[83] However, there can be no liability for authorisation if the person in question did not know or have any reason to suspect that infringements were taking place.[84] It must also be established that an act of infringement has in fact taken place, before any question of authorisation can arise.[85] In recent years the issue of authorisation of infringement has particularly arisen in two contexts: home taping of audio material and photocopying in educational institutions, both discussed in more detail

---

79. The main hope of getting an injunction to restrain the sale of the compact discs and cassettes lay in fair trading legislation or the tort of passing off, but since the packaging carried large, bold, red print disclaimers to the effect that the recordings were unauthorised and might not be of good quality, any association with the performer or the recording company was negated: see [17.10].
80. For further comment on the effects of piracy see WIPO, *Background Reading*, para 8.8.2; P Brazil, 'Infringement of Copyright and the Problem of "Piracy"' (1987) 61 *ALJ* 12.
81. See also Chapter 9.
82. *University of New South Wales v Moorhouse* (1975) 133 CLR 1; *WEA International Inc v Hanimex Corp Ltd* (1987) 10 IPR 349 at 353–368; *APRA Ltd v Jain* (1990) 18 IPR 663; *Nationwide News Pty Ltd v Copyright Agency Ltd* (1996) 34 IPR 53.
83. See eg *APRA v Jain*, ibid.
84. See eg *Microsoft Corp v Marks* (1995) 33 IPR 15. Note that the separate question of whether such a person is *jointly* responsible for any infringement committed by the organisation is decided according to the common law principles relating to joint tortfeasors: see eg *King v Milpurrurru* (1996) 34 IPR 11; and see [2.6].
85. *WEA International Inc v Hanimex Corp Ltd* (1987) 10 IPR 349; *Nationwide News Pty Ltd v Copyright Agency Ltd* (1996) 34 IPR 53.

below. 'Authorisation of a performance in public' also provides a useful avenue for pursuing recalcitrant managers of venues offering live or recorded music who decline to enter into appropriate licensing agreements.[86]

[8.17] Home taping. It has only been within the last 15 years that inexpensive high quality copying of audio material has been possible. It is estimated that the Australian music industry loses about $30 million per annum because of home taping off air and directly from other recordings. In the UK it is estimated that total annual loss of sales is about 70% of the value of actual sales.[87] Attempts have been made to make the suppliers of blank tapes liable to copyright owners, but these attempts have been unsuccessful. In *CBS Songs Ltd v Amstrad Consumer Electronics plc*[88] it was argued that the sale of twin-deck tape-recording machines capable of reproducing music cassettes directly onto blank tapes was an authorisation of the practice, and therefore an infringement of copyright on the part of the manufacturers and sellers of such equipment. The House of Lords affirmed the decision of the Court of Appeal[89] to the effect that the sale of such machines did not amount to authorisation of any breach of copyright and refused to grant injunctions preventing the sale of machines with a copying facility. In discussing the meaning of authorisation Lord Templeman (with whom the other Law Lords agreed) applied the definition adopted in previous cases that 'authorise' means 'sanction, approve or countenance' and held that on the facts there was no control over the use to which machines were put once sold. Furthermore, there was no incitement to commit a tort, namely procuring copyright infringement, and nor were Amstrad negligent, since there was no duty to prevent or discourage infringement by others.[90]

[8.18] Photocopying. The main Australian case on authorisation is *University of New South Wales v Moorhouse*.[91] The respondent (plaintiff) suspected that some of the photocopying going on in universities contravened copyright, and alleged that the University had authorised infringing reproductions of works by allowing students free access to photocopying machines installed in the library, while failing to exercise control or supervision over what books were copied and how much of any work was taken. The respondent, an author of a book of short stories to be found in the library, organised a former student of the University to make an infringing copy of one of the stories on the photocopy machines provided. The High Court declared that the University had authorised the breach of copyright by providing an unqualified supply of books and photocopying machines, amounting to an invitation to users of the library to make such use of the machines as they saw fit. Any steps taken to supervise machine use and

86. See eg *APRA Ltd v Canterbury-Bankstown Leagues Clubs Ltd* [1964–5] NSWR 138; *APRA Ltd v Jain* (1990) 18 IPR 663.
87. 40 million sound recordings and 70 million blank tapes were sold in the UK in 1984: *CBS Songs Ltd v Amstrad Consumer Electronics plc* (1988) 11 IPR 1 at 5.
88. (1988) 11 IPR 1.
89. [1987] 3 All ER 751.
90. See [6.41]–[6.42] concerning the fate of amendments to allow home taping for private, domestic use.
91. (1975) 133 CLR 1.

exclude illegal copying were inadequate and directed towards giving students access to machines rather than safeguarding copyright owners' rights.

As a result of this case a new provision, s 39A, was inserted into the Act by the Copyright Amendment Act 1980 to the effect that a library providing photocopying services will not be taken as having authorised the making of infringing copies if a notice bringing the provisions of the Act to the attention of users of the machine is put up near the machine. This has the effect of making it very easy for universities to avoid 'authorising' copyright infringements perpetrated by students and staff. The Act was also amended at the same time to allow educational institutions, on payment of a royalty, to make multiple copies of certain works for the teaching purposes of the institution. This and similar schemes were considered in the previous chapter.[92]

(d) Indirect Infringement

[8.19] Forms of indirect infringement. Indirect infringement is not to be confused with indirect copying,[93] but refers to dealing with unauthorised reproductions of works, rather than actually reproducing the material itself. The main forms of indirect infringement involve infringing copies being imported for the purposes of trade without the licence of the copyright owner (ss 37, 102), or sold, hired out or otherwise made the subject of trade (ss 38, 103). It is necessary to establish that a defendant knew or ought reasonably to have known that the article with which they were dealing was an infringing copy.[94] Permitting a place of public entertainment to be used for a public performance which infringes copyright in a work also constitutes indirect infringement, though only if the defendant should have known that such a performance would infringe and if the permission was given for profit (s 39).[95]

[8.20] Parallel importing. Of the indirect infringement provisions, ss 37 and 102 have been the subject of most debate. They allow a copyright owner or exclusive licensee to control the importation into Australia of works and other subject matter, even if the items in question have been acquired quite lawfully overseas. The establishment of exclusive distribution networks is premised on the prevention of parallel importation. The key words in ss 37 and 102 in this respect are 'without the licence of the owner of the copyright'. The onus is on the party alleging infringement to establish that this licence is lacking. Thus if no evidence is produced as to the attitude of the owner towards the importation, any action under these sections must fail.[96] But so long as the owner is the plaintiff, or is prepared to back up an exclusive licensee who is seeking to prevent parallel

---

92. See [7.19].
93. See [8.6].
94. See *Apple Computer Inc v Computer Edge Pty Ltd* (1984) 53 ALR 225; *Ainsworth Nominees Pty Ltd v Andclar Pty Ltd* (1988) 12 IPR 551; *Star Micronics Pty Ltd v Five Star Computers Pty Ltd* (1990) 18 IPR 225; *Milpurrurru v Indofurn Pty Ltd* (1994) 30 IPR 209.
95. See *APRA Ltd v Miles* (1961) 3 FLR 146. As to what constitutes public performance, see [8.10].
96. *Avel Pty Ltd v Multicoin Amusements Pty Ltd* (1990) 171 CLR 88.

importation, the unauthorised importer cannot rely on the fact that their acquisition of the material was itself perfectly legal. The courts have consistently held that for the purposes of ss 37 and 102, the word 'licence' connotes a *positive* authorisation to import. The fact that at the time of acquisition no prohibition was explicitly imposed on importation into Australia will not protect the parallel importer.

The leading case in this regard is the High Court's decision in *Interstate Parcel Express Co Pty Ltd v Time-Life International (Nederlands) BV.*[97] Angus & Robertson, a retail bookseller owned by the appellant, purchased cookbooks from a book wholesaler in California, and imported them into Australia to sell for $8.95. The respondent, the Time-Life Co, had an exclusive licence from the American publisher of the cookbooks to publish them throughout the world, other than in North America. They sold the books in Australia for $16.95. Time-Life argued that Angus & Robertson's importation of the books into Australia infringed their copyright by virtue of ss 37 and 38 of the Act. Angus & Robertson argued that the importation involved no infringement because they were impliedly licensed to deal with the books, having purchased them legally in the US, and that the sale had contained no restrictive terms as to the use to which the buyer might put the books. It was held that the sale of a book does not involve the sale of the copyright, only the loss of rights in respect of that particular copy of the work as a chattel. Since no positive licence to import had been established, Angus & Robertson were in breach of the Act.

The provisions of ss 37 and 102 have also been utilised in respect of software,[98] records[99] and videotapes. In *Sega Enterprises Ltd v Gottlieb Electronics Pty Ltd*[100] the applicant's video games, involving computer generated images embodied in integrated circuits, were nevertheless regarded as cinematograph films within the Copyright Act and therefore entitled to protection against parallel importing, whereas there is no such prohibition on the importing of integrated circuits under the Circuit Layouts Act 1989.[101]

[8.21] Reform of the parallel importation provisions. Restrictions imposed by copyright owners on the free movement of copyright products allow the division of the world into self-contained market segments so that optimum exploitation of the work throughout the world can occur, maximising profits and restricting or preventing competition in the sale of copyright products of the same type or brand within national boundaries.[102] In the case of books, for example, exclusive rights over the Australian market have traditionally been the preserve of British publishers, even in relation to works originally published in North America. So long as Australian

97.   (1977) 138 CLR 534. See also *Lorenzo & Sons Pty Ltd v Roland Corporation* (1992) 23 IPR 377.
98.   See eg *Computermate Products (Australia) Pty Ltd v Ozi-Soft Pty Ltd* (1988) 12 IPR 487; *Star Micronics Pty Ltd v Five Star Computers Pty Ltd* (1990) 18 IPR 225; *Broderbund Software Inc v Computermate Products (Australia) Pty Ltd* (1991) 22 IPR 215.
99.   See eg *Polygram Records Pty Ltd v Monash Records (Australia) Pty Ltd* (1985) 72 ALR 35; *Chrysalis Records Ltd v Vene* (1982) 43 ALR 440.
100. (1996) 35 IPR 161.
101. As to the circuit layouts legislation, see [9.23] ff.
102. In the case of *R A & A Bailey & Co Ltd v Boccaccio Pty Ltd* (1986) 6 IPR 279, ss 37 and 38 were used to prevent the importation and sale of a product not itself protected by copyright, but whose label was an artistic work: see [20.4].

booksellers were unable to import in competition with these publishers, readers in this country were often forced to wait months for books long since published abroad, and to pay higher prices into the bargain. The same appears to have been true in relation to records and software. Attempts to modify the restriction on parallel importing have tended to centre on these products. An extensive inquiry was made by the CLRC into the question of whether any changes should be made to ss 37, 38, 102 and 103 of the Copyright Act.[103] The CLRC unanimously reached the conclusion that the sections should continue to apply to parallel imports but with certain exceptions, allowing the importation of non-pirated copyright material in certain circumstances, including:

(a)   if the material is not available in Australia;

(b)   if the copyright material is a work comprised in a label or mark attached to a product or its packaging;[104] and

(c)   where a customer places an order with an importer for material which the customer does not require for the purposes of trade or commerce.[105]

In arriving at these conclusions the CLRC provided only a partial answer to the problems of access to and pricing of copyright material which critics of the parallel importing provisions have identified. The CLRC recognised that publishers and distributors of books, records and films are the main beneficiaries of the importation provisions of the Act, benefiting from the rights conferred on authors, composers and other originators of copyright material.[106] The burden of the prohibitions is borne by consumers in the form of higher prices and inhibited access to copyright material.[107] In 1989 the Prices Surveillance Authority (PSA) went further and recommended that territorial copyright should be removed altogether so that the delay in arrival in Australia of books published overseas would be greatly reduced and prices would be lower.[108] The report of the PSA provoked a hostile reaction not only from publishers but also from authors, who perceived detriment from the disruption of existing marketing arrangements.

The CLRC's review was conducted by way of written submissions and public hearings. Representations were made by the major copyright industries, with book publishing, record, film and video and computer software companies all asserting that the importation provisions should be retained or indeed strengthened. One problem for both pro and anti lobby groups was that the arguments as to the economic effects of lifting import barriers were speculative, the only certainty being that in Australia and other common law countries copyright is an economic right. Since the justification for its existence is economic the question of parallel importing must presumably be answered with reference to the question as to the extent to

---

103. *The Importation Provisions of the Copyright Act 1968*, 1988.
104. See [20.4].
105. *The Importation Provisions of the Copyright Act 1968*, pp 3–7.
106. Ibid p 31.
107. Einfeld J referred to this problem in *Ozi-Soft Pty Ltd v Wong* (1988) 10 IPR 520 at 525 and much media comment has pointed to the detriment suffered by the Australian public.
108. *Inquiry into Book Prices: Interim Report*, Report no 24, 1989. The Final Report was issued in January 1990.

which the function of copyright is to promote the efficient allocation of resources.[109] In the *Time-Life* case[110] Murphy J observed that Time-Life's enforcement of its copyright might breach the restrictive practices sections of the Trade Practices Act 1974 (Cth), which are discussed below. This view was also taken by Einfeld J at the trial of the *Ozi-Soft* case, although no evidence was found of a serious breach of the trade practices legislation nor of grave injury to the public if the diskettes in question could not be marketed in Australia.[111]

[8.22] Books: relaxation of prohibition on parallel importing. As a result the Australian government was faced with two conflicting recommendations: abolition of the parallel importing controls being urged by the PSA, as against the CLRC view that the provisions be retained in a modified form. The government's response was to introduce the Copyright Amendment Act 1990. Sections 37 and 38 (dealing with works) were amended by making them subject to a new s 44A, while ss 102 and 103 are similarly restricted in relation to published editions by a new s 112A. The amendments apply only to 'non-infringing books', meaning books which are legitimately manufactured in their country of origin. Specifically excluded (and therefore still subject to the existing regime) are books consisting mainly of musical scores, as well as computer software manuals and periodicals. In 1995 the CLRC in its final report on computer software protection recommended that the restrictions on parallel importing of computer programs remain in place, but computer manuals produced separately be subject to the general regime in place for books.[112] Interestingly, the CLRC moved from its position in the draft report, where the majority had recommended lifting the prohibitions on parallel importation for all software and manuals. Following industry submissions to the effect that the availability of computer programs is not a 'pressing problem'[113] and the Law Council of Australia's recommendation that the law should not change until it is clear that there will be some advantage resulting from the change, the CLRC opted to leave the existing system in place with respect to computer software.

Sections 44A and 112A draw a crucial distinction between books first published overseas and books first published in Australia. In the case of the former, the importation provisions do not apply, allowing foreign books to be imported without restriction. Where on the other hand a book is first published in Australia, or is first published overseas prior to the amendments taking effect, the importation provisions have been only partially relaxed. In the first place, a single copy of such a book may be imported at any time for a customer who has ordered it and undertaken not to make it the subject of commercial dealings; and one or more copies may be imported to fill an order from a non-profit library. Second, some

---

109. As to which, see generally W M Landes and R A Posner, 'An Economic Analysis of Copyright Law' (1989) 18 *J of Leg Studies* 325; cf A Fels and J Walker, 'The Market for Books and the Importation Provisions of the Copyright Act 1968' (1990) 17 *MULR* 566.
110. (1977) 138 CLR 534 at 560.
111. *Ozi-Soft Pty Ltd v Wong* (1988) 10 IPR 520 at 525.
112. *Computer Software Protection*, rec 2.39.
113. Ibid at [2.38].

commercial importation is allowed, but only where necessary to satisfy local orders which have remained unfilled for at least 90 days. The effect of the reforms was intended to be that, in order to preclude unauthorised importation, a publisher or authorised distributor would need to ensure that books are 'first published' in Australia and that reasonable stocks are kept in the country to meet demand. There is an obvious element of discrimination here in favour of the local publishing industry, although it is important to note that foreign publishers do not automatically lose out. As with existing provisions in the Act,[114] 'first publication' is deemed to take place in Australia if a book is published here within 30 days of publication overseas, giving overseas interests at least some opportunity of avoiding an open market in non-infringing copies.

The most obvious consequence of these reforms should be to improve the availability of foreign books. The Act does not attempt to deal with the question of prices, an omission that on balance appears defensible given the difficulty of finding a workable or appropriate regulatory mechanism. It has been difficult to determine the impact of the amendments on the price of books, since the factors determining price include production, distribution and advertising costs, currency fluctuations, freight charges and profit margins. The public expect to pay the 'recommended retail price' (RRP) on every book, except those remaindered or otherwise discounted. It is difficult to compare the price of books before the amendments with those afterwards, but it may be that prices have flattened, and not risen as fast as they used to. On the other hand Australia has recently experienced lower inflation and the 'flatter' prices may be simply part of an economic trend applicable to all products. In 1995 the PSA reviewed the effect of the importation provisions and found that high-volume novels and other best sellers seemed to be closer to overseas prices, but technical and professional books remain relatively expensive.[115] Anecdotal evidence[116] suggests that the service offered by local distributors holding exclusive licences had improved, although others suggest that the 90 days margin still protects inefficient distributors and allows them to maintain minimal stock and poor service. On the other hand, availability is regarded as improved and new releases reach Australia faster. Furthermore, local publishing dates now match overseas release in many cases, making local distributors preferable to parallel importers.

As with the suggested amendments on sound recordings discussed in the next paragraph, the interests of all groups touched by the amendments (authors, publishers, distributors, booksellers and the public) were discussed before the legislation was changed and no one group seems to bear an unfair burden of compliance. This is not to say there has been no effect in terms of changing practices in publishing and promoting books, nor that concerns of remaindering or dumping of books on the Australian market have entirely evaporated.

114. For example, s 29(5): see [6.54].
115. PSA, *Inquiry into Book Prices and Parallel Imports*, Report no 61, 1995.
116. The authors are indebted to Diana Ferry for empirical research reported in her minor thesis *Parallel Imports: An Assessment of the Amendments to the Import Provisions of the Copyright Act 1968 in the Broad Context of Publishing in Australia and in Relation to Wider Intellectual Property and Social Objectives*, UNSW, 1995.

At present, the Act is open to the charge that it places this country in breach of its international obligations under Art 5 of the Berne Convention and Art XX of GATT, which require uniformity of intellectual property rights as far as possible.[117] Equivalent copyright laws to ours arguably allow copyright owners to prevent parallel importing.[118] And despite the government's claim that the reforms are not discriminatory because any national would be free to publish here within a month of first publication overseas, it is also possible that the Act breaches the national treatment principle in the Berne Convention.[119] However, in view of the recognition of the World Trade Organisation (WTO) requirements under the proposed amendments to sound recordings discussed in the next paragraph, the Act may well be 'tidied up' to accommodate these concerns.

[8.23] Sound recordings: legislative proposals. In 1990 the PSA also conducted an inquiry into the price of sound recordings, particularly compact discs, whose importation into Australia is subject to the provisions of the Copyright Act in the same way as books. Once again, it recommended that the prohibition on parallel importing be relaxed.[120] In December 1992 a Copyright Amendment Bill was introduced to achieve that objective in relation to sound recordings, but it lapsed with the March 1993 election. The legislation was not reintroduced, and indeed the government struggled for the next three years to come to any definite decision on the matter. Cabinet was reported to be divided over the proposal, 'with some ministers supporting the interests of consumers in cheaper CDs and other ministers being more solicitous of the recording industry, with particular concern about the impact on local performers and producers'.[121] As with books, a compromise was reached. In February 1996 the Exposure Draft Bill to amend the Act set out in Sch 3 a series of proposed amendments concerning sound recordings in two circumstances:

(a) to allow importation where the copyright owner is unable within 30 days to supply copies of a sound recording that has been published in Australia; and

(b) to allow a retailer, on the firm order of a customer, to import on behalf of the customer a single copy of the sound recording.

The draft amendments take into account Australia's membership of the WTO and permit importation from all members of that organisation. Provision is made for royalties to be paid to the relevant copyright owner of the work and various conditions must be satisfied if the importation is not to be an infringement of copyright. For example, the recording must have been published in Australia, so that copyright owners retain the capacity to decide the timing of the public release of records here. Some of the

---

117. See P Brazil and J Crawford, 'Territorial Copyright — A Treaty Obligation?' (1990) 8(1) *Copyright Reporter* 6; J Harman, 'The Copyright Amendment Act 1991: Some of the Implications for Book Publishers and Sellers' (1993) 4 *AIPJ* 113 at 116.

118. Although the 'exhaustion of rights' doctrine (cf [20.4]) would militate against this in the EEC at least: see J McKeough, 'Intellectual Property Protection and Freedom of Competition: Competing Policies under the Treaty of Rome' (1985) 1 *IPJ* 237.

119. See [21.15]. As to GATT, see [21.8] ff.

120. *Inquiry into the Prices of Sound Recordings*, Report No 35, 1990. See M Davison, 'The Market for Sound Recordings: Open or Closed?' (1992) 20 *ABLR* 30.

121. Ricketson (1994), p 296.

provisions as to notice and payment mirror the compulsory licensing aspects of the Act with respect to sound recordings[122] and the actual mechanics of the proposed amendments have been worked out in a way that reflects industry practice as to ordering of sound recordings and payment of royalties. Section 133 of the present Act was also to be amended in that the penalties for commercial dealing with infringing copies of films would also apply to infringing copies of sound recordings. The increased penalties were designed as a deterrent against using the relaxed importation provisions as a screen for the infringing importation of sound recordings, but also apply to manufacture and distribution of infringing material in Australia.

It would now appear that these provisions will not be part of a revised Bill to amend the Copyright Act. In its 1996 election arts policy statement *For Art's Sake — A Fair Go,* the Liberal/National Government undertook to consult with interested parties on the best means to achieve price reductions on sound recordings sold in Australia. To this end, an Inter-Departmental Committee (IDC) of representatives from various Commonwealth departments was set up in September 1996 to investigate long-term price competitiveness with respect to sound recordings. The matters to be taken into account include the context of general competition policy, Australia's international relations and obligations, the interests of copyright owners and all aspects of the music industry and the impact of new technology delivery systems.

2. DEFENCES

[8.24] The available defences. The rights of copyright owners are not entirely untrammelled, but are subject to considerations of what is fair and reasonable use of material for certain worthwhile purposes. The Act allows certain use of works and other subject matter without the need to get permission (a licence) from the owner of copyright. The defences to infringement:

> may be seen as serving one or more of four laudable objectives ... the administration of justice, the advancement of education, the protection of the public's right to be informed and fixing the limits beyond which it is unreasonable to assert a proprietary right in one's own or another's work.[123]

'Fair dealing' with material for these purposes is allowed by the statute, and there is also a non-statutory defence of publication in the public interest, as discussed below. Beyond that, it is possible that in some cases an action for breach of copyright may fail on the ground that it would be contrary to public policy for the plaintiff to be assisted by the courts, as for example where the work in question is considered obscene.[124] However, the mere fact that the plaintiff's work has been created in breach of another's copyright is not, it would seem, a ground in itself for withholding a remedy.[125]

---

122. See [7.18].
123. Phillips and Firth, para [14.15].
124. See eg *Glyn v Weston Feature Film Co* [1916] 1 Ch 261. Note also that enforcement of laws for the confiscation of proceeds of crime may have the effect of denying copyright to criminal offenders who seek to 'profit' by writing about their experiences: see A Freiberg, 'Confiscating the Literary Proceeds of Crime' [1992] *Crim LR* 96.
125. *ZYX Music GmbH v King* (1995) 31 IPR 207; *A-One Accessory Imports Pty Ltd v Off Roads Imports Pty Ltd (No 2)* (1996) 34 IPR 332: see further [6.35].

[8.25] Research or study: educational use. A variety of provisions permit certain educational uses to be made of copyright material. In the first place, fair dealing is allowed with works for the purposes of research or study (s 40), and/or for criticism or review (s 41). Items may be copied by institutions assisting readers with a print disability or persons with an intellectual disability (ss 135ZN, 135ZQ, 135ZR, 135ZT, 200AA).[126] Certain performances of material in class or in a way limited to the educational purposes of a place of education will be seen as fair dealing (s 28). So will the inclusion of a short extract or adaptation of a published work in a collection of works, as long as the extract was not published for use by places of education in the first place, or if the collection consists principally of non-copyright material. However, sufficient acknowledgment must always be made (s 44). Small extracts from literary and dramatic works may be copied on the premises of educational institutions for the purposes of a course of education at that institution (ss 135ZG, 135ZH). Not more than 1% of any work should be copied under this provision, and subsequent extracts from the work cannot be made within 14 days of the previous copying. Examination questions and answers will not infringe copyright in material reproduced (s 200(1)(b)), and nor will answers in class (s 200(1)(a)). Off-air copying of educational material is also allowed for the instructional purposes of an educational institution (s 200(2)). There is also a notion of fair dealing in Pt XI of the Act concerning performers' rights in that copying for private and domestic use, scientific research, educational copying and the other exceptions relating to reporting news, criticism/review and legal proceedings does not require the performer's permission.[127]

[8.26] Defining fair dealing. In *Hubbard v Vosper*[128] Lord Denning stated that '[i]t is impossible to define what is "fair dealing". It must be a question of degree' and that the tribunal of fact must decide in all the circumstances of the case. In 1980 s 40 was amended to add subss (2), (3) and (4) which now provide vague guidelines as to when 'fair dealing' with a work for the purposes of research or study takes place.

Regard must be had to a range of factors, including the purpose and character of the dealing, the nature of the work in question, its commercial availability, the effect of the dealing on the value of the work and the amount and substantiality of the part copied (s 40(2)). Notwithstanding these considerations, a dealing is deemed to be fair if any or all of an article in a periodical is copied, provided no other article in the same issue and dealing with different subject matter is also copied (s 40(3)(a), (4)). In any other case, the copying of a 'reasonable portion' of the work is deemed to be fair (s 40(3)(b)). Without limiting the phrase, s 10(2) provides that a reasonable portion only of a published edition will have been taken if not more than one chapter or 10% of the edition (whichever is greater) is copied.

There is a distinction to be drawn between the compulsory licensing and fair dealing provisions of the Act. In *Haines v Copyright Agency Ltd*[129] a memorandum from the Director-General of Education for New South

---

126. The 1996 Exposure Draft Bill contains, in Schs 8, 9 and 12, certain minor amendments concerning the administration of the licences under discussion.
127. See the definition of 'exempt recording' in s 248A.
128. [1972] 2 QB 84 at 94.
129. (1982) 42 ALR 549.

Wales entitled 'Further Information on the Copyright Act' was circulated to school principals. This memorandum pointed out that s 40 'allows for virtually the same amount and type of copying [as s 53B or s 53D, the compulsory licensing provisions then in force] without imposing any need to keep records or make payments'. This could arise by a teacher constituting themselves an agent for students and doing multiple photocopying as 'fair dealing' instead of pursuant to the compulsory licensing provisions. However, the Full Federal Court emphasised the distinction between s 40 and s 53B and denied the possibility that s 40 was 'an attractive alternative' to s 53B.[130]

[8.27] Reporting of news. Fair dealing with works is also permissible for the reporting of news (s 42), as is the use of audio-visual material (s 103B). There must, for example, be a sufficient acknowledgment of material copied from a newspaper or periodical. Playing music recorded incidentally in the course of reporting news by means of broadcasting or in a film is protected by s 42, but not if the music is added to the soundtrack and is not part of the news being reported (s 42(3)).[131]

[8.28] Cases on fair dealing. In *Commonwealth v John Fairfax & Sons Ltd*[132] the High Court considered both the defence of fair dealing for purposes of criticism or review (s 41) and the defence of fair dealing for the purpose of reporting of news (s 42). The non-statutory 'public interest' defence was also considered in this case, which arose when the Federal Government became aware that the defendants were about to publish long excerpts of a book entitled *Documents on Australian Defence and Foreign Policy 1968–1975* in *The Age* newspaper. Included were documents produced by the Department of Foreign Affairs, as well as unpublished government memoranda, assessments, briefings and cables. Ex parte injunctions to prevent instalments of this book being published in the defendant's newspaper were granted, and the government sought to continue the injunctions, claiming breach of copyright in the documents. The defendant did not dispute the subsistence of copyright, but argued the fair dealing and public interest defences. The public interest defence[133] was not made out, being confined (in Australia) to allowing the publication of material so as to protect the community from destruction, damage or harm:

> It has been acknowledged that the defence applies to disclosures of things done in breach of national security, in breach of all law (including fraud) and to disclosure of matters which involve danger to the public. So far there is no recorded instance of the defence having been raised in a case such as this where the suggestion is that the advice given by Australia's public servants, particularly its diplomats, should be ventilated, with a view to exposing what is alleged to have been the cynical pursuit of expedient goals ...[134]

130. Ibid at 555. Sections 53B and 53D have now in any event been replaced by provisions which are less onerous in their impact: see [7.19]–[7.21]. See also [8.28].
131. See *Hawkes & Son (London) Ltd v Paramount Film Service Ltd* [1934] Ch 593 for an example of infringement of a musical work by a newsreel before such a provision was introduced into the UK Act.
132. (1980) 147 CLR 39.
133. See [4.17]–[4.21]. See also *Beloff v Pressdram Ltd* [1973] 1 All ER 241. Cf *Collier Constructions Pty Ltd v Foskett Pty Ltd* (1990) 19 IPR 44, where Gummow J declined to recognise the existence of the defence.
134. (1980) 147 CLR 39 at 57.

The other defences fared no better. Mason J held that 'fair dealing' with unpublished work within s 41 would not normally be fair at all, if an author had not released it to be the subject of public criticism or review.[135] Apart from this, any criticism or review was 'merely a veneer', since the reproduction of the plaintiff's documents was to occur on a large scale with little actual comment and in several instalments.[136] Similarly, s 42(1)(a) required rather more selective judgment to be applied to the material than simply reproducing vast tracts of the plaintiff's documents, although this did not mean that 'news' is to be given a narrow meaning confining the concept to reporting of current events.[137]

An extensive discussion of 'fair dealing' also took place in the *Journalists* case,[138] where it was held that the defendant, a press-clipping service, had infringed copyright in newspaper articles belonging to the journalists who wrote them. Every defence conceivable was raised, including all the grounds of fair dealing provided by the Copyright Act. Beaumont J consulted the *Macquarie Dictionary* to ascertain the definition of key words such as 'research', 'study' (s 40), 'criticism', 'review' (s 41) and 'news' (s 42). The overriding purpose of the defendant's retrieval of copyright material was purely commercial, to supply a photocopy of the published material in return for a fee. The dictionary meanings and case law all indicated a private purpose behind research and study on the part of the user of the material, not the supplying of copyright matter to a customer. Criticism or review are cognate terms: 'one is the process and the other is the result of the critical application of mental faculties'.[139] The defendant did not supply this element in collecting material, their purpose being location rather than evaluation of the articles. Reporting of news is for the purpose of conveying information, usually about recent events but not inevitably so;[140] however, having a commercial motive in compiling clips of news material means that the activity is not for the purpose of reporting that news.[141] Further, the defence provided in s 42(1) is only available where the reporting is in a newspaper, magazine or similar periodical, which the press clipping service was not.[142] In any event, quite apart from the primary purpose for which

---

135. Ibid at 56–7. In the US the application of a 'strong' presumption to this effect has generated considerable controversy, with historians and biographers arguing that they cannot work effectively without being able to draw on the unpublished letters, manuscripts etc of public figures. It has been claimed that the practical effect of decisions such as *Salinger v Random House Inc* (1987) 811 F 2d 90 and *New Era Publications International ApS v Henry Holt & Co Inc* (1989) 873 F 2d 576 has merely been to enrich the estates of such figures since they can demand payment for use of those writings.

136. Cf *Time Warner Entertainment Co Ltd v Channel 4 Television Corporation plc* (1993) 28 IPR 439 where a documentary including clips of the film *A Clockwork Orange* was held to be fair dealing since the length of extracts was balanced by commentary. Furthermore, the film had been in the public domain despite being restricted in the UK, and it was not unfair to review it in that way.

137. Ibid at 56. See also *Wigginton v Brisbane TV Ltd* (1992) 25 IPR 58.

138. *De Garis v Neville Jeffress Pidler Pty Ltd* (1990) 95 ALR 625: see [7.4].

139. Ibid at 631.

140. Ibid at 633, citing Mason J in *Commonwealth v John Fairfax & Sons Ltd* (1980) 147 CLR 39 at 56.

141. Ibid at 632, citing *Pacific & Southern Company Inc v Duncan* (1984) 744 F 2d 1490 at 1496.

142. See *John Fairfax & Son Ltd v Deputy Commissioner of Taxation* (1988) 15 NSWLR 620.

these articles were taken failing to come within the statutory grounds of fair dealing, the amount taken (the whole of each work) was certainly not 'a reasonable portion' of the work (s 10(2)) so as to be 'fair'. Similarly, copying articles from journals by research scientists in the course of employment by an oil company has been regarded by an American court as part of the commercial activities of the firm, rather than fair use.[143]

[8.29] Legal advice and judicial proceedings. It is a defence to an action for infringement of copyright to use works or other subject matter for the purposes of giving (or seeking) legal professional advice or for the purpose of a judicial proceeding, or reporting thereof (ss 43, 104). A judicial proceeding is defined in s 10(1) as a proceeding before a court, tribunal or person having by law power to hear, receive and examine evidence on oath.

[8.30] Further considerations on fair dealing. The existing notion of fair dealing reflects cultural values relating to the use of material in the interests of access for the purposes of those concerned with, inter alia, 'the preservation and promotion of learning, culture, knowledge and ideas'.[144] There is no legal system in which freedom of speech, discussion of ideas and further creativity are valued which would abolish any concept of fair dealing. However, digital technology creates a different environment in which fair use of others' material must be considered. Delivery of copyright material via a computer terminal allows users of the material to access and utilise it in a way not available, for example, to a person browsing through a book. The 'threat' posed by the digital environment works both ways. For creators of material the ease of access, wholesale copying, manipulation and amalgamation with other material poses great threats to their economic rights in a copyright system used to regulating the 'reproduction' in 'material form' of a 'substantial part'. The fact is that digital technology subverts underlying assumptions about the nature of the use of works by individuals in a system premised on a traditional public/private dichotomy. 'The effect of these technologies has been to "privatise" the use made of copyright materials, in that individuals now become their own publishers and works can be used and enjoyed on-line and on an individual basis where previously this could only be done as part of a larger group.'[145] The implications for the yet to be introduced moral rights requiring respect for and correct attribution of creative effort can only be imagined.

On the other hand technology may allow monitoring and licensing of individual use of works (even the 'browsing' on-screen analogous to reading a book).

> It has been suggested that because technology now exists to monitor *all* uses made in the electronic environment, it is now appropriate to allow copyright owners to charge for these uses, even where these uses have not traditionally amounted to infringement of copyrights. Thus 'browsing' through a database might attract a charge.[146]

---

143. *American Geophysical Union v Texaco Inc* (1994) 29 IPR 381.
144. CLRC, *Copyright Reform: A Consideration of Rationales, Interests and Objectives,* 1996, p 13.
145. S Ricketson, 'The International Legal Environment: National Laws and the Berne Convention. Enforcement and Sanctions, WIPO and GATT', IFRRO Conference, *Copyright in the Asia Pacific Region: Reprography and Digital Copying,* 17–18 January 1995, p 26.
146. IFFRO Conference, ibid p 22.

The wish of university libraries to conduct their 'reserve' collections (short term loans of prescribed course materials, etc) electronically by scanning in articles and allowing students to read them on a computer screen (and possibly make a single copy) has led to requests from CAL for licensing fees based on uses of the material that go far beyond the fees levied when the material is in 'hard copy'. The relevance of existing notions of fair dealing is also being questioned overseas. The Canadian reprographic rights licensing body CANCOPY (analogous to CAL) suggests that more sophisticated licensing of almost all uses of material is likely to replace fair dealing. Another consideration is the likelihood that service providers may charge for access to services and for the 'search' software, with the content being almost secondary.[147] There is no doubt that the CLRC's review and simplification reference[148] will require consideration of these challenges for owners and users of copyright.

[8.31] **Miscellaneous restrictions on the exercise of copyright.** At present the Act contains some exceptions to infringement in addition to those mentioned above. Again, these various defences allow for freedom of speech and probably do not cause the copyright owner any economic loss by affecting the market for products embodying the material. One of these miscellaneous defences is the right to quote for the purposes of criticism or review (ss 41, 103A), which has been referred to above. Obviously reviews of books and films may actually be to the advantage of the owner of copyright if sales are increased due to the publicity given in a review. Public recitation or reading of a literary, dramatic or musical work, or including this in a broadcast, is also allowable if sufficient acknowledgment is given (s 45). Performance of a literary, dramatic or musical work, or an adaptation thereof 'at premises where persons reside or sleep' is excused under s 46, as is causing a sound recording to be heard on such premises and in clubs (ss 26(3), 106).[149] Performance of works or other subject matter is one of the rights comprised in the copyright and 'performance' has been given a wide interpretation under s 27(1)(a).[150] The effect of s 46 is thus that institutions such as hotels, guest houses, hostels and hospitals may avoid the need to obtain a licence from the owners of these copyrights, usually administered by a collecting society. Similarly, occupiers of such premises will not be liable for copyright infringement in sound recordings or films playing on a television or sound broadcast (s 199). The CCG recommended amending s 199(4) so that the transmission by any means of a broadcast be allowed only to enhance the quality of an original broadcast where the signal is inadequate.[151]

A sculpture or work of artistic craftsmanship permanently exhibited in a public place can be reproduced in two dimensions (for example by

---

147. This is contemplated by the US *White Paper on Intellectual Property and the National Information Infrastructure*, 1995, pp 15–16.
148. See [5.16].
149. The CCG recommended that s 26(3) be repealed as inequitable (CCG Report, para [6.1]), and this is provided for in the Exposure Draft Bill of February 1996, Sch 5.
150. See eg *APRA Ltd v Tolbush Pty Ltd* (1985) 62 ALR 521.
151. Consequential amendments to s 199(5), (6) and (7) will also be made, and complementary amendments to s 212 of the Broadcasting Services Act 1992: CCG, para [4.2]. The text of these suggested amendments appears in Sch 5 of the Exposure Draft Bill, February 1996.

drawing, painting or photographing, without fear of infringement (s 65), and the same is true of buildings or models of buildings (s 66). Also permitted are the incidental filming or televising of such works (ss 67–69), and their reproduction for broadcasting purposes (s 70). It has been suggested that these provisions recognise that control of copying of such works, often found in parks or streets, is not practicable.[152] They 'doubtless exempt twentieth century tourists from the dreadful prospect of having their holiday snaps delivered up for destruction'.[153] The defence does not extend to other artistic works such as drawings, paintings, engravings, prints and photographs so that the photographing of these in an art gallery, for example, will be a breach of copyright.[154] The government is presently reviewing the special exceptions allowing the use of artistic works without permission as provided for in ss 66, 69 and 135ZM.[155]

Artists who reproduce parts or aspects of an artistic work of which they were the author (as defined in s 10(1)) will not infringe copyright in that earlier work as long as the 'main design' of the earlier work is not repeated (s 72(1)). Thus an artist who assigns away copyright will still be able to continue pursuing their creative line of development and may use moulds, casts, sketches, plans, models or studies made for the purposes of the earlier work (s 72(2)). A building may also be reconstructed without copyright being infringed (s 73).

Copyright in a cinematograph film may well expire before copyright in the underlying works (script, music, artwork), since the film copyright is 50 years from first publication (s 94) and work copyrights generally last 50 years from the end of the year in which the author died (s 33(2)). To meet this, the Act provides in s 110(2) that exhibiting an 'old' film does not infringe any work copyright in it. Old news films can also be exhibited in public (but not otherwise dealt with) 50 years after the principal events depicted in the film occurred (s 110(1)). Since this exception is confined to films intended as 'means of communicating news' it is likely that the principal events depicted and publication of the film are very close in time anyway, so the term of copyright protection is not cut short by very much. If, however, the definition of 'news' is wider than just recent or current events,[156] then perhaps a documentary film (for example concerning World War II) would never have enforceable copyright protection against public exhibition.

3. REMEDIES

[8.32]   General. Part V of the Copyright Act provides a range of remedies for infringement of copyright. Proceedings may be commenced either by the copyright owner or by an exclusive licensee (ss 115(1), 119).[157] The

---

152. Lahore, *Copyright,* para [42,030], citing CLRC, *Report of the Copyright Law Review Committee,* 1959, para [219].
153. Phillips and Firth, para [14.19].
154. See Lahore, *Copyright,* para [42,030] for a comment on the inconsistency of this provision.
155. Australian Copyright Council, *Newsletter,* April 1996, p 5. See also [7.19]–[7.21] re use of artistic works by educational (and other) institutions.
156. See eg *Commonwealth v John Fairfax & Sons Ltd* (1980) 147 CLR 39.
157. See [7.12].

main remedies are set out in s 115(2), which provides that a court may award injunctive relief,[158] and either damages or an account of profits in the court's discretion.[158] The Federal Court has stated that the Copyright Act is not exhaustive of available remedies, and that indeed any remedy which a court (hearing a copyright matter) may award in its inherent jurisdiction is available, for example a declaration.[159] If the infringement is deliberate, criminal penalties may be imposed (s 133). Sections 190 and 194 also allow for damages or an injunction where a false attribution of authorship is made.

[8.33] Injunctive relief. Section 115(2) provides that the court may grant an injunction concerning unauthorised use or threatened use of copyright material. The principles upon which interlocutory relief will be available are those applicable in general law.[160] In cases where evidence of copyright infringement may be destroyed the courts may also grant an Anton Piller order to allow a person bringing an action to enter a defendant's premises and seize offending material. In Australia such orders are mainly sought in connection with record, video and software piracy.[161]

[8.34] Damages.[162] The basic measure of damages is the loss in value of the copyright caused by the infringement,[163] although other measures (such as fair remuneration for the use of the plaintiff's work or loss of profits due to the defendant's activities) may be adopted where appropriate.[164] Additional damages of a punitive and/or aggravated nature may be awarded under s 115(4), having regard, inter alia, to the flagrancy of the infringement and to the benefits accruing to the defendant therefrom.[165] The courts have also recognised, on occasions, that copyright infringement involves more than just damage to property and may also be a cause of injury to reputation or feelings.[166] Damages will not be available, however, where the defendant was unaware and had no reasonable grounds for suspecting that the plaintiff's copyright was being infringed (s 115(3)).[167]

---

158. As to the extent of the court's discretion in this regard, see *Robert J Zupanovich Pty Ltd v B & N Beale Nominees Pty Ltd* (1995) 32 IPR 339; *A-One Accessory Imports Pty Ltd v Off Road Imports Pty Ltd (No 2)* (1996) 34 IPR 332.
159. *WEA International Inc v Hanimex Corp Ltd* (1988) 10 IPR 349 at 354.
160. See [2.10]–[2.12].
161. See eg *EMI (Australia) Ltd v Bay Imports* [1980] FSR 328; *EMI Records Ltd v Kudhail* (1983) 4 IPR 513; *IBM Corp v Computer Imports Ltd* (1989) 14 IPR 225.
162. See generally T H W Wells, 'Monetary Remedies for Infringement of Copyright' (1989) 12 *Adel LR* 164; D Miller, 'Restitutionary and Exemplary Damages for Copyright Infringement' (1996) 14 *Aust Bar Rev* 143.
163. *Sutherland Publishing Co Ltd v Caxton Publishing Co Ltd* [1936] Ch 323 at 326; *Prior v Lansdowne Press Pty Ltd* [1977] VR 65.
164. See eg *Interfirm Comparison (Australia) Pty Ltd v Law Society of NSW* (1975) 6 ALR 445; *Autodesk Australia Pty Ltd v Cheung* (1990) 17 IPR 69; *Bailey v Namol Pty Ltd* (1994) 30 IPR 147; *Columbia Pictures Industries Inc v Luckins* (1996) 34 IPR 504.
165. See eg *Concrete Systems Pty Ltd v Devon Symonds Holdings Ltd* (1978) 20 SASR 79; *Prior v Lansdowne Press Pty Ltd* [1977] VR 65; *Wellington Newspapers Ltd v Dealers Guide Ltd* (1984) 4 IPR 417; *Bailey v Namol Pty Ltd* (1994) 30 IPR 147.
166. See eg *Milpurrurru v Indofurn Pty Ltd* (1994) 30 IPR 209 (see [8.36]).
167. See *Z S Projects Pty Ltd v G & R Investments Pty Ltd* (1987) 8 IPR 460; *Golden Editions Pty Ltd v Polygram Pty Ltd* (1996) 34 IPR 84. Section 115(3) provides that the plaintiff remains 'entitled' to an account, though it appears the court retains the discretion to refuse it.

[8.35] Conversion of infringing copies. A further remedy is provided
by s 116, whereby the plaintiff may sue in conversion or detinue in respect
of 'infringing copies' or plates used to make such copies.[168] The plaintiff
may seek either delivery up of the offending items,[169] or damages calculated according to the market value of those items.[170] Such damages are
cumulative with any recovered under s 115,[171] though double counting will
not be permitted.[172] Again, innocence is a defence (s 116(2)). In 1992 the
Act was to be amended to make conversion damages available on a discretionary basis rather than being available as of right. This legislation lapsed
with the calling of the 1993 federal election. Schedule 6 of the Exposure
Draft Bill to amend the Copyright Act would re-introduce these amendments untouched.

[8.36] The Milpurrurru case. *Milpurrurru v Indofurn Pty Ltd*[173] offers a
useful illustration of the different bases on which damages may be awarded
under ss 115 and 116 and the flexible approach to assessment taken by the
courts. The action was brought by or on behalf of eight Aboriginal artists
whose artworks had been reproduced without their permission on carpets
manufactured overseas and imported into Australia by the defendants.[174]
In awarding damages for infringement of copyright von Doussa J accepted
that it would be inappropriate to apply the well established principle of
awarding separate judgment in favour of each applicant, assessed as to individual loss and damage, where Aboriginal law and custom would treat each
of the applicants in the case equally. He agreed that the defendants' liability, although assessed according to the usual rules, should be aggregated
and judgment would be awarded to the plaintiffs as a group. The plaintiffs
were awarded damages on three distinct bases. The first was an amount by
way of conversion damages for the value of the infringing copies, in this
case the carpets. Their value was assessed at an average cost, as if the
carpets were worth $190 per square metre. This came to $90,981.50.

---

168. These terms are defined in s 10(1). Note in particular that a film of a work is not an
'infringing copy' for this purpose. Section 116 appears to catch all those in
possession of infringing copies or plates, even if they have not committed any
infringement (eg an importer who lacks the requisite knowledge under ss 37 or
102): see *Young v Odeon Music House Pty Ltd* (1976) 10 ALR 153; cf *Infabrics Ltd v
Jaytex Shirts Ltd* [1981] 1 All ER 1057.
169. Cf the equitable remedy of delivery up for destruction: see *Sutherland Publishing Co
Ltd v Caxton Publishing Co Ltd* [1936] Ch 323 at 338.
170. See *Caxton Publishing Co Ltd v Sutherland Publishing Co Ltd* [1939] AC 178;
International Writing Institute Inc v Rimila Pty Ltd (1995) 31 IPR 356; *Autodesk Inc v Yee*
(1996) 35 IPR 415. The same measure applies even where part only of the article
consists of infringing matter: see *Infabrics Ltd v Jaytex Shirts Ltd* [1981] 1 All ER
1057; *W H Brine & Co v Whitton* (1982) 55 FLR 440.
171. See *Caxton Publishing Co Ltd v Sutherland Publishing Co Ltd* [1939] AC 178. Cf *Thornton
Hall Manufacturing v Shanton Apparel Ltd* (1982) 12 IPR 48. Damages under s 116 may
not be claimed in conjunction with an account of profits, for the latter involves
waiving the infringement and hence any title to the infringing copies or plates: see
Sutherland Publishing Co Ltd v Caxton Publishing Co Ltd [1936] Ch 323 at 336.
172. See eg *Lewis Trusts v Bamber Stores Ltd* [1983] FSR 453.
173. (1994) 30 IPR 209.
174. Two of the four defendants successfully appealed against the finding that they were
responsible for the infringement: *King v Milpurrurru* (1996) 34 IPR 11 (see [2.7]).
However, the appeal did not involve any challenge to the aspects of the first
instance decision discussed below.

Second, an award was made under s 115(2) to compensate for the loss of value of the plaintiffs' copyright. These damages were assessed at $1500 in respect of each artwork, reflecting the loss of value resulting from the degradation of the artwork and the resulting commercial use to which it had been put by the defendants. Von Doussa J noted that damages awarded under s 115(2) are usually assessed with reference to monetary loss, but may include compensation for anger, distress or personal suffering caused by the copyright infringement, not just on the part of the copyright owner but of 'those around' them.[175] Importantly, he accepted that the 'personal and cultural hurt' suffered by the artists *and* their communities should be compensable. However, he decided not to compensate for this 'pirating of cultural heritage' under s 115(2). Such damages could not be quantified by reference to the liability of the defendants (as had been requested by the plaintiffs), but only by reference to the individual circumstances of each of the plaintiffs. Assessment along those lines, artist by artist, would not have been in accordance with the principle of equality which the judge had agreed to follow. However, the Copyright Act does allow for additional damages for flagrant infringement under s 115(4) and in this instance the copyright infringement was found to be deliberate and calculated. Accordingly the element of 'cultural harm' was reflected in an award under that provision. These additional damages were assessed at $70,000 and would have been higher but for the other damages already granted.

[8.37] Unjustifiable threat of action. Section 202 provides that a person shall not threaten another by an action for infringement of copyright. In the event that such threats are made, any aggrieved person (who need not be the person threatened, but merely someone damaged by the threats),[176] may seek a declaration that the threats are unjustifiable, an injunction and/or damages.[177] It is a complete defence to such a charge that the action in relation to which the threats were made was indeed a breach of copyright (s 202(1)), though it is not enough that the defendant believed this to be the case, no matter how honestly.[178] On the other hand, a person who does no more than give notice as to the existence of a copyright, without threatening proceedings, will not attract liability on this score (s 202(2)).

[8.38] Seizure by customs. In relation to material which is alleged to be imported in breach of copyright, the copyright holder's remedies have recently been strengthened by extending the power of the Comptroller-General of Customs to seize such material and hold it pending a court decision on the question of infringement.[179] Previously the power of seizure had been limited to 'printed copies' of literary, dramatic or musical works,

---

175. (1994) 30 IPR 209 at 244, citing *Williams v Settle* [1960] 1 WLR 1072 at 1086–1087.

176. See *S W Hart & Co Pty Ltd v Edwards Hot Water Systems* (1980) 30 ALR 657.

177. As to the principles for assessing damages in such cases, see *Avel Pty Ltd v Intercontinental Grain Exports Pty Ltd* (1996) 34 IPR 1.

178. *S W Hart & Co Pty Ltd v Edwards Hot Water Systems* (1980) 30 ALR 657. If a breach can be shown, however, it does not matter that the copyright in question belongs to someone other than the defendant: see *Avel Pty Ltd v Multicoin Amusements Pty Ltd* (1990) 171 CLR 88.

179. See Pt V, Div 7, introduced by the Copyright (World Trade Organization Amendments) Act 1994 to replace the former s 135.

whereas the main objects of unauthorised importation tend to be records, films and software. However, the onus is on the person objecting to the importation to commence proceedings for infringement; if this is not done within a stipulated time, the material will be released. The Comptroller-General may also ask the objector for a sum of money to be deposited with the request for seizure in order to cover expenses.

[8.39] Criminal offences.[180] The Copyright Act provides that if an infringer has knowledge that an article is an infringing copy, that a plate (as defined in s 10(1))[181] will be used for making such copies, or that a performance will amount to an infringement, then criminal penalties may be imposed. Importing articles known to be infringing copies is also prohibited (s 133). The penalties provided for will be increased by a factor of three under proposed amendments to help combat piracy of sound recordings, when the parallel importing of such recordings is to be allowed in certain circumstances.[182]

In 1986 amendments to the Copyright Act were made in order to allow copyright owners to combat piracy more effectively. For example, s 132(2A) now provides that hiring out articles is an offence if a person knows or ought reasonably to have known that the article was an infringing copy. In *Pontello v Giannotis*[183] the defendant was charged with having in his possession 67 pre-recorded video tapes which were infringing copies. The major issue was the question of 'knowledge' under the 1986 amendments. It was held that the defendant certainly ought to have known that each of the tapes was an infringing article since he had been informed by solicitors acting for copyright owners that this was so, had been instructed by a member of the Australasian Film and Video Security Office on how to recognise pirated copies, and had in his possession equipment for copying video tapes. A term of imprisonment was considered by Sheppard J, who imposed a fine instead since it was a first conviction. Fines totalling $56,900 were also imposed on an offender who made unauthorised copies of films in *Pontello v Ceselli*.[184] It is clear in this context that a defendant's lack of knowledge based on an error of law is not an excuse.[185]

New offences were also created in 1984 by the Copyright Amendment Act to complement the provisions relating to the protection of computer programs as literary works. Section 133A now provides for an offence of advertising the supply of infringing copies of computer programs where a person knows or ought reasonably to know that the copy is an infringing one. It is also an offence to transmit a computer program where such transmission would result in the creation of an infringing copy of the program when received and recorded. This is deemed to be the supply of an infringing copy (s 133A(2)). The CLRC in its report *Computer Software Protection*

180. See W Kelcey, 'The Offence Provisions of the Copyright Act 1968 — Do They Protect or Punish?' (1995) 6 *AIPJ* 229.
181. A proposed amendment will substitute 'device' for 'plate': Sch 13, Exposure Draft Bill, February 1996.
182. Exposure Draft Bill to amend the Copyright Act, February 1996, Sch 3: See [8.23].
183. (1989) 16 IPR 174.
184. Federal Court of Australia, Wilcox J, 11 May 1989, unreported.
185. *IBM Corp v Computer Imports Ltd* (1989) 14 IPR 225. See also *Irvine v Hanna-Rivero* (1991) 23 IPR 295; *Irvine v Carson* (1991) 22 IPR 107.

recommended that possession of pirated software for business purposes be a separate offence, and that s 132(2A) be accordingly amended. The CLRC also recommended software infringement penalties being brought into line with those applying in respect of unauthorised commercial copying of films — fines ranging from $1500 for individuals and $7500 for corporations for a first offence to $50,000 and $250,000 respectively for repeated offences, with the possibility of imprisonment.[186]

---

186. *Computer Software Protection*, paras [16.31]–[16.37].

Chapter 9

Protection of Computer Technology

1. INTRODUCTION

[9.1] Computers. Computers are electronic machines capable of storing and processing enormous amounts of information. They have revolutionised almost every aspect of life in the developed world. As the developed world enters the 'electronic estate',[1] individuals have access to computer technology for private purposes: home computers, for computer games and word processing, and in the form of calculators and digital watches. Many daily events are regulated by computer technology which is employed to adjust fuel consumption in cars, room temperatures in thermostats and in cash registers to add up purchases and record inventory movements. Computer chips (integrated circuits) have made 'intelligent' buildings possible: office blocks which automatically adjust temperature, lighting and shutters according to the rooms in use and the cycle of the sun.

[9.2] The information superhighway. These examples and the effects on our lives are trivial in comparison with the developments in information technology and communications which have been brought about by computers, word processors and telecommunications and the links that can be established between them. It is possible for almost instantaneous exchange of information to occur on a world wide basis. That information, because it can be stored so readily and in such quantities, has far-reaching implications for privacy, international relations, national security and defence. We are moving from the industrial era into the digital era, where vast quantities of information can be stored, manipulated, and conveyed with great ease.

---

1.   T Barr, *The Electronic Estate: New Communications Media and Australia*, 1985.

This allows the emergence of a different sort of workforce and has implications for most aspects of our lives from leisure activities to, some would say, the type of government we will have in the future. The world of digital images and communications existing only over computer networks is known as 'cyberspace' and it is here that the 'information superhighway' (ISH)[2] or 'info autobahn' is being developed, through the Internet.[3] The term 'information superhighway' is attributed to Al Gore, elected Vice-President of the USA in 1992. In 1979, Gore proposed a nationwide network of fibre optic 'data highways'.[4] Part of the first Clinton/Gore election campaign included a promise to create a network that would 'link every home, business, lab, classroom and library by the year 2015',[5] to be known as the National Information Infrastructure (NII).

[9.3] Digitisation and multimedia. In Chapters 5 and 6 some of the consequences of convergence were referred to, particularly with reference to the effect on communications resulting from changing delivery systems for broadcasting and telecommunications. Categories previously depending on distinct technologies such as broadcast spectrum, telephone, cable, microwave, satellite and indeed print media, may now all be delivered by one method, for example accessed by telephone line using a computer and modem. Apart from methods of delivery converging, the content itself merges into one format with digitisation.

Digitised information can be stored in much greater volume than standard data, although different subject matter takes up different amounts of space. A one megabyte floppy disk can store between 200 and 250 pages of A4 text, or six seconds of music, or a single still image. It requires about 27 floppy disks to play one second of a motion picture,[6] but as high speed micro-processor units and developments in data compression take place, it will be easier to process and apply such high-volume data.

'The basis of our economic world is changing from atoms to bits. In the information age, more and more of what we are selling and buying is not actually made up of things you can touch.'[7] Geographic constraints do not apply on the Internet. Terrestrial governments have no natural sovereignty in cyberspace where regulation of an invisible domain is impossible and the individuals interacting may be citizens of another country, even if identifiable. Governments are becoming concerned about the problems with collecting tax revenue when the tax base is oriented to material goods rather than the exchange of data.[8] 'Notions of property, value, ownership and the nature of wealth itself are changing more fundamentally than at any time since the Sumerians first poked cuneiform into wet clay and called it stored

2.   Among alternative names suggested for the ISH is ELVIS (short for Electronic Light Video Information Services).
3.   For an explanation of the Internet and how services are provided 'on-line', see *Trumpet Software Pty Ltd v OzEmail Pty Ltd* (1996) 34 IPR 481.
4.   F H Cate, 'The National Information Infrastucture: Policymaking and Policymakers' (1994) 6 *Stanford Law and Policy Rev* 43.
5.   Ibid at 44.
6.   Japanese Government Committee, *Exposure '94 — A Proposal of the New Rule on Intellectual Property for Multimedia*, p 2.
7.   J Casimir, 'Battle in Cyberspace', quoting John Perry Barlow, *Sydney Morning Herald*, 29 July 1995, Spectrum 5A.
8.   M Ward, 'All the World Shall be Taxed', *New Scientist*, 20 July 1996, p 14.

grain.'[9] At the same time, it is argued, copyright and the protection of material within the existing legal framework are no longer viable. Indeed, the notion of protecting ideas and creative output by copyright may be inappropriate in the digital environment, since copyright protects set categories of subject matter expressed 'in material form'. Access to the information will be the most important right to protect. Possible solutions include a complete re-conceptualisation of copyright and the subject matter involved. Some would like to see the development of technological billing methods, and enforcement of rights based on encryption technology, with collective enforcement by a central 'clearing house' (as presently exists with respect to print and music industries). On this basis, the key form of legal protection required is not so much copyright, as a prohibition on the development or use of technology (such as decryption software) whose function is to circumvent those payment arrangements.[10] Other suggestions include abandoning existing notions of property and considering new rights such as 'access' or 'disclosure'.[11] 'Accessright' is a means of controlling/permitting access to content, and is said to overcome the problem of defining infringement in a technology specific manner and 'substantial reproduction'. In fact, copying is not the question at all, rather usage and value to the user is the issue.[12] The concept of something approaching an accessright (and consequently a charge for all access) has occurred to the Copyright Law Review Committee (CLRC) and been raised as a matter for discussion.[13] This is also evident in the thinking of the US government's major policy statement on communications and copyright issues.[14]

[9.4] Creative Nation — Australia and the information superhighway. In October 1994 the Prime Minister, Paul Keating, released 'Creative Nation' — the then Federal Government's cultural policy statement which highlighted the government's aim to 'maintain and develop Australian culture', recognising (inter alia) the importance of the arts and copyright industries as exporters.[15] Heavy emphasis was placed upon developing a significant Australian involvement in the international communication superhighway, including the creation of the Australian Multimedia Enterprise to finance the development and marketing of CD-ROMs. The statement recognised the difficulties facing creators of multimedia products in using and protecting copyright material (as well as the issues facing performers and creators of other products) and expressed a commitment to reforming copyright law (and administration) including the implementation of the recommendations of the Copyright Convergence Group (CCG)

---

9. Ibid.
10. Cf T C Vinje, 'A Brave New World of Technical Protection Systems: Will There Still be Room for Copyright?' [1996] 8 EIPR 431.
11. S Olswang, 'Accessright: An Evolutionary Path for Copyright into the Digital Era?' (1995) 5 *EIPR* 215.
12. Ibid, at 217–18.
13. *Copyright Reform: A Consideration of Rationales, Interests and Objectives*, 1996, p 22.
14. Information Infrastructure Taskforce, *Report of the Working Party on Intellectual Property Rights, Intellectual Property and the National Information Infrastructure*, 1995.
15. 'It is difficult to remember a major policy statement purporting to cover government policy in relation to a whole industry sector being accepted with such universal acclaim and so little criticism.' M Cooper, 'The Politics of Culture' (1995) 14(2) *Communications Law Bulletin* 1 at 1.

which reported in August 1994.[16] To this end, the CLRC was assigned the task of reviewing and simplifying the Copyright Act, to report by the end of November 1997. The first matter for report is to concern issues of protectible subject matter, bearing in mind 'convergence of product' since subject matter need no longer be defined according to the medium in which it is expressed or contained.

Although the existing Copyright Act has been described as a 'car, bus and truck' regime, it is copyright law (albeit a new Act, streamlined and updated) which will probably be used to regulate the ISH. The previous Labor Government expressed commitment to copyright owners continuing to have control over their material, and the Coalition Government elected in March 1996 seems equally committed to strengthening copyright as a tool of cultural policy.

[9.5] Global information policy. The work of the CCG and the need to address the policy issues, proprietary rights and matters of access to information inherent in the 'information superhighway' have been receiving attention at the international level. In the US, the setting up of the NII has been energetically pursued, although initially intellectual property issues were secondary to the logistics of broader information policy making, which in the US 'involves every cabinet department, more than 100 executive branch and independent agencies, two dozen congressional committees and expert advisory bodies, the federal courts, 51 state utilities commissions, and literally thousands of local regulators. These figures include none of the international policy making institutions.'[17] However, in 1994 the Working Party on Intellectual Property and the NII began work, producing first a Green Paper (draft) and in September 1995 the final White Paper. This 'exhaustive and exhausting document ... has a distinctive point of view, favouring expanded rights for copyright owners'.[18] This agenda was pursued by the US in December 1996 at a meeting of a Committee of Experts on a possible Protocol to the Berne Convention, intended to clarify matters with respect to issues arising (inter alia) from the development of new technologies. The US regards the White Paper's proposed model for the NII as appropriate for the policy determining intellectual property protection at the international level, the Global Information Infrastructure (GII).[19] Australia played an active role in these discussions. A major consideration for a national importer of copyright material is the expense associated with significant increases in proprietary rights for activities not hitherto caught within copyright law. For example, 'accessright' is a new concept — at present, taking a book from a shelf to browse through it is not an infringement of copyright, although accessing material on-line may become so. Australia successfully resisted the introduction of a new importation right at the December 1996 meetings.[20]

---

16. See [8.12].
17. F H Cate, 'The National Information Infrastructure: Policymaking and Policymakers' (1994) 6 *Stanford Law & Policy Review* 43 at 50.
18. L A Kurtz, 'Copyright and the National Information Infrastructure in the US' [1996] 3 *EIPR* 120 at 120.
19. Information Infrastructure Taskforce, *Report of the Working Party on Intellectual Property Rights, Intellectual Property and the National Information Infrastructure*, 1995, p 131.
20. See [1.19].

[9.6] Problems in cyberspace. Not everyone is enamoured of the information superhighway and life in cyberspace. Some are simply techno-phobic, on the basis that computers are 'antisocial, unnecessary and highly addictive'.[21] Others fear 'loss of cultural dominance' in the 'cultural war-fare between the wired and the unwired'.[22] Although the Internet is capa-ble of creating communities of almost any interest group, some fear the cyberspace community will become a series of ghettos of interest groups, with little or no 'community' of interest at all. There is deep suspicion that 'thus far, the computer revolution is about toys for boys'.[23] Evidence that 90% of use of the Internet is by males is giving way to a greater usage by women. However, despite the fact that the Internet does not require mus-cles, is based on relationships (thus possibly advantaging women) and does not require huge capital outlay, it does mean that, for example, those with-out electricity or telephone lines cannot participate. In central Africa there are seven telephone lines per 1000 people, in China nine, in India five. 'The information superhighway is like a state-of-the-art monorail running across a shanty town. The poor slum dwellers of the Third World will never be able to buy a ticket.'[24] Despite the sentiments expressed in 'Creative Nation' the cost of general access to the 'infobahn' may be prohibitive and further divide the haves from the have nots. In Australia, a notional expenditure of $11,765 would be required per annum for each family of two adults and two children to link that household to the ISH.[25] Even if access is available, is it presently worthwhile? There is nothing to indicate that, for example, students learn more effectively with interactive comput-ing facilities,[26] that there is demand for newspapers 'on-line', or that scroll-ing down a screen will replace reading books. It has been suggested that adequate dental care, literary, visual or performing arts or drought relief may have a higher priority for Australians than getting onto the infobahn.

[9.7] Legal protection for information technology. On the whole, however, disciples of the new technology outweigh the critics, although feeling at times like prophets crying in the wilderness to the uninformed,[27] particularly on the issue of how to or even whether to regulate the informa-tion superhighway, including formulating intellectual property rights. In Australia, creative endeavour, the traditional subject matter of intellectual property, has been assumed to require protection and discussion has cen-tred on how to effect this, rather than whether to. It is not necessarily self evident that such protection is desirable. In many instances it is arguable

---

21. A Slee, 'Cyberspace; Has Technology Gone Too Far?', *Sydney Morning Herald*, 14 July 1995, p 11.
22. J Casimir, 'Battle in Cyberspace', quoting John Perry Barlow, *Sydney Morning Herald*, 29 July 1995, Spectrum 5A.
23. P Adams, 'The Latest Toys for the Trendiest Boys', *The Weekend Australian* , 5–6 August 1995, Review, p 2.
24. B Faust, 'Computer Rage Here', *The Weekend Australian*, 5–6 August 1995, p 28.
25. B Faust, 'Breakdown on the IT Highway', *The Weekend Australian*, 29–30 October 1994, p 28.
26. Ibid.
27. Or even 'I feel like Jesus among the Pharisees every time I talk to these guys' (that is, US Government officials): J P Barlow, quoted in Jon Casimir, 'Battle in Cyberspace', *Sydney Morning Herald*, 29 July 1995, Spectrum 5A. Although presumably it is ignorance rather than hypocrisy of which Barlow is complaining.

that the legal monopolies conferred by intellectual property rights are at least as likely to stifle innovation in the field of information technology as they are to encourage it — quite apart from any impact they may have on freedom of expression and access to information.

Nevertheless, over the past ten to 15 years there has been a clear willingness on the part of law makers to expand the rights accorded to innovators in this field, and conversely to find ways of 'punishing' those who seek to exploit 'pirated' technology. In Chapter 6, one example of this was discussed: the CCG's recommendations to meet the challenge of digital delivery systems by casting rights in 'technology neutral' form, so as to close any gaps in copyright protection. The remainder of this chapter is devoted to a further series of issues in relation to which the same tendency to expand rights is apparent. Hence there is a discussion of the use of copyright law to protect computer programs and multimedia works. This is followed by an examination of the special legislative regime created for integrated circuits, as well as other forms of legal protection, notably under the patent system. In many of these cases the US, aggressively concerned to protect the interests of large companies such as IBM, Microsoft and the like, has been a powerful force, using the threat of trade sanctions to compel other countries to adopt legal regimes which 'match up' to US laws.[28] It remains to be seen whether these regimes prove to be as beneficial to the countries upon whom they have been forced as they apparently are to the US information technology giants.

2. COPYRIGHT

(a) Recognition of Copyright in Computer Programs

[9.8] Introduction. Since 1984 Australian law has protected the underlying programs which cause computers to perform. In 1995 the CLRC completed an extensive review of protection of software and made various recommendations discussed in this chapter.[29] The most important kind of computer software are programs, which govern the operation of the computer according to the objects to be achieved: storage and updating of information, calculations based on data held, control of the processes described above. A committee of experts meeting under the auspices of the World Intellectual Property Organisation in June 1983 to consider the question of protection of computer software concluded that it was premature to take a stand on the question of the best form of protection to recommend as an international model, since the conceptual basis for that protection was not yet clear.[30] Since that time, however, the protection of computer programs as literary works under a copyright regime has become the accepted international norm due largely to pressure from the US.[31] The existence of this norm is specifically confirmed by Art 10(1) of the TRIPS Agreement, which states that computer programs are to be

28.   See further [21.11].
29.   See *Computer Software Protection*.
30.   WIPO, 'Legal Protection of Computer Software' (1983) 17 *J World Trade Law* 537 at 544–5.
31.   See *Computer Software Protection*, paras [3.22]–[3.25].

protected under the Berne Convention. Commentators have argued that it would be more appropriate from a conceptual point of view to create a special or *sui generis* regime for the protection of software, as has been done for integrated circuits.[32] As will be apparent from the paragraphs which follow on the evolution of copyright protection for computer programs in Australia, copyright is far from an ideal 'fit' and there remain many difficult questions as to how its fundamental concepts can and should be applied in relation to software. Nevertheless, it appears that we are stuck with it.

[9.9] The Apple litigation in Australia. It was always generally assumed that copyright would protect software, but in late 1983 the well-known Apple programs were held at trial not to be literary works within the Copyright Act 1968 and therefore unprotected by that statute.[33] In that case, Apple sought an injunction, damages and an account of profits based on allegations that Computer Edge had imported into and sold in Australia a computer manufactured in Taiwan known as a 'Wombat', which sold for less than half the price of the Apple II computer of which it was a copy. The software or programs for the Wombat system were also copied. The only difference in a printout produced from each program was that 'Wombat' appeared where the word 'Apple' had appeared in the plaintiff's program. For the purposes of the copyright issue, the unauthorised copying of software had occurred overseas and was thus allegedly an indirect infringement within ss 37 and 38 of the Copyright Act.

[9.10] Background. To infringe the Copyright Act the infringing item must be copied from a recognised category of subject matter which is embodied in a material form. In the software area, for reasons of basic copyright law, the software must be characterised as a 'literary work' if it is to be protected. A 'literary work' in s 10(1) of the Act includes a written table or compilation, and writing is defined in s 10(1) as 'a mode of representing or reproducing words, figures or symbols in a visible form and "written" has a corresponding meaning'. Thus the definition of writing in the Act depends in turn upon what 'a visible form' means, and may also depend upon what is regarded as 'material form', since this is only partially defined (s 21(1)).[34]

The *Apple* case dealt with computer programs in both source code and object code. The programs were embodied in ROMs or EPROMs or a combination thereof. The two types of program in question were 'Applesoft' programs written in Assembly Language 6502, known as 'Applesoft Source', or in machine language, known as 'Applesoft Object'. Similarly, a program known as 'Autostart' was expressed in both languages. The *Apple* case did not concern a higher level language. These types of computer program have different functions to perform in the operation of a computer.[35] Some programs can be stored permanently in a memory device called ROM (Read-Only Memory) embodied in a silicon chip. These are placed inside the computer when manufactured, but can be replaced. They

---

32. See eg A Christie, 'Towards a New Copyright for the New Information Age' (1995) 6 *AIPJ* 145.
33. *Apple Computer Inc v Computer Edge Pty Ltd* (1983) 50 ALR 581.
34. See [6.3].
35. For an explanation of these terms, see *Apple Computer Inc v Computer Edge Pty Ltd* (1984) 53 ALR 225 at 230–4, from which this passage is derived.

cannot be altered and the information or 'memory' is not lost when the computer is turned off. This type of memory is usually used to hold data which must be available to the computer when the power is turned on. Other programs or information are made available to the computer when a magnetic disk comprising a program is placed into the disk drive unit. The RAM (Random Access Memory) stores this program while the computer is on, but does not retain it. Another memory device is called an EPROM (Erasable Programmable Read Only Memory), which is variable: information may be retained or erased.

The original program or set of instructions for the Apple II computer was written in source code, that is, a computer language understood by trained persons but not by the computer, which understands electrical impulses. By typing a source program into a computer the appropriate electrical impulses are recorded (with the use of an 'assembler' or 'compilation' program) which allows the machine to operate. This program is then expressed in object or machine readable code. Apple claimed that three of the silicon chips in the Wombat were not what they appeared to be, that is, devices for controlling the operation of a computer, but were in fact literary works subject to copyright. These silicon chips were said by Apple to be 'in writing' because their content could be deciphered through an electron microscope.

[9.11] The decisions. It was held at trial that none of the programs were literary works within the 1968 Copyright Act because of the definition adopted by Beaumont J that a 'literary work' is something intended to afford information, instruction or pleasure in the form of literary enjoyment.[36] A computer program merely drives a machine, that is, controls the sequence of operations carried out by the computer without performing these other functions. On appeal, Apple's claim to copyright in their computer programs was upheld by a majority of the Full Federal Court.[37] It was held that the source code was copyright as a literary work and that the object code was an adaptation thereof within s 31(1)(a)(vi) of the Copyright Act, since it could be viewed as a translation. The source code conveyed a meaning to suitably trained people and there is a distinction between the functioning of the machine due to electro-magnetic instructions for the storage and reproduction of knowledge.

On further appeal to the High Court, the trial judge's decision was restored.[38] The court did find that Apple's programs in source code were 'original literary works' in which copyright subsisted, since they were apt to afford information or instruction (perhaps even pleasure?) to a qualified reader, the operator keying instructions into the machine to enable the machine to convert source code to object code. Since writing the programs in source code involved skill, labour and experience on the part of the programmers, they also satisfied the requirement of originality. However, the object code was held not to be a literary work, and nor could it be regarded as a reproduction or adaptation of source code.[39]

---

36. *Apple Computer Inc v Computer Edge Pty Ltd* (1983) 50 ALR 581 at 591. See *Exxon Corporation v Exxon Insurance Consultants International Ltd* [1982] RPC 69 at 88.
37. *Apple Computer Inc v Computer Edge Pty Ltd* (1984) 53 ALR 225.
38. *Computer Edge Pty Ltd v Apple Computer Inc* (1986) 161 CLR 171.
39. For more detailed discussion of the decision, see [6.16], [6.34]. See also J McKeough, 'Semi Conductor Chip Protection: Copyright or Sui Generis?' (1986) 9 *UNSWLJ* 101.

[9.12] Reaction to Apple: the 1984 amendments. Even before the High Court heard the appeal in the *Apple* case the furore caused by Beaumont J's judgment at first instance prompted the Federal Government to legislate to amend the effect of the decision. This followed a symposium held in Canberra to learn industry views on the desirability of protecting computer software from copiers.[40] As a result, amendments to the Copyright Act were made to confer 'literary work' status on computer programs.[41] 'Computer program' is defined in s 10(1) to mean:

> an expression in any language, code or notation of a set of instructions (whether with or without related information) intended, either directly or after either or both of the following:
>
> (1) conversion to another language, code or notation,
> (2) reproduction in a different material form,
>
> to cause a device having digital information processing capabilities to perform a particular function.

In the *Apple* case the High Court interpreted 'language' and 'code' as describing forms of expression which can be perceived by human senses.[42] Therefore object code could not be a 'computer program' in itself, since the electrical form of object code was not a 'language, code or notation'. The 1984 amendments also provide that in relation to a computer program an 'adaptation' now means:

> a version of the work (whether or not in the language, code or notation in which the work was originally expressed) not being a reproduction of the work.

However, according to the *Apple* case adaptations of works must themselves be works. If for that reason an adaptation must in fact be in a 'language code or notation', then object code in electrical form will not be regarded as an adaptation either, despite the terms of the definition.

The 1984 amendments were intended to provide a short-term solution to the inadequacies of copyright law as revealed in *Apple*, eventually being amended to provide more accurate and appropriate protection. In fact, the amendments have proved surprisingly durable.

(b) The Scope of Copyright in Computer Programs

[9.13] The Autodesk case. Prior to the effectiveness of the 1984 amendments being tested in litigation, it had been assumed that computer programs were now protected by copyright,[43] a commercially expedient assumption which allowed firms to pursue their remedies without too much concern about their underlying rights.[44] In 1989 the definition of 'computer program' was considered for the first time in the Federal Court in the *Autodesk* case. The complaint of the applicant, Autodesk Inc, was that

---

40. *National Symposium on Legal Protection of Computer Software*, 15–16 March 1984.
41. See [6.17].
42. *Computer Edge Pty Ltd v Apple Computer Inc* (1986) 161 CLR 171.
43. See eg *Barson Computers Australasia Ltd v Southern Technology Pty Ltd* (1988) 10 IPR 597; *Ozi-Soft Pty Ltd v Wong* (1988) 10 IPR 520; *Computermate Products (Australia) Pty Ltd v Ozi-Soft* (1988) 12 IPR 487.
44. Indeed the assumption before Beaumont J's decision had been that copyright did somehow protect software, the subsequent view being that Apple had done the industry a disservice by having the issue resolved contrary to this point of view.

the respondent had broken a code and produced a device which could be used to allow the applicant's computer program to run on any suitable computer, without using a lock device which was normally necessary to allow Autodesk's program to run. The software in question, AutoCAD, was a very sophisticated program designed to facilitate the drafting of architectural and engineering plans and designs. The letters 'CAD' stood for 'computer assisted drafting'. AutoCAD cost about $5200 to purchase. In order to deter copying of the program, the applicants developed a method of limiting its use to one computer at a time. This method involved the use of an AutoCAD hardware lock, a device which had to be in place for the program to run. Copies of the program would not run without a lock either. It was hoped by Autodesk that this would encourage further sales of their program by rendering copying ineffective. Once the respondents had produced a device known as the 'Auto-Key lock' to enable AutoCAD to run without the lock, they began to advertise and sell the device for $499. The respondents believed that manufacture and sale of the Auto-Key was not an infringement of copyright law, but must have suspected it was sharp practice as they went to great lengths to conceal their identity.[45]

A part of the AutoCAD program (known as 'Widget C') contained instructions to the computer on which it was run, requiring the computer to send a 'challenge' to the AutoCAD lock.[46] On receipt of the challenge, the lock would 'answer' and, if correct, the AutoCAD program would continue to run. The respondents managed to simulate the function of the lock with their Auto-Key, but argued that the lock did not constitute or incorporate computer programs. The central issues in the case were (i) whether or not the computer program contained in AutoCAD was in part contained within the AutoCAD lock, and (ii) whether the Auto-Key was a reproduction in material form or an adaptation of the AutoCAD program.

[9.14] **The decision at first instance.** In discussing the definition of 'computer program', Northrop J said there was little doubt that each lock was 'a device having digital information processing capabilities' and also devised 'to perform a particular function'.[47] On this point the judge noted that the performance of a function is a new concept in copyright in a literary work and removes the necessity to consider whether a literary work could be understood by a human being, or whether it needs to convey pleasure or information: in other words, being intended to perform a function is the mark of a computer program. Furthermore, the encoding of digital information on the shift register (as used by the AutoCAD lock) or the EPROM (used in the Auto-Key lock), which allowed the locks to function, constituted an expression in a 'language, code or notation'. On the question of whether the Auto-Key lock was a reproduction of the AutoCAD lock and therefore an infringement of the copyright of Autodesk in the lock (being a computer program), Northrop J considered ss 13 and 14 of the Copyright Act, and referred to the views of Gibbs CJ in the *Apple* case that reproduction of a substantial part of the work involves two elements — 'that the infringing work sufficiently resembles the copyright work and that

---

45. *Autodesk Inc v Dyason* (1989) 15 IPR 1 at 8.
46. See ibid at 14 for detail on the working of the AutoCAD hardware lock summarised here.
47. Ibid at 21.

it was produced by the use of the copyright work'.[48] Obviously the second element was clearly established in this case. The difference in form between the hardware within the AutoCAD lock and the Auto-Key lock (that is, between shift register and EPROM) did not deter Northrop J from a finding of sufficient similarity, for:

> Each performs the same function. It is this function which is the essential aspect of each lock. Function has a particular importance in the definition of a computer program and regard must be given to this concept of function in considering the question of whether there is a 'sufficient degree of objective similarity' between the two locks.[49]

The method of operation by which a device having digital information processing capabilities performs a particular function was not really relevant in deciding whether the Auto-Key lock sufficiently resembled the AutoCAD lock. The fact that the result could be reproduced by processes adopted in the Auto-Key lock was sufficient for Northrop J to find infringement here.

The approach taken by Northrop J could be classified as a type of 'look and feel' analysis (as discussed below), in that the way the program works is not as important as what it does: it is the end result for the user that is considered in assessing whether reproduction has occurred. This approach appears to ignore the idea/expression dichotomy, in that the reproduction of an idea (result or function) is taken to amount to copying the expression of that idea, irrespective of any differences in form.[50]

[9.15] Autodesk on appeal. The result in the trial of *Autodesk*, while generally welcomed by the computer industry, was overturned on appeal to the Full Federal Court.[51] All three judges disagreed with the proposition that the lock itself either contained or constituted a program. The Full Court went on to hold that AutoCAD had not been reproduced, nor adapted, but that the alternative Auto-Key was a development of an original idea to produce a cheaper computer product entirely different from Auto-CAD despite the fact that it produced the same result. In so finding the judges adhered to the traditional 'form' requirement of copyright protection which does not allow protection of an underlying idea.

The Full Federal Court's decision provoked an outcry similar to that unleashed after the trial of *Apple*. Opinion was not uniform. Some commentators approved the result, arguing that the decision would promote a dynamic software industry[52] by allowing scrutiny of and improvement upon original ideas and the manufacture of compatible products and accessories.[53] On the other hand, industry representatives expressed shock at the decision, alleging it would stifle development, limit the choice of product and affect the quality of support enjoyed by users.[54]

---

48.   (1986) 161 CLR 171 at 186.
49.   (1989) 15 IPR 1 at 27.
50.   Cf G Greenleaf, 'Software Copyright: Form Follows Function, OK?' (1990) 64 *ALJ* 160.
51.   *Dyason v Autodesk Inc* (1990) 18 IPR 109..
52.   See H Meredith, 'Ruling Heads Off Computer Battle', *The Australian*, 17 September 1990, p 5.
53.   See B Head and C Fox, 'Court's Decision Reduces Reverse Engineering Risk', *Financial Review*, 17 September 1990, p 54.
54.   See 'Decision in Autodesk Hardware Lock Case', *PC Week*, 27 September 1990, p 39; D Frith, 'Law Reform Call After Court Ruling', *Sun-Herald*, 7 October 1990, p 50.

[9.16]   Autodesk in the High Court. The High Court held (per Dawson J, with whom the rest of the court agreed) that, in creating a device to interact with Widget C which allowed the AutoCAD program to run, this resulted in copyright infringement as a substantial part of a literary work (Widget C's message from the 'look-up table') had been reproduced.[55] Despite the fact that the look-up table was not a computer program itself, because it was not a set of instructions, it was still a 'substantial, indeed essential part' of the computer program comprised in Widget C.

In August 1992 an application was made to the High Court to re-open the *Autodesk* case.[56] The respondents sought to have the matter re-argued on the grounds that:

(i)   the look-up table in Widget C did not amount to a set of instructions but was simply data; and

(ii) the look-up table was not a substantial part of the Widget C program.

The application was dismissed by the majority (Brennan, Dawson and Gaudron JJ, Mason CJ and Deane J dissenting) who considered (inter alia) that the respondents had been given ample opportunity to be heard. In his dissenting judgment, Mason CJ rejected the idea that the functional aspect of a program determines its substantiality and said that in copyright law the emphasis is on originality of the part allegedly taken.[57] However, the emphasis on the *function* of a computer program as determining what is a 'substantial part' was maintained by the majority.

Commentators on the *Autodesk* decision have suggested that the High Court's decision confers protection on the function of the program, showing a tendency to protect the idea rather than the expression of the idea (despite a 'ritual incantation' of basic copyright principles).[58] The CLRC states that:

> The conclusion that the look-up table was a substantial part of the Widget C program, with the result that copying of the look-up table constituted copying of the program, causes the Committee some concern. Further, the conclusion that the creation of the look-up table in Autokey from observation of the operation of Widget C and the AutoCAD lock was a copying of the look-up table in Widget C, even though the maker of Autokey (Mr Kelly) never saw the table, is also viewed by the Committee as a far-reaching and questionable extension of copyright.[59]

Autodesk was applied in *Data Access Corporation v Powerflex Services Pty Ltd*,[60] concerning a program which produced identical file structure (organisation of files) to that of an original program with which it was compatible.

55. *Autodesk Inc v Dyason* (1992) 173 CLR 330.
56. *Autodesk Inc v Dyason (No 2)* (1993) 176 CLR 300.
57. *Autodesk Inc v Dyason (No 2)* (1993) 176 CLR 300 at 305; see further *Total Information Processing Systems Ltd v Daman Ltd* (1991) 22 IPR 71; *Computer Associates International Inc v Altai Inc* (1992) 23 IPR 385; *John Richardson Computers Ltd v Flanders* (1993) 26 IPR 367; *Accounting Systems 2000 (Developments) Pty Ltd v CCH Australia Ltd* (1993) 27 IPR 133. These cases tend to support the reasoning of Mason CJ as to what comprises a 'substantial part' of a computer program.
58. J Lahore, 'Intellectual Property Rights and Unfair Copying: Old Concepts, New Ideas' [1992] 12 *EIPR* 428. See also G Greenleaf, 'Autodesk (No 2) — The Uncertain Role of "Function" in Software Copyright' (1993) 67 *ALJ* 445.
59. *Computer Software Protection*, para [5.25].
60. (1996) 33 IPR 194.

The programming language of the application development system (DataFlex) was found to be a computer program within the meaning of the Copyright Act, although it was argued that the allegedly infringing PFX plus system 'adopted ... the meaning and function of each of the words ... but the expression ... is completely different'.[61] Jenkinson J held that 'The expression given in the Dataflex table is but one of many possible expressions',[62] and that 'each of the words of the DataFlex language is in my opinion an expression of a set of instructions intended to cause a device having digital information processing capabilities to perform a similar function'.[63] The decision is controversial and has been widely criticised. The applicants have appealed.

[9.17] 'Look and feel' cases. One of the factors which determines the market success of a computer system is a favourable proprietary user interface. The audio-visual screen displays generated by a program constitute the means by which the user conducts a dialogue with the computer. Once users have mastered one way of coping with a computer they may be loath to change,[64] but it is exactly this 'look and feel' or sequence, structure and organisation of the original program which is likely to be copied by competitors. 'Infringers' say they take only the idea of a program, but do not copy the program itself, relying on the idea/expression dichotomy to render their activities legal since completely different programming may lead to very similar output from the user's point of view.

The early 1980s saw the recognition of computer programs as protectable subject matter under copyright law. The 'first generation'[65] cases involved questions as to whether copyright protection extends to operation as well as application systems, to object code as well as source code, and software fixed on read-only memory chips (ROMs). The 'second generation' cases dealt with the issue of under what circumstances, if any, a competitor of a successful software developer may adapt and market a functionally equivalent work without infringing the basic program.

In the US, a series of cases beginning with *Whelan Associates v Jaslow Dental Laboratory Inc*[66] conferred protection on the 'look and feel' of a computer program, although that term was not used in the case. In *Whelan* the programs in question were used to manage dental laboratories. The court held that copyright infringement may occur despite the absence of copying from either the source or object code. This approach essentially extended protection beyond the literal elements of the program to the organisation and structure of the software. In *Whelan* the court relied heavily upon evidence of the visual similarity of the screen outputs and considered that all operations of the computer, including the screen output, were related to the operating program. The next major case to adopt the *Whelan* principles was *Broderbund Software Inc v Unison World Inc*,[67] where copyright was held to

---

61. Ibid at 197.
62. Ibid at 203.
63. Ibid at 197.
64. See *Lotus Development Corp v Borland International Inc* (1995) 33 IPR 233 at 247.
65. S Soltysinski, 'Protection of Computer Programs: Comparative and International Aspects' (1990) 21 *IIC* 1.
66. (1986) 797 F 2d 1222.
67. (1986) 7 IPR 193.

exist in the audio-visual displays of a computer program (audio-visual works are separately defined and protected by US copyright law). This was expressly extended to the overall appearance, sequencing and arrangement of the screen display.

'Look and feel' litigation continued to develop with the decision of *Digital Communications Associates Inc v Softklone Distributing Corp*.[68] Again it was found that there was copyright infringement of a software screen despite the absence of program code copying. This case recognised that even in a basic cloning situation the design and expression of the software is of fundamental importance.[69] The court determined that there were a number of ways to express the information in the status screen, that a number of features of the plaintiff's screen (such as the specific placement, arrangement and design of the parameter/command terms) resulted from extensive original human authorship, rather than being arbitrary or predetermined, and that the status screen was therefore a compilation subject to copyright protection to the extent of its arrangement and design.

These cases deeply divided the US software industry and attracted much adverse comment. It was argued by smaller firms (in particular) that protecting the user interface amounts to monopolisation of the user's experience, and that there are only so many ways to format certain programs so it is unfair to allow exclusive rights over such things.[70] It would certainly seem that the idea/expression dichotomy was not maintained either in *Whelan* or in *Softklone*, where status screen outputs were deemed to be separate works.[71] Indeed the decision at first instance in *Autodesk* has been described as 'look and feel with knobs on' for failing to maintain a clear distinction between idea and form.[72]

The US courts have not agreed among themselves on the limits of copyrightable expression. In *Lotus Development Corp v Paperback Software International*[73] a federal district court held that a Lotus 1-2-3 user interface consisting of a specific menu command system was protected as expression of an idea rather than the idea itself. However, in *Apple Computer Inc v Microsoft Corp* a federal district court held that a screen display could not be protected.[74] Apple achieved great success in the 1980s with the introduction of icons or symbols to represent information, the use of pull-down menus or lists of commands, use of windows to display information, and the ability to

68. (1987) 10 IPR 1.
69. See M Dailey, 'Case Comment — *Digital Communications Associates Inc v Softklone Distributing Corp*—The "Look and Feel" of Copyrightable Expression' [1987] 8 *EIPR* 234.
70. See M Radcliffe, 'Recent US Developments in Copyright Law related to Computer Software' [1986] 2 *EIPR* 43; R Stern, 'The Centre Will Not Hold — Recent Developments in Protecting "Idea" Aspects of Computer Software' [1987] 5 *EIPR* 128; L Spivack, 'Does Form Follow Function?' (1988) 35 *UCLA L Rev* 723.
71. See J Pinheiro and G Lacroix, 'Comment — Protecting the "Look and Feel" of Computer Software' (1987) 1 *High Tech L J* 410.
72. B Head and C Fox, 'Court's Decision Reduces Reverse Engineering Risk', *Financial Review*, 17 September 1990, p 54.
73. (1990) 740 F Supp 37.
74. (1992) 24 IPR 225. *Whelan v Jaslow* (1986) 797 F 2d 1222, *Broderbund Software Inc v Unison World Inc* (1986) 7 IPR 193 and *Digital Communications Associates Inc v Softklone Distributing Corp* (1987) 10 IPR 1 were not followed.

move, resize, open or close windows to retrieve, put away or modify information. Microsoft developed the Windows software, compatible with the IBM microcomputer standard and with visual displays greatly resembling those in the Apple Macintosh. The court held that an arrangement of purely functional items, or a combination thereof, are as far beyond the reach of copyright as other examples of user interfaces or arrangements of individual elements such as the dials, knobs and remote control devices of a television or VCR, or the buttons or clocks of an oven or stove, or the dashboard, steering wheel, gear shift, brakes, clutch and accelerator pedals of a car:[75]

> The similarity of such functional elements of a user interface or their arrangement in products of like kind does not suggest unlawful copying, but standardisation across competing products for functional considerations. Standardisation of the visual features in a computer's interface helps to achieve its purpose, a point which Apple learned early on when it insisted on interface uniformity for Macintosh applications and which has also been implicitly recognised by this court ... Some visual displays are or become so closely tied to the functional purpose of the article that they become standard. If 'market factors play a significant factor in determining the sequence and organisation' of a computer program, then those patterns may well be termed ideas beyond the ownership of one seller.

The trend of cases away from allowing protection for the expressive elements of computer programs has been applauded by commentators.[76] The CLRC discussed the concept of 'look and feel' aspects of a computer program and what that term actually means. After looking at developments in the US (not including *Apple v Microsoft*, discussed above) it concluded:

> the need for standardisation and need for efficient user interfaces to be used and developed outweighs the need to grant authors copyright protection in the 'look and feel' of their program's behaviour ... no amendments should be made to the Act to establish additional protection for the 'look and feel' of computer programs.[77]

[9.18] The CLRC software reference. In 1988 the CLRC was asked to inquire into whether the Copyright Act adequately protects computer programs, works created by or with computer programs, and works stored in computer memory. The CLRC reported in 1995, and found that the 1984 'sunset' provisions for the protection of software have been surprisingly durable, but recommended some changes to clarify the definition of 'computer program' and somewhat extend the notion of 'reproduction' with respect to computer programs.[78] Despite calls from some commentators to remove computer software from the copyright regime in favour of *sui generis* protection,[79] the CLRC considered that it would be unrealistic for Australia unilaterally to decide to embark on such a course, particularly in light of the USA's propensity to place Australia on a Priority Watch List if

---

75. (1992) 24 IPR 225 at 238.
76. See eg R Stern, 'Is the Centre Beginning to Hold on US Software Copyright Law?' [1993] 2 *EIPR* 39; G Rinck, 'The Maturing US Law on Copyright Protection for Computer Programs: *Computer Associates v Altai* and Other Recent Developments' [1992] 10 *EIPR* 351.
77. *Computer Software Protection*, para [9.42].
78. See [6.17], [8.2].
79. See eg A Christie, 'Designing Appropriate Protection for Computer Programs' [1994] 11 *EIPR* 486.

copyright protection is considered inadequate. The Committee concluded that due to the strong and entrenched views held in the US and EU, 'protection of computer programs as literary works is the appropriate form of protection'.[80] A number of other desirable amendments to the law were also put forward by the CLRC, as discussed in the next section.

(c) Other Copyright Issues

[9.19] Protection of program locks. The Autodesk company has been at the forefront of moves to have the Copyright Act further amended to protect computer technology and submissions were made to the CLRC during the course of its review of software protection to the effect that Australian law should be changed to prevent the removal or circumvention of devices designed to prevent copying, a measure introduced in the UK by the Copyright Designs and Patents Act 1988 and the subject of an EC Directive. The CLRC recommends that modification of a locked computer program for the purpose of circumventing the lock should be prohibited, and also subsequent copying of such modified programs.[81] In Europe, debate concerning reverse engineering and decompilation has highlighted the interests of two different groups. The European Council for Interoperative Systems (ECIS), composed of systems manufacturers such as Unisys, Sun Microsystems, Amdahl, Bull, Olivetti and Fujitsu, lobbied for inclusion in the Directive of specific permission to reverse engineer software to see how it works in order to be able to create competing products (or interfacing products, for example printers) using the same ideas but not the literal aspects of any program. This was vigorously opposed by the Software Action Group for Europe (SAGE), which includes IBM, Digital, Microsoft and Lotus.[82] The CLRC points out that decompilation may occur for a number of reasons, including correction of error, achieving interoperability and for legitimate inspection of ideas in software and should be allowed to some extent, as indeed the ideas in conventional literary works can be accessed without necessarily being 'copied'.[83] A compromise position is also what is embodied in the EC Directive.[84]

[9.20] Databases. Databases are large assemblies of information stored in computer memory. Information stored in centralised data banks is accessible by home computer over telephone and cable networks and through over-the-air broadcasting via networks or satellites. It has been thought unreasonable that no sanction attaches to these databases being searched by third party users without paying the appropriate fee to the owner of copyright in the databases, even if the computer from which the information is accessed does not belong to that owner. However, much of the information on databases, although voluminous, does not qualify for copyright

---

80. *Computer Software Protection*, para [4.14].
81. Subject to allowing back up copying and error decompilation: ibid, recs 2.29 and 10.94.
82. See P Waters and P Leonard, 'The Lessons of Recent EC and US Developments for Protection of Computer Software in Australia' [1991] 4 *EIPR* 124.
83. *Computer Software Protection*, paras [10.70]–[10.73].
84. D Mackenzie, 'Europe lays down the law on software', *New Scientist*, 22 June 1991, p 14; S Chalton, 'The Amended Database Directive: A Commentary and Synopsis' [1994] 7 *EIPR* 94.

protection on its own merits. The Copyright Act provides that a compilation of material including computer programs is subject to copyright, as
indeed compilations of material have always been protected within the definition of 'literary work' (s 10). The problem is that the compilation of
material must be put together with the requisite amount of 'originality' or
expenditure of a sufficient degree of labour, skill, judgment, intellectual
effort, etc in the arrangement of material comprising the work.[85] It is the
combination or arrangement of material that is protected, rather than the
underlying information. Although the standard of originality is 'fairly
low'[86] under Australian law, there is a minimum threshold to be met and
the investment of time, money and effort alone does not make a database
worthy of copyright protection, however much entrepreneurial effort has
gone into compiling it.

In *Feist Publications Inc v Rural Telephone Service Co Inc*[87] the white pages
telephone book was held by the US Supreme Court not to reach the
required threshold of originality in order to qualify for copyright protection. This case rejected the 'sweat of the brow' doctrine under which effort
and investment in compiling information is protected and came as something of a surprise as copyright in directories had long been acknowledged.
The question of what is 'unprotectable' data and what is 'protectable'
expression is not easy to answer. In *Feist*, 'selection and organisation' of the
raw data was required, over and above a simple alphabetical compilation of
subscribers' names and addresses.

The CLRC comments that 'electronically stored databases themselves
are not fundamentally different from databases that have been compiled
through vastly slower, non-electronic means in times past'.[88] However,
access to, use and reproduction of a computer database, particularly
through networks, distinguish them from collections of data stored only as
hard copy and make the computer database more useful and therefore
more valuable. Apart from this, many databases would qualify for copyright
protection under general principles as original compilations.

Although the need for protection of compilations of works which are
themselves the object of copyright is fairly obvious, in 1988 the European
Commission began considering protection for databases composed of non-
original material.[89] The resulting Directive on Legal Protection of Databases and accompanying memorandum described databases as 'hypermar-
kets of the future' where vast amounts of information are easily accessible
and can be 'sorted' into useful formats. For example, the telephone white
pages, an alphabetical list of subscribers and not 'original' in copyright
terms, may still be unfairly searched, used or re-arranged by someone who
did not supply the financial investment and effort required to compile the
database. The CLRC discussed the EC Directive and the recommended
right of 'unfair extraction' for original and non-original databases, but
recommended deferring a decision of adopting such a right until the Directive is considered in its final form.[90] Article 10 of the TRIPS Agreement

---

85. See [6.12].
86. *Computer Software Protection*, para [14.31].
87. (1991) 20 IPR 129.
88. *Computer Software Protection*, para [14.03].
89. *Green Paper on Copyright and the Challenge of Technology*, 1988, p 215.

explicitly requires protection for databases (as well as computer programs) and the protection of such non-original but worthy compilations seems to be firmly on the international agenda.

[9.21] **Works created by computers.** Because of the requirement that a copyright work be 'original', it might be thought that using a computer to create works may not lead to copyright subsisting in material developed through the use of, for example, computer graphics, spreadsheets or random allocation of numbers. However, this is not necessarily the case. For example, in *Express Newspapers plc v Liverpool Daily Post & Echo plc*[91] a set of computer selected numbers, arranged in grid form on a card published by a daily newspaper to enable their readers to play a form of bingo, was held to be a literary work. Although the plaintiffs had used a computer to arrive at the sequence of letters and grids, this was merely a tool of the person devising the grid. The CLRC recommends[92] that copyright protection be afforded to 'computer generated material' as a new class of subject matter other than works. Material created using a computer as a tool (that is, a word processor) would be subject to usual principles of protection, but in circumstances where no human author is involved there will be questions of 'originality' and arguments that the reader has displaced the author as the active participant.[93]

> Perhaps the simplest example to consider is that of satellite images of things such as weather patterns, vegetation and geological formations. In many cases the data that makes up the images is collected automatically by remote sensors on satellites. The information is automatically processed by specialised computer programs and the final image down loaded or printed out in hard copy either automatically or at the press of a button.[94]

Expert systems may also generate reports without any original contribution or selection of data by a human author. Since the notion of an author or creator does not apply to such material, and increased interactivity allows users to play a role, copyright may need to be limited or contain some notion of 'access' to material, rather than rely on the present rights listed in s 31.[95] The CLRC's recommendation recognises the entrepreneurial effort rather than authorship, as is presently the case with the Part IV copyrights.

[9.22] **Protection for multimedia.** Under existing concepts of copyright protection, multimedia may be regarded as a collection of separate components comprising existing works or other subject matter.[96] The law is familiar with the concept of multiple copyrights subsisting in one medium. For example, a broadcast has its own protection and may involve a film which itself embodies literary, dramatic, musical, artistic and sound recording material. The problems of identifying and dealing with all the possible

---

90. *Computer Software Protection*, paras [14.75] ff.
91. [1985] FSR 306.
92. *Computer Software Protection*, rec 2.42.
93. W Greisdorf, 'The Laugh of the Hypertext' (1994) 9 *IPJ* 1.
94. *Computer Software Protection*, para [13.11]; see also M Franzoni and G de Sanctis, 'Moral Rights and New Technology: Are Copyright and Patents Converging?' [1995] 2 *EIPR* 396.
95. A Christie, 'Towards a New Copyright for the Information Age' (1995) 6 *AIPJ* 145.
96. The CLRC was left with the 'strong impression' that 'a multimedia production is essentially a collective production combining a number of items of copyright material': *Computer Software Protection*, para [14.83].

creators of material embodied in a multimedia product are manifest. One possible solution is a multimedia collecting society. In a review of Australian collecting societies it was recommended that multimedia rights 'be administered collectively, possibly through existing collecting societies and based on a statutory licence to grant access to copyright material for the purpose of multimedia exploitation'.[97]

Quite apart from existing notions of copyright and their practicability in a digital environment where thousands of component copyrights might be involved, there is arguably an act of authorship necessary in creating the links and elements and arranging the material. While the 'compilation' of existing material may carry its own copyright, the application of the authorship/ rights copyright template to multimedia is coming under question. The CLRC made no recommendation on additional or different protection for hypertext, the interconnecting 'links' between elements of a multimedia product.

Multimedia may be more than the sum of its parts in the sense that there is a greater range of possible inputs and it may be used in a non-linear way since different people may use different parts of it and digitisation makes the product more accessible, more easily copied, transformed or used in a variety of ways.[98] The opportunity to infringe copyright is much greater when using multimedia networked material but the CLRC[99] and the CCG[100] have declined to single out multimedia for special treatment outside the existing copyright framework; on-line services were not discussed at all by the CLRC. It may be that the overhaul of the Copyright Act, the subject of the present CLRC reference, may result in subsuming categories of material and rights into a broader conceptual framework, such as allowing rights of access/distribution/transmission rather than relying on existing concepts of reproduction/performance/diffusion, for example.

One area of concern is the application of moral rights with respect to multimedia, acknowledged as an important aspect for a medium where use and alteration is so easy.[101] If moral rights require the existence of copyright in the subject matter, the copyright status of multimedia needs clarification. Film producers, but not record producers, will be accorded moral rights pursuant to the scheme outlined in the June 1994 Discussion Paper 'Proposed Moral Rights for Copyright Creators' and now in draft form in the 1996 Exposure Draft Bill to amend the Copyright Act.[102] The CCG canvassed the suggestion that a new category of 'audio-visual work' be introduced which would incorporate film and include multimedia.[103] In the meantime, contractual arrangements go a long way towards determining who benefits financially from multimedia technology, although the traditional fights between publishers and authors have tended to break out.[104]

---

97. Simpson, para [31.1.1]. The CCG, however, has noted an international trend away from compulsory licensing: CCG, para [7.8].
98. P Leonard, 'Beyond the Future — Multimedia and the Law' (1994) 7 *IP Law Bull* 105.
99. *Computer Software Protection*, para [2.63].
100. CCG, para [7.8].
101. I Collie, 'Moral Rights and Multimedia' (1995) 20 *Alt LJ* 166.
102. See [5.14]–[5.15].
103. CCG, para [7.4].
104. S Wyndham, 'Disks put Publishers in a Spin', *The Weekend Australian*, 24–25 December 1994, Review, p 6.

3. INTEGRATED CIRCUIT LEGISLATION

[9.23] **Circuit Layouts Act 1989.** The 1984 Copyright Act amendments recognising copyright in computer programs were supplemented by the Circuit Layouts Act 1989 (Cth), which provides *sui generis* copyright-style protection for integrated circuits or semiconductor chips. There is no possibility of dual protection under the Copyright or Designs Acts.[105] The Act, passed in May 1989 and proclaimed to take effect on 1 October 1990,[106] allowed Australia to join the WIPO Treaty on the Protection of Intellectual Property in respect of Integrated Circuits (the Washington Treaty) which was declared in April 1989.[107] Protection for member countries to the Treaty is provided on the national treatment principle familiar to members of the Berne Convention.

[9.24] **Nature of eligible layout rights.** The Circuit Layouts Act overcomes the problem that copying electronic circuitry may not be caught by the 1984 Copyright Act amendments,[108] but only where the layout is in an integrated circuit (silicon chip) rather than stored on a floppy disk. Protection applies automatically when an eligible layout is made, as defined in s 5. An 'eligible layout' (EL) is an original circuit layout, the maker[109] of which was an eligible person[110] at the time the layout was made, or else the layout was first commercially exploitable in Australia or in an eligible foreign country.[111] A 'circuit layout' is a 'representation, fixed in any material form, of the three-dimensional section of the active and passive elements and interconnections making up an integrated circuit'. 'Integrated circuit' is in turn defined to mean 'a circuit, whether in final form or an intermediate form, the purpose, or one of the purposes, of which is to perform an electronic function, being a circuit in which the active and positive elements, and any of the interconnections, are integrally formed in or on a piece of material'.

Other key definitions include 'original' and 'commercial exploitation'. In s 11 of the Act it is provided that a circuit layout is not original if it involved no creative contribution by the maker, was commonplace at the time it was made, or its features are dictated solely by the function it is required to perform. Commercial exploitation involves selling, hiring, distributing by way of trade or offering to do so, as well as importing a layout

---

105. As an artistic work or design, as to which see J McKeough, 'Semi Conductor Chip Protection: Copyright or Sui Generis?' (1986) 9 *UNSWLJ* 101 at 112–14. The ALRC has recommended in its final report on the reform of designs law that circuit layouts continue to be excluded from registration, although not necessarily their outer casing: *Designs*, para [4.24].
106. Almost immediately after coming into force, some of the definitional provisions were amended by the Law and Justice Legislation Amendment Act 1990 (Cth).
107. See [21.23]. In view of the TRIPS affirmation that computer software is to be protected as a literary work, circuit layouts legislation will continue to take second place in the international scheme of protection of computer technology.
108. See G L Hughes and A Sharpe, *Computer Contracts: Principles and Precedents*, 1987, p 88.
109. A person will be the 'maker' of a layout even if a computer was used to design it (s 10(a)).
110. An Australian citizen, resident or protected person, a body corporate incorporated in Australia, or such a person from an eligible foreign country (s 5).
111. Foreign countries will only be declared eligible if they are parties to a relevant convention to which Australia is also party or if they extend reciprocal protection to Australian layouts (s 42).

or integrated circuit made in accordance with the layout (s 8). The creator enjoys the exclusive rights to copy the layout, that is, the 'plan' for the chip; to make a chip in accordance with the layout; to be the first to commercially exploit the layout or a chip made in accordance with such a layout; or to authorise any of these acts (ss 17, 9). The 'protection period' lasts for a minimum period of ten years calculated, in general, from the time when the layout is first commercially exploited (s 5). EL rights are personal property and are transmissible by assignment, by will and by devolution by operation of law (s 45(1)). Assignments, which must be in writing, may be total or partial: that is, an owner may limit an assignment to some only of the rights, or to a certain area or for a certain period (s 45(2), (3)). The grant of a licence, which may be exclusive, binds the grantor's successors (s 45(4)). Provision is also made for agreements in relation to the assignment or licensing of future EL rights (s 44).

[9.25] Infringement of eligible layout rights. An infringement of EL rights occurs when a person, acting without the owner's authority, does anything substantially falling within the scope of the owner's exclusive rights: though the right of commercial exploitation is only infringed if the person knows or should reasonably know that the owner has given no authorisation (ss 19, 13). In *Nintendo Co Ltd v Centronics Systems Pty Ltd*[112] the High Court held that it is not enough that the defendant be aware that the plaintiff has given no authorisation for their use of the layout: for infringement to be established, the defendant must also know or have reason to believe that the plaintiff is in fact the owner of the layout rights. On the other hand, the High Court also indicated that a person who had that knowledge would be guilty of infringement even if they were unaware that their particular use of the layout amounted to a commercial exploitation and thus fell within the scope of the owner's exclusive rights. In other words, ignorance of the existence of layout rights or the identity of their owner may constitute a defence; but ignorance as to the *extent* of those rights may not.

Certain acts are not to be taken as infringements. These include commercial exploitation, where at the time the layout was acquired or the circuit made, the person did not know and could not reasonably be expected to have known that EL rights subsisted in the layout, and provided equitable remuneration is paid to the owner or exclusive licensee of the rights from the time of awareness (s 20); copying for private use or for research or teaching purposes (ss 21, 22); reverse engineering of a layout, including the use or exploitation of any original circuit layout created as a result (s 23);[113] and use for defence or security purposes (s 25). Commercial exploitation of a copy of a layout or of a circuit made in accordance with the layout is also excused where the copy or circuit has been acquired as a result of authorised commercial exploitation of the layout here or overseas (s 24(1)). Thus unlike conventional copyright protection, the owner cannot prevent parallel importation.[114] However, in *Sega Enterprises Ltd*

---

112. (1994) 181 CLR 134.
113. See *Nintendo Co Ltd v Centronics Systems Pty Ltd* (1991) 23 IPR 119.
114. Note also that the parallel importation provisions applicable to copyright articles (see [7.12]) are explicitly excluded from application to copyright work contained in a circuit, so long as the EL rights in question are not being infringed (s 24(2)): see *Avel Pty Ltd v Wells* (1992) 23 IPR 353.

v Galaxy Electronics Pty Ltd[115] the applicant's video games, involving computer-generated images, were classified as 'cinematograph films' under s 10(1) of the Copyright Act and were thus protected against parallel importing.

Where an infringement can be made out, the owner (or an exclusive licensee) may obtain an injunction and either damages (including exemplary damages) or an account of profits; except that damages may not be awarded against a person who neither knew nor reasonably should have known that they were committing an infringement (s 27(2)–(4)).

[9.26] **International precursors.** The regime of protection for topographical layouts broadly follows the pattern of similar legislation enacted in recent years in the US, Japan, Scandinavia and Europe. The US Semiconductor Chip Protection Act 1984 was the first example of such *sui generis* legislation for a new technology. The first attempts to pass such legislation foundered because of disagreement as to the form and extent of appropriate protection, with some arguing that there should be no protection at all since competition in the industry provided the impetus which made America the world's leader in chip innovation. The Act attempted to accommodate these different points of view, and similar features appear in the Australian Circuit Layouts Act. For example the chip monopoly is limited in several ways, perhaps most significantly in the Act's recognition of reverse engineering, analogous to the doctrine of 'fair use'. This allows the exchange of new information in the industry in that reverse engineering is permissible for the purpose of teaching, analysing, or evaluating the concepts or techniques embodied in the mask work. The information thus gained can be used in new designs, but not to replicate the original chip. Chips must be 'original', that is, not consist of 'staple familiar or commonplace designs' before protection will be given under the Act. The scope of this requirement of originality in the US legislation is not clear and the Circuit Layouts Act shares this uncertainty: hence the references in s 5 to what is not original, rather than what is.

One practical effect of the US tailormade chip protection (which took semiconductors outside the ambit of copyright legislation) was that no obligation arose under the Universal Copyright Convention 1952 to grant equivalent protection to foreign chips under the doctrine of national treatment. Congress was concerned that amendments to the Copyright Act would, under the Universal Copyright Convention or other treaties, mean that foreign chips were protected in the US, but American chips would not be protected by the inadequate copyright laws in other countries. A policy of comity rather than national treatment was included in the Act, requiring reciprocal mask work protection for US chips before foreign chips could be protected by the Semiconductor Chip Protection Act At the final reading of the Act to the Senate it was envisaged that the international comity provisions would 'go far to encouraging a prompt and positive response in Japan, Western Europe and elsewhere'.[116] This comment seems to have

---

115. (1996) 35 IPR 161. See also *Nintendo Co Ltd v Golden China TV — Game Centre* (1993) 28 IPR 313, a South African decision in which a computer generated video game was also held to be a film.
116. R Roberts, 'Protection of Semiconductor Chip Design Under Canadian Copyright Law: Will Canada Follow the Lead of the US?' (1985) 23 *U West Ont LR* 101 at 108, quoting Senator Mathias.

been accurate in that Japan has introduced legislation aimed at establishing comity with the US, and the European Commission drafted a Directive on the protection of semiconductor chips in response to the requirement of reciprocity.[117] WIPO also held discussions on a draft treaty to protect integrated circuits,[118] which culminated in the declaration of the Washington Treaty in April 1989, which the EC signed as a contracting party.

4.   ALTERNATIVE FORMS OF PROTECTION

[9.27]   The call for protection. Even before the *Apple* litigation made it clear that computer software possessed no intangible or incorporeal right falling within a recognised category to which legal or equitable protection attached, the computer industry nevertheless held the view that software should be treated as property,[119] a view which government and legislative policy supported. The realisation that computer software is a valuable commodity with regard to both export and indigenous markets and the fact that skill and resources must be devoted to its production tended to pre-empt any debate on the desirability of extending protection to this species of intellectual or industrial property: rather the debate has centred upon the most appropriate form of such protection.

[9.28]   Software liberation. One alternative to copyright style protection, while still promoting the funding of software development, is proposed by the Software Liberation Lobby.[120] This group claims that most activity in the Australian software industry is in the sphere of tailoring or contract work for which adequate legal protection is provided by licence agreements based on contract and trade law. The proposed alternative to copyright protection is public funding of microcomputer software packages (the software which is sold retail to a mass market of unknown users), through a levy on disks and chips which would be paid to producers of software. This sort of scheme was to be introduced with respect to sound recordings by the levying of a 'royalty' on blank tapes, in return for which non-commercial home taping would be permitted.[121] Reciprocal arrangements with other countries producing microsoftware (mainly the US) may be inevitable, but less desirable than returning moneys collected to Australian software houses, in return for which overseas users would have free use of Australian developed software.[122] It is argued that mass market packaged software has more in common with broadcast and diffusion than with 'goods', since once the product has been released there is no advantage in restricting its reception if some way of paying for it can be found. Another analogy is with other 'public goods' such as roads or scientific research.

117. Ibid.
118. *Report Adopted by the Committee of Experts on Intellectual Property in Respect of Integrated Circuits*, 1985.
119. See Australian Computer Retailers Association, 'Draft Submission to Conference on Software Protection', *National Symposium on Legal Protection of Computer Software*, 1984, Report 70.
120. The Lobby is led by Albert Langer. See B Taylor, 'Statement for Software Liberation', *National Symposium on Legal Protection for Computer Software*, 1984.
121. See [6.41]–[6.42]. Although ruled unconstitutional, the scheme is expected to be revived in tax legislation.
122. *National Symposium on Legal Protection for Computer Software*, 1984, p 5.

Furthermore, copyright law has made major concessions because of relatively cheap home copying of video and audio material and easy access to
photocopying. Since software is so easily copied any copyright is unenforceable; imitation is not prevented by copyright but has similar economic
effects since the cost of redeveloping a successful package, even without
copying it, is only a fraction of the original cost and undermines recovery of
the original investment in the same way as copying. 'Cloning' of software is
widespread and follows very closely upon the market success of a 'new'
package.

Nevertheless, the Copyright Act as amended in 1984 (to be supplemented by the introduction of the CLRC's recommendations, when implemented) is still the main source of protection for computer programs.
Although legal protection exists for the narrow market packages provided
by mainframe suppliers who also offer continuous support and have contractual agreements concerning use and confidentiality of software and
source codes, easily copied mass-produced microsoftware is unprotected in
any practical sense from the home copier.[123]

[9.29] 'Copyright is dead'. A related policy to software liberation promotes complete abolition of the copyright regime with respect to digitised
material. This has been advocated by John Perry Barlow, on the basis that
copyright protects 'the bottle, not the wine', and the bottle is disappearing,
even in the form of floppy disks, CD-ROMs and other discrete 'bit-pack-
ages'.[124] Users of the Internet, like users of 'shareware', have become
accustomed to sharing information at no cost and enjoy the lack of regulation in cyberspace, which is not subject to the constraints of 'meatspace'.
However, although copyright seeks to protect expression 'in material form',
a redundant concept in cyberspace, it does have the imprimatur of international acceptance, and has in fact been used to make operators of bulletin
boards liable for infringement by users.[125] Even if supplemented by 'accessright', contractual arrangements, compulsory licences or technological
solutions such as encryption, the fundamental aim of encouraging creation
through enforcing boundaries between the public domain and proprietary
interests will continue to animate legislators. Even the most radical proponents of the 'copyright is dead' line admit that regulation is likely to occur
in a form desired by the relevant community, and where the provision of
content depends upon reward being paid to the creators, some means of
enforcing the right to remuneration will be sought.[126]

[9.30] Patent protection for computer programs. The UK and
European Patent offices exclude computer programs from patentability, an

---

123. See however *Irvine v Carson* (1991) 22 IPR 107 and *Irvine v Hanna Rivero* (1991)
     23 IPR 295 where criminal penalties were imposed for 'home copying' of software.
124. J P Barlow, 'Selling Wine Without Bottles, The Economy of Mind on the Global
     Net' (1994) 7 *Aust IP Law Bull* (Supplement Issue).
125. See *Playboy Enterprises Inc v Frena* (1993) 839 F Supp 1552; *Sega Enterprises v Maphia*
     (1994) 857 F Supp 679 discussed in N Elkin-Koren 'Copyright Law and Social
     Dialogue on the Information Superhighway: The Case Against Copyright Liability
     of Bulletin Board Providers' (1995) 13 *Cardozo Arts and Ent LJ* 2.
126. John Perry Barlow himself is happy to admit that when he receives a cheque for
     explaining his views, 'I alone will cash it': Postscript to 'Selling Wine Without
     Bottles, The Economy of Mind on the Global Net' (1994) 7 *Aust IP Law Bull*
     (Supplement Issue).

attitude stemming from the conception that programs are nothing more than instructions for performing intellectual exercises and involving the application of programming techniques to a particular problem. These techniques are usually within the common professional expertise of those working in the field and therefore, in patent law terms, lack novelty and/or are obvious.[127] The Australian Patent Office has also denied patentability to computer programs for similar reasons to those articulated overseas: that computer programs per se are generally no more than methods of calculating mathematical problems and are simply schemes or instructions on how to use a computer in a particular manner.[128] This is not to say that the *application* of computer programs in a way that fulfils the requirement of amounting to a 'manner of manufacture' will be refused a patent. Thus an improved method of drawing a curve using sophisticated software has been held patentable,[129] as has an ingenious method of allowing Chinese characters to be constructed using a word processing program.[130]

There has been a good deal of debate over the issue of patenting software lately, as the US has granted hundreds of patents each year for programming techniques or algorithms. This has led to 'uproar' from programmers who say that 'things we would regard as totally obvious are getting patents'.[131] This trend is interfering with software development as patents are granted for techniques which, in the time between filing the application and grant, 'hundreds of programmers around the world may have independently created ... thus infringing the patent'.[132] Sorting out conflicting claims will be time consuming and expensive, discouraging newcomers from entering the field and requiring the payment of royalties to those who assert ownership over widely used technology. Small companies have begun to terrorise larger concerns through the wielding of patent monopolies over such basic technology as spreadsheets[133] or three-dimensional displays,[134] and for familiar processes such as generating footnotes and comparing documents.[135] Indeed, even basic semiconductor chip technology was patented by a 'Silicon Valley garage shop' inventor, who obtained the patent in July 1990 and acquired the legal basis for claims that 'could drain hundreds of millions of dollars from chip-company coffers'.[136] Although there was fierce opposition to this patent from companies like Intel, Motorola and Texas Instruments, as well as hundreds of smaller concerns working with microprocessor technology, many corporations prefer to pay licence fees rather than face the expense and vagaries of patent

---

127. See Cornish, pp 142–3; Phillips and Firth, para [4.11]. As to the requirements of novelty and lack of obviousness under the patent regime, see [12.13]–[12.24].
128. Australian Patent Office, *Guidelines for Considering the Patentability of Computer Program Related Inventions*, 1986. See also J Worthy, 'Software Patents in the UK After Merrill Lynch' [1989] 10 *EIPR* 380.
129. *IBM Corp v Commissioner of Patents* (1991) 22 IPR 417.
130. *CCOM Pty Ltd v Jiejing Pty Ltd* (1994) 28 IPR 481.
131. D Charles, 'Rights and Wrongs of Software' *New Scientist*, 29 September 1990, p 34 at p 38. See generally R H Stern, 'Patenting Algorithms in America (Parts I and II)' [1990] 8 *EIPR* 292; [1990] 9 *EIPR* 321.
132. Charles, ibid.
133. See 'Software Patents: Law of the Jungle', *Economist*, 18 August 1990, p 54.
134. Charles, ibid, p 38.
135. B Kahin, 'The Software Patent Crisis', *Technology Rev*, April 1990, p 75 at p 80.
136. *Financial Review*, 17 September 1990, p 51.

litigation. By the time rights are granted the patented software may well be redundant, the industry as a whole having moved on; nevertheless they may be asked to pay for technology used in the past, no longer productive and which no one may have guessed there would be patent rights over.

The costs of maintaining a system of protection of intellectual property based on patent law are enormous, even for software developers and publishers who do not wish to patent their products but must bear the costs of operating under the system. The software industry is highly decentralised, programming requires no special materials, facilities or tools, and barriers to entry are low. An industry locked into patent law protection requires that before a program can be written the prior art must be analysed in order to avoid infringement, something which requires an (expensive) search to be done. One problem emerging is that the US patent office has accepted the deposit of software (in the same way as micro-organisms)[137] to satisfy the requirement of full disclosure rather than requiring documentary disclosure.

> Software documents its own design, in contrast to physical processes, which require written documentation. Also, software is usually distributed without source code under licences that forbid reverse engineering. This may amount to suppressing or concealing the invention and therefore prevent the program from qualifying as prior art. The search for prior art may require securing oral testimony from people who developed software at universities many years ago, an expensive proposition.[138]

These searching costs are in addition to the direct costs of the patent monopoly, a necessity for those whose work may otherwise be monopolised, since the patent system does not allow for co-existence of independently created material. 'Software developers who understand the impact of patents are demoralised.'[139] The US software industry had been a 'model of creative enterprise'[140] before the rush of patenting, and the whole history of the computer industry is testimony to the fact that the traditional 'incentive' function[141] of patent protection is unnecessary in this instance. If the trend towards patenting continues, the stranglehold the system imposes on research and development of software may have to be relieved by generous compulsory licensing or fair-use rules. The more likely solution to protecting computer programs continues to be through copyright law, a more flexible and forgiving medium in terms of the independent creativity of other persons.

The CLRC briefly discussed patent protection for software but detected almost no support for this alternative in submissions made to it.[142] While computer programs are not expressly excluded from patent protection in Australia there must be disclosure of a 'manner of manufacture' rather than simply presenting or performing an algorithm.[143]

---

137. See [12.27].
138. Kahin, ibid, p 77.
139. Ibid, p 80.
140. Ibid, p 78.
141. See [11.4], [11.6].
142. *Computer Software Protection*, paras [4.07]–[4.09]. For discussion of the potential for patent protection of software, see *CCOM Pty Ltd v Jiejing Pty Ltd* (1994) 28 IPR 481.
143. See *Re Application by Honeywell Bull Inc* (1991) 22 IPR 463; cf *IBM Corp v Commissioner of Patents* (1991) 22 IPR 417.

Chapter 10

Designs

1. INTRODUCTION

[10.1]   General. In September 1995 the Australian Law Reform Commission (ALRC) produced its final report on designs law following an investigation into the registered designs system, particularly its adequacy and appropriateness in terms of providing protection and remedies for users of the system.[1] The ALRC was also asked to modernise and simplify the existing legislation and remove difficulties that had arisen in the operation of the Designs Act 1906 (Cth).[2] It is anticipated that there will be new legislation to be called the Designs (Visual Features) Act. This chapter will outline the existing regime, commenting on likely changes resulting from the ALRC report.

At the moment the Designs Act 1906 establishes a system for the protection of registered industrial designs. The design monopoly protects the appearance of articles to which a distinctive shape, ornamentation or pattern can be given. Because consumers show distinct preferences for certain styles and colours good design is important for all sorts of items, ranging from kitchenware and bathroom accessories to cars, spare parts, toys, furniture, computer keyboards, pens, trains, telephones and light fittings. In fact, the appearance of a whole range of manufactured articles may be protected by the Act. Good design aims at making products easy to manufacture, ergonomically sound and 'user friendly' and is crucial to the market success of most everyday items. The importance of industrial design is increasing as the primary sector can no longer be regarded as the mainstay of the Australian economy. Designing products that the manufacturing industry can sell overseas creates new export markets and reduces the bill

---

1.   See *Designs*.
2.   All references in this chapter to legislation and sections are to this Act. The recommendations of the ALRC are referred to as rec (number).

for imported products. Companies such as Decor, Sebel, Ford, Teletronics and Sunbeam have been successful at doing this. It is this link between innovative product design and economic success that provides the most obvious justification for having a system for registering new designs. Despite the absence of any concrete evidence as to the net economic benefits of such a system, it seems to be generally assumed that, without some legal protection against unauthorised copying by competitors, there would be less incentive for such firms to commit resources to the creation of innovative designs.[3] Nevertheless, the question remains as to the scope of such protection, and in particular whether it should be possible to secure monopoly rights over designs which are concerned with the functioning of a product rather than its visual appearance.

[10.2] Existing scope of design rights: protecting visual appearance. Design protection became important when the Industrial Revolution made possible the mass production of articles previously produced individually. When England began to lose its pre-eminence as a producer of industrial goods (particularly fabrics), parliament in an attempt to stimulate and protect manufacturing activity, conferred a 'copyright' upon the owner of designs which satisfied certain criteria of novelty or originality. The first designs statute was the Designing and Printing of Linens (etc) Act 1787, which gave protection to designs for certain textiles such as linens, cottons, calicos and muslins. From this developed other statutes giving protection in respect of the ornamentation of any 'article of manufacture' as well as the shape and configuration of any such article. The present Designs Act is based on the considerations which led to the first such legislation, but designers now work in a world of interactive graphics, computer aided design and networking, allowing design and manufacturing teams to work cooperatively and with reference to a variety of considerations beyond basic visual appeal. The ALRC report points out that a 'mismatch' between modern designs and available legal protection has occurred as the scope of industrial designs has expanded. It may not be sensible to distinguish between, for example, engineering design, fashion design, graphic design, environmental design and systems and processes to achieve a certain end. Where objects and our surroundings are contrived with particular attributes of structure, appearance, safety, function (and others) it is not appropriate to conceive of design protection as confined to simple visual features.[4] Nevertheless, the Designs Act 1906 as it stands is specifically aimed at preserving 'to the owner of the design the commercial value resulting from customers preferring the appearance of articles which have that design to that of those which do not have it'.[5] If a design does not have a distinctive visual appeal, it is not registrable. It is not possible to obtain monopoly rights over a 'design' which is concerned with how a product is constructed, or how it works, or what safety features it has. This is not to say that it is impossible to use the designs system to protect the 'functional' aspects of a product. At least since 1981, the fact that a design includes

---

3.   See Bureau of Industry Economics, *The Economics of Intellectual Property Rights for Designs*, Occasional Paper 27, 1995; *Designs*, paras [3.10]–[3.23].

4.   See *Designs*, ch 2. See further S Ricketson, 'Towards a Rational Basis for the Protection of Industrial Design in Australia' (1994) 5 *AIPJ* 193.

5.   *AMP Inc v Utilux Pty Ltd* [1972] RPC 103 at 108.

features which serve a functional purpose has not operated as a bar to regis-trability.[6] Nevertheless, the focus must still be on visual appearance. If that appearance is not new and original, there can be no design right. Moreover there is nothing to stop a competitor copying the functional aspects of a registered design without infringement, provided that a different visual appearance is given to the rival product. Thus the protection given to the functional features of designs under the current system is indirect at best.

[10.3] Extending protection to functional features? As the ALRC noted in its review, this limitation of the registered designs system has attracted much criticism from designers and manufacturers.[7] What many firms want is protection against their designs being copied and losing the benefits of their hard work, whether those designs relate to the visual appearance or to the functioning of their products — or indeed some underlying engineering principle that has guided the creation of those products. The notion of broadening design rights at least some way beyond the more aesthetic aspects of product appearance has certainly attracted considerable support, and finds precedents in the designs regimes of other countries, especially in Europe.[8]

Nevertheless, the ALRC's recommendation was that the focus of the designs system continue to be the protection of visual features. It took the view that to provide designs protection for all forms of functional innova-tion would run the risk of undermining other intellectual property regimes, especially in terms of the level of innovation required to obtain patent rights over a product or process. Any extension to protection should only be countenanced after a broad-ranging review of intellectual property rights in general, or at least of the patent system. Accordingly the Commis-sion recommended that the review of the petty patent system, which was then in progress, should address the problem of how to overcome any 'gap' in protection for functional innovation.[9] The recommendations of that review are considered in the next chapter.[10] The Commission adopted a similar stance in relation to an alternative approach which had been sug-gested as a way of providing appropriate protection for the broader aspects of industrial designs: the creation of an anti-copying right, either to supple-ment or replace the registered design system, and either limited to designs or more broadly embracing 'unfair copying' of any type. As noted in Chap-ter 1, the Commission contented itself with a recommendation that a review be commissioned as to the advantages and disadvantages of intro-ducing such a right.[11] In the meantime, it saw its own task to be one of strengthening the present system, not radically recasting it.

---

6.   See [10.14].
7.   *Designs,* para [2.44]. It is also the subject of much ignorance. Many respondents to the ALRC's design users survey were under the mistaken belief that the designs system confers protection on the way a product works: ibid, para [4.44].
8.   See European Commission, *Green Paper on the Legal Protection of Industrial Designs,* 1991; L J Duncan, 'Improvement of International Protection of Designs and Models' (1993) 4 *AIPJ* 32; S Ricketson, 'Towards a Rational Basis for the Protection of Industrial Design in Australia' (1994) 5 *AIPJ* 193; Bureau of Industry Economics, *The Economics of Intellectual Property Rights for Designs,* Occasional Paper 27, 1995.
9.   *Designs,* paras [3.36]–[3.58].
10. See [11.8].
11. *Designs,* paras [3.59]–[3.71]: see [1.15].

[10.4] Designs and copyright. It is not just the potential overlap between the designs and patent systems which may create controversy. Where a design is based upon an artistic work, or indeed constitutes such a work, copyright protection may also be available for that work, something which has always presented difficulties. The legislature's attempts to prevent dual protection have had, at times, unintended consequences; amendments in 1989, designed to straighten out some of the anomalies, have created their own problems and this is one of the issues the ALRC was asked to address in its designs reference. The provisions dealing with the design/copyright overlap are considered at the end of this chapter.[12]

2. THE REGISTRATION PROCESS

[10.5] Application for registration. The designs system is administered by the Australian Intellectual Property Office (AIPO) under the auspices of a Registrar of Designs. Under s 20 the owner or co-owners of a design may apply for its registration. Normally the owner of an unregistered design will be its 'author' (s 19(1)), that is, the person who conceives the design and reduces it to material form.[13] That rule is displaced, however, in favour of a person who commissions a design (s 19(2)), the employer of an author acting in the course of employment (s 19(3)) or a person to whom ownership of a design has been assigned in writing (s 19(4)). The ALRC recommends that the legislation should provide that the designer be the owner, subject to the rights of employers and those commissioning designs, and that this be spelled out in the new Act.[14]

Applications must be in the prescribed form and accompanied by the prescribed number of representations (drawings, specimens, etc) of the article to which the design is applied (s 20(3)): separate applications are required for each article in question, unless part of a set (s 20(6), (7)). The application may also be accompanied by, or the Registrar may request, a statement of monopoly and/or a statement of novelty. As defined in s 4(1), these set out the features of the representations in respect of which the applicant claims a monopoly and/or novelty or originality.[15] The ALRC recommends that the statement of monopoly as an optional aspect of the system be replaced with a requirement that applicants identify new or distinctive features of the design (rec 47), which will be given significance in any assessment of infringement (rec 49). Failure to provide this will confine the court to considering the overall appearance of the product rather than the new and distinctive features (rec 50).[16]

---

12. See [10.24] ff.
13. See *Chris Ford Enterprises Pty Ltd v B H & J R Badenhop Pty Ltd* (1985) 4 IPR 485 at 491. A person who merely follows another's instructions in producing a drawing or model, etc does not displace that other as the author: see eg *Pearson v Morris Wilkinson & Co* (1906) 23 RPC 738.
14. *Designs*, ch 7.
15. A monopoly statement may also include disclaimers by the applicant, that is, statements as to those features for which a monopoly is *not* being claimed: cf *Re Beerens' Application* (1986) 7 IPR 413.
16. Cf *Richsell Pty Ltd v Khoury* (1995) 32 IPR 289.

Section 49 also provides for applications in respect of designs for which protection has been sought within the previous six months[17] in a 'convention country'. A country falls into this category when it is prescribed as such under s 48: those currently prescribed are members of the Union established by the Paris Convention for the Protection of Industrial Property, originally made in 1883. A Convention application must be supported by the documentation relating to the foreign application (s 49(4)). The priority date for such an application is the date of the foreign application (s 49(1)). In the case of an ordinary application the priority date is that of lodgment of the application at the Designs Office (s 21). This 'priority date' is all important because, as will be seen, any design rights subsequently granted are retrospectively deemed to commence on the priority date of the original application, so that any infringements after that date may be pursued.

Many aspects of the registration system will remain the same under the ALRC's proposed amendments; in particular the requirements regarding Convention applications should not be amended, based as they are upon international practice (rec 86).

[10.6] Processing the application. An application is presently considered by the Registrar, who, having conducted any searches deemed necessary, must be satisfied that the design is registrable and that the applicant is entitled to apply (s 23).[18] No application will be refused until the applicant has been given the chance to be heard (s 24). Amendments to the application may be allowed by the Registrar, but not so as to cause the application to include matter not in substance originally disclosed (s 22B).[19] Where an amendment has the effect of excluding a design, that design may be the subject of a further application at any time up to the grant or refusal of the original application (s 22C(1)). Any such further application is known as a 'divisional application', and it will be deemed to have been lodged on the date of the original application, that date becoming its priority date also (s 22C(2)). The ALRC is in favour of retaining this provision for preserving the priority of designs 'divided out' from initial applications (rec 85).

When an application is granted, the applicant will be issued with a certificate and details of the design will be entered on the Register (s 26), at which point the applicant's documentation will become open to public inspection (s 27). Where an applicant has died prior to registration, the applicant's legal personal representative may be registered as the owner of the design (s 22A).

---

17. Where applications have been made in more than one such country, the relevant date is that of the earliest (s 49(3)); though the Registrar may disregard applications which have been withdrawn before becoming open to public inspection (s 50).
18. See [10.10] for discussion of the proposed system allowing a choice of non-publication of designs. At the moment, design details are published at the time of filing the application. This would not occur under an optional publication/registration system as it would defeat the purpose of making the choice (rec 95).
19. See *Chris Ford Enterprises Pty Ltd v B H & J R Badenhop Pty Ltd* (1985) 4 IPR 485. The ability of applicants to amend applications as set out now in s 22B should be retained in any new designs legislation (rec 83).

[10.7] **The Register.** The Register of Designs records all relevant particulars relating to registered designs (s 33). Any assignee or transmittee of a registered design will, on application, be registered as its owner (s 38), as will the legal personal representative of a deceased owner (s 38AA). Provision is also made for the interests of persons such as mortgagees or licensees to be noted (s 38A), though not trusts (s 34). An unregistered instrument relating to a registered design will not be admissible in any proceedings as proof of title to the design or an interest therein (s 38B). The one exception arises under s 39, whereby 'any person aggrieved' may apply to a prescribed court to have the Register rectified to correct an error. Section 39 plays a particularly significant role in the system, in that it may be invoked by way of counterclaim to an action for infringement (s 32) and thereby used as a vehicle for challenging the validity of a registered design by seeking to have it expunged from the Register.[20] In keeping with computerisation of records and the use of databases by land titles and share registries, the ALRC recommends (rec 98) that the Register itself be evidence of any particular entered upon it, rather than certificates of registration being prima facie evidence of the facts stated therein. Procedures for correcting the Register and offences concerning false entries are to be retained and in some cases extended.[21]

[10.8] **Period of protection.** Section 27A provides for a maximum period of protection of 16 years, made up of an initial period of 12 months from the date of registration, an extension until the expiration of six years from the priority date of the application (which of course will be earlier than the date of registration, so that this 'extension' effectively includes the initial 12 months), and two further five-year extensions. The two five-year extensions will be granted on application (within six months of the expiration of the period as previously extended). The critical procedure relates to the first extension. This extension, which must be sought during the initial registration period, may be refused by the Registrar on the ground that the design lacked novelty or originality at its priority date. Although there is no procedure as such for formally opposing the extension, any person may draw the Registrar's attention to any publication of a document in Australia before the priority date which is considered to be relevant to the issue of novelty or originality (s 27A(4)). Where registration lapses owing to a failure to apply for an extension, an application for restoration may be made (s 27B). This will be granted if the Registrar is satisfied that the failure to seek an extension was unintentional and that no 'undue delay'[22] has occurred. On the other hand, registration may at any time be cancelled by a prescribed court on application from 'any person interested' on the ground that the design has been published in Australia prior to the priority date of the relevant application (s 28(a)).

The present process was intended to provide for an inexpensive and quick opposition to the continued registration of a design. However, the ALRC found confusion among design users resulting from the linking of the administration of the renewal system with procedures for removal of designs from the Register. To this end, the initial one year period of

---

20. Cf *Macrae Knitting Mills Ltd v Lowes Ltd* (1936) 55 CLR 725.
21. *Designs,* ch 9.
22. See *Board of Control of Michigan Technological University v Commissioner of Patents* (1982) 56 ALJR 616.

registration is to be removed (rec 104), making the term of protection 15 years. New procedures to challenge the validity of a registered design (by initiating examination proceedings, rec 118) are suggested in Chapter 11 of the ALRC report.

[10.9] Subsequent registration in respect of other articles. Under s 25D, a person who owns a design which is registered in respect of one article may seek to register that design or one that is an obvious adaptation thereof in respect of another article; or to register, in respect of the same or another article, a design that differs from the original design only in immaterial details or in features commonly used in the relevant trade.[23] Such an application will not be refused by reason of registration, publication or use of the original design after its priority date. Where registration is granted on this basis, it is deemed to take effect from the date of application and remains in force only while the original design's registration subsists. Where the original design's registration is cancelled under s 28(a), however, the subsequent registration continues to subsist in its own right, unless the court specifies otherwise.

[10.10] Choosing publication. Although in the future protection of designs will continue to be based on a registration system, as this is supported by industry and patent attorneys and has a number of advantages,[24] the ALRC recommends an optional publication or registration system, with publication to destroy novelty and prevent anyone else registering (including the publisher of the design).[25] This is to provide an alternative to registration which, with its costs, delay and uncertainty, has been criticised by users of the designs system. It would be especially suitable for textile or fashion designers who have large numbers of designs or seasonal/short life products for which registration is too slow. Under the proposed system, an application would still be filed in the usual way, but the applicant could then elect to have the design published rather than go through with the process of registration. Although no protection would be given under the designs legislation, the applicant would be safe from any later attempt by someone else to register the same design (which would now lack novelty), and could still rely on copyright protection where appropriate. It is interesting to note that a proposed 'unregistered design right', which *would* have offered some protection as an alternative to registration, and which had been suggested in the ALRC's earlier discussion paper, was abandoned by the ALRC in its final report.[26]

3. REGISTRABLE DESIGNS

[10.11] General. The Act requires a number of criteria to be satisfied for a design to be registrable. For the most part they fall into two categories: those going to the definition of design and those going to novelty or originality. These will continue to be crucial under any new regime. The question of whether a design is registrable may be raised at various stages: when the Registrar considers an application (s 23(1)); when a first extension of the

23. These terms are also used in s 17(1), discussed below: see [10.18]–[10.19].
24. See *Designs*, ch 8.
25. Ibid, paras [8.11]–[8.14].
26. Ibid, para [8.15].

registration period is sought (s 27A(9)); when cancellation of registration is sought on the ground of prior publication (s 28(a));[27] or when rectification of the Register is sought to expunge a design which, it is claimed, could not have been registered (s 39(1)(b)). As already noted, this latter procedure is commonly invoked by way of defence in proceedings for infringement.

(a) Definition of Design

[10.12] Design defined. 'Design' is defined in s 4(1) to mean 'features of shape, configuration, pattern or ornamentation applicable to an article, being features that, in the finished article, can be judged by the eye, but does not include a method or principle of construction'. Taking the elements of this definition in turn, the terms *shape, configuration, pattern or ornamentation* refer, in a composite way, to features both two- and three-dimensional.[28] While colour is not specifically mentioned in the definition, the particular colour(s) in which a design is expressed may in some instances be an integral part of that design.[29] *Article* is defined to mean 'any article of manufacture and includes a part of such an article if made separately' (s 4(1)).[30] The term also includes a set of articles and/or each article in that set (s 4(2)). The definition thus excludes naturally occurring substances and it has further been held that the relevant article must have some function other than that of merely carrying the design.[31] Buildings and fixtures have also been taken to be outside the scope of the term 'article',[32] except where they are portable and manufactured elsewhere prior to delivery.[33] On the other hand, it is no objection to the validity of a design that the article in question is of indefinite extent in one or two dimensions (s 18(2)).[34]

As to the requirement that a design be *applicable* to an article, this suggests that it is not the article itself that is protected, but rather a conception of visual appearance that may be applied to that article.[35]

27. Note however the narrow scope of this provision: see *Wolanski's Registered Design* (1953) 88 CLR 278 at 280.
28. See *Rollason's Registered Design* (1898) 15 RPC 441 at 446; *Wolanski's Registered Design* (1953) 88 CLR 278 at 280.
29. See *Smith, Kline and French Laboratories Ltd's Design Application* [1974] RPC 253.
30. The definition goes on specifically to exclude 'an integrated circuit, or part of an integrated circuit, within the meaning of the Circuit Layouts Act 1989, or a mask used to make such a circuit'. As to that Act, see [9.23]–[9.25]. See further Designs Act s 7.
31. See *King Features Syndicate Inc v O & M Kleeman* [1941] AC 417; *Edwards Hot Water Systems v S W Hart & Co Pty Ltd* (1983) 1 IPR 228.
32. *Re Concrete Ltd's Application* (1940) 57 RPC 121; *Inala Industries Pty Ltd v Associated Enterprises Pty Ltd* [1960] Qd R 562.
33. See eg *Tefex Pty Ltd v Bowler* (1982) 40 ALR 326. See also *Shacklady v Atkins* (1994) 30 IPR 387 (yacht held to be an 'article').
34. This provision was introduced by the Industry, Technology and Commerce Act 1992 in order to overcome the effect of the decisions in *Bondor Pty Ltd v National Panels Pty Ltd* (1991) 102 ALR 65 and *Brisbane Aluminium Fabricators and Supplies Pty Ltd v Techni Interiors Pty Ltd* (1991) 23 IPR 107, which held that designs for articles of uniform cross-section but indefinite length would not be registrable. In an unusual move, provision was also made to protect those who may have relied on those decisions and acquired designs whose registration they believed to be invalid, by permitting them to apply for a licence to use the designs: s 18(3); regs 29AA–29B.
35. See *Re Clarke's Registered Design* (1896) 13 RPC 351 at 358; *Wolanski's Registered Design* (1953) 88 CLR 278 at 279.

Where three-dimensional features are concerned (shape and configuration), this entails distinguishing between the 'fundamental form' of an article — its shape as an article of that type — and features which are introduced in order to give it a particular and individual appearance.[36] Finally, the design's features must be capable of being *judged by the eye*. The individuality of any design must lie in some striking and distinctive visual appearance, though it need not be aesthetically appealing.[37] Although the Act is not completely clear, it would seem that it is the eye of the court that must judge the issue, not that of a hypothetical customer.[38]

[10.13] Proposed definition of design. The ALRC agrees that all aspects of a product's visual appearance should be capable of protection. The new definition of design is to be 'one or more visual features of a product' (rec 7). Visual features are to include shape, configuration, pattern, ornamentation, colour and surface (rec 8). A 'product' (regarded as a more contemporary word than 'article') is anything manufactured, thus retaining much of the meaning of the existing provisions. Designs or models of buildings will be capable of protection (rec 14); also packaging (rec 16) and designs for products with one indefinite dimension, such as extruded roof guttering manufactured in a continuous process (rec 15). Circuit layouts will be excluded from design registration, although not their external housing (rec 18). Screen displays on computers will also not be eligible on general principles as the screen display itself is not a product, but results from use of a product (rec 20).

[10.14] Functional aspects of a registered design. Originally, the shape of an article was not treated as registrable as a design if it had a utilitarian function only, that is, if the shape was dictated by the requirement that the article perform a certain task.[39] In 1981 s 18 was inserted into the Designs Act, providing that a design is not invalid by reason only that it 'consists of, or includes, features of shape or configuration that serve, or serve only, a functional purpose'. As Franki J pointed out in *Edwards Hot Water Systems v S W Hart & Co Pty Ltd*,[40] there still needs to be an element of appeal to the eye when an article is also functional. This view was also taken in *Ogden Industries Pty Ltd v Kis (Australia) Pty Ltd*,[41] where key blanks were held to have sufficient individuality and appeal in appearance to constitute designs, although their appearance was dictated solely by their function. In *Fire Nymph Products Ltd v Jalco Products (WA) Pty Ltd*,[42] s 18 did not apply, the circumstances of the case having arisen prior to the 1981 amendments taking effect. This had the result of excluding from design registration a

---

36.   *Malleys Ltd v J W Tomlin Pty Ltd* (1961) 35 ALJR 352; *Mangraviti v Vardi* (1976) 12 ALR 355; *Dalgety Australia Operations Ltd v F F Seeley Nominees Pty Ltd* (1985) 5 IPR 97; *Firmagroup Australia Pty Ltd v Byrne & Davidson Doors (Vic) Pty Ltd* (1987) 9 IPR 353; *Interlego AG v Croner Trading Pty Ltd* (1992) 25 IPR 65.
37.   *Re Bayer's Design* (1907) 24 RPC 65 at 77; *Malleys Ltd v J W Tomlin Pty Ltd* (1961) 35 ALJR 352; *AMP Inc v Utilux Pty Ltd* [1972] RPC 103 at 121.
38.   *L J Fisher & Co Ltd v Fabtile Industries Pty Ltd* (1979) 49 AOJP 3611; *Dart Industries Inc v Decor Corp Pty Ltd* (1989) 15 IPR 403 at 408–9.
39.   See eg *AMP Inc v Utilux Pty Ltd* [1972] RPC 103; *Hosokawa Micron International Inc v Fortune* (1990) 19 IPR 531; *Interlego AG v Croner Trading Pty Ltd* (1992) 25 IPR 65.
40.   (1983) 49 ALR 605 at 634–5.
41.   [1982] 2 NSWLR 283.
42.   (1983) 47 ALR 355.

fireplace which, although aesthetically pleasing, had a shape and configuration dictated solely by function. However, since design registration was inapplicable, copyright protection could continue despite s 77 of the Copyright Act. This is no longer the case. To begin with, functional but attractive aspects of the fireplaces would, since 1981, now be registrable and, as will be seen, the new s 77 introduced in the 1989 amendments provides for loss of copyright protection even for unregistrable designs (such as plans for hot water systems, slurry pumps or car exhaust systems).[43]

The ALRC discussed the role of attractiveness in design protection as 'judged by the eye', noting that since the definition of design refers to the visual features of a product, it is unnecessary to include the words 'judged by the eye' any longer (rec 21). As far as requiring some attractive or aesthetic quality for the design, although the statute does not require this at the moment the case law suggests that aesthetic or sensory criteria may be relevant to registrability. The Commission recommends that there be no requirement for designs to be distinguished on the basis of attractiveness, sensory perceptions or aesthetic sensation (rec 22). Furthermore, s 18(1) should be retained (rec 24) and a design should not be refused registration because a feature has a functional purpose. However, as noted earlier, the Commission did not consider that the designs system should be extended to provide more than the indirect protection s 18(1) offers in relation to the functional features of designs.

[10.15] Methods or principles of construction. Methods or principles of construction are specifically excluded in the definition of 'design', a principle well established prior to the 1981 amendment of the definition to that effect.[44] Thus in *Re Wolanski's Registered Design*[45] a 'neck-tie support' could not be registered because the shape defined the article. Similarly in *Kestos Ltd v Kempat Ltd*[46] a brassiere could not be registered as a design when the article itself could not be distinguished from the design. The Designs Act gives a monopoly in design only and not to the trading of the article to which it is applied: 'If something said to be a design does not by appeal to the eye take the article beyond the fundamental form of the class of article under consideration it is not a registrable design'.[47] In discussing the express exclusion from registrability of 'methods or principles of construction' the ALRC recommended deleting these words from any new definition of design (rec 26) on the basis that they are redundant, adding little to the current (and proposed) definition and creating problems of interpretation which have 'rendered design protection inappropriately narrow for utilitarian products such as locks and pumps'.[48]

[10.16] Spare parts. There has always been contention as to whether spare parts are or should be protected by designs law.[49] At the moment

43. See [10.27].
44. See *Pugh v Riley Cycle Co Ltd* [1912] 1 Ch 613; *Malleys Ltd v J W Tomlin Pty Ltd* (1961) 35 ALJR 352 at 353; *Weir Pumps Ltd v CML Pumps Ltd* (1983) 2 IPR 129.
45. (1953) 88 CLR 278.
46. (1935) 53 RPC 139.
47. *Dalgety Australia Operations v F F Seeley Nominees Pty Ltd* (1985) 5 IPR 97 at 109.
48. *Designs*, para [4.51].
49. See eg A Horton, 'European Design Law and the Spare Parts Dilemma: The Proposed Regulation and Directive' [1994] 2 *EIPR* 51.

bumper bars, tyre tread patterns, motor vehicle body parts and indeed many other bits and pieces of cars may possess the appropriate criteria for registration as designs. Until 1989 many parts may have had copyright protection despite being unregistrable as designs, being too pedestrian or not having 'eye appeal'.[50] However, concern has often been expressed as to the potential monopoly effects of protecting spare parts, particularly where the relevant market relates only to that part, for example, if a make of car must be fitted with a particular exhaust system, bumper bar, or door panel. The market for car spare parts in Australia is estimated at $800 million a year.[51] Submissions supporting both design protection and its abolition were received by the ALRC, the economic and competition issues hotly debated on both sides. The ALRC recommends (rec 165) that new designs legislation should include a procedure for referral of potentially anti-competitive designs to the Australian Competition and Consumer Commission,[52] which would then assess whether the granting of design rights would have the effect of substantially lessening competition in a market. Potentially anti-competitive designs would be identified by a number of characteristics (rec 166). These are: (a) the design is a design of a component part; (b) the component part is to be used to repair a product that is durable, likely to require repair during its expected life, and assembled from many component parts; and (c) the component part is manufactured by or under licence from the product manufacturer or importer. If the Commission decides that the grant of a design right would be anti-competitive, registration may be excluded, or allowed subject to certain conditions being met.[53]

[10.17] Literary or artistic articles. Section 17(2) provides for regulations to be made excluding designs for articles that are 'primarily literary or artistic in character'. To this end reg 11 of the Designs Regulations 1982 lists book-jackets; calendars; certificates or other documents; dressmaking patterns; greeting cards; labels; leaflets; maps; plans; post cards; stamps and transfers. In *Re Application by TDK Electronics*,[54] for example, a cassette wrapper was excluded from registration as being within reg 11(1). It has been held that an article of a kind that appears on the list in reg 11 may nevertheless fall outside the exclusion contemplated by s 17(2), on the ground that the article in question is not in fact 'primarily literary or artistic'.[55] This view has, however, been disputed and is just one of a number of points on which reg 11 is far from clear.[56]

---

50. See [10.25].
51. *Designs*, para [16.11], citing NRMA and RACV submissions.
52. Previously the Trade Practices Commission: see the Hilmer Report, *National Competition Policy Review*, 1993.
53. The ALRC also discussed the role of s 51(3) of the Trade Practices Act (exempting the exercise of intellectual property rights from some of the restrictions on anti-competitive behaviour in that Act): *Designs*, paras [6.55]–[6.59]; and see [22.31]. The ALRC concluded that a further separate review of s 51(3) is required with respect to the range of intellectual property rights, and commented that few submissions and little information regarding the effect of s 51(3) were presented to the Commission.
54. (1983) 1 IPR 529. See also *RA & A Bailey & Co Ltd v Boccaccio Pty Ltd* (1986) 6 IPR 279.
55. *Re Australian Postal Corp* [1992] AIPC 90–857.
56. See J Phillips, *Protecting Designs: Law and Litigation*, 1994, pp 165–76.

(b) Novelty and Originality

[10.18] The innovation threshold: 'new or original'. Australia, like most countries, requires a minimum standard of novelty before a design may be registered. Article 21 of the TRIPS Agreement uses the formulation 'new or original' found in the present legislation. The ALRC recommends some modification of the present test but not so as to conflict with Australia's obligations under GATT.[57]

Under the 1906 Act, designs must be new or original in order to be registered (s 17(1)), but need not be both.[58] A new design is one that has not been known or used before; an original design is presumably then an old design which is creatively given some novel application.[59] It is unclear how much difference from the prior art is required for a design to be new or original. It has been said that to be registrable a design must be 'substantially different' from what has gone before, so as to possess some 'individuality of appearance'.[60] In practice, however, quite subtle distinguishing features may be considered sufficient, especially where the article to which the design has been applied is a fairly common object (such as an item of furniture) and it would be difficult to conceive of a wholly new design.[61] In any event, a design will not be disqualified from registration merely because it has been adapted from something not new or original. In *Saunders v Wiel*[62] a design for a spoon handle made to represent Westminster Abbey was held to have been validly registered; the fact that it was taken from a source to which all the world could resort did not destroy the novelty of the design as applied to an article of that sort.

The ALRC recommends a two-step test of novelty *and* distinctiveness be adopted to assess the eligibility of a design for registration (rec 32). The first part of the test, novelty, will ensure that the design is different from those known before. The distinctiveness aspect expresses a requirement for something more. 'Special', 'noticeable', 'captures and appeals to the eye', 'bold', 'different' is how the cases have explained such a quality.[63] The distinctiveness test does not focus on individual specific aspects of appearance and the overall impression created by the design would be important, as assessed by an informed user, 'a person who is reasonably familiar with the nature, appearance and use of products of the relevant kind' (recs 33, 34). The tests for distinctiveness and infringement are to correspond, 'so that an infringing design is not a distinctive design and vice versa'.[64]

[10.19] Prior use or publication. In an attempt to clarify the requirements of novelty or originality, s 17(1) at present goes on to provide that the requirements are not satisfied in the case of a design which (a) differs

---

57. *Designs*, para [5.4].
58. *Malleys Ltd v J W Tomlin Pty Ltd* (1961) 35 ALJR 352.
59. See *Dover Ltd v Nurnberger Celluloidwaren Fabrik Cebruder Wolff* [1910] 2 Ch 25 at 29.
60. *Malleys Ltd v J W Tomlin Pty Ltd* (1961) 35 ALJR 352 at 352–3.
61. See eg *D Sebel & Co Ltd v National Art Metal Co Ltd* (1965) 10 FLR 224; though cf *Richsell Pty Ltd v Khoury* (1995) 32 IPR 289.
62. (1892) 10 RPC 29.
63. *Designs*, paras [5.7]–[5.9].
64. Ibid, para [5.22].

only in 'immaterial details'[65] or in 'features commonly used in the relevant trade'[66] from a previous design in respect of the same article; or (b) is an 'obvious adaptation'[67] of a previous design in respect of any other article. In each case the previous design must have been registered, published or used in Australia before the priority date of the application for registration of the design under challenge. No definition is given of what constitutes prior use or publication, which must accordingly be determined on a case by case basis.[68]

As in patent law, prior publication includes use in 'trade magazines, textbooks, dictionaries, pamphlets, patent specifications or any similar document. This broad interpretation should be maintained'.[69] Consideration is being given to introducing an absolute novelty requirement rather than assessing novelty within Australia only, as is the case now. In any event, design originality is to be contrasted with the concept in copyright law, which is found in the application of independent skill and effort;[70] even unrelated creation of a design already used or published, or for which registration has been sought or obtained, will pre-empt registration.[71] The existing law on defeating novelty will continue under the ALRC recommendations. However, it is proposed that for the purposes of the distinctiveness test the prior art base should be limited to prior registration and should not extend to prior publications generally: 'This will appropriately allow for the protection of designs that are inspired by designs that appeared in past publications but are not a slavish copy of them.'[72]

The present Act indicates that certain publications or uses are *not* to be taken to preclude novelty or originality. These include secret use (s 17(1A)); publication or use after the priority date (s 22); publication or use in breach of the design owner's confidence, provided registration is applied for with reasonable diligence when the publication or use becomes known (s 46A); and exhibition or publication at an 'official or officially recognised international exhibition' within six months before application for registration (s 47). These provisions will basically continue under new legislation, with some tidying up of detail. Special provision is also made in s 17A for designs which have been taken from artistic works. Where copyright subsists in an artistic work under the Copyright Act 1968 and an application is made by the owner (or with the owner's consent)[73] to register a corresponding design, that design will not be treated as having been anticipated by use of the artistic work unless that use consisted of commercial dealings by or with the owner's consent with articles to which

---

65.   See *Re Calder Vale Manufacturing Co Ltd* (1935) 52 RPC 117 at 125; *Sebel & Co Ltd v National Art Metal Co Pty Ltd* (1965) 10 FLR 224.
66.   See *Phillips v Harbro Rubber Co* (1920) 37 RPC 233 at 240; *Dalgety Australia Operations Ltd v F F Seeley Nominees Pty Ltd* (1985) 5 IPR 97; *J Rapee & Co Ltd v Kas Cushions Pty Ltd* (1989) 15 IPR 577; *Conrol Pty Ltd v Meco McCallum Pty Ltd* (1996) 34 IPR 517.
67.   See *D A Lewis & Co Ltd v Trade Winds Furniture Ltd* (1985) 4 IPR 621.
68.   See eg *J Rapee & Co Ltd v Kas Cushions Pty Ltd* (1989) 15 IPR 577.
69.   *Designs*, para [5.37].
70.   See [6.11].
71.   See eg *D A Lewis v Trade Winds Furniture* (1985) 4 IPR 621.
72.   *Designs*, para [5.38].
73.   See *Tefex Pty Ltd v Bowler* (1982) 40 ALR 326.

the design had been applied industrially.[74] Thus, for instance, an artist who
draws a cartoon character will be able to publish drawings (artistic works)
in newspapers, books, magazines or make a film depicting the character,
without prejudicing any subsequent application for registration of a design
based on the character. It should be noted, however, that a design which is
only registrable by reason of s 17A cannot remain registered after copyright
in the relevant artistic work expires (s 27A(16)).

4. THE DESIGN OWNER'S RIGHTS

[10.20] Infringement. The present Act confers on the owner of a registered design a monopoly on that design (s 25) and permits an action to be
brought against any person who infringes that monopoly (s 30(2)). Since
registration is deemed to commence from the date on which the application was lodged (s 27A(1)), the owner may sue in respect of infringements
occurring prior to the application being accepted, though the action itself
may only be brought after acceptance.[75] Direct infringement will occur
when a person, without the owner's licence or authority, 'applies the design
or any fraudulent or obvious imitation of it to any article in respect of
which the design is registered' (s 30(1)(a)). According to the High Court in
Malleys Ltd v J W Tomlin Pty Ltd,[76] this means that infringement may occur in
one of three ways: where use is made of the same design; where use is made
of an obvious imitation, that is, 'a copy apparent to the eye notwithstanding
slight differences'; and where use is made of a fraudulent imitation, that is,
'a copy with differences which are both apparent and not so slight as to be
insubstantial but which have been made merely to disguise the copying'.[77]
A deliberate imitation of a registered design may be 'fraudulent' in this
sense notwithstanding the lack of any intention to deceive,[78] though the
imitator must usually have known or had reason to believe at the time of
the copying that a design right already existed or that an application for
such a right was pending.[79] It is also important to appreciate that a person
may quite deliberately use a registered design as the basis for their own
design without infringing, so long as what is copied is merely the 'idea' of the
registered design and the two designs do differ in significant respects.[80]

74. See *Press-Form Ltd v Henderson's Ltd* (1993) 26 IPR 113. The terms 'corresponding
     design' (s 4(1)) and 'applied industrially' (s 17A(2)) are given the same meaning as
     in the Copyright Act 1968: see further [10.27].
75. See *Glamagard Pty Ltd v Enderslea Productions Pty Ltd* (1985) 59 ALR 740.
76. (1961) 35 ALJR 352.
77. Ibid at 354. See also *Monier Ltd v Metalwork Tiling Co* (1984) 73 FLR 105; *Dalgety
     Australia Operations Ltd v F F Seeley Nominees Pty Ltd* (1985) 5 IPR 97; *Firmagroup
     Australia Pty Ltd v Byrne & Davidson Doors (Vic) Pty Ltd* (1987) 9 IPR 353; *Turbo Tek
     Enterprises Inc v Sperling Enterprises Pty Ltd* (1989) 15 IPR 617; *Fisher & Paykel
     Healthcare Pty Ltd v Avion Engineering Pty Ltd* (1991) 22 IPR 1.
78. *Dart Industries Inc v Decor Corp Pty Ltd* (1989) 15 IPR 403 at 412.
79. *Turbo Tek Enterprises Inc v Sperling Enterprises Pty Ltd* (1989) 15 IPR 617 at 635. It may
     be sufficient that the imitator knew or had reason to believe that other intellectual
     property rights (such as a patent) existed or were being sought in relation to the
     design: see *Elconnex Pty Ltd v Gerard Industries Pty Ltd* (1992) 22 IPR 551 at 565-6;
     Lift Verkaufsgerate GmbH v Fischer Plastics Pty Ltd (1993) 27 IPR 187 at 200-1.
80. See eg *Malleys Ltd v J W Tomlin Pty Ltd* (1961) 35 ALJR 352; *Turbo Tek Enterprises Inc v
     Sperling Enterprises Pty Ltd* (1989) 15 IPR 617; *Wilson v Hollywood Toys (Australia) Pty
     Ltd* (1996) 34 IPR 293.

In deciding whether imitation has occurred, the court must make a visual comparison of the two designs, if necessary with the aid of expert evidence.[81] In making the necessary comparison a degree of 'imperfect recollection' is allowed for: this assumes a comparison on the basis of having seen the registered design, 'then having gone away and come back and perhaps been put in a position of deciding whether some other article is the one you originally saw'.[82] Copying as such does not have to be established.[83] The extent to which the design allegedly infringed is novel or original may be an important factor: thus where the novel or original aspects of the plaintiff's design consist of only slight variations from the prior art, the defendant's design need only be slightly different again in those same respects for infringement to be avoided.[84]

The Act also provides for indirect infringement in the form of commercial importation or dealing with infringing articles, whether innocent or not, without the owner's licence or authority (s 30(1)(b), (c)).

Part of the terms of reference to the ALRC refer to difficulties that have arisen in the operation of the present legislation, interpretation of which has led to undesirable narrowing of the scope of protection and failure to prevent fairly blatant copying.[85] The Commission recommends an infringement test of 'substantially similar in overall impression' (rec 45). The terminology is designed to incorporate a notion of qualitative analysis such as the courts are used to applying when assessing infringement in copyright law and to move away from a close analysis of individual aspects of the design.[86] The suggested test also accords with the recommended test for registrability where the overall 'distinctiveness' of the design will be assessed. Both registrability and infringement are to be assessed by an 'informed' user. The ALRC recommends against widening the concept of infringement to include a concept of 'exploiting' the design, as in patent law (rec 61), nor were moral rights considered appropriate under any new legislation (rec 62).

[10.21]   Remedies. Actions for infringement may be instituted in a prescribed court (s 31), in which event the Registrar may be given leave to appear (s 32A). The relief that a court may grant includes an injunction and, at the plaintiff's option, either damages or an account of profits (s 32S(1)). The latter remedies may be refused, however, where at the time of infringement the defendant was unaware that the design was registered and had taken all reasonable steps to ascertain whether a monopoly in the design existed (s 32S(2)).[87] Where damages are awarded, various measures may be employed so as to compensate the plaintiff for loss in fact suffered

---

81. See *L J Fisher & Co Ltd v Fabtile Industries Pty Ltd* (1979) 49 AOJP 3611; *Dart Industries Inc v Decor Pty Ltd* (1989) 15 IPR 403 at 408–9.
82. *Valor Heating Co Ltd v Main Gas Appliances Ltd* [1972] FSR 497 at 502.
83. *Dunlop Rubber Co Ltd v Golf Ball Developments Ltd* (1931) 48 RPC 268 at 279.
84. *Hecla Foundry Co v Walker Hunter & Co* (1889) 6 RPC 554 at 558; *Sebel & Co Ltd v National Art Metal Co Pty Ltd* (1965) 10 FLR 224 at 228–9; *Mangraviti v Vardi* (1976) 12 ALR 355.
85. *Designs*, paras [6.3]–[6.5]. See further Ricketson (1994), p 424, listing a series of major cases in which plaintiffs were unable to establish infringement; and see also T Golder, 'Should Designs be Better Protected?' (1990) 1 *IPJ* 107.
86. *Designs*, para [6.5].
87. See *Khawam & Co v Chellaram & Sons (Nigeria) Ltd* [1964] RPC 337.

as a result of the infringement.[88] As with the copyright legislation,[89] action may be taken against unjustified threats of infringement proceedings (ss 32C–32G).

The ALRC Report discusses damages in Chapter 14, reviewing the current state of the law and endorsing many aspects of present practice. The Report recommends against introducing conversion damages for infringement (rec 156) but favours additional damages in cases of flagrant infringement, following the Copyright Act s 115(c) in this respect (rec 151).

[10.22] Dispute resolution. Part of the ALRC reference was to ensure design protection is adequate, quick, effective and inexpensive. In 1995 the Labor Government issued a Justice Statement promoting the aim of a 'simpler, cheaper and more accessible justice system'. Chapter 13 of the *Designs* report reviews enforcement and dispute resolution, noting that many of the problems with delay and expense are hardly confined to the designs area. However, of registered design owners who had been involved in litigation, 75% were unhappy with the outcome.[90] A variety of measures to educate designers in using the system (along with the suggested substantive changes to the legislation) were canvassed. The suggestion that a specialist intellectual property court be set up was rejected, with the expertise of the Federal Court in design law (and all intellectual property matters) being noted.[91] No changes to the current jurisdiction of federal, state and territory courts in matters arising under designs legislation was thought necessary, although flexible use of procedure and expert advice in pre-trial proceedings to expedite designs litigation were recommended. Seeking an opinion from the Registrar of designs on factual issues relating to validity is suggested (rec 140) although not the establishment of an AIPO tribunal. The increasing trend towards mediation and alternative dispute resolution was noted, and this was urged as a first option (rec 148), as well as being in line with the WIPO forum for the resolution of intellectual property disputes.[92] Submissions received on the role of arbitration tended to be negative on the basis of its lack of determinative value.[93]

[10.23] Ownership, transmission and licensing. The rights of an owner with respect to a registered design are personal property and thus may be assigned or transmitted by operation of law (s 25C(1)). Any assignment must be in writing signed by or on behalf of the owner (s 25C(3)). Licences, on the other hand, require no formality. Where a registered design is owned by more than one person, it is held by them in equal shares (and thus as tenants in common), with each entitled to make use of it without accounting to the others, though forbidden to grant a licence or assignment without their consent (s 25A). Each of these provisions is, however, subject to contrary agreement. Any disputes arising between co-owners may be settled by the Registrar giving directions pursuant to s 25B.

An application for a compulsory licence of a registered design may also be made to a prescribed court by 'any person interested' (s 28(b)). The

---

88. See *P B Cow Ltd v Cannon Rubber Manufacturers Ltd* [1961] RPC 236.
89. See [8.29].
90. *Designs*, para [13.5].
91. See [2.18].
92. *Designs*, para [13.76].
93. *Designs*, para [13.74].

applicant must establish that the design is being applied overseas by manufacture to any article and is not being applied to a reasonable extent in Australia. Another form of compulsory licensing allows a design to be used for the services of the Commonwealth or a state (s 40A). The Commonwealth may also compulsorily acquire a design (s 40D) or take an assignment thereof (s 40E). Apart from recommending modification of the provisions concerning Crown use, sale or acquisition of designs, the ALRC, while considering aspects of ownership and notification of interests on the Register, did not propose major changes to the existing scheme.[94]

5.   INTERFACE BETWEEN COPYRIGHT AND DESIGN PROTECTION

[10.24]   General. One of the most troublesome areas in the entire field of intellectual property has been the relationship between copyright protection for artistic works under the Copyright Act 1968 and protection for registered designs under the Designs Act 1906. The problem arises because the rights of a copyright owner in a two-dimensional artistic work (typically, engineering drawings or plans) include the right to reproduce the work in a three-dimensional form (Copyright Act s 21(3)).[95] As a result, copyright potentially protects all commercial and industrial products which originate as drawings. Examples include solar hot water systems, pumps and machinery, spare parts and also integrated circuits. Indeed, as has been seen,[96] s 17A of the Designs Act provides that prior use of an artistic work will not necessarily deprive a later design based on that work of novelty. In order to prevent copyright owners acquiring what may be considered to be excessive rights to control the industrial application of their artistic works, ss 74–77 of the Copyright Act 1968, as amended by the Copyright Amendment Act 1989, limit copyright protection for works which are applied industrially as designs.[97] In their original form, these provisions were criticised for their complexity and for creating anomalies, particularly with respect to unregistrable designs, copyright protection for which remained intact despite mass production of articles made according to the plan or design. The particular anomaly arose because copyright continued to protect an artistic work which did not for some reason qualify for design registration. If, for example, that artistic work could be regarded as a method or principle of construction (rather than being applicable to an article to provide shape or pattern within the definition of 'design' under s 4(1) of the Designs Act), it would be unregistrable as a design. Obviously, engineering drawings and blueprints are not capable of being designs, but rather provide instructions for building or constructing machinery, spare parts, and so on. This anomaly, which had led to copyright protection

---

94. No examples of the Crown's power being exercised were discovered by the ALRC, and it is recommended that the provisions in question not be retained (rec 75): see *Designs,* paras [7.23]–[7.28].
95. See the discussion of indirect reproduction at [8.6]–[8.7].
96. See [10.19].
97. These provisions do not apply to works created before the Copyright Act took effect on 1 May 1969, which are instead covered by s 218 of the Copyright Act: see J Phillips, *Protecting Designs: Law and Litigation,* 1994, pp 48–50.

being retained for mass-produced items such as spare parts, was dealt with by the Copyright Amendment Act 1989, which largely removed the possibility of copyright protection for three-dimensional industrial applications of designs, whether or not those designs are registrable. The changes, which took effect on 1 October 1990, were introduced following a review of the provisions by the Attorney-General's Department,[98] and are largely those recommended by the Franki Committee.[99] However, 'there is an unacceptable degree of confusion surrounding the designs/copyright overlap'[100] and the ALRC recommends reform of this area by introducing into the copyright legislation an 'adaptation right' for owners of artistic works, or if this is not accepted, modification of the Copyright Act to clarify existing policy.

[10.25] The original provisions. Under the original form of ss 74–77, most commercial use of artistic works used as designs and applied to articles resulted in an initial loss of copyright protection in relation to unauthorised reproduction of the articles in question, so long as the corresponding design had been registered or was registrable. In the case of registered designs, this loss of copyright protection lasted for the period of registration: in the case of unregistered (but registrable) designs, for 16 years from the date of the relevant articles being marketed. Thereafter, in each case, the loss of protection was extended further: no infringement of copyright in the underlying work would occur in respect of any act falling within the widest possible design monopoly that could have been acquired by registering every other related design under s 25D of the Designs Act.[101]

Apart from their complexity the most notable feature of these provisions, as mentioned, was that unregistrable designs retained full copyright protection.[102] The one statutory mechanism designed to cut down protection for mass-produced machinery and the like was the so-called 'non-expert defence' in s 71 of the Copyright Act. This provided that a representation of an artistic work in another dimension would not infringe copyright in that artistic work 'if the object would not appear to persons who are not experts in relation to objects of that kind to be a reproduction of the artistic work'. The 'non-expert' in question was the judge hearing a copyright infringement action, who would have to apply the defence once experts had shown that there had in fact been reproduction of the artistic work in question. Decided cases revealed judges who could not recognise a dress having been derived from a sketch[103] and, at the other extreme, members of the High Court of Australia who could recognise a solar hot water system as having been derived from the underlying engineering

---

98. *Copyright Protection for Artistic Works Industrially Applied,* Discussion Paper, 1987.
99. Designs Law Review Committee, *Report on the Law Relating to Designs,* 1973.
100. *Designs,* para [17.3].
101. See [10.9].
102. This included designs excluded from registration under s 17(2) of the Designs Act (see [10.17]), as well as designs otherwise incapable of registration (see *Edwards Hot Water Systems v S W Hart & Co Pty Ltd* (1983) 1 IPR 228 at 255–6). However, a design unregistrable by reason only of a lack of novelty or originality would still be caught by s 77, so that copyright protection would be lost: *Kevlacat Pty Ltd v Trailcraft Marine Pty Ltd* (1987) 11 IPR 77; *Interlego AG v Croner Trading Pty Ltd* (1992) 23 IPR 65.
103. *Burke & Margot Burke Ltd v Spicers Dress Designs* [1936] Ch 400.

drawings.[104] In any event, s 71 was repealed by the Copyright Amendment Act 1989 as part of the overhaul of the design/copyright interface, which introduced amendments to ss 74–77 to limit the design/copyright overlap by making a distinction between use of artistic works and manufacture of industrial products.[105]

[10.26] The current provisions: registered designs. As the Copyright Act now stands, s 75 covers the situation where there has in fact been registration of a 'corresponding design'. The latter refers to any design which, when applied to an article, results in a reproduction of an artistic work, except where the design consists solely of features of two-dimensional pattern or ornament applicable to a surface of an article (s 74).[106] As soon as the design is registered, any copyright in the work is not infringed by its reproduction in the course of applying that or any other corresponding design to an article (s 75). The owner must therefore rely on the design registration (assuming it has not been taken out by someone else with consent) for protection, though copyright protection is retained in respect of uses of the work falling outside the design monopoly and, more particularly, two-dimensional use of the work. Thus commercial application of a flat or surface design will be disregarded and copyright protection retained.[107] Furthermore, no account is taken under s 75 of any design falsely registered without the consent of the owner of the design (s 76).

[10.27] The current provisions: unregistered and unregistrable designs. Where a corresponding design has not been registered, s 77 provides that copyright protection will still be lost if the design is applied industrially by or with the licence of the copyright owner and the resulting articles are marketed in Australia or elsewhere. A design is deemed to have been 'applied industrially' when it is applied to more than 50 articles or to one or more articles manufactured in lengths or pieces (s 77(4); Copyright Regulations, reg 17): in other situations it will be a question of fact.[108] From the first date on which the articles are marketed, any copyright in the relevant artistic work (other than a building, a model of a building, or a

---

104. *S W Hart & Co Pty Ltd v Edwards Hot Water Systems* (1985) 159 CLR 466. Although in that case the majority in the Federal Court (Fox and Franki JJ) had decided that the defence did apply and that the drawings were too difficult to be understood by a non-expert ((1983) 49 ALR 605 at 617), this was ascribed by Gibbs CJ in the High Court to 'a subconscious compensation for their own expertise in this regard' (159 CLR 466 at 478).

105. No transitional provisions were provided by these amendments, which has created some confusion: see *Designs*, paras [17.42]–[17.44]. It appears, however, that the new ss 74–77 should be regarded as applicable to any acts of (what would otherwise be) copyright infringement occurring after those sections took effect on 1 October 1990, even if the design in question had been created or first industrially applied prior to that date: *Ametex Fabrics Inc v C & F Fabrics Pty Ltd* (1992) 111 ALR 565; *Interlego AG v Croner Trading Pty Ltd* (1992) 25 IPR 65; *Shacklady v Atkins* (1994) 30 IPR 387; but cf *Roland Corp v Lorenzo and Sons Pty Ltd* (1991) 22 IPR 245.

106. Although 'design' is not defined in the Copyright Act, it has been held to have the same meaning as in the Designs Act: *Edwards Hot Water Systems v S W Hart & Co Pty Ltd* (1983) 49 ALR 605 at 632; *Hosokawa Micron International Inc v Fortune* (1990) 19 IPR 531 at 534–5.

107. See eg *Ametex Fabrics Inc v C & F Fabrics Pty Ltd* (1992) 111 ALR 565.

108. See *Safe Sport Australia Pty Ltd v Puma Australia Pty Ltd* (1985) 4 IPR 20; *Press-Form Pty Ltd v Henderson's Ltd* (1993) 26 IPR 113; *Shacklady v Atkins* (1994) 30 IPR 387.

work of artistic craftsmanship) is not infringed by its reproduction in the course of applying that or any other corresponding design to an article (s 77(2)).

An example of loss of copyright protection for an unregistered design is found in *Hutchence v South Seas Bubble Co Pty Ltd.*[109] In that case the pop group INXS had applied designs to T-shirts, which were sold at concerts. The respondents copied the designs and sold them on T-shirts at markets. The effect of s 77(2) of the Copyright Act was to deprive the applicants of any copyright protection in respect of the designs, as applied to the same articles (T-shirts), since the applicants themselves had 'industrially applied' the designs. Since the designs were not registered, the Designs Act afforded no protection either.[110] The interrelationship of copyright and designs legislation was described in the *INXS* case as a 'troublesome matter'.[111] The particular circumstances of that case would no longer cause a loss of copyright (for the artistic works used on T-shirts), since the design in question was a 'flat design'. Wilcox J distinguished such designs from three-dimensional ones when he said:

> The fundamental reasons for excepting industrial designs from the protection of copyright law are to avoid uncertainty in the industrial world and to avoid hindrance to the improvement of the design of manufactured articles. It is difficult to see that these reasons have much relevance to a two dimensional artistic work printed onto clothing which, at a glance, will appear as somebody's original creation.[112]

No account is to be taken under s 77 of a design excluded from registration by regulations made under s 17(2) of the Designs Act.[113] However, designs which are in other respects unregistrable are now subject to loss of copyright protection. In introducing the Copyright Amendment Act 1989 the Attorney-General, Lionel Bowen, said that industrial works were 'excessively protected' by the Copyright Act, and that this protection was uncertain and its effects 'often inequitable'.[114] After the amendments someone wishing to copy a mass-produced item need only search the Design Register to discover whether there is protection for the item.

[10.28] Alternatives for reform. The 1989 amendments for the most part achieved the desired objective of avoiding dual protection for artistic works commercially applied as designs on three-dimensional articles. But there are a number of areas in which the operation of ss 74–77 is far from certain.[115] For example, does the exception for two-dimensional or flat designs 'applicable to the surface of an article' cover embossed or woven

---

109. (1986) 6 IPR 473.
110. It should be noted that copyright protection was still available for one of the designs, an album cover ('The Swing') which INXS had not used on T-shirts. There was also found to be a serious question to be tried regarding passing off and ss 52 and 53(c) of the Trade Practices Act 1974 (Cth), in that the respondents' merchandise would be assumed by purchasers to be approved by the applicants: see [16.27].
111. (1986) 6 IPR 473 at 485.
112. Ibid.
113. See [10.17].
114. Second reading speech, 8 November 1988.
115. See generally A Bates, 'Artistic Works Industrially Applied: A Comparison of Copyright/Designs Law in Australia and New Zealand' (1993) 17 *UQLJ* 247; J Phillips, *Protecting Designs: Law and Litigation, 1994*, pp 23–48.

designs? The practical difficulties encountered in interpreting ss 74–77, as well as lingering uncertainty as to whether the provisions set an appropriate boundary between copyright and design protection, have led to two major reviews this decade. In 1991 the Lahore Committee, which had been established by the Minister for Industry, Technology and Commerce to investigate changes to this and certain other aspects of design law, proposed a number of amendments to clarify ss 74–77.[116] However, the Committee was hampered in this respect by its limited terms of reference, and it felt unable to explore more far-reaching changes. That task has now fallen to the ALRC in its *Designs* report.

The ALRC reviewed a number of options, ranging from one extreme, repealing the sections outright and allowing full copyright and design protection for all designs, to the other extreme of removing all copyright protection for commercially exploited artistic works by limiting the term of copyright. The favoured option is to repeal ss 74–77 and s 21(3), expressly provide that a two-dimensional work is not reproduced by the production of a three-dimensional version, and introduce an adaptation right for artistic works into the Copyright Act. The ALRC is clearly of the view that copyright is inappropriate to protect more than copying the drawing, and should not extend to control of marketing of products as such, unless these are artistic works, being works of artistic craftsmanship, buildings or models. The proposed adaptation right 'gives the copyright owner the right to industrially apply a version of the copyright work that is itself an artistic work in three dimensions. The adaptation right should also apply in relation to two-dimensional versions of three-dimensional artistic works.'[117] The effect will be to reserve copyright for artistic works while more functional products receive only design protection. 'For example, a sculpture made from a drawing or a sculpture would infringe copyright but a pump made from an engineering drawing would not.'[118] The ALRC also proposed that the incidental reproduction of an artistic work in two dimensions in the course of or for the purposes of industrial application should not amount to an infringement of copyright. Suppose for example that A manufactured a pump from engineering drawings and B copied it. The repeal of s 21(3) would prevent B's pump from being considered an infringement of copyright in A's drawings; A's adaptation right would not be infringed, since B's pump would not be an artistic work in itself. However, if B then made a drawing of their own pumps, this would indirectly reproduce A's drawings and thus infringe A's copyright, allowing A to get around the repeal of s 21(3), were it not for the ALRC's additional proposal.[119]

This scheme does not address 'gaps' in protection which may occur before registration of a design, nor the 'gap' which exists for unregistrable designs for 'the way things work'. Nevertheless, it does appear to be a sensible approach to a difficult problem. The ALRC's fallback option, should its preferred approach not be implemented, is to retain ss 74–77 with modifications to existing policy, including an adaptation right.

---

116. *Inquiry into Intellectual Property Protection for Designs*, 1991.
117. *Designs*, para [17.9].
118. Ibid.
119. Cf *Amalgamated Mining Services Pty Ltd v Warman International Ltd* (1992) 24 IPR 461.

PART IV

Patents

Chapter 11

The Patent System

1. HISTORY[1]

[11.1] Early patents. The common law has traditionally demonstrated antipathy to monopolies of any description. Freedom of competition has been considered desirable to prevent the development of rigid structures in the economy, which may fail to adapt promptly to changing conditions, thus becoming inefficient and having a deleterious effect on prices and product quality. Nevertheless, from the time a market economy began to develop in Europe, the conferring of monopolies in certain areas has been regarded as necessary to balance the need of society for new inventions with the need of the inventor for some scope for reward. A Venetian law of 1474 granted privileges for ten years to inventors of new arts and machines so that devices 'of utility and benefit' would be built;[2] and in England, the boroughs and guilds of the Middle Ages began to emerge with exclusive trading privileges and control of the market and training of craftsmen. In the time of Elizabeth I the Crown adopted the continental practice of granting monopolies to individuals who introduced new inventions into the realm. Elizabeth was also in the habit of granting other monopolies, such as the exclusive right to conduct trade in a foreign country or area, and it was not long before the known world was parcelled out to the Merchant Venturers, the Russia Company (1553), the Levant Company (1581) and the East India Company (1600). The Crown reaped great profit from these sixteenth century monopolies. Besides the sums demanded in return for the initial grant of the monopoly, royalties (a portion of the proceeds) were also paid for the exploitation of the right conferred. The official documents conferring the right or privilege were called letters patent.

---

1. See generally Ricketson, pp 859–68; Cornish, pp 66–71.
2. See G Mandich, 'Venetian Patents (1450–1550)' (1948) 30 *J Patent Office Soc* 166 at 171. The aim was also to encourage innovators to come to Venice.

[11.2] Monopolies under challenge. By the end of Elizabeth's reign there was a large number of monopolies, and the prerogative power of the Crown to grant monopolies had become a grave constitutional issue (as indeed was the prerogative power of the Crown generally). In 1601 a parliamentary debate on monopolies took place at which outrage was expressed concerning 'divers patents granted since the last parliament', including those for currants, iron, powder, cards, ox shin-bones, train oil, transportation of leather, lists of cloth, ashes, aniseed, vinegar, sea-coals, steel, aqua vitae, brushes, pots, saltpetre, lead, as well as others already in existence, such as those for dice, starch, cards and salt.[3] It was claimed that the grant of such patents was 'grievous' to the subjects of the Queen, that 'great oppressions' were wrought by the holders of monopoly rights in the trade of such commodities, and that 'from the thraldom of those monopolies ... there was no town, city or country free'.[4] In 1602 *Darcy v Allen*,[5] otherwise known as the *Case of Monopolies,* was decided. Darcy had been granted the sole right to import foreign playing cards, and he sued Thomas Allen for infringing his letters patent by ordering and selling playing cards. The court declared the patent void and gave judgment for the defendant. Monopolies were declared to be generally invalid because they operated in restraint of trade and tended to increase prices and reduce quality.

[11.3] Statute of Monopolies. James I continued Elizabeth's habit of granting monopolies, but was unable to withstand the Commons as well as his predecessor. In 1624 the Statute of Monopolies was passed which declared void all monopolies for the sole buying, selling, making or using of anything in the realm. There was an exception to this, however: inventions. Patents for the 'sole working or making of any manner of new manufacture' could be granted for 14 or not more than 21 years to 'the first and true inventor'. An 'inventor' in 1624 was taken to include a person who imported an invention from abroad, the English being at that stage technically backwards compared with France and Holland. It was an important feature of the early patent systems that they were designed to encourage the importation of foreign innovation, increasing trade, employment and perhaps foreign investment. Indeed, this is still an aim of patent systems today, especially for developing countries.

[11.4] Evolution of the patent system. Patents continued to be granted in increasing numbers under the royal prerogative, as limited by the Statute of Monopolies, particularly as the Industrial Revolution got under way. As the system evolved, a key feature gradually emerged: the need for an inventor to file 'specifications' in support of an application. The specification was (and still is) a technical document which described the invention and claimed an area over which the patentee would have exclusive domain for the term of the patent. During the eighteenth century judges began to express the idea that the object of patent law was to secure the revelation of beneficial secrets which could be generally exploited when the inventor's term of protection expired. This required the inventor to prepare a specification sufficient to allow the invention to be used by

---

3.   M Evans and R I Jack, *Sources of English Legal and Constitutional History,* 1984, p 256.
4.   Ibid, p 257.
5.   (1602) 11 Co Rep 84; 74 ER 1131.

posterity. Patentees had begun to enrol statements of their inventions with the Court of Chancery around this time. Although this began as a device to help protect against infringers, the courts came to require a sufficient statement of the patent as 'consideration' for the monopoly conferred. In *Attorney-General (Cth) v Adelaide Steamship Co*[6] Lord Parker said:

> The right of the Crown to grant monopolies is now regulated by the Statute of Monopolies, but it was always strictly limited at common law. A monopoly being a derogation from the common right of freedom of trade could not be granted without consideration moving to the public, just as a toll, being a derogation from the public right of passage, could not be granted without the like consideration. In the case of new inventions the consideration was found either in the interest of the public to encourage inventive ingenuity or more probably in the disclosure made to the public of a new and useful article or process.

Much of patent law revolves around the issues of what is patentable, whether the specification is adequate, whether the monopoly claimed is supported by the documentation, and whether the supposed invention is novel and inventive. All these issues are relevant to the balancing act at which the patent system aims: that is, the encouragement of innovation for the mutual benefit of inventor and public, while at the same time not tying up areas of industry and technology by having the right to exploit inventions belonging to any individual for a long period of time. After a patent expires, the invention enters the public domain and can be used freely by anyone. The patent specification was therefore required to give sufficient detail to allow an expert to perform the invention. Indeed even before the filing of specifications became usual practice it had been intended that inventors should pass on their knowledge. Thus the patent term of 14 years provided for by the Statute of Monopolies was set to span two apprenticeship periods, during which time apprentices would be instructed in the technology.[7]

[11.5] Modern legislation. By the mid-nineteenth century the procedures for both obtaining and enforcing patent rights had become cumbersome in the extreme. Legislation was accordingly introduced in Britain to simplify and in turn codify the relevant processes, providing the model on which the current system is founded.[8] As with other areas in intellectual property, Australian legislation tended to follow the British lead. Thus the Patents Act 1952 (Cth),[9] which until 1991 was the operative statute in this country, was based on the Patents Act 1949 (UK); although the link was subsequently broken with the considerable changes made to the British system by the Patents Act 1977 (UK). The 1952 Act established a system whereby patents could be granted for a term of 16 years. Apart from domestic applicants, protection might also be extended in certain circumstances to those who had obtained, or were in the process of obtaining, an overseas or international patent. The system was

6.   [1913] AC 781 at 793. See also *Liardet v Johnson* (1778) 1 WPC 53; 62 ER 1000.
7.   See T S Eisenschitz, 'The Information Function of Patents' [1987] *Patent World* 38.
8.   Patent Law Amendment Act 1852; Patents, Designs and Trademarks Act 1883.
9.   The Act replaced the Patents Act 1903 (Cth) and was based on the report of the Dean Committee: Committee Appointed by the Attorney-General of the Commonwealth to Consider what Alterations are Desirable to the Patent Law of the Commonwealth, *Report*, 1952.

administered by the Patent Office, headed by the Commissioner of Patents, which processed applications and maintained a Register of Patents.

[11.6] The IPAC review and the economic impact of the patent system. In 1984 a review of the Australian patent system was undertaken from an economic perspective by the Industrial Property Advisory Committee.[10] IPAC's report recommended that the patent system continue to operate in Australia, but that changes should be made to enhance the fostering of indigenous innovation and the development of export markets, to reduce anti-competitive conduct involving patents, and to improve the efficiency of the patent system with a consequent reduction of direct costs through the streamlining of procedures. It should be noted that one of the experts on the Committee, Professor Lamberton, dissented from the majority's findings on a number of central issues and co-wrote a separate report.[11] Neither report was unequivocally in favour of or opposed to the patent system, although the minority characterised any benefits as being tenuous and subtle, with a probable negative overall cost/benefit ratio.[12]

A more recent review by the Bureau of Industry Economics, while agreeing with the general thrust of IPAC's assessment, has sounded a slightly more positive note. It points out that the patent system makes at least some contribution to narrowing the gap between private returns and social returns on investment in research and development, increasing the incentive for such investment in a reasonably cost-effective way.[13] True, it is only some industries which make extensive use of the system. While patents are regularly used in relation to pharmaceutical products and some chemicals (which are costly to develop but often relatively easy to imitate), it is rarer for all but the simplest engineering innovations to be patented, with new engineering processes typically being protected as trade secrets.[14] The review also comments on the significance of the fact that more than 90% of Australian patents are granted to non-residents:

> This is indicative that the majority of patents are used to protect foreign suppliers from imitations either from domestic or overseas sources. In other words, the patent system enables foreign patentees to charge 'monopoly' prices in Australia without being exposed to competition by imitators.[15]

However, the review cautions against any temptation for Australia to modify its patent laws to favour local interests, or indeed to abandon the patent regime altogether. Such moves would breach Australia's international obligations under the TRIPS Agreement, inviting retaliation from other countries and from some of the large multi-nationals which use the patent

10. *Patents, Innovation and Competition in Australia*, 1984.
11. T D Mandeville, D M Lamberton and E J Bishop, *Economic Effects of the Australian Patent System*, 1982.
12. Ibid. Some commentators believe that too much is made of the cost/benefit equation: see eg N R Norman, 'Patent Law Revision — Some Economic Considerations' (1984) 12 *ABLR* 226 at 229.
13. *The Economics of Patents*, Occasional Paper 18, 1994.
14. Ibid, pp 24–6, 35; and see [3.10], [13.11] as to the relationship between trade secrets law and the patents system.
15. Ibid, p 47.

system, and potentially denying local industry some of the imported technology on which it is so dependent.[16]

[11.7] **Patents Act 1990.** For the foreseeable future, therefore,
Australia will almost certainly continue to have a patent system. The
present regime is governed by the Patents Act 1990,[17] which was enacted to
implement a number of policy changes flowing from the IPAC review. In
fact the 1990 Act made relatively few substantive changes to the system
established by the 1952 statute, though it did bring the legislation into line
with existing practice in the Patent Office. The new Act is also notable for
'relegating' to regulations many matters of detail formerly contained in the
text of the 1952 Act. Although the Patents Regulations 1991 have to date
contained few departures from the procedures established under the
previous statute, the effect is that the patents system may in future be
altered in quite significant ways without any recourse to parliament. This
'unconstitutional' approach to law-making is just one of a number of
aspects of the new legislation which have been criticised by
commentators.[18] There has been particular concern with the drafting of
both the Act and the Regulations, parts of which fall a long way short of
meeting any reasonable standards of 'plain language'.[19] This is all the more
ironic in light of its drafters' stated intent to bring 'the language and
structure of the Act down to earth, so that mere mortals without law
degrees have some chance of understanding what it is all about — at least
in general terms'.[20] As a subsequent report to the Prime Minister's Science
and Engineering Council put it:[21]

> The Patents Act (1990) was drafted in a 'Plain English' style that was obvi-
> ously intended to make this area of law more comprehensible to users of the
> patent system. Unfortunately, this laudable object has not been achieved and
> concepts that were previously clear under the old law are now more difficult
> to understand and apply. A good example of this can be illustrated with
> regard to the question of obviousness and inventive step: under the Patents
> Act (1952), a five line provision set out the ground of obviousness for the
> purposes of revocation, but under the Patents Act (1990) the application of
> this concept now requires the reader to 'track' through three separate sec-
> tions of the Act, refer to the Dictionary in Schedule 1, refer to the Acts Inter-
> pretation Act, and read more than fifty lines of text.

The Patents Act 1990 took effect on 1 May 1991. Under transitional
arrangements set out in Ch 23 of the Act, any patent granted or application
made under the 1952 Act is treated as if it had been granted or made under
the new legislation, with the important rider that no ground of objection or
invalidity may be raised against such a patent or application that was not

---

16. Ibid, pp 47–50. See further [11.27] as to the impact of extending the standard
    patent term to 20 years, something forced on Australia by the TRIPS Agreement.
17. All references in this and the next three chapters are to the 1990 Act and the
    Patents Regulations 1991, unless otherwise stated.
18. See eg C Marsh, 'The Patents Act 1990 — Is the Tail of Bureaucratic Convenience
    Wagging the Legislative Dog?' (1993) 4 *AIPJ* 142; D Speagle and M Dowling, 'The
    1990 Patents Act: Unfinished Reform' (1993) 4 *AIPJ* 166.
19. Indeed, 'there is an informal but widely held view that the 1990 Act is so poorly
    drafted that a new Act will be required': Speagle and Dowling, ibid at 180.
20. Barry Jones, Minister for Science, Customs and Small Business, Hansard, 1 June
    1989, p 3479.
21. *The Role of Intellectual Property in Innovation — Vol 2, Perspectives*, 1993, p 80.

available under the former Act (s 233(4)).[22] Since its enactment the 1990 Act has been amended on a number of occasions, notably in 1995 when the term of a standard patent was extended from 16 to 20 years in accordance with Australia's obligations under the TRIPS Agreement.[23]

[11.8]   Petty patents. In 1979, in line with international trends, the Patents Act 1952 was amended to introduce petty patents, known as utility models in Germany and Japan, or patents brevet in France.[24] These are designed to provide protection for small-scale innovations with a short commercial life, such as gadgets, small appliances and accessories. Obtaining a petty patent is cheaper and quicker than for a full scale or 'standard' patent and the term of protection is shorter, being limited to a maximum of six years. The expense and length of time required to obtain a standard patent is more appropriate where there is greater investment in the invention and the possibility of export sales. Although the substantive requirements of patent law are applicable to petty patents, they are meant to be somewhat easier to obtain and are assessed for novelty against what is known or used domestically rather than being judged by international patent standards. Unlike standard patents, most petty patents are obtained by Australian residents.

A recent review by the Advisory Council on Industrial Property (ACIP), however, has identified a number of drawbacks in the petty patent system.[25] Chief among these is that the present system does not do enough to fill what it perceived as a significant gap in intellectual property protection. This gap, which was also identified by the Australian Law Reform Commission in its review of the registered designs system,[26] 'relates to functional innovations that are not sufficiently inventive under the present standard or petty patent system to warrant protection, and are not protectable under the designs system which protects the appearance of articles, but not "the way they work"'.[27] Although acknowledging the success of the petty patent system in being relatively cheap and easy to use, ACIP noted:

> a widely held perception among the patent attorney profession that in the Patent Office there is relatively little difference between the inventive height required to obtain a standard and a petty patent ... [and] that under normal circumstances there is little reason to apply for a petty patent as a standard patent can be obtained for a slightly higher cost and for a much longer term.[28]

To meet this problem, ACIP has recommended that petty patents be replaced by 'innovation patents', to provide a 'second tier' of patent protection that

---

22. As to the interpretation of the transitional provisions, which have caused no little difficulty in practice, see *N V Philips Gloeilampenfabrieken v Mirabella International Pty Ltd* (1993) 26 IPR 513; *Re Franke and Commissioner of Patents* (1993) 29 ALD 801; *Murex Diagnostics Australia Pty Ltd v Chiron Corp* (1995) 30 IPR 277; and see further D Speagle and M Dowling, 'The 1990 Patents Act: Unfinished Reform' (1993) 4 *AIPJ* 166 at 177–80.

23. See [11.27]. Note also the Patents Amendment Bill 1995, which proposed a number of technical amendments to the 1990 Act, and the Patents Amendment Bill 1996, which is intended to restrict the patentability of genetic information (see [15.7]). The 1995 Bill lapsed when the 1996 federal election was called, but is expected to be reintroduced in the future.

24. Patents Amendment Act 1979 (Cth).

25. *Review of the Petty Patent System*, 1995.

26. See [10.3].

27. *Review of the Petty Patent System*, p 5.

28. Ibid, p 24.

would be significantly different from that offered by standard patents and more effective in meeting the needs of small and medium Australian businesses. Innovation patents would specifically be aimed at 'minor or incremental innovations' and would have a duration of eight years rather than six. Importantly, the inventive level required would be lower than that for standard patents. The latter are only granted where the invention in question is not only novel, but would not have been 'obvious' to a skilled person in light of the general state of knowledge in their field.[29] ACIP's proposal is that provided an invention were novel, it could be the subject of an innovation patent unless it varied 'from a previously publicly available article, product or process only in ways which [made] no substantial contribution to the effect of the product or working of the article or process'.[30]

The Minister for Science and Technology announced in February 1997 that ACIP's proposals will be implemented and an innovation patent system introduced. The only recommendation rejected by the government was that it should be possible to take out both an innovation patent and a standard patent for the same invention, something currently forbidden in relation to petty patents by s 64 of the 1990 Act.

2. OBTAINING A PATENT

[11.9] Procedural requirements of patenting. Various aspects of patent law are easier to grasp if the procedure for obtaining registration is understood. The 1990 Act was designed to streamline the procedural aspects of obtaining a patent by improving the efficiency of the administration of the system. To this end s 4 of the Act has flowcharts illustrating typical steps involved in getting and maintaining patents with reference to appropriate sections. The system is still administered by the Patent Office, which as noted earlier is now part of the Australian Industrial Property Organisation.[31]

(a) Applying for a Patent

[11.10] Who may apply. Any person at all may apply for a patent (s 29(1)), but s 15(1) strictly limits the class of persons to whom a patent may be granted. Thus an application, no matter who made it, would always need to specify such a person as the ultimate recipient of any grant. The potential grantee must be a person who:

(a)   is the inventor;

(b)   would, on the grant of a patent for the invention, be entitled to have the patent assigned to them;

(c)   derives title to the invention from either of the above;[32] or

(d)   is the legal representative of a deceased person who falls into one of the previous categories.

In practice most inventions are owned by corporations, as persons entitled to take an assignment from the actual inventor(s). The provision covering this class of applicant was added to the 1952 Act in 1960 and reflects the

---

29.   See [12.13] ff.
30.   *Review of the Petty Patent System*, rec 2.
31.   See [1.10].
32.   See *George C Warner Laboratories Pty Ltd v Chemspray Pty Ltd* (1967) 41 ALJR 75.

operation of express or implied provisions in employment contracts which give employers the right to claim ownership of inventions made by workers during the course of their employment.[33] It should also be noted that it is possible to make joint applications and to hold a patent jointly (ss 31, 63).[34]

[11.11]   The application. An application may be for a standard patent or a petty patent, though it is possible to convert one to the other prior to acceptance. The applicant must file a patent request and such other documents as are prescribed (s 29(1); reg 3.1). The application must be either a provisional application, accompanied by a provisional specification, or a complete application, accompanied by a complete specification (s 29(2)–(4)). A provisional application is made where the applicant wishes to secure a 'priority date' (see below) as soon as possible. A provisional specification need only 'describe the invention' (s 40(1)), with the applicant then having 12 months in which to lodge a complete application in relation to the same matter (s 38; reg 3.10). By contrast, a complete specification must provide more detailed information (s 40(2)–(4)). It must fully describe the invention, including the best method of performing it known to the applicant, and end with a claim or claims (one only in the case of petty patents) defining the invention. These claims must be clear, succinct and fairly based on the matter described.

A 'divisional' application may also be made in order to allow an applicant to make a further application in respect of an invention already disclosed in a complete specification but not previously claimed as such (s 39).

[11.12]   Priority date. Lodging a specification secures a priority date for the invention. This is extremely important as patent rights, if eventually granted, will subsist from this date and the applicant will have priority over any later applications. The priority date of a claim made in a specification is usually the date on which the complete specification is lodged. However, where such a specification is fairly based on matter disclosed in a provisional specification, it is the *earlier* date on which the provisional specification was lodged that constitutes the priority date (s 43; regs 3.12–3.13).[35]

[11.13]   Convention and PCT applications. A priority date may also be secured in connection with a patent application filed in another country. This may occur in one of two ways. In the first place a 'Convention application' may be made (ss 94–96; regs 3.12, 8.5–8.7). Where an application has previously been made in a country which, like Australia, is a party to the Paris Convention for the Protection of Industrial Property, the applicant may also seek protection in Australia. Provided the convention application is made within 12 months of the original foreign application, the Act provides that the date of the latter is taken to be the priority date for Australian purposes. A convention application must, however, be accompanied by a complete specification and by a certified copy of the foreign specification.

Alternatively, a 'PCT application' may be made under the terms of the Patent Co-operation Treaty 1970 (ss 88–93; regs 3.12, 8.1–8.4). A convention application is essentially founded on the notion of reciprocity between

33.   See [13.2]–[13.6].
34.   See further [13.12].
35.   As to the effect that the making of amendments may have on the priority date of a claim, see s 114, reg 3.14.

member nations, with lodgment of an application in one country effectively creating a priority period in which protection may be sought in others. By contrast, the PCT seeks to establish a more genuinely international system. A single PCT application is made within any contracting state. If the application designates Australia as a country in which patent protection is sought, and if the application has been given an international filing date, it will be treated as an application under the domestic legislation and the international filing date will become its priority date for domestic purposes. From this point on the application will, as far as Australia is concerned, be governed by our own legislation. Nevertheless certain formalities are dispensed with — although this does not include the specification requirements or the basic prerequisites for patentability. The terms of the PCT further require that an international search be conducted to identify prior discoveries and publications bearing upon the issue of patentability, and that WIPO publish the application. An international preliminary examination may also be sought in order for a tentative conclusion to be reached on patentability. Although such searches and examinations have no binding effect in relation to the success of the application under domestic law, they might be expected to be of significant aid to the domestic authorities.

Apart from being used by foreign corporations to secure patent protection in Australia, PCT applications have also proved to be fairly popular with local inventors. They offer a useful way of reducing the complexity of seeking patent protection both in Australia and in the other leading industrialised nations — something which is increasingly being seen as necessary, especially by those who wish to take their innovations into the larger (and potentially more profitable) markets in the northern hemisphere.[36] The PCT system also has the advantage that, after payment of an initial processing fee, filing fees for the countries designated in the application need not be paid until at least 18 months after the priority dates. Nevertheless, few Australian inventors will venture lightly into the international patent system, given the costs involved. It has been estimated that even if an application is limited to a select number of the major overseas markets, such as the US, Japan and Germany, the costs (including filing and renewal fees and patent attorney charges) may rise to as much as $100,000 over the life of the patent, compared to a typical figure of about $15,000 for a patent limited to Australia.[37] And that does not, of course, take account of the much larger figures that may need to be budgeted to cover the cost of pursuing infringers and defending the patent against challenges to its validity.[38]

[11.14] Patents of addition. Patents of addition to standard (but not petty) patents may also be granted to protect improvements to or modifications of the invention (ss 80–82). Such a patent is not open to challenge on the ground of obviousness, even if the improvement is not an inventive step

---

36. The PCT system is less useful for those who wish to obtain patent protection in the expanding South-East Asian markets, since many of the countries in question are not contracting states. This is a state of affairs which it would clearly be in Australia's interests to change: see *The Role of Intellectual Property in Innovation — Vol 1, Strategic Overview*, Prime Minister's Science and Engineering Council, 1993, pp 27–9.

37. *Review of the Regulatory Regime for Patent Attorneys*, Report to the Minister for Science and Technology, 1996, pp 22–9.

38. See [14.9].

in light of the main invention (s 25). If granted, a patent of addition will remain in force for as long as the term of the patent for the main invention (s 83(1)). A patent of addition may remain in force even if the main patent is revoked, subsisting thereafter as an independent patent for the unexpired term of the main patent (s 85).

[11.15] **Role of patent attorneys.** Patent attorneys play a key role in the formulation of patent applications. Under the regime established by Ch 20 of the Act, these professionals are required to have a technical qualification in science or engineering. They must also pass a series of examinations, administered by the Patent Attorneys Professional Standards Board, which cover the legal and practical aspects of the patent system, as well as the trade marks and registered designs systems (in relation to both of which they are also regularly consulted). Only registered patent attorneys are permitted to carry on the business of preparing patent documentation and prosecuting applications (ss 200(1), 201), though inventors may always take the (often unwise) step of acting for themselves. Solicitors are specifically prohibited from drafting specifications (a task which has been described as 'an exercise in draftsmanship, prophecy, scientific exegesis and delimitation'),[39] unless they are also patent attorneys or acting under the instructions thereof (s 202). Their statutory monopoly in relation to specifications has helped patent attorneys to assume a general role of providing advice in relation to the entire process of patenting. However, a recent review for the Federal Government, while not recommending the breaking of that monopoly, has proposed various changes to the regulatory regime which would encourage greater competition in the provision of other patent-related services, as well as revamping the system for becoming registered as a patent attorney.[40] The Minister for Science and Technology has announced that most of the changes recommended in the review will be implemented.

(b) Processing of Standard Patent Applications

[11.16] **Examination.** The patent system operates in such a way that the Patents Office will process applications only as requested, although the Commissioner may nudge applicants along by directing applicants to ask for examination of their patent request and complete specification (ss 44(2)–(4)). This examination will be carried out by a patent examiner. In practice, many inventors do not proceed with examination of their specification, either because they have lost interest in obtaining a patent or else because they are in the course of developing some other aspect of their research which is not necessarily relevant to the application already filed. If the Patent Office examined every application made, without waiting for the applicants to indicate whether they intended to proceed, it would still be processing applications made in 1902. In fact, the time lapse between lodgment and examination tends to be between six and nine months.

[11.17] **Criteria for examination.** Section 45 and reg 3.18(2) require the Patent Examiner who makes the examination to report on whether the

39. C J Bannon, *Australian Patent Law*, 1984, para [96].
40. *Review of the Regulatory Regime for Patent Attorneys*, Report to the Minister for Science and Technology, 1996.

application and specification comply with the Act's requirements, including whether the content of the specification complies with s 40; whether the invention is a 'manner of new manufacture' which is both novel and inventive;[41] whether the invention is excluded from patentability under s 18(2) or the application is capable of being refused under s 51;[42] and whether the person to be granted the patent is eligible under s 15. Provision exists for modified (and effectively less rigorous) examinations in the case of a convention application, or where a patent has been granted in a prescribed foreign country in respect of a comparable application (ss 46–48).[43]

Chapter 9 of the Act also provides for a process of re-examination to determine whether the invention lacks novelty or inventiveness.[44] This must be arranged by the Commissioner, on application, where the grant of a patent is opposed or at any time after a patent has been granted. Alternatively the Commissioner may be directed to re-examine by a court which is considering the validity of a patent.

[11.18] **The searching procedure.** Before examination takes place the invention is classified according to the International Patent Classification and abstracts are prepared for search material. The search list provides a list of 'prior art' considered relevant to the issues of novelty and inventiveness. This includes previous patent specifications (including those published after the priority date of the claim in question) and certain other publications to which the examiners are directed to have regard by the Commissioner. The applicant will obviously check the search report and review the material cited to see if anything which may threaten the validity of one or more of the claims is revealed. The Patent Office will not, at this stage, comment as to whether the cited prior art precludes the invention being novel or inventive, although applicants may wish to amend their application in order to cut out any claim or part thereof which has been anticipated: this is discussed below. The application will then proceed to a formal examination.

[11.19] **Significance of the examination process.** While the examination is a necessary hurdle for any application to clear, it is important to realise that success by no means assures the validity of any resulting patent. For one thing, the prior art base against which inventions are ultimately assessed for novelty and inventiveness will usually be wider than the subject matter searched by the Patent Office. There is indeed no absolute guarantee of the validity of a patent even once granted (s 20). In this sense the system is basically self-enforcing, in that competitors may oppose the grant or seek revocation of a patent despite the Patent Office finding no fault. Obviously it is impossible for the Patent Office to discover all possible disclosures of an invention, particularly on a worldwide basis,[45] since an article written in a foreign scientific journal may make public information which discloses an invention. In fact it has been said that the majority of patents

41. See [12.1] ff.
42. See [12.8], [12.10]–[12.11].
43. The prescribed countries presently listed in reg 3.21 are the US, Canada, NZ and the signatories to the European Patent Convention.
44. Note that for the purpose of such a re-examination the relevant 'prior art base' is restrictively defined: see [12.14].
45. See [12.14], [12.23].

granted are either invalid for want of novelty or could be described as such if enough money were spent on the search of their antecedents.[46]

[11.20] Amendments. In the event of an adverse report after an examination, procedures are established whereby the applicant may propose amendments to the application or specification for the examiner's consideration, again either voluntarily or at the Commissioner's direction. An applicant or patentee may also request an amendment at any other time, or be directed to do so by the Commissioner or by a court whenever it appears that a patent or a patent application would otherwise have to be treated as invalid (ss 104–107). However, restrictions are in each of these instances placed on the nature of the amendments which may be proposed: in particular, an amendment will be disallowed if its effect would be to have the specification claim matter not in substance disclosed in the specification as originally filed (s 102(1)).

[11.21] Acceptance and publication. A favourable report to the effect that there is no lawful ground of objection to a patent request and specification will lead to them being accepted (s 49). An applicant may request that acceptance be delayed (s 49(3)), although not indefinitely, as outlined below. Once a patent application and specification are accepted, this fact is advertised in the *Australian Official Journal of Patents, Trade Marks and Designs,* and various documents associated with the application become open to public inspection (ss 53–58; regs 4.1–4.3). Almost all relevant documentation is published in this way, with the exception of examiners' reports.

[11.22] Restrictions on publication. Not every invention is one that the public *should* have available. Some years ago it was disclosed in the British press that patents for chemical warfare agents were available to the public in the Patent Office Library. The detail in the specifications would have allowed any competent chemist to prepare highly lethal nerve gases using readily available chemicals and simple apparatus. The patents were originally granted to the Ministry of Defence under a secrecy order (the purpose of the applications was not revealed) but had eventually been published. The patent documents were withdrawn from the library and access would presumably not now be granted on the grounds that their publication would encourage antisocial behaviour.[47] In 1987 the Nuclear Non Proliferation (Safeguards) Act (Cth) amended the Patents Act 1952 to allow appropriate safeguards to prohibit or restrict publication of the information contained in a patent specification for an invention applicable to enrichment of nuclear material, reprocessing of irradiated nuclear material, production of heavy water or nuclear weapons, or nuclear information that is covered by an international agreement and declared by the Minister to be information relating to 'associated technology'. These provisions are reproduced in Ch 15 of the 1990 Act.

[11.23] Opposition. Once disclosed, the invention will be scrutinised by competitors and the opportunity to oppose the grant of the patent will arise.[48] Opposition may come from the minister or 'any other person' within three months from the date of advertisement of acceptance (s 59;

46. Phillips and Firth, para [5.5].
47. For an account of this, see Grubb, p 39.

reg 5.3.1). The Commissioner is then required to decide the case, hearing both applicant and opponent if they desire, with an appeal lying to the Federal Court (s 60). Under s 59, a grant may only be opposed on the grounds that the nominated person is not entitled to a grant of a patent for the invention, that the invention is not a 'manner of manufacture' which is both novel and inventive, or that the content of the specification filed in respect of the complete application does not meet the statutory requirements. Nothing else is a ground of opposition, so that matters such as inutility, secret use or other objections to the specification[49] are not to be raised at the opposition stage.

To reiterate a point made earlier, it is important to appreciate that even when opposition is unsuccessful and the patent is subsequently granted, this does not by any means make the patent immune from further challenge. As will be seen, the patent may subsequently be revoked on a wider variety of grounds than are available to an opponent at the opposition stage.[50] However, an important advantage for the patentee resisting revocation is the reversal of onus which occurs once the patent is sealed. Before grant the patentee has to make out the validity of the patent and adequacy of the documentation. Afterwards, the presumption is that the requirements of the Act have been fulfilled and the person seeking revocation has the onus of making out the grounds upon which they rely.

(c) Processing of Petty Patent Applications

[11.24] **Petty patent procedures.** Although many of the features described above in relation to standard patents apply to the consideration of petty patent applications, two important differences exist which effectively simplify and shorten the process of obtaining a petty patent. In the first place, there is no examination as such. The Commissioner is merely required to make such 'investigations' as seem appropriate to determine whether the application complies with the legislative requirements, or whether there is a 'lawful ground of objection' (which would include all issues going to patentability). If no ground of objection is found, or if such a ground is overcome by amendment of the application or accompanying specifications, the application will be accepted (s 50). On sealing of the patent, though not before, the relevant documents become available for public inspection on notification in the *Journal* under the provisions mentioned earlier. The second distinctive feature of the petty patent procedure is that no formal opportunity is provided for an application to be opposed, although any person may notify the Commissioner of matters affecting the validity of any patent which might be granted (s 28). However, the initial grant of a petty patent is for a term of one year only and the

---

48. For a fuller discussion of the opposition procedure, see T J Collins, 'Patents Act 1990: Opposition to Grant of a Standard Patent' (1993) 4 *AIPJ* 147. Note also the provision for a person, after publication of a complete specification, to notify the Commissioner of reasons for the belief that the invention is not patentable (s 27).
49. See [12.25] ff.
50. See [11.29]. Cf *Commissioner of Patents v Microcell Ltd* (1959) 102 CLR 232 at 244–5, stressing that for this reason the Commissioner should not refuse to accept an application unless it is 'practically certain' that the patent would be invalid.

patentee will normally wish to seek an extension. It is at this point, when an extension is considered, that provision is made for opposition.[51]

It was noted earlier that ACIP has recommended that petty patents be replaced by 'innovation patents'.[52] The key changes in terms of procedure are that innovation patents would subsist for a single term of eight years, thus eliminating the 'administratively clumsy and confusing' extension arrangements;[53] all applications would be required to undergo a substantive examination, though the applicant would have up to three years from the date of filing to request it; and applications would be published three months after filing, irrespective of whether they were ultimately successful.

(d) Lapse and Restoration of Applications

[11.25] Circumstances in which applications may lapse. Section 142 provides for a number of situations in which a patent application will be taken to lapse. These include:

- where a provisional specification has been lodged, failure to lodge a complete specification within 12 months (as required by reg 3.10);
- failure to request an examination within five years of lodging a complete specification or within six months of a direction to that effect by the Commissioner (see regs 3.15–3.16);
- failure to pay the prescribed continuation fee; and
- where an application is not accepted within 12 months (or up to 21 months if an extension is granted) of the applicant receiving the first examiner's report (see reg 13.4).

Provision is made under s 223 for extensions of time to be granted in various circumstances, with a general power to cover any situation where a time limit has been exceeded by reason of some error on the part of the Patent Office or the person affected, or by reason of circumstances beyond that person's control. Where an extension of time is given in respect of a period which has already expired, the application is taken to have been restored (s 223(7),(8)).

3.   GRANT AND SUBSISTENCE OF PATENTS

[11.26] Grant of patent. Once an application has been accepted and, in the case of a standard patent application, any opposition overcome, the patent will be sealed (ss 61, 62). This will happen immediately in the case of a petty patent. Where a standard patent is concerned, it must occur within three to six months of the acceptance being advertised, though extensions may be granted (reg 6.2). If the right to patent the invention has been assigned prior to sealing or the person nominated as the grantee of the patent has died, the patent will be granted to the assignee or the applicant's legal representative respectively (ss 113, 215). The Act also deals with a number of situations in which it becomes apparent that a person other than the applicant for or existing holder of a patent is entitled to obtain a patent in respect of the relevant invention. This might come to light in

---

51. See [11.28].
52. See [11.8].
53. *Review of the Petty Patent System*, 1995, p 37.

court proceedings relating to the patent, following revocation of the patent, or on the non-acceptance of a request and complete specification. In each instance the person identified to be eligible may, on making a complete application, be granted the patent (ss 34–36).

[11.27] Term of standard patent. The term of a standard patent runs from the 'date of the patent' (s 67), which in most cases is the date on which the complete specification was lodged (s 65; reg 6.3). Prior to 1995 that term was set at 16 years, with the possibility in some cases of an extension being granted. The 1952 Act originally allowed for an extension of either five or ten years on the grounds of inadequate remuneration due to no fault of the patentee, or (less commonly) because its exploitation had been inhibited due to war. In 1989 the Act was amended, doing away with extension of term for any products other than pharmaceutical substances for human therapeutic use, and limiting the extension to four years. Drug patents were singled out for special treatment because the drugs concerned tend to be expensive to manufacture and take a long time to get approval and become available for use, thus shortening the 'effective term' of the patents. The 1990 Act also adopted these provisions.

With the enactment of the Patents (World Trade Organization Amendments) Act 1994, however, all standard patents granted after 1 July 1995 will last for 20 years, as will patents granted before that date but due to expire after it. There is now no provision at all for standard patent terms to be extended. The change was prompted by Art 33 of the TRIPS Agreement, which requires a minimum of 20 years for patent terms. As a signatory to the Agreement, Australia was obliged to bring its laws into compliance. Whether the change proves to be beneficial to the national economy is quite another matter. A paper prepared for the Industry Commission has estimated that, as a net importer of patented products and processes, Australia stands to lose anywhere up to $3.8 billion over the next 30 years in additional licence fees, even after offsetting the additional revenue that will accrue to Australian patent holders.[54] The cost of extending the standard patent term may be further increased if the pharmaceutical companies (which are overwhelmingly based outside this country) are successful in their push to have restored the special provisions for extending the term of drug patents.

[11.28] Term of petty patent. The term of a petty patent is 12 months from the date on which the patent was sealed (s 68(a)), though this may be extended by the Commissioner for a further period of five years. To obtain an extension, the patentee must apply at least a month before the expiration of the initial 12 month term (ss 68(b), 69; reg 6.5). The assumption is that an extension will always be granted to the term of a petty patent unless it is clearly apparent that the patent is invalid. Thus the extension will be granted unless the Commissioner is satisfied that the patentee was not entitled to the patent, the invention claimed does not constitute a 'manner of new manufacture' that is both novel and inventive, or that the specification does not comply with the requirements of s 40 (s 69(2); reg 6.6). Allegations that any of these grounds exist may be notified to the Commissioner by any

---

54.   N Gruen, I Bruce and G Prior, *Extending Patent Life: Is it in Australia's Economic Interests?*, 1996.

person up to 11 months after the sealing of the patent (s 28(1); reg 2.6) and in that event the Commissioner is required to give a hearing to the opponent and the patentee (s 69(3)). Given that there is no formal equivalent to the procedures for examination and opposition that apply to the granting of a standard patent, it is clear that it is at this point that the issue of a petty patent's validity will be routinely raised.

[11.29] Revocation. A patent may be revoked either by a prescribed court or by the Commissioner. A court may act either on a petition by the Minister or any other person (s 138), or on a counterclaim for revocation by a defendant accused of infringing the patentee's rights (s 121). The grounds for revocation are set out in s 138(3). They are that:

(a)   the patentee is not entitled to the patent;

(b)   the invention is not patentable;

(c)   the patentee has contravened a condition in the patent;

(d)   the patent was obtained by fraud or misrepresentation;

(e)   an amendment to the request or specification was made or obtained by fraud or misrepresentation; or

(f)   the specification does not comply with the requirements of s 40.

The court may either revoke the whole patent or, in the case of a standard patent, one or more of the claims in the complete specification.

The Commissioner may revoke a patent in a number of situations. In the first place, this may be done where the patentee has offered to surrender the patent, though if any revocation or infringement proceedings are pending, the leave of the court and the consent of the parties must be sought (s 137). Second, where a patent covers an invention that is an improvement in or modification of an invention covered by another patent held by the same patentee, an application may be made to have the former patent revoked and a patent of addition granted instead (s 82). Third, the Commissioner may be asked to revoke a standard patent for non-working, a compulsory licence having earlier been granted (s 134).[55] Finally, where an adverse report has been received after a re-examination,[56] the Commissioner may revoke the patent in whole or in part, though the patentee must be given a hearing and no action is possible while court proceedings in relation to the patent are pending (s 101).

---

55. See [13.21].
56. See [11.17].

Chapter 12

Validity of Patents

[12.1]   General. A patent application and the invention on which it is based will be scrutinised to ascertain whether the statutory criteria for patentability have been met. Those criteria must be addressed during the process of examination, re-examination or opposition to an application.[1] Most importantly, the validity of a patent will be thoroughly tested when its revocation is sought, either on application or by reason of a counterclaim during infringement proceedings.[2] The various issues which may be raised in relation to validity are the subject of this chapter. Section 18(1) of the 1990 Act specifically lists the requirements of a 'patentable' invention. These requirements are that the invention:

(a)   is a 'manner of manufacture within the meaning of s 6 of the Statute of Monopolies';

(b)   is novel and inventive;

(c)   is useful; and

(d)   has not been the subject of secret use.

Furthermore, human beings are not patentable (s 18(2)). Section 18 is not exhaustive on the subject of patent validity, since there are other requirements whose non-fulfilment may affect the grant or subsistence of a patent: for example, those relating to the content and form of a specification.

1.   INVENTION: THE STATUTE OF MONOPOLIES DEFINITION

(a) Manner of New Manufacture

[12.2]   The relevance of the Statute of Monopolies. The Patents Act 1952 defined an invention in s 6 as 'any manner of new manufacture the

---

1.   See [11.16]–[11.17], [11.23]–[11.24].
2.   See [11.29], [14.10].

subject of letters patent and grant of privilege within s 6 of the Statute of Monopolies, and [including] an alleged invention'. A patent application had to relate to a 'manner of new manufacture' and the same point could have been raised as a ground of opposition and of revocation. Despite the 'plain English' drafting of the Patents Act 1990, the previous definition of 'invention' is retained (Sch 1), and s 18(1)(a) also stipulates that an invention must be a 'manner of manufacture' for it to be patentable. Over the years the phrase 'manner of new manufacture' has been the subject of a great deal of judicial attention and indeed has 'assumed a life and meaning of its own, one that flows far beyond the boundaries of conventional meaning'.[3] Out of cases such as *NRDC* (see below) has evolved a detailed set of principles which have effectively been used to limit the types of 'innovation' that may qualify for the grant of a monopoly. The reason for the continued reference to the 1624 Statute in the 1990 Act was presumably then to import those principles into the new legislation. In *N V Philips Gloeilampenfabrieken v Mirabella International Pty Ltd*,[4] which is discussed in more detail below, the High Court confirmed this conclusion. The consequence is that in order to be patentable, the subject matter of a claim must first satisfy the threshold requirement imposed by 'traditional' principles of patent law — that is, that the claim disclose a 'manner of new manufacture'. Only if that requirement can be satisfied is it necessary to move on to the further requirements of novelty, inventiveness, and so on.

[12.3]   Industrial application: the NRDC case. The words 'manner of manufacture' have come to denote either a *product* which can be produced by following the instructions in the patent specification; or a *process* or method which, similarly, can be used to achieve certain results by following the specification. However, products or processes cannot be patented unless they are capable of 'industrial application'. The leading decision on this point is *National Research Development Corp v Commissioner of Patents* (the *NRDC* case).[5] The applicant applied for a patent for a method of killing weeds growing in fodder crops, leaving the useful plants unharmed. The Deputy Commissioner of Patents had directed that three of the claims be deleted on the grounds that they did not disclose an 'invention'. The claims rejected described the action of the substance developed by NRDC in eradicating weeds growing among broad-leaf crops, without harming the fodder plants. The patent examiner had decided that this was outside the scope of what is known as an invention:

> The Commissioner, adopting certain judicial pronouncements ... emphasises the word 'manufacture' and contends for an interpretation of it which, though not narrow, is restricted to vendible products and processes for their production, and excludes all agricultural and horticultural processes. On the grounds both of the suggested restriction and of the suggested exclusion he denies that a process for killing weeds can be within the relevant concept of invention.[6]

---

3.   Ricketson (1994), p 590.
4.   (1995) 183 CLR 655: see [12.9]. See also *Anaesthetic Supplies Pty Ltd v Rescare Ltd* (1994) 28 IPR 383; *CCOM Pty Ltd v Jiejing Pty Ltd* (1994) 28 IPR 481; *Ramset Fasteners (Aust) Pty Ltd v Advanced Building Systems Pty Ltd* (1996) 34 IPR 256.
5.   (1959) 102 CLR 252.
6.   Ibid at 268.

The appellant argued that, because the process produced a useful physical result in relation to a material or tangible entity, it was the proper subject matter of a patent.

In discussing the concept of 'manner of manufacture', the High Court pointed out that the relevant inquiry was into the breadth of the concept rather than the meaning of particular words.[7] 'Manufacture' could be taken to refer to the production of tangible goods because that is its connotation in everyday speech. The case law on the subject showed, however, that not only products but also processes had long been regarded as comprehended within the term 'manufacture' as used in s 6 of the Statute of Monopolies.[8] Reference was made to the important case of *Re GEC's Application*,[9] in which the view was firmly advanced that processes and not just products are proper subject matter for patent protection. There Morton J proposed that a process or method is patentable if it leads to the production, improvement or preservation of a vendible product.[10] This enunciation of what have come to be known as the 'Morton Rules', while actually expanding on a narrow interpretation of 'manufacture', did tend to restrict the development of the concept by reference to the effect being upon a 'vendible product'. The examiner of NRDC's patent had decided that the three claims in question failed to reveal a process which acted upon a vendible product (the land itself upon which the weeds grew not being a product that was produced, improved or restored by having the weeds killed). However, the High Court looked beyond the expression 'vendible product' and pointed out that:

> What is meant by a 'product' in relation to a process is only something in which the new and useful effect may be observed ... [T]he 'something' need not be a 'thing' in the sense of an article; it may be any physical phenomenon in which the effect, be it creation or alteration may be observed [including a tract or stratum of land].[11]

Thus the proper emphasis to be derived from the Morton Rules is that there should be some industrial or commercial or trading character about the process. What is patentable is the application of ingenuity in the field of economic endeavour — specifically, in this case, in an artificially created state of affairs which results in an important improvement in the conditions in which the crop is to grow.

[12.4] Agricultural and horticultural processes. The objection to the claims in *NRDC* was not only that they fell outside intrinsic restrictions on patentable subject matter, but also that claims for agricultural or horticultural processes are excluded from patentability. The Patent Office had developed a practice of denying patents in these areas of endeavour. Upon investigating this reluctance to issue such patents, the High Court detected several overlapping considerations. In the normal agricultural or horticultural realm there may more readily be confusion between an invention and a 'mere discovery' of the laws of nature, which, as will be seen, is not

7.   Ibid at 269.
8.   Ibid at 269–70, citing *Boulton v Pull* (1795) 1 Hy Bl 433; 126 ER 651; *Crane v Price* (1842) 1 Web PC 393; 134 ER 239; *Hornblower v Boulton* (1799) 8 TR 95; 101 ER 1258.
9.   (1942) 60 RPC 1.
10. Ibid at 4.
11. (1959) 102 CLR 252 at 276.

patentable. It may be easier to establish that a product or process lacks novelty when the area of use is one with a long history of human endeavour. Furthermore, there is a reluctance, partly based on statutory provisions,[12] to allow monopolies in areas concerned with human or animal foodstuffs. The result of these overlapping concerns had been to establish a principle that agricultural or horticultural processes could not be a manner of new manufacture. This was according to the High Court, 'a generalisation not supported by the reasons leading to the conclusions in the particular instances from which the generalisation is drawn'.[13] Accordingly there is no consideration wrapped up in the label 'agricultural or horticultural' which necessarily takes a process outside the area of patentability, as long as the process is novel and of sufficient inventiveness.

[12.5] Discoveries excluded from patentability. A further objection taken to the claims in *NRDC* was that the company had merely made a discovery, and that discoveries are excluded from being a manner of manufacture since the observation of certain physical properties or the finding of a previously unknown but naturally occurring substance is not something that should be monopolised by any individual or company. The chemicals involved in the weed killing process were not newly compounded but were already known: it was the process for which they were being used which was the invention — or was it only a discovery? As the court pointed out, while acknowledging that 'mere' discoveries are not patentable, '[t]he truth is that the distinction between discovery and invention is not precise'.[14] The applicant's research in *NRDC* had led to the discovery that a useful result could be attained beyond the previously known uses to which the chemicals could be put. It was the translation of a discovery into something new and useful which supplied the relevant factor for patentability. An application of scientific ingenuity combining knowledge, thought and experimentation led to an appreciation that the chemical reacted differently on different plants, according to their enzyme system. It was this 'discovery' which led to the invention — selective weed control based on a new principle.[15]

The principle that the discovery of an existing naturally occurring substance cannot be patented has implications for the isolation of desirable substances. Although the process of obtaining such useful substances as tissue plasminogen activator or human growth hormone may be patentable, the product itself may not be.[16] Furthermore, scientific theories or

---

12. See [12.8].
13. (1959) 102 CLR 252 at 278. Plant varieties are now protected by separate legislation: see [15.20]–[15.24].
14. (1959) 102 CLR 252 at 264.
15. 'The newly discovered factor is that there is such a relationship between the enzyme make-up of the tissues of some plants and a certain type of hormone herbicide derived from straight-chain aliphatic acids higher in the series than acetic acid that in these plants the herbicide is not degraded to the active acetic derivatives, although it is so degraded within the tissues of many common weeds normally found in association with these plants. The consequence is that this type of herbicide kills the weeds in which it is so degraded but has no deleterious effect on the plants in which it is not.' (ibid at 266.)
16. *Genentech Inc v Wellcome Foundation Ltd* [1989] RPC 147. See the discussion on biological patents in Chapter 15. Note further that if the technology for isolating or cloning the substances is known, then the process may not be patentable either.

intellectual information without application to some end which will 'add to the sum of human art'[17] are not patentable for the same reasons that 'mere' discoveries are not: there must be some application of the theory or information to economically significant ends.[18] The requirement that information is only patentable when embodied in some practical, technical or industrial application, as well as satisfying the further criteria of novelty and inventiveness, is intended to prevent whole areas of research being tied up by one organisation and to ensure that ideas per se are not protected — just as ideas must be in 'material form' before copyright protection will crystallise around them.[19] There would also be difficulty in identifying the boundaries of the idea or information in order to define the patent monopoly.[20]

[12.6] Presentation of information and computer software. Just as information itself (for example, a scientific formula) cannot be patented, so it is often said that a product or process which involves the presentation of information cannot be the subject of a patent. The case law on 'manner of new manufacture' is certainly littered with examples of arrangements and methods of presenting information (including product packaging) being denied patents.[21] However, it is unclear whether there is any distinct principle at work in these cases, or whether the 'inventions' concerned simply failed to meet the *NRDC* requirement that there be 'a mode or manner of achieving an end result which is an artificially created state of affairs of utility in the field of economic endeavour'.[22] There have certainly been a number of recent cases in which, by focusing on this general proposition, Australian courts have overcome what was previously regarded as a reluctance (at least on the part of the Patents Office) to accept applications involving computer software.[23] One difficulty in patenting computer technology has been that computer programs may in some instances be regarded as merely 'reciting a mathematical algorithm'.[24] If, however, the algorithm (a formula which is itself unpatentable) is applied to some defined purpose, that may amount to a 'manner of manufacture'. An invention relating to an improved method and equipment for producing curved images in computer graphics displays has been allowed.[25] An invention involving the use of a word processor to assemble text in Chinese characters has also been held to be a 'manner of manufacture' where the operation of the keyboard led to the computer program searching in such

17. *Neilson v Minister of Public Works (NSW)* (1914) 18 CLR 423 at 429.
18. See *Lane-Fox v Kensington and Knightsbridge Electric Lighting Co* (1892) 2 RPC 413; *Otto v Linford* (1862) 46 LT 35; *Reynolds v Herbert Smith & Co* (1902) 20 RPC 123; *Slee and Harris' Application* [1966] RPC 194.
19. See [6.3].
20. Note however the role played by the action for breach of confidence in protecting valuable but not necessarily patentable information, much of which will be created in the course of developing inventions: see [3.10], [13.11].
21. See eg *Re Virginia-Carolina Chemicals Corp's Application* [1958] RPC 38; *Wellcome Foundation Ltd v Commissioner of Patents* (1980) 145 CLR 520; and see further Lahore, *Patents*, para [12,420] ff.
22. *CCOM Pty Ltd v Jiejing Pty Ltd* (1994) 28 IPR 481 at 514.
23. See further [9.30].
24. See *Re Application by Honeywell Bull Inc* (1991) 22 IPR 463 at 468.
25. *IBM Corp v Commissioner of Patents* (1991) 22 IPR 417.

a way as to retrieve and display all Chinese characters relevant to the search criteria entered.[26] Previously, the 6000 characters of the Chinese language (3000 for 'everyday' vocabulary) had either been assembled separately using many keystrokes or a digital pad had to be attached to the computer.

[12.7] A 'human treatment' exception? The British Patents Act 1977 s 4(2) and the European Patent Convention Art 52(4) both provide that a method of treatment of the human or animal body by surgery or therapy or of diagnosis practised on the human or animal body shall not be taken to be capable of industrial application, not therefore fitting within the conception of patentable subject matter. This statutory provision codifies a rule long observed in British and Australian courts in refusing to allow patents for methods of treatment of disease in humans. This rule, although previously applied in Australian courts, has never had a statutory basis in Australia and in *Anaesthetic Supplies Pty Ltd v Rescare Ltd*[27] it was rejected as a ground for refusing patent protection for a method (and a device) for the prevention of sleep apnoea. It was concluded by Gummow J at trial that there was no sensible reason for maintaining the 'human treatment' exception.[28] The majority of the Full Federal Court (Lockhart and Wilcox JJ) upheld this decision. However, Sheppard J dissented, following the reasoning of previous decisions that allowing monopolies over beneficial treatment techniques and processes is 'generally inconvenient',[29] and pointing out that under the TRIPS Agreement (Articles 27.2 and 27.3) members are permitted to exclude certain inventions and methods for the treatment of humans and animals, and that this reflects a substantial body of international thinking on the undesirability of such patents.[30]

Apart from being 'generally inconvenient' on social policy grounds to allow patenting of methods of treatment, many such methods may simply lack other basic criteria of patent validity. In *NRDC* the High Court said that 'the exclusion of methods of surgery and other processes may well lie outside the concept of invention because the whole subject is conceived as essentially non economic'.[31] However, this reluctance to regard medical advances as having economic significance has been under question for some time. For many years the leading Australian decision on the human treatment exception was *Joos v Commissioner of Patents*.[32] There the High Court defined treatment as 'the arrest or cure of a disease or diseased condition or the correction of some malfunction or the amelioration of some incapacity or disability'.[33] In *Joos* the Examiner of Patents had reported adversely on an application for a patent for an invention titled 'Process for improving strength and elasticity of keratinous material' such as hair and nails. The process was claimed to be beneficial to bleached, permed and dyed hair. The Deputy Commissioner decided that the application should

---

26. *CCOM Pty Ltd v Jiejing Pty Ltd* (1994) 28 IPR 481.
27. (1994) 28 IPR 383. In fact in *Rescare* much of the patent was invalid as several claims were not fairly based on the provisional specification: see [12.28].
28. *Rescare Ltd v Anaesthetic Supplies Pty Ltd* (1992) 25 IPR 119.
29. See [12.11].
30. Ibid at 418; see P Loughlin, 'Of Patents and Patients: New Monopolies in Medical Methods' (1995) 6 *AIPJ* 5.
31. (1959) 102 CLR 252 at 275, citing *Maeder v Busch* (1938) 59 CLR 684.
32. (1972) 46 ALJR 438.
33. Ibid at 441.

not proceed because it was for a process for the treatment of parts of the human body whilst attached to or growing upon the body. On appeal, Barwick CJ decided that the process had economic virtue or significance and commercial application in the hairdressing field so as to be within *NRDC's* definition of 'invention'.[34] Furthermore, there were significant economic benefits in effective treatments or surgery, including the repair and rehabilitation of the workforce and the subsequent impact on workers' compensation, invalid pensions and rehabilitation costs to the community. Thus the exclusion from patentability of medical advances in the form of 'treatment' was obviously not solely on the grounds that the activity had no economic relevance in the requisite sense.

In fact, as a matter of practice the Patent Commissioner began to accept methods or processes for human treatment for patenting on the basis that Barwick CJ in the *Joos* case had expressed doubt as to the exclusion of such subject matter from patenting. This change in practice, and the authorities on the 'human treatment exception' were reviewed by Gummow J at trial in the *Rescare* case. The dissenting judgment of Sheppard J in the *Rescare* appeal also reviewed the historical and ethical basis of the 'human treatment' exception to patentability. The exception seems to have originated in *Re C & W's Application*,[35] where a process for extracting lead from human bodies was held not to be patentable.[36] The statutes under which this and other cases were decided were similar to the present legislation, in that they did not specifically address the issue of patentability of human treatments, the exception thus being supplied by the courts. In New Zealand the exception has been doubted,[37] but was endorsed by the Court of Appeal in *Commissioner of Patents v Wellcome Foundation Ltd*.[38] The claim in question concerned a method of treating or preventing meningeal leukaemia by the internal administration of drugs. The compound was already known as a treatment for malaria. The Assistant Commissioner of Patents, following an adverse examiner's report, had decided that the claims did not disclose an 'invention' because they related to a method of treatment of human beings. The High Court of New Zealand held that there was no reason per se why such a process should not be patentable.[39] From that decision the Commissioner appealed to the Court of Appeal where it was decided that the weight of authority was against patenting. Although there might be no intrinsic reason as to why human treatment should not be considered a manner of new manufacture, the treatment of human ailment did possess a special character and it might be unwarranted to allow patent monopolies in the field of alleviation of human disease and suffering. In light of the decision in *Rescare* and the High Court's refusal to grant leave to appeal from the Full Court's decision, however, it must be assumed that the

---

34. Ibid at 440.
35. (1914) 31 RPC 235.
36. See also *Upjohn's Application* [1977] RPC 94; *Unisearch Ltd's Application* (1965) 35 AOJP 465.
37. *Wellcome Foundation Ltd v Plantex* [1974] RPC 514; *Wellcome Foundation Ltd's (Hitchings) Application* [1980] RPC 305.
38. (1983) 2 IPR 156.
39. Assuming that the application of the substance to the new use was otherwise within the conception of 'manner of manufacture' and was novel and inventive.

human treatment exception no longer has any force in Australia. It remains to be seen whether it might be re-introduced by legislation.

[12.8] Patenting of drugs. It is to be noted that the statutory prohibition on the patenting of methods of treatment in the British Act and in the European Patent Convention is not extended to drugs, that is, 'a product consisting of a substance or composition'. In other words, substances developed for use in treatment are protectable 'as such'. On the other hand, while a new drug will be patentable, subsequent medical uses of the drug will not be, even if research, testing and effort beyond 'mere discovery' is required to develop subsequent uses.[40] The Australian legislation does say that the Commissioner has a discretion not to grant a patent for a substance capable of being used as medicine (or food) where that substance is a mere mixture of known ingredients or a process producing such a substance by mere admixture (s 51(b)).[41] However, a drug composed of existing ingredients may be more than a mere 'admixture' if a synergistic effect is produced which takes it outside the statutory prohibition, or if it fits within the requirements of a 'selection' patent, as discussed below.[42]

[12.9] The need for 'newness' and 'inventiveness'. As we have seen, the phrase 'manner of new manufacture' has been interpreted to mean that the subject matter of a patent claim must have an industrial application, and must also have been 'invented' rather than merely 'discovered'. A further restriction on patentability developed by the courts out of the Statute of Monopolies formula hinges on the adjective 'new'. It has been repeatedly emphasised that a patent cannot be granted for putting a known substance with known properties to some new use for which those known properties made it suitable.[43] What is lacking in such a case is any quality of 'inventiveness', or the use of ingenuity to add to the sum of human knowledge. It is a different story if, as in *NRDC*, the 'new use that is proposed consists in taking advantage of a hitherto unknown or unsuspected property of the material' to produce a useful result.[44] The same is true of a 'mere collocation of known integers' (that is, the grouping together of features or components which are each well established).[45] In order to be patentable the combination itself must be more than the sum of its parts: there must have been an element of inventiveness in the decision to assemble the particular components to create something new and useful.[46]

---

40. As was the case in *NRDC*, where hitherto unknown properties of existing chemicals were being claimed.
41. Note that s 4(3) of the Patents Act 1977 (UK) provides that the prohibition of methods of treatment does not operate to prevent any substance or composition used in the method being capable of industrial application and therefore patentable.
42. See Australian Patent Office, *Patent Examiner's Manual*, 1984, para [155.10]. It may be very difficult to prove a synergistic effect: see Grubb, p 144.
43. *Commissioner of Patents v Microcell Ltd* (1959) 102 CLR 232; *NRDC* (1959) 102 CLR 252 at 262; *W R Grace & Co v Asahi Kasei Kogyo Kabushiki Kaisha* (1993) 25 IPR 481.
44. (1959) 102 CLR 252 at 262.
45. See eg *Ramset Fasteners (Aust) Pty Ltd v Advanced Building Systems Pty Ltd* (1996) 34 IPR 256.
46. See eg *Welch Perrin & Co Pty Ltd v Worrel* (1961) 106 CLR 588; *Minnesota Mining & Manufacturing Co v Beiersdorf (Australia) Ltd* (1980) 144 CLR 253. See [12.19] for more on 'combination patents'.

Section 18(1)(b) of the 1990 Act does now specify 'novelty' and some 'inventive step', as measured against a defined 'prior art base', as separate requirements of patentability.[47] In *N V Philips Gloeilampenfabrieken v Mirabella International Pty Ltd*[48] it was argued that accordingly there is no longer any 'residual requirement of newness' imposed by the retention of the Statute of Monopolies definition, and that any questions of 'newness' or 'inventiveness' can only be pursued under s 18(1)(b). This contention is supported by the absence of the adjective 'new' in s 18(1)(a), which refers only to the need for a 'manner of manufacture' (which would presumably still import the requirement for an industrial application). However, the argument was rejected by the High Court, albeit by a bare 3–2 majority. Brennan, Deane and Toohey JJ held that the use of the term 'invention' (defined in Schedule 1 to mean a 'manner of new manufacture') in the opening words of s 18(1) was sufficient to import the requirement of 'inventiveness' developed in earlier decisions. This meant that the patent concerned, which was for compact fluorescent lamps, could be held invalid as involving no more than a new use for a known substance (phosphors) without any reference to s 18(1)(b) and the relevant prior art base. As the majority explained:[49]

> That does not mean that the threshold requirement of 'an alleged invention' corresponds with or renders otiose the more specific requirements of novelty or inventive step (when compared with the prior art base) contained in s 18(1)(b). It simply means that, if it is apparent on the face of the specification that the quality of inventiveness necessary for there to be a proper subject of letters patent under the Statute of Monopolies is absent, one need go further.

(b) Other Restrictions

[12.10] **General.** Section 6 of the Statute of Monopolies, besides requiring a manner of new manufacture, also contained a rider to the effect that no patents should be granted in respect of inventions that were 'contrary to the law [or] mischievous to the State ... or hurt of trade, or generallie inconvenient'. This embargo has allowed the courts to make value judgments on issues of social advantage as part of their consideration of the patentability of an invention. Besides being incorporated into the definition of 'invention' through its reference to the 1624 Statute, one part of the restriction is explicitly reinforced by the Australian legislation, in that the Commissioner has the discretion to refuse to accept an application in respect of an invention 'the use of which would be contrary to law' (s 51(a)).

[12.11] **'Generallie inconvenient'.** The 'treatment' exception to patentability discussed in the previous section (and still relevant in Europe) was based in part upon the idea that it would be generally inconvenient to allow monopolies over methods of curing disease or alleviating suffering.[50] Other considerations relevant to the assessment of general convenience

47. See [12.13]–[12.24].
48. (1995) 183 CLR 655.
49. Ibid at 664.
50. See *Commissioner of Patents v Wellcome Foundation Ltd* (1983) 2 IPR 156 at 164; cf *Anaesthetic Supplies Pty Ltd v Rescare Ltd* (1994) 28 IPR 383 at 399.

include whether granting a patent would preclude the undertaking of normal activities.[51] Thus the Patent Office will not allow general claims which merely involve faster production, cheaper manufacture, safer operation or automatisation,[52] unless a particular process or machine for achieving any of these things is the invention being claimed.

In Britain and Europe the general convenience of the public is expressed in terms of whether inventions are in a category 'the publication or exploitation of which would be generally expected to encourage offensive, immoral or antisocial behaviour'. This phrase is found in s 1(3)(a) of the Patents Act 1977 (UK) and is similar to the provision in the European Patent Convention excluding inventions contrary to 'ordre public' (Art 53(a)), described by Phillips and Firth as an 'untranslatable French term',[53] but equivalent to 'morality' according to Cornish.[54] In the past, patents for contraceptives were refused on this ground.[55] It may be that there is little scope today for refusing patents on grounds of immorality, but one issue is whether patents should be granted for new animal varieties, the genetic manipulation and bio-engineering techniques used to achieve this being seen by some as being highly undesirable.[56] The Australian legislation does not explicitly prohibit patents issuing for animals, although the European and UK legislation does.

On the other hand, the patenting of 'human beings and the biological processes for their production' is now explicitly prohibited following the enactment of s 18(2) of the 1990 Act. This prohibition was inserted by the Senate Standing Committee on Industry, Science and Technology, although a wider amendment to exclude all patents for life and life forms was not adopted. More recently, the Patents Amendment Bill 1996 has been introduced into parliament by the Australian Democrats. If passed, the bill would restrict the patentability of genetic information.[57]

[**12.12**]   **Contrary to law.** It would seem that the phrase 'contrary to law' may be distinguished from the concept of general inconvenience as having a more precise meaning. This is not necessarily the case as the two seem to overlap, particularly in Europe where the provisions in the British Patents Act and European Patent Convention mentioned in the previous paragraph correspond to an earlier enactment which contained the phrase 'contrary to law or morality'.[58] The meaning of 'contrary to law' has in fact

---

51.   See *Rolls Royce Ltd's Application* [1963] RPC 251; *Re Application by Beecham Group Ltd* (1984) 3 IPR 26.

52.   See *British United Shoe Machinery Co v Simon Collier Ltd* (1909) 26 RPC 21.

53.   Phillips and Firth, para [5.29].

54.   Cornish, p 150. Article 53(a) of the European Patent Convention is echoed by Art 2.3 of the EC Directive on Biotechnological Inventions which prohibits the patenting of the human body, parts of the body, processes for modifying the genetic identity of humans where this would be contrary to human dignity, and processes for modifying the genetic identity of animals which are likely to cause suffering or handicaps without any substantial benefit resulting.

55.   See *Riddlesbarger's Application* (1936) 53 RPC 57.

56.   For example, Jeremy Rivkin of the Foundation for Economic Trends, who has been described as 'an implacable foe of genetic engineering': C Wallis, 'Should Animals be Patented?', *Time (Australia)*, 4 May 1987, p 74. See also [15.17].

57.   See [15.7].

58.   Patents Act 1949 (UK) ss 10(1)(b), 32(1)(k).

received almost no judicial attention.[59] It seems to be assumed by the Patent Office that the phrase refers to inventions the primary use of which would amount to a criminal offence, for example bombs intended for surreptitious use or an explosive safe designed to kill burglars.[60] It is interesting in this connection to note the application by Novatech Energy Systems, a New York (USA) company, for two patents in respect of an invention with alarming overtones.[61] The invention is a potentially lethal water pistol which ejects jets of water with opposite electrical charges. When the jets are directed at a plant, current flows through the droplets that fall on its leaves. A current of 5 milliamps kills insects. The second patent application is for the use of the device to control crowds, the current being switchable between 'sting mode' and 'stun mode', although the proposal also suggests that 'kill mode' could be achieved with a charge of 100 milliamps or more. The filing of two applications in this example was to allow one to proceed but not the other.

2. NOVELTY

[12.13] **General.** The need for a manner of manufacture to be 'new' finds separate expression in the requirement that any invention claimed in a patent application must be 'novel' (s 18(1)(b)(i)). Novelty is obviously a basic requirement of the patent system, since the consideration moving to the public in return for the monopoly is the revelation of something hitherto unknown. Furthermore, to allow patents for inventions already known and possibly in use would be to deprive the public of rights previously being exercised and would be unjust. In 1901 the Fry Committee[62] demonstrated that 40% or more of patents granted at that time were already described in earlier British specifications. This led to the requirement that applications be examined for novelty by the patent authorities.

[12.14] **Assessment of novelty and the 'prior art base'.** The assessment of novelty basically requires an investigation to establish whether the alleged invention has been anticipated, judged as at the time of its priority date. A priority date, as seen in the previous chapter, is generally secured by lodging a specification. Anticipation may principally occur through prior publication or prior use.[63] The 1990 Act provides that the novelty of any claim is to be assessed 'when compared with the prior art base as it existed immediately before the priority date of that claim' (s 18(1)(b)). The 'prior art base' for this purpose is defined in Sch 1 to include information which is publicly available anywhere in the patent area (that is, Australia), either in documentary form or through the doing of an act.[64] In the case of a standard patent, it also includes information in a document publicly

---

59. But see *Dow Chemical Co v Ishihara Sangyo Kaisha Ltd* (1985) 5 IPR 415.
60. See *Patent Examiner's Manual*, 1984, para [55.2].
61. B Fox, 'Patents', *New Scientist*, 28 October 1989, p 20.
62. Committee appointed by the Board of Trade to inquire into the working of the Patents Acts on certain specified questions, *Report*, Cmnd 506, 1901.
63. See *Griffin v Isaacs* (1938) 12 AOJP 739.
64. Note however that where novelty is assessed during a re-examination, the prior art base is to be taken *not* to include information made publicly available by the doing of an act: s 98(2). Thus the Examiner is in this instance confined to looking at prior documentary publication. Why this restriction should apply in relation to re-examination, though not the original examination, is somewhat hard to fathom.

available outside the patent area.[65] Besides dispensing with any separate objection based on prior publication, the new statute's provisions on the novelty issue involve an important substantive change to the patents regime. The effect is that, at least as far as standard patents are concerned, novelty is to be assessed by reference to disclosures in documentary form anywhere in the world. This change brings Australia into line with most of its trading partners, the idea being that export oriented companies will benefit from closer parity between Australian patent laws and international developments. The criterion of 'absolute' rather than 'domestic' novelty was, for example, introduced in the UK in 1979 in order to bring British law into line with the European Patent Convention.[66] However, it should be noted that the effect of the 1990 Act is only to impose a test of absolute novelty in respect of documentary disclosure, and then only for standard patents. Domestic or 'national' novelty remains the criterion in respect of use or other revelations of the invention; and petty patents continue to be tested only against the local prior art base.

[12.15] What constitutes anticipation. Apart from dictating a wider information base against which to assess standard patent specifications, the 1990 Act appears to contemplate that the criteria for determining whether anticipation has occurred will remain as they were under the 1952 Act. This means continuing to apply the 'reverse infringement test':

> The basic test for anticipation or want of novelty is the same as that for infringement and generally one can properly ask oneself whether the alleged anticipation would, if the patent were valid, constitute an infringement.[67]

Thus, for example, the fact that the invention as claimed contains variations from an earlier publication will not preclude anticipation being found unless those variations contain additional information of a significant nature and amount to more than just 'mechanical equivalents'.[68] If there *are* significant variations from the prior art base, however, it would appear that the requirement of novelty will be satisfied even if the variations themselves lack 'ingenuity' or 'inventiveness'. In *R D Werner & Co Inc v Bailey Aluminium Products Pty Ltd*[69] the Full Court of the Federal Court pointed out that under modern patents legislation a clear distinction is drawn between lack of novelty and lack of inventive step. Thus if an invention as claimed differs in significant respects from a particular prior publication, there is no anticipation. The fact that an expert reading that publication would have needed no great ingenuity to come up with the invention in question will be irrelevant, unless the publication can be said to form part of 'common general knowledge' for the purpose of the separate rules relating to the inventive step requirement.[70]

---

65. Note that 'document' here could include a computerised database: see Acts Interpretation Act 1961 (Cth) s 25.
66. Patents Act 1977 (UK) s 2(2).
67. *Meyers Taylor Pty Ltd v Vicarr Industries Ltd* (1977) 137 CLR 228 at 235.
68. *Griffin v Isaacs* (1938) 12 AOJP 739; *R D Werner & Co Inc v Bailey Aluminium Products Pty Ltd* (1989) 13 IPR 513; *Nicaro Holdings Pty Ltd v Martin Engineering Co* (1990) 16 IPR 545.
69. (1989) 13 IPR 513. Cf *Griffin v Isaacs* (1938) 12 AOJP 739 at 740; *Windsurfing International Inc v Petit* [1984] 2 NSWLR 196 at 226.
70. See further [12.23].

Section 7(1) provides that novelty is to be assessed by comparing an invention with the prior art base, but specifically in the light of any one of three types of information, each of which must be considered separately. The three kinds of information are single documents or acts revealing the invention, another patent specification, or a combination of documents or acts which a 'person skilled in the relevant art' would treat as a single source. Thus each publication or act must be looked at separately to see whether it anticipates the alleged invention. This provision seems to reflect judicial opinion, to the effect that an invention is not to be regarded as lacking novelty simply because someone could have put together all the aspects of the invention from a variety of unconnected sources. Such a process, of making a 'mosaic' of pieces of information which are not otherwise cross-referenced, has not been permitted in assessing novelty even under the former legislation.[71]

[12.16] Public knowledge. The 1990 Act refers to information being 'publicly available'. Again, the intention is presumably to import the learning on the meaning of 'public knowledge' which the courts have already developed. In this connection, publication has been said to involve adding to the stock of knowledge which the public has or can acquire.[72] If even one person has the invention revealed to them then novelty will be lost, unless there is some obligation on the recipient to keep the invention confidential. The authorities show that:

> whenever a document describing a method of manufacture … was placed where the public had access to it and whenever an article was used in such circumstances, the whole of the information contained in the document or revealed by the use of the articles became part of public general knowledge.[73]

Similarly, it has been said that:

> A description in an obscure publication would suffice to destroy novelty, provided it was a publication, that is to say that the document, whether or not it was read generally by the public, had been available to the public and similar considerations applied to publication by user.[74]

Even if no one but an expert can understand a publication,[75] disclosure will still form part of the prior art because it has been made available to the public 'even though the man on the Clapham omnibus would have no idea that it had been made available to him'.[76] Disclosure will have occurred even if a document is in a foreign language. This has always been true but will be particularly relevant when Australian patent law tests novelty against a worldwide documentary prior art base. In *Dennison Manufacturing Co v Monarch Marketing Systems Inc*[77] an invention entitled 'Connecter for Holding Articles Together' (being a plastic tag used to attach price labels to clothing and other merchandise) was compared with a French specification

---

71. See *Acme Bedstead Co Ltd v Newlands Bros Ltd* (1937) 58 CLR 689 at 703–4; *Nicaro Holdings Pty Ltd v Martin Engineering Co* (1990) 16 IPR 545; *Winner v Ammar Holdings Pty Ltd* (1993) 25 IPR 273. Cf *George C Warner Laboratories Pty Ltd v Chemspray Pty Ltd* (1967) 41 ALJR 75.
72. *Gadd & Mason v Manchester Corp* (1892) 9 RPC 516 at 527.
73. *HPM Industries Pty Ltd v Gerard Industries Ltd* (1957) 98 CLR 424 at 437.
74. *Sunbeam Corp v Morphy-Richards (Aust) Pty Ltd* (1961) 35 ALJR 212 at 218.
75. *General Tire & Rubber Co v Firestone Tyre & Rubber Co Ltd* [1972] RPC 457.
76. Phillips and Firth, para [5.2].
77. (1983) 1 IPR 431.

recently filed in the Australian Patent Office. This document, 'resting qui- etly in the French language in Canberra',[78] was held by two of three Fed- eral Court judges to have disclosed all integers of the claimed invention.

Other examples of anticipation through slight exposure include the improved ball point pen which was given to members of a government depart- ment as a friendly gesture (without any obligation to keep the invention confidential);[79] the use of a new type of hospital bed in a hospital before the priority date;[80] and use of a seed collecting machine in the district where the inventor lived.[81] Publishing photographs of inventions can anticipate them if enough detail is shown. For example, the publication in a magazine of a photograph showing a mechanical hay rake was held to anticipate the novel feature claimed.[82] So, too, a sailboard was anticipated by a photograph appearing in a magazine.[83] Just one sale of an item before the priority date may amount to anticipation, or even demonstrating an invention with some commercial purpose in mind.[84] It has been held, however, that use of a prod- uct must be 'informative' prior use, so it will become part of the prior art only in so far as all necessary information about the invention is revealed.[85]

[12.17] **Prior claiming.** The situation may arise where competitors file similar patent applications within quick succession, so that although one secures an earlier priority date, their application is not yet published at the time the second applicant lodges a specification. In such a situation, the second claim cannot be said to have been anticipated by prior publication. However, one of the most fundamental principles of patent law is that not more than one patent should be granted for the same invention. On the other hand the second applicant has presumably worked hard to produce their invention without the benefit of having had the invention already revealed in the prior art. In order to be as fair as possible to both appli- cants, the 1952 Act recognised a separate ground of invalidity known as 'prior claiming'. This occurred whenever an invention was found to have been claimed in a claim of earlier priority date contained in a complete or petty patent specification, the application having been made or the patent granted in Australia. In the case of examination and opposition, prior claiming would not invalidate an application if the earlier application or patent had lapsed, expired or been refused. In determining whether prior claiming had occurred, courts tended to take a lenient view. Generally speaking, unless the two claims were identical the earlier would not be taken to invalidate the later, even if the invention revealed was substantially the same.[86] This reduced the effectiveness of the objection and also resulted in 'highly recondite judicial decisions'.[87]

---

78. Ibid at 435.
79. *Fomento Industrial SA v Mentmore Manufacturing Co Ltd* [1956] RPC 87.
80. *Acme Bedstead Co Ltd v Newlands Bros Ltd* (1937) 58 CLR 689.
81. *Longworth v Emerton* (1951) 83 CLR 539.
82. *Van der Lely NV v Bamfords Ltd* [1963] RPC 61.
83. *Windsurfing International Inc v Petit* [1984] 2 NSWLR 196.
84. *Re Wheatley's Patent Application* (1984) 2 IPR 450; *Innovative Agriculture Products Pty Ltd v Cranshaw* (1996) 35 IPR 643.
85. *Hope v Heggies Bulkhaul Ltd* (1996) 34 IPR 584.
86. See eg *Ethyl Corp (Cook's) Patent* [1970] RPC 227; *Re Kromschroder's Patent* [1960] RPC 75.
87. Committee to Examine the Patent System and Patent Law, *Report*, Cmnd 4407, 1970, p 2 ('Banks Report').

Under the 1990 Act a different approach is taken, with prior claiming no longer a separate ground of invalidity. Instead the 'prior art base' against which novelty is to be assessed is defined to include information contained in a complete specification for a claim with an earlier priority date which was unpublished at the priority date of the patent or application under challenge.[88] This makes for a much more straightforward position: instead of being treated as a distinct issue, the effect of an unpublished specification on a later-filed specification simply becomes one of anticipation in the same way as any other prior publication or prior use. In adopting this 'whole contents' approach, the new Act corresponds to the Patents Act 1977 (UK) and the European Patent Convention. When this change was introduced in the UK the comment was made that:

> [I]n so re-defining novelty the 1977 Act has finally got rid of the ground of invalidity known as prior claiming, a change which can only be welcomed in view of the chaotic state of the law relating to that ground.[89]

It should be noted that the reference in the 1990 Act's definition of 'prior art base' to specifications unpublished on the priority date of the application in question applies only to considerations of novelty and not to the question of whether there is an inventive step. In other words, the existence of an earlier unpublished application can destroy the novelty of an invention but cannot be used to argue that the invention is obvious. Therefore the two concepts remain distinct, as under the 1952 Act, although in some respects the material to be considered overlaps.

[12.18] Publications and uses not precluding novelty. There are a variety of circumstances in which it would be inappropriate and/or unfair for a prior disclosure to prejudice the patentability of an invention. Besides providing, presumably out of abundant caution, that a claim is not affected by publication or use of the relevant invention after the claim's priority date, or by the grant of another patent of the same or a later priority date which claims the same invention (s 23), the Act sets out in s 24 matters not affecting the validity of a patent. Publication without the patentee's consent and disclosure to public authorities are explicitly mentioned, but the remainder are left to regulations to prescribe. These are set out in reg 2.2 and include:

- the showing or use of the invention at a recognised exhibition;
- the publication of the invention while a recognised exhibition is being held;
- the publication of an invention in a paper written by the inventor and read before a learned society, or published with the inventor's consent by or on behalf of a learned society;
- the working in public of the invention within one year before the priority date of a claim for the invention for the purpose of a reasonable trial, provided that, because of the nature of the invention, it is reasonably necessary for the working to be in public.

The inventor must report the nature of the exhibition and that the invention has been so displayed at the time of filing for patent rights in order for the exceptions to prior publication to apply. The explanatory memorandum for the 1990 Act suggests that a 'wider range of circumstances may be

---

88. See eg *Alcatel NV v Commissioner of Patents* (1996) 35 IPR 255.
89. W Aldous et al, *Terrell on the Law of Patents*, 13th ed, 1982, para [742].

prescribed at some stage, however, particularly if international moves to recognise a "grace period" before the application date proceed'.

[12.19] Combination patents. Before leaving the topic of novelty it should be realised that there is a type of invention which draws on existing elements but can still be regarded as novel. A claim for a combination of integers, some or all of which are known, may be patentable if a new result is achieved by the combination, provided the objection of obviousness (discussed below) can be overcome. The essential aspect conferring validity for a combination patent is that the components interact to produce a better result. The emphasis is on what the combination achieves through the interaction of the integers with each other. For example, non-irritating sticking plaster which both covered the wound effectively while allowing air to penetrate and aid healing was the subject of a valid combination patent.[90] Although sticking plaster was already known, a thin breathable translucent surgical tape of this sort, possessing the advantages it did, had not been part of the prior art. Similarly a device for cleaning conveyer belts in mines was held to be valid because, although composed of well-known elements, when combined they resulted in a machine which cleaned more effectively, was easier to maintain, minimised loss of productive operation of the conveyer belt and was operative in unusually confined spaces.[91] A collection of elements which continue to perform their own function but do not combine to produce a new result is known as a mere collocation (or a 'sausage machine' after the case of *Williams v Nye*,[92] where a more efficient sausage machine was made by combining a mincer and filler: these separate parts were already in use and simply putting them together did not amount to a patentable invention).

[12.20] Selection patents. Another type of patent over existing material is known as a selection patent, which may be allowed for an invention which selects out a group of members from a known class. The main use of selection patents is in cases concerning chemical substances where it is shown that the sub-class selected has some advantage over the class as a whole.[93] The classic formulation of the requirements of a selection patent was given by Maugham J in *I G Farben Industrie's Patents*.[94] The patents before the court concerned a particular class of dyestuffs known as ozo dyes, formed by coupling diazo compounds (already known substances) with other compounds to produce a particularly effective dye, resistant to Kier-boiling, a process of boiling cottons in caustic soda to remove impurities. It was held that for a selection patent to be valid, (i) it must be based on some substantial advantage to be secured by the use of the selected members; and (ii) all the selected members must possess the advantage (or the patent could be misleading and fail for insufficiency and inutility, two

90. *Minnesota Mining & Manufacturing Co v Beiersdorf (Australia) Ltd* (1980) 144 CLR 253.
91. *Martin Engineering Co v Trison Holdings Pty Ltd* (1989) 14 IPR 330. See also *Welch Perrin & Co v Worrel* (1961) 106 CLR 588; *Shave v H V McKay Massey Harris Pty Ltd* (1935) 52 CLR 701; *Purcell v Haase* (1967) 37 AOJP 215.
92. (1890) 7 RPC 62. See also *Re Application by Schering's Aktiengesellschaft* (1991) 22 IPR 632; *Ramset Fasteners (Aust) Pty Ltd v Advanced Building Systems Pty Ltd* (1996) 34 IPR 256.
93. See Grubb, pp 131–4 for a discussion of chemical selection patents.
94. (1930) 47 RPC 289 at 321.

objections to validity discussed below). The quality for which the selection is made must be of a special character, not one which those skilled in the art would expect to find in a large number of the members: 'the citadel must be defended, there is no reward if the gates have been opened at the first blast of the trumpet'.[95] As this last point reveals, the issues concerning selection and combination patents are not confined to considerations of novelty but also concern inventiveness, as well as utility.

3.   INVENTIVENESS

[12.21]   The objection of obviousness. It is not enough for an invention to be novel to become patentable. The patent system would be overwhelmed if every new product or process which nobody had previously bothered to bring into existence could be patented. Accordingly an invention must have 'subject matter', in the sense that it involves a real advance on the state of the relevant art rather than being 'obvious'. The 1990 Act puts the matter positively, with involvement of an 'inventive step' being a requirement of patentability (s 18(1)(b)(ii)). Once again, the intention is presumably to incorporate the previous learning on 'obviousness'. Besides being a ground for opposition (s 59(b)) or revocation (s 138(3)(b)), inventiveness is also made a relevant matter at the stages of both examination (s 45(1)(b)) and re-examination (s 98).

[12.22]   Inventiveness distinguished from novelty. There is no doubt that, while the concepts of novelty and inventiveness are separate, they may overlap with each other in that an invention which differs too little from the prior art to be inventive may also have been made public. On the other hand, something already revealed to the public is not necessarily obvious to those working in the field, unless that public knowledge is also part of the 'common general knowledge' in the trade. Apart from the *R D Werner* case[96] which has already been discussed, numerous cases illustrate this point, notably the High Court's decision in *Minnesota Mining & Manufacturing Co v Beiersdorf (Australia) Ltd.*[97] In *Sunbeam Corp v Morphy-Richards (Australia) Pty Ltd*[98] Windeyer J said that in assessing novelty the question to ask is whether an invention has been already disclosed, whether to many or few people, a description in an obscure publication sufficing to destroy novelty and similar considerations applying to publication by user. On the other hand, if inventiveness is at issue the question is whether the new thing or process is obvious, or whether it had required an exercise of the inventive faculties to produce it. That question is to be asked in relation to a person skilled in the art to which the invention relates and has to be determined in the light of common general knowledge in that art. For example, a patent specification which has been published is part of 'public knowledge', but not necessarily 'common knowledge' if skilled persons in the field are not in the habit of consulting such specifications.[99]

---

95.   Ibid.
96.   *R D Werner & Co Inc v Bailey Aluminium Products Pty Ltd* (1989) 13 IPR 513: see [12.15].
97.   (1980) 144 CLR 253.
98.   (1961) 35 ALJR 212 at 213.
99.   See eg *Minnesota Mining & Manufacturing Co v Beiersdorf (Australia) Ltd* (1980) 144 CLR 253; *Dennison Manufacturing Co v Monarch Marketing Systems Inc* (1983) 1 IPR 431.

[12.23] Common knowledge and the prior art base. The 1952 Act referred to inventiveness being assessed 'having regard to what was known or used in Australia on or before the priority date of the claim'. As indicated in the previous paragraph, the courts have taken the view that this is to be understood as referring to 'common general knowledge'. This has been described as:

> that which is known or used by those in the relevant trade. It forms the background knowledge and experience which is available to all in the trade in considering the making of new products or the making of improvements in old, and it must be treated as being used by an individual as a general body of knowledge.[100]

This learning is effectively incorporated into the terms of the 1990 Act. Section 7(2) indicates that inventiveness is to be taken to be present 'unless the invention would have been obvious to a person skilled in the relevant art'. This is to be determined in the light of 'common general knowledge' in Australia as at the invention's priority date, together with 'prior art information' that the aforementioned skilled person could be reasonably expected to have ascertained, understood and regarded as relevant to work in the relevant art in Australia (s 7(2), (3)). As with novelty, such information must be publicly available; individual pieces of information must be considered separately, rather than being 'mosaiced' to establish the necessary common knowledge;[101] and no account is to be taken of the various sources of information set out in ss 23–24 and reg 2.2, which apply to the consideration of inventiveness as much as to the issue of novelty.[102] One important change effected by the 1990 Act, however, arises through the reference in s 7(2) and (3) to 'prior art information'. The 'prior art base' to which regard must be had for this purpose is, with one exception, identical to that which is relevant for the purposes of novelty (Sch 1).[103] Accordingly documents published anywhere in the world are now a relevant source of information, at least where standard patents are concerned, although the 'common general knowledge' in question is still that of a skilled person in the relevant field in Australia. The exception, to which reference has already been made,[104] is that the part of the definition of 'prior art base' which refers to unpublished specifications applies only to considerations of novelty and not to the question of whether there is an inventive step. The IPAC report *Patents, Innovation and Competition in Australia* in August 1984 recommended widening the prior art base for assessing obviousness. The 1990 Act does not go as far as suggested but allows inventive step to be assessed in the light of common general knowledge in Australia *plus* a single prior document (or more documents, if connected) or act in Australia which the skilled person could reasonably have been expected to have ascertained, understood and regarded as relevant to work in the relevant art in Australia.

The 1990 Act has been described as a 'lost opportunity' to invoke a more 'international' prior art base for use in assessing obviousness, which, it is

---

100. *Minnesota Mining*, ibid at 292.
101. See [12.15].
102. See [12.18].
103. See [12.14]. This includes the restrictive definition of 'prior art base' for the purpose of re-examination (s 98(2)).
104. See [12.17].

suggested, (along with the prior art base for novelty) should include all publicly available documentary material, regardless of geographical source.[105] The prior art base at present is narrower than that consulted in the US (Patents Act 1952, s 103) or Europe (European Patent Convention, Article 56). 'The United States, United Kingdom and the EC all presume an omniscient person skilled in the relevant art when assessing obviousness. They also allow, in limited circumstances, the combination of documents which are not part of the common general knowledge. The new Australian standard falls far short of the prior art base in those jurisdictions.'[106]

[12.24] Assessing inventiveness. The requirement that inventions involve an inventive step is a legal one, but the assessment of this quality requires a scientific comparison of the invention claimed against the existing prior art. Establishing:

(i)   who is skilled in the art,

(ii)   what they are expected to know, and

(iii) whether in the light of this skilled person's knowledge at the relevant time an inventive step is exhibited by the invention,

requires competent witnesses. This is one of the features which makes patent litigation so lengthy and expensive, since the evidence required to establish these factors is obviously voluminous and extremely technical.

Having established what is common knowledge in the field, the question of inventive step involves asking whether a 'non-inventive' or 'not particularly imaginative' skilled worker would have found it obvious to take the step actually chosen by the inventor.[107] Obviously thinking of something entirely new is inventive,[108] but invention may also lie in providing the practical solution to a problem which no one has yet been able to overcome,[109] in the suggestion of a new method of using known substances,[110] or in the satisfaction of a long felt need.[111] On the other hand, simply exercising tenacity, skill and managerial efficiency in order to achieve a known goal using familiar theory and practice towards that end, is not inventive. Thus, for example, it was obvious to try recombinant DNA technology as a means of producing human tissue plasminogen activator.[112] By contrast, in the English court hearing the *Chiron* case, dealing with rights to a

---

105. D Speagle and M Dowling, 'The 1990 Patents Act: Unfinished Reform' (1993) 4 *AIPJ* 166.
106. Ibid at 174.
107. *Minnesota Mining & Manufacturing Co v Beiersdorf (Australia) Ltd* (1980) 144 CLR 253 at 293; *Wellcome Foundation Ltd v VR Laboratories (Australia) Pty Ltd* (1981) 148 CLR 262 at 270; *W R Grace & Co v Asahi Kashi Kogyo Kabushiki Kaisha* (1993) 25 IPR 481 at 492; *Leonardis v Sartas No 1 Pty Ltd* (1996) 35 IPR 23.
108. *Hicklen's Patent* (1909) 26 RPC 339.
109. *Washex Machinery Corp v Roy Burton & Co Pty Ltd* (1974) 49 ALJR 12 at 16. See *Martin Engineering Co v Trison Holdings Pty Ltd* (1989) 14 IPR 330.
110. *National Research Development Corp v Commissioner of Patents* (1959) 102 CLR 252 at 254, where the inventive step lay in the application of scientific ingenuity combining knowledge, thought and experimentation in relation to certain chemicals but also the enzyme systems of certain weeds and plants.
111. *Parks-Cramer Co v G W Thornton & Sons Ltd* [1966] RPC 407 at 418; *Elconnex Pty Ltd v Gerard Industries Pty Ltd* (1992) 25 IPR 173 at 182, *Winner v Ammar Holdings Pty Ltd* (1993) 25 IPR 273 at 282.
112. *Genentech Inc v Wellcome Foundation Ltd* [1989] RPC 147.

diagnostic kit used in detection of Hepatitis C in blood donations, the invention was not obvious although it was argued that identification of the Hepatitis C virus and its genome was achieved by an obvious course of investigation, and the route taken was a 'relatively straightforward one with few options'.[113] The fact that the plaintiffs had spent '30 man years' achieving the result, and that teams around the world had been trying to identify the agent causing the disease for ten years, strongly suggested that an inventive step had taken place. (Aldous J declined to find, as argued by the defendants, that this length of time suggested incompetence in the plaintiff's researchers rather than the great difficulty of the task.)[114] Other factors which may (though will not necessarily) point to an invention not being obvious include the commercial success of the invention or of a product which is based on it, as well as the willingness of the inventor's rivals to move quickly to put an imitation on the market.[115]

What makes obviousness so hard in practice for examiners and judges is the fact they must perforce assess the significance of an innovation *after* the event. As Sheppard J put it in *Elconnex Pty Ltd v Gerard Industries Pty Ltd*:[116]

> Questions of obviousness are frequently difficult because it is very easy to fall into the trap of using hindsight. Once an innovation which is useful comes on to the market, there is an inclination not only for lawyers but also for those in the relevant industry to treat it as the norm and as something which might have been easily thought of by any reasonably competent worker in the industry.

It also needs to be borne in mind that some answers may appear obvious, but only once the right question is asked. In such cases 'it may be that the perception of the true nature of the problem was the inventive step which, once taken, revealed that straightforward experiments will provide the solution'.[117] Reflective road markings provide a good example. Providing them 'appears simple and obvious, if the problem is stated as being one of indicating to the driver of a motor vehicle at night the line of the road ahead by using the light from the vehicle itself'.[118]

Given the dangers posed by hindsight, it is all the more significant that courts have stressed that there need only be a 'scintilla of invention' for a particular step not to be obvious,[119] and that the simplicity of an idea does not prevent it from being inventive if it is an effective solution to a problem.[120] 'Though small, there must be some difficulty overcome, some barrier crossed.'[121] Thus a combination patent may be granted where there is inventiveness in the use or combination of known devices or substances

113. *Chiron Corp v Organon Teknika Ltd (No 3)* [1994] FSR 202 at 229. See further [15.12].
114. These issues have not been resolved in Australia as the *Chiron* litigation was settled in September 1996 on a world wide basis (after several weeks of hearing in the Federal Court in Sydney).
115. Cf *Elconnex Pty Ltd v Gerard Industries Pty Ltd* (1992) 25 IPR 173.
116. Ibid at 193–4. See also *Commonwealth Industrial Gases Ltd v W G Holdings Pty Ltd* (1970) 44 ALJR 385 at 386–7; *Allsop Inc v Bintang Ltd* (1989) 15 IPR 686 at 701.
117. *Wellcome Foundation Ltd v V R Laboratories (Aust) Pty Ltd* (1981) 148 CLR 262 at 281.
118. *Leonardis v Sartas No 1 Pty Ltd* (1996) 35 IPR 23 at 45, citing Cornish, p 129.
119. *Samuel Parks & Co Ltd v Cocker Bros Ltd* (1929) 46 RPC 241 at 248; *Meyers Taylor Pty Ltd v Vicarr Industries Ltd* (1977) 137 CLR 228 at 249.
120. See eg *Leonardis v Sartas No 1 Pty Ltd* (1996) 35 IPR 23.
121. *R D Werner & Co Inc v Bailey Aluminium Products Pty Ltd* (1989) 13 IPR 513 at 523.

to produce some new effect.[122] Similarly, the selection of some of a larger number of possibilities thrown up by earlier published research may be considered inventive.[123] In each case, however, the combination or selection must involve at least some particular ingenuity.

4. OTHER REQUIREMENTS FOR PATENTABILITY

[12.25] Utility. The Act provides that an invention must be useful in order to be patentable (ss 18(1)(c); 138(3)(b)). The concept of utility in patent law does not mean that an invention must be socially useful in the sense of fulfilling some desirable function, but simply that the result claimed is capable of being achieved by following the instructions in the specification. Thus a process of subjecting flour to electrically charged air which was claimed to reduce the carbohydrate content and increase the protein content of flour was held not to be patentable for want of utility since the treatment of the flour in the way described did not give the results claimed.[124]

One form which objections based on lack of utility may take is to say that the specification describes apparatus or means of achieving the claimed result which would not work as claimed. In *Welch Perrin & Co Pty Ltd v Worrel*[125] it was argued that a specification for a hay rake was bad because it referred to the raking wheel being 'angularly displaced' from the normal direction of movement of the frame. 'The lack of utility alleged did not go beyond the suggestion that the claims were so general that an unworkable machine could be made in conformity therewith.'[126] However, no one reading the specification would interpret it with complete disregard for what could be considered a workable angle and thus build a non-workable machine. The purposeful adoption of a form of the invention as would obviously malfunction is not the way to interpret a specification,[127] but rather the claims should be read in the light of the specification as a whole according to what an intelligent person skilled in the relevant art and desirous of making use of the invention would do.[128]

[12.26] Sufficiency of specification. At this stage the discussion of 'patentable invention' digresses from substantive requirements to the requirements of a complete specification. This is because there is a close overlap between utility and the sufficiency of the specification. A complete specification must describe the invention fully, including the best method known to the applicant of performing the invention (s 40(2)(a)). Failure to fulfil this requirement is known as 'insufficiency' and a great many cases

---

122. See eg *British United Shoe Machinery Co Ltd v A Fussell & Sons Ltd* (1908) 25 RPC 631; *Willmann v Petersen* (1904) 2 CLR 1; *Minnesota Mining & Manufacturing Co v Beiersdorf (Australia) Ltd* (1980) 144 CLR 253. Cf *Fallshaw Holdings Pty Ltd v Flexello Casters and Wheels plc* (1993) 26 IPR 565.
123. See eg *E I Du Pont de Nemours & Co (Witsiepe's) Application* [1982] FSR 303.
124. *Alsop's Patent* (1907) 24 RPC 733. See also *Pracdes Pty Ltd v Stanilite Electronics Pty Ltd* (1995) 35 IPR 259.
125. (1961) 106 CLR 588.
126. Ibid at 622.
127. *Washex Machinery Corp v Roy Burton & Co Pty Ltd* (1974) 49 ALJR 12 at 20. See also *Martin v Scribal Pty Ltd* (1954) 92 CLR 17 at 97: 'It is right to construe a claim with an eye benevolent to the inventor and with a view to making the invention work.'
128. *Martin Engineering Co v Trison Holdings Pty Ltd* (1989) 14 IPR 330 at 339.

are concerned with this issue, which may be closely allied to inutility. Nevertheless there is a distinction between the two issues. Insufficiency is found where the invention is not described fully enough to allow an informed reader with reasonable skill in the trade to perform the invention.[129] This is distinguished from inutility in this way:

> If you cannot achieve the promised result because of deficiencies in the information given in the specifications, there is insufficiency. But if, following that information and having achieved mechanically that which the specification promises you will achieve by so following it, the end product will not of itself achieve that promise, then that is inutility.[130]

[12.27] Sufficiency and micro-organisms. If the invention is or involves the use, modification or cultivation of a micro-organism and a person skilled in the art could not reasonably be expected to perform the invention without having a sample of the micro-organism, a sufficient description will require the deposit of the micro-organism in a prescribed depository institution, along with all relevant information about the characteristics of the organism known to the applicant for the patent (ss 41–42). The prescribed institution will not necessarily be in Australia, but nevertheless a micro-organism deposited according to the deposit requirements will be regarded as reasonably available. The deposit requirements exist because it is practically impossible to define a strain of micro-organism unambiguously by a written description, and even if a complete description were possible this would not put the public in possession of the invention:

> Anyone who wished to carry out the process of the invention would first have to catch his [sic] bacterium; he could perhaps tell when he had got the right one, but to get it, by search in nature or random mutation, might take years or might take forever.[131]

Section 41 incorporates changes made to Australian patent law in 1988 when the Budapest Treaty 1977 was incorporated into domestic law. This came into force in 1980 and most developed countries now require deposit of strains in a viable state as instituted by the Treaty. There are several International Deposit Authorities and a single deposit made at any of these will satisfy the sufficiency requirements of all signatory states.

[12.28] Ambiguity and fair basing. Besides being sufficient, claims must be clear and succinct and fairly based on the matter described in the specification (s 40(3)). Failure to fulfil the 'clear and succinct' requirement is known as ambiguity. This is part of the overriding requirement that the public has a right to know what it may or may not do and this has to be clearly delineated by the patentee. The specification and claims are to be read in the light of common knowledge at the priority date of each claim and using the common sense that would be applied by a person skilled in the particular art.[132] Claims must also be fairly based upon the material revealed in the specification to ensure that a wider monopoly than that justified by the specification is not being asked for. Sometimes a complete

129. *Samuel Taylor Pty Ltd v SA Brush Co Ltd* (1950) 83 CLR 617.
130. *Tetra Molectric Ltd's Application* [1976] FSR 424 at 432.
131. Grubb, p 153.
132. *Welch Perrin & Co Pty Ltd v Worrel* (1961) 106 CLR 588. Cf *Interlego AG v Toltoys Pty Ltd* (1973) 130 CLR 461; *Decor Corporation Pty Ltd v Dart Industries Inc* (1988) 13 IPR 385; *Elconnex Pty Ltd v Gerard Industries Pty Ltd* (1992) 25 IPR 173. See further [14.6].

specification will improve upon a provisional one in such a way that the later document makes claims not supported by the original disclosure. The requirement of fair basing is therefore to ensure conformity between a provisional specification (which secures a priority date for an invention) and the claims made which may be based on further development.[133]

The courts have formulated various tests to assist the process of determining whether a claim is fairly based.[134] For example, the oft-cited *Mond Nickel* test asks the following three questions:[135]

> (1) Is the alleged invention as claimed broadly (that is, in a general sense) described in the basic application? (2) Is there anything in the basic application which is inconsistent with the alleged invention as claimed? (3) Does the claim include as a characteristic of the invention a feature as to which the basic application is wholly silent?

However, as Gibbs J pointed out in *F Hoffman-La Roche & Co Aktiengesellschaft v Commissioner of Patents*,[136] while these questions are intended to assist courts in applying the statutory test, they 'are not a substitute for that test'. Ultimately, the question is simply whether the provisional specification contains 'a real and reasonably clear disclosure' of the alleged invention as subsequently claimed in the complete application.[137] It is also important to remember that all the provisional specification has to do is 'to describe generally and fairly the nature of the invention, and not to enter into all the minute details as to the manner in which the invention is to be carried out'.[138]

Although these principles suggest a reasonably liberal view of what will constitute fair basing, it is notable all the same just how many patents have been struck down in the courts in recent times on this ground.[139] This has drawn criticism from the Advisory Council on Industrial Property (ACIP), which has described the Federal Court as adopting 'a restrictive and highly constructionist approach'.[140] It went on to note that a number of the cases in question concerned:

> Australian applicants who had relied on the filing of a provisional application to afford priority whilst publicly testing and developing the invention. In each case the consequence was the loss of valuable rights. ACIP considers these cases to run contrary to the interests of Australian industry and inventors. ACIP recommends that action be taken to foster a less restrictive approach to the granting of priority based on disclosure in a provisional specification.[141]

[12.29]   Secret use. Secret use of an invention by a patentee before the priority date of the relevant claim was a ground for revocation of the patent

---

133. See *Fabwerke Hoechst AC v Commissioner of Patents* (1971) 124 CLR 654; *Atlas Power Co v ICI Australia Operations Pty Ltd* (1989) 15 IPR 34.
134. See *CCOM Pty Ltd v Jiejing Pty Ltd* (1994) 28 IPR 481 at 496–501.
135. *F Hoffman-La Roche & Co Aktiengesellschaft v Commissioner of Patents* (1971) 123 CLR 529 at 538, citing *Re Mond Nickel Co Ltd's Application* (1956) RPC 189 at 194.
136. (1971) 123 CLR 529 at 538.
137. *Societe des Usines Chimiques Rhone-Poulenc v Commissioner of Patents* (1958) 100 CLR 5 at 11; *Leonardis v Sartas No 1 Pty Ltd* (1996) 35 IPR 23.
138. *Anaesthetic Supplies Pty Ltd v Rescare Ltd* (1994) 28 IPR 383 at 401.
139. See eg *Interact Machine Tools (NSW) Pty Ltd v Yamazaki Mazak Corp* (1993) 27 IPR 83; *Anaesthetic Supplies Pty Ltd v Rescare Ltd* (1994) 28 IPR 383; *CCOM Pty Ltd v Jiejing Pty Ltd* (1994) 28 IPR 481; though cf *Leonardis v Sartas No 1 Pty Ltd* (1996) 35 IPR 23.
140. *Review of the Petty Patent System*, 1995, p 47.
141. Ibid.

under the 1952 Act, but has never been a ground of opposition. The 1990 Act preserves this position, making the absence of secret use its final criterion for patentability (s 18(1)(d)), but excluding its relevance at any stage other than revocation (s 138(3)(b)). Secret use is 'use unknown to the public and not discoverable by the public'.[142] This does not mean accidental or experimental use, but use with an intention to keep the information concealed.[143]

In order to avoid the situation where a patentee is deprived of their rights by perfectly appropriate uses of the invention during a developmental stage prior to application, certain acts will not invalidate a patent. In this context the Act allows use for the purpose of reasonable trial and experiment, use by a public authority to whom the patentee has disclosed the invention, use pursuant to a confidential disclosure, and any other use of the invention for a purpose other than trade or commerce (s 9).

[12.30] Obtaining and false suggestion. Finally, two other grounds of invalidity should be noted. Under the 1952 Act a patent could be opposed or revoked on the ground that the invention claimed had been obtained from another, whether fraudulently or innocently.[144] The equivalent sections in the 1990 Act provide for opposition or revocation on the ground that the patentee is not 'entitled' to the patent (ss 59(a), 138(3)(a)). As has already been noted, provision is made in this type of case for the patent to be granted to the person who is in fact entitled to it.[145] More generally, a patent 'obtained by fraud, false suggestion or misrepresentation' may also be revoked (s 138(3)(d)). While this may overlap with other grounds such as inutility, obtaining and lack of fair claiming, it covers any material deception which results in a patent being granted.[146]

---

142. *Bristol-Myers Co v Beecham Group Ltd* [1974] 2 WLR 79 at 93. See also *Re Wheatley's Patent Application* (1984) 2 IPR 450.
143. Ibid at 103; *Melbourne v Terry Fluids Control Pty Ltd* (1993) 26 IPR 292.
144. See *Dabscheck v Hecla Electrics Pty Ltd* (1936) 57 CLR 418.
145. See [11.26].
146. See *Prestige Group (Australia) Pty Ltd v Dart Industries Inc* (1990) 19 IPR 275; *Pracdes Pty Ltd v Stanilite Electronics Pty Ltd* (1995) 35 IPR 259; M Gething, 'Patents Obtained by Fraud, False Suggestion or Misrepresentation' (1994) 5 *AIPJ* 152.

Chapter 13

Ownership and Exploitation of Patent Rights

[13.1] **Nature of patent rights.** The grant of a patent under the Patents Act 1990 confers on the patentee the exclusive right to 'exploit' the invention (s 13(1)). The dictionary in Sch 1 defines 'exploit' as 'make, use sell or otherwise dispose of the product' or offer to do so, 'import it or keep it for the purpose of doing any of those things', or use a patented process or method to achieve any of those ends. This strongly echoes the language of the Patents Act 1952 which gave the patentee the exclusive right to 'make, use, exercise or vend' the invention. The content of the patentee's exclusive rights is examined in the following chapter in the context of infringement. The present chapter is devoted to the nature of patent rights and the ways in which they may be exploited. It is specifically provided in the legislation that the rights granted to a patentee 'are personal property and are capable of assignment and of devolution by operation of law' (s 13(2)). Furthermore, the application provisions implicitly recognise that rights in an invention may be owned, assigned and otherwise transmitted *prior* to the grant of a patent.[1] Various issues that flow out of these propositions, and various provisions of the legislation which reflect them, are considered in the sections which follow.

1. OWNERSHIP

(a) Employees' Inventions

[13.2] **Background.** The general assumption made by the patents legislation is plainly that it is the inventor, the person responsible for supplying

---

1.   See [11.10].

the spark of creativity, who 'owns' an invention in the sense of being prima facie entitled to patent it. This is not to say that the inventor will be the applicant. Apart from the possibility that someone else may apply on the inventor's behalf, the understanding being that at the end of the process the inventor will receive the letters patent, the legislation also contemplates that someone else may have acquired the rights to the invention prior to any application. Where this happens, whether by assignment or devolution, the new owner is permitted to apply for a patent. Alternatively, the inventor or some other person may make the application, with the new owner being understood to be the ultimate patentee if the application is successful.

All this is straightforward enough where the inventor voluntarily assigns the rights to an invention, or bequeaths them to successors in title. However, more difficult considerations may arise when, as is often the case, an employee produces an invention whose benefit is then claimed by their employer. These days inventions are seldom stumbled across by accident, although this can of course happen. More usually, though, they arise out of planned research. Management sets goals for teams of researchers, and laboratory assistants and other technical staff run tests and carry out procedures. It has been estimated, for instance, that over 80% of all patentable inventions in the UK are made by salaried employees.[2] Often inventions will be arrived at 'in committee'.[3] In most cases these employees will have been engaged for the very purpose of creating patentable matter, and will have used the employer's resources to achieve the inventive result. Assuming that the inventor or inventors can in fact be identified, can they take advantage of the position in law of the inventor as owner principle and go on to take out a patent?

[13.3] Legislative provisions. The 1990 Act does not explicitly deal with an employer's rights to inventions made by its employees (and nor did the 1952 legislation). However, s 34(1)(fa) of the 1952 Act provided that one category of persons entitled to apply for a patent was 'a person who would, if a patent were granted upon an application made by a person referred to in any of the preceding paragraphs, be entitled to have the patent assigned to him'. The 'persons previously referred to' included the actual inventor or their assignee or legal representative. This provision was added to the 1952 Act in 1960 specifically in order to cover employment contracts under which employers might be entitled to take assignments of inventions made by employees.[4] Its practical effect was to dispense with the need for an actual assignment of rights to an invention to be made prior to the patent being granted: provided a person, including an employer, had an enforceable right to take an assignment, they could go ahead and obtain a patent. The same provision is, in effect, made by the 1990 Act which puts no limit on the class of persons who may apply for a patent, but lists instead those to whom a patent may be granted: this list also includes those who would, on the grant of a patent, be entitled to take an assignment (s 15(1)(b)).

2.   J Phillips and M J Hoolahan, *Employees' Inventions in the United Kingdom: Law and Practice*, 1982, p 3.
3.   See eg *Speed Seal Products Ltd v Paddington* [1986] 1 All ER 91.
4.   *Patent Office Examiner's Manual*, 1970, para [34.27], cited in Ricketson, pp 882–3.

[13.4] **Role of the employment contract.** Accordingly it is the contractual relationship between an employer and employee that will be the basic determinant of matters concerning the ownership of inventions and the right to seek patents, for in the absence of any express or implied provision on the matter the employer will have no legal claim to an invention. In the simplest situation, ownership of the employee's intellectual activities may be determined by way of an express 'pre assignment clause', whereby the employee promises to assign to the employer any rights in an invention not yet made. This will typically include a provision as to non-disclosure of the details of an invention, but will be construed strictly against the employer if any element of restraint of trade is present. In *Electrolux Ltd v Hudson,*[5] for example, Whitford J refused to enforce a pre-assignment term against a storekeeper who worked for the plaintiff company, which manufactured vacuum cleaners. The defendant and his wife devised an adaptor to fit a bag to a vacuum cleaner. They did this outside work hours in their own home, applied for a patent and assigned the invention to a third party. The court held unenforceable a clause in the storekeeper's conditions of employment which purported to give the employer ownership of any process, invention or improvement relating to almost any article manufactured or not by the company: the width of the clause was considered to create an unreasonable restraint of trade.

[13.5] **The implied duty to assign inventions.** In the absence of an express contractual provision dealing with the subject of ownership of inventions, the matter falls to be determined according to the terms implied by law into a contract of employment. In this respect the courts have basically tended to favour employer ownership. Any invention will impliedly belong to the employer, so long as it is arrived at in the course of duties the employee is engaged to perform.[6] Thus an employee who is hired 'to design or draft' can normally expect that anything they produce in the ordinary course of their work will be taken to be their employer's.[7] This recognition that 'what [a worker] produces by the strength of his [sic] arm or the skill of his hand or the exercise of his inventive faculty shall become the property of his employer'[8] dates from what Cornish refers to as the 'age of corporate capitalism'.[9] It relies to some extent upon the notion of a general duty of fidelity owed by the employee,[10] particularly (though by no means exclusively) where the employee is in a senior or managerial position. A good example of the principle is provided by *Triplex Safety Glass Co v Scorah.*[11] The employee, a chemist involved in improving the properties of glass, patented an invention involving the use of acrylic acid as an adhesive for glass in car windscreens. The employee left Triplex before applying for the patent but had been employed there while developing it. The company had sought a patent for the invention only to find one had

---

5. [1977] FSR 312.
6. *Charles Selz Ltd's Application* (1954) 71 RPC 158 at 164; *Sterling Engineering Co Ltd v Patchett* [1955] AC 534 at 543–4, 547.
7. *Aneeta Window Systems (Vic) Pty Ltd v K Shugg Industries Pty Ltd* (1996) 34 IPR 95 at 106; *Vokes Ltd v Heather* (1945) 62 RPC 135 at 136.
8. *Sterling Engineering Co Ltd v Patchett* [1955] AC 534 at 544.
9. Cornish, p 177.
10. See [4.34].
11. (1938) 55 RPC 237.

already been granted to their former employee. It was held that the employer was entitled to the patent. A notable feature of this decision is that a term was implied to that effect despite the fact that express terms regarding employee inventions in the contract of employment were unreasonable and unenforceable. Thus the employer has two bites at the cherry, so to speak: if an express term drafted to deal with the matter proves to offend the restraint of trade doctrine, it is possible to fall back on the implied obligation. While this principle is now well established it is questionable whether it is appropriate, given that it provides no incentive to employers to be moderate in the drafting of their employment contracts.

[13.6] Scope of the implied duty. In any event there are limits to the operation of the implied duty upon employees to assign inventions to their employers. Where an employee is not engaged to invent in a specific field, then the results of any inventive activity may well accrue to the employee, allowing them to license the invention to others. Thus in *Electrolux Ltd v Hudson* Whitford J, having held the express provision unenforceable, went on to find that the employer could not invoke the implied obligation either. Since the storekeeper was not employed to invent and had made the adaptor outside working hours and without using the employer's materials, there was no implied covenant that the invention should belong to or be held on trust for the employer. This was a fairly clear situation in which the employee had not really acted in the course of their duties. The same can be said of *Kwan v Queensland Corrective Services Commission*,[12] in which two prisoners, while working in the prison kitchen and poultry farm, devised a new method of laminating vegetable matter (such as dried flowers) on a card and obtained a patent. It was held that they were not employees of the Commission, and that even if they were the invention was not made in the course of their normal duties. However, as *British Syphon Co Ltd v Homewood*[13] illustrates, this may not always be easy for an employee to establish. There the defendant, chief technician in charge of design and development for the plaintiff's business and employed, among other things, to give advice on design and development of soda syphons, was held accountable for an invention relating to a 'low-pressure system of soda water distribution' for which the company had neither asked nor sought his advice on developing. The defendant assumed that, because his work for the company was no longer connected with soda syphon tops, therefore they had no relevant interest in the invention and he could take it with him to his new job. It was held that the technician had a duty to give the employer the best possible advice and this required that any inventions made during his time of employment should belong to the employer if at all related to the plaintiff's business.

[13.7] Alternative suggestions on patent ownership of employee inventions. The development of the law on the issue of ownership of employee inventions has long been criticised. Even in 1949 the British parliament felt that employee inventors were being unfairly treated and the Patents Act 1949 (UK) attempted to remedy matters by making provision for the apportionment of rights between the employer and employee. The provisions were rendered nugatory, however, by the House of Lords in

12.   (1994) 31 IPR 25.
13.   [1956] RPC 225.

Sterling Engineering Co Ltd v Patchett,[14] where it was held that apportionment of rights under the Patents Act could only apply when the invention did not, as a matter of law, belong wholly to one party or the other. In almost every case express contractual terms or the common law could be used to give one party or another the whole rights to the invention. Subsequently the Patents Act 1977 (UK) introduced a further scheme designed to clarify the rules for determining ownership of inventions, restrict the power of employers to impair employees' rights and establish a statutory scheme for rewarding inventive creativity at work.[15] The legal origin of the master and servant relationship has significantly influenced the development of these statutory rules governing rights in inventions produced during employment. As regards ownership of patent rights the old common law rule was reformulated. It now stands that the invention belongs to the employee unless it was made in the course of duties specifically assigned to him or her, and the circumstances were such that an invention might reasonably be expected to result from the carrying out of those duties, or the employee had a special obligation to further the interests of the employer's undertaking. Furthermore, any contract purporting to limit the employee's rights in any future invention is rendered unenforceable.

The effect of the 1977 Act is that the only inventions which belong to the employer are those made in the course of the employee's duties if such duties are expected to result in inventions: the employer can no longer legally require an employee to assign all inventions. The common law will still inform the concept of 'the course of duties' of the employee, although the employer may give more thought to the definition of normal duties in order to clarify which inventions belong to the company.[16] Even where an employee invention does become the employer's property, there is also now provision for compensation for employee-inventors if the patent is 'of outstanding benefit to the employer', having regard to the size and nature of the employer's undertaking. The scope of this provision has not yet been tested to any extent.[17] It should be noted that the right of an employee-inventor to file a patent application on his or her own behalf does not mean that confidential information of the employer may be revealed: the duty of confidentiality remains intact.

By contrast, in the US the concern has been more to safeguard the employer's interests where an employee produces an invention to which, on ordinary principles, the employer would not be entitled. The courts have developed an equitable 'shopright' doctrine, which in certain circumstances allows the employer a licence to use inventions arising out of efforts which are not within the terms of employment.[18] However, the employer has no general power to stop the employee exploiting the invention to their own ends.

---

14. [1955] AC 534.
15. S Saxby, 'Employees' Inventions and English Law' in J Phillips, *Employees' Inventions: A Comparative Study,* 1981, p 13.
16. See Grubb, p 188. Grubb also points out that some companies still require employees to sign contracts which completely ignore the provisions of the Patents Act 1977, purporting to assign any discovery, invention, secret process etc to the employer.
17. Ibid. See also Cornish, pp 177–82.
18. R M Milgrim, *Trade Secrets,* 1987, pp 55–7.

[13.8] **Inventions in universities.** Universities are a major employer and by their nature an important source of innovation and invention. Academic staff, particularly those in the scientific and technical faculties, will in the course of their work make discoveries which are suitable for patent protection. The University of New South Wales is one of many institutions which have recognised this fact and responded by establishing a research and development company. The University development arm is known as Unisearch Ltd. Its activities provide a good illustration of the issues that may arise in relation to academics' inventions.

Unisearch is a company limited by guarantee and exclusively owned by the University. An important aspect of its work is the administration and commercial exploitation of intellectual property rights generated through University research. Its income from patents in 1993 was $870,000 and in 1994 $851,000. The actual and potential importance of patents to the University is therefore significant. Furthermore the likelihood of increases in corporate sponsorship and involvement in university research has implications for the University's administration of intellectual property rights. One recent example of technology developed within the University and licensed out is a high efficiency laser grooved buried contact solar cell. A team in micro electronics has produced the most efficient solar module in the world.[19] Such modules can be used to power telephones, level crossings, water pumps and machinery in remote areas and provide electricity in developing countries at a small fraction of the cost and inconvenience of supplying mains electricity. The solar modules are also useful on satellites, oil rigs in the ocean and other remote locations. The buried contact solar cell technology has been patented through Unisearch Ltd and licensed by several solar cell manufacturers, including the large German corporation AEG. In 1994 negotiations with Pacific Power led to the establishment of a company to develop thin film solar cell technology. The rights to the technology were assigned for $19 million.[20]

[13.9] **Ownership of university inventions.** As noted in Chapter 1, universities are becoming much more aware of intellectual property issues, including ownership as between staff, students and the institution.[21] Development of appropriate policies is required of institutions, even to the extent that external funding and rating of universities may be linked to the requirement of having suitable policies in place. In determining the rights to inventions made within a university, reference must first be made to the contractual relationship between the university and the inventor. Again using the University of New South Wales as an example, the contract of employment for lecturing staff contains a clause dealing with intellectual property. In relation to patents this clause states:

> The University requires that appropriate protection of any discovery, invention or process improvement or original design produced by or under the supervision of a staff member is arranged through the University's research and development Company, Unisearch Limited.[22]

19. The module is 17% efficient compared with 10–13% for previous commercial solar modules.
20. Unisearch Ltd, *Annual Report*, 1994.
21. See [1.29].
22. University of New South Wales, General Conditions of Appointment, p 5. The University is presently finalising a general intellectual property policy.

While this clause imposes obligations on employees as to their dealings with and disclosure of any potentially patentable inventions, it does not seem to have any effect on the ownership of such inventions. On the other hand, given the nature of academic employment, in particular the emphasis placed on freedom to choose areas of research, it seems likely that any invention made would be made within the course of employment. It would only be in rare circumstances that no significant connection with the University or its facilities could be established. Nevertheless the combination of the contractual clause above and the width of the academics' course of employment would suggest that any inventions made will belong to the University.

[13.10] Rewards for academic inventors. The practice of Unisearch is to give the inventor a one-third beneficial interest in any profits derived through the patenting and development of the invention. This is an ex gratia payment and where there is more than one possible inventor the amount of compensation may be adjusted appropriately. In the context of joint research projects it is potentially a difficult process to ascertain the amount of compensation to which participants should be entitled. However, the total share payable to joint inventors will not usually exceed the one-third level. In September 1986 the Australian Democrats announced that they planned to introduce legislation to give researchers a share of patent royalties, when the research is done in a government funded institution such as a university. The proposal was to give 50% to the funding body, 25% to the university, CSIRO or other research institution, 12.5% to the university department and 12.5% to the research team.[23] To date, this proposal has not come to fruition. However, it is increasingly common for university intellectual property policies to set out agreed percentages for the division of patent returns.

[13.11] Confidentiality and the patent process. A final point to make in the context of employee inventors relates to the issue of confidentiality. The employee who works on developing inventions will owe a duty to the employer at every stage of development. Until a patent application is filed that obligation coincides with the general duty to keep confidential any information about the work which amounts to more than mere general knowledge or skill.[24] To recapitulate some of the points made in Chapter 4, the difficulty is to distinguish between discrete technical secrets which will be protected by an obligation of confidence and 'general' or 'subjective' knowledge which the employee is free to use. Relying on a general obligation of confidence requires a sorting out of information which is protected, that which is not, and that which may be safeguarded by an appropriate express covenant. Of course, once a patent is applied for, the specification spells out exactly what aspects of the invention are to be protected. However, non-patented 'trade secrets' of the employer which are ancillary to the invention remain subject to the employee's duty of confidence.

---

23. 'Democrats Propose New Patents Law', *Federation of Australian Universities Staff Association News*, 2 September 1986, p 8.
24. See [4.33]–[4.34].

(b) Co-ownership

[13.12] The position of co-owners. Where a patent is granted to two or more persons, they take equal shares and thus hold the patents as tenants in common. Each is entitled to work the patent without accounting to the others, although none of them may grant a licence or assign an interest in the patent without the consent of all (s 16(1)). Each of these provisions is subject to contrary agreement, however, and the difficulties that may arise make it highly advisable that a co-ownership agreement be negotiated to define the parties' respective rights and liabilities. Any disputes arising between co-owners may in any event be the subject of an application to the Commissioner seeking directions as to the relevant matters (s 17).

2. TRANSMISSION AND REGISTRATION

[13.13] Transmission of patent interests. Since patent rights are property, they can be dealt with in the same way as any other chose in action. Thus they can be sold, leased, mortgaged, bequeathed in a will or given away. A patent is expressly permitted to be assigned for a place in or part of Australia (s 14(2)). This has the important effect that a patent right may be divided up geographically, with one assignee having the right to exploit the patent in one area, and another (or the original patentee) possessing that right elsewhere, and so on. Assignments of patents (and presumably also of part-interests therein) must be in writing and signed by or on behalf of both the assignor and the assignee (s 14(1)).

[13.14] Register of patents. Chapter 19 of the 1990 Act provides for a Register of Patents, on which are recorded particulars of patents in force and a range of other matters. The Register can be inspected by any person during office hours at the Patent Office (s 190). The details to be maintained in respect of each patent include the name of the patentee and any other person who has an interest in it or who has dealt with it. Thus assignees and other transmittees are required to apply for registration as proprietor of the patent concerned, and mortgagees and licensees are also required to register their interests (s 187; reg 19(1)). By contrast, express, implied and constructive trusts relating to a patent or to a licence thereof are not to be registered (s 188), though this does not preclude the registration of agreements to grant patents or interests therein.[25] The significance of the Register may be gauged from the provision that the patentee, defined in Schedule 1 as 'the person for the time being entered in the Register as the grantee or proprietor of a patent', may deal as absolute owner with the patent, subject to any rights appearing in the Register to be vested in any other person (s 189(1)). On the other hand, unregistered interests are by no means completely unprotected. A person will only be able to acquire a patent free of unregistered interests if they deal with the patentee as a purchaser in good faith for value and without notice of any fraud on the part of the patentee (s 189(2)). Furthermore equities in relation to a patent may be enforced against the patentee, except to the prejudice of a purchaser in good faith for value (s 189(3)). However, an unregistered instrument is inadmissible in any proceedings in proof of title to a patent

---

25. See *Stewart v Casey* (1892) 9 RPC 9.

or patent interest, except at the direction of the relevant court or tribunal, or where the proceedings relate to rectification of the Register or the enforcement of an equity in relation to a patent or licence (s 196).

3.   LICENSING

[13.15]   General. The exploitation of patent rights is an integral part of many businesses where patentable inventions form the stock in trade. Most large companies engaging in research and development operate a policy of licensing out the results and licensing in new technology as needed. These companies integrate licensing matters into the overall running of their business. Overall sales and marketing strategies, funding of research projects for new and existing markets and areas of pure and applied research may all be subject to the strategic aspects of exploiting and protecting the products of research through suitable licensing arrangements. Often these firms have inhouse legal and licensing experts who assist in identifying and facilitating licensing opportunities.[26] In legal practice the exploitation of patent rights will inevitably take precedence over the establishment and maintenance of those rights, which fall mainly within the province of a patent attorney.[27]

[13.16]   Express licences. A licence granted by a patentee need not be in writing to be effective. The legislation does not distinguish between different types of licence, other than to allow an exclusive licensee to sue for infringement (s 120). An 'exclusive licensee' is narrowly defined to mean a person who is accorded rights with respect to the whole of a patent throughout Australia, and which are exclusive of those of any other person, including the patentee (s 6; Sch 1). Thus while licences may come in all shapes and sizes, being limited either on a territorial or a temporal basis or both, it is only where a licensee is given the sole right to exploit the invention anywhere in Australia that they may stand in the patentee's shoes for the purposes of pursuing an infringement.

[13.17]   Restrictive conditions in licences. It is common to find conditions attached to the grant of a licence which limit the uses to which the licensee may put the invention. However, certain restrictions on these conditions should be noted. In the first place, the legislation proscribes 'tying' arrangements relating to patents, including those which require a licensee not to deal in certain respects with persons other than the licensor (s 144).[28] An example of such a clause is one compelling a licensee to purchase unpatented materials from the licensor, or insisting that royalty payments continue after the patent expires. However, the prohibition will not apply where the licensee could have engaged in the relevant dealings on reasonable terms without agreeing to such an arrangement and where the licensee has the opportunity to escape from the arrangement on reasonable notice.[29] Second, the effect of the restrictive dealing provisions of the

---

26.   See T Black, *Intellectual Property in Industry*, 1989, ch 2. The pharmaceutical industry is particularly proficient at licensing: see Grubb, ch 18.
27.   See [11.15].
28.   These provisions also apply to contracts relating to the sale or lease of patented inventions.
29.   *Transfield Pty Ltd v Arlo International Ltd* (1980) 30 ALR 201.

Trade Practices Act 1974, discussed in Chapter 22, should be borne in mind.

[13.18] Implied licences. A licence to exploit an invention may be implied in certain circumstances. Since using a patented process or a product resulting from the use of a patented process is plainly within the patent owner's exclusive prerogative, a purchaser of such a process or product must, in order to be able to use it, have a licence to do so. To meet this problem, the courts have been prepared to imply that a legitimate sale of goods embodying an invention carries an implied licence to use these goods.[30] Similarly, an implied licence to repair patented goods is allowed as long as the line between repair and making a new article is not crossed.[31]

[13.19] Compulsory licences. It is considered to be an abuse of patent monopoly rights to fail to make an invention available on the market at a reasonable cost. Since the exclusive rights of the patentee are granted in consideration of the disclosure to the public of information about new technology, those working in the field are likely to know of new developments and want to use them. There could be complaints if the technology is, in effect, suppressed by the patentee failing to work the patent.[32] The patent system, 'displaying great prudence in its judgment, has so ordered its priorities as to provide machinery which has the potential to prevent the occurrence of such abuses of the monopoly grant'.[33] This mechanism is the compulsory licence.

A person may, after three years from the date of sealing a patent, petition a prescribed court for the grant of a compulsory licence in regard to the patent on such terms as the court considers just (s 133; reg 12.1). The applicant must satisfy the court that the 'reasonable requirements of the public' (see below) have not been satisfied with respect to the patented invention; that the patentee has given no satisfactory reason for failing to exploit the patent;[34] and that the applicant has made reasonable efforts to obtain an authorisation from the patentee to work the invention.[35] Any licence that is granted cannot be exclusive, and may only be assigned if the business holding it is sold. Where the applicant would not be able to work the patented invention without infringing a separate patent over another

---

30. *National Phonograph Co of Australia Ltd v Menck* [1911] AC 336 at 353. See also the discussion of *Interstate Parcel Express Co Ltd v Time-Life International (Nederlands) BV* (1977) 138 CLR 534 at [8.20].
31. *Weir Pumps Ltd v CML Pumps Ltd* (1983) 2 IPR 129; *Dunlop Pneumatic Tyre Co Ltd v Neal* (1899) 16 RPC 247; *Solar Thomson Engineering Co Ltd v Barton* [1977] RPC 537. See further [7.13].
32. There have, however, been some remarkably successful examples of patent suppression which have delayed (or prevented) the release of such inventions as fluorescent lighting: see R Dunford, 'Is the Development of Technology Helped or Hindered by Patent Law — Can Antitrust Provide the Solution?' (1986) 9 *UNSWLJ* 117.
33. Phillips and Firth, para [7.16].
34. See *Fastening Supplies Pty Ltd v Olin Mathieson Chemical Corp* (1969) 119 CLR 572.
35. This third condition was not originally imposed by the 1990 Act, but was added by the Patents (World Trade Organization) Amendments Act 1994, as was the provision described later in the paragraph dealing with the grant of an additional compulsory licence. Both were intended to meet requirements imposed by Art 31 of the TRIPS Agreement.

invention, the court must also grant the applicant a licence over that invention as well, though only on reasonable terms and only if the patented invention 'involves an important technical advance of considerable economic significance' on the other invention.

[13.20] 'Reasonable requirements'. The 'reasonable requirements of the public' will not be met if a trade or industry in Australia requires the article or process, but there is a failure to manufacture it to an adequate extent, supply it on reasonable terms or grant licences on reasonable terms (s 135(1)(a), (b)). This in itself provides an incentive to negotiate licence agreements, because the practice of refusing licences to certain parties, or of insisting on stringent conditions of the sort that may fall foul of the restrictions mentioned earlier, may be considered unreasonable and could lead to the court granting licences to persons the patentee hoped to exclude. Where the demand for an invention is being met by importation, but it could be worked commercially in Australia, this also means the reasonable requirements of the public have not been met This reflects the fact that one of the objects of the compulsory licensing system is to foster Australian manufacturing.[36] However, if the court considers that the three-year period is not sufficient to set up commercial working of the patent in Australia, it may adjourn the proceedings so as to afford the patentee time to commence operations in this country (s 135(2)).

[13.21] Revocation following compulsory licence. Where a compulsory licence is granted, a further procedure exists, after two years have elapsed, for seeking revocation of the patent for non-working (s 134). Again, it must be shown that the reasonable requirements of the public have not been met and that the patentee has no satisfactory explanation. The 1990 Act dispenses with the requirement, imposed by the 1952 Act, that a petitioner proceed through the Commissioner and seek to reach an arrangement with the patentee prior to requesting a prescribed court to grant the revocation order.

[13.22] Crown use of inventions.[37] Patents, since they are granted by the government, can be offered on whatever terms thought appropriate. One aspect of this is the wide power that the government possesses to reserve patents for itself and to exploit them for its own purposes. Besides the fact that the Commonwealth may compulsorily acquire a patent (s 171) or take an assignment (s 172), the legislation also provides for what is effectively a compulsory licence in favour of public authorities. Thus the Commonwealth or a state[38] can exploit a patent (or a patent pending) without infringement or authorise another person to do so (s 163). However, the use of a patent in this manner must be 'for the services of the Commonwealth or State'. The meaning of this phrase has generated some uncertainty, though some indication of what it comprehends can be gathered from decisions authorising the use by a state rail authority of an invention for the construction of rail carriages,[39] and the use by a local government

---

36.   *Fastening Supplies Pty Ltd v Olin Mathison Chemical Corp* (1969) 119 CLR 572 at 574.
37.   See also the discussion of Crown use of copyright works at [7.24].
38.   Under s 162, a reference to the Commonwealth or a state includes a Commonwealth or state 'authority': see *General Steel Industries Inc v Commissioner of Railways (NSW)* (1964) 112 CLR 125; *Stack v Brisbane City Council* (1995) 32 IPR 69.
39.   *General Steel Industries Inc v Commissioner of Railways (NSW)* (1964) 112 CLR 125.

authority of a meter in connection with the measurement of water supply.[40] Following a 1994 amendment, s 163(3) now 'clarifies' the matter by providing that an invention is taken to be exploited for the services of the Commonwealth or a state if exploitation of the invention is 'necessary for the proper provision of those services'.[41] It is hard to see exactly what this adds, though presumably the intention was to exclude any possibility of inventions being used for purely commercial or wholly incidental purposes. Another amendment made in 1994 was to add a procedure in effect allowing a patentee to seek the revocation of any compulsory licence obtained under s 163. Section 165A now permits a prescribed court to declare that the exploitation of the patentee's invention is no longer necessary for the proper provision of the relevant services.

Where a patent is compulsorily acquired by the Commonwealth, compensation must be paid to the patentee and to any other person with an interest in the patent: this is to be determined by agreement with the relevant authority or, failing that, by a prescribed court (s 171(4)). A similar procedure applies to the fixing of the terms on which a patent may be compulsorily licensed by or on behalf of the Commonwealth or a state (s 165(2)); while the patentee's entitlement to remuneration is not spelled out so clearly, the 'terms' in question are specifically stated to include provision for such remuneration.[42]

40. *Stack v Brisbane City Council* (1995) 32 IPR 69.
41. See also s 168, dealing with the supply of products to foreign countries for defence purposes.
42. Note that 'patentee' for this purpose includes an exclusive licensee (s 161).

Chapter 14

Infringement of Patent Rights

1. WHAT CONSTITUTES INFRINGEMENT

[14.1] General. Under the Patents Act 1990, a patent will be infringed whenever a person, acting without the patentee's authorisation, does something in relation to the invention which falls within the scope of the patentee's exclusive rights. These rights extend throughout Australia (s 13(3)) and may be infringed by any conduct after the date of publication of the complete or petty patent specification (s 57), though proceedings may only be instituted after the patent has actually been granted (s 57(3)). Knowledge is not required, so that innocence will be no defence as such: although it may, as will be seen, have some bearing upon the remedies available to the plaintiff.

[14.2] 'Make, use, exercise and vend'. Under the 1952 Act, the exclusive rights conferred by a patent were to 'make, use, exercise and vend' the invention, so that the patentee should 'have and enjoy the whole profit and advantage accruing by reason of the invention during the term of the patent'. Although the various components might be treated separately, the phrase 'make, use, exercise and vend' was generally regarded by the courts as a composite phrase which covered most commercial dealings with inventions, including for instance dealings with the products of patented processes.[1] On the other hand, it was held to be no infringement merely to deal in parts of a patented product,[2] unless all the parts were sold together.[3]

[14.3] 'Exploit'. The terminology used in the 1952 Act to describe the patentee's rights came under criticism from those concerned with the need for plain English in drafting. It was described as comprising 'archaic words with hidden meanings' by the then Minister for Science, Customs and Small Business, Barry Jones, in his second reading speech for the Patents Bill 1989.[4] Reflecting this view, the exclusive rights conferred on a patent

---

1. See eg *Beecham Group Ltd v Bristol Laboratories Ltd* [1978] RPC 153.
2. *Walker v Alemite Corp* (1933) 49 CLR 643.
3. See eg *Windsurfing International Inc v Petit* [1984] 2 NSWLR 196.
4. *Hansard*, 1 June 1989, p 3479.

owner under the 1990 Act are 'to exploit the invention and to authorise another person to exploit the invention' (s 13(1)). The term 'exploit' was apparently chosen because it 'bears a sensible, usual meaning'.[5] Nevertheless there are some inherent complexities in the term which the definition in Sch 1 of the 1990 Act attempts to clear up. There 'exploit', in relation to an invention, is specified to include:

(1) where the invention is a product — make, hire, sell or otherwise dispose of the product, offer to make, sell, hire or otherwise dispose of it, use or import it, or keep it for the purpose of doing any of those things; or

(2) where the invention is a method or process — use the method or process or do any act mentioned in paragraph (a) in respect of a product resulting from such use.

Apart from the echoes of archaic words found in the current legislation, this definition will undoubtedly be interpreted in the light of developed case law concerning the 'hidden meanings' of the 1952 Act. The main principle seems to be a simple one: that the owner of the patent should be able to control use and commercial exploitation of the invention during the term of the patent.

[14.4] Contributory infringement. One area in which the 1990 Act was apparently intended to extend the patentee's rights is that of 'contributory infringement' in relation to patented processes. Suppose that B supplies C with a certain product together with instructions to use it in a way that infringes a patent held by A. For example, the product might be a well known chemical which has hitherto unsuspected properties that allows it to be used in a certain way to act as a cleaning agent: it is the method of using it that A has patented, not the product itself. C's use of A's patented process is plainly an infringement, falling within para (b) of the definition of 'exploit' quoted above. But if C is one of many individual customers of B, each with relatively few resources to meet any judgment obtained by A, there will be little point in A suing them. A would obviously prefer to sue the supplier, B, who in a sense is more obviously responsible for the infringement (and who is likely to have deeper pockets). But B has not used A's process, and the product itself is not patented, so B has not personally 'exploited' the invention.[6]

One possibility is for A to argue that B is a joint tortfeasor with C, on the basis that they have acted in concert as part of a 'common design'.[7] However, for a person to be a joint tortfeasor there must be 'participation, rather than mere facilitation',[8] and it is not clear that merely supplying a product with appropriate instructions can truly be said to involve a common design.[9] Alternatively, it may be argued that B is liable in tort for inciting or procuring the infringement.[10] However, there is some doubt as to

5. Ibid.
6. *Townsend v Haworth* (1875) 12 Ch D 831; *Walker v Alemite Corp* (1933) 49 CLR 643 at 658; *Dow Chemical AG v Spence Bryson & Co Ltd* [1982] FSR 397.
7. See eg *Morton-Norwich Products Inc v Intercen Ltd* [1978] RPC 501; *BEST Australia Ltd v Aquagas Marketing Pty Ltd* (1988) 12 IPR 143; *Murex Diagnostics Australia Pty Ltd v Chiron Corp* (1995) 30 IPR 277; and see further [2.6].
8. *BEST Australia Ltd v Aquagas Marketing Pty Ltd* (1988) 12 IPR 143 at 147.
9. See *CCOM Pty Ltd v Jiejing Pty Ltd* (1993) 27 IPR 577; *Advanced Building Systems Pty Ltd v Ramset Fasteners (Aust) Pty Ltd* [1995] AIPC 91–129.
10. See eg *Innes v Short & Beal* (1898) 15 RPC 449.

the scope of any such principle under Australian law;[11] and in any event the view has been expressed in recent decisions that, once again, something more would be required than merely supplying a product with instructions.[12]

To meet this apparent lack of a doctrine of contributory infringement under the common law, the Industrial Property Advisory Committee (IPAC) recommended that the patents legislation be amended to impose liability on the supplier in this situation.[13] Accordingly s 117 of the 1990 Act provides that where use of a product would infringe a patent, and the supplier of the product is not the patentee or a licensee, the supplier is guilty of infringement if: (a) the infringing use is the only use of which the product is reasonably capable; or (b) the supplier had reason to believe the customer would put it to an infringing use and the product is not a 'staple commercial product'; or (c) the infringing use is in accordance with any instructions for the use of the product or any inducement to use the product emanating from the supplier. This provision would seem clear enough, especially as the explanatory memorandum for the Act makes it plain that s 117 was intended to give effect to the IPAC recommendation. However, at first instance in *Rescare Ltd v Anaesthetic Supplies Pty Ltd*[14] Gummow J adopted the curious view that where the patent in question is for a process, s 117 only applies in relation to a product which is itself created as a result of that patented process. In the example given above, the chemical supplied is not a product of the patented process: it is merely something which is used in that process. Accordingly on Gummow's view, which was approved in the Full Court without discussion,[15] B's conduct would not fall within s 117. As Monotti points out, this interpretation plainly misconstrues the legislation.[16] Its effect is to negate the effect of s 117 completely: if the product that is supplied *is* the result of a patented process, the supplier is in any event 'exploiting' the invention and there is no need to use s 117 to establish infringement. If the courts persist with Gummow's interpretation, it seems likely that the Act will be amended to put the basis for contributory infringement beyond doubt.

In *Rescare* Gummow J also considered another new feature of the 1990 Act, which is that under s 13(1) the patentee is given the exclusive right to 'authorise' any exploitation of the invention. In the situation under consideration, could it be said that B is 'authorising' C's infringing use by supplying the product? Gummow J referred to authorities on the meaning of 'authorise' under copyright law[17] and, without expressing a concluded view, indicated that the supplier could avoid any liability by warning customers of the need to obtain a licence from the patentee.[18] When the same

11. See *Walker v Alemite Corp* (1933) 49 CLR 643 at 658; *Firth Industries Ltd v Polyglas Engineering Pty Ltd* (1975) 132 CLR 489 at 497.
12. See *Ryan v Lum* (1989) 14 IPR 513 at 522; *CCOM Pty Ltd v Jiejing Pty Ltd* (1993) 27 IPR 577 at 627.
13. *Patents, Innovation and Competition in Australia*, 1984, pp 66–8.
14. (1992) 25 IPR 119.
15. *Anaesthetic Supplies Pty Ltd v Rescare Ltd* (1994) 28 IPR 383 at 405.
16. A Monotti, 'Contributory Infringement of a Process Patent under the Patents Act 1990: Does it Exist after Rescare?' (1995) 6 *AIPJ* 217.
17. See [8.16]–[8.18].
18. (1992) 25 IPR 119 at 115

issue arose in *Advanced Building Systems Pty Ltd v Ramset Fasteners (Aust) Pty Ltd*[19] Hill J was prepared to be more definite on the authorisation point, holding that 'a mere countenancing or enabling of infringement by another does not constitute an authorisation'.[20] He then went on, however, to find the supplier guilty of misleading or deceptive conduct under s 52 of the Trade Practices Act 1974 for *failing* to warn its customers of the very real possibility that use of the supplier's products would infringe the plaintiff's patented process.

[14.5] Burden of proof. Ordinarily the burden is on the patentee (or exclusive licensee) to establish that the defendant's conduct amounts to infringement. However, in 1994 the Act was amended to add s 121A, which applies where a defendant has been able to create a product identical to that resulting from a patented process. If the court is satisfied that it is 'very likely' that the defendant has used that process, and the plaintiff has made reasonable but unsuccessful attempts to discover what process the defendant has actually used, the burden switches to the defendant to prove that some other process has been used. The change was required in order to comply with Article 34 of the TRIPS Agreement.

[14.6] Interpreting the specification. Infringement will only occur when the invention as claimed has been the subject of the defendant's activities. The first step is thus to decide what the invention consists of and the second to compare the infringing article or process. This requires that the relevant complete or petty patent specification be carefully construed in order to establish the extent of the territory that the patentee has marked out. The question of how narrowly or generously claims in patent specifications should be interpreted thus becomes a crucial one and in this regard the courts have been far from unanimous as to the most appropriate way to proceed. In the past a literal reading of the specification was often the approach employed.[21] On this view the monopoly outlined was considered to be narrowly circumscribed by the words chosen to describe it, so that only an item or process exactly matching that described would infringe. This considerably diminished the potential to establish infringement. A less restrictive approach was to ask whether the 'pith and marrow' of the invention had been taken, this being the essential elements of the invention, with less essential parts being omitted or replaced by a 'mechanical equivalent' which would perform the same function.[22] In so far as this approach concentrated on the essential integers of the invention, it at least made it possible to identify infringement where, although differing in minor details, the defendant's article or process involved the essence of the plaintiff's invention.

---

19.   [1995] AIPC 91–129. The decision on this issue was not dealt with on appeal, the Full Court holding the patent to be invalid: *Ramset Fasteners (Aust) Pty Ltd v Advanced Building Systems Pty Ltd* (1996) 34 IPR 256.

20.   See also *Sartas No 1 Pty Ltd v Koukourou & Partners Pty Ltd* (1994) 30 IPR 479, where Gummow J was by now prepared to reach the same conclusion.

21.   See eg *Rodi & Weinenberger AG v Henry Showell Ltd* [1969] RPC 367; *Van der Lely NV v Bamfords Ltd* [1963] RPC 61 and the (dissenting) judgment of Menzies J in *Interlego AG v Toltoys Pty Ltd* (1973) 130 CLR 461.

22.   *Clark v Adie* (1877) 2 App Cas 315; *Marconi v British Radio Telegraph & Telephone Co* (1911) 28 RPC 181.

[14.7] **The purposive approach.** In recent years, however, the most popular approach taken by English and Australian judges in reading patent specifications has been the 'purposive' approach articulated by Lord Diplock (with whom the other members of the House of Lords agreed) in *Catnic Components Ltd v Hill & Smith Ltd.*[23] Besides endorsing the need to identify the 'pith and marrow' of an invention, this approach focuses on the question of the patentee's intention in drafting the specification:

> [A] patent specification is a unilateral statement by the patentee, in words of his [sic] own choosing, addressed to those likely to have a practical interest in the subject matter of his invention (ie 'skilled in the art'), by which he informs them what he claims to be the essential features of the new product or process for which the letters patent grant him a monopoly. It is those novel features only that he claims to be essential that constitute the so-called 'pith and marrow' of the claim. A patent specification should be given a purposive construction rather than a purely literal one derived from applying to it the kind of meticulous verbal analysis in which lawyers are too often tempted by their training to indulge.[24]

In the *Catnic* case the invention allegedly infringed was a lintel for use in spanning the spaces above window and door openings. The first claim referred to a supporting back plate 'extending vertically' from the base. The defendants copied the lintel but moved the back plate 6 degrees from the vertical, with no significant change in strength or function. The House of Lords held the patent to have been infringed. The reason for making the back plate vertical was that this best supported the load, and a back plate close to the vertical was just as effective in fulfilling the purpose. A literal approach (confining an embodiment of the invention to a lintel with a right angle) would have confined the patentee to a monopoly over an invention which could fairly easily be reproduced. Lord Diplock emphasised that the addressee of the specification was a person in the field, in this case, a builder. If the term 'vertical' was used by a geometer addressing himself to follow geometers then it would be understood as a word of precision only, but when used in a description of a manufactured building product the expression 'extending vertically' was 'perfectly capable of meaning positioned near enough to the exact geometrical vertical to enable it in actual use to perform satisfactorily all the functions that it could perform if it were precisely vertical'.[25]

The purposive approach to interpreting patent specifications is now firmly established in Australia, but it is important to appreciate its limitations. Although *Catnic* was applied in *Populin v HB Nominees Pty Ltd,*[26] for example, infringement was not found in that case since certain essential elements of the invention were not taken by the respondent. The Full Court of the Federal Court, echoing Lord Diplock, stressed that:

> The complete specification must not be read in the abstract but in the light of common knowledge in the art before the priority date, bearing in mind that what is being construed is a public instrument which must, if it is to be valid, define a monopoly in such a way that it is not reasonably capable of being misunderstood (see generally *Welch Perrin & Co Pty Ltd v Worrel* (1961) 106 CLR 588 at 610). The essential features of the product or process for

---

23. [1981] FSR 60.
24. Ibid at 67.
25. Ibid.
26. (1982) 41 ALR 471.

which it claims a monopoly are to be determined not as a matter of abstract uninformed construction but by a common sense assessment of what the words used convey in the context of then-existing public knowledge.[27]

However, despite a purposive reading of the specification, the Federal Court did not consider the respondent's machine to have adopted mere 'mechanical equivalents' of inessential features of the appellants' sugar cane planting machine. The patented machine moved cane billets from a large supply bin to a small bin using a conveyor belt which caused the billets to align themselves so they could be planted. The respondent's machine did not employ two separate containers although 'what happens in operation of both machines regarding orientation of the cane billets is very similar'.[28] The appellants had claimed the separate bins as vital to the working and efficacy of this invention. The court observed that:

> Because of the requirement of provisions such as s 40, it has become the practice to set out in the claim, sometimes at great length, the element or integers of the invention. As in this case it is also common for the first claim to be added to or varied in the subsequent claims. This progressively adds elements to the combination, which tend to make an attack upon the grounds of want of subject matter or want of novelty more difficult. The effect is to progressively narrow the area of monopoly claimed.[29]

In effect here the appellants, by defining their invention in the way they had, had 'left open' what the alleged infringer had done and could not get round 'the fundamental rule that there will be no infringement unless the alleged infringer has taken all of the essential features or integers of the patentee's claim'.[30] This notion that the patentee is bound by what they have chosen to claim is also reflected in the principle that it is not permissible to refer to the body of the specification to vary or qualify the meaning of any 'plain and unambiguous' words used in a claim; only if the claim is unclear on its face is recourse to the specification as a whole permitted.[31]

[14.8] Exemptions from infringement. The legislation provides in certain instances that conduct that would otherwise infringe a patent is not to be taken as doing so. One such exemption excuses the use of an invention on board a foreign vessel, or in the construction or working of a foreign aircraft or land vehicle, where that vessel, aircraft or vehicle temporarily or accidentally comes into Australia (s 118). The aim of this provision is to preclude a vessel (etc) from a country which is a party to the Paris Convention being forced to secure a patent licence every time it enters another Convention country. The definitions of 'foreign vessel', etc in the 1990 Act refer to a 'prescribed foreign country' (Sch 1) to allow for prescription of member countries of the Paris Convention, to ensure the required degree

---

27. Ibid at 476. See also *Decor Corp Pty Ltd v Dart Industries Inc* (1988) 13 IPR 385 at 399–400.
28. (1982) 41 ALR 471 at 474.
29. Ibid at 476.
30. *Olin Corp v Super Cartridge Co Pty Ltd* (1977) 180 CLR 236 at 246. See also *Allsop Inc v Bintang Ltd* (1989) 15 IPR 686; *Fisher & Paykel Healthcare Pty Ltd v Avion Engineering Pty Ltd* (1991) 22 IPR 1; *Leonardis v Sartas No 1 Pty Ltd* (1996) 35 IPR 23.
31. *Welch Perrin & Co Pty Ltd v Worrel* (1961) 106 CLR 588 at 610; *Interlego AG v Toltoys Pty Ltd* (1973) 130 CLR 461 at 478–9. For some recent examples of this principle being applied where the meaning of a patent claim was in dispute, see *Melbourne v Terry Fluid Controls Pty Ltd* (1994) 28 IPR 302; *Freeman v T J & F L Pohlner Pty Ltd* (1994) 30 IPR 377; *Lantech Inc v First Green Park Pty Ltd* (1995) 31 IPR 327.

of reciprocity. A further exemption in the 1952 Act related to use during a period in which a patent had lapsed but was subsequently restored. Since the 1990 Act largely fails to provide for procedures for restoration as such,[32] the only similar provisions in it appear in relation to retrospectively operating extensions of time (s 223(10)) and applications in respect of 'associated technology' (s 150(5)). However, the new Act does add another ground of exemption, addressing the situation where the invention is already in use immediately before the priority date of a claim (s 119). The user will not be able to rely on this provision if the invention was revealed to such a user by the patentee or a predecessor in title, or if the use had been permanently discontinued. In some ways the provision is a strange one, since it would normally be the case that proof of such prior use would in any event result in the patent being invalidated on the ground of lack of novelty.

Finally, it is possible to obtain a non-infringement declaration which allows exploitation of an invention where there may be some question as to infringement (ss 125–127). Such a declaration will only be given after the applicant has notified the patentee of the proposed use and offered to pay for advice as to whether the proposed use would infringe or not. The effect of a declaration is to give users of technology which may be on the fringes of patentability the safeguard of not being liable for damages or an account of profits in respect of activities undertaken while the declaration is in force, should it be subsequently found that the use actually amounts to trespassing within the patent area.

2. PROCEEDINGS FOR INFRINGEMENT

[14.9] **Who dares, sues.** Infringement proceedings may be started in a prescribed court or another court having jurisdiction to hear and determine the matter (s 120(1)). The proceedings may be brought either by the patentee or by an exclusive licensee, although in the latter instance the patentee must be joined as a party to the proceedings, either as a co-plaintiff or as a defendant (s 120(2)).[33] Patent litigation is usually an expensive and lengthy process; the amount of evidence required to allow the tribunal to assess the various issues is legendary.[34] Estimates as to the average cost of a patent infringement case in Australia 'range from as low as $20,000 to over $1,000,000, although a general estimate is that typical costs per party range from $50,000 to $250,000'.[35] It is during a full-blown infringement action that it becomes apparent that patent litigation is a game for big players. The stakes may be enormous, however, as in *Genentech Inc v Wellcome Foundation Ltd*[36] where the potential market for the product in issue (tissue plasminogen activator, or TPA) was worth billions of dollars per annum.

---

32. See [11.25].
33. As to the capacity of a person with an equitable interest in a patent to sue for infringement, see *Stack v Brisbane City Council* (1996) 35 IPR 296.
34. See eg *Unger v Sugg* (1891) 9 RPC 113 at 116; *Weir Pumps Ltd v CML Pumps Ltd* (1983) 2 IPR 129 at 154.
35. *The Role of Intellectual Property in Innovation — Vol 1, Strategic Overview*, Prime Minister's Science and Engineering Council, 1993, p 19. For reform proposals addressing the cost and complexity of patent litigation, see [2.3].
36. [1989] RPC 147: see [15.12].

[14.10] Infringement proceedings and issues of patent validity.
One of the reasons why patent litigation tends to be so complex is that the
defendant almost invariably counterclaims for revocation of the patent, a
tactic specifically condoned by the legislation (s 121). Phillips and Firth
remind us that:

> It is ... a fact of life that revocation is generally raised, not in abstract by
> some kind and disinterested soul who wishes to rid the economy of an unde-
> served monopoly, but by an infringing defendant against whom the full legal
> force of the patent has been unleashed and whose only realistic means of
> escaping liability is by killing the plaintiff's monopoly before it kills him
> [sic].[37]

As noted in earlier chapters, the validity of a patent is never guaranteed, no
matter how carefully it has been assessed by the Patent Office during the
course of an examination or of opposition proceedings (s 20). Validity is
always a matter to be determined by the courts, and even success in a contested suit does not prevent some other infringer subsequently challenging
the validity of a claim. It is possible, however, for a patentee whose claims
have survived litigation contesting their validity to obtain a certificate of
validity (s 19). Although still not providing protection against an adverse
finding, this does certify that the validity of a claim was questioned. Should
some hardy litigant subsequently dare to throw down the gauntlet where
another has failed and in turn be rebuffed, the holder of the certificate will
ordinarily obtain costs as between solicitor and client in these further proceedings.

[14.11] Remedies. The remedies generally open to a successful plaintiff
in patent infringement proceedings are an injunction and either damages
or an account of profits at the plaintiff's option (s 122(1)). Injunctive relief
to restrain the infringement will always be available in the court's discretion. There was previously some reluctance to impose interlocutory
restraints upon an alleged infringer unless the patent in question had been
held to be valid or had stood unchallenged for some years.[38] However, the
approach now appears to be that with the more stringent procedures that
have gradually been adopted for assessing patent applications, patents
should at least prima facie be assumed to be valid: accordingly an interlocutory injunction should not be withheld merely because the defendant puts
the validity of the patent at issue.[39] It is not at all clear that patents *are* in
fact more likely to be found to be valid these days, but in any event it seems
that applications for interlocutory relief will now simply be assessed according to the general principles that govern such proceedings.[40]

The pecuniary remedies, on the other hand, may not always be pursued.
One such situation that has already been mentioned is that of conduct
during the subsistence of a non-infringement declaration.[41] They are also
unavailable where the infringement pre-dated an amendment to a published claim, unless the original claim was framed in good faith and with

37. Phillips and Firth, para [8.1].
38. See eg *Beecham Group Ltd v Bristol Laboratories Pty Ltd* (1968) 118 CLR 618.
39. See eg *Martin Engineering Co v Trison Holdings Pty Ltd* (1988) 11 IPR 611; *Tidy Tea
     Ltd v Unilever Australia Ltd* (1995) 32 IPR 405; *A B Hassle v Pharmacia (Australia) Pty
     Ltd* (1995) 33 IPR 63.
40. See [2.10]–[2.12].
41. See [14.8].

reasonable skill and knowledge or the amendment resulted in the disclosure of new matter (s 115). More generally, damages or an account of profits may be refused by a court where the infringement is innocent, in the sense that at the relevant time the defendant neither knew nor had reason to believe that a patent existed for the invention (s 123(1)). However if products are marked so as to indicate they are patented and have been sold or used to a substantial extent in Australia before the date of infringement, the defendant is taken to have been aware of the existence of the patent unless the contrary is proved (s 123(2)).

Where damages are available, the basic measure is the restoration of the plaintiff to the status quo ante.[42] Depending on the particular facts, this may for instance entail looking to the plaintiff's lost manufacturing profits, or alternatively assessing a fair royalty that would have been payable.[43] If an account of profits is chosen instead of a claim for damages, the profits made by the defendant as a result of the infringement will be assessed according to the principles already described.[44]

Aside from the remedies listed in s 122(1), a court hearing a patent infringement action also has an inherent power to order the delivery up of any products which have resulted from the infringing conduct.[45]

[14.12] Action for threats. Given the length, expense and vagaries of patent litigation, it might be considered worthwhile for a patentee or someone with a patent pending to threaten infringement proceedings and obtain compliance from the 'infringer' without all the trouble entailed in actually suing. It is not permissible to threaten idly, however, since a person aggrieved by circulars, advertisements or other communications is entitled to retaliate with a suit for unjustifiable threats, and obtain a declaration that the threats are unjustified, an injunction against their continuation and the recovery of any damages sustained by the applicant as a result of the threats (s 128).[46] The business of a manufacturer whose goods are unfairly alleged to infringe may be seriously damaged, not only from ceasing to make and sell the allegedly infringing technology themselves, but also if customers are frightened away by being told they are not entitled to purchase from the alleged infringer.

The mere notification of the existence of a patent or a patent application does not amount to a threat for this purpose (s 131). Thus a polite letter informing a person that the writer is the holder of a patent, and possibly offering a licence to use the invention, will not contravene. Ultimately, however, whether a particular communication amounts to a threat depends on 'whether the language would convey to any reasonable person that the author ... intended to bring proceedings for infringement'.[47] Where there

---

42.   *General Tire & Rubber Co v Firestone Tyre & Rubber Co Ltd* [1976] RPC 197.
43.   See eg *Pearce v Paul Kingston Pty Ltd* (1992) 25 IPR 591.
44.   See [2.16].
45.   See eg *Roussel Uclaf v Pan Laboratories Pty Ltd* (1994) 29 IPR 556; and see further [2.14].
46.   See eg *Meth v Norbert Steinhard & Son Ltd* (1962) 107 CLR 187; *Townsend Controls Pty Ltd v Gilead* (1989) 16 IPR 469; (1990) 21 IPR 520; see generally Lahore, *Patents*, para [18,030] ff. Note that such an action may not be mounted against a legal practitioner or patent attorney acting on behalf of a client (s 132).
47.   *U & I Global Trading (Australia) Pty Ltd v Tasman-Warajay Pty Ltd* (1995) 32 IPR 494 at 500.

has been a threat in the relevant sense, the applicant will be granted relief unless the defendant can show that the acts complained of amounted or would amount to an infringement of a patent claim, whose validity the applicant has not been able to challenge (s 129). As with the equivalent provisions in the Copyright Act,[48] it is no excuse that the defendant honestly believed that the activity complained of amounted to an infringement.[49] Thus an action for threats ultimately comes down to whether the defendant can indeed establish infringement, or whether the applicant may be able to preclude such a finding by showing the patent's invalidity. Reflecting this, provision is made for the defendant, if they are the patentee or an exclusive licensee, to counterclaim for infringement; and for the applicant to 'counter-counterclaim' for revocation (s 130).

---

48.   See [8.37].
49.   *Skinner & Co v Perry* (1893) 10 RPC 1.

Chapter 15

Biotechnology

[15.1] **Introduction.** One of the most interesting and controversial issues in recent years has been the extent to which living material can be patented and the extent to which information about genes, or even genes themselves, can be monopolised. In fact processes using or resulting in the production of micro-organisms have long been held to be patentable.[1] The questions now arising concern the application of biotechnological techniques to developing new animals and plants and whether these are to be considered 'manners of new manufacture' which are both novel and inventive. The human genome project, an international effort to work out the coded sequence and determine the function of all human genes, has led to arguments concerning the patenting of sections of the genome and products resulting from use of that information. This chapter reviews the various issues, as well as looking at the treatment accorded under special legislation to plant varieties.

1. BACKGROUND

[15.2] **Biotechnology.** Biotechnology may be loosely defined as the production of useful products by living micro-organisms and cell cultures.[2] In this sense it has been known to us at least since ethanol was first produced from yeast cells to provide alcoholic beverages. The production of various industrial chemicals and antibiotics by fermentation processes has been achieved more recently, as well as the isolation of antibiotic products from selected strains of micro-organisms. Within the last 20 years there has arisen a 'new biotechnology',[3] distinct from classical fermentation technology, which allows the production of modified micro-organisms or cell lines, generally

---

1.   See Ricketson, p 924 for examples.
2.   See Grubb, p 150.
3.   Ibid.

by one of two basic techniques. The first of these is recombinant DNA technology, also referred to as gene splicing or genetic engineering, in which genetic material from an external source is inserted into a cell so as to cause production of a desired protein by that cell. The other method is hybridoma technology, which is based upon the workings of the immune system rather than upon molecular genetics. Different types of immune cells are fused together to form a hybrid cell line producing monoclonal antibodies.[4] There are four possible ways of producing specific human antibodies. Although not all are developed yet, they involve manipulation of genetic material and are intended to provide mass-produced antibodies for medical purposes. All require a great deal of research experimentation and investment.[5] Combining 'new' and 'old' biotechnology may occur, as when bacteria are modified by splicing into their DNA clusters of genes which cause the bacteria to make desirable products which are variations on the chemicals produced by the unmodified bacteria. In this way tailormade drugs can be produced.[6]

[15.3] The significance of legal protection. Industrial application of biological material is the basis of the biotechnology industry.[7] Without the assurance of patent protection or some other proprietary right few firms would be willing to spend millions of dollars on such research. In this regard it is significant that the return on research and development in the US fell from 12% in 1960 to as low as 3.3% in the late 1980s.[8] Costs to second entrants to industries, where know-how rather than equipment is a major ingredient, are only a small percentage of the original developer's costs. This makes the information a valuable asset and requires firms to protect it while at the same time exploiting it and training personnel in the 'secret' art.

[15.4] Recombinant DNA. Recombinant DNA technology and research is the subject of intense public debate. Some fear the escape of new pathogens, others the application of the techniques to our own species. While the structure of DNA has been known since 1953,[9] recombinant DNA (rDNA) technology was introduced in 1972 with the first cloning experiments.[10] Such technology allows not only the creation of new substances, plants, micro-organisms and animals by the manipulation of DNA and the modification of genetic material, but also the controlled reproduction of the exact item (cloning). Transgenic animals can also be produced by rDNA technology through the joining of pieces of DNA in a laboratory to create organisms combining genes from more than one species. This has been described as rivalling the discovery of fire in importance:

> '[T]he eighth day of creation' had begun. Man could now 'play God', disarranging and recombining gene fragments of unrelated species at will to design, for better or worse, new organisms for utilitarian ends.[11]

---

4.   Ibid.
5.   'Antibodies of Mice and Men', *Economist*, 3 March 1990, p 91.
6.   P Ball, 'Give Bacteria the Tools and They'll do the Job', *New Scientist*, 17 June 1995, p 16.
7.   This discussion of biotechnology is derived from K Bozicevic, 'Distinguishing "Products of Nature" from "Products Derived from Nature"' (1987) 69 *J of Patent & Trade Mark Office Soc* 415; Straus; I P Cooper, *Trade Secrets and Biotechnology*, 1982.
8.   I P Cooper, *Trade Secrets and Biotechnology*, 1982, p 15.
9.   Straus, p 23.
10. Ibid, p 25.
11. N Perlas, 'Biotechnology and Anthroposophy' [1987] *J of Anthroposophy* 5 at 7.

[15.5] Uses of biologically engineered products. The inventive
work within the scope of recombinant DNA technology concerns many
areas, some of paramount economic or social importance. Over a decade
ago it was claimed that up to 40% of manufactured products were based on
biological technology.[12] The main users of biotechnology are the chemical,
pharmaceutical, medical and agricultural industries. In 1983, for the first
time, human insulin produced by rDNA technology reached the market,[13]
soon to be followed by other 'regulatory proteins' such as human growth
hormones, interferons (cancer-attacking substances) and other artificially
produced amino acids which have a great impact on medical treatment.
Other pharmaceutical applications of rDNA technology include the
availability of large quantities of identical and pure supplies of blood
products, vaccines and antibodies. One great success has been the cloning
of 'Factor VIII', which is used to treat haemophiliacs.[14] Another has been
the production of human growth hormone used to treat children with
poorly developed pituitary glands. Until the mid-1980s this was derived
from pituitary glands taken from cadavers. A thousand cadavers were
needed to make enough growth hormone to treat one child and it
sometimes contained viruses which had been present in the donors'
brains.[15] The progress of motor neurone disease has been slowed by a drug
which is a genetically engineered version of a chemical produced in
muscles.[16]

[15.6] Agricultural uses. In the area of animal agriculture rDNA is
applied to the diagnosis, prevention and control of animal diseases, animal
nutrition and growth promotion as well as the genetic improvement of animal breeds. Animal breeding in developing countries is being revolutionised by a system of transferring embryos produced by prize bulls and cows
to surrogate mothers. Animal hormones are used so that the cows produce
multiple fertile eggs. The European animals bred for meat or milk production acquire resistance to the diseases encountered in developing countries
from their surrogate mothers. This system is being used to transform the
poor quality herds of Egypt and India.[17] The modification of hereditary
material allowed by rDNA is also being applied to the improvement of
plants, particularly food crops, to fish culturing and the prevention and
control of fish diseases, to the area of food additives (since many flavours
and other attributes of food can be cloned and thus be advertised as 'natural' products) and in the treatment of toxic waste and pollution control.
Some have expressed fears that the development of new animals and plants
(with monopoly rights over their exploitation) will harm the developing
world rather than offer new hope of improved crops and food sources. The
concept of a 'farmer's privilege' is a feature of plant varieties protection
legislation which may allow farmers to use seed or otherwise propagate

12. F Beier, R Crespi and J Straus, *Biotechnology and Patent Protection: An International Review*, 1985, p 10.
13. Straus, p 25.
14. Ibid, p 11, citing Fishlock, 'The Cloning of Factor VIII', *Financial Times*, 30 November 1984, p 10.
15. 'Stretch Genes Clinic', *Sydney Morning Herald*, 17 March 1990, p 1.
16. A Coghlan, 'New Factor Slows Wasting Disease', *New Scientist*, 17 June 1995, p 24.
17. I Marsh, 'Embryo Transplants Could Replace Artificial Insemination — Calves "Settle In" the Wombs', *Financial Times*, 25 January 1985, p 8.

protected plant varieties,[18] and a more radical form of this extending to transgenic animals has been proposed for insertion into the EC Directive on Biotechnological Inventions.[19] Farmers say that patents on new crops threaten their livelihoods as the rights to keep and re-sow crops are not allowed under patent law, and animals bred from a patented animal cannot be used by the farmer. Opposing patents is a lengthy and time-consuming process, and the holders of rights are usually large industrial corporations who can afford to resist challenges. Furthermore, crops engineered by biotechnology are often based on DNA obtained from species used in the developing world. 'If the industry were then to sell its engineered crops back to the developing world, it would be threatening the heritage of the very countries from which they obtained the extra gene in the first place.'[20] A related concern is the loss of biodiversity as commercial crops come to dominate the market. Factors such as consumer demand for a certain appearance or uniform ripening (or even flavour) for the convenience of growers lead to the abandoning of traditional varieties in favour of hybrids, possibly leading to the loss of some varieties entirely.

Dramatic examples of damage to vulnerable economies depending on very few cash crops have been provided by the genetic engineering of plants which are superior in some way or will grow in climates where they do not usually thrive. In June 1995 the first crop of a genetically altered rapeseed plant was harvested in the US. The plant has been altered to produce an oil more usually extracted from coconuts and palm kernels, a vital cash crop for several developing nations.[21] The Philippines sugar industry has been affected by the development of high-fructose varieties of corn produced by American plant breeders. The promise offered by biotechnology, of feeding more people and increasing productivity in developing countries, may prove to be entirely hollow if their existing livelihood is undermined.

[15.7] Human genes. Although somewhat beyond the scope of this chapter, it should be noted that a major intellectual property issue for indigenous people has arisen recently with the report that the US patent office has issued a patent over the genetic material of a foreign citizen, an indigenous man of the Hagahai people of Papua New Guinea.[22] The patent claims a cell line containing unmodified Hagahai DNA and several methods for its use in detecting certain retroviruses. Although this patenting activity is being seriously opposed on a number of grounds, the legality of patenting 'naturally occurring' information such as a stretch of DNA is greatly in doubt, without even considering the serious ethical and moral aspects of allowing third party (and foreign) ownership of someone's very genes. The issues raised concern the fundamental questions of to what extent 'biocolonialism' and commodification of human life should be allowed, and at the other end of the spectrum the usual commercial issues

---

18.   See [15.23].
19.   R Nott, 'The Proposed Directive on Biotechnological Inventions' [1994] 5 *EIPR* 191.
20.   B Watts, 'A Matter of Life and Patents', *New Scientist*, 12 January 1991, p 38.
21.   K Kleiner, 'Altered Crop Threatens Poor Nations', *New Scientist*, 17 June 1995, p 10.
22.   P Mooney, 'Indigenous Person from Papua New Guinea claimed in US Government Patent', Press Release, Rural Advancement Foundation International, 30 November 1995.

as to what compensation, royalties or other remuneration may be allowed to the originators of the raw material, since there is 'no concrete provision for the Hagahai to receive any compensation for becoming the property of the US Government'.[23]

The impetus towards patenting genetic material has arisen out of the Human Genome Project (HGP), the aim of which is to map and sequence over a 15-year period the estimated 100,000 genes which comprise the human genome, with the intention of obtaining sufficient understanding so that any gene whose alteration is responsible for a disease will be easily identified and analysed. It may also be possible to use the information to manufacture diagnostic tests, and therapeutic proteins to identify and treat genetic disorders. In 1995 an international group of scientists embarked upon the Human Genome Diversity Project (HGDP) which aims to draw blood and tissue samples from as many indigenous groups in the world as possible. This has been dubbed the 'Vampire Project' by its opponents, of which there are many, including the Sami indigenous women from the Nordic countries, who denounced the project at the Beijing Women's Conference in August 1995. While the HGP has highlighted the issues of patenting of gene sequences, gene therapies and other aspects of human life, the HGDP appears to be pursuing an aggressive patenting policy which, furthermore, has the overtones of all the worst aspects of colonialism.

The National Institute of Human Genome Research opened at the National Institute of Health (NIH) in Washington in 1990. Although coordinated from the US, many developed countries are involved in sequencing the genome. Sequencing human genes has been performed by molecular geneticists since the early 1980s, but the HGP has the express aim of improving the coordination of international efforts to achieve the sequencing. The patentability of the gene sequences being determined has become one of the most divisive issues surrounding the project. In 1991 a researcher at the NIH decided to file patent applications for the first fruits of the research, 2600 DNA strands related to certain genes from the human brain. The US patent office rejected the applications on the basis that the sequences lacked novelty, utility and were 'obvious' in that they could be derived from existing data.[24]

Patent offices around the world have not yet decided whether stretches of DNA amount to an invention or are merely 'discovery' of a sequence of genes. If specifications are suitably drafted patenting may be possible, and certainly the manufactured therapeutic and diagnostic products may be inventions. The issues are not simply legal ones, however, and even among the researchers there is disagreement. The first Director of the HGP, James Watson (winner of the Nobel prize for his seminal work, with Francis Crick, in identifying the DNA 'spiral' while researching at Cambridge University in the 1950s) resigned, at least partly in order to express his opposition to the NIH decision to file for patent rights which he denounces as 'sheer lunacy'.[25] The argument put by those in favour of applying for patent

23. Ibid, p 1. In the event, the researchers agreed to share the benefits with the Hagahai people.
24. C Anderson, 'NIH cDNA Patent Rejected: Backers Want to Amend Law' (1992) 359 *Nature* 263.
25. J Maddox, 'The Case for the Human Genome' (1991) 352 *Nature* 14 at 14.

rights is to secure any property rights which may be forthcoming,[26] because failure to obtain the rights in the first place may make them unretrievable later on. In self defence, the British Medical Research Council reluctantly began applying for patents on stretches of DNA. This policy was abandoned at the end of 1993, and the heads of four leading professional organisations of clinical geneticists wrote a joint letter to the European Patent Office and to senior UK government ministers asking for a prohibition on the patenting of human genes, arguing that it is morally unacceptable to patent an entity found in a natural state in the human body (even if legally possible) and that the HGP is a cooperative worldwide effort but the NIH's actions were making researchers increasingly reluctant to share information.[27]

Some of these fears began to be realised when a UK hospital received a demand for US$6000 to use a gene for cystic fibrosis employed to screen patients for the disorder. Although any patent rights had not yet been granted anywhere, the Toronto Hospital for Sick Children, where the gene was identified and sequenced, intended that those using the information pay royalties and licence fees.[28]

While the Australian patent office takes the position that it will grant a patent to anything within legal limits, s 18(2) of the Patents Act 1990 expressly prohibits patents for human beings or biological processes for their creation. It is not clear whether a stretch of DNA is a 'human being' or an isolated part thereof which should be patentable. The proposed EC Directive on Biotechnological Inventions contains (in Art 2.3) a very similar provision to s 18(2), following Art 53(a) of the European Patent Convention. However, the Legal Affairs Committee of the European Parliament after considering the Biotechnology Directive proposed a dramatic departure from the text by asking for an absolute ban on patenting human genes and gene therapies (on which much current medical and pharmaceutical research is based).[29] The final version of the Directive was expected at the end of December 1995, but has floundered due to considerable opposition to patenting life in any form from various lobby groups across the European Community. A bill to disallow the patenting of genes or genetic information was introduced by the Democrats into the Australian parliament in September 1996.[30] It remains to be seen whether this will be passed, or whether the general principles applicable to patenting will prohibit genetic information as such being patentable under usual criteria (requiring a manner of manufacture which is novel and inventive).

The 'gene wars' have escalated and the issues have escaped beyond the confines of the patent system. In October 1994 the US firm Human Genome Systems (HGS) announced that if scientists want to use the information held by the company on fragments of 35,000 human genes they must enter into a contract to give HGS rights to commercial products

---

26.   C Anderson, 'Patents, Round Two' (1992) 355 *Nature* 665.
27.   D Dickson, 'UK Geneticists ask for Ban on Patenting of Human Genes' (1993) 366 *Nature* 391.
28.   A Coghlan, 'Patents', *New Scientist*, 23 January 1993, p 4.
29.   R Nott, 'The Proposed EC Directive on Biotechnological Inventions' [1994] 5 *EIPR* 191 at 194.
30.   Patents Amendment Bill 1996.

developed using the data.[31] Thus the willingness to regard the information as property and exploit it as such is not dependent on obtaining patent rights, although this would greatly reinforce the position of those seeking to assert such proprietary notions over the building blocks of human life.

Not only human genetic material is targeted by 'gene hunters'. An important aspect of Aboriginal heritage is knowledge of harvesting techniques and uses for traditional foods, for example abalone, now a keenly sought food among the wider community. The obtaining of genetic material from animals and plants and acquiring monopoly rights over the organisms or some genetically altered version thereof, or some product derived therefrom, is also becoming a common practice. A US patent on a pesticide derived from the seeds of the neem tree (*Azadirachta indica*, a native of India) is being opposed by a coalition of pressure groups as its pesticidal properties have been used for centuries by the people living where the tree grows. If nothing else, it seems that the patent must fail for want of novelty! 'The patent, owned by the giant seed company W R Grace, has become a cause celebre in the fight to prevent rich nations from plundering the biological resources and traditional knowledge of developing countries.' [32]

2.   LEGAL ISSUES IN PATENTING LIFE FORMS

[15.8]   Obstacles to patentability. Patent protection may not be a suitable tool for protection of the knowledge upon which biotechnology is based. The patent laws of most countries, including Australia, exclude 'discoveries' from patent protection.[33] The paramount criterion of patentability is that the patent should issue for an 'invention', or 'manner of new manufacture' within s 6 of the Statute of Monopolies. Mere discoveries do not fit within this formula unless they can be applied to some useful end and, despite the uses to which biotechnology has been put, much of the work in the area may not move far enough away from the 'discovery' stage to be eligible for patent protection. Furthermore in so far as biotechnology also encompasses traditional methods of plant and animal breeding and traditional industrial microbiology,[34] the question of whether a development is 'novel' in the patent sense may arise. Different categories of biotechnological inventions exhibit a high degree of interrelationship and interdependency,[35] and the issue of how far the use of known techniques invalidates a claim of novelty with regard to a patent application is a separate but possibly overlapping issue with that of whether the result is patentable, or excluded as being a 'discovery'.

---

31.   L Dayton, 'A Precarious Climb on the DNA Ladder', *Sydney Morning Herald*, 7 January 1995, p 14.
32.   K Kleiner, 'Pesticide Tree ends up in Court', *New Scientist*, 16 September 1995, p 7. See further E Da Casta e Silva, 'The Protection of Intellectual Property for Local and Indigenous Communities' [1995] 11 *EIPR* 546; M Doucas, 'Intellectual Property Law — Indigenous People's Concerns' (1995) 12 *Can IP Rev* 1; M J Huft, 'Indigenous Peoples and Drug Discovery Research: A Question of Intellectual Property Rights' (1995) 89 *Northwestern ULR* 1678; H Fourmile, 'Protecting Indigenous Property Rights in Biodiversity' (1996) 72(5) *Curr Aff Bull* 36.
33.   See [12.5].
34.   Straus, p 32.
35.   Ibid, p 43.

[15.9]   Of nature or derived from nature? The new technologies in
the field of biotechnology are mostly based on numerous 'discoveries' in
the sense of scientific findings of no immediate practical use. Furthermore
the basic working material of the biotechnologist is living matter — plant,
animal, micro-organism or plasmid — and the question arises whether the
outcome of the work may still be considered as a discovery or something
found in nature. The courts in the US have drawn a distinction between
non-patentable discoveries or products of nature (based on a law of nature
that has been learned by a scientist) and the application of a discovery so
that a patentable 'product derived from nature' is arrived at. The rule in
the US is that a 'product of nature' is not patentable, whereas a 'product
derived from nature' may well be. Objections raised by clinical geneticists
in the UK to the patent applications for gene fragments, applied for by the
NIH researchers in the US, have included the grounds that it is legally
questionable to patent an entity found in a natural state in the human
body.[36]

[15.10]   Obviousness. Apart from problems of novelty, obviousness may
present yet another objection to patenting recombinant DNA products.[37]
The question of obviousness involves asking whether or not something for
which a patent is applied involves an inventive step, and to some extent
judgment of what is or is not obvious is a subjective matter. There have
been a great many patent cases in which obviousness has been at issue, the
consensus of judicial opinion being that the person to whom the invention
must be non-obvious for patent purposes is a person 'skilled in the art', a
competent worker but without imagination or inventive capability.[38] Like
most issues in a patent case, obviousness is 'a type of jury question'[39] and
although the court ultimately makes the decision it will require a great deal
of evidence to establish the inventive step which makes the patent valid and
keeps it from being struck down for obviousness.

It is the argument that many biotechnological inventions are 'obvious'
within patent concepts which has led one commentator to say that 'viewed
globally, the patenting of a recombinant DNA product having the activity of
a known protein is in a mess'.[40] Although large numbers of applications for
the cloning and expression of genes coding for known proteins are being
filed in these jurisdictions, few are emerging as patents, principally because
of the patent examiners' objection that the recombinant protein and DNA
encoding it are inherently 'obvious': the argument being that everyone
knows that the protein is desirable and therefore attempting to make it by
standard recombinant methods is obvious. In view of the fact that the aim
of the patent system is to provide a monopoly to inventors in exchange for
'consideration' in the form of knowledge revealed in the specification, it

36. D Dickson, 'UK Clinical Geneticists ask for Ban on Patenting of Human Genes'
     (1993) 366 *Nature* 391.
37. See eg P E Montague, 'Biotechnology Patents and the Problem of Obviousness'
     (1993) 4 *AIPJ* 3.
38. See [12.23]–[12.24].
39. C J Bannon, *Australian Patent Law*, 1984, p 54.
40. K Percy, 'The Obvious Difference' (1988) 334 *Nature* 21 reviewing S A Bent,
     R L Schwaab, D G Conlin and D D Jeffrey, *Intellectual Property Rights in Biotechnology
     Worldwide*, 1987.

is inappropriate to allow patents for products produced by 'obvious' techniques, since to do so would tie up particular areas of technology and inhibit development by other firms. The NIH's patent applications discussed above have been characterised as 'basic science that does not meet the threshold requirements for a patent' by the top legal official of the Department of Health and Human Services, who vigorously opposed the filing of the applications.[41]

[15.11] Trade secret protection. An alternative to applying for a patent is to keep the invention secret and characterise it as confidential information, detestable as this option is to academic scientists who would wish to publish their work. Of course, if the technique or product is totally obvious then it would not be regarded by the law as a secret worth protecting. It would seem, however, that there is a gap between what is 'obvious' in the patent sense and obvious in the colloquial sense, so that an invention may be lacking an inventive step (obvious) but still not generally known and thus retain trade secret protection. It has been suggested that whereas in the US a patent has been granted for a transgenic mouse,[42] protection in England (and possibly Australia) may need to be secured by installing an electric fence.[43] The action for breach of confidence would thus be available should the secret 'jump the fence'. Disadvantages are seen with using trade secret protection, which in demanding secrecy would slow research, with inventors, academics and industrialists withholding knowledge to the detriment of the overall research community. Enforcing confidentiality may also have the effect of stifling debate and reducing public insight, which would predispose the research community to constant challenge by the misinformed, the mischievous and the malicious. Those seeking to pioneer genetic medicine might usefully reflect on the fate of the nuclear power industry and the consequences of failure to educate and inform a concerned public.[44]

[15.12] Litigation on patent claims. One of the best known examples of a patent being refused for the results of rDNA technology is Genentech's application for British patents in respect of tissue plasminogen activator (TPA).[45] TPA converts plasminogen into plasmin, the enzyme that breaks down fibrin clots formed during heart attacks. The potential market for this is enormous, as are the benefits of using it early in the treatment of coronary thrombosis. TPA is a protein occurring in very small amounts in the body and its DNA could be analysed and reproduced by rDNA methods. Genentech made 20 different claims, covering all known ways of making TPA. The Patent Court rejected its claims, as did the Court of Appeal, finding that TPA was not an invention, that the structure of the DNA was an unpatentable discovery, and that the product itself and its desirable

41. L Roberts, 'Top HHS Lawyer Seeks to Block NIH' *Science* (1992) 258, p 209.
42. See [15.16].
43. K Percy, 'The Obvious Difference' (1988) 334 *Nature* 21 at 22. Note, however, that Australia does not prohibit animal patents per se, and the EPO may be changing its attitude too: see H Garaghan, 'Europe Changes Tack on Transgenic Animals', *New Scientist*, 20 October 1990, p 5; and see further [15.16].
44. G Poste, 'The Case For Genomic Patenting' (1995) 378 *Nature* 534.
45. *Genentech Inc v Wellcome Foundation Ltd* [1989] RPC 147. See also R S Crespi, 'Claims on Tissue Plasminogen Activator' (1989) 337 *Nature* 317.

properties had been known already. Furthermore others in the field had recognised that it was desirable to produce TPA in quantities by rDNA methods. All the steps taken by Genentech in finding out the composition and applying that knowledge to produce the product were applications of known technology, and no step was inventive,[46] although a remarkable job involving laborious and costly effort had been achieved.[47] Another genetically engineered substance, recombinant erythropoietin (EPO), has been the subject of what has been described as 'one of biotechnology's longest-running battles'.[48] EPO is a kidney cell protein which stimulates bone marrow red blood cell production, with expected annual sales between US$250 million and US$1000 million. Two companies both laid claim to the product and the methods of producing it, but neither was found to have a clear right to patents over the product or the processes for obtaining it.

In what seems to be a contrasting decision to the *Genentech* case, claims to the Hepatitis C virus and products for detecting it have been upheld in the UK in *Chiron Corp v Organon Teknika Ltd (No 3)*[49] where the issue of inventiveness of a claim to a DNA sequence was central to the decision. Proceedings for revocation of the patent in Australia commenced with litigation on procedural aspects;[50] however, in September 1996, after several weeks of hearing in the Federal Court, the legal issues were left unresolved following a worldwide settlement between the parties. The patent concerns a product used in detecting the Hepatitis C virus by means of an immunoassay test kit using what is known to pathologists as the ELISA test, and also the DNA sequence of the virus itself, which was very difficult to isolate and too fragile to work with under normal conditions. The product is commercially valuable and of public importance since every blood donation used in transfusions in developed countries is tested using the kit.

> The claimed invention is not only valuable; it arose out of scientific investigation aimed at the identification of the Hepatitis C virus which, if not inventive in the relevant sense — a matter to be determined — was at any rate prolonged, expensive and sophisticated.[51]

The UK Court accepted that the claims for the Hepatitis C virus, the diagnostic kit developed using it, vaccines against the virus and tissue culture systems for propagating the virus were inventive. As in the *Genentech* case, many research groups were trying to solve the problem at around the same time, and some were using the ELISA technique (but had been unsuccessful). In *Chiron*, only one team in fact achieved the goal and had shown exceptional talent in overcoming a previously insoluble problem.

[15.13] **Structural problems.** There are other problems associated with obtaining patent protection for biotechnological developments and these have to do with the structure of the biotechnology industry, which is composed of a large number of small venture capital companies. This contrasts with the pharmaceutical industry, which is made up of a small number of

46. Ibid at 242–8, 276, 286.
47. Ibid at 280.
48. D Genshon, 'Court Battle Ends at the Start' (1989) 342 *Nature* 846. See further [22.26].
49. [1994] FSR 202.
50. *Murex Diagnostics Australia Pty Ltd v Chiron Corp* (1995) 30 IPR 277.
51. Ibid at 279.

giant multi-nationals. Since the biotechnology companies do not have the capability at present to launch products on the market themselves, the products are typically licensed out to pharmaceutical companies on terms that are not always favourable to the smaller concern. The small companies may often be faced with the choice between bankruptcy and being taken over by larger companies or becoming mere contract research centres for the pharmaceutical giants. One of the major expenses facing these firms is the cost of obtaining and litigating patent rights. The problems are increased by the market power techniques of patent consolidation and 'patent blitzkrieg'[52] employed by big companies. This involves gaining control of key patents through research and development and also through buying up such patents, which may mean the purchase of the companies engaged in the research holding the relevant patents. Abjuring the realm of patent protection and relying on trade secret protection may be the sensible solution for small companies in such an environment. However, if others are patenting the technology then these firms may not be able to avoid infringement. It is obvious that the system is ill-suited to protect ideas and research at an early stage, particularly when the holder of the information is not a large company experienced at playing the patent game.

[15.14] Patenting life forms in Australia: micro-organisms. So far as Australia is concerned, inventions involving the use of micro-organisms are patentable under normal principles. The Australian Patent Office's practice rests upon the decision in *Rank Hovis McDougall Ltd's Application*,[53] where the Commissioner allowed the patenting of a process for isolating a micro-organism and of the variations in the organism induced by the inventor, although the organism itself could not be protected because it occurred naturally and was not therefore novel. Barry Jones, then Federal Science Minister, noted in the second reading speech for the Patents Amendment Bill 1984 that the Patent Office had long regarded biological processes and micro-organisms themselves as patentable, provided they satisfied the usual preconditions for obtaining a patent: that is, they must be novel and inventive, industrially useful and fully described in the patent specification.[54] The 1984 amendments gave effect to the provisions of the Budapest Treaty on the International Recognition of the Deposit of Micro-Organisms for the Purposes of Patent Procedure, signed on 28 April 1977. As noted in an earlier chapter, this provides for the deposit of new strains in recognised culture collections to be made available to the public, in order to fulfil the full and sufficient disclosure requirements.[55] Such disclosure is regarded by some as too extensive, 'superdisclosure' in fact, leaving the owner of the micro-organism nothing to sell in the form of 'know-how'.[56]

[15.15] Other higher life forms. The concept of invention in Australian patent law embraces more complex life forms than micro-organisms, although there is a prohibition in s 18(2) on patenting human beings and

52. R Dunford, 'Is the Development of Technology Helped or Hindered by Patent Law — Can Antitrust Laws Provide the Solution?' (1986) 9 *UNSWLJ* 117.
53. (1976) 46 AOJP 3915.
54. *Hansard*, Commonwealth Parliament Debates, HR, 28 March 1984, p 897.
55. See [12.27] and see further [21.28].
56. See W L Casey and L S Moss, 'Intellectual Property Rights and Biotechnology' (1987) 4 *IDEA* 251.

biological methods of producing them. 'Invention' is of such a 'wide, elastic and amorphous character as to cover almost all newly-created subject matters or processes, provided that the conditions otherwise specified in the Act are met'.[57] The early attitude that any invention of medical, agricultural or horticultural significance could not be patented has been modified in favour of a much more liberal patenting policy.[58] In 1988 the Australian Patent Office received its first patent application from a German company, Transgene, to cover a method developed to produce new animals through recombinant DNA technology. This was soon followed by a report that an Adelaide University research group was seeking a patent for a transgenic pig.[59] The transgenic pig is capable of reaching market weight seven weeks earlier than normal pigs, resulting from the presence in its cells of a second copy of a normal pig growth hormone gene. The economic rewards for more efficient pork, lamb and wool production are potentially enormous if Australia can maintain its world leadership in transgenic technology. Obviously, corporate executives investing tens of millions of dollars in the development of new animals with the expectation of being provided with a degree of market exclusivity through the granting of a patent may be disappointed if patenting of such material is not allowed, or it is at least uncertain as to whether a patent application will be successful. It has been suggested that new forms of animal may be more appropriately protected by a form of 'animal breeder's rights'.[60] The patents proceeded to grant but there has been considerable consumer resistance to the transgenic pork and it has not been commercially successful, with at least one large supermarket chain refusing to stock the meat.

[15.16] The debate overseas. Section 51(3) of the UK Patents Act 1977 excludes from patentability 'any variety of animal or plant, or any essentially biological process for the production of animals or plants, not being a microbiological process or the product of such a process'. This provision is replicated in Art 53 of the European Patent Convention, although the TRIPS Agreement in Art 27.2 is not so restrictive and would allow animals to be patented according to the usual criteria of validity. In 1988 WIPO issued an expert opinion deciding that any international harmonisation of patent laws (on which the organisation has been working since 1977) should exclude animal varieties from patent protection in the same terms as the UK legislation and European Patent Convention.[61] However, the view espoused in the European Patent Convention has effectively been challenged by the European Commission, the executive body of the

---

57. J G Starke, 'The Patenting of Animal Forms with New Traits' (1987) 61 *ALJ* 324 at 325–6. See also Patent Office Notice (1980) 50 AOJP 1162 which states: 'The criteria to be met before an application concerned with living organisms will be accepted are precisely the same as those for any other application, ie no distinction is to be made solely on the basis that a claimed product or process is, or contains or uses, a living organism. Higher life-forms will not be treated any differently from lower life-forms such as micro-organisms.'
58. See [12.3]–[12.4].
59. 'This Little (Transgenic) Piggy Goes to Market', *Sydney Morning Herald*, 15 April 1988, p 1.
60. N Peace and A Christie, 'Intellectual Property Protection for the Products of Animal Breeding' [1996] 4 *EIPR* 213.
61. 'No Animal Patents Please, We're European', *New Scientist*, 26 August 1989, p 11.

European Community, which has issued a proposal calling for more patent
protection of biotechnological discoveries, including animals and plants
altered through genetic engineering.[62] This was extremely controversial,
given that 13 countries are signatories to the Convention. West Germany in
particular has been exceptionally sensitive to the ethics of any manipulation of life. In fact, suggested amendments to the EC Directive on Biotechnological Inventions would go much further and ban patenting human
genes and gene therapies altogether.[63]

The anti-patenting stance taken by British and European authorities, not
to mention WIPO, has by no means attracted universal support. In 1987 the
US Patent Office announced that it would allow non-naturally occurring
non-human multicellular living organisms (including animals) to be patentable subject matter. The first patent application was for the 'Harvard
Mouse' (an oncomouse, that is a mouse with a modified gene making it very
susceptible to cancer-causing agents) thus highlighting important legal and
ideological differences between Europe and the US in this respect. In June
1989 the European Patent Office in Munich rejected an application to patent the oncomouse, but in May 1992 the EPO finally granted a patent for
the mouse, following lengthy talks between the applicants and the EPO.
This first European patent for a transgenic animal caused distress among
animal welfare groups which called for the patent to be revoked, and led to
debate within the European Parliament, resulting in major amendments to
the draft Directive, referred to above. The Green and animal welfare lobby-
ists have made a point of opposing patents for animals, plants or genetic
sequences,[64] including applications from Australian researchers.[65]

[15.17] The ethical dimension. Restrictions on the subject matter of
patenting are only one form of regulation concerning the ownership and
manipulation of life. Any sort of genetic manipulation is closely monitored.
In a parliamentary debate in Germany in 1989, for instance, a Green Party
member demanded that all genetic engineering be banned because it
could be 'even more of a threat to mankind than nuclear energy'.[66] This
type of comment highlights the important ethical dimension to the present
debate as to the wisdom or desirability of patenting higher life forms.[67]
Those who are increasingly voicing moral and ethical concerns on this
issue are by no means confined to Europe. In the United States a coalition
of animal welfare and public policy groups led by the Humane Society has
been formed to oppose the policy of patenting genetically engineered
animals that do fulfil the criteria of being non-obvious 'inventions'. The

62. See R Whaite and N Jones, 'Biotechnological Patents in Europe — The Draft
    Directive' [1989] 5 *EIPR* 145. The Draft Directive recommends a narrow
    interpretation of Art 53(b) so that 'variety' and 'biological process' are not taken to
    include animals produced by means other than classical breeding processes, thus
    allowing patenting of many genetically engineered higher life forms. See
    'Oncomouse Seeks European Protection' (1989) 340 *Nature* 85.
63. R Nott, 'The Proposed Directive on Biotechnological Inventions' [1994] 5 *EIPR* 191.
64. A Abbott, 'EPO Rejects bid to Revoke First Plant Patent' (1992) 357 *Nature* 525.
65. L Dayton, 'A Precarious Climb on the DNA Ladder', *Sydney Morning Herald*, 7
    January 1995, p 14.
66. 'Genetic Engineering: West Germany Eases Law' (1989) 340 *Nature* 85.
67. See eg A Wells, 'Patenting New Life Forms: An Ecological Perspective' [1994]
    3 *EIPR* 111.

major objection is that 'the entire creative process in higher forms of life, including human life, is going to be redirected or controlled to satisfy purely human ends'.[68] In the same vein, animal liberationists in Australia have described the patenting of animal breeds as 'an imperialistic and material-istic attitude towards living beings that denies any recognition of their inherent nature' and which may result in increased suffering: for example, chickens bred to grow so fast that their legs collapse or break, and 'super' pigs with genetic faults such as leg weaknesses, stomach ulcers and soft exu-dative flesh.[69] Religious groups voice similar concerns with regard to the protection and sanctity of human life, as do philosophers.[70] These fears may turn out to be well grounded, as the patenting of human life forms has been countenanced by the US Commissioner of Patents;[71] although as noted above that possibility has now been precluded in Australia by s 18(2) of the Patents Act 1990. It is not to be denied that there would be enor-mous value to society in the cloning of human genetic material to produce, for example, insulin or other products which could cure cancer, Alzheimer's disease or AIDS. However, it remains to be seen whether the price that is arguably paid in moral terms for such advances proves to be too high.

3. PLANT BREEDER'S RIGHTS

[15.18] Uses of plant varieties. The application of biotechnology to plants has already resulted in 'designer' vegetables and grains being 'manu-factured' so that gourmands may now enjoy crunchier carrots, meatier tomatoes and even beverages made from a hybrid coffee-cocoa bean.[72] The other big advantage is that of disease-free or even frost-resistant crops, as well as more uniform tasting food. In order to achieve these results, tissue culture techniques and gene mapping are used to grow whole plants from single cells. Recombinant DNA technology is also being used to create new genetic strains, perhaps combining species into new sorts of material or inserting genes to produce or enhance particular characteristics. For exam-ple, the 'Flavr Savr' tomato has a 'mirror image' of the gene that controls softening to allow the fruit to ripen longer on the vine without softening. These developments are opposed just as vigorously as those relating to the manipulation of animals and their genes through biotechnological tech-niques.[73] The 'Flavr Savr' tomato, approved for sale in the US in May 1994, has as a result of its genetic alteration become resistant to certain antibiot-ics. It is feared that this resistance may be passed on to humans who eat the tomato and a consumer boycott of the product (and others of Campbell Co which developed the tomato) has been urged by activist Jeremy Rivkin.[74]

---

68. *New York Times*, 17 April 1987, p D15.
69. C Townend, Letter to the Editor, *Sydney Morning Herald*, 24 February 1988, p 18.
70. See N Perlas, 'Biotechnology and Anthroposophy' [1987] *J of Anthroposophy* 5; J Rivkin, quoted in C Wallis, 'Should Animals be Patented?', *Time Australia*, 4 May 1987, p 74.
71. D Quigg, as reported on *Compass* (ABC Television), 22 May 1988.
72. K Springen, 'Improving on Mother Nature', *Bulletin and Newsweek*, 27 January 1987, p 99.
73. See N Perlas, *Biotechnology and Anthroposophy*, 1987, p 54.
74. C Ripe, '"Flavr Savrs" spell disaster', *The Weekend Australian*, 27–28 March 1993, Review, p 6.

However, the major pharmaceutical and chemical companies are realising the commercial value of plant varieties with desirable traits and have spent billions of dollars buying up or entering into research and joint ventures with seed companies.[75] To take one example, in 1990 an Australian company, Calgene Pacific Pty Ltd, entered into a joint venture with the huge Japanese brewing company Suntory Ltd, which is a big investor in research in biotechnology and pharmacology. The deal is intended to result in the production of a blue rose produced by transferring a gene for blue colour, taken from a petunia, to a rose, without changing the shape or smell. The blue rose should be on the market by 1997 and is expected to sell for about $100 per stem, the figure that market research has indicated that Japanese purchasers would be willing to pay. Roses account for about 20% of all cut flowers sold, with a worldwide market of more than $1.6 billion. Calgene has estimated that the wholesale market for a blue rose would be worth about $300 million. Other research into the colour manipulation of flowers is concentrated on gerberas, carnations and chrysanthemums, which are the top selling cut flowers along with the rose.[76] Further examples of the use of biotechnology involve disease-free plants. Each year about 40% of crops worldwide are lost to disease.[77] Chemical sprays are expensive, may be difficult to apply and are environmentally undesirable, apart from which they do not effectively combat bacteria and viruses. To meet that problem, disease-resistant crops are being developed through genetic engineering. For instance, Monsanto has developed tomatoes, petunias and tobacco plants with disease-resisting traits; and the US Department of Agriculture has produced a variety of peach tree which resists the previously lethal and incurable leaf spot disease.[78]

[15.19] Patent protection. The large corporations who increasingly control the plant industry have agitated for legal protection for this sort of technology. Unlike the UK and European patent legislation mentioned earlier, Australian patent law does not deny protection to plant varieties. Some plant breeding techniques are plainly suitable for patenting, including tissue culture, cell and protoplast culture and genetic engineering techniques, and several patents involving the introduction of new genetic information into plants have been granted in Australia. The Patent Office has also been prepared to allow patents to be obtained in respect of new varieties, so long as they meet the criteria of novelty and industrial applicability (that is, there must be a manner of new manufacture), and so long as the application shows human intervention to produce a non-obvious and non-naturally occurring result.[79]

---

75. A Christie, 'Patents for Plant Innovation' [1989] 11 *EIPR* 394.
76. M Skulley, 'Local Company Heads the Search for the Blue Rose', *Sydney Morning Herald*, 21 May 1990, p 30.
77. K Springen, 'Improving on Mother Nature', *Bulletin and Newsweek*, 27 January 1987, p 99.
78. Ibid.
79. Australian Patent Office, *Background Paper on Australian Patents for Plants*, 1989. This explains how the Australian Patent Office applies the criteria of the Patents Act to plant material, including the satisfaction of s 40 requirements as to description of the variety which involve lodging photographs, supplying an anatomical description of the plant and providing a distinction of the plant from related varieties.

In 1989 the American company Lubrizol obtained the first European patent for a method of genetically engineering plants. The method involves inserting a gene which boosts the ability to store proteins and the company has applied the technique to the fodder plant alfalfa, although almost any plant could be altered in the same way. A legal challenge was mounted to this, on the basis that the European Patent Convention does not allow patents for plant varieties. The European Patent Office was of the opinion that the claim was for a technique, rather than a variety of alfalfa as such, and was therefore patentable (the view the Australian Patent Office takes). The opposing party, a Swedish political group, claimed that the granting of such a patent was an 'outrageous' attempt to 'force new principles of intellectual property rights through a system that was not devised for that purpose'.[80]

[15.20]   Plant Breeder's Rights Act 1994. Protection for new plants is also available under specific legislation which does not require the plant or method of producing it to be novel, inventive or otherwise fulfil the onerous criteria of patentability. The Plant Breeder's Rights Act 1994 replaced the Plant Variety Rights Act 1987,[81] which was based on the International Convention for the Protection of New Varieties of Plants 1961 (UPOV). The drafters of UPOV in the early 1960s were concerned with protecting the results of conventional biological plant breeding. It was revised in 1991 in an attempt to bring the law into line with contemporary technological developments, and the Plant Breeder's Rights Act reflects the more up to date approach and ensures that Australian law still complies with the Convention. As originally worded, UPOV envisaged the patent and plant variety systems to be separate and mutually exclusive.[82] However, a revised text was signed in October 1978 which allowed countries to offer both patent and plant variety rights to the same invention if this was contemplated by domestic law at the time of ratification. This allowed the US and Australia, the only two countries to have dual protection, to join the Convention.[83]

[15.21]   What is a plant variety? A plant variety is defined in s 4 of the 1994 Act as a plant grouping (including a hybrid) contained within a single botanical taxon (classification) of the lowest known rank. A variety must be distinguishable from other varieties, and may be defined by genotype characteristics as expressed by the plant. There must be at least one expressed characteristic distinguishing the variety from other plant groupings. The plant must be able to be propagated unchanged, by sexual or asexual means beyond 'cloning'. Genetically modified plants are included, even when the genome has been altered by the introduction of non-plant genetic material (s 6). In order to be protected under the Act, a variety must also have been produced by 'breeding', since only a 'breeder' (or someone who is their successor in title) may apply for rights under the

---

80. S Kingman, 'Plant Patent Faces New Legal Challenge', *New Scientist,* 16 December 1989, p 4. Environmentalists and farmers continued the fight to have the patent revoked after the EPO rejected earlier attempts: A Abbott, 'EPO rejects bid to revoke first plant patent' (1992) 357 *Nature* 525.
81. The Plant Breeder's Rights Act 1994 took effect on 10 November 1994. Transitional provisions are set out in Pt 9.
82. A Christie, 'Patents for Plant Innovation' [1989] 11 *EIPR* 394 at 396.
83. See Cornish, p 519.

legislation.[84] 'Breeding', however, is defined to include 'the discovery of a plant together with its use in selective propagation so as to enable the development of the new plant variety' (s 5).

[15.22] Obtaining plant breeder's rights. The legislation operates in a way which is very similar to the patent system. Applications are made by breeders to the Secretary of the Department of Primary Industries and Energy (ss 24, 26), whose powers may be delegated to a Registrar of Plant Breeder's Rights (ss 58–59). The original application need only contain a brief description (and possibly a photograph) of a plant which is sufficient to establish a prima facie case that the variety is distinct from other varieties of common knowledge (s 26(2)(e)). However, if the application is accepted, the applicant must as soon as possible furnish a detailed description which will be made public (s 34). There are also requirements to deposit propagating material for the variety with an approved genetic resource centre (s 44(1)(b)(vii)), to supply a specimen plant to an official herbarium (s 44(2)), and to give the variety a name which complies with various requirements (s 27). As with patents, applications are given a priority date (ss 28–29) and a procedure is established for objections to rights being granted (s 35), as well as for revocation (s 50). In order to be registrable,[85] a variety must satisfy the following criteria (s 43):

- it must have a breeder;
- it must be 'distinct', in the sense of being clearly distinguishable from any other variety whose existence is a matter of common knowledge;
- it must be 'uniform' in its relevant characteristics on propagation;
- it must be 'stable' — its relevant characteristics must remain unchanged after repeated propagation; and
- it must not have been 'exploited' through the sale of propagating or harvested material in Australia more than a year before the date the application was lodged, or in another country that is also a member of UPOV more than four years before that date (six in the case of trees or vines).

If doubts arise as to whether a variety satisfies the legislative criteria, a test growing may be ordered (ss 37–38, 41).

[15.23] Scope of plant breeder's rights. The general nature of plant breeder's rights (PBR) is set out in s 11. PBR is the exclusive right to do, or license another person to do, any of the following in relation to propagating material of the variety: produce or reproduce that material; condition it for propagation; sell, import or export it; or stock it for any of the foregoing purposes. PBR covers certain 'dependent varieties' (s 13) of the initial variety, as well as material harvested or products created as a result of unauthorised production or reproduction of the propagating material (ss 14–15). It may also extend to 'essentially derived varieties' for which PBR has

---

84. Note that where a variety is bred by a person 'in the course of performing duties or functions as a member or employee of a body (whether corporate or unincorporate)', that body is taken to be the breeder (s 3(1)).
85. Note that certain varieties may be excluded by regulations from being registrable (s 42).

been obtained or sought by another person (ss 4, 12, 40). However, there are important limits to PBR:

- it is possible to experiment with protected plant varieties, to use them for breeding other varieties, and indeed to do anything with them of a private and non-commercial nature (which would presumably allow home gardeners to use the seed they gather from protected plants) (s 16);

- the 'farmer's privilege' or 'farm-saved seed exemption' allows farmers to harvest and use legitimately obtained seed (s 17);

- propagating material may be used as a food, food ingredient or fuel, or for any other purpose that does not involve production or reproduction of the material (s 18);

- 'reasonable public access' to protected plant varieties is required, something which is satisfied by making propagating material available free or at a reasonable price in sufficient quantities to meet demand (s 19);[86] and

- once propagating material has been sold by the right owner or with the right owner's consent, PBR is 'exhausted' to the extent that the material may lawfully be sold or imported thereafter, though it still cannot be used for further production or reproduction of the material (s 23).

The rights conferred by the Act subsist for 20 years, or for 25 years in the case of trees or vines, from the date of acceptance of the application (s 22). PBR is personal property (s 20), as is the right to apply for PBR (s 25).

PBR in a plant variety is infringed by (a) doing something which only the right owner is entitled to do under s 11, without that person's authority; (b) falsely claiming to have the right to do such a thing; or (c) using a protected variety's name for another variety or plant (s 53). An action for infringement of PBR may be commenced in the Federal Court; and again, just as under the patents system, the defendant may counterclaim for revocation (s 54). Where infringement is established the relief that the court may grant includes an injunction, and either damages or an account of profits at the plaintiff's option (s 56(3)). The latter remedies may be withheld where the defendant can establish that at the time of infringement they did not know of the existence of the rights in question and had no reasonable grounds for suspecting their existence; though where propagating material has been labelled to indicate the existence of PBR and sold to a substantial extent in Australia, such knowledge will be presumed unless the defendant can prove otherwise (s 57).

[15.24] Patents or plant breeder's rights? It has been seen that the fact that a patent application concerns living subject matter is not a barrier to patentability in Australia. Even before the High Court in the *NRDC* case[87] broadened the scope of patentable subject matter to include horticultural and agricultural processes, patents for processes involving microorganisms had been granted. Thus, as discussed above, patent protection is to some extent available for plant varieties under Australian law. There is

---

86. If this is not done, a compulsory licence to sell or produce propagating material may be granted (s 19(3)–(10)).
87. (1959) 102 CLR 252: see [12.3]–[12.4].

growing recognition that the patent system is indeed better equipped to protect plant biotechnology, with the plant variety rights system being more suited to the protection of plants at the varietal level. However, the incorporation of biotechnology in a plant variety, as in the Lubrizol patent which involved transfer of a gene boosting the ability to store protein,[88] gives rise to complications about the degree of protection provided by the plant variety rights system. Generally speaking, it is thought desirable to have both systems acting together to provide protection for plant biotechnology and its incorporation into marketable products: the plant varieties themselves. Retention of this dual system was indeed supported by a report commissioned by the Federal Government in 1990.[89] In theory, a plant breeder could apply for protection under both regimes, but in practical terms a choice is generally made, depending on the aspects of the innovation requiring protection and the scope of protection required.[90]

One advantage of the plant variety rights scheme is that the rights are relatively cheap and easy to secure, and may cover material not suited to patent protection, such as a naturally occurring breed (resulting from natural mutation) that someone 'discovers', or a variety produced by age-old breeding techniques. On the other hand, firms using advanced biotechnological methods may prefer to obtain patent rights, whereby techniques or processes can be protected instead of just the end-product. Moreover while the plant breeders rights legislation, as noted above, excuses a range of conduct that would otherwise amount to infringement, the patent monopoly is rather more extensive. The Patent Office has indicated that 'infringement of a patented plant variety occurs whenever use of a patented product or process is made, which would deprive a patentee of the natural profit and advantage of the invention'.[91] These uses include the sale of patented seed plant or plant products without the licence of the patentee, as well as the use of a patented gene in a way that is unavailable at the time of grant of the first patent (in which case the new use will only be available upon obtaining a licence to use the patented gene for the new purpose). However, if bona fide experimentation produces a new variety from a patented variety, then no infringement occurs if the patented variety is not repeatedly used.

---

88. See [15.19].
89. N J Byrne, *Legal Protection of Plants in Australia under Patent and Plant Variety Rights Legislation*, 1990.
90. S Irvine, 'Intellectual Property Protection for Plant Innovations in Australia', *Blake Dawson Waldron Reporter,* April 1990, p 10 at p 14; see also R B Jarvis, 'Plant Patent, Plant Variety Right — or Both?' (1993) 4 *AIPJ* 211.
91. *Background Paper on Australian Patents for Plants*, 1989, p 113.

PART V

Business Reputation

Chapter 16

Misappropriation of Business Reputation: General Principles

1. INTRODUCTION

[16.1] Business reputation as industrial property. The copyright, design and patent regimes each confer protection on the direct products of creative effort. Successful commercial use or exploitation of such effort in turn generates something which has come to be regarded as worthy of protection: the 'benefit and advantage of the good name, reputation and connection of a business … the attractive force which brings in custom'.[1] The ways in which the integrity of the connection between a business and its consumers may be safeguarded are the subject of this and the following chapters. The fact that this topic has traditionally been regarded as part of the framework of intellectual property regulation is further evidence of the emphasis given in Anglo-Australian law to encouraging and protecting commercial investment in intellectual effort, as much if not more than such effort itself.

[16.2] History. However, while the modern law in regard to business reputation can conveniently be rationalised by treating such reputation as 'industrial property', and thus akin to patents and designs in particular, the history of its development tells a rather different story.[2] In its early stages the emphasis was very much on preventing or punishing fraudulent business practices. The fact that this benefited merchants whose goodwill was damaged by such practices seems not to have been the dominant concern of the courts, who were doing little more than extending established notions of right and wrong into the commercial arena.[3] Likewise the

---

1. *Inland Revenue Commissioners v Muller & Co's Margarine Ltd* [1901] AC 217 at 223–4.
2. See Cornish, pp 393–5.

current emphasis on consumer protection, which in the last 30 years has come to pervade much of the relevant law, sees injured traders more or less as incidental beneficiaries of regulation designed to ensure that the public is not disadvantaged by deceptive marketing.[4]

Nevertheless, the notion that traders should be recognised as having some proprietary interest in the goodwill built up by their efforts was plainly influential in the formative period in the mid- to late nineteenth century. Up to this point the tort of 'passing off' had been confined to fraudulent attempts by traders to pass off their goods as those of another. The equity courts, ultimately analysing the injured trader's interest as proprietary in nature, effectively extended the tort by being willing to grant injunctions to restrain such conduct even in the absence of malice.[5] The emphasis thus shifted, if not entirely away from the wrongful conduct of the deceptive trader, at least towards the concept of rights attaching to the 'marks' used by traders to identify their goods. Against this background, it was entirely natural for the British parliament to respond to calls for greater protection against imitators by establishing a system for the registration of trade marks rather than by proscribing a wider range of competitive practices.[6] The trade mark system, subsequently adopted in Australia, allows the proprietor of a distinctive mark to acquire a monopoly over its use and is described in detail in Chapters 19–20.

[16.3] **Modern scope of the common law.** The enactment of trade marks legislation did not by any means see the end of common law development in relation to the protection of business reputation. For one thing, the fact that a mark has been or may be registered does not preclude action being taken in passing off to protect it.[7] More importantly, the tort was steadily expanded by the courts beyond the original situation which produced its name. Instead of traders being perceived as having property in a particular mark or name, the action was ultimately rationalised as protecting a proprietary right in the *goodwill* built up by the use of that mark or name, or indeed by any other means.[8] As matters now stand, the tort comes close to encompassing all forms of deceptive misappropriation by one trader of another's reputation. Nevertheless the tort has in the most important respect remained close to its roots, in that it is still necessary to identify

---

3.   See eg *Southern v How* (1618) Pop 143; 79 ER 1243.
4.   See [16.38].
5.   See eg *Millington v Fox* (1838) 3 My & Cr 338; 40 ER 956; *Edelsten v Edelsten* (1863) 1 De G J & S 185; 46 ER 72.
6.   See Trade Marks Registration Act 1875 (UK).
7.   *Great Tower Street Tea Co v Langford & Co* (1888) 5 RPC; and see Trade Marks Act 1995 (Cth) s 230(1). Note also that, so long as the elements of passing off are otherwise established, an action may be maintained against the user of a registered mark notwithstanding their statutory rights: *Van Zeller v Mason Cattley* (1907) 25 RPC 37; *NSW Dairy Corp v Murray Goulburn Co-op Co Ltd* (1989) 14 IPR 26 at 48. Cf Trade Marks Act 1995 (Cth) s 230(2), which effectively confirms the right to sue in passing off while limiting the damages recoverable where a registered mark is involved (see [16.19]).
8.   *A G Spalding & Bros v A W Gamage Ltd* (1915) 32 RPC 273 at 284; *Star Industrial Co Ltd v Yap Kwee Kor* [1976] FSR 256 at 269. The term 'goodwill' has a broader meaning in this context than the one it may carry for the purposes of revenue law: *Conagra Inc v McCain Foods (Aust) Pty Ltd* (1992) 23 IPR 193 at 231–2, 265; and see further [17.13].

a misrepresentation by the offending trader. As Lockhart J put it in *Conagra Inc v McCain Foods (Aust) Pty Ltd*:[9]

> [T]he basis of the cause of action lies squarely in misrepresentation, for its underlying rationale is to prevent commercial dishonesty. The tort of passing off protects the business of the plaintiff with its many facets: its assets, goodwill and reputation. It stops persons gaining a commercial advantage through wrongfully taking the attributes of another's business if it causes or is likely to cause that other person's business some damage.

Despite (mostly covert) attempts by some judges to fashion a broader tort, the requirement of misrepresentation means that non-deceptive appropriation of reputation still remains largely untouched by the common law.[10]

On the other hand, although misrepresentation or deception is a necessary element in the tort of passing off, it is not sufficient in itself. The tort does not, for example, encompass statements by one business about a competitor's product which, although false, do not imply any connection between the two businesses. Such statements are instead the realm of the tort of injurious falsehood.[11] However, that cause of action has remained much more limited than passing off in important respects. For one thing, the courts have been unwilling to forgo the need for malice to be established on the part of the defendant, who must be shown either to have been aware of the statement's falsity or to have intended to damage the plaintiff.[12] The statement must also relate to the plaintiff or the plaintiff's product. This means that deliberately false descriptions of the defendant's own product are not actionable, even if they damage the plaintiff by drawing away trade.[13] These limitations, together with a determination to disregard 'puffery' or patently hyperbolic claims,[14] have ensured that it is only in the most exceptional cases under the common law that the courts have become embroiled in judging the quality or competing claims of businesses and their products and services.

[16.4] Emphasis on misappropriation. Those functions are now conferred upon by the courts in unequivocal terms by Pt V of the Trade Practices Act 1974 and by equivalent state legislation, which cover a broad range of misrepresentations made in the course of trade. Nevertheless, this and the following chapters are confined to examining passing off and those statutory provisions (principally s 52 of the 1974 Act) which deal with comparable types of wrongdoing, rather than all facets of competitive misbehaviour. In one sense this might be regarded as illogical. The modern law of passing off and of trade marks is concerned first and foremost with marketing. In that light it seems strange to exclude consideration of the legality of all marketing practices, deceptive and otherwise, which injure another trader's goodwill. However, as noted in the first chapter, if there is a theme which links the areas traditionally treated as falling under the rubric 'intellectual and industrial property', it is that of 'reaping without sowing', or *misappropriation* of another's effort. Accordingly, attention is confined to those

---

9.   (1992) 23 IPR 193 at 231.
10.   See [16.20]ff.
11.   See Ricketson, pp 588–91; Cornish, pp 427–31.
12.   *Wilts United Dairies Ltd v Thomas Robinson Sons & Co Ltd* [1957] RPC 222 at 237.
13.   *White v Mellin* [1895] AC 154.
14.   See eg *De Beers Abrasive Products Ltd v International General Electric Co of New York Ltd* [1975] 1 WLR 972. Cf *Schindler Lifts Australia Pty Ltd v Debelak* (1989) 15 IPR 129.

commercial practices which seek to appropriate someone else's goodwill, as opposed to the wider range of conduct that may directly or indirectly involve injury to that goodwill. The treatment commences by outlining the two heads of liability principally invoked in misappropriation cases, the tort of passing off and the statutory prohibition on misleading or deceptive conduct. This is followed in subsequent chapters by an analysis of various issues or difficulties that may arise when a plaintiff seeks in either context to establish a protectable reputation and the existence or threat of deceptive conduct.

2.   THE TORT OF PASSING OFF

[16.5]   The basic requirements. Few judges have had the temerity to attempt a complete definition of the tort of passing off. Indeed it has been said that the law 'contains sufficient nooks and crannies to make it difficult to formulate any satisfactory definition in short form'.[15] Nevertheless, reference is often made to the five characteristics indicated by Lord Diplock in the *Advocaat* case[16] to be required of a successful action:

> (1) a misrepresentation; (2) made by a trader in the course of trade; (3) to prospective customers of his [sic] or ultimate consumers of his goods or services supplied by him; (4) which is calculated to injure the business or goodwill of another trader (in the sense that this is a reasonably foreseeable consequence); and (5) which causes actual damage to a business or goodwill of the trader by whom the action is brought or (in a quia timet action) will probably do so.

The fact that this is not a complete definition, a point stressed by Lord Diplock himself, detracts from its usefulness; and even within its own terms it appears to be inaccurate, with the third requirement in particular being unduly restrictive.[17] Nonetheless it is helpful in emphasising the three key elements in a passing off suit, sometimes described as the 'classical trinity'.[18] These are (a) the subsistence of some reputation or goodwill on the part of the plaintiff; (b) deceptive conduct on the part of the defendant; and (c) the existence or threat of damage to the plaintiff as a result of that conduct.[19]

(a) Reputation

[16.6]   General. Over the years the courts have taken a liberal view both as to the persons who may be said to possess a protectable reputation and as to the material to which that goodwill may attach. As to the former, virtually any form of even vaguely 'commercial' activity may suffice to attract protection. It has been held, for instance, that professional associations[20]

---

15. *Conagra Inc v McCain Foods (Aust) Pty Ltd* (1992) 23 IPR 193 at 247.
16. *Erven Warnink v J Townsend & Sons (Hull) Ltd* [1979] AC 731 at 742.
17. See eg *Associated Newspapers plc v Insert Media Ltd* [1991] 1 WLR 571.
18. *Consorzio del Prosciutto di Parma v Marks & Spencer plc* [1991] RPC 351 at 368–9.
19. See also *Reckitt & Colman Products Ltd v Borden Inc* [1990] 1 WLR 491 at 499 where Lord Oliver constructed his own definition of passing off around these three elements. Although still incomplete (in the sense that the language used is directed to some but by no means all of the fact situations which the tort covers), it has been said by the Full Court of the Federal Court to provide a 'workable test': *Vieright Pty Ltd v Myer Stores Ltd* (1995) 31 IPR 361 at 369.
20. See eg *Australian Society of Accountants v Federation of Australian Accountants Inc* (1987) 9 IPR 282.

and even charities[21] may restrain persons from claiming accreditation from or affiliation with those bodies. Indeed in a recent case the New South Wales Court of Appeal went so far as to accept that for a church to call itself the 'Ancient Church of the East', a name associated with another church, could amount to passing off, on the basis that the latter's reputation was 'essentially indistinguishable from commercial goodwill'.[22]

As to the ways in which reputation may become fixed in the minds of the relevant section of the public, it has been noted that

> [T]he tort is no longer anchored, as in its early nineteenth century formulation, to the name or trade mark of a product or business. It is wide enough to encompass other descriptive material, such as slogans or visual images, which radio, television or newspaper advertising campaigns can lead the market to associate with a plaintiff's product, provided always that such descriptive material has become part of the goodwill of the product. And the test is whether the product has derived from the advertising a distinctive character which the market recognises.[23]

As this passage highlights, passing off is far from being merely concerned with common law trade marks. While a good many of the reported cases are still concerned with the names or devices used by the parties in relation to their products or businesses, as many more involve the 'get-up' or packaging of goods, or images created in the course of advertising. It is the existence of a reputation which counts: the means by which that reputation is garnered or exploited is relevant only to the factual issue of establishing whether any misappropriation has occurred.

[16.7] The source question. One important point the courts have stressed is that so long as the plaintiff can show that goodwill has been established, it does not matter that the plaintiff is personally unknown to the relevant consumers.[24] The plaintiff's identity is irrelevant, in other words, provided the public associate that product or business with a particular *source* which in fact turns out to be the plaintiff. Thus in a case where the public had over a number of years grown used to purchasing one brand only of 'Yorkshire Relish', its maker was entitled to restrain another firm from marketing a similar product under the same name, notwithstanding its own anonymity.[25] Nonetheless it would be a foolhardy business which, hoping to corner a new market, made no attempt to advertise its identity. In the *Yorkshire Relish* case the plaintiff had had the market to itself for a number of years. In the more fiercely competitive world of today, the trader who puts a new product or service on the market without aggressively marketing its connection thereto runs the risk that, before it has built up a distinctive reputation as the supplier of the product or service, imitators

---

21. See eg *Dr Barnardo's Homes v Barnardo Amalgamated Industries Ltd* (1949) 66 RPC 103.
22. *Holy Apostolic and Catholic Church of the East (Assyrian) Australia NSW Parish Association v Attorney-General (NSW); ex rel Elisha* (1989) 16 IPR 619 at 620. The court also indicated its dispproval of the decision in *Kean v McGiven* [1982] FSR 119 that a political party cannot bring such proceedings in similar circumstances.
23. *Cadbury Schweppes Pty Ltd v Pub Squash Pty Ltd* [1980] 2 NSWLR 851 at 858.
24. Thus it does not matter, for instance, that the plaintiff is known through a pseudonym: see eg *Landa v Greenberg* (1908) 24 TLR 441; *Sykes v John Fairfax & Sons Ltd* [1977] 1 NSWLR 415. Cf *Lovatt v Consolidated Magazines Pty Ltd* (1988) 12 IPR 261.
25. *Birmingham Vinegar Brewery Co Ltd v Powell* [1897] AC 710. See also *Emrik Sporting Goods Pty Ltd v Stellar International Sporting Goods Pty Ltd* (1981) 53 FLR 319; *Komesaroff v Mickle* [1987] VR 703.

will move in to take advantage of its success. This occurred in relation to the 'Rubik's Cube'. A successful marketing campaign created huge demand when this popular puzzle was first released. Its manufacturers and marketers, Politoys and Ideal respectively, subsequently sought to prevent cheap Taiwanese copies of the Cube being imported into Britain. However, their passing off action failed. Although the plaintiffs had created great interest in the Cube as a product, they had not done enough to associate it in the public's mind with a particular manufacturer: there was little to suggest that purchasers were aware that the Cube came from one source alone.[26]

[16.8] No need for individual exclusivity. Although the plaintiff must be identified by the relevant public as a source of the business in question, it is now recognised that the plaintiff need not be *the* source. The plaintiff may be just one of a number of traders who share a reputation, either because they are all part of a class of producers to whom goodwill attaches,[27] or because they have concurrently used a particular mark or name in such a way that it cannot be definitively identified with any one of them.[28] Nonetheless while they may not sue each other, they may all take independent action to protect their own interest.[29] The emergence of this principle has important ramifications where the use of a mark or name to which goodwill attaches is licensed to another, or where the product in question passes through the hands of a distributor. The licensee or distributor may wish to join in any action taken to protect the goodwill — possibly they may be the only plaintiff, where the original source is a foreign entity with no local business presence under its immediate control.[30] Traditionally, such intermediaries could only sue if they could show that the public had come to regard *them* as the source of the product, a process which would by definition exclude any rights formerly or ever possessed by the manufacturer or licensor.[31] Today, however, it seems that all those able to establish a commercial stake in the relevant business or product are allowed to bring proceedings, so long as they are more than a mere link in the distribution or retail chain.[32]

---

26. *Politechnika Ipari Szovetkezet v Dallas Print Transfers Inc* [1982] FSR 529. Note that the plaintiffs did, however, succeed in establishing infringement of copyright. Cf *John Engelander & Co Pty Ltd v Ideal Toy Corp* [1981] ATPR 40–218, where in similar proceedings in Australia, although the plaintiff was also unable to show deception, it seems to have been assumed the result would have been different if the defendant had not been as careful in adopting a distinctive name and packaging for its version of the Cube. For further discussion of the issue of 'source motivation', see *Tot Toys Ltd v Mitchell* [1993] 1 NZLR 325.

27. See [16.13].

28. See [16.41].

29. *GE Trade Mark* [1973] RPC 297 at 326; *Erven Warnink v J Townsend & Sons (Hull) Ltd* [1979] AC 731 at 742.

30. Cf [17.13].

31. See eg *Oertli AG v Bowman (London) Ltd* [1959] RPC I. Cf cases in which the licensor has been held to retain their goodwill: see eg *J H Coles Pty Ltd v Need* [1934] AC 82; *Apand Pty Ltd v Kettle Chip Co Pty Ltd* (1994) 30 IPR 337; *Ariaans v Hastings* (1996) 36 IPR 211.

32. See eg *Children's Television Workshop Inc v Woolworths (NSW) Pty Ltd* [1981] 1 NSWLR 273; *Erven Warnink v J Townsend & Sons (Hull) Ltd* [1979] AC 731; *Hutchence v South Seas Bubble Co Pty Ltd* (1986) 64 ALR 330; *Ocean Pacific Sunwear Ltd v Ocean Pacific Enterprises Pty Ltd* (1990) 17 IPR 405. Cf *Thai World Import & Export Co Ltd v Shuey Shing Pty Ltd* (1989) 17 IPR 289 at 296.

[16.9] Other issues relating to reputation. A range of other questions may arise when a plaintiff seeks to establish a protectable reputation. These include the location and duration of business activity needed to satisfy the requirements of the action, whether reputation may be claimed in 'descriptive' material or 'functional' elements, and whether there is any relevance in the plaintiff's reputation arising out of a different 'field of activity' to that in which the defendant is trading. Since these issues also tend to arise in regard to actions brought under the legislative provisions dealing with misleading or deceptive conduct, detailed discussion is left to the following chapter.

(b) Deception

[16.10] The relevance of intention to deceive. For liability to arise in passing off there must be a misrepresentation which is 'calculated to deceive' the relevant public.[33] Again, a more extensive analysis of the approaches taken by the courts to this question, and of the type of evidence required to be presented so as to establish deception, is deferred to Chapter 18. However, certain general points may be made at this juncture. The first is that, at least as far as injunctive relief is concerned, the plaintiff is not required to show that the defendant acted with an intention to deceive. It is enough that the behaviour in question may foreseeably produce deception. On the other hand, this does not mean that the defendant's intention is completely irrelevant. As will be seen, fraud must be established before substantial damages will be awarded.[34] More significantly, it has been stressed time and again that proof of an intention to deceive will carry the plaintiff a long way towards showing that the intent was successful.[35] As it was once said, 'if you find a defendant who is a knave, you may presume he [sic] is not a fool'.[36] This principle is particularly important in cases where the parties have similar products on the market, or use similar get-ups or names, and there is some doubt whether the plaintiff's product (or get-up or name) has acquired a distinctive reputation. There can be no question that proof of deliberate copying may tip the balance towards a finding that the defendant has taken advantage of an association already established in the mind of consumers between that particular product (or get-up or name) and the plaintiff's business.[37]

Nevertheless, there are limits to the use to which an established intent to copy can be put, as the Full Court of the Federal Court has emphasised in a number of cases over recent years. In *Conagra Inc v McCain Foods (Aust) Pty Ltd*[38] the defendant launched in Australia a range of 'Healthy Choice' frozen food products, having taken the name and idea from an established line of products in the United States. The US producer failed in its attempt to sue for passing off. It was held that even if it could be shown that the defendant was trying to 'dig a pit' in the path of a foreign trader's entry

---

33. *A G Spalding & Bros v A W Gamage Ltd* (1915) 32 RPC 273 at 284.
34. See [16.19].
35. See eg *Australian Woollen Mills Ltd v F S Walton & Co Ltd* (1937) 58 CLR 641 at 657; *Ronson Products Ltd v James Ronson Pty Ltd* [1957] VR 731 at 739–40; *Cadbury Schweppes Pty Ltd v Pub Squash Pty Ltd* [1980] 2 NSWLR 851 at 861.
36. *Claudius Ash, Sons & Co Ltd v Invicta Manufacturing Co Ltd* (1911) 28 RPC 597 at 603.
37. See eg *Telmak Teleproducts (Australia) Pty Ltd v Coles Myer Ltd* (1989) 15 IPR 362.
38. (1992) 23 IPR 193.

into the Australian market,[39] the plaintiff could not establish that it had developed a reputation for its products in this country. Without such a reputation to protect, no amount of wicked intent could create a cause of action.[40] In any event, as both Lockhart and Gummow JJ pointed out, the evidence did not establish that the defendant here intended to mislead the Australian public. As the former put it:[41]

> [D]eliberate copying of the plaintiff's goods does not always evidence an intention to deceive; it may indicate nothing more than realisation that the plaintiff has a useful idea which the defendant can turn to his [sic] own advantage, though not intending to pass off his goods as those of the plaintiff.

The same point was stressed in *Apand Pty Ltd v Kettle Chip Co Pty Ltd*,[42] dealing with 'continuously' or 'kettle' cooked potato chips. The defendant had adopted the name 'Country Kettle' for its product where previously the plaintiff and its licensees had been in the market with 'Kettle Chips'. The court accepted that the defendant's intention was to 'gain the benefit of the favourable impression shared by consumers that a "Kettle Chip" was a better chip produced by a different process than most mass produced chips; but not to lead people to believe that the [defendant's] product was linked or associated with the [plaintiff's] product'.[43] Thus no intent to deceive could be imputed to the defendant, though in this case the plaintiff did succeed in obtaining a declaration that passing off had occurred: unlike *Conagra*, the plaintiff had developed a reputation among the relevant group of consumers and it was found that the defendant's use of the term 'Kettle' in its product name might indeed mislead consumers into inferring a connection between the two traders.

[16.11] Types of misrepresentation. Perhaps the most significant aspect of the 'definition' of passing off given by Lord Diplock in the *Advocaat* case is that, while stressing that there must be a misrepresentation by the defendant, it does not indicate what *type* of misrepresentation is required. In some ways this is a wise omission. The history of the tort has been marked, as Deane J noted in *Moorgate Tobacco Co Ltd v Philip Morris Ltd (No 2)*,[44] by its adaptation

> to meet new circumstances involving the deceptive or confusing use of names, descriptive terms or other indicia to persuade purchasers or customers to believe that goods or services have an association, quality or endorsement which belongs or would belong to goods or services of, or associated with, another or others ...

The roots of this developmental process can be traced to Lord Halsbury's assertion in *Reddaway v Banham* that 'nobody has the right to *represent* his [sic] goods as the goods of somebody else'.[45] Prior to this, passing off had generally been regarded as the act of putting off goods for sale as those of a rival trader.[46] Whether intended or not, the reference to the need for a

---

39. See *Turner v General Motors (Australia) Pty Ltd* (1929) 42 CLR 352 at 364.
40. See further [17.13].
41. (1992) 23 IPR 193 at 236.
42. (1994) 30 IPR 337.
43. Ibid at 356–7. See also *Vieright Pty Ltd v Myer Stores Ltd* (1995) 31 IPR 361 at 370–1.
44. (1984) 156 CLR 414 at 445–6.
45. [1896] AC 199 at 204 (emphasis added).
46. See eg *Leather Cloth Co v American Leather Cloth Co* (1865) 11 HLC 523 at 538; 11 ER 1435 at 1442.

representation opened the way for the courts to expand the doctrine, since the tort could be extended to cover situations where other types of representation were made.[47] In the 'classic' situation for which the tort was developed, the defendant's (mis)representation is effectively 'the plaintiff manufactured these goods'. Over time, however, each of the elements of that representation came to be seen as replaceable. For example, the representation might be 'the plaintiff was responsible for these services'; or, in a more complex variation, 'the plaintiff produced the original sketch on which this film is based'.[48]

Although the creation of a belief that the defendant's product is that of the plaintiff has remained the paradigm of passing off, the tort has now come to cover virtually all situations where the defendant expressly or implicitly misrepresents the existence or scope of some connection between its business and that of the plaintiff.[49] Thus it has been applied where a name or marketing device used by the defendant would lead consumers to infer some affiliation with or sponsorship by the plaintiff;[50] where the defendant markets one class of the plaintiff's product as if it were another;[51] and in situations of 'inverse' passing off, where a product of the plaintiff is represented to be that of the defendant (rather than the other way around, which is more usually the case).[52]

[16.12]   Misrepresentations as to quality. A development which illustrates the expansion of the tort, and which has attracted particular comment, relates to the situation where the defendant falsely claims that its product or business possesses a certain quality. Ordinarily this would be a matter only for the legislative restrictions on deceptive trading. However, if the quality is one which is in fact distinctively possessed by the plaintiff, it is possible to spell out of the defendant's conduct a misrepresentation as to a link with the plaintiff which does not exist, viz, common membership of that class of products or businesses in exclusive possession of the relevant quality. Viewed in that way, there can be little doubt that passing off has occurred. This proposition was not accepted without some hesitation and a number of earlier decisions appeared to be plainly against it.[53] However, it could be detected in cases in which a product had been represented as having been tested and sold,[54] or as being 'as shown on television',[55] the products which satisfied the description in fact being those of the plaintiff.

---

47.   See generally W L Morison, 'Unfair Competition and "Passing Off": The Flexibility of a Formula' (1956) 2 *Syd LR* 50.
48.   See eg *Samuelson v Producers Distributing Co Ltd* [1932] 1 Ch 201.
49.   As to the possibility of a person being liable for misrepresenting a connection between the plaintiff and *someone else's* business (as for example in the case of an innocent retailer of a deceptively similar product), see [18.2].
50.   See eg *Walter v Ashton* [1902] 2 Ch 282; *Harrods Ltd v R Harrod Ltd* (1924) 41 RPC 74; *Henderson v Radio Corp Pty Ltd* (1960) 60 SR (NSW) 576.
51.   See eg *A G Spalding & Bros v A W Gamage Ltd* (1915) 32 RPC 273.
52.   See eg *Testro Bros v Tennant* (1984) 2 IPR 469; *Bristol Conservatories Ltd v Conservatories Custom Built Ltd* [1989] RPC 455.
53.   See eg *Tallerman v Dowsing Radiant Heat Co* [1900] 1 Ch 1; *Cambridge University Press v University Tutorial Press* (1928) 45 RPC 335.
54.   *Plomien Fuel Economiser Co Ltd v National School of Salesmanship Ltd* (1943) 60 RPC 209.
55.   *Copydex Ltd v Noso Products Ltd* (1952) 69 RPC 38.

[16.13] The Spanish Champagne case. Nevertheless, despite being logically capable of accommodation within existing principles of passing off, it was only as a result of a series of English cases involving wines and spirits that this type of behaviour was unambiguously identified as actionable. The most famous of these involved 'Spanish Champagne', a sparkling wine made in Spain and marketed by the defendant. The plaintiffs, Bollinger and 11 other producers from the Champagne district in France, sought an injunction restraining the sale of this wine, contending that the public were being deceived into thinking that it was the 'genuine article' — wine produced in the Champagne district by the true 'methode champenoise'. In a preliminary decision Danckwerts J held that if the plaintiffs could indeed establish that consumers would be deceived in this way they would have a good cause of action. The defendant simply had no right to attach to its product a description which was part of the plaintiffs' goodwill.[56] It was subsequently found that a significant number of people would indeed be deceived by the name. Although any real wine buff would be aware that the Champagne district is in France and would thus be alerted by the term 'Spanish' that this was a different product, this could not be said of the many persons 'whose life or education has not taught them much about the nature and production of wine' and who wanted to experience a taste of the famous champagne.[57]

One significant point to emerge from the decision was that a group of plaintiffs may sue as and on behalf of a class of producers, notwithstanding that other members of that class are not represented.[58] More importantly, however, the decision confirmed that it is unlawful to misappropriate a person's goodwill by falsely claiming for one's product a quality which is exclusively possessed by that other, even though no false statement is directly made about the plaintiff's business. This proposition was subsequently reaffirmed in a range of English cases involving other wines or spirits, including the House of Lords' decision in *Advocaat*.[59] There seems no reason not to regard it as of general application.

[16.14] Geographical indications of wines: special legislation. It is convenient at this point to mention the provisions of Pt VIB of the Australian Wine and Brandy Corporation Act 1980 (Cth), introduced in 1993 to give effect to Australia's bilateral agreement with the European Community on appellations of origin for wine.[60] The main purpose of

56. *J Bollinger v Costa Brava Wine Co Ltd* [1960] Ch 263.
57. *J Bollinger v Costa Brava Wine Co Ltd (No 2)* [1961] 1 All ER 561 at 567. A similar (though more dubious) conclusion has more recently been reached by the English Court of Appeal in relation to the marketing of a non-alcoholic carbonated drink known as 'Elderflower Champagne': *Taittinger v Allbev Ltd* [1994] 4 All ER 75.
58. See also *Erven Warnink v J Townsend & Sons (Hull) Ltd* [1979] AC 731; *Scott v Tuff-Kote (Australia) Pty Ltd* [1975] 1 NSWLR 537.
59. *Erven Warnink v J Townsend & Sons (Hull) Ltd* [1979] AC 731. See also *Vine Products Ltd v MacKenzie* [1969] RPC 1 (sherry); *John Walker & Sons v Henry Ost & Co Ltd* [1970] RPC 489 (scotch whisky).
60. See D Ryan, 'The Protection of Geographical Indications in Australia under the EC/Australia Wine Agreement' [1994] 12 *EIPR* 521; M Wallman, 'Recent Developments in Australian Intellectual Property Law: The Protection of Geographical Indications of Wines' (1994) 5 *AIPJ* 113; and see further [19.31], [21.38].

the Wine Agreement was to bring to an end the common practice in this country of using established European (and especially French) terms, generally derived from specific localities, to denote certain styles of wine. Thus the Act now provides that a person must not knowingly sell, export or import wine with a false or misleading description or presentation (ss 40C, 40E).[61] A description or presentation is false or misleading for this purpose if it uses or suggests a link to a locality (or an expression derived from that locality) which is registered under the Act, without having in fact originated from that locality (ss 40D, 40F). The Register of Protected Names maintained under s 40ZC reflects the Agreement, and in particular provides for the phasing out in three stages of the use of certain European geographical indications in relation to Australian wines. In the first group, prohibited from the end of 1993, are terms such as 'beaujolais' and 'frascati'. The second group of terms, to be discontinued from the end of 1997, includes 'chianti', 'frontignan' and 'madeira'. The third group contains many terms which have been in common use in Australia, such as 'burgundy', 'chablis', 'champagne', 'claret', 'moselle', 'port', 'sauternes' and 'sherry'. The date from which these terms are no longer to be used (save in regard to existing stocks) is to be the subject of further negotiations between the EC and Australia before 1998.

The fact that the Agreement was pursued so aggressively by the EC on behalf of its wine producers reflects the inability of those producers to rely on other intellectual property laws to protect some of the appellations in question. A number of terms in the third group in particular have been used so extensively in this country that they have become generic, in the sense that nobody would believe that in buying a wine under that name they were getting a product originating from the relevant part of Europe. Champagne is certainly in that category, as the French producers discovered in 1981 when they failed in their attempt to replicate in this country their success in the *Spanish Champagne* case. It was held that since the term 'champagne' had come to connote any wine produced by something approximating the methode champenoise, whether in the Champagne district or not, Australian consumers would not be deceived by its use in connection with wines made outside that district.[62] Under the new legislation, by contrast, deception is irrelevant; Australian producers will simply have to find new terms to distinguish some of their wines.

(c) Damage

[16.15]   Necessity of establishing damage. In theory the tort of passing off is complete as soon as the relevant misrepresentation is made, so that there is no need for the plaintiff to show that any damage has been

---

61. As to the requirement of knowledge, see *Comite Interprofessionel des Cotes de Provence v Bryce* (1996) 35 IPR 170.
62. *Comite Interprofessionel du Vin de Champagne v NL Burton Pty Ltd* (1981) 38 ALR 664. Interestingly, the New Zealand Court of Appeal has reached the opposite conclusion where that country is concerned, with Cooke P rather snootily dismissing anyone using the term generically as indulging in a 'white lie' for reasons of 'pretension or tact or the constraints of one's purse': *Wineworths Group Ltd v Comite Interprofessionel du Vin de Champagne* (1991) 23 IPR 435 at 440.

suffered to their reputation.[63] In practical terms, however, it is a different story. If more than nominal damages are to be obtained, the plaintiff must of course establish compensable loss.[64] More importantly the availability of injunctive relief, the usual remedy in passing off cases, is dependent upon the plaintiff establishing actual damage or the real prospect of such damage as the result of the defendant's continuing activities.[65]

[16.16] Types of damage: loss of existing trade. In the great majority of cases the damage which a plaintiff in a passing off suit will claim to be suffering involves a devaluation of their existing goodwill through a loss of trade. In the most obvious situation the complaint will be that business is being diverted to the defendant as consumers act under the mistaken impression that the two businesses (or the specific products involved) are one and the same, or share the same features. Alternatively the plaintiff may seek to show that the negative implications of association with the defendant's business or product will result in its reputation being 'diluted' and trade being lost (even if the customers in question do not switch to the defendant). There may, for example, be a disparity in quality and price between the relevant products, leading the plaintiff (as in the champagne cases) to fear that the exclusivity and success of their product will suffer through the association.[66] The dilution argument is particularly important in situations where the parties are engaged in different trading activities, where it may be impossible to infer direct diversion of custom.[67]

[16.17] Loss of potential to exploit goodwill. Although loss of existing trade is the most obvious form of damage for a plaintiff to plead, it now seems clear that it is by no means the only one. In *Henderson v Radio Corp Pty Ltd*[68] the defendant put out a record of ballroom dancing music, showing a dancing couple on the cover. These were recognisable as the plaintiffs, who were well-known professional ballroom dancers. Their claim in passing off succeeded in the New South Wales Supreme Court, on the basis that the defendant had falsely represented that the plaintiffs were sponsoring the record. At first instance Sugerman J had held that being associated with the defendant might damage the plaintiffs' standing, making this a straightforward case of damage to existing goodwill. However this was rejected on appeal by the Full Court, who found instead that what had been damaged here was not the plaintiffs' present goodwill as such, but rather their potential to exploit that goodwill. Their recommendation was theirs to bestow at will

---

63. *Henderson v Radio Corp Pty Ltd* (1960) 60 SR (NSW) 576 at 593–4; *Pacific Dunlop Ltd v Hogan* (1989) 14 IPR 398 at 428. Cf *Petersville Sleigh Ltd v Sugerman* (1987) 10 IPR 501.
64. See [16.19].
65. *Henderson v Radio Corp Pty Ltd* (1960) 60 SR (NSW) 576 at 594; *Erven Warnink v J Townsend & Sons (Hull) Ltd* [1979] AC 731 at 742.
66. See eg *Taittinger v Allbev Ltd* [1994] 4 All ER 75; and see also *Flamingo Park Pty Ltd v Dolly Dolly Creations Pty Ltd* (1986) 6 IPR 431; *Conagra Inc v McCain Foods (Aust) Pty Ltd* (1992) 23 IPR 193 at 260. Cf H Carty, 'Heads of Damage in Passing Off' [1996] 9 *EIPR* 487, advocating a much narrower view of the concept of damage to goodwill, and hence of the tort itself.
67. See eg *Harrods Ltd v R Harrod Ltd* (1924) 41 RPC 74; *Totalizator Agency Board v Turf News Pty Ltd* [1967] VR 605; *Nicholas v Borg* (1986) 7 IPR 1; and cf *Harrods Ltd v Harrodian School* (1996) 35 IPR 355. As to 'common field of activity', see further [17.18]–[17.19].
68. (1960) 60 SR (NSW) 576.

and could not be appropriated without payment. This decision effectively opened the way for 'appropriation of personality' suits, where a famous identity sues to prevent their name or professional image being used without payment to secure their consent. These actions, together with the related area of 'character merchandising', are considered in more detail below.

[16.18]   Business expansion. Although the significance of *Henderson* should not be underestimated, the notion of identifying damage in lost potential for exploitation of goodwill had already been recognised in a slightly different context. In certain instances a plaintiff might establish that the defendant's activities would create a belief that the two businesses were linked, yet be unable to show a loss of existing trade because, for instance, the two were operating in different locations or in different fields of activity. Nevertheless, even if the plaintiff's reputation could not be shown to be diluted by association with an inferior business, damage might still be identified in terms of the plaintiff's lost potential to expand its business into the defendant's location or field of activity.[69] Thus in *Lego System v Lego M Lemelstrich Ltd*[70] the plaintiff, the company responsible for the well-known toy building blocks, was able to restrain a similarly named Israeli firm from marketing irrigation equipment in Britain. Having found that the public would be confused by the defendant's use of the LEGO mark into inferring a connection between the parties,[71] Falconer J held, citing *Henderson* with approval, that the damage threatened was the plaintiff's loss of opportunity to take advantage of the familiarity of its mark by going into the irrigation equipment business itself — or, more likely, by granting a licence or franchise to someone else to use the mark for that purpose.

The principal difficulty with accepting lost opportunity for expansion as a recognised head of damage centres on the question of proof. A number of authorities suggest that the plaintiff must show that plans to make such an expansion are already in train, or that an expansion is at least likely in the near future.[72] However, in *Lego* Falconer J imposed no such requirement, and on balance this would appear to be the better view. If a plaintiff's name or image is so well entrenched in the relevant public's mind that deception is likely to result from the defendant's activities, even if those activities are confined to a different locality or activity to that in which the plaintiff presently operates, then both consumer protection and full recognition of the value of the plaintiff's goodwill dictate that the court intervene.[73] In so far as the notion of the plaintiff expanding into the defendant's locality or field is an implausible one, then it is hard to see how consumers could have been deceived in the first place.[74] Moreover in many instances (though not in *Lego*) the defendant has deliberately copied the plaintiff's name or image: why else would this have been done if not to cash in on the plaintiff's goodwill? So long as the defendant can be seen to be

---

69.   See eg *Eastman Photographic Materials Co Ltd v John Griffiths Cycle Corp Ltd* (1898) 15 RPC 105.
70.   [1983] FSR 155.
71.   See [18.20].
72.   See eg *Taco Co of Australia Inc v Taco Bell Pty Ltd* (1982) 42 ALR 177 at 196; *Conagra Inc v McCain Foods (Aust) Pty Ltd* (1992) 23 IPR 193 at 234.
73.   Note also in this connection the registrability of defensive trade marks: see [19.55].
74.   Though cf *Stringfellow v McCain Foods (GB) Ltd* [1984] RPC 501.

deceptively misappropriating that reputation, it is difficult to see the justification for refusing relief. As to the argument that it is undesirable to confer an effective monopoly in a name or image, even outside the plaintiff's sphere of operations, it must be remembered that the defendant need only remodel its marketing activities to make it clear that no connection exists with the plaintiff. It should also be noted that relief may be refused to a plaintiff who, in the opinion of the court, is seeking to keep the defendant out of business altogether while it effects an uncontested expansion into the new field or locality.[75]

(d) Remedies

[16.19]   Available remedies. The principal form of redress sought in a passing off action involves the defendant being restrained from engaging or continuing to engage in the conduct which has triggered the suit. The principles applicable to the grant of injunctive relief have already been discussed in Chapter 2 and need not be repeated here.[76] In terms of pecuniary remedies, the plaintiff has the usual election between damages and an account of profits. The latter is unavailable in respect of profits earned while the defendant was innocent of any knowledge of wrongdoing;[77] and in any event the practical difficulties of taking an account appear to deter the great majority of plaintiffs, who will look instead to damages. There has been some doubt as to whether substantial damages may be recovered in the absence of fraud by the defendant. The High Court left the question open in *BM Auto Sales Pty Ltd v Budget Rent A Car System Pty Ltd*,[78] and some judges still shy away from considering the point to be settled.[79] However, the balance of authority (or at least a series of judgments mostly involving Gummow J) now favours the view that, as with an account of profits, fraud must be shown.[80] 'Fraud' in this context does not equate to the mental element required in the tort of deceit, but simply means 'persistence after notice'.[81] Even if this view were to be overturned, it would seem likely that some effort would be made to protect innocent defendants, particularly retailers who find themselves engaged in passing off which has effectively been caused by the activities of those further up the supply chain.[82] It

---

75.   See *Nationwide Building Society v Nationwide Estate Agents Ltd* (1987) 8 IPR 609.
76.   As to the particular forms that injunctions may take in passing off cases, see Kerly, pp 423–6.
77.   *Apand Pty Ltd v Kettle Chip Co Pty Ltd* (1994) 30 IPR 337 at 358; and see [2.16].
78.   (1976) 51 ALJR 254 at 258.
79.   See eg *Conagra Inc v McCain Foods (Aust) Pty Ltd* (1992) 23 IPR 193 at 236.
80.   See eg *10th Cantonae Pty Ltd v Shoshana Pty Ltd* (1987) 10 IPR 289 at 310–14; *Hogan v Koala Dundee Pty Ltd* (1988) 12 IPR 508; *Star Micronics Pty Ltd v Five Star Computers Pty Ltd* (1991) 22 IPR 473; *Conagra Inc v McCain Foods (Aust) Pty Ltd* (1992) 23 IPR 193 at 254–5. Note, however, that damages may undoubtedly be awarded against an innocent defendant where the passing off amounts to a breach of contract: see eg *Flamingo Park Pty Ltd v Dolly Dolly Creations Pty Ltd* (1986) 6 IPR 431.
81.   *Turner v General Motors (Australia) Ltd* (1929) 42 CLR 352 at 362; *Conagra Inc v McCain Foods (Aust) Pty Ltd* (1992) 23 IPR 193 at 254–5; *Apand Pty Ltd v Kettle Chip Co Pty Ltd* (1994) 30 IPR 337 at 358.
82.   See eg *Flamingo Park Pty Ltd v Dolly Dolly Creations Pty Ltd* (1986) 6 IPR 431 (retailer entitled to indemnity against supplier for not revealing authorship of product); *Prince Manufacturing Inc v ABAC Corp Australia Pty Ltd* (1984) 4 IPR 104 (retailer held liable only for small part of plaintiff's loss).

should also be noted that the proprietor or authorised user of a registered trade mark which is substantially identical with or deceptively similar to another mark and who is sued in passing off by the owner of that other mark is in any event not to be liable in damages for any period when reasonably unaware of the plaintiff's mark.[83]

As to the measure of damages that will be awarded, this must depend on the type of loss pleaded by the plaintiff. Where, as is typically the case, that loss consists of profits forgone as a result of the defendant's activities, the plaintiff is not required to adduce precise evidence of lost sales or business. If such damage can reasonably be inferred, compensation will be awarded notwithstanding any difficulties in calculation.[84] Moreover, there is no reason why the same approach should not be taken where the loss concerned is of a different nature. Thus where the passing off has the effect of diminishing the plaintiff's reputation for quality products or personal standing, such loss should be reflected in an award.[85] Similarly, where the plaintiff has been denied the opportunity to charge for their sponsorship, a reasonable fee should be assessed.[86] Exemplary damages may also be awarded, it would seem, where there has been a particularly blatant disregard for the plaintiff's rights.[87]

(e) Beyond Passing Off: Unfair Competition

[16.20] The limits of passing off. Decisions such as *Spanish Champagne*[88] and *Henderson*[89] illustrate the development of the tort of passing off into an action which provides protection against most forms of misappropriation of valuable goodwill. In particular, it is now clear that the tort protects not only the business and customer connections actually generated by a trader ('goodwill' in its narrowest sense), but the trader's ability to exploit their reputation by licensing others to make use of any name, mark or image by which that trader has come to be known to the public ('goodwill' in the broad sense).

Nevertheless certain 'gaps' remain, as the *Babycham*[90] and *Pub Squash*[91] cases demonstrate. In the former, the champagne producers were again litigating to protect their goodwill, this time in relation to 'Babycham', a drink variously described as 'champagne perry' or 'champagne cider'. The drink was marketed in such a way as to attract young females, with advertising stressing a 'glamorous' image similar to that associated with champagne. In the latter case, the plaintiffs were the producers of 'Solo', a tangy

---

83. Trade Marks Act 1995 (Cth) s 230(2). As to the meaning of the terms 'substantially identical' and 'deceptively similar', see [20.5]–[20.6].
84. *Draper v Trist* (1939) 56 RPC 429; *Prince Manufacturing Inc v ABAC Corp Australia Pty Ltd* (1984) 4 IPR 104 at 111; *Star Micronics Pty Ltd v Five Star Computers Pty Ltd* (1991) 22 IPR 473. Cf *Winning Appliances Pty Ltd v Dean Appliances Pty Ltd* (1995) 32 IPR 65.
85. *Flamingo Park Pty Ltd v Dolly Dolly Creations Pty Ltd* (1986) 6 IPR 431; *Surge Licensing Inc v Pearson* (1991) 21 IPR 228.
86. See eg *Shoshana Pty Ltd v 10th Cantonae Pty Ltd* (1987) 11 IPR 249. Cf *Hogan v Koala Dundee Pty Ltd* (1988) 12 IPR 508.
87. *Flamingo Park Pty Ltd v Dolly Dolly Creations Pty Ltd* (1986) 6 IPR 431 at 456–7.
88. *J Bollinger v Costa Brava Wine Co Ltd* [1960] Ch 263: see [16.13].
89. *Henderson v Radio Corp Pty Ltd* (1960) 60 SR (NSW) 576: see [16.17].
90. *H P Bulmer Ltd v J Bollinger SA* [1978] RPC 79.
91. *Cadbury Schweppes Pty Ltd v Pub Squash Pty Ltd* [1980] 2 NSWLR 851.

lemon drink sold in a yellow can with a medallion design. Apart from being marketed with the general theme of being for 'real men', the advertising campaign for Solo specifically sought to evoke nostalgic memories of similar drinks that used to be made in pubs, known as 'pub squash'. The defendants responded by marketing 'Pub Squash', a similar drink sold in a yellow can with a medallion design. In both instances the passing off claims failed, it being found that consumers would not have been deceived into inferring a connection between the respective drinks or their producers.

If we accept the admittedly dubious conclusions that no deception had taken place,[92] no great mystery attaches to these decisions. They involved conduct which is simply beyond the reach of passing off, and which will remain so for as long as the tort is regarded as one of *deceptive* misappropriation. Although the past century has seen considerable expansion in the range of misrepresentations which may trigger intervention, some element of deception remains essential. If non-deceptive misappropriation is ever to be rendered unlawful, this would seem to require the recognition of a tort which goes beyond passing off as currently understood. Suggestions along these lines have generally centred around the concept of a general wrong of 'unfair competition'.[93] Besides being an integral part of many European systems,[94] the idea has considerable currency in the United States, though the level of support for it has waxed and waned over the years. The highpoint came in *International News Service v Associated Press*,[95] in which the defendant had taken war news from the plaintiff's east coast newspapers and, taking advantage of the time difference, published it on the west coast in competition with the plaintiff's outlets there. The US Supreme Court found this to be unlawful, describing it as

> an unauthorised interference with the normal operation of complainant's legitimate business precisely at the point where the profit is to be reaped, in order to divert a material portion of the profit from those who have earned it to those who have not.[96]

[16.21] Rejection of the tort of unfair competition in Australia.

However, despite the support found in other systems for a general wrong of unfair competition, the idea has failed to gain currency in this country, or for that matter in England. Although its adoption had occasionally been

---

92. As to the finding in this respect in *Pub Squash*, see [18.15]. In *Babycham* Waller LJ dissented on the deception issue, while Goff LJ appeared to rule against the champagne producers only because of their failure to tender any evidence as to deception having occurred.
93. See generally W R Cornish, 'Unfair Competition? A Progress Report' (1972) 12 *JSPTL* 126; and see further [1.32]–[1.35].
94. See Beier, 'The Law of Unfair Competition in the European Community' (1985) 16 *IIC* 139.
95. (1918) 248 US 215. See S Chafee, 'Unfair Competition' (1940) 53 *Harv LR* 1289; D G Baird, 'Common Law Intellectual Property and the Legacy of *International News Service v Associated Press*' (1983) 50 *U Chi LR* 411.
96. (1918) 248 US 215 at 240. Note that the formalities necessary in the United States for acquiring copyright had not been observed by the plaintiff, so that no claim could be mounted on that ground. On the other hand, the defendant's conduct did appear to amount to 'inverse' passing off (see [16.11]), in that the defendant appeared to be misrepresenting the plaintiff's product to be its own work. This was the ground on which Holmes J decided the case, and would probably (along with copyright) be the basis for a similar result in this country today.

advocated,[97] any suggestion that the law should recognise such a tort was firmly quashed by the High Court in *Moorgate Tobacco Co Ltd v Philip Morris Ltd*,[98] thus bearing out Morison's observation that our law is not 'susceptible to the facile generation of new torts'.[99] Deane J put the matter thus:

> The rejection of a general action for 'unfair competition' involves no more than a recognition of the fact that the existence of such an action is inconsistent with the established limits of the traditional and statutory causes of action which are available to a trader in respect of damage caused or threatened by a competitor. Those limits, which define the boundary between the area of legal and equitable restraint and protection and the area of untrammelled competition, increasingly reflect what the responsible Parliament or Parliaments have determined to be the appropriate balance between competing claims and policies. Neither legal principle nor social utility requires or warrants the obliteration of that boundary by the importation of a cause of action whose main characteristic is the scope it allows, under high-sounding generalisations, for judicial indulgence of idiosyncratic notions of what is fair in the marketplace.[100]

[16.22] Problems with an unfair competition analysis. Doubtless many of the objections expressed by Deane J may be quite sensibly countered.[101] Nevertheless, the decision appears to be a sensible one. There are considerable problems with the assumptions made by those who have propounded the need to recognise unfair competition as tortious. One such assumption is that conduct of the sort found in the *Babycham* and *Pub Squash* cases is self-evidently unfair and ought to be wrongful, even if no deception occurs. Now there is no question that the defendants in those cases in effect were 'reaping without having sown', in that they were plainly trading off a reputation built up by someone else. But this does not mean they were *misappropriating* goodwill. It is easy to say that a trader who deceives consumers into inferring a connection that does not exist, no matter how innocently, is behaving wrongly. Spence advances two reasons why this should be so:[102]

> First, a community that claims to value truthfulness must be reluctant to allow one party to suffer harm, or indeed another party to benefit, as a consequence of an untruthful statement … Second, … the misrepresentation that the law of passing off seeks to restrain is a particularly pernicious one, because it strikes at the heart of an individual's autonomy in society. When an individual misrepresents his [sic] products to be those of another, or misrepresents himself as having that other's endorsement, he is not simply borrowing that other's reputation. By effectively claiming to speak as the other, he is more fundamentally assuming that other's identity.

It is much harder to make such a judgment about a trader who cashes in on another's hard work without misleading anybody. From one point of view such behaviour could be regarded as *clever,* not unfair, competition.

---

97. See eg *Hexagon Pty Ltd v Australian Broadcasting Commission* (1975) 7 ALR 233 at 251–2.
98. (1984) 156 CLR 414. See also *Cadbury Schweppes Pty Ltd v Pub Squash Pty Ltd* [1980] 2 NSWLR 851 at 868–9.
99. 'Unfair Competition and "Passing Off": The Flexibility of a Formula' (1956) 2 *Syd LR* 50 at 60.
100. (1984) 156 CLR 414 at 445–6.
101. See eg A Terry, 'Unfair Competition and the Misappropriation of a Competitor's Trade Values' (1988) 51 *MLR* 296 at 306 ff.
102. M Spence, 'Passing Off and the Misappropriation of Valuable Intangibles' (1996) 112 *LQR* 472 at 497.

More importantly, and leaving such difficult ethical judgments aside, there appears to have been a consistent failure to establish precisely what public interest would be served by conferring protection on traders against the non-deceptive appropriation of their goodwill. It must not be forgotten that such protection may effectively create a monopoly over material or methods which are not secret or patentable, which cannot be registered as designs or trade marks, and which are not subject to copyright. Nor, as is the case with the protection generated by passing off (and its legislative equivalents), could this monopoly be overcome by a clear disclaimer as to the plaintiff's involvement in or links with the defendant's business.[103] To shift the balance of intellectual property protection in this way should require powerful evidence, it might be thought. On balance, that evidence appears to be lacking. The point can be illustrated by considering three types of conduct which, according to Ricketson, should arguably be caught by a general prohibition against 'misappropriation'.[104] These are product simulation, image stealing and importing a reference.

[16.23] Product simulation. The case for protection is by far the weakest in this first situation. Bearing in mind that *deceptive* product simulation is (or ought to be) already caught by passing off,[105] and that distinctive design features may be registered if they are new or original, there seems to be a clear danger in prohibiting one trader from reacting to another's success by rushing their own version of the same product onto the market: that danger of course being that the first into a market may use the prohibition to bar or at least delay others from competing.[106] No doubt there are cases where the second trader's imitation is so slavish — though almost all reverse engineering requires at least *some* skill and effort — that it might be appropriate to intervene. However the process of identifying these cases, while ensuring that the public would not be deprived of the benefits of product competition, would require a difficult balancing exercise. As Cornish points out:[107]

> [A] positive demand that all sides be evaluated must lead — particularly within our judicial systems — to endless complications of evidence and long-winded presentations which deprive many situations of any legal certainty and leave survival to the litigiously fittest. Given the wealth of options already available to the would-be product monopolist, notwithstanding recent legislative and judicial attempts to restrict the use of copyright as an anti-competitive device, it is difficult to discern the necessity of going to so much trouble to penalise lazy traders.

[16.24] Image stealing. Much the same argument can be mounted, though rather less emphatically, in relation to the copying of an image or 'feel' created to sell a product or business. It was this type of conduct which escaped censure in the *Babycham* and *Pub Squash* cases. The monopoly fear is much reduced here, since there may be 'an infinite number of marketing techniques' available to promote a given product or service.[108] Nevertheless

103. See further [17.10].
104. '"Reaping Without Sowing": Unfair Competition and Intellectual Property Rights in Anglo Australian Law' (1984) 7 *UNSWLJ* 1 at 23–39: see [1.32].
105. See [17.7]–[17.10].
106. As Ricketson has himself acknowledged elsewhere: see Ricketson, pp 596–7.
107. 'Unfair Competition Under Common Law and Statute' (1985) 10 *Adel LR* 32 at 40. Cf C Fellner, *The Future of Legal Protection for Industrial Design*, 1985, pp 199–201.
108. A Terry, 'Unfair Competition and the Misappropriation of a Competitor's Trade Values' (1988) 51 *MLR* 296 at 308.

difficulties remain. How different (or original?) must the defendant's advertising campaign be, given that it would not be sufficient merely to make it clear that no link with the plaintiff's product or business existed? More importantly, it may be questioned whether there is any obvious public interest in protecting the clever marketer from the clever (and non-deceptive) imitator. There is considerable room for the belief that firms already over-invest in marketing, and that if anything the law should be encouraging more resources to be devoted to product development rather than to expensive promotional campaigns. A firm which cannot gain a competitive edge through its advertising budget might be expected to seek to enhance its market share by measures which are more obviously to the public benefit, such as price reduction or quality improvement. Stripped of the assumption that variety in advertising techniques is important to the efficient operation of a market, the case for preventing image stealing almost comes down to the natural law argument that marketing effort should be rewarded.

[16.25] Importing a reference. The third type of 'unfair' conduct noted by Ricketson involves an attempt by one trader to 'feed on' another's success by suggesting that the former's product is a substitute for the latter, or may be used in connection with it, and so on. Assuming again that no deception is thereby practised on consumers, whether as to the nature or quality of either product or as to their compatibility, this practice is entirely lawful.[109] Once again, even if it is accepted that there is something inherently wrongful in such behaviour, practical problems arise in determining when conduct is to be regarded as purely 'parasitical'. Presumably there is no desire to prevent firms developing and marketing socially useful products and services which are ancillary to, or cheaper substitutes for, established goods and services.

[16.26] Character merchandising. If there is a case to be made for moving towards a general tort of unfair competition or misappropriation of trade values, it might be that such a move would compel the courts to bring out into the open fundamental policy questions raised by certain forms of trading. Under the present law of passing off (and under the legislative provisions discussed in the next section), attention is constantly focused on the need to establish deception. In some instances, it is apparent that courts will strain to find conduct deceptive where they consider that conduct to transgress the limits on 'fair' competition. This has been particularly true in regard to 'character merchandising'.[110] Although this has been described as the practice of using 'the reputation of a well-known

---

109. See eg *Harrods Ltd v Schwartz-Sackin & Co Ltd* [1986] FSR 490; *Interlego AG v Croner Trading Pty Ltd* (1992) 25 IPR 65. Cf Trade Marks Act 1938 (UK) s 4(1) ('importing a reference' prohibited in certain instances in relation to registered marks): see Cornish, pp 479–81; Kerly, pp 276–8. The Dean Committee recommended against the introduction of such a provision in Australia: Committee Appointed by the Attorney-General of the Commonwealth to Consider What Alterations are Desirable in the Trade Marks Law of the Commonwealth, *Report*, 1954, p 11.
110. See generally J McKeough, 'Character Merchandising: Legal Protection in Today's Marketplace' (1984) 7 *UNSWLJ* 97; IPAC, *Legal Protection of Character Merchandising in Australia*, 1988; A Terry, 'Proprietary Rights in Character Merchandising Marks' (1990) 18 *ABLR* 229; S Ricketson, 'Character Merchandising in Australia: Its Benefits and Burdens' (1990) 1 *IPJ* 191; B F Katekar, 'Coping with Character Merchandising — Passing Off Unsurpassed' (1996) 7 *AIPJ* 178.

fictitious character like Mickey Mouse or Superman to give a name to, and add to the popularity of, goods not otherwise connected with that character',[111] it might also be considered to extend to the activities of entertainers trading under invented and/or collective names, such as rock bands. Such merchandising tends to take two forms. In the first place, those who have invented or are responsible for the relevant character may wish to market merchandise (T-shirts, posters, toys, etc) which involves direct representations of the character, or of some device or slogan associated with the character. Production of these promotional items is usually carried out pursuant to a series of licensing arrangements, the aim typically being to exploit the desire of fans to proclaim their approval of the character or to surround themselves with appropriate icons. Second, the creators/ owners may wish to license the use of the character by other businesses, who may see some advantage as far as the marketing of their own product is concerned. Promotion of the character in this situation is more or less incidental to the basic desire to profit from the sponsorship deal.

[16.27] Promotional merchandise. As far as the first type of merchandising is concerned, Australian courts have been willing to confer protection against the activities of those who market 'unauthorised' items.[112] Relief has, for example, been granted in respect of toys representing 'Muppet' characters from the 'Sesame Street' television series,[113] and T-shirts celebrating albums and tours by the rock band INXS.[114] In both of these cases it was stressed that the public are generally aware of the licensing activities that go on with respect to promotional merchandise. This can hardly be contested, given the publicity now given to the range of merchandise accompanying each new 'hot' product. What might be doubted is the consequent assumption that consumers *care* as to whether they are getting authorised or unauthorised merchandise. Contrary to the courts' perceptions in the *Muppets* and *INXS* cases, it would seem likely that many purchasers of merchandise, even if alerted to the fact that they were getting cheap and unauthorised copies rather than the 'real thing', would still feel satisfied at getting the product they wanted for a good price. To say that deception occurs in such a case is to stretch the facts so as to catch what is perceived as an act of piracy.

[16.28] Sponsorship arrangements. Turning to sponsorship arrangements, those involving characters are merely one part of a burgeoning trend in marketing towards the use of established identities and images to help sell products. Again, Australian judges have been willing to protect the

---

111. *IPC Magazines Ltd v Black and White Music Corp* [1983] FSR 348 at 350.
112. The English courts have in the past been much less generous in this regard: see eg *Lyngstad v Anabas Products Ltd* [1977] FSR 62; *Wombles Ltd v Wombles Skips Ltd* [1977] RPC 99. However, the decision in *Mirage Studios v Counter-Feat Clothing Co* [1991] FSR 145, in which action was successfully taken in relation to 'Teenage Mutant Ninja Turtles' merchandise, employs an approach more akin to that adopted in Australia: see further M Elmslie and M Lewis, 'Passing Off and Image Marketing in the UK' [1992] 8 *EIPR* 270.
113. *Children's Television Workshop Inc v Woolworths (NSW) Ltd* [1981] 1 NSWLR 273. See also *Surge Licensing Inc v Pearson* (1991) 21 IPR 228 ('Teenage Mutant Ninja Turtles'); *Anheuser-Busch Inc v Castlebrae Pty Ltd* (1991) 21 IPR 54 ('Spuds MacKenzie').
114. *Hutchence v South Seas Bubble Co Pty Ltd* (1986) 6 IPR 473. See also the successful litigation by Bruce Springsteen and Dire Straits described in Murumba, pp 122–4.

capacity of those involved to charge for their services. It has been clear since *Henderson*[115] that a well-known person or creator/licensee of a character may restrain a trader from misrepresenting their connection with or approval of the trader's business, even if that trader is operating in an entirely different commercial field.[116] There may be some doubt as to whether a person who is not trading at all can take action;[117] although given that loss of potential exploitation of reputation is recognised as constituting damage,[118] it is hard to see why such a restriction should apply. The real point would surely be that if the plaintiff is perceived not to be engaging in any form of trade, it might be difficult to show that the public would be deceived into inferring a commercial link with the defendant.[119] As far indeed as the key issue of proving deception as to sponsorship is concerned, recent cases have gone either way on their facts.[120] However, it is the litigation involving Paul Hogan and his *Crocodile Dundee* movie which graphically illustrates the willingness of some courts to find a way of intervening where a defendant is considered to be blatantly attempting to trade off another's fame.

[16.29] The Hogan litigation. The phenomenal success of *Crocodile Dundee* and the popularity of its eponymous character, played by Hogan, prompted a number of businesses to incorporate images or titles from the film into their advertising or product names. In *Pacific Dunlop Ltd v Hogan*[121] Hogan took action to restrain and seek compensation for the screening of a television advertisement for Grosby Leatherz shoes. The advertisement plainly parodied the famous 'knife scene' from the film: equally plainly the actor used, though resembling Hogan, could not have been mistaken for him. Nevertheless the Full Court of the Federal Court upheld the trial judge's finding that those watching the advertisement would have been deceived into inferring that Hogan had given his approval for the use of the *Crocodile Dundee* characters and images pursuant to some commercial arrangement with the defendant.

The artificiality of this sort of finding was highlighted by Pincus J in *Hogan v Koala Dundee Pty Ltd.*[122] Holding that a clothing firm had engaged in passing off by using names and images from the film in its products and their marketing, he commented upon

---

115. *Henderson v Radio Corp Pty Ltd* (1960) 60 SR (NSW) 576: see [16.17].

116. See further [17.18]–[17.19]. Cf *Wickham v Associated Pool Builders Pty Ltd* (1988) 12 IPR 567, which appears to be wrongly decided on this point.

117. See *Henderson v Radio Corp Pty Ltd* (1960) 60 SR (NSW) 576 at 593; *Kaye v Robertson* [1991] FSR 62.

118. See [16.17]–[16.18].

119. See eg *Honey v Australian Airlines Ltd* (1990) 18 IPR 185 (see [16.30]).

120. Besides the cases discussed in the ensuing paragraphs, see eg *Paracidal Pty Ltd v Herctum Pty Ltd* (1983) 4 IPR 201 (deceptive use of photograph of well-known horsemaster); *Newton-John v Scholl-Plough (Australia) Ltd* [1986] ATPR 40–697 (non-deceptive use of celebrity 'lookalike' where celebrity's non-involvement made clear); *10th Cantonae Pty Ltd v Shoshana Pty Ltd* (1987) 10 IPR 289 (non-deceptive use of character in advertisement with same name as, though no physical resemblance to, television personality); *Wickham v Associated Pool Builders Pty Ltd* (1988) 12 IPR 567 (deceptive use of swimmer's endorsement after endorsement arrangement ceased); *The Really Useful Group Ltd v Gordon & Gotch Ltd* (1994) 29 IPR 19 (non-deceptive publication of magazine about musical show written and produced by plaintiffs).

121. (1989) 14 IPR 398.

122. (1988) 12 IPR 508.

the incongruity of basing this sort of suit on the issue whether the public has been misled about licensing arrangements. In practice, the ideas of the buying public as to licensing arrangements are very much in the back of their minds and necessarily vague and inaccurate. They have no reason to be interested in the question of licensing. Unlike a representation as to the origin or quality of goods, use of mere images in advertising, though presumably effective to generate sales, does not necessarily do so by creating, or relying on, any specific conclusions in the minds of the buying public.[123]

The judge went on to make the point that nobody would seriously believe that a celebrity used to promote a product was actually giving it a personal endorsement.[124]

The tenor of these remarks was echoed by Burchett J in the *Pacific Dunlop* case where, stressing the need for the techniques used in television advertising to be given special consideration, he suggested:[125]

> Character merchandising through television advertisements should not be seen as setting off a logical train of thought in the minds of television viewers … An association of some desirable character with the product proceeds more subtly to foster favourable inclination towards it, a good feeling about it, an emotional attachment to it. No logic tells the consumer that boots are better because Crocodile Dundee wears them … The whole importance of character merchandising is the creation of an association of the product with the character; not the making of precise representations.

Despite these observations, Burchett J was content to find that deception had occurred through the stimulation of a belief, albeit subtly suggested, that Hogan had approved the advertisement. A similar finding was made by Tamberlin J in the *Duff Beer* case,[126] in which the producers of the popular television series 'The Simpsons' successfully sued to prevent the marketing of a beer under that name. It was held that a significant section of the public would associate the name with the fictional beer drunk by Homer Simpson in the series. The judge, who cited with approval the comments made by Burchett J in *Pacific Dunlop*, admitted that 'it would be artificial to anticipate that every person buying Duff Beer would take the time to analyse the subtle legal or merchandising overtones and connotations and ask specifically whether the beer is made with the license or permission of the applicant'.[127] Nevertheless, the judge was satisfied that use of the name would create an 'impression' of a connection which did not in fact exist. It was significant that there had been widespread (authorised) merchandising of characters and images from the series, so that consumers might well

---

123. Ibid at 517. See further [18.16], discussing the problem of circularity of reasoning in such a case.
124. Ibid at 519; and see also *10th Cantonae Pty Ltd v Shoshana Pty Ltd* (1987) 10 IPR 289 at 295–6. Indeed, in so far as celebrities claim protection against misappropriation of their sponsorship by arguing that they maintain high standards as to the products they promote, it might be thought that they should be liable for any failure to check the quality of a defective product which, thanks to their involvement, is successfully marketed: see eg *Re Cooga Mooga Inc* (1978) 92 FTC 310, a US case in which the actor Pat Boone was held to be liable in this way under false advertising laws; and see further S Barnes and M Blakeney, *Advertising Regulation*, 1982, pp 237–43; J S Kogan, 'Celebrity Endorsement: Recognition of a Duty' (1987) 21 *John Marshall L Rev* 47.
125. (1989) 14 IPR 398 at 429.
126. *Twentieth Century Fox Film Corp v South Australian Brewing Co Ltd* (1996) 34 IPR 225.
127. Ibid at 242.

assume that when they saw the familiar name 'it was just another product permitted by the producers'.[128]

By contrast, in *Koala Dundee* Pincus J was prepared to take the plunge and find that the wrong committed in this sort of case was that there had been 'wrongful appropriation of a reputation or, more widely, wrongful association of goods with an image properly belonging to the [plaintiff]', rather than a misrepresentation as to licensing or sponsorship.[129] There is little support for this view in the case law; and it is a little hard to see why celebrities and those behind famous characters should be protected against non-deceptive appropriation of their images when other traders, such as the drinks producers in *Pub Squash* and *Babycham*, are apparently not so favoured. However, the Pincus formulation does at least have the merit that it brings the issue of 'image filching' out into the open, rather than concealing it beneath the spurious question of consumers' impressions as to licensing deals.[130]

[16.30] Appropriation of personality. An alternative suggestion is that, rather than 'stretching' passing off to accommodate non-deceptive appropriation of reputation, a separate tort of 'appropriation of personality' should be adopted.[131] Such an action would protect what the United States courts have come to term the right of publicity — 'the right of every person to control the commercial use of his or her own identity'.[132] If a person's name or image is used to help market a product without their permission, the right is considered to be infringed — whether or not they are a celebrity, and whether or not the public are deceived or confused as to whether the person is endorsing the product. Crucially, however, the right does not extend to fictional characters.

There is no immediate sign that Australian courts are ready to embrace a tort of appropriation of personality or a right of publicity: 'the proposition that such a cause of action exists is little more than a glint in the eye of counsel'.[133] Thus even though the tort of passing off protects what is rationalised as a proprietary interest in the potential to turn fame into money through sponsorship arrangements, the broader interest which a person may have in restraining commercially motivated invasions of their privacy has been ignored.[134] How fine the line can be is illustrated by comparing the decisions in *Honey v Australian Airlines Ltd*[135] and *Talmax Pty Ltd*

---

128. Ibid at 243.
129. (1988) 12 IPR 508 at 520.
130. See *Tot Toys Ltd v Mitchell* [1993] 1 NZLR 325 for a sustained attack on the propensity of Australian courts to 'force the square peg of character merchandising into the round hole of passing off' (at 363).
131. See eg R G Howell, 'Personality Rights: A Canadian Perspective: Some Comparisons with Australia' (1990) 1 *IPJ* 212. See also T Frazer, 'Appropriation of Personality: A New Tort?' (1983) 99 *LQR* 281; C L Pannam, 'Unauthorized Use of Names or Photographs in Advertisements' (1966) 40 *ALJ* 4.
132. J T McCarthy, 'The Human Persona as Commercial Property: The Right of Publicity' (1996) 7 *AIPJ* 20 at 21.
133. *Sony Music Australia Ltd v Tansing* (1993) 27 IPR 649 at 656. Cf *Tot Toys Ltd v Mitchell* [1993] 1 NZLR 325 at 363.
134. See *10th Cantonae Pty Ltd v Shoshana Pty Ltd* (1987) 10 IPR 289 at 307–8; *Kaye v Robertson* [1991] FSR 62; and see generally Murumba. Where confidentiality is infringed, there may be a remedy: see eg *Pollard v Photographic Co* (1888) 40 Ch D 345; and see further [3.9], [4.11].
135. (1990) 18 IPR 185.

v Telstra Corp Ltd.[136] In the former case the plaintiff, a long jump champion, was pictured in action on a poster produced by Australian Airlines to promote sport generally. This photograph was subsequently used, with Australian's consent, on the front cover of a book entitled *How to Live the Kind of Life You've Always Wanted to Live* published by a religious organisation. The plaintiff, whose permission had not been sought in either instance, took action, but was held to be unable to show that those seeing the poster or book would be deceived into inferring that he had some link with either organisation. Thus what was plainly an unauthorised use of a person's identity and image failed for lack of proven deception, just as it would have failed if the plaintiff had not been well known.

By contrast in *Talmax* another Olympic athlete, the swimmer Kieren Perkins, successfully sued Telstra for breach of the statutory prohibition on misleading and deceptive conduct.[137] The telecommunications company produced an advertising supplement for a newspaper which, besides urging consumers to choose Telstra over its main competitor Optus for long distance telephone calls, contained a feature on the Australian swimming championships. Perkins was pictured in a swimming cap with a Telstra logo and discussed in an 'article' which referred to the Telstra-sponsored Australian swimming team. The Queensland Court of Appeal held that people reading the supplement would be deceived into thinking that Perkins himself was sponsored by Telstra, that he had endorsed the advertising, and that he supported the company over Optus in the choice of long distance carrier. There seems little doubt that the publicity given to Perkins' ability to 'cash in' on his success in the pool would have helped the court reach this conclusion. Unlike athletes such as Honey, Perkins' name and face has become as well known from TV appearances and advertising as it has from his feats in competition. Hence the more the public is aware of a celebrity and their endorsements, the more likely it is that appropriations of their personality will be caught by the tort of passing off or the law of misleading and deceptive conduct.

3. MISLEADING AND DECEPTIVE CONDUCT:
STATUTORY PROVISIONS

(a) Relevant Provisions

[16.31] Section 52. Division 1 of Pt V of the Trade Practices Act 1974 (Cth) proscribes a range of unfair practices detrimental to the interests of consumers.[138] Most important of these provisions is s 52:

(1) A corporation shall not, in trade or commerce, engage in conduct that is misleading or deceptive or is likely to mislead or deceive.

136. (1996) 36 IPR 46.
137. No action for passing off was apparently brought, though it seems clear the result would have been the same.
138. See generally J Goldring, L W Maher and J McKeough, *Consumer Protection Law in Australia*, 4th ed, 1993, ch 7; A Hurley and G Wiffen, *Outline of Trade Practices and Consumer Protection Law*, 1994, chs 8, 9, 12; J D Heydon, *Trade Practices Law*, chs 11, 12, 18; CCH, *Australian Trade Practices Reporter*, para 20–010 ff.

(2) Nothing in the succeeding provisions of this Division shall be taken as limiting by implication the generality of sub-section (1).

Section 52 acts as the 'catch-all' prohibition in the Division, so that while proceedings may also be commenced for breach of the more specific provisions that follow, in practice these are almost invariably brought in conjunction with a s 52 action. Indeed it is not uncommon for s 52 alone to be relied upon, although since fines cannot be imposed in respect of any breach (s 79), criminal proceedings must necessarily involve the other provisions. Most significantly for present purposes, the phrase 'misleading or deceptive conduct' is wide enough to encompass all forms of commercial conduct which would constitute passing off. For reasons which are explained below, s 52 has indeed come to supplant the tort as the dominant form of redress against misappropriation of business reputation in Australia.

[16.32] Definitions and restrictions. Before going on to look at the relationship between s 52 and passing off, it is necessary to say something about the meaning and significance of the various components of the prohibition in subs (1):

a corporation — The Trade Practices Act is primarily enacted under s 51(xx) of the Constitution, the corporations power. Hence 'corporation' is defined in s 4(1) to mean a trading, financial or overseas corporation (the types of corporation referred to in s 51(xx)),[139] as well as corporations formed in a territory, and holding companies of any of the above kinds of corporation. The extension to territory corporations is achieved through use of the Commonwealth's legislative power over the territories under s 122 of the Constitution. Other constitutional heads of power are also used to extend the reach of the Act, including those relating to international and interstate trade and commerce (s 51(i)), and postal, telegraphic and telephonic services (s 51(v)). Thus while on its face s 52 of the Trade Practices Act applies only to conduct by a 'corporation', s 6 provides that this is to be taken to include a natural person in certain situations. These are where the conduct (a) is carried on the course of interstate or overseas trade, or trade within or involving a territory; (b) is carried on in the course of trade with a Commonwealth instrumentality; (c) involves the use of postal, telegraphic or telephonic services;[140] or (d) occurs in a territory in the course of the 'promotional activities of a professional person'.

in trade or commerce — This phrase, which is not exhaustively defined in the Act, has generally been given an expansive interpretation by the courts. It has been said, for example, that:

> The terms 'trade' and 'commerce' are not terms of art. They are expressions of fact and terms of common knowledge ... [T]he terms are clearly of the widest import ... [T]hey are not restricted to dealings or communications which can properly be described as being at arms length in the sense that they are within open markets or between strangers or have a dominant objective of profit-making.[141]

---

139. As to the meaning of these terms, see P Hanks, *Constitutional Law in Australia*, 1991, pp 291–5; L Zines, *The High Court and the Constitution*, 3rd ed, 1992, pp 74–9.
140. As to this particular extension, see eg *Handley v Snoid* [1981] ATPR 40–219; *Snyman v Cooper* (1990) 19 IPR 471.
141. *Re Ku-ring-gai Co-operative Building Society Ltd* (1978) 36 FLR 134 at 167.

However, while this indicates that many activities are to be regarded as 'commercial' for this purpose,[142] this does not necessarily mean that s 52 catches all deceptive conduct by a person who is carrying on trade or commerce. It must still be established that the relevant conduct occurred *in* trade or commerce, a point emphasised by the High Court's decision in *Concrete Constructions (NSW) Pty Ltd v Nelson*[143] that a representation as to the safety of a workplace made by one employee to another could not fall within the prohibition. According to the majority in that case:

> What the section is concerned with is the conduct of a corporation towards persons, be they consumers or not, with whom it (or those whose interests it represents or is seeking to promote) has or may have dealings in the course of those activities or transactions which, of their nature, bear a trading or commercial character.[144]

The distinction which the decision requires, between conduct which is part of a person's trading activities and conduct which is merely incidental thereto, is far from easy to apply in practice. On the other hand it is difficult to conceive that the type of conduct relevant in the present context, misappropriation of business reputation, would ever fall on the incidental side of the line. *Nelson* notwithstanding, passing off cases are likely to continue to be caught by the section, other than in those rare cases where the 'goodwill' protected is not of a commercial nature at all, as in the *Ancient Church of the East* case.[145]

engage in conduct — This is defined very broadly in s 4(2), so that for instance even inadvertent omissions may be covered.[146]

misleading or deceptive — No definition is provided for these crucial adjectives, whose meaning has accordingly been developed in the case law. The basic notion is clear enough: conduct is misleading or deceptive if it 'leads into error',[147] or is likely to do so.[148] The process of fleshing out that notion has been marked by a judicial tendency to utilise concepts drawn from existing common law doctrines — and the passing off type of cases, as will be seen, have been no exception. All that need be said at this point is that, save in one instance, the contravener's state of mind or intention is irrelevant, liability being strict;[149] although as in passing off, proof of an

---

142. See eg *Australian Society of Accountants v Federation of Australian Accountants Inc* (1987) 9 IPR 282.
143. (1990) 169 CLR 594.
144. Ibid at 604.
145. See [16.6]. At first instance, it was indeed held that no action could be maintained under s 52, despite the availability of passing off: *Re Attorney-General (NSW); ex rel Elisha* (1989) 14 IPR 609. The point was not taken on appeal, though the first instance judgment was in any event affirmed: (1989) 16 IPR 619.
146. As to the responsibility of a corporation for the conduct of its servants, agents and directors, and the question of proving corporate intent, see s 84; and see eg *Snyman v Cooper* (1990) 19 IPR 471.
147. *Weitmann v Katies Ltd* (1977) 29 FLR 336 at 343; *Parkdale Custom Built Furniture Pty Ltd v Puxu Pty Ltd* (1982) 149 CLR 191 at 198. See further [18.8]ff.
148. Likely' here requires a 'real or not remote chance or possibility regardless of whether it is less or more than fifty per cent': *Global Sportsman Ltd v Mirror Newspapers Ltd* (1984) 55 ALR 25 at 30, quoting *Tillmans Butcheries Pty Ltd v Australasian Meat Industry Employees' Union* (1979) 27 ALR 367 at 380.
149. *Hornsby Building Information Centre Pty Ltd v Sydney Building Information Centre Ltd* (1978) 140 CLR 216 at 223. But cf [18.11].

intention to mislead or deceive will be of considerable assistance in establishing the success of that design.[150] The exception is that where a statement is made as to the future, it will only be deceptive if the maker has no reasonable grounds for making it, though the onus in this respect is on the maker to establish such grounds (s 51A). In practice, passing off type cases rarely involve such representations, being squarely based on issues of present fact.

[16.33] **Prescribed information providers.** One limitation on the operation of s 52 is provided by s 65A, which exempts 'prescribed information providers' (newspapers, magazines, television and radio stations, etc) from liability. Thus an information provider is not directly liable for deceptive conduct in the course of reporting news, though it would seem that it may still be liable for 'aiding or abetting' a contravention and thus be subject to an injunction or damages.[151] The exemption does not extend to advertisements or other promotional material connected with the supply of goods, services (including the provider's own services)[152] or interests in land, though these may in turn become the subject of the 'publisher's defence' in s 85(3). This protects a publisher from liability under Pt V in respect of any advertisement accepted in the ordinary course of business, so long as the publisher had no reason to suspect that the publication would be in contravention of the Act.[153]

[16.34] **Remedies.** Section 52 is one of the few provisions in Div 1 of Pt V of the Act *not* to attract criminal penalties (s 79). However, a range of civil remedies are available. First and foremost, the Australian Competition and Consumer Commission or 'any other person' may obtain an injunction to restrain a contravention, or conduct which amounts to aiding, abetting, inducing or being knowingly concerned in such a contravention (s 80).[154] It has been held that the court's power to grant injunctive relief extends to making orders for corrective advertising to undo the effect of the conduct, notwithstanding the existence of a separate provision (s 80A) which specifically allows the Minister or the Commission (but no others) to seek such an order.[155]

Second, a person who has suffered loss or damage as a result of a contravention may recover damages in respect of that loss from the contravener or from any person involved in the contravention (s 82).[156] Where misleading or deceptive conduct is concerned, damages under s 82 are generally assessed on the same basis as damages in tort.[157] Thus where a misappropriation of business reputation is involved, the principles developed in

---

150. *Rhone-Poulenc Agrochimie SA v UIM Chemical Services Pty Ltd* (1986) 12 FCR 477 at 488, 503–4; *Telmak Teleproducts (Australia) Pty Ltd v Coles Myer Ltd* (1989) 15 IPR 362 at 383.
151. *Advanced Hair Studio Pty Ltd v TVW Enterprises Ltd* (1987) 18 FCR 1. See further [18.2].
152. See eg *Sun Earth Homes Pty Ltd v Australian Broadcasting Corp* (1990) 19 IPR 201.
153. See eg *Universal Telecasters Queensland Ltd v Guthrie* (1978) 32 FLR 360.
154. See generally H Jordan, 'The Injunction Against Misleading Conduct — The Quiet Achiever' (1992) 20 *ABLR* 244.
155. *Janssen Pharmaceuticals Ltd v Pfizer Pty Ltd* [1986] ATPR 40–654; *HCF Australia Ltd v Switzerland Australia Health Fund Pty Ltd* (1988) 78 ALR 483 at 491.
156. As to the meaning of 'involved in the contravention', see s 75B; and see further [18.2].
157. *Gates v City Mutual Life Assurance Society Ltd* (1986) 160 CLR 1; *Wardley Australia Ltd v Western Australia* (1992) 175 CLR 514; *Poseidon Ltd v Adelaide Petroleum NL* (1994) 179 CLR 332.

relation to passing off will usually be applicable.[158] Given the emphasis on compensation, however, it would seem that exemplary damages may not be awarded.[159] On the other hand, s 82 does not carry any requirement as to intent, so that (in contrast to the position in passing off) damages will be available even in the absence of fraud.[160]

Third, the court has the power to make a variety of remedial orders, which may be ancillary to the grant of an injunction or damages or sought in their own right, provided it is considered they will compensate the applicant for loss or damage suffered, or prevent or reduce that loss or damage (s 87). These include orders to avoid or vary contracts, to refund money or return property, to repair goods, and so on. Section 87, unlike s 82, can be used to seek compensation for loss or damage likely to be suffered in the future, even if it has not yet occurred.[161] However, it is unclear whether the provision is wide enough to authorise a restitutionary remedy in the nature of an account of profits.[162]

[16.35] Specific prohibitions. As already mentioned, Div 1 of Pt V contains a number of other provisions which proscribe specific manifestations of misleading or deceptive behaviour. Besides the remedies just mentioned, they may also be the subject of a criminal prosecution (s 79), though criminal liability may be avoided by establishing that the contravention resulted from a reasonable mistake, reasonable reliance on information supplied by another, the act of some other person (excluding a director, servant or agent of the defendant), or an accident or event outside the defendant's control (s 85). Some of these provisions are capable of encompassing allegations of misappropriation of business reputation, most notably two paragraphs in s 53. This section provides, where relevant, that:

> A corporation[163] shall not, in trade or commerce, in connexion with the supply or possible supply of goods or services or in connexion with the promotion by any means of the supply or use of goods or services — ...
>
> (c) represent that goods or services have sponsorship, approval, performance characteristics, accessories, uses or benefits they do not have;
>
> (d) represent that the corporation has a sponsorship, approval or affiliation that it does not have ...

These provisions can plainly be, and have been, used to criminalise behaviour which would otherwise amount to passing off.[164] It is possible that use could also be made in this context of two further sections. Section 55

---

158. *Prince Manufacturing Inc v ABAC Corp Australia Pty Ltd* (1984) 57 ALR 159; and see eg *Talmax Pty Ltd v Telstra Corp Ltd* (1996) 36 IPR 46 (damages for loss of opportunity to exploit commercial advantage). Cf *Winning Appliances Pty Ltd v Dean Appliances Pty Ltd* (1995) 32 IPR 65 (damages not awarded because no evidence of actual loss).
159. *Snyman v Cooper* (1989) 16 IPR 585. The point was apparently not pursued on appeal: (1990) 19 IPR 471.
160. *Shoshana Pty Ltd v 10th Cantonae Pty Ltd* (1987) 11 IPR 249; *10th Cantonae Pty Ltd v Shoshana Pty Ltd* (1987) 10 IPR 289 at 310.
161. *Wardley Australia Ltd v Western Australia* (1992) 175 CLR 514 at 527, 543–4, 551.
162. *Apand Pty Ltd v Kettle Chip Co Pty Ltd* (1994) 30 IPR 337 at 358.
163. Note that s 6 gives 'corporation' here the same extended meaning as in s 52: see [16.32].
164. See eg *Apple Computer Inc v Computer Edge Pty Ltd* (1984) 53 ALR 225; *Paragon Shoes Pty Ltd v Paragini Distributors (NSW) Pty Ltd* (1988) 13 IPR 323.

prohibits a person from engaging in conduct, in trade or commerce, that is liable to mislead the public as to a number of matters, including the 'nature' or 'characteristics' of goods.[165] Section 55A imposes a similar liability upon corporations in respect of services.

[16.36]   State fair trading legislation. Although the provisions in Div 1 of Pt V of the Trade Practices Act catch most instances of deceptive conduct in the course of trade or commerce, there remain situations which do not involve a 'corporation' as the contravener, even taking that term in the extended sense already discussed. It is in part to meet that problem that the states have enacted their own fair trading legislation. Each of these statutes replicates the federal provisions, except in so far as they refer merely to a 'person' engaging in the prohibited conduct.[166] This now ensures that in those situations where the 1974 Act cannot be invoked for lack of a 'corporation', proceedings may be instituted under the comparable state provisions.[167]

(b) Relationship With Passing Off

[16.37]   Advantages of a statutory claim. It is comparatively rare these days in Australia for a suit alleging misappropriation of business reputation to rest solely on the common law. Generally, such an action will be pursued under the Trade Practices Act (or if necessary under state fair trading legislation), either with or without an associated claim in passing off.[168] The attractions of such a course are obvious. By invoking the statute, the applicant may be able to obtain remedies (such as the consequent orders under s 87 of the federal Act) which are not available under the common law. It is also possible, as will be seen, that liability may be found under the statute which would not attach at common law. But most importantly in practice, a claim under the Trade Practices Act gives the applicant automatic access to the Federal Court, where cases can often be resolved more quickly than in the state courts.

[16.38]   Capacity of traders to bring statutory proceedings. The fact that those whose business reputation is threatened by misleading or deceptive conduct may see clear advantages in using the statutory provisions to protect themselves is not in itself sufficient justification for allowing them to do so. It is easy to overlook the fact that the legislation's principal objective is to protect consumers, not traders. Nevertheless in *Hornsby Building Information Centre Pty Ltd v Sydney Building Information Centre Ltd*[169] the High Court confirmed that a trader whose reputation is threatened by

---

165. The provision is able to apply in all instances to natural persons because it is based on the Paris Convention for the Protection of Industrial Property and is thus supported by the federal legislative power over external affairs (Constitution, s 51(xxix)): *Mildura Fruit Juices Pty Ltd v Bannerman* (1983) 1 IPR 56.
166. For equivalents to ss 52 and 53 in particular, see Fair Trading Act 1987 (NSW) ss 42, 44; Fair Trading Act 1985 (Vic) ss 11, 12; Fair Trading Act 1989 (Qld) ss 38, 40; Fair Trading Act 1987 (SA) ss 56, 58; Fair Trading Act 1987 (WA) ss 10, 12; Fair Trading Act 1990 (Tas) ss 14, 16. See also Fair Trading Act 1992 (ACT) ss 12, 14; Consumer Affairs and Fair Trading Act 1990 (NT) ss 42, 44.
167. See eg *Komesaroff v Mickle* (1986) 7 IPR 295; *Lutze v Barrett* (1996) 34 IPR 606.
168. As to jurisdictional issues here, see [2.20].
169. (1978) 140 CLR 216.

another's deceptive conduct may sue to protect both private and public interests. The majority stressed that the generality of s 52 should not be limited by the fact that it appears in Pt V of the Act, headed 'Consumer Protection'. Although, as Stephen J conceded, the purpose of s 52 is not *directly* to protect business reputation, but rather to protect the public against deceptive conduct, it is equally obvious that traders whose reputation has been misappropriated will indirectly benefit from any protection given to the public. It is particularly important to bear in mind that 'any person' can seek an injunction under s 80 to restrain a contravention — and 'any person' includes a trader as much as a consumer.

The notion that traders should be accorded standing to vindicate what is in theory a purely public interest in consumer protection can be defended on policy grounds. After all, self-interested traders are in a much better position to sue than deceived consumers when the question of resources is taken into account, so that in practice the prohibitions on deceptive conduct are far more likely to be enforced. A counter-argument to this would be that a system of civil enforcement by competitors, rather than relying on criminal prosecutions, runs the risk of encouraging 'competition by litigation', where the threat of action is used to disrupt a rival's business at a tactically significant moment (such as the launch of an advertising campaign for a new product), or as a vehicle for securing a licensing arrangement. Such a system, it has been argued, is no match for one strongly and consistently policed by public authorities or consumer groups.[170] It may also be significant that in the *Nelson* decision[171] three members of the High Court were prepared to infer from the heading to Pt V that only conduct which is deceptive of 'consumers' is caught by s 52; and even the majority were prepared to say that the heading had some influence on their construction of the terms 'in trade or commerce'. Although having no direct bearing on the *Hornsby* decision, *Nelson* reflects a desire by the court to prevent s 52 becoming an all-purpose vehicle for commercial litigation (a horse which many would say has already bolted).[172] Nevertheless it seems unlikely that the availability of trade practices or fair trading proceedings as a viable alternative to passing off will be taken away in the foreseeable future by either the courts or the legislatures.

[16.39] Assimilation of passing off principles. The logic underlying the *Hornsby* decision helps to explain why it is that in practice the law of passing off has been so important in claims mounted under s 52 and its equivalents. Section 52 has of course a much wider sphere of operation than passing off, for it encompasses deceptive behaviour of all descriptions (subject of course to the 'trade or commerce' requirement). But where misappropriation of business reputation is concerned, in most cases both passing off and s 52 require that the same two questions be asked: whether the plaintiff has a distinctive reputation; and whether the relevant public have been deceived by the defendant's conduct. In passing off the focus is

---

170. See W R Cornish, 'Unfair Competition Under Common Law and Statute' (1985) 10 *Adel LR* 32 at 33–7.
171. *Concrete Constructions (NSW) Pty Ltd v Nelson* (1990) 169 CLR 594: see [16.32].
172. Cf W Pengilley, 'Section 52 of the Trade Practices Act: A Plaintiff's New Exocet?' (1987) 15 *ABLR* 247; P H Clarke, 'The Hegemony of Misleading or Deceptive Conduct in Contract, Tort and Restitution' (1989) 5 *Aust Bar Rev* 109.

nominally on the question of a protectable reputation: but only misrepresentations are remediable, and there can only be a misrepresentation where someone is misled or deceived. Under s 52 the focus is of course on deception — but the most obvious way to establish that the public is being deceived about the connection between different businesses is to determine whether there is an established public perception of one of those businesses. Thus in most cases — though not all — the extent of the complainant's pre-existing reputation becomes the key reference point on the deception issue.[173] This explains why it is that concepts and principles developed in the context of the tort action are so freely applied by courts when dealing with the statutory provision, for at bottom in these type of cases the inquiry tends to be the same.

The extent of this process of assimilation has by no means been fully acknowledged by the courts. In the earlier s 52 cases in particular, the standard judicial line appeared to be that while the law of passing off 'should not be disregarded', it 'may not always provide any safe guide' to the interpretation and application of the statutory provision.[174] In the *Taco Bell* case Deane and Fitzgerald JJ put the matter more strongly:[175]

> The backgrounds of s 52 and the law of passing off are quite different. Their respective purposes and the interests which they primarily protect are contrasting. Their areas of operation do not coincide. The indiscriminate importation into s 52 cases of principles and concepts involved in passing off … is likely to be productive of error and to give rise to arguments founded on false assumptions.

Quite apart from the fact that this ignores the basic thrust of the *Hornsby* decision, *Taco Bell* neatly bears out Blakeney's observation that 'in each case in which a warning of the potential inappropriateness of passing off principles is made, the final decision has been based on the application of some technical passing off rule'.[176] In that case each party sued each other in passing off and under s 52. After solemnly considering each of the separate claims and counterclaims, the court reached a common conclusion which was plainly dictated by notions developed under the common law.[177] That result is typical of the courts' approach to s 52, if not necessarily their rhetoric; although there is perhaps a trend in the more recent cases to acknowledge the link with passing off more openly. Thus in *Vieright Pty Ltd v Myer Stores Ltd*[178] the Full Court of the Federal Court said:

> The settled course of authority holds that, as in the passing off claim, the essential question [for the purpose of the Trade Practices Act] is largely one of fact: is, in all the circumstances, the [defendant's] conduct likely to mislead? In the present kind of case, it will usually be the situation that if a passing off claim is established, it will be so by reason of a finding of a misrepresentation of the type discussed in the authorities. Such a misrepresentation will usually

173. See eg *Conagra Inc v McCain Foods (Aust) Pty Ltd* (1992) 23 IPR 193 at 244, 269.
174. *Hornsby Building Information Centre Pty Ltd v Sydney Building Information Centre Ltd* (1978) 140 CLR 216 at 227.
175. *Taco Co of Australia Inc v Taco Bell Pty Ltd* (1982) 42 ALR 177 at 199.
176. M L Blakeney, 'Old Wine in New Bottles: Influence of the Common Law on the Interpretation of Section 52 of the Trade Practices Act' (1984) 58 *ALJ* 316 at 317.
177. See [17.13].
178. (1995) 31 IPR 361 at 373. See also *Telmak Teleproducts (Australia) Pty Ltd v Coles Myer Ltd* (1989) 15 IPR 362 at 381; *Equity Access Pty Ltd v Westpac Banking Corp* (1989) 16 IPR 431 at 440.

constitute a contravention of s 52, and possibly s 53, of the Trade Practices Act. Conversely, if no misrepresentation is found, it will usually follow that the Trade Practices Act claim will also fail.

It is precisely for this reason that in applying s 52, authorities on passing off 'provide guidance by analogy as to the type of conduct which would be likely to mislead or deceive the public'.[179]

[16.40]   The case against assimilation. The question is whether the use of passing off principles in this way is desirable. Blakeney, for one, has lamented the way in which this process has 'eliminated the difference between the private proprietary tort action and the public interest concerns which ought to have animated the pro-consumer statutory action' and frustrated 'the attempt by the proponents of the Trade Practices Act 1974 to replace the caveat emptor philosophy of the common law with a pro-consumer policy'.[180] Much of his criticism of the way in which s 52 has been applied in practice is well-founded, as will become clear from the course of the discussion in the following chapters. However, as that discussion will also reveal, the problem does not lie with the assimilation process as such. Once the congruence of the issues involved in most passing off and s 52 claims is accepted, there is nothing inherently unsatisfactory about using the same set of principles.[181] The real target should be the principles themselves, which in many instances impose unnecessary technicalities where a simple, factual approach would suffice, and with the handling by the courts of the whole issue of proving consumer deception. These defects affect passing off and s 52 alike. To argue, for instance, that a particular passing off case should be decided differently under s 52 may well miss the true point: that the passing off decision is wrong in its own terms.[182]

[16.41]   Points of difference. Inevitably, however, there will be cases which on any view must be decided differently under the two forms of action. Assuming that the *Koala Dundee* extension to passing off is rejected and the need for a misrepresentation maintained,[183] it is safe to assume (as the Full Court did in *Vieright*) that any finding of passing off in a commercial case[184] should also militate a finding that s 52 (or a state equivalent) has been contravened. But while the converse is usually true, it is not always necessarily so. Even if attention is confined to cases involving a misrepresented connection with another business, there will be some situations where a s 52 action might succeed where a passing off claim would inevitably fail. In the first place, there may be cases where the plaintiff can establish that the defendant is deceiving the public as to the existence of such a connection, but does not possess the established reputation necessary to succeed in passing off. The classic instance here is the *Sunday Territorian* case,[185] where two rival newspaper groups more or less simultaneously

---

179. *R & C Products Pty Ltd v S C Johnson & Sons Pty Ltd* (1993) 26 IPR 98 at 102.
180. (1984) 58 *ALJ* 316 at 318, 325.
181. Cf the views of Lord Diplock in the *Advocaat* case as to the desirability of developments in legislative policy informing the modernisation of common law principles in this area: *Erven Warnink v J Townsend & Sons (Hull) Ltd* [1979] AC 731 at 742–3.
182. Or vice versa: see eg the *Lego* cases, discussed at [18.20].
183. See [16.29].
184. Cf the *Ancient Church of the East* litigation: see [16.6], [16.32].
185. *Peter Isaacson Publications Pty Ltd v Nationwide News Pty Ltd* (1984) 56 ALR 595.

launched a Sunday paper of that name for the Northern Territory. Since each had been preparing in secret until almost the last moment, neither had built up the reputation needed to challenge the other in passing off. However, each was able to restrain the other under the Trade Practices Act from marketing their product without clear differentiation. A variation on this problem occurs where a trader with an established reputation allows another to build up goodwill in the same name or mark. The former's acquiescence may suffice to preclude any passing off action, on the basis that the parties must now be taken to have a concurrent reputation.[186] Again, a s 52 action ought in principle to be available to prevent consumers being deceived. The same applies where the defendant is found to be suggesting a connection with some third party, not the plaintiff. In the absence of strict standing requirements, this would not matter under the Act, but is fatal under the common law.[187]

There may also be instances where the plaintiff can establish deception, but not damage to its reputation. While a claim for injunctive relief in passing off will thereby fail, there is no reason (subject to the court's discretion) why it should not be granted under the statute.[188] In the same way, as noted earlier, a claim for damages might fail at common law for lack of proof of fraud on the defendant's part, yet succeed under the legislation.

---

186. See eg *Habib Bank Ltd v Habib Bank AG Zurich* [1982] RPC l; *Dominion Rent A Car Ltd v Budget Rent A Car System (1970) Ltd* (1987) 9 IPR 367. Cf *Ausdoc Office Pty Ltd v Complete Office Supplies Pty Ltd* (1996) 34 IPR 151.
187. Cf *Evian (CB) Ltd v Bowles* [1965] RPC 327; *Rolls Razor Ltd v Rolls (Lighters) Ltd* (1949) 66 RPC 299. See also *Elders IXL Ltd v Australian Estates Pty Ltd* (1987) 10 IPR 575: see [17.17].
188. See eg *Central Equity Ltd v Central Corp Pty Ltd* (1995) 32 IPR 481.

Chapter 17

Misappropriation: Establishing a Reputation

[17.1]   General. As the previous chapter explained, the tort of passing off requires that the plaintiff establish a distinctive reputation attaching to its business or products. Similarly, where an action is mounted under s 52 of the Trade Practices Act 1974 (or a comparable provision), and that action relates to an alleged misappropriation of business reputation, the applicant will in most instances seek to support its case by advancing evidence as to the existence of such a reputation. Unfortunately the courts have in both these contexts turned what ought to be a simple inquiry into a legal minefield. The basic thesis of this chapter is that whether the relevant section of the public has some perception of the plaintiff's business, and if so how far that perception extends, is essentially a question of fact. It cannot be pretended that these questions are easy to answer, for there are an infinite variety of situations and hard cases abound. The courts' task is made no easier by the problems of finding reliable evidence, both as to the existence of a reputation and the likelihood of deception, a matter which is discussed in the following chapter. Nevertheless, there can be little justification for the extensive use of legal precedents that characterises much of the litigation in this field, nor for the desire of some commentators to explain every decision in terms of a legal principle rather than a factual conclusion. Many of the decisions cited relate to fact situations which can almost always be distinguished in some way or another and which are rarely helpful for that reason. Although this point was refreshingly emphasised by Lord Oliver in the House of Lords in the *Jif Lemon* case,[1] it unfortunately still manages to elude many courts in both England and Australia.[2] More dangerously, the development of the law of passing off and its importation into

---

1.   *Reckitt & Colman Products Ltd v Borden Inc* [1990] 1 WLR 491 at 499.

the learning attached to s 52 has seen the evolution of a number of wholly unnecessary principles relating to various characteristics or manifestations of business reputation. Some of these, such as the approach to 'descriptive words', merely involve the elevation of common sense assumptions to the status of legal tenets. But others, such as the principles governing foreign reputations, or the suggested need for a 'common field of activity', have at times created inappropriate and ill-conceived restrictions. The persistence of these notions represents an unfortunate intrusion of legal technicality where very little is in truth warranted.

1. REPUTATION IN DESCRIPTIVE TERMS AND FUNCTIONAL CHARACTERISTICS

[17.2] The monopoly concern. The first set of issues to be examined relates to the capacity of a trader to establish a protectable reputation in descriptive terms and functional characteristics. These are the aspects of a product or business, or the presentation thereof, which are dictated more by the inherent nature of the product or business than by any ingenuity on the trader's part. The courts have demonstrated a strong concern about the consequences of allowing one trader to restrain another from using the same common description for its product or business, or from incorporating the same functional features. Great danger has been perceived in effectively conferring a monopoly over matters which ought to be available to everyone.[3] On closer analysis, however, this apparently tough stance turns out to have very little substance to it.

(a) Descriptive Terms

[17.3] Descriptive terms: the orthodox approach. This is illustrated by considering the situation where the alleged misappropriation consists of the description by the defendant of its product or business in terms similar to those employed by the plaintiff. Countless decisions have asserted that a protectable reputation cannot be established in an ordinary, obvious or factual description, unless that description has acquired a 'secondary meaning' by becoming distinctively associated with the plaintiff's product or business. This principle requires two questions to be asked. The first is whether the terms employed (usually words, though this need not always be the case) are indeed 'merely descriptive' in the sense indicated. Terms are descriptive if they are inevitably suggested by some quality of the product or business, such as its purpose, method of performance, geographical location or origin, and so on. This is to be contrasted with the use of 'fancy' or invented terms, as well as with the use of ordinary terms in a context in which their usual meaning is

---

2.   That said, Lord Oliver's comments have been cited with approval by Australian courts: see eg *Morgan & Banks Pty Ltd v Select Personnel Pty Ltd* (1991) 20 IPR 289 at 293; *Vieright Pty Ltd v Myer Stores Ltd* (1995) 31 IPR 361 at 369, 371. See also *Twentieth Century Fox Film Corp v South Australian Brewing Co Ltd* (1996) 34 IPR 247 at 251.

3.   See eg *Hornsby Building Information Centre Pty Ltd v Sydney Building Information Centre Ltd* (1978) 140 CLR 216 at 229; *Telmak Teleproducts (Australia) Pty Ltd v Coles Myer Ltd* (1989) 15 IPR 362 at 378.

inapplicable.[4] Generally speaking, it is fairly easy to ascertain the category into which particular terms fall. Even in those instances where a new product is concerned, the use of familiar terms to suggest its principal characteristics will tend to be regarded as falling on the descriptive side of the line.[5] The more difficult issue is that posed by the second question: assuming the relevant terms eg indeed descriptive, may the plaintiff nevertheless claim to protect them on the basis that they have become distinctively associated with the plaintiff's business or product? This is simply a question of fact: the plaintiff must show that it has been using those terms over such a period and in such a way that the terms would suggest to the relevant public not just any product or business with the requisite quality, but the plaintiff's product or business.

[17.4] Examples. Out of the many, many cases that could be selected, two High Court decisions suffice to illustrate the operation of these principles. *Hornsby Building Information Centre Pty Ltd v Sydney Building Information Centre Ltd*[6] furnishes an example of an unsuccessful attempt to establish a reputation in descriptive words. The plaintiffs operated the Sydney Building Information Centre, a showcase for building materials and techniques and a general source of information for those contemplating building work. Despite having been in business for some 30 years, they were held to be unable to restrain the defendants from establishing a similar centre in the suburb of Hornsby, not having established a distinctive reputation in the descriptive words 'building information centre'. As Stephen J pointed out, this was an instance of the 'price to be paid for the advantages flowing from the possession of an eloquently descriptive trade name'.[7] By choosing to use terms which would be equally applicable to any similar business, a trader must accept that quite small differences in the trade name adopted by a rival will render that name unchallengeable. As the House of Lords had earlier pointed out, any risk of consumer confusion in such a case must be accepted.[8] Presumably though the plaintiffs could have succeeded had the defendants exactly copied the name Sydney Building Information Centre, since it would be difficult to believe that 30 years of trading had not resulted in a reputation being acquired in the precise name, descriptive or not. Indeed even if no such reputation were established and an action in passing off were thus unavailable, the use of the same name would surely amount to deceptive conduct under s 52, as in the *Sunday Territorian* case.[9]

---

4. Although note the possibility that an invented term may become so successfully associated with a particular type of product that, paradoxically, it acquires the status of a generic description for that product, thus lessening the chance of a successful suit: see eg *Linoleum Co v Nairn* (1878) 7 Ch D 834. See further [19.29] in relation to registered trade marks.

5. See eg *McCain International Ltd v Country Fair Foods Ltd* [1981] RPC 69 ('oven chips'); *Lumley Life Ltd v IOOF of Victoria Friendly Society* (1989) 16 IPR 316 ('flexibond').

6. (1978) 140 CLR 216. For other unsuccessful claims in respect of descriptive words, see eg *Telmak Teleproducts (Australia) Pty Ltd v Coles Myer Ltd* (1989) 15 IPR 362 ('dry-fry convection oven pan with lid'); *Dodds Family Investments Pty Ltd v Lane Industries Pty Ltd* (1993) 26 IPR 261 ('solar tint' for windows).

7. (1978) 140 CLR 216 at 229.

8. *Office Cleaning Services Ltd v Westminster Window & General Cleaners Ltd* (1946) 63 RPC 39 at 43. See further [18.9].

9. *Peter Isaacson Publications Pty Ltd v Nationwide News Pty Ltd* (1984) 56 ALR 595: see [16.39].

The second High Court case, and one in which the plaintiff's claim did succeed, is *B M Auto Sales Pty Ltd v Budget Rent A Car System Pty Ltd.*[10] Here Budget, the car hire firm, was able to establish that despite its descriptive name it had built up so distinctive a reputation in the period 1965–1968 that it could restrain others from using the adjective 'budget' in relation to car hire services. This reputation was held to extend even to the Northern Territory, the location of the defendant's activities, where Budget's business activities had at the relevant date been slight. This aspect of the decision is considered further below.

[17.5] A realistic view. The orthodox approach to descriptive terms suggests a process of rule and exception, with clear evidence needed to overcome the courts' reluctance to grant what are perceived to be monopoly rights. In reality, however, the only question is whether the plaintiff can establish a sufficient reputation by reference to which deception may be established. Whatever their rhetoric might suggest, the courts have in practice been quite happy to concede a 'monopoly' over terms which have become distinctively associated with the plaintiff's business. On this basis the 'principles' so frequently enunciated boil down to no more than this common sense proposition: that the use of descriptive terms, while carrying advantages in terms of making the product or business self-explanatory, has the corresponding disadvantage that it will require more effort than would be the case with non-descriptive terms to establish a public perception of the plaintiff as the distinctive source of the product or business so described. As Hill J has noted, there is in reality a 'continuum', ranging from purely descriptive names at one end to completely invented names at the other: the further along the continuum towards the fancy name one goes, the easier it is to establish a distinctive reputation.[11] Looked at in this way the monopoly issue is irrelevant, for everything comes down to being able to establish a reputation, just as in any other case.

[17.6] Business names. Before leaving the issue of descriptive terms, the special position of business names needs to be addressed. As a general rule, any person is entitled to trade under their own name, even if confusion is thereby caused in relation to some other established business or product, so long as they behave entirely honestly.[12] Thus the retailer David Jones would have no right, for instance, to prevent a person of that name attaching it to their own business. However, this is subject to two important qualifications. The first is that it does not apply with the same force where an invented company name is concerned. Although the use of such a name over a period of time has been said to create some sort of 'natural' entitlement to its use,[13] this is probably better regarded as an instance of a

---

10.   (1976) 51 ALJR 254. For other successful claims, see eg *Abundant Earth Pty Ltd v R & C Products Pty Ltd* (1985) 4 IPR 387 ('pure & simple'); *Apand Pty Ltd v Kettle Chip Co Pty Ltd* (1994) 30 IPR 337 ('kettle (cooked) chips').

11.   *Equity Access Pty Ltd v Westpac Banking Corp* (1989) 16 IPR 431 at 448, cited with approval in *Dodds Family Investments Pty Ltd v Lane Industries Pty Ltd* (1993) 26 IPR 261 at 269.

12.   *Parker-Knoll Ltd v Knoll International Ltd* [1962] RPC 265; *Greg Cotton Motors Pty Ltd v Neil & Ross Neilson Pty Ltd* (1984) 2 IPR 214. The principle does not apply to nicknames: *Biba Group Ltd v Biba Boutique* [1980] RPC 413.

13.   *Parker-Knoll Ltd v Knoll International Ltd*, ibid.

distinctive reputation being protected in the normal way. Even registration of a company or business name under state or territory legislation[14] will be insufficient to preclude action being taken to restrain its use by a person with an established reputation whose product or business name is deceptively similar.[15] As Young J explained:[16]

> The purpose of the [legislation] is not to create property in a name, but to record for the public protection the identity of the person using the name ... Although the mere fact that a name is registered under the Act creates some de facto protection because the registrar will not register a similar name, that is a side effect of the operation of the Act.

Second, even a natural person has no absolute right to use their own name. It is one thing to trade under that name, but quite another to attach it to a product or use it in advertising in a deceptive fashion. Thus for instance in *Bradmill Industries Ltd v B & S Products Pty Ltd*[17] Bradmill, a company with a distinctive reputation in the manufacture and marketing of textile products, successfully restrained B & S from using the name 'Bart-Mills' on its goods. Although B & S were operated by a Mr Bart and his son, the fact that their goods had also been packaged in a manner very similar to Bradmill's products led Lockhart J to reject the argument that the family name could be used.

(b) Functional Characteristics

[17.7] Product simulation and the case against protection. The courts' concern about the possibility of misappropriation actions being used to secure or protect a monopolistic position has if anything been even stronger in relation to cases of product simulation than where descriptive material is concerned. On the face of it, the logic of passing off and the principles developed under s 52 suggest that it should be unlawful to put a product on the market whose functional features so resemble that of the plaintiff that consumers would infer that they were the same product or at least emanated from the same source. However, a number of authorities deny this possibility, insisting that there can be no liability for the mere copying of the shape or appearance of a product.[18] Thus in *Interlego AC v Tyco Industries Inc*[19] the plaintiffs, makers of Lego toy building blocks, were refused relief in the Hong Kong Court of Appeal against the marketing of identical blocks, on the basis that the only distinctive features of the plaintiff's product were functional characteristics dictated solely by utility.

---

14. See eg Business Names Act 1962 (NSW); and see further Ricketson, ch 41.
15. See eg *B M Auto Sales Pty Ltd v Budget Rent A Car System Pty Ltd* (1976) 51 ALJR 254; *Burswood Management Ltd v Burswood Casino View Motel/Hotel Pty Ltd* [1987] ATPR 40–824.
16. *Wallace v Baulkham Hills Smash Repairs Pty Ltd* (1995) 32 IPR 443 at 446.
17. (1980) 53 FLR 385. See also *Halloran v Henry F Halloran & Co Pty Ltd* [1985] ATPR 40–501; *Gollel Holdings Pty Ltd v Kenneth Maurer Funerals Pty Ltd* (1987) 9 IPR 109; *B R Gamer (Investments) Pty Ltd v Gamer* [1993] ATPR 41–200.
18. See eg *Benchairs Ltd v Chair Centre Ltd* [1974] RPC 429; *Paragon Shoes Pty Ltd v Paragini Distributors (NSW) Pty Ltd* (1988) 13 IPR 323.
19. (1985) 7 IPR 417. Cf the later proceedings in Australia between the same parties, where no such principle is apparent in the decision of the Full Court of the Federal Court: *Interlego AG v Croner Trading Pty Ltd* (1992) 25 IPR 65. It was held on the facts that purchasers of Tyco bricks would not be deceived into thinking they were Lego bricks or licensed by Lego; although the defendant's claim that their product 'worked with' the Lego bricks was found to be misleading and deceptive.

In *Parkdale Custom Built Furniture Pty Ltd v Puxu Pty Ltd*[20] the High Court was faced with a situation where the defendant was responsible for a range of furniture which was virtually identical to a range manufactured and promoted by the plaintiff. The court, with Murphy J dissenting, rejected the plaintiff's s 52 claim. Brennan J based his decision squarely on the principle that, where a design is involved which cannot attract protection under the Designs Act, neither the common law nor s 52 should afford its owner a means of creating a monopoly over its use. Such a result, he indicated, would destroy the 'careful balance' established by the patents and designs legislation.[21]

[17.8]   Paramountcy of consumer protection. The 'no liability in mere copying' approach has created significant difficulties in practice. In particular, it requires that a distinction be made between the functional features of a product, copying of which should be permissible, and its 'get-up', which cannot necessarily be taken with impunity. Get-up here is taken to mean any 'capricious addition'[22] made to the product for the purpose of packaging and/or marketing it. As might be imagined this distinction, described by a leading commentator as perhaps belonging 'more to the realms of metaphysics than of commercial design',[23] can be enormously difficult to apply. More fundamentally, it is questionable whether the monopoly concern deserves to be elevated to these sort of heights. The point was forcefully made by Mason J in *Parkdale*. He rejected the argument that the pro-competition policy evident in Pt IV of the Trade Practices Act dictated that s 52 be construed so as to avoid the creation of monopolies:[24]

> [I]n a collision between the general policy of encouraging freedom of competition and the specific purpose of protecting the consumer from misleading or deceptive conduct it is only right that the latter should prevail. It would be wrong to attribute to the Parliament an intention that the indirect and intangible benefits of unbridled competition are to be preferred to the protection of the consumer from the misleading or deceptive conduct which may be an incidental concomitant of that competition.

Mason J also went on to reject the notion that the scope of the patents and designs systems marked off an area in which no monopolies should be allowed to subsist in functional matters.

[17.9]   Establishing deception in product simulation cases. In any event, to adopt an absolute principle that copying the functional aspects of a product cannot be unlawful is to ignore the fact that the concern is solely with deceptive copying, not copying per se. Even on an orthodox application of misappropriation law, a plaintiff will rarely succeed who seeks to rely solely on simulation of the product itself, rather than its name, labelling, advertising, and so on. Just as with descriptive terms, common sense suggests that a long or at least particularly visible period of use would be necessary before any distinctive reputation is acquired in the functional or

---

20.   (1982) 149 CLR 191.
21.   Ibid at 219–26. See also *UPL Group Ltd v Dux Engineers Ltd* (1988) 13 IPR 15 at 27–8; *Seekers Nominees Ltd v Target Australia Pty Ltd* (1995) 32 IPR 372 at 379; J M Evans, 'Passing-Off and the Problem of Product Simulation' (1968) 31 *MLR* 642.
22.   *J B Williams Co v H Bronnley & Co Ltd* (1909) 26 RPC 765 at 773. Cf *William Edge & Sons Ltd v William Niccolls & Sons Ltd* [1911] AC 693.
23.   Kerly, p 403.
24.   (1982) 149 CLR 191 at 205. See also *Targetts Pty Ltd v Target Australia Pty Ltd* (1993) 26 IPR 51 at 68.

non-capricious aspects of a product's appearance.[25] As the House of Lords decision in the *Jif Lemon* case[26] demonstrates, if the evidence is strong enough to support the conclusion that the public would be deceived, then liability should be established. For 30 years the plaintiffs had been marketing to British consumers their product, Jif lemon juice, in a container with the size, shape and colour of a real lemon. The defendants, who were also well established in the lemon juice market, now sought to use the same sort of container: in doing so, they were held to be passing their product off as that of the plaintiff. While Lords Oliver and Jauncey, giving the leading judgments, took the view that the choice of container was part of the get-up of the product, both strongly rejected arguments founded on the 'monopoly assumption'. Lord Jauncey indeed went out of his way to reject any notion that copying the shape or configuration of goods may not amount to passing off. If the thrust of this decision is followed in Australia, as it should be, a further technical and unnecessary restriction on the law of misappropriation will have been removed.[27]

[17.10] Disclaimers. It is also important to appreciate, as indeed Lord Jauncey pointed out in *Jif Lemon*, that where one trader has established a reputation in a particular product, rival firms are not absolutely precluded from entering the market — merely from doing so without taking adequate steps to distinguish their own product. Cases abound where a defendant has been able to escape any liability by establishing that their product has been marketed with some form of disclaimer or other distinguishing material that would preclude confusion between the two products, or indeed any other form of deceptive association.[28] Thus in the *Apple* case, for example, the defendants were able to import clones of the plaintiff's computers without attracting liability because they were clearly marked as 'Wombat' micro-computers.[29] Similarly in *Parkdale* the finding by Gibbs CJ and Mason J that no deception had occurred turned on the presence of a distinguishing label on the defendant's furniture.[30] A particularly striking example was furnished by the importation and distribution of cassettes and CDs containing live recordings obtained without the consent of the artists concerned. The defendants escaped liability for passing off and misleading or deceptive conduct, because in each case the cover of the disc or cassette was stamped with the word 'Unauthorised' in prominent lettering.[31]

---

25.   See eg *F Hoffman-La Roche & Co AG v DDSA Pharmaceuticals Ltd* [1972] RPC 1; *Komesaroff v Mickle* (1986) 7 IPR 295.

26.   *Reckitt & Colman Products Ltd v Borden Inc* [1990] 1 WLR 491. See also *Chris Ford Enterprises Pty Ltd v B H & J R Badenhop Pty Ltd* (1985) 4 IPR 485.

27.   The decision also signals the abandonment of a hitherto well established 'rule of thumb' — that an action based on the copying of get-up will only tend to succeed if the get-up is complicated and highly distinctive, or if an intention to deceive is established, or preferably both: see C Wadlow, 'Passing Off Enters the Supermarket Age' [1990] 3 *EIPR* 104.

28.   See generally A Terry, 'Disclaimers and Deceptive Conduct' (1986) 14 *ABLR* 478.

29.   *Apple Computer Inc v Computer Edge Pty Ltd* (1983) 50 ALR 581. On appeal the decision that s 52 had not been infringed was overturned, but only because of the defendant's conduct in supplying Apple manuals together with its own computers: (1984) 53 ALR 225.

30.   But see [18.15].

31.   *Sony Music Australia Ltd v Tansing* (1993) 27 IPR 649.

The only problem with relying on a disclaimer is that there will be circumstances where, because of the nature of the product or the way in which consumers tend to acquire it, it is unlikely that any notice will be taken of it.[32] An unusual example of an ineffective disclaimer occurred in the *Duff Beer* case. Faced with a finding that their use of the name 'Duff Beer' would deceive people into inferring a connection with the producers of the television series 'The Simpsons',[33] the defendants then argued they should be allowed to market beer under that name in cans containing the word 'Unauthorised' and other disclaimers. Unlike the example of the sound recordings, however, it was held that this would not be sufficient to avoid deception.[34] One reason for this, as Tamberlin J explained, was that:[35]

> [G]iven the evidence that 'The Simpsons' program makes a point of 'sending up' in a comic manner other advertisers and advertisements, and given the irreverent nature of the content of the series, it is by no means beyond reasonable argument that the disclaimers would reinforce, rather than negate or diminish, any association with the series.

Where a disclaimer is ineffective, there may in practice be no way of avoiding confusion and thus of entering the market lawfully with an exact copy. On the other hand, this tends to underrate the marketing ingenuity that abounds in the commercial world. In any event, it may simply have to be tolerated as part of the price for protecting the public.

2. LOCATION AND DURATION OF REPUTATION

[17.11] Territorial nature of goodwill. In *Star Industrial Co Ltd v Yap Kwee Kor*[36] Lord Diplock emphasised the territorial nature of goodwill when he described it as 'local in character and divisible'. While this is something of an overstatement, as will be seen, it does draw attention to the undoubted need on the plaintiff's part to establish a reputation in the relevant area at the relevant time. The relevant area is not necessarily where the plaintiff's trading activities are primarily based, but rather in the particular location in which the defendant's conduct is alleged to be taking effect. Typically, though by no means inevitably,[37] this will be the jurisdiction in which the action is commenced, or some specific part of it.

This principle is starkly illustrated by *Dairy Vale Metro Co-operative Ltd v Brownes Dairy Ltd.*[38] Dairy Vale, which had established a market in South Australia for 'Eve' yoghurt, was now looking to launch the product in Western Australia. Together with a licensee, it spent more than $200,000 on a promotional and sales campaign for that state. Two days before the launch, the defendant began marketing its own brand of yoghurt, 'Temptation'. This appeared in a similar carton to 'Eve' and, as with its rival, was promoted in

---

32. See eg *Abundant Earth Pty Ltd v R & C Products Pty Ltd* (1985) 4 IPR 387; *Reckitt & Colman Products Ltd v Borden Inc* [1990] 1 WLR 491.
33. See [16.29].
34. *Twentieth Century Fox Film Corp v South Australian Brewing Co Ltd* (1996) 34 IPR 247.
35. Ibid at 254.
36. [1976] FSR 256 at 269.
37. Cf *Alfred Dunhill Ltd v Sunoptic SA* [1979] FSR 337; *Tan-Ichi Co Ltd v Jancar Ltd* [1990] FSR 151: see further [21.1].
38. (1981) 54 FLR 423.

television advertisements which featured an apparently naked woman
'ecstatically' eating the product. The s 52 claim by Dairy Vale and its licensee to restrain the defendant's activities was unsuccessful. It was held that
Western Australian consumers could not have been misled or deceived into
inferring that the defendant's business was connected with the plaintiffs',
since at the time when 'Temptation' appeared nobody had heard of 'Eve'.

[17.12]   **Spreading a reputation in Australia.** Unfortunately for Dairy
Vale, that was as clear a case as could be imagined. More often, it happens
that a business which is primarily trading elsewhere has *some* sort of reputation in the relevant locality: the question is, how extensive must that reputation be? As far as cases relating to different parts of Australia are
concerned, it is evident that there are some businesses, both local and
(more especially) multi-national, with a reputation which genuinely
extends across the country and which, leaving out of account some of the
offshore territories, would undoubtedly be protectable everywhere. On the
other hand, there are many more traders who cannot claim to possess this
national exposure and who may thus struggle to show that their reputation
has spread from its home base. The decided cases on this point show that
everything turns on the particular circumstances, but especially the nature
of the business and the manner of its marketing. In some instances, a
spread of reputation has been accomplished fairly readily. In the *Budget*
case,[39] for instance, the plaintiff had a fairly easy time in proving that its
reputation had extended to the Northern Territory, for it found a ready
market there for its car rental services amongst travellers from other states
who were already aware of the business. In other situations, however, where
the business involved does not of its nature involve interstate movement or
communications, the task may be considerably harder.[40] The geographical
isolation of the major population centres in this country makes it far more
difficult to establish the sort of mobility of goodwill that appears, for
instance, to exist in the United Kingdom.[41] This is exacerbated by the relative scarcity of national advertising outlets, particularly in the print and
radio media which are the staple source of promotion for medium and
small businesses.

[17.13]   **Foreign traders.** Most of the cases relating to the spread of reputation within the relevant country are decided on a predominantly factual
basis. In other words, the courts weigh up the evidence to determine
whether a reputation has been established in the appropriate location,
without being overly concerned to establish or apply legal rules. Unfortunately, the same has not always been true of those cases where a trader
based in another country and without a substantial local presence has nevertheless sought to restrain conduct by a local trader. Here there has been a
regrettable tendency to formulate restrictive principles which have arguably contributed to incorrect results being reached. The principles concerned have generally centred around the assertion that a foreign trader

39.   *B M Auto Sales Pty Ltd v Budget Rent A Car System Pty Ltd* (1976) 51 ALJR 254.
40.   See eg *Snoid v Handley* (1981) 38 ALR 383; *Motorcharge Pty Ltd v Motorcard Pty Ltd*
[1982] ATPR 40–302; *Targetts Pty Ltd v Target Australia Pty Ltd* (1993) 26 IPR 51.
41.   See eg *Chelsea Man Menswear Ltd v Chelsea Girl Ltd* [1987] RPC 189. Cf the position
in New Zealand: see eg *Auckland Harbour Cruise Co Ltd v Fullers Captain Cook Cruises
Ltd* (1986) 8 IPR 185.

may only obtain relief for passing off if it can show some form of tangible 'business activity' within the jurisdiction, which at the very least must mean having actual customers who deal with the trader within the country concerned.[42]

Although mainly articulated by English judges, this restrictive approach has at times attracted support in Australia. In *Taco Co of Australia Inc v Taco Bell Pty Ltd*,[43] for instance, the defendant was an American company which operated a well-known chain of Mexican-style restaurants in that country under the name 'Taco Bell'. When in 1981 it opened two outlets in Sydney, it found itself being sued in passing off and under s 52 by the plaintiff, who had since 1970 operated a Mexican restaurant in the Sydney suburb of Bondi, first under the name 'Taco Bill's' and then as 'Taco Bell's Casa'. The defendant counterclaimed in respect of the plaintiff's pre-1981 activities, but failed, thus leaving the way open for the plaintiff's action to succeed on the understandable basis that it had built up its own legitimate reputation during the 1970s which it was entitled to protect against the defendant's incursion. The interesting question, of course, is as to why the counterclaim did not succeed in the first place. In the Full Court of the Federal Court Franki J accepted that the business activity test must be satisfied. On this basis he held that the defendant could not succeed in passing off for lack of local customers: the fact that those who had been to the United States might have heard of or been customers of the American business was not enough. Deane and Fitzgerald JJ on the other hand did not decide this point, preferring instead to reject the defendant's claim for lack of likely damage, there being no evidence that the defendant had any intention of expanding into Australia at the time the plaintiff first opened its restaurant.[44]

However, the business activity requirement has now been firmly rejected by the Full Court of the Federal Court in *Conagra Inc v McCain Foods (Aust) Pty Ltd*.[45] After an exhaustive review of the authorities (especially by Lockhart J), it was held that it is sufficient for a trader to show that it has developed a reputation in the relevant jurisdiction, in the sense that its product or business is known to a 'substantial number' of persons. How that reputation is acquired is irrelevant, as Lockhart J stressed:[46]

> [R]eputation within the jurisdiction may be proved by a variety of means including advertisements on television or radio or in magazines and newspapers within the forum. It may be established by showing constant travel of people between other countries and the forum, and that people within the forum (whether residents there or persons simply visiting there from other countries) are exposed to the goods of the overseas owner ...

The Full Court's view was that so long as the trader has a sufficient reputation in the jurisdiction, and can show damage to that reputation, it may sue

---

42. *Athletes Foot Marketing Associates Inc v Cobra Sports Ltd* [1980] RPC 343 at 349–57; *Anheuser-Busch Inc v Budejovicky Budvar NP* [1984] FSR 413.
43. (1982) 42 ALR 177. See also *Merv Brown Pty Ltd v Dovid Jones (Australia) Pty Ltd* (1987) 9 IPR 321.
44. Note that this appears to overlook the proposition that loss of the capacity to *license* goodwill may constitute damage for the purposes of passing off: see [16.18].
45. (1992) 23 IPR 193. See F Martin, 'Protection of International Business Reputation in Australia' (1993) 21 *ABLR* 317.
46. (1992) 23 IPR 193 at 234.

in passing off to protect it. It is irrelevant that the trader has no actual customers in the jurisdiction, since what the tort protects is a valuable reputation, not 'goodwill' in the narrow sense of current trading activities. On the facts of this case, as mentioned earlier,[47] the plaintiff failed to show the necessary reputation: there was simply insufficient evidence that, at the time the defendant launched its range of 'Healthy Choice' frozen food products in this country, more than a small number of people were aware of the plaintiff's 'original' line of products in the United States.

The effect of *Conagra* therefore is that as far as passing off is concerned, the crucial issue is a purely factual one: whether sufficient people are aware of the foreign trader's business or product to be deceived by the defendant's activities. This must in any event be the only question to be asked in relation to a statutory claim against misleading or deceptive conduct, neither damage nor the presence of local business activities having any relevance at all. So much was recognised in *Taco Bell*, where the Full Court went on to dismiss the counterclaim based on s 52 on the basis that the few who knew of the defendant's US operations would not have been deceived into supposing any connection with the plaintiff.

[17.14] The 'internationalisation' of reputation. Although *Conagra* has certainly clarified matters, the broad view of protectable reputation adopted by the Full Court was by no means without precedent. In particular, a number of Australian decisions had suggested that goodwill might be established merely by extensive publicity. As far back as 1929, for example, the High Court held that an American company could create a reputation here by publicising its decision to set up business in this country.[48] More recently, it has become fashionable to emphasise the 'internationalisation' of commerce and, consequently, of business reputations. With markets increasingly seen in world terms, and with much faster and more effective travel and communications, it becomes so much more appropriate to regard the 'slop over' of publicity from one jurisdiction as sufficient to create goodwill in another.[49] This notion has for instance found favour with the New Zealand courts, particularly where Australian businesses are concerned.[50] In *Dominion Rent A Car Ltd v Budget Rent A Car System (1970) Ltd*[51] Cooke P went so far as to question the notion that a separate goodwill must be taken to subsist in each country:

> The weight of judicial opinion appears to recognise the possibility that an international business may have one individual international goodwill, the reputation of any local branch or agency being that of association with the international organisation

47. See [16.10].
48. *Turner v General Motors (Australia) Pty Ltd* (1929) 42 CLR 352. See also *Fletcher Challenge Ltd v Fletcher Challenge Pty Ltd* [1981] 1 NSWLR 196, discussed below.
49. See J Dwyer, 'Reputation Slopover' *Intellectual Property Forum*, Issue 4, March 1986, p 2; F Mostert, 'Is Goodwill Territorial or International?' [1989] 12 *EIPR* 440.
50. See eg *Esanda Ltd v Esanda Ltd* (1983) 2 IPR 182; *Crusader Oil NL v Crusader Minerals NZ Ltd* (1984) 3 IPR 171.
51. (1987) 9 IPR 367 at 379.

In Australia the clearest expression of this view has come from Wilcox J in *Chase Manhattan Overseas Corp v Chase Corp Ltd.*[52]

> Many markets are international in nature. Communications are speedy and comprehensive. Just as an overseas company may have a 'slopover' reputation sufficient to sustain a passing off action in a country where it does not trade ... there may be cases in which a reputation precedes the newcomer so that, upon the commencement of its operations, it is recognised for what it is. This is likely particularly to be the case where the newcomer is a significant and well-known company in a country with close links with Australia, such as New Zealand.

With the development of the Internet as a medium on which to transact business, it can indeed be expected that more and more traders will be able quite speedily to develop reputations which 'slop' around the world, no matter where their (physical) centre of operations.

[17.15] Establishing a new reputation. In *Chase Manhattan* Wilcox J drew a distinction between an established trader looking to extend its sphere of activities and a business coming into the market for the first time. In the former, it may be possible to garner a protectable reputation in a very short time indeed. This is most strikingly illustrated by *Fletcher Challenge Ltd v Fletcher Challenge Pty Ltd,*[53] where the publicity surrounding the announcement by a well-known New Zealand company of its intention to commence operations in New South Wales was held at least prima facie to create within a matter of hours a protectable reputation in that state. By contrast, it might be expected that it would take some considerable time for a firm starting from scratch to reach the stage of having a sufficient market profile. In some instances a headstart may be provided by the product or personalities involved being particularly visible, as is often the case with merchandise based on instantly successful films, or with businesses started by celebrities. Even in these instances, however, goodwill does not spring into full-grown existence. It is interesting then to note that in some instances courts have been willing to protect plaintiffs who have done no more than launch a trade campaign (directed to members of the relevant industry and specialist media rather than to the public) to promote the upcoming launch of their business.[54] The explanation here seems to lie in the courts' distaste at a defendant deliberately seeking to pre-empt the plaintiff by getting in first with a copied idea or name, a factor also plainly present in *Fletcher Challenge*. In so far, however, as it is difficult in these cases to say that anyone is really being deceived — certainly the public, who actually hear of the defendant first, can hardly be said to be misled — the suppression of such 'copycat' activities looks suspiciously like an instance of an 'unfair competition' theory at work.[55]

[17.16] Survival of reputation. At the other end of the spectrum are cases where a reputation has been built up over time, but the trader in

---

52. (1985) 9 FCR 129 at 140–1; and see also *Conagra Inc v McCain Foods (Aust) Pty Ltd* (1992) 23 IPR 193 at 232–3. Cf *TV-am plc v Amalgamated Television Services Pty Ltd* (1988) 12 IPR 85.
53. [1981] 1 NSWLR 196.
54. See eg *Elida Gibbs Ltd v Colgate-Palmolive Ltd* [1983] FSR 95; *My Kinda Bones Ltd v Dr Pepper's Stove Co Ltd* [1984] FSR 289. Cf *Dairy Vale Metro Co-operative Ltd v Brownes Dairy Ltd* (1981) 54 FLR 423: see [17.11].
55. See [16.20] ff.

question ceases business activities. For at least some time after this happens a misappropriation action may still be maintained by whoever retains or has acquired the relevant goodwill, since it is obvious that until the business fades from public memory a potential remains for deception. In *Ballarat Products Ltd v Farmers Smallgoods Co Pty Ltd*[56] the fact that by the date of trial the plaintiff had been out of business for seven years did not prevent relief being granted against another trader, although it was emphasised that the closure was 'temporary' and that the plaintiff intended at some point to re-open. Since this was a passing off action, it was necessary to show such an intention in order to defeat any claim that the reputation had been abandoned, as well as satisfying the requirement of probable damage as a result of the defendant's activities. Where a s 52 claim is concerned, on the other hand, no such intention to recommence trading need be established: so long as the public would be deceived, in principle it ought not to matter that there has been an indefinite cessation of business.

[17.17] Assignment of goodwill. This last point was confirmed in *Elders IXL Ltd v Australian Estates Pty Ltd,*[57] which also illustrates the possible pitfalls where an attempt is made to exploit rights which have been purportedly acquired from a trader who has built up goodwill. There is no doubt that goodwill may be acquired by assignment, so that the assignee becomes entitled to take action in passing off, even against the assignor.[58] However, contrary to the position that may obtain with registered trade marks,[59] an assignment merely of the name, mark or other indicia whose use have created the reputation will not in itself confer any property in the assignee. Thus no right to bring passing off proceedings is obtained where, prior to the assignment of an unregistered mark, the assignor had ceased trading on a permanent basis;[60] or where the assignee, although acquiring all rights to the assignor's established business, takes no steps to keep it going and has no intention of so doing. This is what happened in *Elders IXL*, although the plaintiffs were still able to restrain the defendant under the Trade Practices Act from making deceptive use of the well-established name of the acquired business.[61] The decision on the passing off point was distinguished in *ACI Australia Ltd v Glamour Glaze Pty Ltd,*[62] where a business was assigned under an agreement which explicitly stated that no goodwill was being transferred. Despite this provision, it was held that the assignee had indeed acquired the established goodwill in the name of the business, since every other facet of the business had been transferred and this inevitably included the reputation attaching to it. Furthermore, in contrast with *Elders IXL*, the assignee here had continued to market products featuring the name of the acquired business.

---

56.   [1957] VR 104. See also *Ad-Lib Club Ltd v Granville* [1972] RPC 673.
57.   (1987) 10 IPR 575.
58.   See eg *Adrema v Adrema-Werke* [1958] RPC 323.
59.   See [20.12].
60.   *Star Industrial Co Ltd v Yap Kwee Kor* [1976] FSR 256.
61.   See also *Winning Appliances Pty Ltd v Dean Appliances Pty Ltd* (1995) 32 IPR 43.
62.   (1988) 11 IPR 269.

3. FIELDS OF ACTIVITY

[17.18]   A requirement of 'common field of activity'? In *McCullough v Lewis A May (Produce Distributors) Ltd*[63] Wynn-Parry J formulated the most artificial and absurd restriction of all on the capacity of a plaintiff to establish a protectable reputation:

> I am satisfied that there is discoverable in all those [cases] in which the Court has intervened this factor, namely that there was a common field of activity in which, however remotely, both the Plaintiff and the Defendant were engaged and that it was the presence of that factor that accounted for the jurisdiction of the Court.

On that basis relief was refused to the plaintiff, a broadcaster popular with children under the sobriquet 'Uncle Mac', against the makers of a breakfast cereal, also called 'Uncle Mac' and promoting a (fictional) avuncular character of that name. The implication of the judgment is that a reputation which has been built up by trade in one area of commerce cannot be taken as extending to a different area, no matter how clear it might be that consumers would be deceived by the activities of a person in that other field. To that extent the decision is plainly inconsistent with other British cases, both before and since, which have held that a well-known firm may protect itself against those who would deceptively suggest an association with it, even if the fields of activity involved are entirely distinct.[64] Given such decisions, it is scarcely surprising that the courts in that country have substantially retreated from the *Uncle Mac* formulation.[65] The dominant view now is that the fact that the parties are operating in widely different fields is merely an important and highly relevant consideration, though by no means definitive, in assessing the likelihood of the relevant consumers being deceived.[66]

[17.19]   The Australian approach. With the possible exception of the Victorian Supreme Court, which has at times appeared to flirt with the common field requirement,[67] that notion has scarcely taken root in Australia. The *Uncle Mac* judgment was decisively rejected in *Henderson v Radio Corp Pty Ltd*,[68] and subsequent decisions have for the most part seen this view strongly reaffirmed.[69] Even where there has been some inclination to see an absence of common field as relevant, courts have been adept at finding the parties' fields of activity to be sufficiently related as to defeat

63.   (1947) 65 RPC 58 at 66–7.
64.   See eg *Eastman Photographic Materials Co Ltd v John Griffiths Cycle Corp Ltd* (1898)15 RPC 105; *Harrods Ltd v R Harrod Ltd* (1924) 41 RPC 74; *Lego System v Lego M Lemelstrich Ltd* [1983] FSR 155 (see [18.20]).
65.   See generally J Phillips and A Coleman, 'Passing Off and the "Common Field of Activity"' (1985) 101 *LQR* 242.
66.   *Stringfellow v McCain Foods (GB) Ltd* [1984] RPC 501; *Harrods Ltd v Harrodian School* (1996) 35 IPR 355.
67.   See eg *Ronson Products Ltd v James Ronson Pty Ltd* [1957] VR 731; *FMC Engineering Pty Ltd v FMC (Australia) Ltd* [1966] VR 529; *Petersville Sleigh Ltd v Sugarman* (1987) 10 IPR 501. See also *Cue Design Pty Ltd v Playboy Enterprises Pty Ltd* (1983) 43 ALR 535.
68.   (1960) 60 SR (NSW) 576: see [16.17].
69.   See eg *Totalizator Agency Board v Turf News Pty Ltd* [1967] VR 605; *Hutchence v South Seas Bubble Co Pty Ltd* (1986) 6 IPR 473; *Nicholas v Borg* (1986) 7 IPR 1; *Fido Dido Inc v Venture Stores (Retailers) Pty Ltd* (1988) 16 IPR 365.

any objection based on that point.[70] Moreover while in Britain the question of common field may quite legitimately come into play even where deception is established, in that it may be impossible for the plaintiff to establish damage where the defendant is not in any sense a competitor,[71] this will not tend to be the case here. This is in part due to the adoption in *Henderson* and other cases of a broad conception of damage, which includes the loss of licensing potential,[72] but is more particularly a function of the statutory remedies against misappropriation, which do not require damage to be established at all. Nevertheless there is nothing intrinsically wrong with the approach now adopted by the British courts, for it can hardly be denied that the further apart the parties' activities, the harder it will be to establish that the public would infer a connection between the two. As with all the 'principles' discussed in this chapter, that should simply be a factual observation based on common sense.

---

70. See eg *Children's Television Workshop Inc v Woolworths (NSW) Pty Ltd* [1981] 1 NSWLR 273 ('owners' of fictional characters and toy retailers); *Abundant Earth Pty Ltd v R & C Products Pty Ltd* (1985) 4 IPR 387 (cooking oil and health food); *Chase Manhattan Overseas Corp v Chase Corp* (1986) 8 IPR 69 (banking and property investment).
71. See eg *Stringfellow v McCain Foods (GB) Ltd* [1984] RPC 501.
72. See [16.17]–[16.18].

Chapter 18

Misappropriation: Establishing Deception

1. BASIC PRINCIPLES

[18.1] Introduction. The tort of passing off, as we have seen, is made out if the defendant can be shown to have misrepresented a connection of some sort between the defendant's and the plaintiff's business or product. Obviously there can be no misrepresentation unless someone is misled or deceived as to the connection. Similarly, statutory liability under s 52 of the Trade Practices Act and its state equivalents depends on showing that conduct in trade or commerce is misleading or deceptive. Whether the tests used in determining whether deception has occurred or is likely to occur under common law and statute are identical is a matter that is taken up in the next section. That discussion, which focuses in particular on the supposed distinction between 'confusion' and 'deception', is followed by an examination of the assumptions made by judges in this context as to the knowledge and behaviour patterns of consumers. Before going on though, some basic principles that govern the process of establishing deception in court may be identified.

[18.2] Source of the deception. The first step, obviously, is to identify the source of the deception. Some problems arise where, as is commonly the case, the offending product or service reaches the relevant consumers via a distribution chain. Where this is so, it seems that any trader in the chain, no matter how innocent, is potentially a defendant in a misappropriation suit. Thus if A manufactures a product whose name or get-up suggests an affiliation with the business of X, and that product is imported by B, sold to the public by C and advertised by D, X would seem to have an action in passing off against A, B, C and D.[1] Why this is so, however, is not entirely

---

1. See eg *Children's Television Workshop Inc v Woolworths (NSW) Ltd* [1981] 1 NSWLR 273; *Star Micronics Pty Ltd v Five Star Computers Pty Ltd* (1990) 18 IPR 225.

clear. Are B, C and D to be taken as falsely suggesting a connection between *their own* business and that of X? Or are they liable for their part in suggesting a connection between A and X, no matter how innocent that role?[2] The matter is more straightforward under the Trade Practices Act. While it is a general principle that a trader is not directly liable under s 52 merely for passing on a representation without in any way verifying or lending support to it,[3] the Act provides that those 'involved in a contravention' are liable to be enjoined under s 80 and/or to be sued for damages under s 82. Thus even if an innocent member in the chain could not be held directly responsible for the relevant misrepresentation, they could be treated as an 'accessory'.[4] As against that, it would seem unlikely in most instances that action would be taken against retailers and others in the 'chain' unless they were intimately involved in the product (as opposed to merely promoting it or providing one of many outlets) or the only available defendant. In any event, it will continue to be assumed for the purpose of this treatment that the defendant is the person whose business is being deceptively linked to that of the plaintiff.

In some instances it may be the original manufacturer who seeks to escape liability by pleading that any deception is the work of those further down the chain, even though the end result is still that a connection is suggested between the plaintiff and the manufacturer. In order to succeed with such an argument, it must be apparent that the retailer (or other trader in the chain) has brought about the deception by 'tampering' with the product or presenting it in a misleading way. Where the manufacturer has supplied the 'means of deception' by producing a product whose name, get-up or characteristics are likely to cause problems, responsibility for the retailer's conduct cannot be escaped unless the manufacturer has taken clear steps to guard against deceptive presentation by instructing the retailer as to how to avoid any problems.[5] Nor can a deceptive manufacturer necessarily rely on any deception having been corrected at the point of sale: if the consumers in question have already been deceived (for instance by advertising) into considering acquisition or use of the product, some courts at least have suggested that any correction of the misleading impression at the retail outlet may be too late.[6]

[18.3] Identifying the targets of deception. Once the appropriate defendant(s) have been identified, it must be determined whether the

---

2.   If they can be said to have deliberately participated in a 'common design', they may in any event be liable as joint tortfeasors: see [2.6].
3.   *Yorke v Lucas* (1985) 158 CLR 661 at 666.
4.   The term 'involved in a contravention' is expanded in s 75B(1) to include those who aid, abet, counsel, procure, induce or are knowingly concerned in a contravention. Proof of intent is not necessary; it is enough that the 'accessory' be aware of the circumstances giving rise to the contravention: *Yorke v Lucas* (1985) 158 CLR 661. As to the special position of 'information providers', see [16.33].
5.   *Braemar Appliances Pty Ltd v Rank Electric Housewares Pty Ltd* (1983) 2 IPR 77.
6.   *Taco Co of Australia Inc v Taco Bell Pty Ltd* (1982) 42 ALR 177 at 197–9; *Tec & Tomas (Aust) Pty Ltd v Matsumiya Computer Co Pty Ltd* (1984) 2 IPR 81; and see also *State Government Insurance Corp v Government Insurance Office of New South Wales* (1991) 21 IPR 65 at 118. Cf *Cadbury Schweppes Pty Ltd v Pub Squash Pty Ltd* [1980] 2 NSWLR 851; *Parkdale Custom Built Furniture Pty Ltd v Puxu Pty Ltd* (1982) 149 CLR 191.

relevant persons have indeed been deceived or would be likely to be deceived. The relevant persons here are those who are or will be exposed to the defendant's business activities. As far as 'classic' passing off is concerned, where one trader's product is passed off for that of another, the need to establish damage in the form of lost custom means that the relevant consumers must be actual or potential customers of the plaintiff's business as well. In many of the 'extended' instances of the tort, however, and also under the statutory provisions, this is unnecessary: it is enough if those reached by the defendant's conduct are sufficiently aware of the plaintiff as to infer a connection between the two businesses. As noted in the previous chapter, it may often be necessary to look separately at the effect of the defendant's conduct in different localities.[7] If nobody within the jurisdiction in which the action is brought has been deceived, no liability will usually ensue.[8] Alternatively, it may be that deception is made out in some localities but not others, in which case injunctive relief will be tailored accordingly.[9]

[18.4] A matter for the court to decide. It is plainly unnecessary to show that all of the relevant class of consumers would be deceived. Equally, the deception must be identified in more than a few. The yardstick here is by definition imprecise, some judges talking of a 'substantial' number,[10] others of a 'reasonably significant' or 'significant' number or section of the public.[11] In practice this is rarely a major issue, for the plaintiff's case does not stand or fall according to the number of actual instances of deception established by the evidence. It has been reiterated time and again that it is for the court itself, having reviewed the defendant's conduct, to determine whether that conduct is calculated to deceive.[12] To do this the court must put itself in the place of a typical consumer and assess the (objective) effect of what the defendant has done. This will involve taking careful account of how the consumer comes into contact with the defendant's conduct. What is deceptive in one situation may not be in another. For instance the larger and/or more expensive the product, the more time the consumer has to take over the transaction or to study the relevant material, the extent to which any similarity between the parties' products or businesses lies in peripheral rather than central elements or features — all these factors militate against a finding of deception, particularly where some conscious effort has been taken by the defendant to avoid the confusion.[13] Allowance must on the other hand be made for the possibility of 'imperfect recollection'. The fact that the names or appearance of two products may readily be distinguished when laid side by side (literally or figuratively) does not mean that deception will not occur when consumers come across one of them in

---

7. See [17.11]ff.
8. Cf use of private international law concepts: see [21.1].
9. See eg *Snoid v Handley* (1981) 38 ALR 383.
10. *Norman Kark Publications Ltd v Odhams Press Ltd* [1962] RPC 163 at 168.
11. See eg *Weitmann v Katies Ltd* (1977) 29 FLR 336 at 343; *Siddons Pty Ltd v Stanley Works Pty Ltd* (1991) 20 IPR 1 at 7–8, 11.
12. *A G Spalding & Bros v A W Gamage Ltd* (1915) 32 RPC 273 at 286; *Taco Co of Australia Ltd v Taco Bell Pty Ltd* (1982) 42 ALR 177 at 202–3; *Interlego AG v Croner Trading Pty Ltd* (1992) 25 IPR 65 at 105.
13. See eg the cases discussed or cited in [17.10].

isolation and confuse it with what they think they know or remember of the other.[14]

[18.5] Evidentiary issues. While the issue of deception is one for the court to decide, the parties will inevitably attempt to lead evidence with a view to influencing the court's view of the matter. Besides addressing the question of deception, such evidence may also seek to establish (or deny, as the case may be) that the relevant public has an established perception of the plaintiff's business. Proof of reputation is of course essential in a passing off action, while it may often in practice be important if deception is to be made out under s 52. Whether concerned with deception or reputation, the evidence submitted to the court may take a number of forms. Much of it will be straightforward and uncontested, being concerned to set out the nature of the businesses and products in question and the way they reach the relevant public. Where controversy may arise is in relation to attempts to establish the beliefs and perceptions entertained by those coming into contact with the defendant's conduct.

[18.6] Evidence of individual consumers. It is common for one or other side to produce trade witnesses, persons experienced in the relevant industry or business who can help to fill out the picture for the court of the parties' activities. While providing useful background or technical information and perhaps of assistance in determining the scope of the plaintiff's reputation, they are rarely helpful in relation to the specific question of deception.[15] To that end, individuals with no particular expertise (other than that needed to belong to the appropriate class of consumers) will typically be called to testify as to their own experiences. In practice the time and expense involved, not to mention the court's patience, ordinarily dictate that only a fraction of the whole class can be heard in court. Moreover the suspicion is always present, whether warranted or not, that such witnesses are carefully coached and provide far from an unbiased view: they would hardly be chosen, after all, if they were not favourable to the litigant calling them. Given that the question is whether a number (varying between 'significant' and 'substantial') of the relevant class would be deceived, it might then be thought that evidence as to what a handful of individuals believe would have very little probative value. It has indeed been stressed often enough that proof of actual deception (or of a lack thereof) is no substitute for the court's exercise of independent judgment.[16] Nevertheless litigants persist in seeking to bolster their argument in this way, reasoning no doubt that it cannot hurt to seek to tip the case in their favour. As French J explained:[17]

> Generally speaking ... evidence from consumers that they have been misled by the impugned conduct is of limited utility. It has no statistical significance

---

14. See eg *Freeman Cosmetic Corp v Jenola Trial Pty Ltd* [1993] ATPR 41–270; *Apand Pty Ltd v Kettle Chip Co Pty Ltd* (1994) 30 IPR 337. Many of the cases illustrating this principle at work involve registered trade marks: see [19.37].
15. See eg *Cadbury Schweppes Pty Ltd v Pub Squash Pty Ltd* [1980] 2 NSWLR 851 at 866.
16. See eg *Taco Co of Australia Ltd v Taco Bell Pty Ltd* (1982) 42 ALR 177 at 202; *Lego Australia Pty Ltd v Paul's (Merchants) Pty Ltd* (1982) 42 ALR 344; *Parkdale Custom Built Furniture Pty Ltd v Puxu Pty Ltd* (1982) 149 CLR 191.
17. *State Government Insurance Corp v Government Insurance Office of New South Wales* (1991) 21 IPR 65 at 84.

and the court cannot draw inferences from it that any section or fraction of the population will have similar reactions. But if the inference is open, independently of such testimonial evidence, that the conduct is misleading or deceptive or likely to mislead or deceive, then it may be that the evidence of consumers that they have been misled can strengthen that inference.

Some witnesses testify to actual circumstances in which they have or have not been deceived; others, more dubiously, recount their reactions under test conditions. A variation is to secure 'trap' purchases, in which it is shown that a request for one product has resulted in the supply of another, though again the results may be easily discounted.[18]

[18.7]   Survey evidence.[19] The obvious drawbacks with individual testimony might seem to cry out for expert evidence based on scientifically administered surveys of public opinion to be used as the primary form of supporting evidence in a case for or against deception. In fact, survey evidence has come nowhere near attaining in this country the status it has in the United States where, it has been said, 'a failure to adduce such evidence, particularly where well-financed companies are involved, can result in adverse inferences by the court'.[20] It used to be treated as inadmissible hearsay for the conductors of a survey to report on the responses of those questioned, without the respondents being personally available to appear in court.[21] However, this objection was comprehensively rebutted by Mahon J of the Supreme Court of New Zealand in *Customglass Boats Ltd v Salthouse Bros Ltd*,[22] and the Full Court of the Federal Court has now accepted that survey evidence either should not be regarded as falling within the hearsay rule at all, or may in any event be admitted in the court's discretion.[23] Nevertheless problems remain. Those responsible for a survey must be available for cross-examination, so that the court may be satisfied that the survey has been fairly designed and carried out. Courts have shown themselves particularly willing to discount survey results on the basis that the sample chosen is unrepresentative,[24] or that the questions chosen are improperly weighted or unrealistic.[25] It has also been said that where the methodology utilised in a survey is disputed, no reliance should be placed on the results obtained, at least for the purpose of interlocutory proceedings.[26]

Even where the methodology of a survey is accepted, there remains the question of whether the court will pay any heed to the results. In *Interlego*

18. See eg *Keith Harris & Co Ltd v Bryant* (1980) 30 ALR 663.
19. See generally J Farmer, 'The Admissibility of Survey Evidence in Intellectual Property Cases' (1984) 7 *UNSWLJ* 57; P G M Pattinson, 'Market Research Surveys — Money Well Spent? The Use of Survey Evidence in Passing Off Proceedings in the UK' [1990] 3 *EIPR* 99; R Langton and L Trotman, 'An Empirical Study of the Weight of Survey Evidence in Deceptive Advertising Litigation' (1992) 5 *Cant LR* 147.
20. Pattinson, ibid at 103.
21. See eg *McDonald's System of Australia Pty Ltd v McWilliam's Wines Pty Ltd* (1979) 41 FLR 429. See also *Mobil Oil Corp v Registrar of Trade Marks* (1983) 51 ALR 735.
22. [1976] RPC 589.
23. *Arnott's Ltd v Trade Practices Commission* (1990) 97 ALR 555.
24. See eg *Chase Manhattan Overseas Corp v Chase Corp Ltd* (1985) 63 ALR 345; *TV-am plc v Amalgamated Television Services Pty Ltd* (1988) 12 IPR 85.
25. See eg *State Government Insurance Corp v Government Insurance Office of New South Wales* (1991) 21 IPR 65.
26. See eg *Nationwide Building Society v Nationwide Estate Agents Ltd* (1987) 8 IPR 609.

AG v Croner Trading Pty Ltd[27] Gummow J, speaking with the concurrence of the other members of the Full Court of the Federal Court, indicated that survey evidence (and indeed evidence from individual consumers) may be adduced to show that deception has in fact occurred. However, except in the case of a 'specialised market',[28] such evidence may *not* be presented to show that prospective consumers would be deceived if they were presented with certain conduct. This, according to Gummow J, is 'the very issue which the court has to determine'.[29] As Langton points out,[30] in itself this sort of response

> would not surprise the innocent bystander since, in her [sic] view, all issues in a court case are for the court to decide. She would, however, be surprised if the central question at the trial was answered by first excluding the evidence that was most directly relevant to the issue.

The bottom line is that many judges appear downright hostile to any form of survey evidence,[31] or would at least prefer it to be backed up by substantial individual testimony.[32] Some appear to believe that the magic of cross-examination is capable of verifying the views of an entire class of consumers: though why those selected to appear in court should be treated as representative is a complete mystery.[33] Whether or not the reluctance of judges to embrace survey evidence is caused by a fear of having their power to make findings as to reputation or deception in some sense usurped, the result is unfortunate. In many cases a scientifically conducted survey, even one based on hypothetical responses to an imagined situation, should be regarded as a superior form of evidence to a judge's own and possibly atypical experiences as a consumer.[34]

2.   DECEPTION AND CONFUSION

[18.8]   The different senses of 'confusion'. The essence of deception is that someone is led into error. This does not mean that the representation made by the defendant or implicit in their conduct must always be false, for a statement may be literally true and yet, when taken in context, capable of misleading.[35] Nor, by the same token, are all false representations deceptive, for it may be that no reasonable person would be expected to rely on them. This explains why traders may get away with 'puffery' in the form of exaggerated statements as to the quality of their product ('the

---

27.   (1992) 25 IPR 65.
28.   *Re GE Trade Mark* [1973] RPC 297 at 321.
29.   (1992) 25 IPR 65 at 107.
30.   R Langton, 'Judicial Attitudes to Survey Evidence in Recent Australasian Intellectual Property Cases', Australasian Law Teachers Association Conference, Intellectual Property Interest Group, 1993, p 23.
31.   See eg *Stringfellow v McCain Foods (CB) Ltd* [1984] RPC 501; *Mothercare UK Ltd v Penguin Books Ltd* [1988] RPC 113.
32.   See eg *Reckitt & Colman Products Ltd v Borden Inc* [1990] 1 WLR 491 at 500–1.
33.   Cf *Conagra Inc v McCain Foods (Aust) Pty Ltd* (1992) 23 IPR 193, where individual testimony was discounted on the basis that the persons concerned were atypical of the relevant class of consumers.
34.   See further [18.17].
35.   This is the case, for instance, with the accurate use of a descriptive term which has become distinctively associated with another trader: see *Hornsby Building Information Centre Pty Ltd v Sydney Building Information Centre Ltd* (1978) 140 CLR 216 at 227.

best in the world' etc), for consumers are taken to understand that such hyperbole is part and parcel of commercial promotion and not to be taken seriously.[36] Of course one might well ask why traders bother to make such claims if it is so obvious that nobody is likely to believe them: there is much force in the comment that 'it is for the Act to control advertisers and not for what are claimed to be present advertising standards to mould the law'.[37] In any event, these are straightforward propositions. Where difficulty arises is in distinguishing between conduct that misleads and conduct that is merely confusing. Over the years the term 'confusion' has amply lived up to its name. In the context of passing off, and latterly s 52, it has been used in at least four different senses:

(i)   as a synonym for deception;[38]

(ii)   as referring to a situation where consumers mistake one product or business for that of another, as opposed to inferring some unspecified connection between the two;[39]

(iii) as signifying conduct which, while capable of leading people into error, does not attract liability; and

(iv)   as signifying conduct which merely creates uncertainty rather than amounting to deception.

This ambiguity makes the term one which, ideally, should be avoided at all costs. Unfortunately, the courts persist in using it. That being so, it becomes necessary to look in more detail at two of the usages identified, the third and fourth.

[18.9] 'Tolerable' confusion. In some instances courts have identified conduct which, while potentially deceptive, must be excused. The explanation commonly given is that any risk of confusion on the part of consumers must be tolerated as an acceptable price for keeping misappropriation liability within reasonable bounds. An example of this thinking was encountered in the previous chapter in relation to descriptive names which are almost but not quite identical,[40] it being said that the minor differences are enough to preclude liability even if consumers might be misled.[41] To the extent that passing off protection is not available to a trader who has not established a distinctive reputation, the point is unremarkable. Where two traders start trading at the same time under the same name, for example, no action would lie under the common law. On the other hand, there is no reason why those traders should not both be statutorily liable for deceiving

---

36.   See eg *Schindler Lifts Australia Pty Ltd v Debelak* (1989) 15 IPR 129.

37.   *CRW Pty Ltd v Sneddon* [1972] AR (NSW) 17 at 37.

38.   See eg *Cadbury Schweppes Pty Ltd v Pub Squash Pty Ltd* [1980] 2 NSWLR 851. Cf Trade Marks Act 1995 (Cth) s 43, forbidding the registration of marks whose use 'would be likely to deceive or cause confusion': see [19.37]ff.

39.   See Murumba, p 36 ff, who makes much of the difference between 'confusion' in this sense and what he regards as the wider notion of 'deception'. While confusion undoubtedly can be used in this sense (see eg *McWilliam's Wines Pty Ltd v McDonald's System of Australia Pty Ltd* (1980) 33 ALR 394 at 412; *CPC (United Kingdom) Ltd v Keenan* [1986] FSR 527) it is just as frequently used in one of the other senses, making the utility of the analysis doubtful.

40.   See [17.4].

41.   *Office Cleaning Services Ltd v Westminster Window & General Cleaners Ltd* (1946) 63 RPC 39 at 43.

each other's customers, as was indeed found to be the case in the *Sunday Territorian* decision.[42] Closer examination of some of the 'tolerable confusion' cases, however, reveals a broader notion at work: that it is important not to allow a trader to acquire a de facto monopoly over the use of a particular name, mark, get-up, etc. Not only does this suggest that passing off protection should be denied even if the plaintiff has developed a distinctive reputation, it can also be used to resist a finding of deceptive conduct under s 52. Thus in *Chase Manhattan Overseas Corp v Chase Corp*[43] the plaintiffs, the well-established banking group, were unable to prevent the defendant, a New Zealand real estate and investment business, from entering the Australian market under the name 'Chase'. Lockhart and Neaves JJ stressed that the plaintiffs should not be allowed to claim any monopoly over that name merely because people commonly used it as shorthand for 'Chase Manhattan'. The minor differences in the full names of the parties, together with the fact that they were operating in slightly different fields, was enough to defeat any claim of deception.

The problem with this reasoning is that it places too high a value on the monopoly concern, as noted earlier in discussing liability for product simulation.[44] Stripped of any such assumption, the case would seem to have been a fairly straightforward instance of deception, given the prominence of the plaintiff. A more realistic decision in this context is provided by the earlier case of *Bridge Stockbrokers Ltd v Bridges*.[45] Again the Federal Court was faced with the conduct of a firm wishing to provide financial services under a name similar, though not identical, to that of an established firm. Here though the court held the new firm liable, stressing that although it had acted in good faith, it had made no reasonable effort to find a way of using the term 'Bridge' without disassociating itself from the plaintiff. It was conceded that the case fell 'close to the borderline between conduct which is misleading and deceptive within the meaning of the Act and conduct which is merely confusing'.[46] In this instance, however, the term 'confusing' was evidently being used in a different sense, the fourth of those set out above: to refer to conduct which merely creates uncertainty rather than deception. This has been the dominant use of the term in recent Australian decisions and indeed it was also used in that way by the majority judges in *Chase*.

[18.10] Confusion as uncertainty. In *Parkdale v Puxu*[47] Mason J, despite stressing that the 'clear words' of s 52 should not be read down, nevertheless stated:

> Conduct does not breach s 52(1) merely because members of the public would be caused to wonder whether it might not be the case that two products come from the same source ... Under s 52 the onus is on the plaintiff to

---

42. *Peter Isaacson Publications Pty Ltd v Nationwide News Pty Ltd* (1984) 56 ALR 595: see [16.41].
43. (1986) 8 IPR 69.
44. See [17.8].
45. (1984) 5 IPR 81.
46. Ibid at 89. See also *Street v Jedsminster Pty Ltd* (1988) 11 IPR 520.
47. (1982) 149 CLR 191 at 209–10. See also *Mc William's Wines Pty Ltd v McDonald's System of Australia Pty Ltd* (1980) 33 ALR 394; *Taco Co of Australia Inc v Taco Bell Pty Ltd* (1982) 42 ALR 177 at 201. Cf the test used under s 43 of the Trade Marks Act 1995 (Cth) to determine whether a mark is deceptive or confusing: see [19.37]–[19.38] and cases there cited.

show that the conduct is likely to mislead or deceive. Therefore conduct which merely causes some uncertainty in the minds of relevant members of the public does not breach s 52.

In the *Bridge* case Lockhart J made a valiant attempt to explain this distinction, using the example of a shopper faced with a new brand of soap which is very similar to an established brand. If the shopper, having been caused to wonder whether they are from the same source, subsequently *concludes* that they are, deception has occurred. That would not be the case, however, if the shopper merely wonders about the connection, decides that they don't know the answer, but buys the new brand anyway.[48] As Murumba observes, however, 'it is difficult to visualise, much less to measure, degrees of intensity of uncertainty on a sliding scale from a state of doubt at one end to a state of misguided certainty at the other'.[49] Moreover this approach is founded on the dubious premise, highlighted earlier in relation to the character merchandising cases,[50] that the mental processes of consumers can readily be reduced to a series of rational steps.

[18.11] Creating uncertainty: the 'cheating' analysis. It is indeed a little difficult to work out just why Australian judges have felt impelled to adopt this distinction between deceiving consumers and merely causing them to 'wonder', which would also appear to apply to a claim in passing off.[51] Nonetheless there are signs of a slightly more liberal version emerging. In his judgment in *Bridge* Lockhart J, while accepting that the distinction might be logical, went on to 'question whether this approach accords with reality and the legislative policy that underlies section 52'.[52] Returning to his example, he noted the possibility that the maker of the new brand of soap might have deliberately set out to create uncertainty:

> The corporation would know that a not insignificant number of people would buy its product in those circumstances. It is not straining credulity too much, or indeed at all, to conceive of such a corporation, with ready access to competent marketing advice, planning its marketing strategy so that it could not be said that the public would think that the two products in fact came from the same source. But the corporation would know that, by stopping short of such conduct at the point where the public is merely confused or uncertain, it will nevertheless increase its sales and market share at the expense of the established product. In my view the corporation is guilty of misleading or deceptive conduct within s 52. It is cheating.[53]

On this basis the creation of 'mere' confusion *would* be unlawful if done with intent, but not otherwise, since it would amount to deceptive (though not misleading) conduct.[54] This of course sits ill with the established view that s 52 necessarily involves strict liability,[55] and it would be better if the courts

---

48.   (1984) 5 IPR 81 at 93–4. See eg *Fire Nymph Products Ltd v Jalco Products (WA) Pty Ltd* (1983) 1 IPR 79; *Irish Distillers Ltd v S Smith & Son Pty Ltd* (1986) 7 IPR 509.
49.   Murumba, p 113.
50.   See [16.29].
51.   See eg *Fire Nymph Products Ltd v Jalco Products (WA) Pty Ltd* (1983) 1 IPR 79; *Morgan & Banks Pty Ltd v Select Personnel Pty Ltd* (1991) 20 IPR 289. This was certainly assumed to be the case in *Chase* and a number of other such cases where actions in passing off were taken to stand or fall with the s 52 claims.
52.   (1984) 5 IPR 81 at 94.
53.   Ibid.
54.   Cf *Parkdale Custom Built Furniture Pty Ltd v Puxu Pty Ltd* (1982) 149 CLR 191 at 198, where Gibbs CJ stated that the two terms are to be treated as synonymous.
55.   See [16.32].

dropped the deception/confusion distinction altogether. However, given that the distinction seems firmly embedded in Australian misappropriation law, the Lockhart approach should be welcomed. Those who choose to sail close to the wind should have no complaint if they are caught out in this way. Although the approach is yet to be definitively adopted by the higher courts, it was referred to without apparent disapproval by the Full Court of the Federal Court in *Murray Goulburn Co-operative Co Ltd v NSW Dairy Corp.*[56] In that case it was held that although the defendant's conduct in marketing 'Moo' dairy products might create uncertainty as to their relationship with the plaintiff's 'Moove' line of flavoured milks, the plaintiff had not acted fraudulently in this regard and thus could not be liable under s 52.

3. ASSUMPTIONS AS TO CONSUMER BEHAVIOUR

[18.12] **Characteristics of the target audience.** Thus far one crucial issue has been put to one side. Given that it is for the court to decide whether deception has occurred or is likely to occur, and given the lack of faith traditionally shown in more 'scientific' forms of evidence, just what are the assumptions that judges make as to the behaviour of the targeted consumers? The typical characteristics of a member of the relevant group are sometimes made easier to pin down by the presence of common expertise, as for instance where the group is exclusively composed of medical practitioners.[57] More often than not, however, the defendant's activities reach a wide cross-section of the community. Reference to some of the factors mentioned earlier may be important: such as how the public comes into contact with what the defendant is doing, or the extent to which any similarities in the parties' products relate to central or peripheral elements. But at the end of the day the court must make some assumption as to the intelligence and/or vigilance of the people into whose place it is putting itself for the purpose of the decision on deception.

[18.13] **The broad approach.** Most courts addressing this point have stressed the need to take account of all those who come within the relevant class of persons affected, excepting only those at the extremes. On this basis, so long as the conduct would deceive a reasonable number of those towards the lower end of the range in terms of intelligence or vigilance, deception would be established. The following is a collection of observations on this point:

> The advertiser must be assumed to know that the readers will include both the shrewd and the ingenuous, the educated and the uneducated and the experienced and the inexperienced in commercial transactions ... An advertisement may be misleading even though it fails to deceive more wary readers.[58]

> [O]nce the relevant section of the public is established, the matter is to be considered by reference to all who come within it, 'including the astute and the gullible, the intelligent and the not so intelligent, the well educated as

---

56. (1990) 16 IPR 289 at 307–8. See also *Pacific Dunlop Ltd v Hogan* (1989) 14 IPR 398 at 418; *Telmak Teleproducts (Australia) Pty Ltd v Coles Myer Ltd* (1989) 12 IPR 297 at 308; *Interlego AG v Croner Trading Pty Ltd* (1991) 21 IPR 373 at 416–7.
57. See eg *Stuart Pharmaceuticals Ltd v Rona Laboratories Ltd* [1981] FSR 20.
58. *CRW Pty Ltd v Sneddon* [1972] AR (NSW) 17 at 28.

well as the poorly educated, men and women of various ages pursuing a variety of vocations'.[59]

The essence of the action for passing off is a deceit practised upon the public and it can be no answer, in a case where it is demonstrable that the public has been or will be deceived, that they would not have been if they had been more careful, more literate or more perspicacious. Customers have to be taken as they are found.[60]

The court should consider customers of ordinary intelligence with ordinary powers of observation, disregarding both the unusually stupid and unobservant and those who might make a minute inspection of the [respective businesses or products] to note points of similarity and dissimilarity.[61]

[18.14]   A duty on consumers to take reasonable care? It is apparent that not all judges share the views disclosed in those observations. It has been suggested from time to time that consumers should be assumed or expected to take 'reasonable care' in their responses and transactions. Thus in *Parkdale Custom Built Furniture Pty Ltd v Puxu Pty Ltd*[62] Gibbs CJ commented:

> Although it is true, as has often been said, that ordinarily a class of consumers may include the inexperienced as well as the astute, [section 52] must, in my opinion, be regarded as contemplating the effect of the conduct on reasonable members of the class. The heavy burdens which the section creates cannot have been intended to be imposed for the benefit of persons who fail to take reasonable care of their own interests.

By any standards, that is a peculiar statement to make in this day and age. The whole point of consumer protection legislation, including Pt V of the Trade Practices Act, is that people do *not* take reasonable care of their own interests, that traders need to be restrained from taking advantage of the innate susceptibility of so many of us to modern marketing methods. No doubt there are those who would argue that such an approach should be discarded as unduly paternalistic, or that the focus should be on consumer education rather than on the often futile attempt to regulate advertising and product design. Whatever the merits of that debate, however, there is a clear legislative policy in place in all jurisdictions whose starting point is that many people, ordinary or otherwise, need to be protected from their tendency to believe what they are told (both overtly and subliminally) in advertisements, to make transactions on impulse or under carefully exerted pressure, to omit careful scrutiny of the details on labels or in the fine print of contracts, and generally to fail to make 'rational' calculations as to their present or future well-being. If there were not so many 'morons in a hurry',[63] we would not need consumer protection laws.

---

59. *Taco Co of Australia Ltd v Taco Bell Pty Ltd* (1982) 42 ALR 177 at 202, quoting *Puxu Pty Ltd v Parkdale Custom Built Furniture Pty Ltd* (1980) 43 FLR 405 at 424.
60. *Reckitt & Colman Products Ltd v Borden Inc* [1990] 1 WLR 491 at 508.
61. *New Zealand Natural Pty Ltd v Granny's Natural New Zealand Ice Cream Pty Ltd* (1990) 19 IPR 214 at 220.
62. (1982) 149 CLR 191 at 199.
63. This was the derogatory phrase used in *Morning Star Co-operative Society Ltd v Express Newspapers Ltd* [1977] FSR 113 at 117 to explain away any instances of one newspaper being confused with another, the two having similar names but otherwise being completely different.

This seems to have been accepted by the Full Court of the Federal Court, which in *Siddons Pty Ltd v Stanley Works Pty Ltd*[64] specifically rejected the 'restrictive approach' adopted by Gibbs CJ. As Wilcox and Heerey JJ pointed out, 'in practice, applicants who failed to take reasonable care of their own interests have frequently succeeded in s 52 claims'.[65] Nevertheless, until perhaps the matter is resolved by the High Court, the 'reasonable consumer' approach may continue to be adopted in some instances.

[18.15] Examples of insistence on reasonable care. Two leading cases illustrate the consequences that may flow from the assumption that consumers should be aware of the need for vigilance. The facts of the *Pub Squash* case have already been set out in an earlier chapter.[66] Given that the makers of 'Pub Squash' could not be liable merely for copying the marketing image established for 'Solo', there remained the fact that the defendant had produced a similar soft drink in a similar can. Anyone examining the defendant's product closely would not be deceived, for it was clearly marked 'Pub Squash'. Realistically, though, how many people do look closely at a can which they have grabbed out of a fridge in a supermarket, deli or milk bar? Powell J, whose judgment was affirmed on appeal by the Privy Council, recognised the existence of this 'casual' attitude on the part of purchasers. Nevertheless he found that no deception would take place, relying on the evidence of a handful of 'confused' witnesses who admitted to realising their mistake by the time they came to pay for the can. The plain inference is that consumers cannot complain if they make quick purchases and do not take the trouble to examine what they have bought before paying for it.[67] This strange view of the realities of modern shopping stands in sharp contrast to the attitude taken more recently by the House of Lords in the *Jif Lemon* case,[68] where no attempt was made to castigate customers for their inattention when shopping for lemon juice. And even if customers are to be expected to exercise vigilance, their standard of care should surely be minimal where low-priced articles are involved, a point that Jenkinson J in particular has been at pains to emphasise in the Federal Court.[69]

The relevance of this last factor was accepted in *Parkdale v Puxu* itself, where the defendant's range of furniture was found not to be deceptively similar to that of the plaintiff. Despite the close resemblance between the two lines, the High Court held that a purchaser of furniture costing as much as $1500 could be reasonably expected to check for a label or some

64. (1991) 20 IPR 1.
65. Ibid at 5. See also *Talmax Pty Ltd v Telstra Corp Ltd* (1996) 36 IPR 46 (see [16.30]), where the Queensland Court of Appeal expressly rejected the trial judge's view that the effect of the defendant's advertising had to be tested on 'careful' readers.
66. *Cadbury Schweppes Pty Ltd v Pub Squash Pty Ltd* [1980] 2 NSWLR 851: see [16.20].
67. See also *Stuart Alexander & Co (Interstate) Pty Ltd v Blenders Pty Ltd* (1981) 53 FLR 307.
68. *Reckitt & Colman Products Ltd v Borden Inc* [1990] 1 WLR 491: see [17.9].
69. See eg *Hunters Products Pty Ltd v R & C Products Pty Ltd* (1987) 8 IPR 591; *Berzins Specialty Bakeries Pty Ltd v Monty's Continental Bakery (Vic) Pty Ltd* (1987) 12 IPR 38. See also *Abundant Earth Pty Ltd v R & C Products Pty Ltd* (1985) 4 IPR 387; *Siddons Pty Ltd v Stanley Works Pty Ltd* (1991) 20 IPR 1; *R & C Products Pty Ltd v S C Johnson & Sons Pty Ltd* (1993) 26 IPR 98. Cf *Andritz Sprout-Bauer Australia Pty Ltd v Rowland Engineering Sales Pty Ltd* (1993) 28 IPR 29 at 50.

other mark to make sure it was the one they wanted. The defendant had attached to their chairs a label which identified the brand and this was held to be sufficient to avoid any deception. However, while the defendant could certainly not be held responsible for the activities of any retailer who removed this label,[70] it is pertinent to note that a purchaser would usually have to lift the chair's cushion merely in order to find it. How many of us would really go to that length? Once again, the court's conception of typical consumer behaviour seems at odds with reality.

[18.16] Erroneous assumptions and self-deception. The most extreme version of the reasonable care notion is to be found in a case in which McDonalds, the burger giant, unsuccessfully sued McWilliam's for describing one of their wines in an advertisement as 'the Big Mac'.[71] The Full Court of the Federal Court indicated that the use of this term, so obviously associated with the plaintiff, would at most create confusion, in the sense discussed above of uncertainty. If any consumers did conclude that the two firms were in some way related, this should be attributed to their own 'erroneous assumption' that the plaintiff had the exclusive right to the use of the phrase 'Big Mac' and that anyone using it must be doing so under some sort of agreement or joint venture. Such deception as might have occurred, in other words, resulted from the consumers' own ignorance and not from any conduct on the part of the defendant.

On the facts of the case, the conclusion that McWilliam's had not misled the public appeared to be correct. But the reasoning employed to reach that conclusion is more than a little suspect. In particular, it ignores the fact that any person who is deceived must begin with *some* form of erroneous assumption. This much was conceded by Deane and Fitzgerald JJ in *Taco Bell*[72] when they attempted to 'clarify' the *Big Mac* judgments. Nevertheless, they maintained the view that the operation of a 'fanciful assumption' on the part of consumers could preclude a finding of deception, so long as the defendant was not obviously attempting to play on that belief.[73] There are echoes here of the Lockhart approach described above, in that a trader whose evident desire is to create and profit from confusion is to be treated less leniently than one who, as was assumed to be the case with McWilliam's, merely overestimates the intelligence or perceptiveness of the public.

There is an intriguing contrast between the reasoning in the *Big Mac* case and the approach taken in some of the character merchandising and 'appropriation of personality' cases discussed in Chapter 16.[74] In *Big Mac* anyone who thought that only McDonalds was entitled to use the name 'Big Mac' was dismissed as making an erroneous assumption as to the 'true' legal position. But in cases such as *Pacific Dunlop*[75] and *Duff Beer*[76] the actionable misrepresentation identified by the courts was that the name or image used by the defendant had been 'approved' or licensed by the

70. See [18.2].
71. *McWilliam's Wines Pty Ltd v McDonald's System of Australia Pty Ltd* (1980) 33 ALR 394. See also *Perceptual Development Corp v Versi Pty Ltd* (1987) 11 IPR 358.
72. *Taco Co of Australia Inc v Taco Bell Pty Ltd* (1982) 42 ALR 177 at 200.
73. Ibid.
74. See [16.26]–[16.30].
75. *Pacific Dunlop Ltd v Hogan* (1989) 14 IPR 398.
76. *Twentieth Century Fox Film Corp v South Australian Brewing Co Ltd* (1996) 34 IPR 225.

plaintiff. Now logically, this could only be a misrepresentation if a significant number of the public actually believed that such approval was necessary. In other words, if enough people thought that the plaintiff's permission was needed, it would be needed since otherwise there would be deceptive conduct. As Pendleton notes, 'there is an inevitable circularity in impressing a public perception of what the law of actionable misrepresentation requires into service as the benchmark of what is an actionable misrepresentation'.[77] What appears to be a 'chicken and egg' dilemma is resolved, however, by bearing in mind that what the law is protecting (directly in the case of passing off, indirectly with s 52) is a trader's reputation. If that reputation, coupled with what the public know or think they know about licensing activities, leads to an incorrect belief that the trader has approved or is somehow linked with another product or business, then the public has been deceived and liability should follow.[78] The more that certain kinds of reputation are known to be exploited by licensing the use of names or images, the more likely it is that this conclusion will be reached — and the greater the control the trader has over those names and images. So on that basis character merchandisers such as Paul Hogan and the creators of 'The Simpsons' are perhaps more likely to succeed in establishing deception than a company such as McDonalds which, for all that its imagery is so pervasive in our society, is not generally known for allowing any traders other than its franchisees to use that imagery. If though it could be established that people did indeed believe that only McDonalds could use the term 'Big Mac', and that accordingly they assumed anyone else using the term must be connected with McDonalds in some way, the logic of the merchandising cases is that there would be an actionable misrepresentation. The question of 'erroneous assumption' is accordingly irrelevant to the real issue: whether there has been a misrepresentation (passing off) or misleading or deceptive conduct (s 52).[79]

[18.17] Judges and consumer behaviour. Returning to the question of the standards expected of consumer behaviour, it is one thing for a judge to recognise that the defendant's conduct must be (hypothetically) tested on someone who is, if anything, of below average intelligence, and quite another for that judge to have a real appreciation of what it means to be a 'typical' consumer, let alone a less than vigilant one. One basic problem is that the personal views, lifestyle, knowledge and experiences of the 'typical' judge are often far removed from those of the hypothetical person whose reactions are being postulated. This is something the courts themselves have recognised. Lord Diplock, for example, in describing the issue of deception as a 'jury question', commented:[80]

> The judge's approach to the question should be the same as that of a jury.
> He [sic], too, would be a potential buyer of the goods. He should, of course,

77. M D Pendleton, 'Character Merchandising and Intellectual Property' (1990) 1 *IPJ* 242 at 242. See also *Hogan v Koala Dundee Pty Ltd* (1988) 12 IPR 508 at 519–20.
78. See B F Katekar, 'Coping with Character Merchandising — Passing Off Unsurpassed' (1996) 7 *AIPJ* 178 at 191–2.
79. See eg *Hogan v Pacific Dunlop Ltd* (1988) 12 IPR 225 at 253; *Pacific Dunlop Ltd v Hogan* (1989) 14 IPR 398 at 428, 431–2.
80. *Re GE Trade Mark* [1973] RPC 297 at 321–2. This passage is frequently cited with approval: see eg *Pacific Dunlop Ltd v Hogan* (1989) 14 IPR 398 at 412; *Interlego AG v Croner Trading Pty Ltd* (1992) 25 IPR 65 at 105.

be alert to the danger of allowing his own idiosyncratic knowledge or temperament to influence his decision, but the whole of his training in the practice of the law should have accustomed him to this, and this should provide the safety which in the case of a jury is provided by their number.

It may be that any gulf between judges and 'ordinary people' is not as wide as it used to be, and that in any event Australian judges are rather more in touch than their British counterparts. Still, without labouring this perennial point of discussion, it is pertinent to wonder how a male judge, born into a comfortable middle-class background and immersed in the closed environment of legal practice for the greater part of his life, can relate to the day-to-day experiences of, say, a migrant woman living in the western suburbs of Melbourne or Sydney.

[18.18] **The difficulty of imagining deception.** Even if it is unfair to emphasise this stereotypical judicial image, it remains the case that all those involved in the process of arguing and deciding issues of deception, not to mention the authors and readers of this book, are almost by definition far from ordinary consumers. Moreover there is something inherently difficult in imagining the effect a particular practice might have if one were exposed to it. Take the use of 'feel good' images in advertising. Once aware of the message the advertiser is trying to convey (such as that consumption of a popular soft drink will render the consumer young, fit, suntanned, attractive to the opposite gender and generally overwhelmed by fun and health), how easy is it to calculate the effect of that message on those who are not cynical or knowledgeable enough to be aware of it? Again, attention has been given to the cunning techniques used by supermarkets and other retailers to lure customers into purchases — such as placing items attractive to small children down at their eye level, using filters and lighting to enhance the appearance of fresh meat, fruit and vegetables, and placing staple products in places which require the shopper to walk through as much of the shop as possible. Having listened to an explanation of those techniques, how does a judge assess the reactions of a person who has not heard the explanation and who might not even comprehend or believe it?

[18.19] **A solution?** It is hard to be too critical of the judges faced with the task of making these decisions, except where they lose sight altogether of the point of consumer protection by emphasising the need for reasonable care. Given the inherent difficulties of the task, courts can surely be excused if they sometimes reach conclusions which many would consider to be erroneous. The real problem lies with putting the decision more or less exclusively in the hands of the court in the first place. If ever there was an inquiry which should be dominated by expert evidence, it is this one. Subjective judicial impression cannot substitute for a properly conducted survey designed to assess, as accurately as possible, the reaction of real life consumers in real life situations.[81] The reliability of such evidence, as

---

81. In *Hutchence v South Seas Bubble Co Pty Ltd* (1986) 6 IPR 473, for example, Wilcox J decided a crucial point on the assumption that INXS fans shopping for T-shirts of the band would not understand the term 'bootleg', which he described as a word which was not 'in everyday parlance'. The only evidence offered to support this observation was that one of a total of three witnesses approached in the street had not heard of the term. How could the judge really be sure of his conclusion without some sort of survey, particularly since the target audience here consisted mostly of teenagers?

conceded earlier, is by no means established: indeed its use throws up all the general difficulties associated with reliance on expert testimony in an adversarial system. Nevertheless much would be gained by attempting to overcome these problems, so that judges can to some extent at least be relieved of the pressure of making what are often impossibly hard decisions.

[18.20] The Lego cases. As a final illustration of the points made in this chapter, it is instructive to compare two decisions handed down by the Full Court of the Federal Court of Australia and by Falconer J in the English High Court. Each concerned an application by Lego, makers of the famous colourful plastic building blocks, to restrain the marketing of irrigation equipment under the name 'Lego'. The defendant was a well-established Israeli company which had always used that name. Nevertheless the equipment was made of colourful plastic and it was the plaintiff's contention that consumers would suppose from these similarities and from the use of the same name that the plaintiff had branched out into a different field. In the Australian proceedings, the Federal Court rejected this argument.[82] By contrast, Falconer J was prepared to accept that many people would indeed be deceived into making this assumption.[83] How are these decisions to be reconciled? Contrary to the English judge's convenient excuse for distinguishing the earlier Australian decision, the fact that one action was brought in passing off and the other under s 52 should not have made any difference at all, for reasons which should be abundantly clear by now. The real explanation lies in the differing approaches taken on the factual issue of deception. The Federal Court scarcely bothered to inquire what consumers would actually think, stressing the need to take an 'objective' approach. On that basis, nobody could 'reasonably' infer or assume a connection between the two companies; anyone who did so only had themselves to blame. Falconer J, on the other hand, was far more concerned to look at the evidence before him, both from individual consumers and, significantly, from market surveys. This showed, in his opinion, that people would confuse the two, no matter how startling that perception might seem to the more knowledgeable amongst us. It is ironic that this realistic attitude to the way people behave is to be found in a passing off case concerned only, in theory, with the interests of rival traders; whereas it is under the consumer protection statute that ordinary consumers are condemned for their foolishness.

---

82. *Lego Australia Pty Ltd v Paul's (Merchants) Pty Ltd* (1982) 42 ALR 344.
83. *Lego System Aktieselskab v Lego M Lemelstrich Ltd* [1983] FSR 155.

Chapter 19

Registration of Trade Marks

---

1. INTRODUCTION

[19.1] Functions of trade marks. Trade marks signify the origin of goods or services and may say something about their quality, as well as serving to advertise the product. Thus they serve a commercial function, rather than act as an incentive to creativity, inventiveness or good design in the way that copyright, patent and design laws are intended. Trade marks obviously protect the interests of traders, much as passing off does, but are also regarded as providing consumers with a certain level of information and therefore protection.[1] Consumers can use trade marks to choose among competing products or services and will come to rely upon the fact that goods and services sold under a particular mark originate from the same source as they always have done, so that even if a mark is used on a variety of products, ultimately some person or enterprise is responsible for their consistency and quality. The informational role of trade marks may be expanding as the use of marks in Internet domain names becomes usual practice.[2]

The development of national and international mass advertising and distribution of goods and services has made trade marks increasingly valuable for advertising, and serves to stimulate and retain consumer demand for one brand over another. This is demonstrated by the fact that, of America's top 22 brands in 1925, 19 still led their product categories in 1990.[3] In Britain the top ten grocery brands have an average age of 42 years.[4] This is

---

1. See P A Smith, 'Role and Function of Trade Marks', WIPO Seminar on Trade Marks and Patents in Trade and Industry, Singapore, October 1984. For a contrary view, see M Pendleton, 'Excising Consumer Protection — The Key to Reforming Trade Mark Law' (1992) 3 *AIPJ* 110.
2. See [20.8].
3. 'Brand-Stretching Can be Fun and Dangerous', *Economist*, 5 May 1990, p 73.
4. Ibid.

despite the plethora of new products of the same description which have been launched during the past half-century. Furthermore, a new product bearing an existing mark has much more chance of success than a totally new brand, and considerably less advertising expenditure is incurred in persuading consumers to try new products.[5] In its 1994 Annual Report, Pacific Dunlop valued its brands and trade marks at $319 million.[6] Even products which, one would think, depend upon the user's specialised knowledge of specific merits possessed by the goods may rely heavily upon a trade name in order to become successful in the relevant market. A prime example is pharmaceuticals. Although such products are supposed to sell on scientifically verifiable effectiveness, not fashion, the pharmaceutical industry appears to be just as reliant on brand name loyalty as any other product. In Britain, for example, the average doctor prescribes from a repertoire of about 100 drugs,[7] although there are some 50,000 available. A trade marked product which is familiar to the doctor will be prescribed often and the market share of that drug will be protected by the brand name after any patent rights expire.

Obviously trade marks can be extremely valuable in achieving sales and possible market dominance for a particular brand of product despite the availability of alternative, possibly identical goods or services. The costs and effort of achieving this market position are borne by the manufacturer of the branded goods who has an interest in protecting the trade marks to which the goodwill is attached. The registration of a mark protects it by preventing others who produce goods or provide services of the same type from using the mark as an easy ride to market success for their own product.

[19.2] Trade Marks Act 1995. On 1 January 1996 the Trade Marks Act 1995 (Cth) came into force, repealing and replacing the Trade Marks Act 1955 (Cth). The new Act also repealed the Trade Marks Act 1994 (Cth), which was passed in some haste in order to enable Australia to accept the WTO agreement following the conclusion of the TRIPS negotiations, but which never came into force. Many of the provisions of the 1994 Act are present in the 1995 legislation which exhibits, however, a more considered approach to trade mark reform and takes into account the views of interested parties, which was not possible before the enaction of the 1994 Act. Although some important substantive and procedural changes have been made to trade mark law, many existing concepts remain in place and most cases decided under the 1955 Act will still be relevant. The 1995 legislation results from the deliberations of a Working Party to Review the Trade Marks Legislation, which took into account international developments including the TRIPS negotiations, the WTO agreement and the WIPO Trademark Law Treaty settled in October 1994.[8] Extensive transitional

---

5. Ibid. Research shows 36% less advertising costs for a brand 'stretched' to a new product. Examples of this include Quaker Oats extending their trade mark to microwaveable sandwiches; McDonalds launching Chicken McNuggets and McPizzas; or Arnotts or Westons introducing a new biscuit under their existing name.
6. Cited in Second Reading Speech to the Trade Marks Bill 1995.
7. 'Take a Dose of Backward Man', *Economist,* 5 May 1990, p 74.
8. Diplomatic Conference for the Conclusion of the Trade Mark Law Treaty, Geneva, 10–28 October 1994.

provisions are set out in Pt 22 of the 1995 Act.[9] The most important of these is s 233, which provides that all marks registered under the 1955 statute continue in force as registered marks for the purposes of the new legislation.

[19.3] Comparison with passing off.[10] Like passing off, a trade mark is a right associated with the protection of reputation established by a trader in respect of goods or services originating from a particular source. In fact, passing off from its earliest days, in its classic form, protected trade marks, albeit unregistered or 'common law' trade marks.[11] One difference between the protection offered by the tort of passing off and the registered trade mark system is that a registered mark is protected, as from the date of application for registration, without the necessity of proving reputation in the mark. Passing off, on the other hand, provides protection for a much wider variety of material indicative of reputation beyond that included in the definition of a registrable mark.[12] This reputation may be obtained by trading in marked goods and services and without the bother and expense of applying for and maintaining trade mark registration. On the other hand proof of infringement of a registered mark is more conveniently achieved than proving reputation for passing off purposes. Not all marks are registrable, although they may in fact have a gigantic reputation which could be protected in passing off.[13] The protection conferred by registration of a trade mark also tends to operate throughout Australia, rather than being geographically defined as is more usually the case with passing off protection.[14]

2.   WHAT IS A TRADE MARK?

(a) General

[19.4] The statutory definition. For the purposes of the statutory regime, s 17 of the 1995 Trade Marks Act defines a 'trade mark' as:

> a sign used, or intended to be used, to distinguish goods or services dealt with or provided in the course of trade by a person from goods or services so dealt with or provided by any other person.

A 'sign' in s 6 includes any letter, word, name, signature, numeral, device, brand, heading, label, ticket, aspect of packaging, shape, colour, sound or scent. This is similar to, but more extensive than the previous definition in s 6(1) of the 1955 Act, which defined 'mark' as including 'a device, brand, heading, label, ticket, name, signature, word, letter or numeral, or any combination thereof'. 'Word' is specifically stated in s 6 to include 'an

---

9.   See R McLean, 'The Transitional Provisions of the Trade Marks Act 1995' (1996) 7 *AIPJ* 106.
10. See *NSW Dairy Corp v Murray Goulbourn Co-operative Co Ltd* (1989) 14 IPR 26 at 45–8.
11. See eg *Reddaway v Banham* [1896] AC 199. See Chapter 16.
12. See [16.6].
13. For example, WATERFORD for crystal, which was refused registration as a trade mark, being a geographic name (*Re Waterford Glass Group Ltd* (1987) 9 IPR 339: see [19.30]), but would presumably 'belong' to the company producing cut crystal in so far as used for such products.
14. See [17.11].

abbreviation of a word'. The key additions in the 1995 definition are discussed in more detail in the sections that follow.

[19.5] **Workers' marks and the Union Label case.** As discussed in Chapter 1, s 51(xviii) of the Constitution confers legislative power on the Commonwealth with respect to 'trade marks'. A discussion of the meaning of the term in this context occurred in the *Union Label* case in 1908.[15] The Brewery Employees Union of New South Wales had registered its own union label as a workers' trade mark, the function of which was to identify that certain members of the community (ie non-unionists) had not been engaged in the production of the goods. The mark was registered in respect of beer, porter, malt, mineral and aerated waters, cordials, hop beer, ginger beer and cider. The employers of the unionists did not want their drinks endorsed with the union label since many customers were opposed to this display of union power. A constitutional challenge was mounted on the grounds that a workers' mark was not a trade mark within s 51(xviii) and therefore that parliament had exceeded its power in providing for the registration of workers' marks in the Trade Marks Act 1905. This challenge was successful. Griffith CJ stated that for the purposes of s 51(xviii) of the Constitution, a 'trade mark' is:

> a mark which is the visible symbol of a particular kind of incorporeal or industrial property consisting in the right of a person engaged in trade to distinguish by a special mark goods in which he [sic] deals, or with which he has dealt, from the goods of other persons. This concept includes in my opinion five distinct elements:
>
> (1) A right which is in the nature of property;
> (2) The owner of the right must be a person, natural or artificial, engaged in trade;
> (3) The right is appurtenant or incident to the dealing with goods in the course of his trade;
> (4) The owner has such an independent dominion over the goods to which the mark is to be affixed as to entitle him to affix it to them; (It is not material whether this right is incident to his possession of the goods or arises under an agreement with the owner of them.)
> (5) The mark distinguishes the goods as having been dealt with by some particular person or persons engaged in trade . . .[16]

The majority of the court (Griffith CJ, Barton and O'Connor JJ; Isaacs and Higgins JJ dissenting) found that the workers' mark did not fulfil the essential functions of a trade mark and that the relevant part of the Act was therefore *ultra vires*. Workers' marks such as the ones successfully challenged in the *Union Label* case had been adopted from the American practice of allowing such marks to be registered and used to indicate that 'sweated' labour was not used in producing goods. The 1905 Act also provided for a 'Commonwealth Mark' which was to be used in a similar way to the workers' marks of individual unions — to indicate that goods to which such a mark was attached had been manufactured within the Commonwealth of Australia under certain conditions as to the remuneration of labour. In 1948 the relevant provisions were repealed, the Commonwealth Mark never having been used, since on the reasoning of the *Union Label* case it would also have been unconstitutional. However, the 1995 Act has now introduced the concept of a collective mark, to be used by members of

---

15. *Attorney-General NSW v Brewery Employees Union of NSW* (1908) 6 CLR 469.
16. Ibid at 513.

an association to distinguish goods and services from those provided by people who are not members of their association.[17] The constitutional validity of the collective mark is supported by the external affairs power since such marks are provided for in the TRIPS Agreement.

[19.6] Service marks. In 1978 the Trade Marks Act 1955 was amended to allow for the registration of marks used to denote the business or services offered by the proprietor of a mark, instead of confining registered marks to those appurtenant only to goods.[18] There are now eight classes of services for which marks may be registered in Sch 1 of the Trade Mark Regulations 1995. These include advertising and business services (class 35), insurance and financial services (class 36), construction and repair services (class 37), communication services (class 38), transport and storage services (class 39), material treatment services (class 40), educational and entertainment services (class 41) and miscellaneous services, that is to say, services not described in classes 35–42 (class 42). Doubt has been cast on the constitutionality of service marks,[19] but such a mark does indicate the trade origin of services and is not therefore caught by the reasoning in the *Union Label* case. Furthermore, Art 6 of the Paris Convention for the Protection of Industrial Property (1883), to which Australia is a contracting country, provides for the registration of service marks, as does the TRIPS Agreement. Accordingly the external affairs power in s 51(xxix) of the Constitution would allow the enactment of such provisions into domestic law, even if s 51(xviii) did not. It would be anomalous if a right in incorporeal property must be attached only to chattels rather than intangibles.

[19.7] The former classes of registration. Under the 1955 Act, trade marks were registered in four different classes. Certification marks (which appeared in Pt C of the Register) and defensive marks (Pt D) are still found in the 1995 Act, and are discussed at the end of this chapter together with the new class of collective marks.[20] However, the new statute has done away with the old distinction between Pt A and Pt B marks. Previously, marks already considered 'distinctive' were registered in Pt A, while Pt B provided a home for marks not yet 'adapted to distinguish' goods or services but *capable* of becoming distinctive at some point in the future (at which point they could be transferred to Pt A).[21] The first major difference was that Pt B marks did not enjoy the presumption of validity that Pt A marks obtained after a certain period of registration. The second difference was that under s 62(2) it was a defence to any action for infringement of a Pt B mark that the defendant's mark would not be likely either to deceive or cause confusion, or to indicate a trade connection with the goods or services with respect to which the plaintiff's mark was registered.[22] Under the transitional provisions in the 1995 Act, Pt B marks on the Register as at 1 January are continued simply as registered marks, without distinction from former Pt A marks (s 233(1)). However, s 254 also has the effect that a person who

---

17. See [19.53].
18. Trade Marks Amendment Act 1978.
19. See eg Shanahan, p 8; cf G Williams, 'Are Service Marks Trade Marks? Commonwealth Power and Intellectual Property' (1995) 6 *AIPJ* 133.
20. See [19.54]–[19.55].
21. As to distinctiveness, see [19.21] ff.
22. See *Marc A Hammond Pty Ltd v Papa Carmine Pty Ltd* (1977) 28 FLR 160.

could have relied on the old s 62(2) defence prior to that date may continue to engage in what would otherwise be infringing conduct.

(b) Elements of the s 17 Definition

[19.8]   'Used or intended to be used'. The property in a mark arises from use or proposed use. In order to be registered, a mark must already be owned through use, or be intended for use when a product range is launched.[23] Lack of intention to use a mark is specifically stated to be a ground on which an application for registration may be opposed (s 59). The Act in s 7 contains provisions which shed light on the meaning of 'use'. Thus s 7(4) states that a reference to use of a mark in relation to goods means to use the mark upon those goods or in physical or other relation to them. The same provision applies to services (s 7(5)). If a trade mark consists of letters, words, names, numerals or any combination thereof, any aural representation of the trade mark is 'use' of the mark (s 7(2)). These provisions are clearly wide enough to cover use in advertising.[24]

Under s 7(3), a requirement that a mark be used may be taken as satisfied by authorised use of a mark. Section 8(1) defines authorised use as use under the control of the owner, control being exercised through quality control (s 8(3)) or financial control (s 8(4)), although the notion of 'control' is not limited to these (s 8(5)). This notion of 'use' by an authorised user relaxes the previous provisions of the 1955 Act, which recognised 'use' only by those formally registered as users.[25] This is particularly significant in the context of an application for removal of a mark for non-use.[26] It means that the owner can rely on use by any licensee of the mark, whether registered or not, so long as the owner retains sufficient 'control' over the licensee's activities. (The control requirement was in any event one of the conditions of becoming a registered user under the old legislation.)

[19.9]   Requirement of bona fide use. The use claimed or proposed must be bona fide commercial use. In one case a cigarette company wished to launch a brand of cigarettes called 'Merit'. When advised that this was probably unregistrable,[27] the name NERIT was registered instead, and 'launched' in the company's staff canteen. This had the benefit of providing protection for the unregistrable mark, since the two were so similar that use of 'Merit' by another cigarette producer would inevitably infringe the registered mark.[28] Registering a mark in order to provide de facto protection for an unregistrable one is called 'ghost marking' and is not permissible since there is no intention to use the registered mark as required by the Act. In this example the limited launch of the NERIT brand was held not to be genuine commercial use of the mark: accordingly the registration was declared to be invalid.[29] Sometimes trade mark

---

23. *Electrolux Ltd v Electrix Ltd* (1953) 71 RPC 23.
24. See *Shell Co of Australia Ltd v Esso Standard Oil (Australia) Ltd* (1963) 109 CLR 407 at 422; *Mark Foy's Ltd v Davies Coop & Co Ltd* (1956) 95 CLR 190.
25. See further [20.14]–[20.15].
26. See [19.52].
27. Presumably on the grounds that a descriptive (or, in this case, misdescriptive) mark is not registrable: see [19.27].
28. See [20.5]–[20.6].
29. *Imperial Group Ltd v Philip Morris & Co Ltd* [1980] 1 FSR 146.

applications may be filed in order to pre-empt another's entry into the local market, or to prevent a competitor expanding their business to include other products or services to which existing marks could be applied. An enterprising person could 'stockpile' trade marks in the hope of selling them off to traders wishing to exploit a popular trend,[30] or intending to begin business activities in the future.[31] This will also fall foul of the requirement of bona fide use.

[19.10] **'To distinguish goods or services'.** The other concept of 'use' relevant to marks is that they must be used *in a certain way* (as well as being in fact used in the sense discussed above). Marks have no life of their own: it is only when used 'to distinguish' goods or services[32] that they fall within the definition in s 17. To borrow a phrase from a passing off case,[33] a mark is a 'capricious addition to the article itself' in that the goods or services as such cannot be monopolised by trade mark registration. Nevertheless, it is significant that the 1995 Act now explicitly permits the 'shape' and 'colour' of goods to be registered as trade marks, both terms being included in the definition of a 'sign' in s 6. Under the previous Act, the case law had decreed that the shape of an item could not be a trade mark: hence the refusal of registration for the round Life Saver sweet, its shape not being something extra or added to the goods, but a characteristic of the item itself.[34] In the same vein, it would seem that previously the colour of a product was not registrable in Australia.[35] However, allowing registration of colours alone as trade marks does not overcome the difficulty in showing that a colour is sufficiently distinctive to found a valid registration.[36] That is not to say that the colour *of* a trade mark (rather than colour *as* a trade mark) previously caused any dilemmas for the Registrar. The 1955 Act specifically provided that a registered mark could be limited to one or more colours, although if it was registered without limitation as to colour it would be deemed to be registered for all colours (s 27). Section 70 of the 1995 Act now provides to like effect.

An 'aspect of packaging' of goods is also now included in the definition of 'sign' and this is evidently intended to overcome the decision in *Coca Cola Trade Marks*[37] to deny trade mark registration for the shape of a container. The House of Lords there refused to allow registration of the well-known 'Coke' bottle, for which protection had been sought after the expiry of design registration and as part of the re-launch of the 'classic' Coke receptacle.

---

30. See eg *Rawhide Trade Mark* [1962] RPC 133; *Pussy Galore Trade Mark* [1967] RPC 265; *Anheuser-Busch Inc v Castlebrae Pty Ltd* (1991) 21 IPR 54.
31. See eg *Michael Sharwood v Fuddruckkers Inc* (1989) 15 IPR 188; *Sizzler Restaurants International Inc v Sabra International Pty Ltd* (1990) 20 IPR 331; *Daimaru Pty Ltd v Kabushiki Kaisha Daimaru* (1990) 19 IPR 129.
32. The 1955 Act used the phrase 'in relation to' goods or services (s 6(1)).
33. *J B Williams Co v H Bronnley & Co Ltd* (1909) 26 RPC 765 at 773, discussing 'get-up': see [17.8].
34. *Life Savers (Australia) Ltd's Application* (1952) 22 AOJP 3106.
35. See *Smith, Kline & French Laboratories (Australia) Ltd v Registrar of Trade Marks* (1967) 116 CLR 628. Cf *Smith Kline & French Laboratories Ltd v Sterling Winthrop Group Ltd* [1976] RPC 511.
36. As to distinctiveness, see [19.21] ff.
37. [1986] RPC 421.

[19.11] 'Dealt with or provided in the course of trade'. The connection in the course of trade which a trade mark indicates is a connection between the relevant goods or services and the person who has the right to use the mark, either as proprietor or authorised user.[38] While excluding private or personal use,[39] this requirement is satisfied by any commercial dealing which indicates a more than temporary connection with the goods or services in question. However, it is not possible to 'reserve' a name or monopolise it in the abstract. An attempt to do this was made in *Re Application by New York Yacht Club*,[40] where the applicant sought to register AMERICA'S CUP for services including 'art galleries and the perpetual promotion of challenge sailing matches'. There were, however, no goods or services to which the mark could be legitimately applied, since the right to conduct the America's Cup series of yacht races does not belong perpetually to one body but passes on to the winner of each series.[41] The public, being well aware of this, would be confused as to the proprietorship of the mark and the connections in the course of trade between the goods and services and the New York Yacht Club: the application was therefore rejected. The *Union Label* case[42] provides a further example of the invalidity of a mark intended to indicate something outside the statutory term 'dealt with or provided in the course of trade'. The 'essential nature of a trade mark' is that it gives an indication of origin and not that someone has dealt with goods in some other way.[43] However, although the trade source function of a mark is often emphasised, it is also possible that the 'trade hands' through which goods pass on their way to market is something which a trade mark may indicate.[44] The 'connections' contemplated under the 1955 Act included the distribution,[45] importation[46] or design[47] of the product.

3.   THE PROCESS OF REGISTRATION

[19.12] Eligibility to seek registration: the concept of proprietorship. The 1995 Act has a flowchart setting out the process for obtaining registration of a trade mark. An application to register a trade mark may be made to the Registrar of Trade Marks by the person who claims to be the owner of the mark (s 27(1)), and one ground of opposition to registration is that the applicant is not the owner (s 58). At common law, the way to

---

38. The 1955 Act used the expression 'so as to indicate a connection in the course of trade' (s 6).
39. See eg *W D & H O Wills (Australia) Ltd v Rothmans Ltd* (1956) 94 CLR 182. Cf *Estex Clothing Manufacturers Pty Ltd v Ellis & Goldstein Ltd* (1967) 116 CLR 254.
40. (1987) 9 IPR 102.
41. Unlike the marks DAVIS CUP and MELBOURNE CUP and the Olympic Symbol, which are organised by official bodies with perpetual rights to organise and promote those events.
42. *Attorney-General (NSW) v Brewery Employees Union of NSW* (1908) 6 CLR 469: see [19.5]
43. *Aristoc Ltd v Rysta Ltd* [1945] AC 68 at 93. In that case a repairer of silk stockings was not allowed to register a mark for the goods (although a service mark would now be registrable in respect of the repairing business). See also *Knickerbox Ltd v Pedita Australia Pty Ltd* (1995) 31 IPR 108.
44. *Powell's Trade Mark* (1893) 10 RPC 195 at 200.
45. See eg *Pioneer Kabushiki Kaisha v Registrar of Trade Marks* (1977) 137 CLR 670.
46. See eg *Defries & Son Ltd v Electric & Ordnance Accessories Co Ltd* (1906) 23 RPC 406.
47. See eg *Barry Artist Trade Mark* [1978] RPC 703.

acquire ownership or property in a mark or name is to use it and acquire reputation in it.[48] In Australia it has long been established that proprietorship of an unused mark arises from 'the combined effect of authorship of the mark, the intention to use it upon or in connexion with the goods [or, since 1978, services] and the applying for registration'.[49] 'Authorship' in this context does not mean that the applicant must 'invent' the mark or show that it is novel, merely that it was first adopted by that person as a trade mark.[50] Therefore the fact that another's idea, word or design has been taken does not preclude an application: the objection that 'I thought of it first' has not of itself been a ground for opposition.[51] A claim to proprietorship is precluded by a better claim but only in respect of a 'substantially identical' mark.[52]

The 1995 Act requires, in addition to the claim of ownership, one of three other criteria (s 27(1)(b)):

(i)   that the applicant is using or intends to use the mark in relation to the goods or services;

(ii) that the applicant has authorised or intends to authorise another's use of the mark in relation to the goods or services; or

(iii) that the applicant intends to assign the trade mark to a body corporate that is about to be formed, with a view to the use by that company of the trade mark in relation to the goods or services.

This largely re-states the position with respect to notions of ownership developed through case law, but the 'use' contemplated in the form of authorising another to use the trade mark relaxes the previous requirement of registered users only making valid use of a trade mark.

[19.13] Adoption of a foreign mark. One of the controversial aspects of ownership of a trade mark has concerned this principle, that the proprietor need not be the originator of the mark. The courts have insisted on viewing the issue in strictly territorial terms. Thus even if a mark was copied from one in use overseas, a first applicant or first user in Australia may become the proprietor of the mark for the purpose of registration in this country. In *Aston v Harlee Manufacturing Co*[53] the Australian applicant for the mark TASTEE FREEZ in respect of iced milk products was found to be entitled to seek registration, despite getting the name during negotiations with a US company which had no trade here but which used the mark in America. It was said that 'the courts frown on these borrowings from abroad' and will accept 'a very small amount of use of the foreign mark' by the foreign owner in Australia as sufficient to establish proprietorship for that person.[54] Nevertheless the court stressed that, in the absence of

---

48. See Chapter 16.
49. *Shell Co of Australia Ltd v Rohm & Haas Co* (1949) 78 CLR 601 at 625.
50. *Shell Co of Australia Ltd v Rohm & Haas Co* (1949) 78 CLR 601. Cf s 124: see [19.45].
51. Ibid; *Aston v Harlee Manufacturing Co* (1960) 103 CLR 391 at 399. Note however that a trade mark may be protected by copyright in appropriate circumstances: see eg *R A & A Bailey & Co Ltd v Boccaccio Pty Ltd* (1986) 6 IPR 279 (see [20.4]).
52. *Carnival Cruise Line Inc v Sitmar Cruises Ltd* (1994) 31 IPR 375; *Comlink Information Systems Inc v Technology One Pty Ltd* (1994) 31 IPR 578.
53. (1960) 103 CLR 391.
54. Ibid at 400, in part quoting Williams J in *Seven Up Co v OT Ltd* (1947) 75 CLR 203 at 211.

fraud[55] or breach of confidence,[56] it is not unlawful for a trader to become the registered proprietor of a mark which has been used, however extensively, by another trader for similar goods in a foreign country. Many other cases testify to this possibility. In 1947, for example, the Seven Up Company were no doubt perturbed to find the High Court of Australia refusing to have expunged from the Register the trade mark 8 UP, which had been registered by a Victorian company in respect of fizzy drinks. The only prior 'use' of the 7 UP mark in Australia by the foreign company was advertising in journals but with no offers to sell their products in Australia.[57] Similarly the registered proprietor in the UK of the mark NEXT for clothing was unable to prevent registration in Australia of that mark for apparel, despite advertising in fashion magazines on sale here;[58] and registration was obtained for the trade mark TIFFANY in respect of jewellery, despite opposition by the famous Tiffany company of New York.[59]

[19.14] Extent of local use in foreign mark cases. Many of these cases in which copying from a foreign mark has occurred turn on the issue of the extent of local use. If the foreign proprietor can establish such use, only they will be entitled to registration here. Conversely, if a local trader can show such use, no amount of use overseas by someone else would preclude that trader from acquiring proprietorship for Australian purposes. In *Moorgate Tobacco Co Ltd v Philip Morris Ltd*[60] a question arose as to who was entitled to register the mark GOLDEN LIGHTS for cigarettes: Philip Morris, the former licensee of the tobacco company Loew's; or Moorgate, the purchaser of the cigarette business carried on by Loew's (and presumably any of its relevant trade marks). The answer depended upon whether Loew's had used the mark in Australia, in which case it belonged to them and could be sold to Moorgate. There was no evidence of 'use', however, since there had been no trade in the goods, only the sending of samples to the former licensees:

> The cases establish that it is not necessary that there be an actual dealing in goods bearing the trade mark before there can be a local use of the mark as a trade mark ... In such cases, however, it is possible to identify an actual trade or offer to trade in the goods bearing the mark or an existing intention to offer or supply goods bearing the mark in trade.[61]

By contrast with the facts in *Moorgate Tobacco,* ordering 'Yanx' cigarettes from England had earlier been held to pre-empt an application by another trader to register the mark YANX, even though the goods had not yet reached Australia: the order was sufficient evidence of an intention to deal in the goods.[62]

Accordingly while local use of a mark may be minimal, it must nevertheless be directed to merchandising in this country, rather than merely

---

55. See *Farley (Australia) Pty Ltd v J R Alexander & Sons Pty Ltd* (1947) 75 CLR 487.
56. See eg *'Gyomin' Trade Mark* [1961] RPC 408.
57. *Seven Up Co v OT Ltd* (1947) 75 CLR 203.
58. *Riviera Leisurewear Pty Ltd v J Hepworth & Son plc* (1987) 9 IPR 305. See also *Flagstaff Investment Pty Ltd v Guess? Inc* (1989) 16 IPR 311; cf *Midas v Mister Figgins Pty Ltd* (1987) 9 IPR 569; *Re Application by Boundy Insulations Pty Ltd* (1987) 9 IPR 345.
59. *First Tiffany Holdings Pty Ltd v Tiffany & Co* (1989) 13 IPR 589.
60. (1984) 156 CLR 414.
61. Ibid at 433–4.
62. *Re Yanx Trade Mark* (1951) 82 CLR 199.

comprising advertising in foreign publications which circulate here.[63] Thus in another case articles in the *Wall Street Journal* referring to the mark FUDRUKKERS (designating a hamburger chain centred in Houston, Texas) did not suffice to establish proprietorship in Australia of that mark so as to preclude an application to register a similar mark, FUDDRUK-ERS.[64] It had been argued that 'most Australians are aware of the US origins of most large (food) franchising activities such as McDonalds and Kentucky Fried Chicken' and that equivalent international trading activities by a company such as the opponent should be recognised as sufficient to support a claim to proprietorship and trade mark protection in Australia.[65] However, the court stressed that it was not relevant that the publicity in the *Wall Street Journal* had created an awareness in the Australian business community of the successful development of the business, nor that visitors to the US would have seen the opponent's restaurants there. The crucial point was whether the evidence established that the mark was used in Australia to designate the restaurant services of the opponent prior to the application date, something which it did not do.

This approach is regarded as out of date and unrealistic in the modern marketplace and some more recent cases have begun to question the position as developed by previous courts. In *Anheuser-Busch Inc v Castlebrae Pty Ltd*[66] the Australian respondent had registered the trade marks SPUDS MACKENZIE, CLOTHES FOR HEROES, SPUDS MCSTUD and a cartoon picture of a bulldog, all used on clothing. At all times the respondent knew that Anheuser-Busch, a US company selling Budweiser beer, had developed and used those trade marks in respect of beer and clothing in the US. When the Anheuser-Busch company applied to register the marks in Australia for beer and clothing, the company sought injunctive relief for alleged misleading and deceptive conduct under s 52 of the Trade Practices Act, despite the fact that 'borrowing from abroad' has traditionally been acceptable to the Australian Trade Mark Office. Davies J pointed to the increase in international travel, media and communications which, coupled with increasing public awareness of the commercial significance of character merchandising, has resulted in a more sophisticated marketplace where consumers are aware of international characters and marks. For this reason, and having regard to the volume of sales of the products of Anheuser-Busch worldwide, it was not possible for the respondent's marks to become distinctive in Australia.[67] Davies J also concluded that the marks were not adapted to distinguish the respondent's goods since they were adopted 'deliberately to take advantage of the notoriety or fame which Spuds Mackenzie had obtained in the US as a trade mark of Anheuser-Busch'.[68]

---

63. It must also be use of the mark as a trade mark: see [19.8] ff.
64. *Michael Sharwood & Partners Pty Ltd v Fuddruckkers Inc* (1989)15 IPR 188. The opposition ultimately succeeded on the separate ground that the applicants were shown to lack an intention to use the mark.
65. Ibid at 193.
66. (1991) 21 IPR 54.
67. In addition, Anheuser-Busch had copyright protection for the bulldog cartoon figure.
68. (1991) 21 IPR 54 at 60. Cf *Conagra Inc v McCain Foods* (1992) 23 IPR 193 (see [17.13].

On the other hand, where the product in question is not an internationally known brand of beer, clothing or the like but one used only within a
certain industry, reputation may not be established with such ease. For
example, the sale of a single drum of PVC compound did not amount to
sufficient use of a mark within Australia so as to defeat the unregistered
user's proprietorship.[69]

[19.15] Well-known marks. One respect in which the 1995 Trade Mark
Act has changed the law is by providing additional protection for marks
'well known' in Australia, even if not used here in strict conformity with the
7 *UP* line of cases. To conform with the TRIPS Agreement, the 1995 Act
introduced a new ground for opposing the registration of a mark if it 'has
acquired a reputation in Australia' and use by the applicant would be likely
to cause confusion or deception (s 60). The meaning of 'acquired a reputation in Australia' is not at all clear. and there are few criteria for identifying
the relevant group of marks. Under Art 16.2 of TRIPS,[70] account is to be
taken of the knowledge of the trade mark in the relevant sector of the public, including knowledge obtained as a result of promotion of the mark.[71]
Whether a mark is well known is left to the local administration and courts
to determine; however, establishing reputation in Australia has been an art
rather than a science. Market surveys are not much used in proving reputation in passing off or under Pt V of the Trade Practices Act and may well be
disregarded by the courts.[72] Section 120(3) provides that a well-known
mark may be infringed by use of that mark on unrelated goods or services.
The distinction (if any) between having a 'well known mark' and one that
has actually been used within Australia requires a departure from established legal principles in that protection of marks has traditionally been
linked to *use* of that mark in a trade mark context and not some vaguer misappropriation analysis. It would seem that a well-known mark is one that
qualifies for registration as a defensive mark,[73] in that even use of dissimilar
goods and services would be misleading to the public.[74]

[19.16] Form of application. An application must be lodged at the
Trade Marks Office in the form prescribed in Pt IV of the Trade Marks Regulations enacted pursuant to the 1995 Act. The application must specify the
goods or services in respect of which registration is sought (s 27(3)). It is
important to note the system for classifying marks set out in Sch 1 of the
Regulations. This classification system, which is derived from an international arrangement to which Australia is party,[75] divides marks into 34 categories for goods and, as set out earlier,[76] eight categories for services. A
mark is registered in respect of any of the goods or services comprised in a

69. *Mulford Plastics Pty Ltd v 3V Partecipazioni Industriali SpA* (1995) 32 IPR 557.
70. See M Blakeney, 'Protection of "Well Known Marks"' [1994] 11 *EIPR* 481.
71. See also Cartagena Agreement (21 October 1993), Common Provisions on
     Industrial Property, Section 84 of Decision No 344.
72. See [18.7]. See also J S Lockhart, 'Handling Trade Practices Cases' (1994) 17
     UNSWLJ 298 at 306.
73. See [19.55].
74. See further F Mostert and T Stevens, 'The Protection of Well-Known Trade Marks
     on Non-Competing Goods' (1996) 7 *AIPJ* 76.
75. Nice Agreement Concerning the International Classification of Goods and Services
     for the Purposes of the Registration of Marks 1957: see [21.35].
76. See [19.6].

prescribed class. An application may relate to one or more classes (s 27(5)). Multi-class filing is a new feature; previously a separate application was required for each class of goods or services for which registration was sought. The 1995 Act attempts to streamline the procedures for obtaining a trade mark; doing away with the need to file separate applications for each class is one such simplification. The Regulations also set out detailed requirements for the representation of the trade mark (reg 4.2 ff).

[19.17] Examination and amendment. The Trade Marks Registry, which is part of the Australian Intellectual Property Office, operates a system of search and examination of all applications for registration of marks made to it in order to determine whether the application is as prescribed and whether there are any grounds of rejection (s 31). In the event of an adverse report by an examiner, the applicant may seek or the Registrar may direct amendments, or the Registrar may accept the application subject to conditions or limitations. There is a presumption of registrability when an application is being examined, so that doubts are to be resolved in favour of the applicant.[77] Before rejecting an application, the Registrar must provide an opportunity for the applicant to be heard (s 33(4)). If the application is eventually rejected or limited, the applicant may appeal to the Federal Court (s 35). The sort of limitations and conditions which may be imposed are dealt with in Pt 6 of the Act and include removing clerical errors or obvious mistakes (s 64), as long as the identity of a published trade mark is not substantially affected (s 65(2)). Mistakes as to classification of goods or services may be rectified (s 65(3)), and indeed all other particulars specified in the application may be amended, unless that would have the effect of extending the applicant's rights (s 65(5)).

[19.18] Acceptance and opposition. Unless the Registrar is satisfied that there is a lawful ground of objection to the application, it must be accepted (s 33(1)): though acceptance may, prior to registration, be withdrawn on the ground of error or in 'special circumstances' (s 38(1)). The acceptance will be advertised in the *Official Journal* (s 34). Provision is made for 'a person' to oppose registration within the prescribed period (s 52(2)), which is three months from the advertisement, or within such further period, not exceeding three months, as the Registrar allows on application during that first three months (regs 5.1, 5.4(5)). After hearing both applicant and opponent the Registrar may register the mark, with or without conditions or limitations, or refuse to do so (s 55). The grounds of opposition may include any grounds on which a trade mark application may be rejected, except the ground that the trade mark cannot be represented graphically (s 57). Grounds of rejection (and therefore opposition) are discussed below.

[19.19] Registration. Except in the case of Convention applications, which are discussed below, registration takes effect from the date of application (s 72(1)). Registration subsists for seven years (s 72(3)) and may be renewed thereafter for an indefinite number of further periods of ten years (s 77(1)). Renewal is subject to payment of prescribed fees, however, and non-payment may result in the mark being removed from the Register (s 78), although a procedure exists for restoration to be sought (s 79). A

---

77. This appears to follow from s 33(1), which indicates that an application must be accepted unless the Registrar is satisfied there is a ground for rejecting it.

mark removed in this way is deemed to be still registered for the purpose of any other person's application within 12 months after expiration of the last registration (s 80).

[19.20] Convention applications. Australia's obligations under the Paris Convention require it, as in other areas of intellectual property, to extend special protection to those obtaining trade mark registration in other member states. Thus where a successful application for registration is made within six months after a similar application in a Convention country (s 29(1)), the date of registration is deemed to be the date of the overseas application (s 29(2)). In all other respects a Convention application is treated in the same way as any other application (s 225(1)). The Regulations may declare a foreign country to be a Convention country under the Act (s 225(1)).[78]

4.   REGISTRABLE MARKS: THE REQUIREMENT OF DISTINCTIVENESS

[19.21]   General. Even if a mark falls within the definition of 'trade mark' discussed above it will not necessarily be registrable. The 1995 Act lists grounds for rejection of a mark in Div 2 of Pt 4. These objections to registrability incorporate much of the previous law and are discussed below. For now, however, it may be stated that the definition of trade mark in s 17 incorporates the requirement that a sign 'distinguish' goods or services from those of any other person. This is reinforced by s 41(2) which requires that a trade mark application be rejected if the trade mark is not capable of distinguishing the applicant's goods or services in respect of which the trade mark is sought to be registered. Because registration of a trade mark amounts to the granting of a potentially perpetual monopoly there is reluctance to give a trader exclusive rights to fence off part of 'that great open common'[79] of the English language when others may wish to wander about on it. The concept of being distinctive is a familiar one in passing off. The whole question of whether a trader can succeed in passing off revolves, as the preceding chapters have shown, around proving protectable goodwill in a mark or in some other indicium of reputation. It must be established that the name or mark, etc, is associated by the relevant public with a particular source, that source in fact being the plaintiff. Obviously trade marks are prima facie registrable if they have such distinctiveness as would support a passing off action. However, the common law concept of distinctiveness has not always overlapped with distinctiveness under the Trade Marks Act.[80] Previously, there were some marks which could not be registered, no matter how strong their acquired or secondary meaning as indicative of a particular business, because they did not fulfil the particular legislative requirements of distinctiveness,[81] one aspect of which was a degree of 'inherent distinctiveness'.

---

78.   See Sch 10 and regulations thereunder.
79.   *Re Dunn's Trade Marks* (1988) 41 Ch D 439 at 455.
80.   See *NSW Dairy Corp v Murray Goulburn Co-operative Co Ltd* (1989) 14 IPR 26 at 47.
81.   See eg *Eutectic Corp v Registrar of Trade Marks* (1980) 32 ALR 211; *Clark Equipment Co v Registrar of Trade Marks* (1964) 111 CLR 511; *Yorkshire Copper Works' Application* (1954) 71 RPC 150; *Liverpool Electric Cable Co's Application* (1929) 46 RPC 99; *Burger King Corp v Registrar of Trade Marks* (1973) 128 CLR 417; *Re Waterford Glass Group Ltd* (1987) 9 IPR 339; *Re Application by Grant* (1987) 9 IPR 57.

[19.22] Acquired and inherent distinctiveness. Distinctiveness under the 1955 statute was generally a combination of these two aspects, acquired and inherent ability to distinguish. Acquired capability to distinguish comes from use of the trade mark in the marketplace, in the way that a reputation in passing off is acquired. Inherent ability to distinguish requires something about the mark itself which makes it unique in the context of application to the applicant's goods or services. The question of whether a trade mark is inherently adapted to distinguish has always been 'whether other traders are likely in the ordinary course of their business and without any improper motive, to desire to use the same mark, or some mark nearly resembling it, upon or in connection with their own goods'.[82] The ascertainment of inherent distinctiveness to some extent involved a policy issue. Thus descriptive words or devices would be treated as inherently unadapted to distinguish if they were so common and their primary meaning so plain that it was inconceivable that they could or should be associated solely with one trader.[83] The 1955 Act was construed by the courts as requiring every trade mark to have some 'inherent adaptability'.[84] Thus no amount of factual or acquired distinctiveness could cure a lack of inherent distinctiveness.[85] This was true in relation to Pt B marks (those with a potential to be distinctive), as much as Pt A marks (those already considered distinctive).[86]

However, the 1995 Act now allows registration of a mark which is entirely factually distinctive. Section 41(3) states that:

> in deciding the question of whether or not a trade mark is capable of distinguishing the designated goods or services from the goods or services of other persons, the Registrar must first take into account the extent to which the trade mark is inherently adapted to distinguish the designated goods or services from the goods or services of other persons.

This is the first inquiry. If 'the Registrar is still unable to decide the question' (s 41(4)), then a 'mixture' of inherent and acquired distinctiveness will be looked at (s 41(5)). This involves considering whether the mark 'does or will' distinguish the applicant's goods or services because of the combined effect of the extent to which the trade mark is inherently adapted to distinguish, the applicant's use or intended use of the mark, and any other circumstances. If the mark is simply not inherently adapted, but the applicant can show that they have already used the mark to such an extent that it 'does distinguish' (s 41(6)), then this will allow it to proceed to registration.

The significance of factual distinctiveness under the new legislation is emphasised by s 88(2)(d). This applies where a mark has been accepted for

---

82. *Eclipse Sleep Products Inc v Registrar of Trade Marks* (1957) 99 CLR 300.
83. See eg *Crosfield & Sons Ltd's Application* (1909) 26 RPC 837; *Electrix Ltd v Electrolux Ltd* [1959] RPC 283; *Eclipse Sleep Products Inc v Registrar of Trade Marks* (1957) 99 CLR 300. See further [19.30] ff.
84. *Eclipse Sleep Products Inc v Registrar of Trade Marks* (1957) 99 CLR 300 at 313; *Clark Equipment Co v Registrar of Trade Marks* (1964) 111 CLR 511 at 513; *F H Faulding & Co Ltd v Imperial Chemical Industries of Australia and New Zealand Ltd* (1965) 112 CLR 537 at 554.
85. Cf *Registrar of Trade Marks v Muller* (1980) 144 CLR 37 at 42, where it seems to be suggested that in exceptional cases factual distinctiveness alone might suffice; but see *Oxford University Press v Registrar of Trade Marks* (1990) 17 IPR 509.
86. See eg *Burger King Corp v Registrar of Trade Marks* (1973) 128 CLR 417.

registration under s 41(5) on the basis of a combination of some degree of inherent distinctiveness and the applicant's intent to use the mark in the future. Where ten years have elapsed since the application was filed, and in that time the mark 'has not been used to an extent sufficient for it to distinguish, in fact, the goods or services of the registered owner', this may be used as a ground for seeking rectification of the Register to expunge the mark. In other words, where a mark is accepted essentially on the basis of potential distinctiveness (as with the old Pt B marks), the owner has ten years to use the mark in such a way as to develop factual distinctiveness.

[19.23] Categories of inherent distinctiveness. Under the previous legislation, the strict requirement of inherent distinctiveness meant that some marks could never be registered. For example, OXFORD for books, tapes, videos and other products from Oxford University Press.[87] In fact, a note to s 41(6) of the 1995 Act indicates that:

> trade marks that are not inherently adapted to distinguish goods or services are mostly trade marks that consist wholly of a sign that is ordinarily used to indicate:
> (1) the kind, quality, quantity, intended purpose, value, geographic origins, or some other characteristics of goods or services; or
> (2) the time of production of goods or the rendering of services.

This echoes s 24 of the previous Act, which set out various categories recognised as inherently capable of distinguishing goods and services of one proprietor from those of another. Those categories and the learning thereon developed by case law are obviously relevant under the 1995 Act, which adopts most of the previous law on the concept of distinctiveness and for the purposes of which it will still be relevant to consider whether a mark is inherently distinctive. The old s 24 categories consisted of:

(a) the name of a person represented in a special or particular manner;
(b) the signature of the applicant for registration or of some predecessor in business;
(c) an invented word;
(d) a word not having direct reference to the character or quality of the goods or services in respect of which registration is sought and not being, according to its ordinary meaning, a geographical name or a surname; or
(e) any other distinctive mark.

The Trade Marks Act 1875 (UK) called these categories of 'essential particulars'.[88] They will be discussed in turn as a considerable amount of case law has developed around them and the concept of an 'inherently distinctive mark' in the 1995 Act is plainly shaped by the previous legislation.

[19.24] Name of a person represented in a special or particular manner. A person here might be a company or other business entity as well as an individual, though in either event their full name had to be used.[89] Where the person concerned was unconnected with the applicant, it was necessary to obtain their consent or, if deceased, that of their legal representative.[90] Because names may be shared by many persons (or businesses of a similar type), they are not necessarily peculiar to the bearer and must

---

87. *Oxford University Press v Registrar of Trade Marks* (1990) 17 IPR 509.
88. See Cornish, p 441.
89. *Mangrovite Belting Ltd v J C Ludowici & Son Ltd* (1938) 61 CLR 149.
90. See now Trade Marks Act 1995 s 18 and regulations thereunder.

therefore have some factor which made the way the name was represented 'special or particular'. What allowed the representation of a name to fulfil the statutory requirement of special or particular manner was that it be 'sufficiently out of the common to strike the eye as being peculiar, and by "peculiar" I mean not likely to occur to somebody who merely wishes to represent the word'.[91] Forming an arch with the letters of the name was not sufficient,[92] for instance, and nor was rendering the name in ordinary block capitals,[93] or an unusual font,[94] even if slightly ornamented.[95]

[19.25] Signature of the applicant. A signature could only be registered if it was genuinely that of the applicant,[96] was legible,[97] and the one normally used by the applicant or the applicant's predecessor in business: a signature customarily used in a firm might be accepted, but a corporation cannot have a signature as such.[98] Some authority suggested that a signature must also be distinctive, for otherwise it might amount to being merely a name in script form.[99] However, the better view is that a signature is in virtually all cases inherently distinctive, so that nothing further need be established.[100]

[19.26] An invented word. To qualify for registration an invented word had not only to be newly constructed but 'clearly and substantially different from any word in common use'.[101] This meant that a word which was new in the sense of not appearing in any dictionary would not be 'invented' if it had a meaning apparent to the section of the community concerned to buy the goods or use the services for which the word was to be used as a trade mark. Where a meaning was apparent from the sound or appearance of a word which was simply misspelt or composed of recognisable segments of existing words, it was 'but an old word or words masquerading under some thin disguise of orthography, abbreviation or pronunciation'.[102] Thus ROHOE was held to be newly coined but not invented, since it would have been understood as an obvious contraction of 'rotary hoe' by farmers and others seeing the mark on agricultural equipment.[103] Similarly HAIR-FUSION (a patented method for fixing hairpieces to the human head) could not be said to be invented,[104] and CEDARAPIDS was held to be a mere conjoining of two constituent words of a place name and therefore still a geographical name.[105] On the other hand, FUDRUKKERS was clearly

91. *Standard Camera Ltd's Application* (1952) 69 RPC 125 at 129.
92. *Fanfold Ltd's Application* (1928) 45 RPC 325.
93. *Re Application by Lavelur* (1989) 15 IPR 217.
94. *Re Application by American Tobacco Company* (1996) 35 IPR 98.
95. *Re Application by Glenleith Holdings Ltd* (1989) 15 IPR 555.
96. *Re Application by Belle Jardiniere* (1989) 14 IPR 159.
97. *'Barry Artist' Trade Mark* [1978] RPC 703.
98. *British Milk Product Co's Application* [1915] 2 Ch 202.
99. See *'Barry Artist' Trade Mark* [1978] RPC 703 at 711.
100. See eg *Parison Fabric Ltd's Application* (1949) 66 RPC 217 at 223.
101. *Howard Auto Cultivators Ltd v Webb Industries Pty Ltd* (1946) 72 CLR 175 at 181 citing *Eastman Photographic Materials Co v Comptroller General of Patents* [1898] AC 571 at 585.
102. Ibid at 182.
103. *Howard Auto Cultivators*, ibid.
104. *Advanced Hair Studio of America Pty Ltd v Registrar of Trade Marks* (1988) 12 IPR 1.
105. *Re Application by Cedarapids Inc* (1988) 13 IPR 297. See also *Mobil Oil Corp v Registrar of Trade Marks* (1983) 51 ALR 735.

an invented word with respect to hamburgers and restaurant services.[106] Foreign words might be 'invented' if they do not convey meaning 'to ordinary Englishmen'[107] or, perhaps in Australia in the 1990s, to a significant section of the community concerned to buy the goods in question.[108]

[19.27] Words not having direct reference to the character or quality of the goods or services, a place name or a surname. The antithesis of a distinctive mark is a descriptive one. The case law surrounding s 24(1)(d) of the previous Act is voluminous, for that prohibited registration of descriptive words or other material. Obviously a 'picture' might be just as descriptive as a word: thus a diagram of a mattress spring was not a distinctive mark for mattresses.[109] Similarly, a kangaroo device was not distinctive of any Australian product,[110] unless perhaps drawn in a very stylised fashion;[111] and a stethoscope twined around a lamp was refused registration for a doctor's after hours service.[112] Initials were considered to be device marks, but sets of initials are not generally distinctive, particularly if amounting to an acronym for a product.[113]

Material excluded under this provision might be descriptive or misdescriptive of the goods or services offered, or of the packaging, mode of operation, price or any other aspect. What was important was that the reference be direct. If the reference to the goods needed to be spelled out rather than being obvious this would probably not exclude words from being registered. In *Mark Foy's Ltd v Davies Coop & Co Ltd*[114] the appellants had registered the mark TUB HAPPY in respect of clothing. When a rival trader was sued for infringement for using the phrase 'tub happy' in their own advertising slogan, it was argued that the words meant 'washable' and that no one clothing manufacturer should be allowed to monopolise such a direct reference to these goods. The High Court found the trade mark to be valid, going no further than

> suggesting in a vague and indefinable way a gladsome carelessness a propos of the tub. They have an emotive tendency, but they do not appear to ... convey any meaning or idea sufficiently tangible to amount to a direct reference to the character or quality of the goods.[115]

As *Tub Happy* illustrates, even registrable words might 'contain a meaning wrapped up in them, if only you can find it'.[116] This continued to encourage applications for marks which would otherwise appear unregistrable, on

---

106. *Michael Sharwood & Partners Pty Ltd v Fuddruckers Inc* (1989) 15 IPR 188.
107. *Philippart v William Whiteley Ltd* [1908] 2 Ch 274 at 279.
108. See eg *Re Applications by Lee Man Tat and Lee Man Lok* (1988) 12 IPR 212 (Chinese surname not an invented word); *Re Applications by Maxam Food Products Pty Ltd* (1991) 20 IPR 381 ('La Deliziosa' an Italian expression conveying laudatory if ungrammatical reference to the supposed character of the goods).
109. *Eclipse Sleep Products Inc v Registrar of Trade Marks* (1957) 99 CLR 300.
110. *Re Brandella Pty Ltd* (1987) 9 IPR 315.
111. Cf *Re Australian National Airlines Commission* (1989) 16 IPR 270.
112. *Re Application by Slaney* (1985) 6 IPR 307 (although in that case the mark MEDICARE presented the main problem).
113. *Re Application by STC plc* (1989) 15 IPR 419: see [19.31].
114. (1956) 95 CLR 190.
115. Ibid at 195.
116. *Eastman Photographic Materials Co v Comptroller General of Patents* [1898] AC 571 at 583.

the basis that some might be allowed through.[117] For example, while TASTEE FREEZ (ice cream) was held unregistrable in the UK,[118] it apparently proceeded to registration in Australia.[119] Examples of marks refused registration because they are directly descriptive include CHEMICAL ABSTRACTS (database of summaries of chemistry articles),[120] JUNIOR (microwave ovens),[121] LITTLE PEOPLE (toy figurines),[122] ALL THE COLOURS IN THE WORLD (knitwear and clothing),[123] NATURAL 8 PLY (knitting yarn),[124] HAIRFUSION (a method of fusing artificial hair to the human head),[125] STATE OF ORIGIN (football matches),[126] BIODYNAMIC SYSTEM (organically produced goods)[127] and THE LEADING EDGE (mail order services).[128] The word TRADEMARK was also refused registration (for wallpaper and other wall coverings) on the basis that it could never be distinctive of any trader.[129]

Initials or acronyms might be directly descriptive and therefore refused registration, for example PDMX for Programmable Digital Multiplexers (equipment used in electronic communications in computer networks).[130] This is particularly relevant in the circumstances of the computer industry where cumbersome names are frequently abbreviated or acronyms employed. Using an alphanumeric telephone number, where the number spells out a phrase, is becoming a useful marketing tool for some businesses. The difficulty in protecting such numbers/phrases is that they are unlikely to become distinctive because the phrase will usually be descriptive. However, the deliberate adoption by a pizza supplier of another's telephone number which included the sequence 241 ('two for one') has been held to amount to passing off.[131]

[19.28] Descriptive but factually distinctive words. It sometimes happens that a descriptive word acquires factual distinctiveness to such a degree that all the people buying or using the goods or services associate the word with a particular source, and in fact the word fulfils the function of a trade mark. Previously a strong degree of direct descriptiveness would still bar such a word from being registered, since under the 1955 Act the acquisition of factual distinctiveness could never make up for a lack of inherent distinctiveness. In *Eutectic Corp v Registrar of Trade Marks*[132] the

---

117. Possibly on the grounds of acquired distinctiveness or potential distinctiveness such as would support Pt B registration (see [19.7]).
118. *Tastee Freez's Application* [1960] RPC 255.
119. *Aston v Harlee Manufacturing Co* (1960) 103 CLR 391.
120. *Re Application by American Chemical Society* (1989) 15 IPR 105.
121. *Re Application by Matshushita Electrical Industrial Co Ltd* (1989) 15 IPR 125.
122. *Re Application by Quaker Oats Co* (1989) 14 IPR 481.
123. *Re Application by Benetton Group SpA* (1989) 14 IPR 198.
124. *Re Application by JGL Investments Pty Ltd* (1989) 13 IPR 347.
125. *Advanced Hair Studio of America Pty Ltd v Registrar of Trade Marks* (1988) 12 IPR 1.
126. *Re Queensland Rugby Football League Ltd* (1994) 28 IPR 603.
127. *Bio-Dynamic Research Institute v Pfizer Inc* (1996) 34 IPR 438.
128. *Re Application by Tatra Nominees Pty Ltd* (1994) 29 IPR 151.
129. *Re Application by Gencorp Inc* (1993) 28 IPR 94.
130. *Re Application by STC plc* (1989) 15 IPR 419. See also *Re Approved Prescription Services Ltd* [1989] AIPC 90–631 (application to register APS in respect of pharmaceutical goods supplied by Approved Prescription Services refused).
131. *Glev Pty Ltd v Foodmakers (1992) Ltd* (1995) 33 IPR 550.
132. (1980) 32 ALR 211.

applicant wished to register EUTECTIC for chemical substances, tools and machinery used in welding and soldering. Eutectic is a technical term in metallurgy which means melting at a low temperature. Despite the fact that most of those engaged in using welding products were unaware of the technical meaning of the word, there was no doubt that it possessed an accurate technical meaning[133] and was an ordinary English word, albeit not in everyday use in the community, and directly referred to the character or quality of the goods. A similarly impressive degree of factual distinctiveness failed to overcome the descriptiveness of the term CHEMICAL ABSTRACTS for abstracts of articles concerning chemistry — and this despite editors, librarians and academics with an average of 32 years experience deposing to the fact that they associated the mark with the particular index for which it was used.[134] Lack of inherent capacity to distinguish does not, of course, only arise from a mark providing direct reference to the character or quality of goods, but also because a name may be a geographic one or a surname.[135] Under the new legislation, however, s 41(6) ensures that such marks may nevertheless be registrable if they have acquired distinctiveness through use.

[19.29] Marks becoming generic. Sometimes a mark that is not initially descriptive of the goods or services for which it is used will become an industry term and thereby acquire a meaning which now makes it descriptive. This is a risk run by manufacturers who introduce a new item or technology into the market, since the name chosen by the maker can become the generic name for the product.[136] A good example of this occurred when the Sony company gave their video cameras and tape recorders the name 'Beta', from the Greek alphabet. Although inherently adapted to distinguish, the word came to indicate a system for video recording and playing apparatus rather than goods emanating from the applicant. When Sony attempted to register BETAMOVIE for their equipment they failed because the name 'Beta' had become a generic term for the goods and was therefore dedicated to public usage. 'Movie' was another generic term, so that the whole mark simply described the goods.[137] Other terms which have acquired generic meanings include 'True-Blue' (truly Australian)[138] and 'Miser' which, although not descriptive of the goods (installations for water supply) because it was merely an emotive use of language,[139] had become common to the trade and therefore lost distinctiveness.[140]

Section 24 of the 1995 Act provides that a mark that consists of or contains a sign which becomes descriptive after registration will lose exclusive trade mark status. Where a mark has become generic by the time of

133. Cf *Manganin Trade Mark* [1967] RPC 271, where a technical word had no well settled meaning.
134. *Re Application by American Chemical Society* (1989) 15 IPR 105.
135. See *Clark Equipment Co v Registrar of Trade Marks* (1964) 111 CLR 511.
136. Cf *McCain International Ltd v Country Fair Foods Ltd* [1981] RPC 69.
137. *Re Sony Kabushiki Kaisha* [1987] AIPC 90–412. See also *Gramophone Co Ltd's Application* (1910) 27 RPC 689.
138. See eg *Re Application by Galaxy International Pty Ltd* (1988) 13 IPR 433 (registration in respect of clothing refused).
139. As in the *Tub Happy* case: *Mark Foy's Ltd v Davies Coop & Co Ltd* (1956) 95 CLR 190 (see [19.27]).
140. *Bowen v Koor Inter-Trade (Asia) Pty Ltd* (1989) 15 IPR 252.

application, the mark will be unregistrable. However, if the usage develops after registration, s 24 applies to the extent that the sign 'becomes generally accepted within the relevant trade as the sign that describes or is the name of an article, substance or service'. Section 25 provides that if the word is the only practicable description of an article or substance formerly subject to a patent and at least two years has elapsed since expiration of the patent, the registration may remain valid. If either of these conditions applies, the registered owner of a mark consisting solely of the relevant word loses exclusive rights to use the mark or to authorise others to use it in respect of that article or goods or services of the same description.[141]

[19.30] Geographical names. Leaving aside false geographic indicators, which are discussed in the next paragraph, there is no express restriction upon registration of geographic names in the 1995 Act as there was in the 1955 legislation. However, such names are obvious examples of non-distinctive marks and in most cases will be rejected under s 41(2). A trader who appropriates a place name as a trade mark may deny it to others quite legitimately wishing to use the name to indicate the source of their goods. This is particularly true if a number of independent traders produce similar goods in a particular region, as was the case with sheepskin slippers from the sheep-farming district around Glastonbury,[142] heavy earth moving equipment from the industrial state of Michigan[143] or wine from the wine producing area of South Australia.[144] All of these examples involved rejection or expungement of trade marks using the name of the geographic source of the goods.

A geographic name is not merely the name of any place: 'a word does not become a geographical name simply because some place upon the earth's surface has been called by it'.[145] A geographic name is one where the primary and obvious meaning of a word supplies a reference to locality. This will be most likely when goods are produced at a place bearing the name for which registration is sought, although for other sorts of goods or services the name could be an 'invented' word. For example, 'Magnolia' is the name of several towns in the USA, but is also the name of a flower and a distinctive mark for heavy industrial machinery.[146] Similarly, '"Monkey" is not proved to be a geographical name by showing merely that a small and by no means generally known island has been called by that name'.[147] On the other hand, the famous Waterford crystal company were refused registration of the trade mark WATERFORD in respect of handmade crystal, despite extensive use of that mark in Australia for 17 years, because 'Waterford is the name of a relatively small county and city, but one which is the seat of manufacture of the goods in question'.[148] Similarly Oxford University Press, another company with an extensive and venerated reputation,

---

141. See eg *'Daiquiri Rum' Trade Mark* [1969] RPC 600.
142. *Bailey v Clark* (1938) 55 RPC 253.
143. *Clark Equipment Co v Registrar of Trade Marks* (1964) 111 CLR 511.
144. *Thomson v B Seppelt & Sons Ltd* (1925) 37 CLR 305; *Re Application by C Trippit & Sons* (1988) 11 IPR 596.
145. *Magnolia Metal Co's Trade Mark* [1892] 2 Ch 371 at 393.
146. Ibid at 378–9. None of the towns called Magnolia were a seat of manufacture of the goods in question.
147. Ibid at 393.
148. *Re Application by Waterford Glass Group Ltd* (1987) 9 IPR 339 at 343.

were unable to register OXFORD in respect of videos, tapes and discs.[149] Some place names are so strongly geographic in nature that registration will be refused even if no manufacturers of the goods in question exist in the place the name is used. In *Re Application by Bristol Myers Co*[150] the well-known pharmaceutical company Bristol-Myers were refused registration of their mark BRISTOL for medicinal and pharmaceutical preparations since Bristol is the name of a city in the UK (as well as two towns in the USA). Presumably OXFORD would also have been refused even if the goods had not originated there.[151]

[19.31] Marks indicating a false geographic origin. Apart from the general requirement of distinctiveness which makes geographic names difficult to register, a trade mark may be opposed on the grounds in s 61, concerning false geographic indicators. Section 6 defines 'geographical indication' in relation to goods originating in a particular country or in a region or locality of that country, meaning a sign recognised in that country as indicating that the goods:

(a) originated in that country, region or locality; and

(b) have a quality, reputation or other characteristic attributable to their geographic origin.

The inclusion in the Trade Marks Act 1995 of an express prohibition on 'false' geographic marks reflects the requirements imposed by the TRIPS negotiations and the EU/Australian Wine Agreement.[152] The opposition may be based on the fact that the mark suggests an origin from a different country, region or locality than the one than the goods actually come from, but will fail if the applicant shows that the relevant goods did originate there (s 61(2)(a)). In that case, however, the mark will not be a 'false geographical indication' but a real one, and presumably barred from registration as a descriptive mark! Opposition on the grounds of false geographic denotion will also fail if the mark has lost its geographical indication function (s 61(2)(b)) or the applicant used the mark in good faith before 1 January 1996, or the day on which the sign was recognised as a geographical indication for the designated goods in their country of origin (s 61(2)(c)). If the mark sought is in respect of wine or spirits, and the name to be used was, on 1 January 1995, the customary name of a variety of grapes used in production of the wine or spirits, that will also lead to the opposition failing (s 61(2)(d)). Again, the use of such a name as a trade mark would seem to invite rejection of an application for lack of distinctiveness. Section 15 defines 'originate' in relation to wine as the wine having been made within a territory or country, or made from grapes grown in that region or locality.

149. *Oxford University Press v Registrar of Trade Marks* (1989) 15 IPR 646; (1990) 17 IPR 509. See also *Re Application by Cedarapids Inc* (1988) 13 IPR 297; *Re Application by C Trippit & Sons* (1988) 11 IPR 596; *Re Application by Fabriques de Tabac Reunies SA* (1987) 10 IPR 124.
150. (1989) 16 IPR 149.
151. See *Yorkshire Copper Works' Application* (1954) 71 RPC 150; *Liverpool Electric Cable Co's Application* (1929) 46 RPC 99; *Clark Equipment Co v Registrar of Trade Marks* (1964) 111 CLR 511; *'Dan River' Trade Mark* [1962] RPC 157; *Boots Pure Drug Co's Application* (1937) 54 RPC 327.
152. Implemented in Australia in other respects through 1993 amendments to The Australian Wine and Brandy Corporation Act 1980 (Cth): see [16.14], [21.38].

[19.32] **Surnames.** Also inhibited from registration under s 24(1)(d) of the 1955 Act were words that, according to their ordinary meaning, are surnames. Since many people may share the same name it is difficult to establish distinctiveness in a surname. Examples of marks refused registration because of their surnomial significance included GLEN (biscuits),[153] ROBBIE BURNS (whisky)[154] and the Chinese character mark for LEE KUM KEE (oyster sauce), because the Chinese characters had surnomial significance to a significant proportion of the population, although the Roman characters comprising a transliteration of the Chinese were capable of becoming distinctive and could be registered.[155] DAVID'S COOKIES was also refused registration for baked goods, confectionery and restaurant services because David is a surname, despite its more common use as a given name.[156] On the other hand, BOGART was allowed registration (for perfumes and cosmetics) because it is chiefly famous for its single significance as the surname of the actor Humphrey Bogart and is not a common surname in Australia.[157] Similarly CASSINI was registrable (for clothing) because, although an Italian surname, it was rare in Australia.[158]

[19.33] **Signs not previously registrable.** Since the introduction of the 1995 Trade Marks Act on 1 January 1996, a number of applications under the expanded definition of 'sign' have been filed. For example, registration has been sought for the distinctive throbbing sound of a Harley Davidson motor bike, the purple colour of Cadbury's chocolate wrappers, the colour red for Australia Post mail delivery services, the 'pips' heard at the beginning of Telstra long distance calls and the smell of beer impregnated in dart feathers.[159] All of the criteria discussed above with respect to distinctiveness apply to registration of such material.

5. OTHER RESTRICTIONS ON REGISTRATION

[19.34] **Trade mark containing prescribed signs.** Section 39(1) prohibits the acceptance of an application for a trade mark which consists of or contains a sign prohibited under regulations made pursuant to s 18, which provides that certain signs may not be used as trade marks. At the time of writing, there were no regulations made under s 18. However, s 39(2) goes on to state that an application *may* be rejected if it contains or consists of a prescribed sign, or a sign so nearly resembling a prescribed sign (or a sign covered by s 18) as to be taken for it. For the purpose of this provision, reg 4.15 prescribes signs such as 'Patent', 'Copyright', 'Plant Breeder's Rights', 'By Royal Letters Patent' and similar indicia of official approval or registration. Also prohibited are representations of flags, seals or Arms of a state, territory or the Commonwealth, emblems of cities or towns in Australia, and representations of marks not entitled to registration under

---

153. *Re Application by Red Tulip Imports Pty Ltd* (1984) 2 IPR 109.
154. *Re Application by Glenleith Holdings Ltd* (1989) 15 IPR 555.
155. *Re Applications by Lee Man Tat and Lee Man Lok* (1988) 12 IPR 212.
156. *Re Application by Liederman* (1989) 16 IPR 241; see also *'Cannon' Trade Mark* [1980] RPC 519.
157. *Amco Wrangler Ltd v Konckier* (1987) 10 IPR 376.
158. *Cassini v Golden Era Shirt Co Pty Ltd* (1985) 10 IPR 247.
159. B Beale, 'Beer-Smelling Darts Make a Sharp Point for Trade Marking', *Sydney Morning Herald,* 23 September 1996, p 3.

international agreements. These sorts of marks were also disallowed under the 1955 Act (s 29), which allowed the Registrar to refuse to accept an application for a mark which consisted of or contained a representation of any member of the Royal family; the Royal Arms, crests or insignia; the national flag of Australia or of any 'part of the Queen's dominions'; or the Arms or emblems of the Commonwealth, any Australian city or town, or any public authority or public institution. The regulations further prohibited such words as 'Coronation', 'Olympic Champion', 'Repatriation', 'Returned Airman' (sailor or soldier) and 'Medicare', as well as initials like NATO, ANZAC and UNESCO.[160]

[19.35] Trade mark that cannot be represented graphically. Although the 1995 Act widens the subject matter of registrable marks to include sounds, smells, shapes, colours or any aspect of packaging, it must be possible to represent these in such a way as to allow the Register to be maintained without becoming a repository of perfumes and a son et lumiere show. To this end, a mark cannot be registered if it cannot be described adequately in writing and/or drawings (s 40). Regulation 4.3 sets out the rules as to representation of trade marks. In particular, reg 4.3(7) states:

> If a trade mark for which registration is sought contains or consists of a sign that is a colour, scent, shape, sound or any aspect of packaging, or any combination of those features, the application for registration of the trade mark must include a concise and accurate description of the trade mark.

The description or representation of the mark must be adequate to allow proper examination (reg 4.3(8)). Perhaps in the future multimedia products will allow users access to smell as well as sounds, text and graphics. In the meantime trade mark agents may need to hone their copywriting skills to be able to describe the sound of a motor bike or the smell of perfume in enough detail to satisfy the Registrar.

[19.36] Scandalous or illegal marks. Section 42 requires the rejection of an application for a mark that contains 'scandalous matter' or whose use would be 'contrary to law'. Most commentators agree that there is little scope for refusing a mark on the grounds that it is scandalous.[161] Examples of marks which have been refused under this category would have offended religious sensibilities, if at all. 'Scandalous' marks may of course be caught under 'contrary to law', for example if they are racist[162] or promote the sale of an illegal substance.

The prohibition on marks contrary to law to some extent raises issues which overlap with those discussed below, since one way in which a trade mark may be 'contrary to law' is by offending against s 43 which prohibits deceptive or confusing marks. Such a mark may also, of course, fall foul of s 52 of the Trade Practices Act 1952 (Cth).[163] Particular statutes prohibit the use of certain words or logos by other than appointed users. These

---

160. See now Trade Mark Regulations 1995 Sch 2.
161. See Shanahan, p 145; Phillips and Firth, para [21.11]; Cornish, p 456; Ricketson, pp 675, 738.
162. As in ABO BRAND for paints or JOLLY NIGGERBOYS for licorice: see Ricketson, p 674.
163. See [16.31] ff.

include the Advance Australia logo[164] and the Olympic symbol.[165] The use of the words 'Bi-Centenary', 'Bi-Centennial' or '200 years' were appropriated by statute so that only licensees of the relevant authority could cash in on the merchandising opportunities presented by the bicentenary of white settlement in Australia in 1988.[166] Similarly, but on a larger scale, a crucial source of revenue to finance the Sydney 2000 Olympic Games is official sponsors who pay for the privilege of associating their goods or services with the Games. The Sydney 2000 Games (Indicia and Images) Protection Act 1996 (Cth) has been introduced to regulate all commercial use of indicia and images associated with the Olympic and Paralympic Games. The Act expires on 31 December 2000 but until then a vast array of words, combinations of words and any visual or aural representations that would suggest a connection with the Sydney 2000 Olympic games or Paralympic Games will be prohibited. A Senate report into protecting the Sydney Games from 'ambush marketing' identified many insidious practices which will not be allowed under the legislation.[167] For example, displaying an advertising banner saying 'Congratulations to our Olympic Athletes' without paying for the privilege.[168]

Other legislation associated with the inauguration of a government body also typically confines use of the appropriate name to the holder of the monopoly. Examples include the Health Legislation Amendment Act 1983 (Cth), which makes the trade use of 'Medicare' an offence,[169] and the State Lotteries Amendment Act 1984 (NSW) which confers a statutory monopoly in the words 'Instant Lottery' on that state's Lotteries Office.[170]

[19.37] **Deceptive or confusing marks.** Section 43 states that an application for registration of a mark in respect of particular goods or services must be rejected if, because of some connotation of the mark or a sign contained in it, the use of the mark would be likely to deceive or cause confusion. As previously noted,[171] s 60 also permits registration to be opposed on the ground that the mark in question is substantially identical or deceptively similar to a 'well known' mark and that, because of the latter's reputation, use of the mark for which registration is sought would be likely to deceive or cause confusion.

There is a well developed body of case law on this point, decided under s 28(a) of the 1955 Act or s 114 of the 1905 Act, which are equivalent provisions to s 43 of the 1995 legislation. A mark may, for instance, be taken as falsely suggesting some quality[172] or geographical origin[173] of the goods

---

164. Advance Australia Logo Protection Act 1984 (Cth): see eg *Re Application by Kelly* (1987) 8 IPR 667.
165. Olympic Insignia Protection Act 1987 (Cth).
166. Australian Bicentennial Authority Act 1980 (Cth).
167. Senate Legal and Constitutional References Committee, *Cashing in on the Sydney Olympics — Protecting the Sydney Olympic Games from Ambush Marketing*, 1995.
168. See *New Zealand Olympic and Commonwealth Games Association Inc v Telecom New Zealand Ltd* (1996) 35 IPR 55 for an example of an attempt to prevent 'ambush marketing' of the Atlanta Olympics.
169. See *Re Application by Slaney* (1985) 6 IPR 307.
170. This did not, however, deter an applicant from seeking registration under the Trade Marks Act: see *Re Application by Grant* (1987) 6 IPR 57.
171. See [19.15].
172. See eg *Schweppes Ltd v E Rowlands Pty Ltd* (1913) 16 CLR 162.
173. See eg *'Advokaat' Trade Mark* [1978] RPC 252.

or services in question, or as implying some form of sponsorship by or connection with another trader.[174] Most commonly, though, any deception or
confusion will arise when the applicant's mark is compared with that of
another trader.[175] It does not matter whether this other trader's mark is
registered or not, so long as evidence of its reputation is presented so as to
show that registration of the applicant's mark would create deception or
confusion among consumers.[176] The principles relevant here are similar to
those considered in Chapter 18 in relation to passing off actions, where the
conduct has to be considered in the context of the target audience. However, there is no need to establish the level of deception necessary to establish passing off: it is enough that there is a tangible danger of confusion.[177]
Moreover the question is not whether the two marks, if compared side by
side, are not noticeably different, but rather whether the ordinary consumer would have the same general impression of the marks when seen at
different times, especially allowing for some measure of imperfect
recollection.[178]

[19.38]   The Southern Cross case. The leading Australian case in this
respect is *Southern Cross Refrigerating Co v Toowoomba Foundry Pty Ltd*,[179] in
which the High Court stated that the nature of the goods in question, their
respective uses and the trade channels through which they are sold are all
matters to be considered in deciding whether the registration of another's
mark would be likely to deceive or cause confusion.[180] The fact that the
applicant's and opponent's goods were not specified by the regulations as
being within the same class of goods did not matter. In the *Southern Cross*
case that well-known mark had been used extensively for a wide range of
agricultural equipment, including windmills, drilling and boring machinery, milking machines and engines. The applicants for the same mark
wished to use it on refrigerators. They were prevented from doing so
because the mark was one of a general character, of a wide and varied significance, and the registered proprietor's articles had long been sold in
country stores where side by side with them domestic refrigerators were

---

174. See eg *Radio Corp Pty Ltd v Disney* (1937) 57 CLR 448.
175. See however J Luck, 'Distinctiveness, Deceptive and Confusing Marks under the
     Trade Marks Act 1995' (1996) 7 *AIPJ* 97 at 100, where it is argued that the wording of
     s 43 is such that 'the connotation must be evident from a mere scrutiny of the mark
     itself and the goods or services for which registration is sought'. If so, marks could *not*
     be considered deceptive and confusing under s 43 solely because of their comparison
     with another trader's marks, as was the case under s 28(a) of the old Act.
176. See eg *Alpine Audio Accoustic v Alpine Electronic Inc* (1985) 4 IPR 258. Note that
     opposition in this type of case could also take the form of objecting to the
     applicant's claim to be 'proprietor' of a mark already used in Australia by another
     trader: see [19.13]–[19.14].
177. *Southern Cross Refrigerating Co v Toowoomba Foundry Pty Ltd* (1954) 91 CLR 592 at 608;
     Jellinek's Application (1946) 63 RPC 59 at 78; *Carnival Cruise Line Inc v Sitmar Cruises
     Ltd* (1994) 31 IPR 375. Cf [18.10]–[18.11].
178. *Jafferjee v Scarlett* (1937) 57 CLR 115; *Australian Woollen Mills Ltd v F S Walton & Co
     Ltd* (1937) 58 CLR 641; *Aristoc Ltd v Rysta Ltd* [1945] AC 68. As to the use of survey
     evidence in this context, see J W Dwyer and B F Katekar, 'Information is Preferable
     to Intuition — But Does Survey Evidence in Trade Mark Cases Provide Any?'
     (1994) 5 *AIPJ* 37.
179. (1954) 91 CLR 592.
180. Ibid at 606.

also stocked and sold. There was a distinct possibility that 'the result of uses of the mark will be that a number of persons will be caused to wonder whether it might not be the case that the two products come from the same source'.[181] A very similar case to *Southern Cross* is *Karachi Aerosol's Application*,[182] where the application to register the mark SUNKIST for air fresheners, disinfectants and germicides was opposed by the registered proprietor of the same mark in respect of fruit juices. The trade marks were almost identical and the goods of both the opponent and the applicant were common household items packaged in similar containers and stacked on supermarket shelves. This case also illustrates the Trade Mark Office practice of not allowing food products and cleaning items to share the same or similar trade marks.[183]

[19.39]   Partial objections. Following the practice developed around s 28(a) of the 1955 Act, in many instances the outcome of a s 43 or s 60 objection will not be that the mark is refused altogether to the applicant, but merely that it should not be registered in respect of the opponent's goods. For example the user of the mark ZOOPER DOOPER for water ices and ice confections objected to the registration of DOOPA in respect of confectionery generally. The opposition was upheld in part so that registration was not allowed in respect of ice confections.[184] Similarly, an application to register WALKABOUT in respect of 'footwear' was confined to fashion shoes, excluding all such footwear in the nature of boots for hiking and similar outdoor activities, when objected to by the proprietor of the mark in respect of camping goods.[185] In a stunning victory for the Victorian Dairy Industry Authority, McDonalds (the US hamburger restaurant chain) were successfully prevented from registering their 'golden arch' stylised M logo for certain goods including milk and fruit juice (but not carbonated drinks), since at the time of the application there could have been some confusion between the opponent's BIG M trade mark and the McDonalds logo.[186] The circumstances of the trade that will be taken into account include whether goods will be sold in the same outlets,[187] but also whether goods are sold in self-serve outlets (so that consumers rely on a visual impression, perhaps a label),[188] and whether the goods will be asked for by name, since some marks are confusing when spoken but not necessarily when in writing, as with BALI and BERLEI,[189] or DECOR and DEEKO.[190]

---

181. Ibid at 608.
182. (1985) 6 IPR 33. See also *Sporoptic Pouilloux SA v Arnet Optic Illusions Inc* (1995) 32 IPR 430.
183. See also *Edward's Application* (1945) 63 RPC 19.
184. *Tavenfar Pty Ltd v Life Savers (Australia) Ltd* (1988) 12 IPR 159.
185. *Walkabout Footwear Pty Ltd v Sunshine Australia Group Pty Ltd* [1987] AIPC 90–402.
186. *Re Applications by McDonalds Corp* (1986) 9 IPR 509. A (then) s 33 objection (see [19.42]) also succeeded against goods in the same class as the Dairy Industry Authority's, being milk shakes and prepared coffee.
187. As in *Southern Cross* and *Re Application by Karachi Aerosol's Co Ltd* (1985) 6 IPR 33.
188. See *Jafferjee v Scarlett* (1937) 57 CLR 115; *Mars GB Ltd v Cadbury Ltd* [1987] RPC 387; *Re Application by Hamish Robertson & Co Ltd* (1988) 13 IPR 69.
189. See *Berlei Hestia Industries Ltd v Bali Co Inc* (1973) 129 CLR 353.
190. See *Deeko Australia Pty Ltd v Decor Corp Pty Ltd* (1988) 11 IPR 531; and see also *Gardenia Overseas Pty Ltd v The Garden Co Ltd* (1994) 29 IPR 485.

[19.40] Marks becoming deceptive. Sometimes a mark, originally distinctive of the proprietor's business, becomes deceptive or confusing over time because another trader is using it in respect of similar goods and the trade mark no longer indicates a particular source. The key point here is that s 28(a) (the equivalent to s 43 in the 1955 Act) was interpreted to have 'an ambulatory effect, so that the tests it propounds may be applied, in relation to a registered trade mark, at any time'.[191] Presumably s 43 and s 60 will also prohibit the continued presence of a mark as well as its original registration.[192]

[19.41] Blameworthy conduct. Section 43 of the 1995 Act re-enacts s 28(a) of the 1955 legislation. It should be noted that s 28 contained three other paragraphs, including s 28(d) which forbade registration of marks 'not otherwise entitled to protection in a court of justice'. Following two major cases,[193] it was established that s 28(a) was to be read as governed by s 28(d), so that s 28(a) only operated to disallow registration of a mark (or its continuation on the Register) if the proprietor of the mark was culpable of 'blameworthy conduct' (for example, by failing to maintain the mark's distinctiveness in the marketplace). Section 28(d) is noticeably absent from the 1995 Act. This will presumably have the effect of disallowing from registration marks which are misleading in some way, without the *additional* requirement of the proprietor needing to have been 'blameworthy'. The same should be said of an objection under s 60.[194]

This is not to say there will be no role for the concept of 'blameworthy conduct' under the 1995 Act. As will be seen, s 89(1) provides that where there is an application to remove a mark from the Register on the ground that it is deceptive or confusing, the lack of any fault on the part of the owner may be a ground for refusing the application.[195] This will be so even where the applicant for removal is arguing that the mark was deceptive at the time of registration. However s 89(1) does not apply to the initial registration of a mark. Thus 'the illogical result is reached where a trade mark that could have been successfully opposed [under ss 43 or 60] may not be removed as a registration wrongly made'.[196]

[19.42] Substantially identical or deceptively similar marks. Section 44 forbids the registration of a mark if it is too similar to another mark which has already been registered by another person, except where there is honest concurrent use or continual prior use of the marks in question.[197] A similar provision was contained in s 33 of the 1955 Act and again, the cases decided under the previous legislation will continue to inform the law

---

191. *HTX International Pty Ltd v Semco Pty Ltd* (1983) 49 ALR 636 at 643. See also *NSW Dairy Corp v Murray Goulburn Co-operative Co Ltd* (1990) 171 CLR 363.
192. See further [19.50].
193. *Riv-Oland Marble Co (Vic) Pty Ltd v Settef SpA* (1988) 12 IPR 321; *NSW Dairy Corp v Murray Goulburn Co-operative Co Ltd* (1990) 171 CLR 363. See R Leahy, 'Competing Trade Marks and Priority to Registration under the Trade Marks Act 1955' (1995) 6 *AIPJ* 160.
194. See argument put in *Lonza Ltd v Kantfield Pty Ltd* (1995) 33 IPR 396. See also *Sporoptic Pouilloux SA v Arnet Optic Illusions Inc* (1995) 32 IPR 430.
195. See [19.50].
196. J Luck, 'Distinctiveness, Deceptive and Confusing Marks under the Trade Marks Act 1995' (1996) 7 *AIPJ* 97 at 102.
197. As to the concurrent and prior use exceptions, see [19.45].

under the 1995 Act. The prohibition applies where an application has previously been made for registration of a similar mark, unless that mark's registration turns out to postdate the date or projected date of registration for the applicant's mark. The similarity between marks envisaged by s 44 is primarily that they be 'substantially identical' or 'deceptively similar'. These terms are also used in s 120 as a basis for determining whether the rights in a registered mark are infringed by the use of another mark: detailed discussion of their meaning can be found in Chapter 20.[198] There is obviously a considerable overlap between s 44 and the prohibition in s 43 on deceptive and confusing marks, though s 44 is both wider and narrower: wider, in that there is no need to show the same extent of use of the other mark that would be necessary to establish deception under s 43; but also narrower, in that it may not be invoked where the similarity is with an unregistered mark (unless registration is in the process of being sought). It is also pertinent to repeat at this point that prior *use* by another person of the same mark may be used to defeat an application for registration, even if that use has resulted neither in potential deception under s 43, nor in an application for registration so as to activate s 44: the argument being, of course, that the prior use defeats the applicant's claim to proprietorship of the mark.[199]

Besides the requirement that the prior registered mark be substantially identical or deceptively similar, the s 44 prohibition will only operate if a further requirement is satisfied. Where the applicant's mark is used in relation to goods, the requirement is that the two marks are or are to be registered in respect of the same goods, or similar goods, or services that are closely related to those goods (s 44(1)). Where a service mark is involved the requirements are the same, with the terms appropriately substituted (s 44(2)). The key phrases here, 'similar' and 'closely related', require further elucidation.

[19.43] 'Similar or closely related' goods or services. Section 44 prohibits registration of marks conflicting with those registered for goods or services which are *similar, or closely related* to the applicant's marks. Section 33 of the 1955 Act, the equivalent provision, used the terminology 'goods of the same description' or goods and services 'closely related' (s 14). The 1995 Act defines 'similar' as 'the same as' or 'of the same description;' however, these terms were not defined in the 1955 Act and it was left to the courts to develop the concepts. The question is one of fact and the cases reveal both a liberal and a cautious approach.[200]

The phrase 'goods of the same description' (used in the 1955 Act) has been described as 'a term of art, implying a relationship between goods such that they would be taken as having the same trade origin if sold under deceptively similar marks'.[201] The factors to be taken into account, at least in relation to goods, were approved by the High Court in the *Southern Cross* case[202] as being the nature of the goods, their uses and the trade channels through which they are sold, although no single consideration is conclusive

---

198. See [20.5]–[20.6].
199. See [19.12]–[19.15].
200. Cornish, p 435, citing *Daiquiri Trade Mark* [1969] RPC 600; *Jellinek's Application* (1946) 63 RPC 59; *Lyon's Application* [1959] RPC 120.
201. Shanahan, p 191.

on its own. In the *Southern Cross* case itself, refrigerators and agricultural equipment were found not to be goods of the same description, so that s 33 of the 1955 Act had no application.[203] The discussion of whether goods should be regarded as being of the same description 'is a question that should be considered in a pragmatic business sense and not on the basis of abstract reasoning'.[204] In discussion of the 'same description' concept it has been found that footwear and camping gear are different,[205] as are packaged cheese and flavoured milk,[206] and synthetic plastic insulating material as compared with semi-processed plastic in pellet or powder form.[207]

[19.44]   'Closely related'. This phrase is not defined by the Act, but the degree of connection between the goods and services considered 'closely related' is that which suggests a common origin, and criteria similar to those used to determine whether goods or services are 'similar' will apply.[208] Examples could include the provision of detergents or equipment (goods) for use by an unrelated carpet cleaning business (service), or clothing and shoes (goods) used in connection with fitness classes (service). The classification in Sch 1 to the Regulations has no bearing on the question, being an administrative tool rather than a conceptual one. This is because a single class may contain goods or services which are not of the same description, while different classes may classify goods or services which *are* of the same description.[209]

[19.45]   Concurrent and prior use. It obviously does happen that traders may in good faith and quite independently of one another develop similar marks. Numerous instances of this came to light when the trade marks register was first established in the UK and unconnected users sought registration for similar marks at the same time.[210] It was decided that concurrent registrations could be granted, but if more than three such applications occurred the mark would be 'common property' in the trade.[211] Under the 1955 Act, where there were concurrent applications for very similar or identical marks the Registrar determined the issue according to the principles of proprietorship already discussed, taking into account any priority gained by virtue of foreign application made under the Paris Convention.[212] However, where the right to register could not

---

202. *Southern Cross Refrigerating Co v Toowoomba Foundry Ltd* (1954) 91 CLR 592 at 606, citing *John Crowther & Sons (Milnsbridge) Ltd's Application* (1948) 65 RPC 369 at 372, discussed in Shanahan, pp 191–2. See also *Walkabout Footwear Pty Ltd v Sunshine Australia Group* (1987) 9 IPR 558 at 561–2.
203. Although the use of the SOUTHERN CROSS mark was nevertheless found to be deceptive under s 28(a): see [19.38].
204. *Lonza Ltd v Kantfield Pty Ltd* (1995) 33 IPR 396 at 402. See also *Polo Textile Industries Pty Ltd v Domestic Textiles Corp Pty Ltd* (1993) 26 IPR 246.
205. *Walkabout Footwear Pty Ltd v Sunshine Australia Group Pty Ltd* (1987) 9 IPR 558.
206. *NSW Dairy Corp v Murray Goulburn Co-operative Co Ltd* (1989) 14 IPR 26.
207. *Lonza Ltd v Kantfield Pty Ltd* (1995) 33 IPR 396.
208. Shanahan, p 193, quoting an address by the Registrar of Trade Marks, F J Smith, 'The Trade Marks Amendment Act 1978' (1979) 53 *ALJ* 118 at 119–20.
209. Shanahan, p 191, citing *Australian Wine Importer's Trade Mark* (1889) 6 RPC 311; *Reckitt & Colman (Australia) Ltd v Boden* (1945) 70 CLR 84.
210. Cornish, p 451.
211. See *Jelley's Application* (1882) 46 LT 381.
212. This gives six months after an overseas application to register in Australia (s 29): see [19.20].

definitively be accorded to one trader because different users had acquired rights in the mark through their trading activities, the Registrar could elect to register them as concurrent marks. Under s 34(1), the Registrar was permitted to accept the registration by different proprietors of substantially identical or deceptively similar marks, subject to any conditions or limitations which the Registrar might choose to impose, where there had been 'honest concurrent use' of those marks. Section 44(3) of the 1995 Act is essentially to the same effect.[213] Factors to be taken into account in this connection included the honesty of the concurrent use, the extent of use in time, area of trade and volume, the degree of likely confusion and the relative inconvenience to the parties.[214]

The concept of acceptable concurrent use is also recognised in s 44(4) of the 1995 Act, which provides that registration is not to be refused by reason of an earlier registration, so long as the applicant's mark has been the subject of continuous prior use by the applicant and any predecessor in title in relation to similar or closely related goods or services. The use must have commenced before the 'priority date' of the earlier registered mark. The priority date is the date from which registration takes effect, usually the date of the application (ss 12, 72). Thus, provided B can show continuous use dating back before A applied to register a substantially identical or deceptively similar mark, B's registration can go ahead. Unlike the equivalent provision in the 1955 Act, s 34(2), it will not matter that A may actually have started using their mark before B commenced any use. In that situation, however, B may be vulnerable to an action by A for infringement, at least for the use of the mark prior to applying for registration. Although s 124 offers a defence of continuous prior use, it only applies where the use predates the first use by the owner of the registered mark or their predecessor in title, or the date of registration, whichever is earlier. Once B's mark is registered, they cannot be sued for any use of the mark after the date of registration (that is, the date of application), since it is a defence to exercise a right to use a mark granted by the Act (s 122(1)(e)).[215]

[19.46] Plant variety names. The name of a plant variety registered under the Plant Breeder's Rights Act 1994 may not be registered as a trade mark. It is an infringement of that Act to use a registered plant variety name in respect of other plants (s 53) and as part of the examination of trade mark application in Class 31 (which includes plants and flowers) the Register of Plant Varieties is searched. The Trade Mark Office has adopted the UK practice of refusing to allow plant varietal names as trade marks, and vice versa. The legal basis of the objection is that such trade marks may be descriptive and therefore not distinctive (s 41(2)), likely to deceive or cause confusion (s 43), or contrary to law (s 42).[216]

[19.47] Associated marks. Trade marks are 'associated' when similar marks are used by the same person for similar goods or services. There is

213. Note that s 44(3) also permits the Registrar to take this course in any 'other circumstances' (the term used in s 34(1) of the old Act was 'other special circumstances').
214. Shanahan, p 203. See also *Alexander Pirie & Sons Ltd's Application* (1933) 50 RPC 147; *Olin Corp v Pacemaker Pool Supplies* (1984) 4 IPR 526.
215. See further [20.9] as to defences to actions for infringement.
216. Trade Mark Office, Official Notice, 28 September 1995.

no provision for formally signifying the association of trade marks under the new Act, following views expressed in submissions to the Trade Mark Working Party that association is an out of date concept in the modern marketing environment. The principal significance of associated marks under the 1955 statute was that they could not be assigned or transmitted separately from each other, the overriding motive being to avoid the consumer deception which might result from the divided ownership of very similar marks for products or services of the same description. If a change in ownership of similar marks for similar products would result in deception or confusion, the validity of the trade mark may now only be challenged under general principles, for example as set out in s 43. The abolition of the concept of associated marks been described as a 'retrograde step',[217] in that it will force assignees to conduct extra searches of the Register to identify other marks they need to acquire, thus increasing the costs of purchasing marks. An assignee is now confronted by the risk that the registration of the mark they are acquiring may be threatened not just by any unregistered marks that may be floating around, but by a registered mark whose existence would under the old system have been notified by the Registrar. It may be possible of course to seek appropriate warranties on the subject from the assignor.

[19.48] Disclaimers. Section 74 of the 1995 Act allows an applicant for a trade mark or a registered owner to disclaim any exclusive right to use or authorise the use of a specified part of a trade mark. This provision is intended to help trade mark owners in resolving conflicts with other parties where the exclusive right of the owner to use part of a trade mark is in dispute by defining the rights of the proprietor. The 1955 Act provided in s 32(1)(b) that the Registrar could insist on a disclaimer in relation to matter 'common to the trade or otherwise not distinctive', such as bunches of grapes on wine bottle labels. Despite the inclusion of such matter, which might also for instance include company names or initials, letters or numerals, a mark may have been registered if the applicant agreed not to claim rights to the exclusive use of such components of the mark. Thus an applicant who sought to register the mark ROARING FORTIES for goods including wines, spirits and liqueurs (Class 33) was required to disclaim any right to the exclusive use of the word 'forties' since, in marks associated with goods included in the classes for which registration was sought, 'numbers are frequently used to convey information on source, year, vat, volume or strength'[218] and other traders might well want to employ the word on their own labels.[219] Under the 1995 Act the Registrar no longer has the power to require applicants to disclaim rights to parts of a trade mark — they are recorded only by request.[220] Disclaimer of non-registrable

---

217. T Golder, 'Disclaimers, Associations, Honest Concurrent Use and Prior Use' (1996) 7 *AIPJ* 93 at 95.
218. *Re Application by McManamey* (1989) 16 IPR 582 at 583. Cf *Pizza Pizza Ltd v Registrar of Trade Marks* (1989) 15 IPR 181 (Canadian decision allowing registration of a telephone number as a trade mark, even though initially rejected by the Registrar).
219. See also *Eclipse Sleep Products Inc v Registrar of Trade Marks* (1957) 99 CLR 300 at 315.
220. Cf T Golder, 'Disclaimers, Associations, Honest Concurrent Use and Prior Use' (1996) 7 *AIPJ* 93 at 95, criticising the removal of 'an appropriate tool given to the Registrar to control the inappropriate width of certain trade mark registrations'.

material allows marks including some non-distinctive matter to be registered, but it is not possible to disclaim the whole mark and still have it registered, as was attempted by an applicant wishing to register JETSYS-TEM for household washing machines whose method of operation was by a system of nozzles or jets.[221]

6. MAINTAINING REGISTRATION

[19.49]   Effects of registration. Initial registration lasts from ten years after the filing date of the application (s 72(3)). Unlike patents, copyright or designs, trade mark registration may last forever, so long as the requisite fee is paid for regular renewal, and no reason for expungement arises. Section 20 provides that registration gives the registered owner the exclusive rights to use the trade mark, to authorise others to use the mark (in respect of goods and services for which it is registered) and to obtain relief for infringement. Renewal fees are to be paid every ten years (s 77(1)). In order for the owner of a mark to justify the exclusive use conferred by registration the mark has to continue to fulfil the criteria expected of a valid trade mark. Registration establishes only prima facie evidence of the validity of a mark, in the same way that patent registration means that, as far as the Patent Office is aware, a patent is valid. In other words, marks remain open to challenge even after registration: thus an action for infringement may be met with the defence that the plaintiff's mark is invalid.

[19.50]   Rectification of the Register. The Registrar may amend or correct any error or omission in the Register on his or her own initiative (s 81) or at the request of the owner, as long as the identity of the trade mark is not substantially affected (s 83). The Registrar may also cancel the registration of a mark at the request of the owner, though not before notifying anyone who is recorded in the Register as claiming an interest in the mark, or who has applied to be so recorded (s 84).

An application for rectification may also be made to a prescribed court under any of ss 85–88. The application must in each instance be made by an 'aggrieved person'. 'Aggrieved' persons in this context denote those with a trading interest to protect rather than persons with a higher motive: for example in *Ellis's Trade Mark*[222] it was held that the Society of Friends (known as the Quakers) did not have locus standi to object to QUAKER remaining registered for spirits.[223] One sure way to cause a person to become 'aggrieved' is to sue them for infringement of a trade mark, upon which event an acceptable tactic at the defendant's disposal is to question the validity of a mark and seek its expungement.[224]

---

221. *Re Application by Industrie Zanussi SpA* (1989) 16 IPR 508. See also *Re Application by Blake* (1989)15 IPR 175; *Re Australian National Airlines Commission* (1989)16 IPR 270; *Bausch & Lomb Inc v Registrar of Trade Marks* (1980) 28 ALR 537.
222. (1904) 21 RPC 619.
223. See also *Shell Co of Australia Ltd v Rohm & Haas* (1949) 78 CLR 601; *Re Walt Disney Productions* (1954) 71 WN (NSW) 334; *Powell's Trade Mark* [1894] AC 8.
224. See *Macrae Knitting Mills Ltd v Lowes Ltd* (1936) 55 CLR 725; *James Watt Constructions Pty Ltd v Circle-E Pty Ltd* [1970] 3 NSWR 481; *Superstar Australia Pty Ltd v Coonan & Denlay Pty Ltd* (1981) 40 ALR 183; *HTX International Pty Ltd v Semco Pty Ltd* (1983) 49 ALR 636.

The grounds for court-ordered rectification include the correction of errors or omissions (s 85); the contravention of a condition or limitation in the Register (s 86); and the contravention of ss 24 or 25, which deal with marks which have become generic or which are linked to expired patents (s 87).[225] More importantly, an application may be made under s 88(1) for registration to be cancelled, or for an entry 'wrongly made or remaining on the Register' to be removed or amended, or for a condition or limitation to be entered. The terms 'wrongly made or remaining', which also appeared in s 22(1) of the 1955 Act, are especially significant. They allow a mark to be challenged not only on the ground that a defect existed in the application at the time it was made which should have led to its rejection, but also on the ground that invalidity has arisen *since* registration. For example, circumstances may have changed since the initial registration and the mark may have become deceptive or confusing.[226] The grounds for challenge under s 88(1) are set out in s 88(2), and include:

- any of the grounds on which the registration of the mark could have been opposed (including that there was no 'mark' within the meaning of the Act; that the applicant was not the proprietor of the mark; or that the mark contained or consisted of improper material, was not distinctive, was deceptive or confusing, or was substantially identical or deceptively similar to another registered mark, etc);

- the use of the mark at the date of the application for rectification being likely to deceive or cause confusion for a reason *other* than circumstances covered by ss 43, 44 or 60 (all grounds for opposition and hence caught by the previous category);

- the obtaining of an entry or an amendment by fraud, false suggestion or misrepresentation; or

- where a mark has been accepted for registration on the basis of potential distinctiveness, the owner's failure to use it over the ensuing ten years in such a way as to make it factually distinctive.[227]

Importantly, however, s 89(1) qualifies the operation of s 87, and also of s 88 in so far as rectification is sought on the ground that the mark is liable to cause deception or confusion. It provides that the court may decide not to grant an application for rectification under these provisions if the owner can establish that the ground relied upon by the applicant has not arisen through any 'act or fault' of the owner. This appears to reintroduce the concept of 'blameworthy conduct' developed by the courts under s 28(a) of the old Act,[228] although the different views expressed by members of the High Court in *NSW Dairy Corp v Murray Goulburn Co-operative Co Ltd*[229] as to what constituted such conduct make it doubtful whether the case law on s 28(a) will be of much assistance in interpreting the terms 'act or fault'. Presumably though, as under s 28(a), it will be relevant to consider whether the owner has stood by and allowed a situation to develop in which

---

225. See [19.29].
226. See [19.40].
227. See [19.22].
228. See [19.41].
229. (1990) 171 CLR 363. As to the difficulty in ascertaining a *ratio decidendi*, see *Nike International Ltd v United Pharmaceutical Industries (Aust) Pty Ltd* (1996) 35 IPR 385 at 400–5.

a similar mark has been used in such a way as to create deception or confusion, or in which the mark has become widely used as an industry term.[230] In any event, it is specifically provided that in determining whether or not to exercise its discretion under s 89(1), the court must take into account any effect on the public interest, whether the circumstances giving rise to the application have ceased, the extent to which the mark was distinctive prior to those circumstances arising, and whether an order other than rectification could be made instead (s 89(2); reg 8.2).

In addition it would seem that, as under s 22 of the old Act, the court retains a general discretion not to order rectification even if one of the other grounds set out in ss 85–88 is established.[231] This seems to follow from the inclusion of the word 'may' in each of those provisions, notwithstanding the enactment of s 89 to confer such a discretion in the specific situations with which it deals.

[19.51] Prescriptive validation. Under the 1955 Act, marks registered in Pt A obtained a certain degree of protection against challenges to the validity of their initial registration after being on the Register for three years (s 60), with greater protection still accruing when the period of registration reached seven years (s 61). The 1995 Act contains no such provisions in relation to marks for which registration is sought under the new regime. However, for Pt A marks which had been registered or accepted for registration prior to 1 January 1996, and whose registration has continued under the new legislation, s 234 effectively re-enacts s 61 of the old Act. Accordingly, once seven years has elapsed the initial registration of such marks may only be challenged on the grounds that the original registration was obtained by fraud, that registration would be contrary to s 28 of the old Act, or that at the date of the relevant proceedings the mark is not distinctive. The continuation in effect of s 28 means that the case law developed around that provision, which is only partially replicated in s 43 of the new Act, will remain relevant, at least in relation to older marks. As already explained,[232] s 28(a) could be used to remove a mark on the ground of deception or confusion, whether as at the time of registration or in light of subsequent developments, but only where there was some 'blameworthy conduct' by the proprietor. Despite the broad terms of s 28(d), however, which referred to marks 'not otherwise entitled to protection', it had been established that neither that provision nor s 28(a) could be used to raise issues of distinctiveness.[233]

[19.52] Removal for non-use. One of the fundamental aspects of a trade mark is that it is in use or is at least intended to be used (s 17). Therefore s 92 provides that a person aggrieved may apply to the Registrar or a court for the removal of a mark from the Register on the ground of non-use. A 'person aggrieved' in this context means 'any person having a real

---

230. See eg *Re GE Trade Mark* [1973] RPC 297; *HTX International Pty Ltd v Semco Pty Ltd* (1983) 1 IPR 403; *Riv-Oland Marble Co (Vic) Pty Ltd v Settef SpA* (1988) 12 IPR 321.
231. See *Ritz Hotel Ltd v Charles of the Ritz Ltd* (1988) 12 IPR 417; *Paragon Shoes Pty Ltd v Paragini Distributors (NSW) Pty Ltd* (1988) 13 IPR 323.
232. See [19.40]–[19.41].
233. *HTX International Pty Ltd v Semco Pty Ltd* (1983) 1 IPR 403; *Riv-Oland Marble Co (Vic) Pty Ltd v Settef SpA* (1988) 12 IPR 321; *NSW Dairy Corp v Murray Goulburn Co-operative Co Ltd* (1990) 171 CLR 363.

interest in having ... the trade mark removed' because of disadvantage in a legal or practical sense from leaving the mark on the Register,[234] for example because the applicant wishes to begin trading in goods or services using that mark.[235] It must be established either that the proprietor had no bona fide intention of using the mark when registration was applied for, and that there has in fact been no use in good faith up to a month before the application (s 92(4)(a)); or that there has been no bona fide use of the mark for a continuous period of at least three years up to a month before the application (s 92(4)(b)). Importantly, any use of the mark by an 'authorised user' will constitute use of the trade mark for this purpose (ss 7(3), 8).[236]

It is significant that an application may specifically be made in respect of 'any or all' of the goods or services in respect of which the mark is registered (s 92(2)(b)). This may be contrasted with the previous legislation, under which an attempt at expungement could be defeated by showing use of the mark in relation to similar goods or services. Under the new regime, it would seem, an owner will need to be able to show use in relation to *each* of the different kinds of goods or services covered by the registration, no matter how closely related they are, or face the registration being 'whittled down'. What is unclear at this stage is how far the courts will go in allowing fine distinctions to be drawn between different products.[237]

Unlike the position under the 1955 Act, where the applicant for removal carried the burden of proof,[238] s 100 provides that the person opposing removal has the onus of rebutting an allegation made under s 92(4). This can be done by showing that the mark has in fact been used by the owner or an authorised user, or that it has been used by an unregistered assignee (provided the Registrar or the court thinks it reasonable to take that into account), or that any non-use was due to 'circumstances (whether affecting traders generally or only the registered owner of the mark) that were an obstacle to the use of the trade mark during that period'.[239] Even if the allegation cannot be rebutted, the Registrar or court retains a discretion not to remove the mark (s 101). However, case law under the previous legislation suggests that this discretion should only be exercised where there is a clear and sufficient reason not to invoke the power to remove.[240]

Section 102 provides that registration of a challenged mark may continue but with restrictions imposed. It might be that both the applicant for removal and the owner of the challenged mark have used the mark (or one very similar to it) in different locations. In that case separate reputations may have been established and the Registrar may apply conditions limiting

---

234. *Ritz Hotel Ltd v Charles of the Ritz Ltd* (1988) 12 IPR 417 at 454; *Kraft Foods Inc v Gaines Pet Foods Corp* (1996) 34 IPR 198.
235. *Peters Foods Australia Pty Ltd v Tip Top Ice Cream Co Ltd* (1996) 33 IPR 475. See also *Murray v Major League Baseball Properties Inc* (1995) 33 IPR 362.
236. See [20.15].
237. See *McHattan v Australian Specialised Vehicle Systems Pty Ltd* (1996) 34 IPR 517 at 542–5.
238. See *Estex Clothing Manufacturers Pty Ltd v Ellis & Goldstein Ltd* (1967) 116 CLR 254 at 258.
239. The equivalent to this last defence in the 1955 Act was the existence of 'special circumstances in the trade' (s 23(4)), a somewhat narrower concept.
240. See *Re Carl Zeiss Pty Ltd's Application* (1969) 122 CLR 1; *Murray Goulburn Co-op Co Ltd v NSW Dairy Corp* (1990) 17 IPR 269. Cf *Peters Foods Australia Pty Ltd v Tip Top Ice Cream Co* (1996) 33 IPR 475.

the registration so that specified areas or markets covered by each registration will be mutually exclusive. Finally, it should be noted that where the opponent of an action for removal prevails, they may obtain from the Registrar or the court a certificate as to the findings of fact made as to the extent of the mark's use, or as to circumstances excusing its non-use. Such a certificate may be used in any future proceedings as evidence of the facts stated in it (s 105).

7. COLLECTIVE MARKS, CERTIFICATION MARKS AND DEFENSIVE MARKS

[19.53] Collective marks. A new type of mark is introduced by Pt 15 of the 1995 Act. A collective mark is a sign used or intended to be used in relation to goods or services dealt with or provided in the course of trade by members of an association to distinguish those goods or services from ones provided by persons not members of the association (s 162). The concept of such a mark was discussed in the *Union Label* case[241] where, as previously discussed, 'workers marks' were ruled unconstitutional in that they asserted proprietary rights not over the goods themselves but the conditions under which they were produced.

[19.54] Certification marks. Part 16 provides for the registration of certification marks, being signs distinguishing goods or services in respect of origin, material, mode of manufacture, accuracy or some other characteristic, from goods or services not so certified (s 169). This allows associations or organisations to register marks which say something about the quality, standard or composition of goods or services offered by authorised traders. Accordingly, applications must be made by the association to which the mark belongs (s 164). Examples of certification marks include the Woolmark, the Standards Association of Australia mark and those indicating that garments fulfil the description of Harris Tweed, Irish Linen and Scottish Cashmere or that Danish Blue Cheese is cultured with the right sort of mould.

The Trade Marks Office determines registrability of the mark on normal principles. If an application is accepted, however, it is passed on to the Australian Competition and Consumer Commission (ACCC, formerly the Trade Practices Commission). An application for registration must be accompanied by draft rules governing the use of the mark (reg 16.1) and the ACCC is required to consider whether they are satisfactory, together with the applicant's competence to perform a certification function and to ensure the public would not suffer detriment (s 175). The rules may subsequently be altered by the ACCC on application from the proprietor (s 178). In considering the rules governing use pursuant to s 175(2)(b), the ACCC will have regard to the principles relating to restrictive trade practices under Pt IV of the Trade Practices Act 1974 (Cth), the principles with respect to unconscionable conduct in Pt IVA of the Trade Practices Act and the principles relating to unfair practices, product safety and information set out in Pt V of that Act (reg 16.6).

---

241. *Attorney General (NSW) v Brewery Employees Union of NSW* (1908) 6 CLR 469. See [19.5].

The Register may be rectified in relation to a certification mark on the grounds that:

(a)   the proprietor is no longer competent to perform the certification function;

(b)   it is no longer to the public advantage that the mark be registered;

(c)   the proprietor has failed to observe a provision of the rules governing use of the mark; or

(d)   it is necessary for the public advantage that those rules be varied (s 181(2)).

Registration has the effect of giving the proprietor the exclusive right to use and to allow others to use the mark in relation to the goods or services for which the mark is registered subject to any conditions or limitations entered in the Register (s 171).[242]

[19.55]   Defensive registration. There are some marks which, because of their considerable reputation, could cause confusion if registered by other than their originators even in respect of different categories of goods or services. Part 17 permits registration of such marks to prevent their use for goods or services not covered by the registration. Examples of defensive marks registered in Australia include: HOLDEN, LEVI'S, CHANEL, GIL-LETTE, KLEENEX, VICKS, SHELL, NUGGET, KELLOGGS, COCA-COLA, ROLLS ROYCE and FAIRY. The applicant seeking defensive registration bears the onus of proving that an existing mark already registered according to general principles has been used in relation to all or any of the goods or services in respect of which it is registered so that the use of the trade mark in relation to other goods or services would be likely to be taken as indicating a connection between those other goods or services and the registered proprietor (s 185(1)). The words 'likely to be taken as indicating' have a similar meaning to 'likely to deceive or cause confusion' within s 43.[243] The registration will not be vulnerable to removal on the ground of non-use (s 186). In most other respects, the Act applies as it would to any other mark.[244] Registration may be cancelled, however, where the requirements of s 185 are no longer satisfied (s 188), or where the proprietor is no longer registered as the proprietor of any other type of mark (s 189). The provision of infringement proceedings for marks 'well known in Australia' (s 120(3)) may be regarded as amounting to de facto defensive registration, as discussed in the next chapter.

---

242. It should be noted that s 170 provides the following do not apply to certification marks: ss 8, 26, 27(1)(b), 33, 34, 41, 82(2)(d), 121, 127, Pt 9, Pt 17.

243. *Re Applications by Mobil Oil Corp* (1995) 32 IPR 535.

244. Under s 186, the provisions of the Act not applying to Pt 17 are: ss 20(1), 27(1)(b), 41, 59, 88(2)(d), 121, 127, Pt 9, Pt 16.

Chapter 20

Protection and Exploitation of Registered Marks

[20.1] **Rights of the registered proprietor.** Under s 20(1) of the Trade Marks Act 1995, the proprietor of a registered mark has the right to the exclusive use of that mark in relation to the goods or services with respect to which it is registered, and also the right to authorise other people to use the mark and obtain relief against infringements. These rights are subject to any conditions or limitations expressly placed on the registration (s 20(2)) and accrue to the owner from the date of registration (s 20(3)).[1] The means by which trade marks may be exploited are considered in the next section. Before that, however, attention needs to be focused on the defensive aspect of trade mark registration: the ability to secure protection against the activities of infringers. The 1995 Act does not provide for registration of users, except on a voluntary basis. Under the 1955 legislation a trade mark was not supposed to be licensed without adherence to strict rules as to the exercise of control of the use of the mark. This was in order to prevent the link between the trade mark owner and the mark itself being weakened and leading to deception of the public who would assume the trade mark owner to be 'in charge' of the products put out under that mark. The registered user provisions were very little used and the market determined question of 'use' of the mark. Hence under the new legislation 'authorised users' may be able to bring actions for infringement, whether or not they are registered.[2]

---

1. The 'date of registration' is usually taken to be the date of application: see [19.19]. Therefore acts done before registration, but after the application was lodged, may constitute infringement.
2. See [20.15].

1. PROTECTION

(a) Establishing Infringement

[20.2] **Infringement provisions.** Section 120(1) provides that a mark is infringed when a person uses as a trade mark a sign which is substantially identical or deceptively similar in relation to the goods or services, in respect of which the trade mark is registered. There is an expansion of the notion of infringement under the 1995 Act, to include use of a substantially identical or deceptively similar sign on goods or services not covered by the registration but 'of the same description' or 'closely related',[3] although it is a defence to establish that such use is not likely to deceive or cause confusion (s 120(2)).

Provision is also made under s 120(3) for the protection of any 'well known' mark against use by others in relation to goods or services unrelated to those in respect of which the mark is registered. If the mark is so well known that use of a substantially identical or deceptively similar sign 'would be likely to be taken as indicating a connection between the unrelated goods or services and the registered owner of the trade mark', this will constitute infringement. Determining whether a trade mark is 'well known in Australia' requires taking account of the extent to which the trade mark is known within the relevant sector of the public, whether as a result of promotion of the trade mark or for any other reason (s 120(4)).

[20.3] **'Use'.** What constitutes use of a mark has already been addressed.[4] In the context of infringement the requisite use must involve the mark being used *as* a mark, so that for instance depiction in the course of comparative advertising by a competitor will not be covered.[5] Nor will a 'descriptive' use such as occurred in *Shell Co of Australia Ltd v Esso Standard Oil (Australia) Ltd,*[6] where Esso's 'humanised oildrop' (Eulenspiegel) trade mark was seen scampering about in a Shell cartoon television commercial. Although the figure was very similar to the registered mark and could have been 'a member of the same tribe', the context in which it was used was not 'as a trade mark' but rather to describe the attributes of the petrol and unite the images presented in the cartoon.[7] Generic use of a registered trade mark in such a way as to avoid infringement occurs when a word or phrase 'is capable of being read as descriptive of a characteristic quality or function of the goods in question'.[8] A generous attitude towards 'descriptive' use of a registered mark has deprived several traders of a remedy. For example, the use of 'kettle cooked' in relation to potato chips did not infringe the mark KETTLE;[9] Coca Cola were unable to prevent the phrase CHILL

---

3. As to the meaning of those terms, see [19.43]–[19.44].
4. See [19.8] ff.
5. See eg *Irving's Yeast-Vite Ltd v Horsenail* (1934) 51 RPC 110; *Berzins Specialty Bakeries Pty Ltd v Monty's Continental Bakery (Vic) Pty Ltd* (1987) 12 IPR 38; *Caterpillar Loader Hire (Holdings) Pty Ltd v Caterpillar Tractor Co* (1983) 48 ALR 511; *Musidor BV v Tansing* (1994) 29 IPR 203. This is now specifically provided by s 122(1)(d) not to constitute infringement: see [20.9].
6. (1963) 109 CLR 407.
7. Ibid at 422.
8. *Top Heavy Pty Ltd v Killin* (1996) 34 IPR 282 at 286.
9. *Pepsico Australia Pty Ltd v Kettle Chip Co Pty Ltd* (1996) 33 IPR 161.

OUT (registered for clothing and footwear) being used on T-shirts since it is a phrase meaning 'calm down, relax';[10] and the use of the word 'caplets' for bullet shaped tablets (ie shaped like a capsule) was held to be descriptive despite registration of that word as a mark for the identical product.[11]

[20.4] **Dealings in genuinely marked goods.** Where a mark has not been applied by or with the consent of the proprietor or a registered user, it is clear that any commercial dealings with goods bearing the mark will constitute infringement, even if the person involved was not the one who unlawfully applied the mark, being for example an innocent retailer, distributor or importer. Suppose, however, that the original marking of the goods was fully authorised: can the proprietor (or registered user) nevertheless argue that a subsequent use of those goods of which they do not approve constitutes an infringement? This issue caused no little difficulty under the 1955 Act, especially in relation to the use of marks on second-hand (used) goods, or on parallel imported goods (that is, goods acquired lawfully overseas but brought into Australia without the consent of the local distributor).[12] In the former case it was eventually resolved, though not without some difficulty, that the marketing of second-hand goods with the original mark still on them would not constitute a use of the mark *as* a mark, even if the goods had been altered in some way.[13] Similarly, although some earlier decisions had reached the conclusion that the unauthorised importation of marked goods would be unlawful even if the goods had been marked with the trade mark owner's consent for distribution overseas,[14] the view eventually emerged that this would not in general constitute infringement.[15] The key in both sets of cases was acceptance of the proposition that a trade mark is not a 'badge of control', but merely a 'badge of origin'.[16] In other words, where a second-hand dealer or parallel importer is openly displaying the mark, there can be no infringement because purchasers are not being deceived as to the origin of the goods. If

---

10. *Top Heavy Pty Ltd v Killin* (1996) 34 IPR 282 at 286.
11. *Johnson & Johnson Australia Pty Ltd v Sterling Pharmaceuticals Pty Ltd* (1991) 21 IPR 1.
12. As to parallel importation, see generally W A Rothnie, 'Gray Privateers Sink Into Black Market: Parallel Imports and Trade Marks' (1990) 1 *IPJ* 72; M J Davison, 'Parallel Importing: Unlawful Use of Trade Marks' (1990) 19 *Fed LR* 420; C Turner, 'Trade Marks and the Parallel Importation of Goods into Australia: Resolved and Unresolved Issues' (1991) 16 *UQLJ* 175.
13. *Fender Australia Pty Ltd v Bevk* (1989) 15 IPR 257; *Wingate Marketing Pty Ltd v Levi Strauss & Co* (1994) 28 IPR 193. See also *Amalgamated Television Services Pty Ltd v Foxtel Digital Cable Television Pty Ltd* (1995) 32 IPR 323, where the same conclusion was reached in relation to the retransmission of television programs containing trade marks belonging to the free-to-air broadcasters.
14. See eg *Pioneer Kabushiki Kaisha v Registrar of Trade Marks* (1977) 137 CLR 670 at 687–8; *Atari Inc v Dick Smith Electronics Pty Ltd* (1980) 33 ALR 20.
15. *Atari Inc v Fairstar Electronics Pty Ltd* (1982) 1 IPR 291; *R A & A Bailey & Co Ltd v Boccaccio Pty Ltd* (1986) 6 IPR 279. Cf *Delphic Wholesalers Pty Ltd v Elco Food Co Pty Ltd* (1987) 8 IPR 545 and *Fender Australia Pty Ltd v Bevk* (1989) 15 IPR 257, where although that proposition was accepted, parallel importation was nevertheless held to infringe: in the former case because the plaintiff was a registered user who was said to have built up an independent reputation in the mark; and in the latter because the mark had been assigned to a local distributor who had not been responsible for marking the goods. Both decisions, each of which have attracted their share of criticism, should now be decided differently under the new s 123, discussed below.
16. *Champagne Heidsieck et Cie v Buxton* [1930] 1 Ch 330 at 341.

there is any other deception taking place, for instance as to the condition or quality of the goods, it must be pursued through the law of passing off or the trade practices legislation.

In any event, s 123 of the 1995 Act now provides that where a person uses a mark in relation to goods or services which are similar to those in respect of which the mark has been registered, this does not constitute infringement if the mark has been applied to or in relation to the goods or services by or with the consent of the registered owner.[17] Thus even if the decisions just referred to were overturned, both second-hand dealers and parallel importers would now be protected. The clear objective of the provision is to introduce into the trade mark legislation the concept of 'exhaustion of rights' that is commonly accepted in other jurisdictions: that is, that the act of marking goods and putting them onto the market 'exhausts' the proprietor's capacity to control any subsequent dealings in those goods.[18]

There is, however, one exception to this. Under s 121, the proprietor or an authorised user may, by notice upon the goods or their container or packaging, prohibit various acts by subsequent owners of the goods in relation to the mark, including alteration, the addition of another mark, and so on. A subsequent owner will infringe the mark by doing or authorising any of these prohibited acts in the course of trade, unless the goods were purchased in good faith without notice of the prohibition or were derived from such a purchaser.

One 'loophole' that remains to be addressed in the aftermath of the enactment of s 123 is the potential for the law of copyright to be used to control the distribution of genuinely marked goods. In *R A & A Bailey & Co Ltd v Boccaccio Pty Ltd*[19] the producers of Bailey's Irish Cream liqueur had a distribution agreement with an Australian company. Boccaccio had imported the liqueur into Australia from Holland, having purchased it from an authorised distributor there. The label (a rural scene) was the trade mark. Having held that no trade mark infringement had occurred, Young J nevertheless found Boccaccio liable for breach of copyright. Besides being a trade mark, the label was also an artistic work for copyright purposes. Applying the *Time Life* decision,[20] Young J refused to view the lawful purchase of the bottles in Holland as carrying with it an implied licence to import these works, and was not prepared to regard this sort of copyright protection merely as a 'loop hole'.[21] Since the decision, however, the Copyright Law Review Committee has recommended that parallel importation of this sort of copyright work be allowed as part of the revamping of the importation provisions of the Copyright Act.[22] Legislation was introduced in 1992 to implement this recommendation, but lapsed when the 1993 Federal Election was called. However, Sch 4 of the Exposure Draft Bill for the

17. Presumably this refers to the person who was the registered owner at the time of the application of the mark: otherwise there is the arbitrary result that any protection given by the section would be lost once the mark was assigned (cf *Fender Australia Pty Ltd v Bevk* (1989) 15 IPR 257).
18. For critical comment, see W A Rothnie, 'Gray Goods Billow onto the Open Main: Section 123 of the Trade Marks Act 1995' (1996) 7 *AIPJ* 87.
19. (1986) 6 IPR 279.
20. See [8.20].
21. (1986) 6 IPR 279 at 290.
22. CLRC, *Report on the Importation Provisions of the Copyright Act 1968*, 1988: see [8.21].

amendment of the Copyright Act, released in February 1996, contains the necessary provisions. If enacted, they would apply to any copyright material embodied in a label, packaging or other 'accessory' (including instructions, warranties or other information) attached to or associated with an imported article. Provided the copyright owner had originally consented to the use of the material on or in relation to the article, neither importation of the article nor any subsequent commercial dealing with it would constitute an infringement of the copyright in the 'accessory'. This would be so even if the importation itself were unauthorised.

[20.5] Substantial identity and deceptive similarity. The tests for assessing substantial identity or deceptive similarity between marks are well established and the use of the same terminology in the 1995 Act signals a clear intention to retain the existing law on this topic. They are independent criteria and are to be judged in different ways.[23] The question of substantial identity is assessed by comparing the marks side by side and assessing the similarities and differences, having regard to the essential features of the marks as identified by the judgment of the court and by evidence. If they differ only in inessential respects, then they are substantially identical. As to deceptive similarity, on the other hand, s 10 deems it to exist when one mark 'so nearly resembles [the other] that it is likely to deceive or cause confusion'. As with the prohibition on deceptive and confusing marks in s 43,[24] therefore, it is a matter of comparing the impression that consumers have of the plaintiff's mark, as based on their (possibly imperfect) recollection of it, and the impression created by use of the defendant's mark. The deceptiveness is to be assessed with reference to the circumstances of the goods, the prospective purchasers, and the market covered by the registered proprietor's monopoly.

[20.6] Examples. In *Polaroid Corporation v Sole N Pty Ltd*[25] the plaintiff was the registered proprietor of the trade mark POLAROID, registered in respect of 'transparent organic plastic material in the form of sheets or blocks'. The defendants advertised their window tinting material under the name 'Solaroid', and were sued for infringement of the POLAROID mark. The marks were held not to be substantially identical in regard to their essential features because the first letter conveyed a difference to the mind of a person considering them side by side. As far as the general impression created, however, the two words were deceptively similar, particularly given the nature of the goods and of the prospective purchasers. As discussed in the preceding chapter,[26] the words 'substantially identical' and 'deceptively similar' also occur in s 44 as grounds for rejecting registration of such marks for goods of the same description. In *Deeko Australia Pty Ltd v Decor Corporation Pty Ltd*[27] the applicant wished to register DEEKO for a wide range of goods (in Classes 15 and 21), including paper napkins, disposable

---

23.   See *Shell Co of Australia Ltd v Esso Standard Oil (Australia) Ltd* (1963) CLR 407 at 414–15; *Pianotist Co's Application* (1906) 23 RPC 774 at 777; *Australian Woollen Mills Ltd v F S Walton & Co Ltd* (1937) 58 CLR 641 at 648; *Societe Francaise des Viandes et Salaisons du Pacifique v Societe des Produits Nestle SA* (1989) 15 IPR 89.
24.   See [19.37] ff.
25.   [1981] 1 NSWLR 49.
26.   See [19.42] ff.
27.   (1988) 11 IPR 531.

cutlery and plates, cups and bowls, drinking straws and paper bags. This application was opposed by a corporation seeking to register its own mark, DECOR, for household or kitchen utensils and containers. These marks were found to be neither substantially identical nor deceptively similar. Side by side they appeared 'as two quite different words: one an ordinary part of the English language (albeit originally from the French), the other an apparently meaningless, invented word'.[28] There was no likelihood of phonetic confusion between the words, reference to the Macquarie Dictionary for guidance on the pronunciation of 'decor' showing that 'one would have to make some very strained or unlikely assumptions in order to conclude that the two could be pronounced sufficiently similarly so as to be mistaken for each other'.[29] Furthermore, the trade marks were clearly displayed on packaging and would be selected by customers from display shelves without needing to ask staff for help, so any phonetic similarity was of less importance than visual (or orthographic) similarity.

However, the sounds of trade marks have often been relevant, despite changes in marketing practices and a move towards self-selection in stores.[30] In *Berlei Hestia Industries Ltd v Bali Co Inc*[31] phonetic likeness was very strong between marks for the same goods which were asked for by name ('Can I have a Berlei bra/Bali bra?') rather than selected by the customer and this overrode any written dissimilarity. Marks for dough-making machines labelled respectively SIMAC and SEMAK were found to be deceptively similar although not substantially identical,[32] and so too MYCOGENTIN (for veterinary pharmaceutical products) and COGENTIN (for a drug to treat Parkinson's disease) were deceptively similar,[33] as was APROVEL for a pharmaceutical product likely to be confused with PROVELLE.[34] On the other hand AGIOLAX and ACTILAX were not too similar for both to be registered for pharmaceuticals.[35]

[20.7] **'Section 20 infringement'.** In the *Tub Happy* case[36] the equivalent of s 120(1), the infringement provision, was said to be 'an appendage' to the equivalent of s 20, which confers the exclusive right to the use of a trade mark upon the registered proprietor. On this basis, the function of s 120(1) is 'to widen the definition of infringement so as to include cases where the defendant does not use the identical trade mark but uses a mark substantially identical with it or so nearly resembling it as to be likely to deceive'.[37] In other words, using the exact words or device could be seen as

28. Ibid at 534.
29. Ibid at 535.
30. *Johnson & Johnson v Kalnin* (1993) 26 IPR 435.
31. (1973) 129 CLR 353.
32. *Re Application by Simac SpA Macchine Alimentari* (1987) 10 IPR 81.
33. *Merck & Co Inc v Syntex Corporation* (1987) 11 IPR 518. Note that the two marks' widely divergent uses and trade channels upon prescription by different professionals meant that they could both be registered without falling foul of s 33 of the 1955 Act, not being products of the same description.
34. *Upjohn Co v Elf Sanof SA* (1995) 33 IPR 573.
35. *Re Application by Polipharm AG* (1989) 15 IPR 237.
36. *Mark Foys Ltd v Davis Coop & Co Ltd* (1956) 95 CLR 190 at 204.
37. Ibid. See also *Shell Co of Australia Ltd v Esso Standard Oil (Australia) Ltd* (1963) 109 CLR 407 at 423.

falling within s 20, not s 120(1), and this was the assumption in *Tub Happy.*[38]

However, this approach was one with which Deane J expressed 'considerable difficulty' in *Angoves Pty Ltd v Johnson,*[39] and in the same case Fitzgerald J noted that there was 'much to be said for according to [s 120(1)] the role of defining what it is which constitutes an infringement of the exclusive right of user granted by [s 20]'.[40] The appellant company in that case was the registered proprietor of the trade mark ST AGNES in respect of beverages, in particular the 'St Agnes' label of brandy. The respondent owned a liquor store in the suburb of St Agnes in Adelaide and called it the 'St Agnes Liquor Store'. The appellant sued for infringement. The majority held that it was not clear from the authorities whether the use of a trade mark in combination with other material would infringe that trade mark. It was possible that the addition of extra material might destroy any suggestion of substantial identity or deceptive similarity, even when the plaintiff's exact mark was used. However, the mere addition of words, for example in this case words descriptive of the nature of the business, would not necessarily prevent a mark from being substantially identical with or deceptively similar to a registered trade mark. Although s 20 provides that the registered proprietor has the right to the exclusive use of the mark, this should probably be confined to the use of the exact mark registered, and no more or no less. It would be anomalous if s 20 made it invariably unlawful to use a registered mark in its exact form as part of another mark, however incidentally and however small a part it might play in the other mark.[41]

Accordingly it is unclear whether s 20 should be construed to make it unlawful to use as a trade mark the exact words of a registered mark, even where those words are accompanied by additions which ensure that the two marks are not substantially identical or deceptively similar. The differing views have been noted in one subsequent case,[42] but otherwise the issue has not been addressed in detail, with courts either ignoring it or simply endorsing the High Court's comments in *Tub Happy.*[43] The 1995 Act retains the same wording as the previous Act in stating the rights of the trade mark owner (s 20) and the scope of infringement (s 120), the legislature giving no indication that the notion of infringement should be confined to the latter section.

[20.8] Internet domain names. A domain name is an Internet address and is allocated through an administrative process, much as business name registration occurs, without necessarily conferring any property rights. Use of trade marks as part of Internet domain names is beginning to occur, and

38.   (1956) 95 CLR 190 at 202.
39.   (1982) 43 ALR 349 at 362.
40.   Ibid at 371. See also *Faessler v Neall* (1994) 29 IPR 1.
41.   In any event, in this case the defence provided by s 122(1)(a)(see [20.9]) was available to the defendant, in that the name of the place of business (St Agnes' Shopping Centre) was being used.
42.   *Caterpillar Loader Hire (Holdings) Pty Ltd v Caterpillar Tractor Co* (1983) 48 ALR 511.
43.   See *R A & A Bailey & Co Ltd v Boccaccio Pty Ltd* (1986) 6 IPR 279 at 286; *Atari Inc v Fairstar Electronics Pty Ltd* (1982) 1 IPR 291.

the person registering the domain name is not always the owner of the registered mark. For example, 'windows.com', 'mcdonalds.com', 'hertz.com', 'coke.com' and numerous other famous trade marks and company names have been registered as domain names by persons other than the corporations most widely associated with those names.[44] Infringement will be established if use of the domain name is use of the trade mark, that is, to distinguish goods or services used in the course of trade from other products. Offering to supply goods or services is obviously use as a trade mark; however, mentioning a company name or mark on a home page may be just non-trade mark use. On the other hand, using another's mark as part of an Internet address may well amount to passing off if the public perceive such use as only possible with the authorisation of the organisation with the established reputation in that name or mark.[45] In *Playboy Enterprises v Frena*,[46] the US District Court (Florida) assumed without discussion that unauthorised distribution of photographs from *Playboy* magazine displaying the PLAYBOY and PLAYMATE trade marks amounted to trade mark infringement.[47]

(b) Defences and Remedies

[20.9] **Statutory defences.** Besides pleading that the mark in question is invalidly registered, a defendant in proceedings for infringement may also have a defence under ss 122 or 124, which permit:

* use in good faith of the defendant's own name or place of business or a predecessor's name or place of business (s 122(1)(a));[48]

* use in good faith of a description of the character or quality, intended purpose, geographical origin or some other characteristic of the defendant's goods or services (s 122(1)(b));[49]

* use of a mark in relation to goods or services of the defendant which are adapted to be parts or accessories for goods in relation to which the mark has been used without infringement, provided the use is reasonably necessary to indicate the adaptation and does not have the purpose or effect of indicating a trade connection that does not exist in fact (s 122(1)(c));[50]

* use of a trade mark for the purposes of comparative advertising (s 122(1)(d));

---

44. J W Marcovitz 'ronald@Mcdonalds.com — 'Owning a Bitchin' Corporate Trademark as an Internet Address — Infringement? ' (1995) 17 *Cardozo L Rev* 85 at 86.
45. See [8.16].
46. (1993) 839 F Supp 1554, cited in Marcovitz at 101.
47. See also D M Kelly and K Kumor, 'Trade Marks: Intellectual Property Protection on the Information Super Highway' [1995] 10 *EIPR* 481.
48. See *Baume & Co Ltd v A H Moore Ltd* [1958] RPC 226 at 235; *Angoves Pty Ltd v Johnson* (1982) 43 ALR 349.
49. See *F H Faulding & Co Ltd v Imperial Chemical Industries of Australia and NZ Ltd* (1965) 112 CLR 537 at 543; *Caterpillar Loader Hire (Holding) Pty Ltd v Caterpillar Tractor Co* (1983) 48 ALR 511. Cf *Cantarella Bros Pty Ltd v Kona Coffee Roastery & Equipment Supplies Pty Ltd* (1993) 28 IPR 176; *Kettle Chip Co Pty Ltd v Pepsico Australia Pty Ltd* (1995) 32 IPR 302.
50. See *Masson Seeley & Co Ltd v Hill Bros (Service) Ltd* (1940) 57 RPC 128.

- use of the mark pursuant to a right granted under the Act (s 122(1)(e));
- use of a mark by a person who would obtain registration in their own name if they applied (s 122(1)(f));[51]
- use of a disclaimed part of a mark (s 122(2)); or
- use of a mark which has been continuously used in relation to similar goods or services by the defendant or a predecessor prior to any use or registration of the plaintiff's mark;(s 124(1)).[52]

[20.10] Remedies. An action for infringement may be brought by the registered owner or, in certain cases, an authorised user.[53] Where infringement is established, a court may grant an injunction and either damages or an account of profits at the plaintiff's option (s 126(b)). Given the discussion of these remedies in earlier chapters little need be said about them here, other than that damages will be assessed and awarded on much the same basis as in passing off cases.[54] Where there has been an application under s 92(3) to remove a mark for non-use, however, damages may not be awarded for an infringement occurring during a period in which the court finds that the mark has not been used in good faith by the owner (s 127).

As with copyright and patents, it is unlawful to threaten that infringement proceedings will be instituted (s 129). However, although the provisions are in other respects similar,[55] the Trade Marks Act is distinctive in providing that if proceedings are commenced and prosecuted 'with due diligence'[56] against the person threatened, no action for threats may lie, whether or not infringement is ultimately established (s 129(5)). Finally, it should be noted that under Pt 13 the Comptroller-General of Customs may be asked by the owner of a registered mark, or in certain cases an authorised user, to seize imported goods which appear to infringe that mark. However, the goods must be released if an action for infringement is not instituted within ten working days (or 20 if an extension is obtained from the Comptroller). If such an action is unsuccessful, the plaintiff may be required to pay compensation to the owner of the goods or any other defendant in the infringement action.

2. EXPLOITATION

[20.11] General. The benefits of trade mark ownership are derived from the marketing advantage of having goodwill in a name or logo. Orthodox trade mark theory has it that a mark is not a commodity in itself, but owners of trade marks may think otherwise and wish to sell or license their marks. It is only with the enactment of the 1995 Act that registered

---

51. Cf the honest concurrent user provisions; see [19.45].
52. See *Hy-Line Chicks Pty Ltd v Swifte* (1966) 115 CLR 159.
53. See [20.15].
54. See *Alexander & Co v Henry & Co* (1895) 12 RPC 360; *Slazenger & Sons v Spalding & Bros* [1910] 1 Ch 257. As to passing off, see [16.19].
55. See [8.37], [14.12]. Note that although s 124 does not specifically state, as the other provisions do, that mere notification of the existence of a trade mark is not a threat, the courts have in any event taken this to be the case: see *Challender v Royal* (1887) 36 Ch D 425.
56. See eg *Dial-An-Angel Pty Ltd v Sagitaar Services Systems Pty Ltd* (1990) 19 IPR 171.

marks have been explicitly recognised as constituting personal property (s 21). Previous legislation provided strict limitations on assignment and licensing, the primary concern being to ensure that the proposed use was not likely to deceive the public as to the quality or origin of goods or services. For this reason it used to be impossible to assign a mark without the goodwill and business with which it was connected,[57] and licensing a mark was not allowed at all until 1948 when the legislation was amended to allow registered users to be licensed to use marks on certain conditions. The registered user system has now been replaced in the 1995 Act by a more liberal approach in which authorised uses may be recognised even in the absence of registration.

[20.12] Assignment of marks. Even last century, traders were demanding the right to be able to treat trade marks as disposable assets.[58] However, legislative response was slow and under the 1955 Act the right to assign was still qualified to some extent. Although s 82 of the Act permitted the assignment of registered marks with or without the goodwill of the business, an assignment without goodwill was invalid if (a) the assignor or a predecessor had not at any time used the mark in good faith in Australia[59] or (b) the assignor continued to use a substantially identical or deceptively similar mark. Section 106 of the 1995 Act has now removed these restrictions. It has also made it possible to assign a mark whose registration is being sought, so that in effect the right to apply for trade mark protection can now be sold. Nevertheless, despite the liberalisation of the assignment provisions, it will remain sensible for both assignors and assignees to tread warily and to observe certain safeguards in order to prevent deception or confusion of the public, or the development of some other ground for rejection or removal of the mark. This is all the more important in light of the abolition of the concept of associated marks, which previously ensured that closely related marks could not be assigned separately.[60]

A person who becomes entitled by assignment (or transmission) to a registered mark, or to a right to apply for registration, is required to apply to the Registrar to be registered as the proprietor of the mark in respect of the goods or services in relation to which the assignment or transmission has effect (ss 107–110). It is possible to have a partial assignment of marks so as to apply to some only of the goods or services in respect of which registration is sought or exists, or limited to a certain area where the mark is used (s 106(2)). An assignment need not be in writing, though the Registrar will require some proof of the assignee's title (reg 10.1). Finally, it should be noted that although the assignment may be with or without the goodwill of the business concerned (s 106(3)), it is generally presumed unless the contrary is shown that the marks used in a business being sold have also been assigned.[61]

---

57.   See eg *Bowden Wine Ltd v Bowden Brake Co Ltd* (1941) 31 RPC 385. Cf the position with unregistered marks: see [17.17].
58.   See Cornish, p 468.
59.   This did not apply where the mark was registered with the intention of assigning it to a corporation to be formed and it had been so assigned, or where it was registered with the intention that it be used by a registered user and this had occurred within six months of registration.
60.   See [19.47].
61.   *'Weston' Trade Mark* [1968] RPC 167 at 183.

[20.13] Licensing. The ability to license trade marks is desirable to enable the proprietor to exploit a mark as part of an overall commercial and marketing strategy. This includes manufacturing goods through a licensee, appointing authorised distributors and franchising. Trade marks and trading identities are vital to franchising, which may be described as selling other people the right to copy your business.[62] Typically, the franchisor insists that the complete persona is adopted, so that the trade marks, get-up and advertising used are all identical, with the franchisee raising their own capital and taking the commercial and financial risks. Franchisors supply not only the persona of the business but also training and support. A successful franchisee will find themselves running a profitable business with a correlative licence fee back to the franchisor. Well-known franchise operations in Australia include McDonalds, Pizza Hut, Mad Barry's, 7-eleven, Snap, Knitwit and RetraVision. Obviously the licensing of trade marks is a vital component of a franchisor's operations.

[20.14] Rationale for controlling licensees. Although historically a trade mark's function has always been to indicate the origin of a product, a view reaffirmed in the parallel import cases,[63] the fact is that many marks today tend to serve more as indicators of product quality than of any single source. This is particularly true where a number of licensees may be manufacturing items. However, there is this risk, that a licensee may be so successful in exploiting the mark that in terms of public perception the mark becomes their own. In so far as the mark then ceases to indicate a trade connection with the proprietor, it may become deceptive and threaten the validity of the registration.[64] In order to preclude this happening, the proprietor should retain some control over the licensee's activities, though this may be as slight as the control exercised by a parent company over a subsidiary.[65] The registered user system under Pt IX of the 1955 Act was indeed limited to licensees who were authorised to use trade marks subject to appropriate quality control mechanisms. Registration was not compulsory, so that an unregistered licence agreement was not in itself invalid. Nevertheless there were certain advantages to registration, notably that use of a mark by a registered user could be relied upon to defeat an action for removal for non-use, even if the proprietor was personally inactive. However where registration of a particular licensee would 'tend to facilitate trafficking', an application for registered user status had to be refused (s 74(2)). According to the House of Lords, discussing a similar provision, trafficking essentially involves using a mark as a commodity in its own right and not primarily for the purpose of identifying or promoting products in which the proprietor is interested.[66] For example, advertising for licensees to exploit the popularity of a fictional character might amount to 'hawking a trade mark around'.[67] Several applications by the American Greetings

---

62. J Phillips, Editorial, *Trade Mark World,* June 1987, p 2. See further [22.28].
63. See [20.4].
64. See *'Bostitch' Trade Mark* [1963] RPC 183; *'GE' Trade Mark* [1970] RPC 339; *Pioneer Kabushiki Kaisha v Registrar of Trade Marks* (1977) 137 CLR 670.
65. See *Pioneer Kabushiki Kaisha v Registrar of Trade Marks* (1977) 137 CLR 670 at 683–4. Cf *Farmer & Co Ltd v Anthony Hordern & Sons Ltd* (1964) 112 CLR 163.
66. *Holly Hobbie Trade Mark* (1984) 1 IPR 486. Cf *Pioneer Kabushiki Kaisha v Registrar of Trade Marks,* ibid at 686–7.
67. *Holly Hobbie,* ibid at 491.

Company were rejected by the House of Lords, where the company wished to license the 'Holly Hobbie' name and image on a wide variety of goods including tableware, lampshades, furniture, sleeping bags, slippers and toys.[68] The prohibition on trafficking attracted a great deal of controversy. The British provision was described in the House of Lords as a 'complete anachronism' in relation to the modern practice of character merchandising,[69] and in 1988 the Industrial Property Advisory Committee recommended the removal of its Australian equivalent.[70] Although not acted upon under the old legislation, that recommendation has been given effect under the 1995 Act with the repeal not just of the trafficking provision but the whole system of registered users. Instead, there is a broader concept of 'authorised use'.

[20.15] Authorised use of trade marks. The 1995 Act does not require parties to a licence agreement to formalise it by having the licensee designated as a registered user for the purposes of the Act, although as discussed below voluntary recording of claims in respect of trade marks is allowed under Pt 11 of the Act. Authorised use of a mark is defined in s 8 as use of the mark under the 'control' of the owner. 'Control' is not defined as such in the Act, although it will be taken to exist where 'quality control' is exercised over goods or services dealt with or provided in the course of trade and in relation to which the mark is used (s 8(3)), or where 'financial control' is exercised over trading activities in relation to which the mark is used (s 8(4)). Two things are apparent from this. One is that the definition of authorised user may extend to a wide range of customers or subsidiaries of a trade mark proprietor, whether or not they have any formal licence agreement to use the mark. Second, however, the new legislation has retained one key element of the old registered user system: the emphasis on the exercise by the owner of some degree of control over what is done with the mark, even if that control is fairly limited.

As noted earlier,[71] authorised use of a mark is taken to be use by the owner (s 7(3)). Section 26 sets out the powers of an authorised user. They include the power to use the mark in relation to the goods or services in respect of which it is registered, subject to any conditions or limitations on that registration; to include with marked goods a notice under s 121 prohibiting various acts in relation to the goods;[72] and to authorise others to apply, alter or remove the mark in relation to the relevant goods or services. An authorised user may also call on the proprietor to institute infringement proceedings and, if this is not done within two months, institute such proceedings personally, joining the proprietor as a defendant in the proceedings. The same applies in regard to the right to demand customs seizure under Pt 13. Importantly, however, each of these powers is subject to the terms of any agreement between the user and the owner.

---

68.   Ibid. See also *Rawhide Trade Mark* [1962] RPC 133; *Pussy Galore Trade Mark* [1967] RPC 265.

69.   *Holly Hobbie,* ibid at 488.

70.   *Legal Protection of Character Merchandising in Australia,* 1988. Cf A Terry, 'Proprietary Rights in Character Merchandising Marks' (1990) 18 *ABLR* 229.

71.   See [19.8].

72.   See [20.4].

[20.16]   Voluntary recording of claims. A new feature in the 1995 legislation is the system under Pt 11 for persons claiming an interest or right in relation to a mark to have their claim recorded in the Register. This can be done in relation to either a mark which is already registered, or one for which registration is in the process of being sought. The fact that a record is made of a claim is not proof of its accuracy (s 116). Nevertheless, the advantage of being recorded on the Register is that it may alert others, especially potential assignees of the mark, that the right or interest is asserted. Conversely, it also ensures that the claimant learns of any assignment. Thus when the Registrar is asked to record an assignment, anyone who has recorded a claim in relation to that mark must be notified (s 111). In practice, the system is likely to be especially useful to licensees, and to those (such as financial institutions) who have a mortgage or some other form of security interest over a mark.[73]

---

73.   See I Zeitler, 'Assignments and Voluntary Recordal of Trade Marks under the Trade Marks Act 1995' (1996) 7 *AIPJ* 103.

PART VI

Other Dimensions

Chapter 21

International Aspects of Intellectual Property Protection

[21.1] Introduction. The capacity to protect work from being pirated overseas is an important aspect of ownership of intellectual property rights. Conversely, being permitted to import foreign books or machinery parts is also important, and without adequate intellectual property protection overseas the owners of rights will not permit the flow of goods into other jurisdictions.

In some instances, the principles of private international law may permit a person to take action in one jurisdiction to vindicate a right obtained in another. However, while this option appears to be available in relation to actions for breach of confidence[1] or passing off,[2] it has been held in Australia (and also in Britain) that no such protection may be claimed for rights arising under foreign statutory regimes, since they have no extra-territorial effect.[3] Where copyright, designs, patents and registered trade

---

1.   See *Attorney-General (UK) v Heinemann Publishers Australia Pty Ltd* (1987) 75 ALR 353 at 374–5, 455. No action may be maintained, however, where the duty of confidence has a sufficiently 'public' character as to bring into play the prohibition on the enforcement of foreign public laws: see eg *Attorney-General (UK) v Heinemann Publishers Australia Ltd* (1988) 165 CLR 30 (see [4.41]).
2.   See eg *Alfred Dunhill Ltd v Sunoptic SA* [1979] FSR 337; *Tan-Ichi Co Ltd v Jancar Ltd* [1990] FSR 151. More usually, of course, a foreign trader is complaining not of a breach of the law applicable in its domicile, but of a breach of the law in the jurisdiction in which the action is commenced, on the basis that its reputation has 'travelled' to that jurisdiction and is protectable there: see [17.11] ff.
3.   *Potter v Broken Hill Proprietary Co Ltd* (1906) 3 CLR 479; *Norbert Steinhardt & Son Ltd v Meth* (1961) 105 CLR 440; *Tyburn Productions Ltd v Conan Doyle* [1990] 3 WLR 167; *LA Gear Inc v Gerard Wholesalers & Sons Ltd* [1991] FSR 670. See Cornish, pp 55–7. Cf E Jooris, 'Infringement of Foreign Copyright and the Jurisdiction of the English Courts' [1996] 3 *EIPR* 127.

marks are concerned, therefore, any protection beyond the original jurisdiction must stem from the implementation of arrangements explicitly designed to confer such a benefit.

[21.2] International arrangements. During the nineteenth century numerous bilateral agreements were entered into, eventually to be replaced by international conventions made between countries with similar require-ments as to protection of intellectual property. Among the first such treaties were the Paris Convention for the Protection of Industrial Property in 1883 dealing with patents, designs and trade marks, and the Berne Con-vention for the Protection of Literary and Artistic Works in 1886, dealing with copyright protection. One of the main principles of these conventions is that of 'national treatment', which requires that signatory nations under-take to protect subject matter produced in other member states to the same extent as their own nationals receive protection. Apart from ensuring reciprocal protection among member countries, another aim of interna-tional conventions is to standardise protection and identify new subject matter which should be protected. Examples of such activity include the recognition of performers' rights,[4] plant variety rights,[5] property in integrated circuits[6] and the problems posed by satellite program distribu-tion.[7] Other international agreements exist not to clarify or confer further protection but in order to facilitate the obtaining of intellectual property rights internationally. For example, the Patent Co-operation Treaty (PCT) of 1970 provides for a single application, search and examination in respect of all nominated member countries, saving the time-consuming and expen-sive duplication of effort involved in filing separate patent applications everywhere that protection is sought. More recently, the focus of inter-national arrangements has shifted to the harmonisation of intellectual property laws, driven by a desire to facilitate international trade. The link between intellectual property rights and trade is the explicit basis for the Trade Related Aspects of Intellectual Property Rights (TRIPS) Agreement, negotiated as part of the Uruguay round of the General Agreement on Trade and Tariffs (GATT). The TRIPS Agreement has a great deal to say about the content and enforcement of national intellectual property laws. With the conclusion of this agreement and its acceptance by most of the major trading nations, it has been said that classical intellectual property law is being absorbed into international economic law with the conse-quence that universal minimum standards are emerging.[8]

[21.3] Regional agreements. Countries in several regions of the world have combined their efforts to set up patent offices serving a number of states. For example, the African Intellectual Property Organisation (OAPI)

---

4.   Rome Convention for the Protection of Performers, Producers of Phonograms and Broadcasting Organisations 1961.
5.   International Convention for the Protection of New Varieties of Plants 1961 (UPOV).
6.   Washington Treaty on the Protection of Intellectual Property in Respect of Integrated Circuits 1989.
7.   Brussels Convention Relating to the Distribution of Programme-Carrying Signals Transmitted by Satellite 1974.
8.   J H Richardson, 'Universal Minimum Standards of Intellectual Property Protection under the TRIPS Component of the WTO Agreement' (1995) 29(2) *The International Lawyer* 345.

consists of a group of 13 French-speaking African nations,[9] while the African Regional Industrial Property Organisation (ARIPO) comprises 12 English-speaking countries.[10] The two organisations enable applicants for patents to obtain rights for each group of states. Of greater immediate relevance to Australia is the European Patent Office (EPO), situated in Munich and established in 1977 by the European Patent Convention (EPC). The EPO presently grants a bundle of patents for member states of the EC, offering a single European Community Patent which allows a single application filed at the EPO to cover all members of the Community, instead of just forming the basis for separate patents in each country. The effect of this has been to diminish further the role of national patent offices in individual European countries, with resulting decreases in employment for patent examiners and ancillary staff and loss of filing fees.

[21.4] **Institutions responsible for intellectual property laws.** The primary sources of intellectual property law are the individual countries which enact those laws and whose judges pronounce upon and develop the protection. These separate sovereign states tend to group together in matters of international trade and form powerful blocs which negotiate between themselves and with other groups of countries to effect their aim of creating a favourable trading environment. Equally important in recent years has been the role of intellectual property in developing countries, whose needs for access to technology are hampered by an inability to develop or pay for goods and services without some degree of foreign aid and cooperation. As international trade increases, the need to develop appropriate and reasonably uniform regulatory mechanisms is felt by both exporters and would-be importers of technology. Countries with a small or otherwise limited domestic market, Australia among them, need to develop export industries, but these in turn may require the importing of complex parts and machinery which there may not be sufficient resources to produce domestically. Lack of corresponding protection between countries seeking to import or export technology to each other will result in friction between different laws, or even wholesale copying if no enforceable regime is in place. The grouping together of countries into international organisations is thus a firmly established aspect of the international protection of industrial and intellectual property. At the forefront of these are the United Nations and its agencies, although their role has perhaps been somewhat lessened in importance with the impact of the GATT TRIPS Agreement.

1. UNITED NATIONS AGENCIES

[21.5] **World Intellectual Property Organisation (WIPO).**[11] This is a specialised agency of the United Nations system of organisations. Although

---

9.   OAPI was established as a result of the Libreville Agreement for the Creation of an African and Malagasy Office of Industrial Property 1962 and the Bangui Agreement Relating to the Creation of an African Intellectual Property Organisation 1982. Its office is situated in Yaounde, Cameroon.

10. ARIPO was set up by the Lusaka Agreement on the Creation of an Industrial Property Organization for English-Speaking Africa (ESARIPO) in 1978, acquiring its present name in 1985. Its headquarters are in Harare, Zimbabwe.

11. See WIPO Background Reading, pp 37–48. The Convention Establishing the World Intellectual Property Organisation was signed at Stockholm in 1967.

active in its present form since the early 1970s, WIPO's origins can be traced back to 1883 when the Paris Convention was adopted, shortly followed by the Berne Convention in 1886. Initially two secretariats were established, one for industrial property and one for copyright, to administer the separate conventions. The offices were merged in 1893. The merged office, administered by the Swiss Federal Government, became known as BIRPI, the acronym of the French language version of its name, United International Bureaux for the Protection of Intellectual Property. The change of name to WIPO coincided with the organisation becoming an intergovernmental body independent of the Swiss Government, and then a specialised agency of the United Nations in 1974.

The most widely accepted definition of 'intellectual property' is that formulated by WIPO[12] and the organisation has been pre-eminent in the field of instituting and facilitating protection. WIPO engages in three types of activity: registration activities; the promotion of intergovernmental cooperation in the administration of intellectual property; and program activities. Registration activities involve processing international applications for patent, design or trade mark registration. Intergovernmental cooperation consists of making patent documents available for search and reference, compiling statistics, conducting regional surveys of the administration of intellectual property and maintaining and updating international classification systems. The major activity undertaken by WIPO lies in substantive or program activities which include promoting wider acceptance of existing treaties, updating and concluding new treaties and organising and participating in development cooperation activities. To these ends WIPO has been extremely active in convening regional seminars on the establishment, teaching, researching and exploitation of intellectual property rights. A major focus of this activity in recent years has been the Asia-Pacific region where intellectual property protection is being introduced at a great rate, due partly to US trade pressure and the desire of countries like China, Singapore, Taiwan, Indonesia and Korea to become part of the international trading community.

WIPO administers three types of treaties: those establishing international protection; those facilitating international protection through international registration and searching; and those establishing classification systems and procedures for improving them and keeping them up to date.

[21.6] United Nations Conference on Trade and Development (UNCTAD).[13] This organ of the General Assembly of the United Nations was founded in 1964. UNCTAD was formed at the behest of the 'Group of 77', a bloc of developing countries wishing to resolve post-colonial problems and emulate GATT by seeking to adjust unfavourable world trade patterns (seen by the Group to operate in favour of industrialised nations). In order to achieve a balance between competing trading interests there are four groups or blocs comprising the UNCTAD board, and a majority of groups must agree on an issue before action will be taken. Group A comprises Afro-Asian countries and the Slavic countries; Group B, developed capitalist economies including Australia, New Zealand, Japan, US, UK,

---

12. See [1.3].
13. See Blakeney, pp 21–4.

Canada, France, Germany and Italy; Group C, Latin American countries; and Group D, the socialist economies (or at least what were formerly the socialist economies) including the former USSR, Poland, Hungary and also Mongolia. The various states may also belong to other groupings which are relevant to trade issues and intellectual property, such as the EC, OAIP or ARIPO, the WTO (see below) and WIPO. A major function of UNCTAD is to establish licensing norms to balance the interests of owners and users of intellectual property in the exploitation of technology. To this end a United Nations Conference on an International Code of Conduct on the Transfer of Technology (TOT Code) was convened in 1978, building on work previously done by an UNCTAD working party beginning in 1970.

[21.7] United Nations Educational, Scientific and Cultural Organisation (UNESCO). This United Nations body is mainly concerned with the dissemination and exploitation of educational and scientific knowledge and materials, the protection of proprietary rights involved being of less importance than making the intellectual property available on reasonable terms. UNESCO's main role in the international intellectual property arena lies in its administration of the Universal Copyright Convention. This role descended upon UNESCO as a result of its concern with the achievement of social and economic progress in developing countries, where progress depends heavily upon easy access to the literary and scientific works of developed countries. The Berne Convention had long been seen as excluding many developing countries from membership (due to the high level of protection insisted upon) and as working to the detriment of such countries. The Universal Copyright Convention was intended to embrace states from all five continents, whatever their level of economic and cultural development.

2.   GATT, WTO AND THE TRIPS AGREEMENT

[21.8] The General Agreement on Trade and Tariffs (GATT). The most significant international intellectual property agreement of recent years has been the TRIPS Agreement, part of the 'Uruguay Round'[14] of GATT, concluded on 15 December 1993 after more than seven years of discussions and negotiations. The TRIPS Agreement created comprehensive new GATT rules to protect intellectual property and govern disputes. The Uruguay Round established a new international institution, the World Trade Organisation (WTO) to administer and oversee the new body of trade rules, including more effective dispute resolution. Established after World War II in an attempt to create a more favourable environment for world trade, GATT is a multilateral treaty subscribed to by almost 100 countries which together account for about 90% of world trade. GATT aims to liberalise and expand world trade and provide a secure and predictable international trading environment through reduction of trade barriers and other measures which distort trade flows. While predominantly a club of western industrialised nations, GATT has espoused market-based rules and the liberalising of trade through reduction of tariffs and domestic subsidisation of farming and manufacturing. GATT members periodically engage in a round or series of negotiations designed to facilitate these aims. The

---

14.   Launched in 1986 in Punta del Este, Uruguay.

Uruguay Round struggled to a conclusion after extensive discussion concerning 14 sectors of world trade, notably trade in services, agriculture (the major sticking point) and TRIPS, the trade related aspects of intellectual property. The desire to know what was being discussed and to influence the outcome if possible led to a number of countries applying to join GATT, including Taiwan, the former Soviet Union, Venezuela, Bulgaria and China.[15] There are other advantages to joining apart from participating in the Uruguay round. These include the favourable trading terms available to GATT members, the access to disputes procedures and the enhancement of economic reform in developing countries which membership of a powerful trading bloc can achieve. Although some concessions are made for developing countries and centrally planned economies, joining GATT involves a commitment to arresting (and eventually reducing) tariff levels and generally opening up trade. The political and economic changes in Eastern Europe in 1989–90 allowed countries like Hungary, Poland, the Czech Republic and Romania to move towards becoming full members of GATT.

The US was a driving force in having GATT produce a code authorising trade sanctions in response to intellectual property violations, and there is much criticism of the coercive nature of TRIPS, which enforces conceptions of property and protection on developing nations where such notions may be incompatible with cultural institutions and invalid under local law and custom. For many indigenous societies, protection exists to protect the sanctity of a process or idea, to preserve cultural patrimony and in particular, to preserve the sacredness of an object or to preserve the sacredness of meaning.[16]

[21.9] Intellectual property and world trade. The interest shown by GATT in intellectual property matters is of relatively recent origin, focusing in the early 1980s on the problems posed by the import of counterfeit trade marked goods, but more recently extending to the trade related aspects of other intellectual property rights, including the availability, scope and effectiveness of national protection in these areas. The reason that intellectual property laws are considered to be relevant to trade is because of the distortions resulting from uneven or inadequate protection in various countries. For example copyright material, such as sound and video recordings, computer programs and books which have been imported into a country without adequate laws, may be vulnerable to widespread pirating. Some countries do not allow patents for foods, chemicals or pharmaceuticals where others do. In some instances, the protection of new technologies including integrated circuits and biotechnological advances is uncertain or completely lacking. Designs law, which may protect any manufactured article, is seen as important in world trade because without adequate design protection textiles, spare parts, aircraft and computer hardware (to name only a few items of international commerce) might all be copied with impunity. Australia's 1989 amendments in this area[17] remain controversial, some manufacturers fearing that overseas suppliers of parts and machinery will

---

15. 'GATT Brief: A Better Deal for Poor Countries', *Economist,* 28 April 1990, p 82.
16. R L Gana, 'Has Creativity Died in the Third World? Some Implications of the Internationalisation of Intellectual Property' (1995) 24 *Denver J of Intl Law and Policy* 109, citing *Milpurrurru v Indofurn Pty Ltd* (1994) 30 IPR 209 (see [8.36]).
17. See [10.24] ff.

refuse to allow them to be imported into Australia now that non-registrable designs are no longer protected by copyright. The legal regimes of protection are only part of the story. Enforcement may be difficult where administrative or procedural problems make it impossible to inhibit pirates even where legal protection theoretically exists, and where remedies and penalties may be inadequate.

[21.10] **The cost of counterfeiting.** The failure of some countries to enact or enforce intellectual property laws, thus allowing widespread reproduction of goods (protected by patents, designs, copyright or trade marks in their country of origin) deters investment and trade in legitimate goods.

> Counterfeiting is an insidious killer of businesses and, for the community, this means the loss of jobs and earnings, as well as taxes and social security contributions unpaid, for counterfeiting is often linked to the 'black economy'.[18]

According to one estimate worldwide losses from counterfeiting exceeded US$60 billion in 1988,[19] at least 15% of the US trade deficit, and up to 750,000 domestic jobs were lost as the result of illegal use of patents, trade marks and copyright.[20] The cost to US industry of piracy in 26 selected countries[21] was estimated to be US$4.63 billion in 1992 alone. The largest loss was in computer software (US$2.2 billion) followed by sound recordings (US$1 billion), motion pictures/videos (US$938 million) and books (US$485 million).[22] The Committee on External Economic Relations of the European Parliament has suggested a figure of 100,000 job losses in EC firms as a direct result of counterfeiting.[23] The Federation de l'Industrie Horlogère Suisse (Swiss Clock and Watchmakers Association) calculates that around 10 million counterfeit Swiss watches are sold every year, for some US$500 million. The losses to European firms manufacturing spare parts for cars are put at US$168 million per annum and Levi Strauss estimate their company's losses at between US$5 and $10 million a year.[24]

Whereas a decade ago American firms were mostly concerned only about the theft of trade marks associated with blue jeans and toys and the illegal copying of books and records, these firms are now being joined in their demands for adequate protection by some of the largest manufacturers in the country, including suppliers of electronic products, ethical drugs, agricultural chemicals and automotive and aerospace products, scientific and photographic equipment, software and other computer technology. The entertainment and fashion industries have long felt the effects of piracy. It is estimated that pirated sound recordings once constituted up to 90% of the market in south east Asia.[25]

The means of duplicating protected works and trade marked goods are becoming easier and cheaper as technology advances. On the other hand

---

18. M-C Piatti, 'Measures to Combat International Piracy' [1989] 7 *EIPR* 239 at 239.
19. K Stanberry, 'Forging a New International Frontier in Intellectual Property Rights' (1990) 13 *World Competition* 105 at 105.
20. Ibid, citing Baldridge and Malcomb, 'Protecting US Intellectual Property Rights' *Business America,* 14 April 1986, p 2.
21. The worst offenders are believed to be Taiwan, Thailand, Italy, PRC, India and Brazil.
22. P C B Liu, 'US Industry's Influence on Intellectual Property and Special 301 Actions' (1994) 13 *Pacific Basin Law J* 87.
23. M-C Piatti, 'Measures to Combat International Piracy' [1989] 7 *EIPR* 239 at 239.
24. Ibid.
25. T Abu-Ghazaleh, 'The GATT and Intellectual Property' (1988) 3 *Economic Impact* 24.

the pirates do not bear the burden of increasing research and development expenses involved in the development of many products that are commonly infringed upon. Some observers may feel that expensive fashion and entertainment items are still available in sufficient quantities with more than adequate returns to their creators, and indeed that the pharmaceutical industry is not suffering too badly. Counterfeiting is now, however, affecting goods on which consumer health and safety are dependent. Examples in recent years include fake fire-fighting systems in Boeing aircraft engines, cardiac pumps with counterfeit components and cars with counterfeit brakes, all of which have been detected due to faulty operation of the fake parts. In the US a dozen or so people died after taking counterfeit amphetamines and the 1979–80 coffee crop in Kenya was destroyed following the use of counterfeit agricultural chemicals bearing the label of a well-known US manufacturer.[26] The Australian experience of losses due to inadequate regimes or enforcement of intellectual property rights is on a correspondingly smaller scale, but a significant impact has been made in our region by US bilateral and unilateral strategy to improve the level of protection.[27]

[21.11] US trade sanctions. Some of the most effective measures for enforcement of intellectual property rights, or indeed inducements to their introduction, lie in the form of US trade laws mandating bilateral and multilateral negotiations and investigations. The Trade Act 1974 (US) provides for enforcement of US rights under trade agreements and covers foreign practices regarding goods, services, investment and the protection of intellectual property rights. The offending practices may take place in the US, in the other country, or in a third country. Section 301 allows the US Trade Representative (USTR) to take any appropriate action against a foreign government which is found to be violating an international trade agreement or engaging in unjustifiable or discriminatory acts. The USTR has exclusive authority to engage in international negotiations on trade issues on behalf of the US.[28] An 'unreasonable act' includes (inter alia) failing to provide adequate and effective intellectual property rights. Section 301 was strengthened by 'super' 301 and 'special' 301 introduced by the Omnibus Trade and Competitiveness Act 1988 (US), allowing for expedited access into the s 301 process for intellectual property matters. It has been said of 'super' 301:

> This is not a breakfast cereal, but rather a measure that requires the USTR each year to promulgate a list of what it unilaterally decides are offenses [sic] committed against our intellectual property by our trading partners and to initiate actions — potentially in contravention of our obligations under GATT and certainly contrary to its spirit — against such countries unless they make satisfactory amends on our timetable in our way.[29]

---

26. Piatti, ibid at 240.
27. I Govey, 'Trade Related Aspects of Intellectual Property Rights (TRIPS)' (1988) 1 *IP* 33.
28. For a discussion of negotiation strategies see P C B Liu, 'US Industry's Influence on Intellectual Property Negotiations and Special 301 Actions' (1994) 13 *Pacific Basin LJ* 87.
29. W P Alford 'How Theory Does — And Does Not — Matter: American Approaches to Intellectual Property Law in East Asia' (1994) 13 *Pacific Basin LJ* 8 at 13. See also D Macleod, 'US Trade Pressure and the Developing Intellectual Property Law of Thailand, Malaysia and Indonesia' (1992) 26 *UBC L Rev* 343; P C B Liu, ibid.

Section 337 of the Tariff Act 1930 (US) allows the fast-track granting of relief from present or potential injury caused by unfairly traded imports. In practice this has often been used in situations involving infringements of intellectual property rights. A GATT panel has ruled that s 337 breaches the national treatment provisions of the TRIPS Agreement and the US has proposed amendment of s 337 in light of this criticism.[30] Nevertheless, the threat of US trade sanctions has proven to be fairly effective in persuading nations such as Japan and the People's Republic of China to upgrade the content and enforcement of their laws. Indeed the creation of the WTO and the conclusion of the TRIPS Agreement have not slowed the US Government's drive to pursue bilateral arrangements. In February 1995, for example, it announced a major agreement with China on the protection of intellectual property in that country.[31] Concerns as to the extent of China's compliance with that agreement have led to a further pact, concluded in June 1996, which requires China to crack down on the counterfeiting of CDs and other material.[32] Other countries too in the Asia-Pacific region have succumbed to the combination of direct US pressure and the requirements of the TRIPS Agreement and been forced to enact or improve intellectual property rights.[33]

US action in placing countries on 'watch lists' for practices detrimental to US commerce is echoed by the EC's annual *Report on US Trade and Investment Barriers*[34] which rehearses long-standing complaints about US unilateral retaliation on matters which displeases it, as amounting to protectionism. However, it is generally recognised that the benefits of the Uruguay Round have included providing a more solid basis for negotiations and a greater amount of common ground for the settlement of disputes.

[21.12] Negotiating TRIPS. TRIPS became one of the most sensitive and controversial issues in the Uruguay Round,[35] owing to the 'extreme positions' taken by the US on one hand and some developing countries on the other, particularly over the issue of pharmaceuticals which the US protected by patent law in situations where other countries would not.[36] Many developing countries were highly suspicious of the whole process, fearing that increased protection for intellectual property rights would strengthen the monopoly power of western multi-nationals, harm development by reducing technology transfer and injure consumers who are already poor

---

30. G Polson, 'Uruguay Round Outcomes: Intellectual Property', Services and Intellectual Property Branch, Trade Negotiations and Organisations Division, Department of Foreign Affairs and Trade, September 1994, p 23.
31. See D Dessler, 'China's Intellectual Property Protection: Prospects for Achieving International Standards' (1995) 19 *Fordham Int LJ* 181; J C Fung, 'Can Mickey Mouse Prevail in the Court of the Monkey King? Enforcing Foreign Intellectual Property Rights in the People's Republic of China' (1996) 18 *Loyola of LA Int Comp LJ* 613.
32. See T Walker, 'US hails China piracy agreement', *The Australian*, 19 June 1996, p 12.
33. See M Blakeney, 'The Impact of the TRIPS Agreement in the Asia-Pacific Region' [1996] 10 *EIPR* 544.
34. See eg 12th Report, 1996, *EU News*, June/July 1996.
35. See M Duffy, 'The Uruguay Round and Trade Related Aspects of Intellectual Property Rights', Intellectual Property Forum, August 1989, p 15; C Arup, 'The Prospective GATT Agreement for Intellectual Property Protection' (1993) 4 *AIPJ* 181.
36. See eg *Genentech Inc v Wellcome Foundation Ltd* [1989] RPC 147, where a British patent for a product/process protected in the US was revoked (see [15.12]).

by raising the prices of essential medicines and other patented goods. On the other side of the equation the developed trading countries argued that foreign investment and technology transfer would be spurred on by the existence and enforcement of protection. In the result, however, many developing countries had little choice but to commit to the GATT/WTO process, given that they would continue to face US pressure no matter what happened. Indeed those countries which had already upgraded their laws in response to the threat of US trade sanctions clearly now had an interest in ensuring they were not undercut by other nations. The Agreement in its final form does make some concessions to the less established trading nations. 'Developing country members' of the WTO and those in the process of transforming centrally planned economies to free market economies are given a five-year transition period (compared to the one year for other members) in which to bring their laws and practices into compliance with the provisions of the Agreement (Art 65). 'Least developed country members' are given a transition period of ten years (Art 66). Developed country members are also required to provide technical and financial cooperation to other members in relation to the formulation of intellectual property laws and the creation of agencies to enforce them (Art 67). To date 130 countries have joined the WTO and thus become bound by the Agreement, with a further 29 (including the Russian Federation and the People's Republic of China) having applied for membership.[37]

Aside from the tensions between the developed and developing nations, more specific issues on which disagreement emerged during TRIPS negotiations included the scope of patent protection for pharmaceuticals, copyright, performers' and broadcast rights, design protection and whether patent rights should be available on a 'first to file' or 'first to invent' basis. In the event, much compromise was entered into on all sides and the US has agreed to move to a 'first to file' model of patent protection, much to the disgruntlement of some US commentators.[38]

[21.13] The provisions of the Agreement.[39] Part I of the TRIPS Agreement sets out a number of general principles. These include the general obligation to give effect to the provisions of the Agreement, subject to the clarification that WTO members may if they wish confer more extensive intellectual property protection than is required by those provisions, unless that is specifically prohibited (Art 1). Article 3 affirms the principle of reciprocity, requiring each member to 'accord to the nationals of other Members treatment no less favourable than that it accords to its own nationals with regard to the protection of each intellectual property'; while Art 4 states that any arrangements for 'most-favoured-nation' status or treatment must 'be accorded immediately and unconditionally to the nationals of all other members'. However, other provisions in Pt I qualify these general obligations by making it clear that entry into the Agreement does not

37. Information obtained from the WTO's website: http://www.wto.org/wto.
38. D Rohrbacher and P Crilly, 'The Case for a Strong Patent System' (1995) 8 *Harv J of Law and Tech* 263.
39. See M Blakeney, Trade Related Aspects of Intellectual Property Rights: A Concise Guide to the TRIPS Agreement, 1996; G E Evans, 'The Principle of National Treatment and the International Protection of Industrial Property' [1996] 3 *EIPR* 149.

derogate from existing obligations or advantages that members may have under various Conventions or other international agreements.

Part II contains minimum standards on copyright and related rights, trade marks, geographical indications, industrial designs, patents, integrated circuit layouts, undisclosed information, and the control of anti-competitive conduct in contractual licences. Part III deals with enforcement, and has particular significance for countries (including a number in Asia) which have traditionally placed little emphasis on the establishment of formal and universally accessible procedures for the vindication of private rights. Enforcement procedures must be effective, fair and equitable, and they must also avoid unnecessary complexity, cost, time limits or delays. Remedies available for the breach of intellectual property rights must include injunctive relief and damages, and provision must also be made for prompt and effective interlocutory relief, as well as for the seizure by customs authorities of imported goods suspected of infringing copyright or trade mark laws. Criminal sanctions must also be imposed at the very least for wilful trade mark counterfeiting or copyright piracy. Part IV confirms that the acquisition or maintenance of intellectual property rights may be made subject to compliance with reasonable procedures or formalities, including of course registration. Part V ensures that members' intellectual property laws and decisions are 'transparent', in the sense of being readily available to other members, and that disputes arising under the Agreement are to be settled under the general procedures established by the WTO Agreement of 1994. These procedures involve disputes being dealt with by panels established by the General Council of the WTO. Part VI contains the transitional provisions already mentioned. Finally, Pt VII deals with other institutional arrangements, including the creation of a Council for TRIPS to monitor the operation of the Agreement.

3.   OTHER INTERNATIONAL CONVENTIONS

[21.14] List of conventions. Apart from the TRIPS Agreement, the conventions listed below confer or regulate international protection for intellectual property rights:

Copyright and neighbouring rights

- Berne Convention for the Protection of Literary and Artistic Works 1886
- Universal Copyright Convention 1952
- Rome Convention for the Protection of Performers, Producers of Phonograms and Broadcasting Organisations 1961
- Geneva Convention for the Protection of Producers of Phonograms against Unauthorized Duplication of their Phonograms 1971
- Brussels Convention Relating to the Distribution of Programme-Carrying Signals Transmitted by Satellite 1974
- Vienna Agreement for the Protection of Typefaces and their International Deposit 1973
- Washington Treaty on the Protection of Intellectual Property in Respect of Integrated Circuits 1989
- Madrid Convention on the Avoidance of Double Taxation of Copyright Royalties 1979

Patents
- Paris Convention for the Protection of Industrial Property 1883
- Patent Co-operation Treaty 1970
- Budapest Treaty on the International Recognition of the Deposit of Microorganisms for the Purposes of Patent Procedure 1977
- Strasbourg Agreement Concerning the International Patent Classification 1971

Plant breeder's rights
- International Convention for the Protection of New Varieties of Plants 1961 (UPOV)

Industrial designs
- Hague Agreement Concerning the International Deposit of Industrial Designs 1925
- Locarno Agreement Establishing an International Classification for Industrial Designs 1968

Trade marks and geographical indications
- Madrid Agreement Concerning the International Registration of Marks 1891
- Nice Agreement Concerning the International Classification of Goods and Services for the Purposes of the Registration of Marks 1957
- Vienna Agreement Establishing an International Classification of the Figurative Elements of Marks 1973
- Trademark Registration Treaty 1973
- Lisbon Agreement for the Protection of Appellations of Origin and their International Registration 1958

(a) Copyright and Neighbouring Rights

[21.15]   Berne Convention For the Protection of Literary and Artistic Works 1886. The main instrument of international copyright cooperation is the Berne Convention, which replaced numerous bilateral treaties, none of which had been totally comprehensive or uniform. The significance of the Convention has been boosted by the TRIPS Agreement, Art 9 of which provides that WTO members must comply with all substantive provisions of the Convention other than those relating to moral rights. This will apply regardless of whether those members have ratified the Convention.

The original text of the Convention has been revised several times,[40] with changes made to accommodate the development of new technologies. Australia has been associated with and bound by Berne since its inception, originally as a result of the ratification by the UK in 1886, and since 1928 in its own right. The member states constitute what is known as the Berne Union for the protection of the rights of authors and owners of protected material. Each member state affords national treatment to work originating in other member countries so that, for example, a book (or other work or

---

40. Notably by the Berlin Revision 1908, Additional Protocol of Berne 1914, Rome Revision 1928, Brussels Revision 1948, Stockholm Revision 1967 and Paris Revision 1971.

subject matter) originating in France will be protected in Australia to the extent that our law provides such protection, and conversely Australian copyright material will be protected in France according to French domestic law. Protection is to be automatic and not subject to any formalities of registration, deposit or the like. The enjoyment and exercise of rights is to be independent of the existence of protection in the country of origin of the work.

[21.16] Scope of protection.[41] The main purpose of the Berne Convention is to protect the rights of authors in respect of literary and artistic works. This is broadly interpreted to cover what Australian legislation would separately designate musical and dramatic works, as well as adaptations, translations, arrangements of music and other alterations of works. The existence or mode of protection of some categories of works is optional, notably the protection of applied art and industrial designs and models, which is a matter for national legislation, as well as the conditions under which the press may reproduce or broadcast news, speeches and other informational material. The Convention intends that authors and successors in title should benefit from the protection offered, although recognition is given to the fact that ownership and exploitation of copyright in some material reflects entrepreneurial rather than creative input. Limitations are imposed on the exercise of rights where 'fair dealing' is concerned and provision for certain compulsory licences is made. Australia's Copyright Act 1968 was designed to accord with the international regime (as determined by the Berne Convention) of the time, and therefore much of the substance of the Convention is in fact reflected by Australian copyright law. Some differences do exist, so that for example the moral rights provided for by Berne have not, to date, been recognised in Australian law. In addition, the introduction of the blank tape royalty (although not presently in force) would have cut into the protection available to works and sound recordings under the Convention but was also intended to operate on a reciprocal basis with countries having a similar scheme, so that the only foreign repertoires remunerated under the scheme would be those where a similar scheme operated to the benefit of Australian musicians. This offends against the national treatment principle which would dictate that the revenue from the blank tape levy be distributed to foreign music owners on the same basis as Australian owners, whether or not a blank tape levy scheme existed in that other country.

[21.17] Developing countries and the Berne Convention. In 1967 the Stockholm Protocol was drawn up, providing that developing countries could adopt the Berne Convention but under certain preferential conditions. This was followed by the Paris Revision 1971, which was concerned to preserve the universal effect of Berne while allowing for the problems faced by developing countries in meeting burgeoning post-war educational needs for which access was required to protected works from abroad. To this end the standards of protection with respect to the translation and reproduction of material from overseas were made subject to non-exclusive

---

41.   See WIPO Background Reading, pp 230–6, S Ricketson, *The Berne Convention for the Protection of Literary and Artistic Works: 1886–1986,* 1987.

and non-transferable compulsory licences to use material for teaching and scholarship purposes.

[21.18] Universal Copyright Convention 1952 (UCC). Some countries have had rather lower levels of protection for copyright material and, as with the US, have required registration to secure those rights — although since the conclusion of the TRIPS Agreement registration is being phased out as part of the world-standardisation process. The UCC is administered by UNESCO and was revised in Paris in 1971 at the same time as the 1971 Berne Revision. As a result it was brought more into line with the Berne Convention, particularly with respect to the special concessions to developing countries. It is possible for nations to join both Conventions, although Berne predominates over the UCC so that two countries which are members of both will abide by Berne. Australia belongs to the UCC as well as to Berne; the US acceded to Berne only in 1989. The copyright symbol © must be applied to works to gain protection under the UCC, but is not required for protection under Berne or domestic Australian law. The formalities of deposit, registration, notice and payment of fees before copyright is afforded to works in certain states belonging to the UCC will be deemed to be satisfied if overseas material has the international notice symbol applied from the first publication along with the name of the copyright owner and year of first publication.[42]

[21.19] Rome Convention for the Protection of Performers, Producers of Phonograms and Broadcasting Organisations 1961. 'Neighbouring rights' to copyright are performers' rights, the rights of phonogram producers in their phonograms (sound recordings) and the rights of broadcast organisations in their radio and television program broadcasts. These rights 'neighbour' on copyright in that the creators of works are helped to disseminate their work to the public. Broadcasters and owners of sound recordings are protected in Pt IV of the Copyright Act 1968 (Cth) but performers' rights were only introduced relatively recently into Australian law, by the Copyright Amendment Act 1989. These rights are regarded as barely fulfilling the minimum protection guaranteed by the Convention, although improved performers' rights are on the agenda, as is the updating of the Rome Convention, which has not been revised since its inception. The incorporation of the TRIPS provisions was discussed at meetings late in 1994,[43] at which Australia referred to the work of the Copyright Convergence Group (CCG) and proposed that the suggested transmission right be discussed by the Committee of Experts for possible inclusion in the revised Treaty.[44] As under the Berne Convention, protection is conferred according to the principle of national treatment so that the protection a state grants under its domestic law will be that enjoyed by performers for performances even if taking place in another contracting state. Similarly, production of phonograms in or transmission of a broadcast from a member state will lead to national treatment of that material in other member states.

---

42. See S M Stewart, *International Copyright and Neighbouring Rights*, 2nd ed, 1990, p 141.
43. Committee of Experts on the Berne Protocol and the New Instrument on the Protection of Performers and Producers of Phonograms, Geneva, December 1994.
44. The transmission right was introduced into the revised treaty in Geneva in December 1996 (see [1.19]).

[21.20] Geneva Convention for the Protection of Producers of Phonograms against Unauthorized Duplication of their Phonograms 1971. The 'Phonograms Convention' was concluded in Geneva in 1971 to protect producers of phonograms against piracy and bootlegging.[45] The agreement supplements the Rome Convention by providing more extensive rights and has had an impressive level of acceptance due to the accelerating increase in international sound recording piracy. As well as this, by identifying phonograms as the subject matter of the convention, countries like Australia have been able to accede to it despite not being eligible to ratify the Rome Convention until the introduction of performers' rights. The Geneva Convention is not based on the principle of national treatment to protect certain rights but rather defines expressly the unlawful acts against which contracting states have to provide effective protection, largely by taking into account all measures already in force under various national laws.

[21.21] Brussels Convention Relating to the Distribution of Programme-Carrying Signals Transmitted by Satellite 1974. The 'Satellites Convention' was concluded in Brussels in 1974 and also protects material within the area of neighbouring rights. The use of satellites in international telecommunications has, since the mid-1960s, presented problems for the protection of broadcasting organisations. The Brussels Convention provides greater protection to such organisations by prohibiting the unlawful distribution of program-carrying signals transmitted by satellites. The definition of broadcasting under the Rome Convention does not encompass transmission of signals not suited to reception by the public, nor when the derived signals are distributed by cable and not by wireless means.[46] Transmission of programs by satellite generally takes place indirectly as electronic signals carrying broadcast material pass through a satellite to reach remote parts of the world which cannot be reached by traditional broadcasting. The program-carrying signals cannot be picked up directly by commercial receivers but must first be picked up by ground stations which make them accessible and distribute them to the public. Although direct transmission from satellites to the public is becoming more common (the signals being demodulated by the satellite itself), the signals transmitted upwards to the satellite remain inaccessible to the public, and may need to pass along a material path (wires) before being beamed back to earth. The Brussels Convention does not protect program material, only the signals emitted by the broadcasting organisation. National treatment is not a principle of the Convention, which merely imposes an obligation on contracting states to take the necessary steps to prevent a certain activity: the distribution of program-carrying signals by any distributor for whom the signals emitted to or passing through the satellite are not intended. No new rights are given by the Convention to broadcasting organisations, nor is it intended to confer any protection on the works or other subject matter comprised in the transmitted program.

[21.22] Vienna Agreement for the Protection of Typefaces and Their International Deposit 1973. As its title suggests, the Vienna Agreement is

---

45. Further discussions have taken place in 1994 and 1996 as part of the New Instrument on the Protection of Performers and Producers of Phonograms mentioned above.
46. See also the definitions in the Copyright Act 1968 (Cth) s 10.

intended to provide protection for what the Australian Copyright Act calls published editions of works. This publisher's copyright in the format and typesetting of books is not one which raises international issues in the same way as the pirating of sound recordings, films and other material, and very few countries have joined the agreement. Australia is not a member.

[21.23] Washington Treaty on the Protection of Intellectual Property in Respect of Integrated Circuits 1989. This treaty was concluded by WIPO at Washington in May 1989. The passing of the Australian Circuit Layouts Act 1989 (Cth) allowed Australia to join this treaty, which, like others concluded under the auspices of WIPO is a multilateral treaty and thus an attractive alternative to the process of negotiating a whole series of bilateral treaties.[47] The need for international protection of integrated circuits was highlighted by the introduction of the US Semiconductor Chip Protection Act 1984 which did not grant national treatment to non-US integrated circuits. Australia (along with the UK, EC, Japan, Sweden and Canada) sought reciprocal protection on the grounds that circuit layouts are artistic works under the Copyright Act and thus US circuit layouts are protected in Australia. In mid-1985 an interim order was issued by the US Secretary of Commerce allowing Australian makers of circuit layouts to apply for registration under the US legislation. The order has been extended on a number of occasions. The US legislation provides reciprocal protection to states which are party to a convention covering circuit layouts and to which the US belongs. The WIPO treaty for the protection of integrated circuits was intended to fulfil this function, but neither the US nor Japan (which between them produce over 90% of the world's integrated circuits) support the Convention, on the basis that some of its provisions, namely those relating to the term of protection and compulsory licensing, are inadequate.[48] The failure of the US to support the Washington Treaty has meant that protection of integrated circuits was one of the issues examined in the TRIPS negotiations of the Uruguay Round of GATT. Article 35 of TRIPS now requires members to provide protection for layout designs in accordance with the Washington Treaty.

(b) Patents, Plant Varieties and Designs

[21.24] Paris Convention for the Protection of Industrial Property 1883. The Paris Convention established an international union (the Paris Union) for the protection of industrial property. It has been revised several times, one of the most significant being the Stockholm Revision of 1967, to which most member countries were party.[49] Like the Berne Convention, the Paris Convention is reinforced by the TRIPS Agreement, with WTO members again required by Art 2 to give effect to its substantive provisions.

---

47. The Act provides sui generis protection for integrated circuits but of a 'copyright style' in that automatic protection is conferred rather than a registration procedure being required: see [9.23]–[9.25].

48. P Treyde, 'The Nature of Intellectual Property: A Copyright Perspective' Intellectual Property Law Seminar for Commonwealth Officers, Canberra, June 1990.

49. The last Revision Conference began in Geneva in 1980 and continued in Nairobi in 1981, Geneva in 1982 and Geneva in 1984.

There are four basic components to the Paris Convention. In the first place, rules of substantive law guarantee national treatment in each member country. Second, there is the right of priority, which means that an applicant filing for patent, design or trade mark rights in a member country may, within a specified period of time,[50] apply for protection in any or all the other member countries and the later applications will be regarded as if they had been filed on the same day as the first application. Third, provisions are made with respect to the establishment of rights and obligations whose aim is to ensure similarity if not total uniformity in the rules laid down by member countries as to matters such as the validity of patents. Finally, there are provisions dealing with the administrative framework of the Convention.

[21.25] Scope of protection. The Paris Convention, in establishing an international union for the protection of industrial property, encompasses not only patents but also trade mark and design rights. An important aspect of protection is the concept of independence. The grant of patent or trade mark rights in one country does not oblige any other member country to grant such rights for the same invention or mark. Conversely, invalidity in one country does not mean that the industrial property will be refused protection or regarded as invalid in another country; their fates will be determined according to domestic law. The Convention deals with issues of importation and compulsory licensing of patents in such a way as to allow domestic law to regulate much of the detail while implementing the overall purpose of the Convention, which is to prevent abuses of the system through failing to work a patent. This promotes industrialisation, since using a patent to block the working of an invention or to monopolise importation of the patented article may inhibit the introduction of new technology into particular countries.

[21.26] Paris Convention and developing countries. In 1974 it was suggested that the Paris Convention be revised in order to promote the interests of developing countries through special provisions to ameliorate aspects of the Convention thought to be advantageous to developed countries. For example, the priority principle 'has been indicted as a disincentive to the initiation and exploitation of new inventions in developing countries because of the possibility of patent rights being invoked in the priority period'.[51] The enormous differences in technological capabilities between developed and less developed countries means that those more advanced in research, development and innovation monopolise the system to their own advantage. The prohibition of discrimination against foreign nationals or in favour of indigenous enterprises inherent in the 'national treatment' provision has the result for many countries of ensuring that most technological and industrial endeavour is owned by overseas interests. In order to accommodate these concerns an Ad Hoc Group of Experts was set up in 1974 to review the Paris Convention. A Declaration of Objectives was adopted and work has continued on amending the Convention to implement the objectives which are:

---

50. Six months for trade marks and designs, 12 months for patents. These periods are today regarded as excessive in view of the speed of modern communications and the availability of patent specifications on computer.
51. Blakeney, p 16.

(i)   to give full recognition to the needs for economic and social develop-
       ment of countries and to ensure a proper balance between these needs
       and the rights granted by patents;
(ii)   to promote the actual working of inventions in each country;
(iii) to facilitate the development of technology by developing countries
       and to improve the conditions for the transfer of technology under fair
       and reasonable terms;
(iv)   to encourage inventive activity in developing countries;
(v)   to increase the potential in developing countries in judging the real
       value of inventions for which protection is requested, in screening and
       controlling licensing contracts and in improving information for local
       industry;
(vi)   to ensure that all forms of industrial property be designed to facilitate
       economic development and to ensure cooperation between countries
       having different systems of industrial property protection.[52]

[21.27] **Patent Co-operation Treaty 1970 (PCT).** The PCT came into
force in 1978. It does not in itself provide for patent rights but is a special
agreement under the Paris Convention which enables the filing of a single
patent application which can be assessed for novelty by a single search
through prior patents and technical literature. The filing of one international application has the same effect as if separate national applications
had been filed in or for all the states which the applicant designates in the
international application. The Treaty sets out detail of formal requirements
and procedural steps to be complied with when filing such applications.
Although the grant of a patent in any particular country depends upon
domestic law (under the principle of independence discussed above),
states designated in the international application may not require further
compliance with requirements as to the form or content of applications
which have observed those provided for by the PCT. Prior to the PCT,
inventors had to file individual applications in each country and pay for
them all to be separately searched. All these applications had to be drafted
in the different languages required by the various countries. By contrast, an
international application need only be in a single language. An international filing date is given and applications are sent to the International
Bureau of WIPO in Geneva (which administers the PCT) and to the International Searching Authority, which subjects the international application
to a state of the art search. A search report is prepared, listing documents
which may have a bearing on the patentability of the claimed invention.
This is published, along with the application, 18 months after the priority
date and the international application is then sent to the national (or
regional) offices of all contracting states designated by the applicant. At
this point national fees are payable, translations may need to be filed and
the application will be assessed according to the domestic law of each state
or region.

[21.28] **Budapest Treaty on the International Recognition of the
Deposit of Microorganisms for the Purposes of Patent Procedure
1977.** The Budapest Treaty is also a special agreement under the Paris
Convention, and like the PCT is designed not so much to determine substantive rights but to facilitate their acquisition. Disclosure of the invention
is a generally recognised requirement for the grant of patents. A legally
sufficient disclosure of a machine or chemical substance may be made in

52.   WIPO Background Reading, p 58.

documentary form, described in writing and diagrams. It is not so easy to describe a genetically engineered organism or a method for using a novel culture unless the organism itself is available. Australia is a signatory to the Budapest Treaty, which specifies deposit, maintenance and distribution standards for patent purposes for depositories in member nations. Patent offices are not generally equipped to handle micro-organisms, however, since storing, preservation and protection (of the organisms and the environment) requires special expertise and equipment. In order to eliminate the duplication of depository requirements in each country, the Budapest Treaty allows for deposit of a micro-organism with any 'international depository authority'. Scientific institutions may be designated international depository authorities by agreeing to comply with certain requirements as to acceptance, storage and furnishing of samples to anyone entitled to them, while also maintaining the necessary secrecy and security. Assurances must be given by relevant authorities that an institution to be designated an international depository authority will not be closed down.

[21.29] Strasbourg Agreement Concerning the International Patent Classification 1971. Australia acceded to this Agreement in 1975, adopting the uniform system of classification of patents and petty patents. Classification is an administrative tool to make the patent information of different national offices more readily accessible and enable easier retrieval and exchange of documents relating to specified areas of technology. WIPO administers the International Patent Classification, in which there are eight broad sections which are subdivided into 118 classes, 617 subclasses and over 55,000 groups. Each of these has a special symbol signifying the category of class, sub-class or group and patent applications are marked with the appropriate symbols to allow retrieval of information according to subject matter.[53] Steps are being taken to create a common pool of patent documents that will be accessible instantly from anywhere in the world. The EPO in Munich, US Patent Office in Washington and Japanese Patent Office in Tokyo have agreed to develop a common standard for the electronic coding of patent documents, so that they can be electronically published. The databases will be issued on CD-ROM. Established patent information referral services include patent gazettes or bulletins published by national patent offices, containing lists of recently published patent documents and sometimes abstracts and first claims, as well as an international service provided by the International Patent Documentation Center (INPADOC), established in 1972. INPADOC stores certain bibliographic data (title of the invention, classification symbol, relevant dates, names and numbers) in a machine readable databank. The data is sent by national patent offices, either in machine readable form or in the original patent gazettes published by those offices.[54]

[21.30] International Convention for the Protection of New Varieties of Plants 1961 (UPOV). Plant breeder's rights are protected under the UPOV Convention to which Australia became a signatory in 1989, and the Plant Variety Rights Act 1987 (Cth) was modelled on its provisions. In 1991 UPOV was updated to take account of new technologies and the Plant

---

53. WIPO Background Reading, p 132.
54. Ibid, p 133.

Breeder's Rights Act 1994 (Cth) was introduced to replace the 1987 legislation, in accordance with the international scheme. The rights provided by UPOV are particularly important in Europe because of an express prohibition on the patenting of new varieties of plants (or animals)[55] under the EPC. Although there has been agitation for the removal of the statutory bar to patenting plants (and animals) in Europe, a lot of opposition exists to any changes which would ease the prohibition on patenting animal breeds, a sensitive issue and a topic on which there is much ethical and moral debate in Europe.[56] Changing the nature of protection for new plant varieties by extending patent law to cover them would also be resisted by those who regard the genetic engineering of new plants as posing a threat to the environment. Approval for the first major release of genetically engineered organisms in Germany was obtained in 1989,[57] but was postponed due to public opposition. The organism in question was a petunia containing genetic material from maize which was to have been test-grown outdoors by the Max Planck Institute in Cologne. The opposition comes from a group known as Burger Beobachten Petunien (Citizens Observing Petunias).[58] Bureaucratic pressure in favour of maintaining UPOV has been brought to bear by WIPO officials in Geneva who administer UPOV and the national officials in the countries which have joined the treaty. Fearing loss of business to the patent systems, those administering UPOV 'have mounted a spirited defence of their territory and counter-attacked the notion of patenting varieties'.[59]

[21.31] **Hague Agreement Concerning the International Deposit of Industrial Designs 1925.** While the Paris Convention secures national treatment for the industrial designs of nationals of member countries, the Hague Agreement allows for the international deposit of designs with the International Bureau of WIPO so that protection may be secured in a number of states with a minimum of formalities and cost. Alternatively, the deposit may be made through the national office of a contracting state if domestic legislation permits. Although Australia is not a member of the Hague Agreement, s 48(3) of the Designs Act 1906 (Cth) provides for the recognition of an international deposit made pursuant to the Agreement as being equivalent to an application made in those Convention countries which are parties to the Agreement. The Hague Agreement undergoes periodic revision and a new Draft Act for design protection is presently under consideration. The Australian Law Reform Commission referred to the Hague Agreement at various points in their Designs Report and assessed proposals with a view to the fact that Australia may join a new Hague Agreement in the future.[60]

---

55. This prohibition does not exist in Australian patent law: see [15.8] ff.
56. Some members of the European Parliament reject the notion of conferring any intellectual property protection on living matter, whether animals or plants: see [15.17].
57. From the Advisory Board for Biological Safety, ZKBS.
58. Environmental groups like this have had a profound effect on political decision-making in Europe, particularly in Germany and Scandinavia, and their views are represented in parliament. This trend is likely to continue and spread to other countries as environmental concerns become the major issue for inhabitants of countries whose health and lifestyle are undermined by environmental damage.
59. N Byrne, 'Protection of Biotechnology' [1990] *JBL* 75 at 76.
60. See *Designs*.

[21.32] Locarno Agreement Establishing an International Classification for Industrial Designs 1968. This Agreement provides for the classification of industrial designs according to internationally agreed criteria, in much the same way as the Strasbourg Agreement does for patents. States which are party to the Agreement form the Locarno Union and industrial property offices of those member states classify designs according to the 31 classes and 211 sub-classes of goods provided in the Agreement into which designs may be incorporated. This facilitates international registration of design rights under the Hague Agreement.

(c) Trade Marks

[21.33] Paris Convention and trade marks. In addition to the usual provisions of national treatment and priority extended to all forms of industrial property with which it deals, the Paris Convention also makes specific provision with respect to trade marks. Since trade mark rights protect the reputation and goodwill of proprietors and serve an informational function, their validity depends upon criteria other than the simple fact of registration. Trade marks also depend heavily upon cultural, social and linguistic influences to a greater degree than other forms of industrial property. The Paris Convention recognises that different countries impose different requirements as to use, licensing, assignment and prohibition of certain marks and erects a framework of regulation within which members of the Paris Union can impose their own requirements. A number of agreements with respect to trade marks have been made under the Paris Convention. Further work on harmonising certain legislative provisions concerning trade marks, particularly the definition of a mark, protection of well-known marks, requirements as to use of a mark and procedural aspects, was begun by a WIPO Committee of Experts in October 1994 in Geneva.[61]

[21.34] Madrid Agreement Concerning the International Registration of Marks 1891. The Madrid Agreement provides for the international registration of marks through the filing of a single application with the International Bureau of WIPO, once registration has been obtained in a country which is a signatory. International applications require the applicant to designate the countries in which protection is sought and a uniform term of 20 years' protection is conferred.[62]

[21.35] Nice Agreement Concerning the International Classification of Goods and Services for the Purposes of the Registration of Marks 1961. This Agreement established the Nice Union, members of which have agreed upon a list of 42 classes of goods and services for which trade marks may be registered. Schedule 1 of the Trade Marks 1995 (Cth) adopts this international classification in its Regulations.

[21.36] Vienna Agreement Establishing an International Classification of the Figurative Elements of Marks 1973. This Agreement entered into force in 1985 and purports to classify all device marks, for

---

61. Diplomatic Conference for the Conclusion of the Trade Mark Law Treaty, Geneva, October 1994.
62. See T Stevens, 'The Madrid Protocol and its Likely Impact on Trade Mark Owners and Trade Mark Practitioners in Australia' (1993) 4 *AIPJ* 48.

example emblems, symbols, pictures or logos, to facilitate searches with respect to existing trade marks containing figurative elements. Whereas the Nice Agreement concerns the goods or services for which trade marks are used, the Vienna Agreement attempts to classify non-word marks themselves. This is an enormous undertaking, given the possible diversity of marks, but is obviously valuable in assisting overseas searching and registration procedures.

[21.37] **Trademark Registration Treaty 1973 (TRT).** This treaty came into force in 1980 and is intended to establish international registration of trade marks without the need to register initially at national level. The TRT has met with limited acceptance because it offers little more than the Madrid Agreement, since single applications lodged directly with the International Bureau of WIPO must still be registered by each individual country. A single international registration procedure would be of more benefit. A WIPO committee of experts was established in 1985 to draft such a treaty. By 1992 a single trade mark application and registration procedure was available for the whole European Community instead of the ten different European trade mark laws which existed previously.

[21.38] **Lisbon Agreement for the Protection of Appellations of Origin and Their International Registration 1958 and the EC/Australia Agreement.** The Lisbon Agreement entered into force in 1966 and is one which Australia has avoided, since it aims to provide protection for geographical indications of source which are also descriptive of products from that source. 'For example, the word "Champagne" is a geographical indication which, while referring to an area in France, has also developed a strongly descriptive meaning with regard to wines.'[63] In Australia the word 'champagne' has been held to mean a style of wine rather than one originating in a certain district of France,[64] although the opposite decision was reached in England,[65] and more recently the New Zealand Court of Appeal has found that to the average New Zealander, apparently far in advance of Australian consumers, 'champagne' means only the French produced wine.[66] French wine producers have long been keen to have Australian, US, Canadian and New Zealand wine producers stop using such terms as champagne, beaujolais, burgundy, chablis, etc for their products. Dispute over the question of protection for appellations of origin was particularly evident in the TRIPS negotiations where the EC's demands for such protection were strongly opposed by the 'former immigrant countries'[67] mentioned, who are regarded as having unfairly gained an advantage for wine producers using descriptive terms which have a geographic provenance. Australia's position in the TRIPS negotiations on this issue was that it was necessary to make a distinction between appellations of origin that have become generic and should be available for use by others, and those which are still indicative of a geographic source. The generic terms are not misleading to the public when they serve to indicate a type of product

---

63. WIPO Background Reading, p 185.
64. *Comite Interprofessionel du Vin de Champagne v N L Burton Pty Ltd* (1981) 38 ALR 664.
65. *J Bollinger v Costa Brava Wine Co Ltd (No 2)* [1961] 1 All ER 561 (see [16.13]).
66. *Wineworths Group Ltd v Comite Interprofessionnel du Vin de Champagne* (1991) 23 IPR 435.
67. W Dullforce, 'Rich Nations Fall Out Over Patents', *Financial Times*, 7 July 1990, p 3.

rather than its actual provenance. The EC thought otherwise, and has urged the adoption of the standards of the Lisbon Agreement.

To a large extent, this has been successful. The TRIPS Agreement contains provisions (Arts 22–24) in respect of geographical indicators so that false suggestions of the origin of products are not allowed and member states agree to enter into negotiations aimed at increasing the protection of individual geographic indicators. To this end, Australia and the EC negotiated a bilateral wine agreement at the end of 1992. The agreement provides for the mutual protection of each country's geographical indicators and traditional expressions and includes the phasing out of European wine names by Australian wine makers, even those that have become generic in this country. For example, champagne, burgundy, beaujolais, chablis, frascati, bordeaux, claret, chianti (and others) must all be phased out according to an agreed timetable.[68] In return for this agreement Australia was granted somewhat easier access to the European market, and Australian wine producers are establishing geographic indicators for their products in certain areas — Hunter Valley, Barossa, Coonawarra, for example.[69]

---

68. For a discussion of the legislation which gives effect to this Agreement, see [16.14], [19.31].

69. In 1992–93 wine exports reached $293 million and are expected to reach $1 billion by 2000: G Polson, 'Uruguay Round Outcomes: Intellectual Property', Services and Intellectual Property Branch, Trade Negotiations and Organisations Division, Department of Foreign Affairs and Trade, September 1994.

Chapter 22

Commercialising Intellectual Property

[22.1] **Technology transfer.** Since ideas are usually embodied in the form of a book, film, sound recording, product design or invention, it is the sale or licensing of such products that creates revenue for right-owners. The process of commercialising intellectual property involves moving the fruits of creative thinking, research and development from the laboratory bench, author's study or designer's computer to the marketplace. This process of diffusing innovations into the community has become known as 'technology transfer'. The term implies the imparting of scientific knowledge, and it is the translation of patent rights, scientific know-how and research and development into marketable industrial components and end products on which this chapter primarily concentrates. Collective administration of copyright is also discussed here.[1]

Technology transfer encompasses both the incorporation of technology into marketable products and the marketing of the end result. The literature on the topic falls into two basic categories, in the first place addressing the methods of technology transfer and assessing the various legal devices used, but also critically assessing these devices and the legal regimes in which they occur, particularly in reference to the cultural impact of technology transfer from developed to lesser developed countries. The present account concentrates on the former aspect of the subject. For lesser developed countries which are not importers of technology, the issue is rather less straightforward, since the capacity to pay for such technology may be limited, existing intellectual property laws to protect the technology may be non-existent or not enforced, and concerns about levels of foreign investment and ownership may lead to foreign licensors being required to

---

1.   See Chapter 7, where assignment and licensing of copyright are discussed.

release the technology into local management or ownership.[2] In addressing the 'digital agenda',[3] the creation of possible new forms of copyright such as 'access' or 'browsing' rights will lead to new forms of exploitation, not presently regulated and which may well require a technological solution to the question of monitoring and paying for such uses.[4] It is not only that new rights may become part of the copyright owner's repertoire, but new products such as multimedia challenge traditional notions of licensing and exploitation of intellectual property.

[22.2] **Legal mechanisms for commercialising intellectual property.** There are a number of business arrangements which may be used to bring about the transfer and commercialising of intellectual property. The three main types are sale or assignment, licensing,[5] or a joint-venture agreement possibly involving reciprocal research collaboration between government and industry or universities and industry. A fourth mechanism which may be identified is the purchase or acquisition of an interest in a company working in a relevant field, so that the technology developed by one firm can be marketed by a larger company with capital and distribution networks. Many business arrangements will exhibit characteristics of more than one of these broad categories. For example, the sale of equipment or capital goods may be accompanied by a licence to manufacture a product using that equipment. In addition to the legal arrangements mentioned, the management and development of technological resources by the owners and developers is an important aspect of commercialising intellectual property, and it is to this that we turn first of all.

1. MANAGEMENT OF INTELLECTUAL PROPERTY

[22.3] **Protecting intellectual property.** Of utmost importance to a policy of successful exploitation of intellectual property is the protection of rights associated with it, so that obtaining patent, design or trade mark registration and preserving the confidentiality of technical information must be an inherent part of running the business. Failing to protect intellectual property has been acknowledged as one of the main mistakes firms make in their commercial efforts,[6] even though it may seem expensive or unnecessary in the first steps of product development. Rights may be jeopardised by carelessness about preserving the novelty of patentable subject matter or

---

2.   T Harper, 'Understanding Technology Transfer' (1988) 10 *Whittier L Rev* 161; R Cai, 'PRC: Importing Technology' (1996) 8 *AsiaLaw* 31.

3.   For example, a draft treaty to amend the Berne Convention to introduce rights with respect to transient or incidental copies and all transmissions of works: 'Basic Proposal for the Substantive Provisions of the Treaty on Certain Questions Concerning the Protection of Literary and Artistic Works to be Considered by the Diplomatic Conference', Geneva, December 1996.

4.   See A Butler, 'Regulation of On-Line Information Services — Can Technology Itself Solve the Problem it has Created?' (1996) 19 *UNSWLJ* 193.

5.   Note that stamp duty will be levied ad valorem on licenses and assignments of intellectual property following the implementation of the 'Stamp Duty Re-Write', possibly during 1997: see P Green, 'Stamp Duty Rewrite — IP Issues' (1996) 19 *UNSWLJ* 72.

6.   See 'Technology Transfer: Commercial Rights and Public Sector R & D', (1990) 10(3) SCITECH 15.

keeping valuable data confidential. Large firms will have in-house legal experts to undertake and advise on obtaining protection, and many smaller firms are coming to realise the importance of getting advice at an early stage. In some fields, particularly pharmaceuticals and biotechnology, patents are of far greater commercial importance than in others, such as engineering or electronics.[7] A new chemical compound may be imitated more easily and with less investment than a complex new machine or semiconductor device and patent infringement is normally easier to establish.[8]

[22.4] Management strategies. Apart from the preliminary step of obtaining appropriate legal advice, large industrial concerns have sales and marketing strategies for identifying markets and funding research and developments projects for new and developing markets, as well as engaging in pure and applied research. Again, it is mainly the pharmaceutical giants who have these procedures in place.[9] A business strategy such as this will require a company to be able to assess accurately its own technological resources (including personnel, know-how, processes, patents, information systems and plant) and whether they are being properly managed, as well as identifying any gaps which may need to be filled by developing or otherwise acquiring equipment or technology. It has been estimated that up to 85% of patents are not exploited due to lack of technical expertise sufficient to use the information protected within the legal infrastructure.

Careful management of technology and intellectual property involves a strategy of 'optimisation, enrichment and safeguarding'.[10] Optimisation means making sure that ideas and inventions are fully investigated and not discarded without their potential being properly assessed. Enrichment involves fighting the obsolescence of all technology by its constant renewal and accurately assessing resources available in terms of personnel, infrastructure, plant, site, power and transport, thus being in a position to identify needs and potential applications of existing technology. Safeguarding refers to the appropriate utilisation of patent laws and keeping informed of all scientific and technological information, making sure it is available to everyone who may need it.

2. ASSIGNMENT

[22.5] Purchase/sale of intellectual property. One way to exploit intellectual property is to sell it, either in the form of a completed product or else as 'raw material'. The simplest example of this is where an author assigns copyright to a publisher, who then supplies the technical and entrepreneurial effort to get the book onto the market. Similarly, a songwriter may assign copyright in musical works to a recording company. Machinery such as motor vehicles may be composed of many patented parts which are sold by different firms. All of this simply affirms the important point that intellectual property rights may be bought and sold like other forms of property. The statutory regimes for copyright, patents, designs, trade

---

7.   See Grubb, p 167.
8.   For other considerations in patenting pharmaceuticals, see [11.27], [12.8].
9.   See T Black, *Intellectual Property in Industry*, 1989, p 22.
10. See C Marback, 'The Management of Technological Resources', WIPO Regional Seminar on Licensing and Other Technology Transfer Arrangements, Seoul, 1987.

marks, plant breeder's rights and circuit layouts all make this clear.[11] As for confidential information, the point has already been made that the courts seem to be leaning towards a proprietary analysis.[12] It is incontrovertible that information, expertise and know-how are exchanged in return for valuable consideration and the drafters of commercial documents do not shy away from speaking of 'the sale of know-how'.[13]

[22.6] Practical importance of assignment. In practice the outright sale or purchase of intellectual property is of far less importance in technology transfer arrangements than the licensing of those rights. The acquisition of capital goods through purchase (or leasing with an option to purchase) will not necessarily be accompanied by the rights to exploit the underlying patents, designs, plant variety rights or copyright. For one thing the vendor, if selling only equipment, will be able to continue selling to other purchasers, whereas any assignment of the underlying rights would have the same result as the sale of any other form of property.[14] The purchase of intellectual property may also require the observance of certain formalities: for example that the assignment be in writing, signed by one or both parties, and possibly registered at the relevant government office. Furthermore, a purchase price tends to be a substantial sum of money, whereas a licence agreement can be tailored to the payment of royalties over the period during which the technology is being exploited.

[22.7] Assignment of copyright and the role of collecting societies. That said, copyright is one area in which intellectual property rights are routinely assigned to another in order to achieve optimum commercialisation. Although it is not unknown, relatively few authors publish their own books: instead a commercial publisher takes on the technical and marketing tasks, usually having the copyright assigned to them in return for royalties payable to the author on books sold. The same is true in relation to music. However, for copyright owners or assignees whose work is exploited in an ephemeral fashion by being played on air, or copied in a way which is difficult to detect (by photocopying, for example), the practical problems of enforcing copyright on the one hand, and getting users to find and pay the owner of copyright on the other, are particularly evident. This is where collecting societies come in. These agencies exist to license out the use of copyrights in return for a fee which is collected and distributed back to the original owners, less administrative costs. In 1994 approximately $85 million was collected in Australia by collecting agencies on behalf of owners of copyright.[15] A 'true' collecting society is a non-profit organisation distributing funds on the basis of payment related to use.[16] Other characteristics of a collecting society include protecting the rights of its members through

---

11. See [7.9], [13.13], [10.23], [20.11]–[20.12], [15.23] and [9.24] respectively.
12. See further [3.14]–[3.17].
13. See G Nicolson, 'Know-How Agreements and Technical Assistance Contracts' (1989) 24 *IPAsia* 15.
14. Note that intellectual property rights can be divided up and dealt with separately. There is no compulsion to sell the whole copyright, for example, to one party: see [5.9].
15. Simpson, p 147.
16. See B Cottle, 'The Role and Management of Collecting Societies in Australia and the Asia Pacific Region', Symposium: Copyright Law and Practice, Sydney, 1983.

litigation where necessary and exercising the right-owner's discretion in fixing fees for use and seeking to increase those fees where appropriate. In Australia collecting societies exist as central organisations licensing copyright in respect of musical and literary works, as well as sound recordings and films. These are briefly described in the following paragraphs.

[22.8] Australasian Performing Rights Association (APRA). APRA was the first collecting society formed in Australia and was incorporated in 1926. It is an association of authors, composers, music publishers and other music copyright owners. The rights assigned to APRA are the broadcast, public performance and diffusion rights in works and sound recordings, known as 'performing rights'.[17] APRA licenses any person or organisation giving or authorising a public performance, broadcast or diffusion of any musical work controlled by the association, whether or not the music is live or recorded and irrespective of whether a charge for admission is made. Premises requiring licences include cinemas, hotels, clubs, restaurants, shops, schools, factories, skating rinks, exercise centres and hairdressing salons, as well as live concert performances, juke boxes and radio stations. The terms of licence agreements and the scale of charges applicable to the grant of licences vary in accordance with the nature and method of performance.[18] Some venues pay an annual licence fee at a set rate; others pay on the 'box office' percentage principle, so that venues for live performances generally pay a percentage (in the region of 1.5–2%) of ticket sales or annual expenditure on performing artists and musicians. Radio stations pay APRA 2% of advertising revenue, and television broadcasters pay per minute of broadcast time. Most of APRA's income is derived from broadcasting and television sources.

The other side of the story concerns the distribution of the $47 million or so collected per annum. APRA has three main procedures for analysing music usage:[19] comprehensive analysis, sampling and analogous performance analysis. A comprehensive analysis is 100% identification of all musical works used in a particular performance and is possible for live concerts where the fees collected can be distributed in accordance with the identification. This technique would be extremely onerous for the broadcasters of musical works, since full record-keeping is involved (and would also be burdensome to audit on APRA's part). A sampling procedure is used to show probable music usage, taking into account factors such as type of medium (radio or television), extent of broadcast, duration of the work and kind of music play (theme or background). Analogous performance analysis is the procedure by which APRA credits members with income from unanalysed sources in accordance with their income from a comparative source. For example, full analysis of juke box performances would be difficult and costly. It is assumed that there is a close parallel between commercial radio and juke box music use (this has been demonstrated by comprehensive analysis), so that juke box income is allocated on a 'follow the dollar' basis with commercial radio sampled usage. Reciprocal agreements exist between APRA and foreign collecting societies, which assign each other's repertoire to the other society for its territory of administration. Thus

---

17. Not to be confused with performers' rights: see [6.20]–[6.24].
18. See J Sturman, 'The Structure and Function of Collecting Societies' [1976] *APRA* 22.
19. See APRA, *Copyright in Music and APRA: A Guide for Licensees.*

APRA owns or controls in Australia the performing rights in a world reper-toire, and belongs to the International Confederation of Societies of Authors and Composers (CISAC) which facilitates the interaction of national collecting societies, not only those in the musical sphere.

[22.9] Australasian Mechanical Copyright Owners' Society (AMCOS). AMCOS represents music publishers, the owners of copyright in published musical works and lyrics, in relation to reproduction licences (not performing rights). These rights are granted to AMCOS under an exclusive licence. The mechanical right is the music industry term denot-ing the right to reproduce a musical work on disc or tape.[20] Putting music on the soundtrack of a film or other audio-visual production also amounts to reproducing the musical work in a material form, and AMCOS is the first point of contact for licences to dub music onto film. If music is specially commissioned for a film the composer will normally give permission directly to the film-maker to reproduce the music in this way (often referred to as the synchronisation right).[21] AMCOS grants licences to broadcasters to *reproduce* music for the purpose of broadcasting. This is to be distinguished from the *broadcasting* licence issued by APRA. Again, AMCOS is party to reciprocal agreements with mechanical right societies around the world.

[22.10] Phonographic Performance Company of Australia Ltd (PPCA). Established in 1969, PPCA represents record producers and manu-facturers in the administration of performing rights in sound recordings, collecting fees (in much the same way as APRA does) for composers and publishers. These fees are collected in respect of broadcasting and public performances, distributed initially to record manufacturers and through them to performers in accordance with contractual arrangements.

[22.11] Copyright Agency Ltd (CAL). Established in 1974, CAL was formed to act as an agent of copyright owners in works being copied by photocopying and printing, particularly in educational institutions, but also by others such as press-clipping services.[22] The advent of photocopiers led to a dramatic drop in income for authors whose works were prescribed texts in schools and universities. Publishers were correspondingly disadvan-taged by the loss in sales caused by multiple copying of works. Changes to copyright law in 1980 introduced statutory licences for photocopying.[23] Under the Copyright Act educational institutions and those assisting handi-capped readers had to keep full records. This was onerous and expensive for both CAL and the institutions, so licensing agreements were negotiated whereby a fee per student was to be paid to CAL and distributed according to a sampling system. In 1989 legislative amendments incorporated volun-tary licence schemes into the Act,[24] and institutions now have a choice as to whether to keep full records of copying or whether to participate in the sampling system, whereby only a limited number of institutions need to

20. See AMCOS, *A Guide to Mechanical Rights.*
21. Note that the composer may have a publishing contract with a music publisher whereby works composed during the agreement are to be assigned to the publisher.
22. See *De Garis v Neville Jeffress Pidler Pty Ltd* (1990) 95 ALR 625, discussed at [7.4], [8.28].
23. See [7.19].
24. See [7.19].

keep records for a period of three months and not more often than every five years. CAL has a Music Rights Division[25] overseeing the copying of sheet music and a Print Rights Division covering literary and dramatic works, as well as artistic works which explain or illustrate works copied under the statutory licence.[26] Despite grave doubts expressed by copyright owners as to CAL's efficiency and level of overheads,[27] substantial amounts have been collected and some distributed. CAL has been very active in expanding the licensing of copying of print material by media monitoring agencies, government departments and businesses of all types. CAL is also investigating the licensing of electronic uses of material in educational institutions, and is positioning itself to administer relevant new rights created for copyright owners for use of 'on-line' material.

[22.12] Audio Visual Collecting Society (AVCS). This collecting society has been active since June 1990 and was set up to administer the scheme for copying off-air material under statutory licence introduced by the Copyright Amendment Act 1989.[28] The scheme operates along the same lines as that for photocopying. Remuneration is collected and distributed on the basis of sampling with a fee to be paid under a licence negotiated with AVCS or in accordance with full record-keeping. It is thought that a sampling system will be less apt to assess copying of broadcast material because of disparity in the type of material copied and the extent of its use as between institutions and educational sectors within the tertiary system. Although the Copyright Act previously provided for copying of broadcast material intended for educational purposes, there was no statutory licence to copy audio-visual material generally. In view of the fact that copying and retaining general broadcast material was unlawful until the introduction of the statutory licence, AVCS offered an indemnity against copyright infringement actions during the six years to 1 January 1990.

[22.13] Christian Music Copyright Collecting Companies. Despite the fact that CAL offers a church music licence, these agencies have recently got together to establish a competing avenue for the collection of royalties and granting of licences in relation to church music. 'It is an interesting proof that where organisations see a niche, competition can follow.'[29]

[22.14] VI$COPY. Following much discussion of the needs of visual artists for a collecting society by groups such as the National Association for Visual Artists (NAVA) and others, the establishment of such a collecting society was endorsed in the Simpson Report,[30] together with the repeal or amendment of s 135ZM of the Copyright Act, which allows an artistic work illustrating text to be copied by educational institutions as part of the compulsory license to copy the literary work, presently administered by CAL. It is expected that VI$COPY will contract CAL's services for sampling the use

---

25. One of few areas where competition exists between collecting agencies: see [22.13].
26. Although a new collecting society has been formed to administer the rights of visual artists: see [22.14].
27. Which were 24.8% of revenue collected in 1993: Simpson, p 202. See P Rolfe, 'In the Money, At Last', *Bulletin*, 29 November 1988, p 145.
28. See [7.20].
29. Simpson, p 21.
30. Ibid, p 263 ff.

of artistic works under the multiple copying compulsory licence for educational purposes. It appears that approximately 2% of material copied by educational institutions contains illustrations (not including graphs, diagrams and maps) and on this basis almost $2 million could be available for visual artists.[31]

Visual artists and craftspeople are not usually well paid for their creative work and frequently lack awareness of copyright and infringement issues generally. Support for VI$COPY is evident from representatives of visual artists, art galleries and other users of such copyright.[32] The possibility of a separate collecting society to represent the interest of Aboriginal and Torres Strait Islander visual artists, possibly in association with VI$COPY and the Aboriginal Arts Management Association (AAMA), is discussed in the Simpson Report.[33]

[22.15] Private Audio Copyright Collecting Society. This collecting society was to have been formed from existing collecting societies representing the owners of copyrights affected by the blank tape levy, which would have applied to the sale of blank cassette tapes used for home taping of musical works.[34] If the blank tape levy is re-introduced as a tax measure, the PACCS will presumably be activated.

[22.16] A multimedia collecting society? Multimedia is a 'convergence' technology that allows the bringing together of material in digital form of text, graphics, film, sound and various subject. Multimedia products may be available on CD-ROM or delivered via the Internet, cable, telephone, television or other telecommunications network. They may contain a vast amount of material collected from thousands of different sources and the digital format means that use (and abuse) of the material by others is correspondingly easier, with no loss of quality if the material is reproduced or adapted. The fact is that for the most part multimedia consists of compilations of material protected by copyright according to traditional theory: after all, a film is a multimedia product and producers must deal with various copyrights.[35] The problems of licensing the use of the material are related mainly to time and volume, in other words the usual practical considerations that collecting societies were formed to overcome apply. The idea of introducing a compulsory licence or special collecting society for multimedia products has not found general acceptance in Australia.[36] Rather, it has been recommended that existing societies set up joint ventures to administer rights in material used in multimedia, or alternatively that the existing collecting societies act individually to administer the relevant rights they presently deal with.[37] Furthermore, the existing collecting societies are demonstrating the ability to look to the future and deal with

---

31. Ibid, p 269.
32. Ibid, p 268.
33. Ibid, pp 266, 270.
34. See [6.41]–[6.42].
35. See discussion at [9.22].
36. There is some discussion of this overseas: see J D Choe, 'Interactive Multimedia: A New Technology Tests the Limits of Copyright Law' (1994) 46 *Rutgers L Rev* 988; Ministry of International Trade and Industry (MITI, Japan), 'Exposure '94 — A Proposal for the New Rule on Intellectual Property for Multimedia'.
37. Simpson, pp 242–3.

new rights should they be introduced, as well as new forms of exercising traditional copyrights. For example, CAL is ready to negotiate licences for use of material 'on-line' in universities and APRA is offering licences to Internet service providers for the supply of music. Eventually, it may be that a technical solution is found through the development of software able to trace and record all uses of material, and facilitate the collection of data to allow owners of rights to collect their dues.

3. LICENSING

[22.17]   General. Throughout the book, various aspects of the licensing of intellectual property have been dealt with in the context of the specific regimes, particularly those issues relating to the formalities required by the various statutes and to compulsory licences.[38] This section is devoted more generally to some of the business considerations in licensing. Granting a licence allows another person (the licensee) to exercise intellectual property rights, while the licensor retains ownership of those rights and can exercise control over many aspects of the ways in which the rights are exploited by imposing appropriate conditions. In the context of technology transfer, licensing involves the licensor giving assistance in the form of know-how, technical or marketing skills and the right to exercise patent, design, copyright, plant variety, integrated circuit and/or other rights. The licensee in return provides compensation in the form of money and may also agree to share with the licensor any developments or improvements they make. Before negotiations begin the parties need to have a clear perception of what sort of agreement they want, since a licence arrangement normally implies an ongoing reciprocal relationship between licensee and licensor. For that reason investigations must be made as to the other party's suitability to provide/exploit the technology and the object of the relationship needs to be clearly identified.[39] The licensee acquires access to technology which would otherwise take a lot of time and effort to develop. Proven technology lowers entrepreneurial risk if a product or end result is already established in the marketplace. On the other side, the licensor's risks are lessened by not bearing the whole cost of commercialising the technology. If the licensor is an individual inventor or academic institution, the only prospect of commercial return may come from licensing. Overall, the licensor will wish to ensure that standards are imposed and maintained and that the licensee observes conditions as to the confidentiality and use of relevant information.

[22.18]   Type and terms of licensing agreements.[40] Licences may be exclusive (where the licensor undertakes not to offer anyone else a licence covering the area of activity), sole (similar to an exclusive licence, but the licensor may reserve the possibility of exploiting the rights in question itself) or non-exclusive (where the licensor retains the right to grant

---

38. See [7.11] ff, [10.23], [13.15] ff, [20.13] ff.
39. See S Niklasson, 'Arrangements for the Acquisition of Technology — Implications for Business Strategy', WIPO Regional Seminar on Licensing and Other Technology Transfer Arrangements, Seoul, 1987, p 21.
40. See generally the various agreements set out in the 'Intellectual Property' section of the *Australian Encyclopaedia of Forms and Precedents*, 3rd ed, vol 7.

licences covering the same object and area to other licensees). On the whole, exclusive licences of patents, designs, copyright and other statutory rights require certain formalities to be complied with, but in any event the contractual provisions regulating the detail of the arrangements should aim to achieve high standards of clarity and certainty in defining the parties' mutual obligations. Typical matters to which attention will be addressed, and which are discussed in the following paragraphs, include the extent of the grant and the field of use, improvements, confidentiality, technical assistance, indemnities, due diligence and remuneration.

[22.19] Extent of the grant and field of use. It is obviously important that the activities the licensee may undertake and those the licensor may retain are clearly understood. The length of time for which the licence is granted also needs to be settled, since the cost to the licensee of the acquisition of the technology inevitably reflects the extent and duration of the rights conferred. As to the particular question of field of use, technology may have a variety of applications and by defining the technical field in which the licensee may operate the licensor will be able to restrict competition against itself or other licensees. For example, if the technology consists of a patent in the field of biotechnology covering a new construction which is useful for expressing proteins at a high level, one licensee might be granted an exclusive licence to use it to make interferon, another to make interleukin 2. Alternatively, if the patent were directed to a cloning technique applicable to plants, one licensee could be granted the right to develop plants with resistance to herbicides, another to produce higher yielding crops.[41] An advantage of granting exclusive licences for a restricted field of application is that the licensee has no fear of competition in that particular area, yet the licensor need not be dependent on a single licensee for obtaining reasonable remuneration. Field of use clauses may also refer to geographical areas and define the territory in which the technology may be used by a licensee. There may well be markets in a number of different countries or regions which can be split up between a number of licensees. It may be important that products produced by one licensee are not sold in another licensee's market, as product quality may differ even where the same 'recipe' is used if raw ingredients vary in quality. One example of this occurred in *Colgate-Palmolive Ltd v Markwell Finance Ltd,*[42] where a US parent company had licensees manufacturing toothpaste in Brazil and the UK and was forced to take action to prevent parallel importation of the Brazilian product into Britain.[43]

[22.20] Improvements. Obviously a licensee developing a product by applying licensed technology may improve upon certain aspects of it, possibly to the point of creating new registrable rights. The licensor may also be continuing to work in the area and make improvements. The question of grant-back to the licensor of licensee improvements and, conversely, the revelation to the licensee of elaborations to the technology supplied by the licensor should be attended to in the agreement. Where the licensor is a

---

41.   See F D Hunter, 'Licensing of Biotechnology', WIPO Regional Seminar on Licensing and Other Technology Transfer Arrangements, Seoul, 1987, p 57 at p 60.
42.   [1989] RPC 497.
43.   See further [20.4].

small company or university department which has no ability to exploit improvements, the agreement will typically have no grant-back provisions, but will provide for the licensee's automatic access to accretions to the technology developed by the licensor.

[22.21]   Confidentiality. Proper and careful management of important business information is vital to the viability of many businesses. Licensees will receive information that may be in the public domain (even if not available for general use if protected by patent or other registration), but will also receive documents revealing know-how and 'show-how' developed by the licensor in respect of the technology. Provision should be made for the preservation of confidential information imparted both in terms of use to which it can be put (which overlaps with field of use clauses) and the persons to whom it may be revealed.[44]

[22.22]   Technical assistance. In order to fulfil the terms of the licence a licensee may need more than just the patent documents, plans, designs or samples detailing the technology, particularly where the licensee is unfamiliar with what is being transferred. While a licence agreement will usually incorporate the transfer of know-how, in some instances because that comprises the relevant intellectual property, the licensor may also have to provide continued technical assistance in the form of personnel or equipment, so that the accumulated experience of the licensor may be made available. Skilled employees of the licensor may impart training, managerial or technical expertise. The agreement should be clear as to the scope, purpose and content of the technical assistance to be provided.

[22.23]   Indemnities. Both parties need to protect themselves against mistakes or circumstances which could cause difficulties to the other. The licensee may be selling end-products incorporating licensed technology which may prove faulty and give rise to product liability claims. In the biotechnology area the possibility of harm to the public or the environment resulting from escaped organisms or faulty products presents real potential for injury or harm. It is prudent to require a licensee (of any intellectual property) to indemnify and hold harmless the licensor from all claims and damages arising out of the licensee's use of the technology, particularly in respect of products based on it. On the other hand the licensor may need to indemnify licensees against faulty materials or incorrect information provided under the agreement, and perhaps undertake to indemnify licensees against the possibility of patent or other rights being held invalid. Alternatively the agreement may be to the effect that no warranties or representations are made as to the validity of patents, patent applications, fitness or merchantability of technology licensed, so that the licensee bears those risks.[45]

[22.24]   Due diligence. A licensor wishing to commercialise the fruits of their intellectual property will expect to see products on the market,

44.   See further Chapters 3–4 for legal issues raised by the enforcement of obligations of confidentiality.

45.   See, however, A Sharpe, 'The Licence Contract — Know-How and High Tech Products', Technology and Know-How Licensing, Taxation, Business and Investment Law Research Centre Seminar, UNSW, 1989 as to which implied legislative terms may or may not be excluded by agreement.

particularly where the sale of end products affects the licensor's remuneration. In order to avoid undue delay on the part of licensees a 'best efforts' clause is often inserted to make the licensee's duty to commercialise products a contractual obligation. Inserting time limits or a 'march-in rights' clause (giving the licensor the right to terminate the agreement if sufficient efforts are not made) will make such clauses more effective. Another mechanism for ensuring due diligence is to require a significant up-front fee which may be offset against subsequent royalties.

[22.25] Remuneration. In addition to up-front fees (also known as down payments) royalties are usually payable to a licensor, calculated as a percentage of net sales or per unit manufactured by the licensee. Indexing for inflation or changing commodity prices may be built in to a per unit fixed price. Other remuneration packages may be negotiated to include offsets, counter trade, stock options or product offtakes.[46] Many industries have guidelines setting out suggested royalty rates to be paid by licensees producing certain products.[47]

One factor in determining the rate of remuneration is to fix it at a level which encourages those interested in exploiting the technology to become licensees rather than opponents in litigation aimed at challenging the validity of the licensor's rights. An example of keeping litigation at bay by granting relatively cheap licences is provided by the Cohen-Boyer patent licences granted by Stanford University in association with the University of California, Berkeley. The universities jointly developed basic recombinant DNA technology, patents on which form the basis of extensive licensing arrangements. Considerable doubts have been expressed as to the validity of the patents but serious challenge has been avoided by a licensing strategy of encouraging potential licensees with a fairly low annual minimum royalty of US$10,000 (or $50,000 for companies with more than 75 employees) and eventual royalties on a commercial product of about 1%.[48] Although this sounds rather low,[49] in 1990 there were over 100 licensees of the Cohen-Boyer patents producing 170 products based on the patented technology which have earned over US$1.5 billion in worldwide sales.[50] The commercial value of the patents to the licensor is enormous but costs individual licensees much less than patent litigation would, thus providing the market with valuable products at prices which have not been inflated by the waste of resources involved in litigating, and saving licensees from the need to consider mounting the public spectacle of 'a commercial firm suing a famous university'.[51]

Provision for auditing and verifying sales, income and other matters affecting the royalties payable will also be included in a licensing contract. Although the parties must proceed on the basis of mutual trust, the ability

46.   See D J Ryan, 'Legal Arrangements for the Commercial Acquisition of Technology' (1989) 24 *IP Asia* 5.
47.   See S Irvine, 'The Commercialisation of Biotechnology: Important Aspects of Technology Licensing', *Blake Dawson Waldron Reporter,* August 1990, p 1 at p 7.
48.   See Grubb, p 174.
49.   Most therapeutic products return a royalty of between 5 and 10% of net sales to the licensor.
50.   S Irvine, 'The Commercialisation of Biotechnology: Important Aspects of Technology Licensing', *Blake Dawson Waldron Reporter,* August 1990, p 1 at p 2, citing *Biotechnology Newswatch,* 19 February 1990.
51.   Grubb, p 174.

to enforce adherence to remuneration formulae provides an important control mechanism for the licensor.[52]

[22.26]   Cross-licensing. The Cohen-Boyer licensing arrangements just described involve a fairly straightforward licensing-out of an invention. However, a firm's licensing policy may not always consist of simply licensing out intellectual property (as licensor) or licensing-in (as licensee). Often a mixture of arrangements will be necessary where no single company owns all the desired technology. Manufacturers may develop a product for sale only to discover that elements of it are covered by someone else's patent, but in the process may have developed aspects which enhance or improve upon the patented technology. In this situation cross-licensing arrangements will prove effective in allowing the parties to continue marketing their version of a product. The result of the dispute over patent rights to a human kidney protein erythropoietin (EPO)[53] illustrates a judicial attempt to force cross-licensing of this sort.[54] Each company's patents were held to be valid and to infringe on particular claims in the other. One party claimed essential elements in producing recombinant EPO, while the other's patent related to a purified form of the substance. The parties were ordered to submit to the court agreements for cross-licensing their versions of the anti-anaemia drug being produced using the EPO technology.

4.   JOINT VENTURES AND FRANCHISING

[22.27]   Joint venture agreements. Cooperation between companies or individuals may take the form of an association between two or more enterprises to combine innovation and developmental, marketing and financing skills. There are two main types of joint venture, contractual or equity joint ventures. Many joint ventures tend to be undertaken to exploit specific market opportunities, their requirements being dictated by the specific goal to be achieved. In these instances the contractual form will be chosen and the contract will define the nature of the contribution which each party will make to the common undertaking. If intellectual property is being exploited in another country there may be restrictions on the foreign ownership of enterprises, so the choice of contractual joint venture will allow expertise to be supplied by the foreigners to an indigenous company.[55] Sometimes though a contractual business association may be a prelude to an equity joint venture, where the participants join to form a new legal entity, separate from any of them. Forming a new company rather than relying on contractual arrangements is appropriate where a longterm project is undertaken and a diversity of functions is to be performed. If wholly-owned subsidiaries of foreign corporations are precluded from operating in certain countries, then equity joint ventures will incorporate whatever local

---

52. See T Black, *Intellectual Property in Industry*, 1989, p 38.
53. *Amgen v Genetics Institute* (1989) 13 USP 2d 1737: see also [15.12].
54. See S Irvine, 'The Commercialisation of Biotechnology: Important Aspects of Technology Licensing', *Blake Dawson Waldron Reporter*, August 1990, p 1 at p 2.
55. See T Harper, 'Understanding 'Technology Transfer' (1988) 10 *Whittier L Rev* 161.

participation and ownership is required.[56] Most of the considerations relevant to licensing will also apply to joint venture agreements.

[22.28]   **Franchising.** A most effective way of supplying a product or service to the marketplace is through franchising, which is a particular business arrangement by which individuals (franchisees) manufacture, distribute or sell a product or run a business initially developed or set up by another (the franchisor). Instead of taking over the whole enterprise, however, franchisees are buying the right to copy another's intellectual property in the form of get-up, trade marks, product and confidential information. In return the franchisor provides support in the forms of training, provision of marketing strategies, group advertising and possibly group purchasing arrangements.[57] Commercial franchising arrangements in Australia were classified by the Swanson Committee[58] into three types of business arrangement:

(i)   *product franchises,* where the franchisee acts as a distributor for a particular product (cars, vacuum cleaners, carpets) or within a particular market;

(ii) *system franchises,* where the franchisee is permitted to run a certain type of business (fast food outlet, homeware store, petrol station); and

(iii) *processing or manufacturing franchises,* where the franchisor provides an essential ingredient or know-how.

Many franchises combine features of two or all three of these sorts of arrangements: for example, a petrol station may sell a certain branded product (petrol and oil), but also presents as a system franchise. Also known as business format franchising,[59] systems franchising has been mainly responsible for the enormous growth in franchising over the last decade, making Australia 'the most franchised nation on earth'.[60] It provides the opportunity for a business to expand without one entrepreneur bearing all the risk and supplying all the capital, offering access to smaller lucrative markets and improving distribution systems. Franchises are perceived as 'ideal survival business for recessionary periods'[61] and the concept is becoming popular with larger non-franchise operations who see the opportunity to convert existing branch distribution systems to franchise by offering each branch as a franchise opportunity to their existing managers. This relieves the central organisation of costs such as superannuation contributions, training and payroll tax levies and payment of wages and overtime for seven-day trading. On the other hand, the franchisee has 'the chance to be in business for themselves but not by themselves'.[62] A known

---

56. See Blakeney, p 45; J Kenny, 'Technology Joint Ventures — Legal Labyrinths Explored' (1989) 3 *Aust Tech Rev* 43 for a discussion of considerations in the legal structuring of a joint venture company.

57. See D Gurnick, 'Intellectual Property in Franchising' (1995) 20 *Oklahoma City ULR* 347.

58. Trade Practices Act Review Committee, *Report,* 1976, para 40.

59. See A Terry, 'Current Developments in Business Format Franchising' Licensing and Franchising: Opportunities, Problems and Taxation, UNSW CLE Seminar, 1990, p 2.

60. P Osborne, 'It's a $13 Billion Industry', *Australian Financial Review,* 5 November 1990, p 41.

61. A Herbert, 'Franchises: The Real Story', *Australian Investment,* September 1990, p 40. See also Osborne, ibid.

62. H Bellin, 'Many Pitfalls for the Unwary', *Australian Financial Review,* 5 November 1990, p 46.

brand name may attract customers more readily and there is usually a greater chance of survival for an established business entity. Franchisees may also be able to get better leasing arrangements or finance on better terms with the help of a franchisor, who will receive a lump sum franchise fee, continuing royalties and possibly an advertising levy.

[22.29] Regulation of franchising. There is little specific legislation regulating franchising in Australia,[63] although the provisions of the Trade Practices Act and Corporations Law apply generally to prohibit false or misleading statements in advertising. Also important in New South Wales is Pt 9 of the Industrial Relations Act 1996, which empowers the local Industrial Relations Commission to grant relief against unfair contracts 'whereby a person performs work in any industry'. This has been held to include a franchise agreement, and an application may assist the franchisee in relation to all aspects of the relationship, from fraud and misrepresentation inducing the contract, to unjust terms included in the agreement and bad faith in its operation.[64] A Franchising Code of Practice commenced in 1993. This is a voluntary self-regulatory code of practice, promulgated by the Franchising Task Force, which features obligations of disclosure, cooling off, dispute resolution and minimum standards of conduct.[65]

5.   RESTRICTIVE TRADE PRACTICES ISSUES

[22.30] Freedom of competition and the Trade Practices Act. As noted in Chapter 1, the granting of monopoly rights over the results of creative effort may be justified on the grounds of promoting innovation and thereby benefiting the community. There are ways in which such rights may be exercised, however, which amount to an abuse of the market power conferred on the owner of a patent, design, copyright, trade mark, trade secret or business reputation. While the actions for breach of confidence and passing off by their very nature tend to recognise the rights of legitimate competition by not allowing monopolisation of publicly available information or words and names in common use, the statutory regimes provide greater scope for monopoly rights to be abused.[66] In Australia the main instrument of regulation of restrictive business practices is the Trade Practices Act 1974 (Cth), itself an amalgam of US and EC competition laws.[67] The functions of this legislation are to promote and preserve workable competition, to promote the interests of small business, and to promote economic efficiency through the rationalisation and restructuring of

---

63. With the exception of the Petroleum Retail Marketing Franchise Act 1980 (Cth).

64. See eg *Swann v Ultratune Australia Pty Ltd* (1983) 5 IR 284; *Majik Markets Pty Ltd v Brake and Service Centre Drummoyne Pty Ltd* (1991) 102 ALR 621, although note that in *Swann* and other cases it is emphasised that where a commercial transaction is entered into at arms' length, relief will not be granted merely because it turns out to be a bad bargain.

65. See A Terry and D Giugni, *Business, Society and the Law,* Harcourt Brace, 1994, pp 601–2.

66. See Ricketson, p 1039 ff; P McCarthy, 'Intellectual Property and Trade Practices Policy: Co-Existence or Conflict? The American Experience' (1985) 13 *ABLR* 198.

67. See M Blakeney, 'Intellectual Property Licensing in Australia and New Zealand and the Impact of the Competition Laws', seminar paper for the Commercial Law Summer School, Queen Mary College, University of London, 1987.

industry with a view to enhancing international competitiveness.[68] One reason for encouraging markets to perform effectively is the belief that this in itself promotes efficiency and community benefit, and protects the interests of consumers, a role endorsed by the High Court in *Queensland Wire Industries v Broken Hill Pty Co Ltd*.[69] The common law doctrine of restraint of trade also operates to allow competition within reasonable limits.[70] The very notion of intellectual property rights assumes that some degree of market exclusivity is beneficial within the broad framework of freedom of competition. However, the exploitation of such property rights may bring about a situation which prevents, restricts or distorts competition beyond what is considered reasonable. There are in fact many standard provisions in assignments, licensing and franchising agreements which may fall foul of Pt IV of the Trade Practices Act.

[22.31]   Part IV provisions. Part IV of the Act, in regulating restrictive trade practices, provides for a 'competition analysis' to be applied in assessing anti-competitive contracts, arrangements or understandings (s 45), and also whether there has been a misuse of market power by a corporation (s 46). Thus before a contravention of these provisions can be established a competition test will be applied to see whether a misuse of a market power by a corporation has resulted in substantial lessening of competition in a market. On the other hand, some practices are considered so inherently anti-competitive that they are prohibited outright. These include price fixing (s 45A), exclusive dealing and exclusionary provisions (ss 45 and 4D) and resale price maintenance (s 48). At a more general level, the assessment of conduct in this regard requires an understanding of the effect of that conduct in the marketplace, since Pt IV is concerned with competition in a market or market power. Behaviour which is prima facie anti-competitive may actually turn out to be pro-competitive in the business context if it allows small firms and shops to remain viable and provides consumers with goods and services which could not be provided by 'open slather' competition. Thus the economic concepts of 'market', 'dominant position', 'abuse', 'substantial degree of market power' and 'lessening of competition' must all be defined and understood by the relevant tribunal and then applied to the conduct in question to determine its effect. The increasing recognition of the importance of economic theory in construing Pt IV[71] and the uncertainty of the outcome makes the giving of advice and decision-making in the restrictive trade practices area an exercise in risk taking, for 'even when the principles are clear there is considerable disagreement regarding their application to specific situations'.[72] As one commentator puts it, 'it is ordained that lawyers must sweat through the jungle of economic theory trying to pin particular arguments to elusive principles'.[73]

---

68.   See S G Corones, *Competition Law and Policy in Australia*, 1990, para 1–05.
69.   (1989) 167 CLR 177. See also G Hay and K McMahon 'The "Duty to Deal" Under Section 46: Panacea or Pandora's Box?' (1994) 17 *UNSWLJ* 54.
70.   Cf M J Trebilcock, *Common Law of Restraint of Trade*, 1986.
71.   See S G Corones, *Competition Law and Policy in Australia*, 1990, ch 3.
72.   R McLean, 'Trade Practices Problems — Restrictions on Supply in Franchises and Licences', Licensing and Franchising: Opportunities, Problems and Taxation, UNSW CLE Seminar, 1990, p 22.
73.   D Shannon, *Franchising in Australia: A Legal Guide*, 1982, p 193.

[22.32] **National competition policy: the Hilmer Report.** Successive federal governments have pursued a national competition policy in the interest of making Australian business more efficient and to this end the Hilmer Report[74] was commissioned. The Report stated that the interaction of intellectual property and competition law is a complex matter, and probably required a separate report on the issue. However, concern was expressed as to whether additional protection for transactions involving intellectual property rights provided for in s 51(3) should continue.[75] It was recognised that there must still be suspension or adjustment of market conduct rules on public interest grounds and that the primary basis for permitting exemptions should continue to be an authorisation process of the kind administered by the Australian Consumer and Competition Commission (ACCC). The public benefit may consist of streamlining the licensing of copyright and reducing what would otherwise be a huge burden on users, and also in allowing the traditional notion of encouragement of creativity, for example by composers of music in Australia.[76]

Furthermore, Pt IIIA, inserted into the Trade Practices Act in November 1995, provides possible compulsory access to services provided by infrastructure facilities of 'national importance'. This 'essential facilities' doctrine has long been known in US competition law,[77] and although a facility of national importance is not defined[78] it may very well include provision of Internet and other communications services, which may in turn affect the use of copyright material constituting the content of the essential facility. Statutory licensing schemes of this sort are well known to copyright law.

[22.33] **Examples of restrictive practices: exclusive dealing.** Perhaps because of this uncertainty and the undoubted pro-competitive effect of certain activities with anti-competitive potential, procedures exist to protect corporations from liability for an infringement of the Act in certain circumstances. Section 51(3) in particular contains a number of exemptions which permit reasonable exploitation of intellectual property by way of assignment and licensing: these are discussed below. On the other hand the power available to right-owners may make it possible for these rights to be dealt with in such a way as to extract extra benefits. For example, a licensor may insist that the supply of a product be tied to an obligation to purchase other products or services. Such a tie-in arrangement breaches s 47, which prohibits 'exclusive dealing' which has the purpose or likely effect of substantially lessening competition.[79] One form of exclusive dealing is full-line

---

74. *Report by the Independent Committee of Inquiry into a National Competition Policy,* 1993 (Hilmer Report). See W Pengilley, 'Hilmer and 'Essential Facilities' (1994) 17 *UNSWLJ* 1.
75. Hilmer Report, ibid, p 150. See [22.38].
76. ACCC, *Draft Determination by the ACCC for Applications for Authorisation and Notification by APRA* (Authorisation Nos A30166 to 30173 and N30714), 16 October 1996.
77. See G Hay and M McMahon, 'The "Duty to Deal" Under Section 46: Panacea or Pandora's Box?' (1994) 17 *UNSWLJ* 54.
78. See Hilmer Report, p 251 for a discussion of the concept.
79. See *Dandy Power Equipment Pty Ltd v Mercury Marine Pty Ltd* (1982) 64 FLR 238 for a discussion of the concept of 'substantially lessening competition'. See also *Radio 2UE Sydney Pty Ltd v Stereo FM Pty Ltd* (1982) 62 FLR 437; *Cool & Sons Pty Ltd v O'Brien Glass Industries Ltd* (1981) 35 ALR 445.

forcing, the supply of a range of products on an all or nothing basis: for instance computers with software, windscreens with all associated products, coffee machines with milk, coffee and tea-bags, or photocopiers with ink, toner and paper. Other examples of exclusive dealing include tying the lease of trading premises to the acquisition of the lessor's products and territorial restrictions. All of these are subject to the 'substantial lessening of competition' test.[80] However, one type of exclusive dealing prohibited per se is third line forcing, or obliging the purchaser of products to obtain other supplies from nominated third parties, usually because the original supplier is getting some pay-back from the third party.[81]

[22.34] Resale price maintenance and price fixing. The desire that a licensor or franchisor may legitimately have for uniformity in pricing creates the temptation to engage in resale price maintenance, requiring the licensee to sell goods at or not below a specified price. This is prohibited under s 48 as being anti-competitive behaviour.[82] Allied to resale price maintenance is price fixing, where competitors agree to maintain standard prices in order to affect price competition (ss 45A, 45C).[83] A distinction is to be made between those arrangements which are intended to affect competition and those which could actually have a pro-competitive effect, such as cooperation between joint buying and selling groups and joint advertising of items for sale, as occurs with chains of chemist shops, hardware stores and the like (s 45A(4)).

[22.35] Restrictive arrangements. General prohibitions exist against 'contracts, arrangements or understandings' restricting dealings or affecting competition (ss 45, 45B). Examples of licence provisions potentially caught include those imposing production limitation quotas, market share and territorial restrictions, the grant back to the licensor of rights to improvements made by the licensee, and undertakings not to dispute matters of validity or ownership of rights. Licensees who attempt to prevent or control the appointment of other licensees may also breach the prohibition.

[22.36] Abuse of market power.[84] Another general prohibition is found in s 46, which prohibits monopolisation, or taking advantage of a substantial degree of power in a market to damage or eliminate competitors, prevent entry into any market or prevent or deter competitive conduct in any market. One critical issue is market definition[85] and what amounts

---

80.   For an argument that intellectual property tie-ins are not necessarily anti-competitive, see J Thorpe, 'In Defence of Intellectual Property Tie-Ins' (1995) 8 *Corp & Bus LJ* 81.

81.   This may not be easy to establish: see *Castlemaine Tooheys Ltd v Williams and Hodgsons Transport Pty Ltd* [1986] ATPR 40–751.

82.   See further s 96(3)(a)–(f), where various forms of resale price maintenance are defined.

83.   See *Radio 2UE Sydney Pty Ltd v Stereo FM Pty Ltd* (1983) 68 FLR 70; *TPC v Australian Autoglass Pty Ltd* [1988] ATPR 40–881.

84.   Trade Practices Commission, 'Section 46 of the Trade Practices Act and Intellectual Property: The Trade Practices Commission View' (1992) 5(4) *Aust IP Law Bull* 37.

85.   'Market' includes substitute goods or services (s 4E): see *Top Performance Motors Pty Ltd v Ira Berk (Qld) Pty Ltd* (1975) 24 FLR 236; *Ah Toy Pty Ltd v Thiess Toyota Pty Ltd* (1980) 30 ALR 271; *Queensland Wire Industries Pty Ltd v Broken Hill Pty Co Ltd* (1989) 167 CLR 177.

to a substantial degree of market power.[86] For instance, s 46 was invoked against a distributor who refused to supply a dealer with Salomon brand Ski boots, which the dealer sold at a discount. Although the distributor was entitled to restrain discounting in order to protect the product name or enhance its image, other discounters were being supplied with the ski boots and so the behaviour was discriminatory.[87]

[22.37] Collecting societies and monopolisation.[88] One way of obtaining market power is to aggregate rights in the way that collecting societies do, thus becoming monopolists over the licensing of the copyrights they acquire. This allows the fixing of prices and conditions upon which licences will be granted, and obviously restricts competition in the marketplace. Australian collecting societies usually obtain an assignment of copyright from the author, rather than the non-exclusive licence typically granted to their American and English counterparts.[89] This pooling of the assigned rights to works and other subject matter makes the collecting society the only possible source of a licence of relevant rights. The monopolistic power held by collecting societies has long been recognised[90] and the Copyright Act 1968, in providing for the establishment of the Copyright Tribunal, gave it jurisdiction over licensing schemes (ss 154, 157). There has only been one case before the Tribunal in which restrictive trade practices issues were raised, and then only in counsel's final address, with no supporting evidence.[91] However APRA's monopoly over the public performance right in musical works and sound recordings through the accumulation of copyright and associated licensing systems was recently challenged under s 46 in *APRA Ltd v Ceridale Pty Ltd*.[92] A dispute arose between APRA and the owners of a Brisbane nightclub over the amount of past licence fees payable in respect of the club's playing of recorded music by a disc jockey. APRA refused to renew the club's licence and sought an injunction restraining the continued public performance of these works. The club argued that this was using market power to collect a debt over which there was a genuine dispute. It was held that APRA's market power was not to be used to enforce agreement with its own demands with respect to a purpose extraneous to the function of licensing copyright users.

[22.38] Exemptions. Section 51(3) provides three limited but important exceptions to the operation of the restrictive practices sections (other than the monopolisation and resale price maintenance provisions in ss 46 or 48). In the first place, effect may be given to a condition in any licence or assignment granted by the proprietor, licensee or owner of a patent, registered design, copyright or eligible layout rights under the Circuit Layouts

---

86. See Trade Practices Commission, *Misuse of Market Power Guidelines and Background Paper,* 1990.
87. *Mark Lyons Pty Ltd v Bursill Sportsgear Pty Ltd* [1987] ATPR 40–809.
88. See J McKeough and S Teece, 'Collectivisation of Copyright Exploitation: Competition Issues' (1994) 17 *UNSWLJ* 251.
89. See L Layton, 'The Impact of the Trade Practices Act on Collecting Societies', Fourth Copyright Law and Practice Symposium, Sydney, 1989.
90. See Spicer Committee: Copyright Law Revision Committee, *Report,* 1959, p 43.
91. *Reference by APRA Ltd; Re Australian Broadcasting Commission* (1985) 5 IPR 449; see also *WEA Records Pty Ltd v Stereo FM Pty Ltd* (1983) 48 ALR 91.
92. (1991) 97 ALR 497; cf *Re Phonographic Performance Co of Australia Ltd* [1991] ATPR 50–105.

Act or by an applicant for a patent or design registration, even where imposition of that condition would otherwise contravene Pt IV. However, the
condition must 'relate' to the relevant invention (or articles made from its
use), goods to which the relevant design is to be applied, the work or other
subject matter in which the relevant copyright subsists, or the relevant eligible layout (s 51(3)(a)).[93] Second, no infringement will flow from the inclusion in a contract or arrangement of a provision authorising use of a
certification trade mark in accordance with Pt XI of the Trade Marks Act
1955 (s 51(3)(b)). Third, it is permissible to include in a contract or
arrangement between the registered proprietor and a registered user of a
trade mark (other than a certification mark) under the 1955 Act a condition relating to the kinds or qualities of goods bearing that mark that may
be produced or supplied (s 51(3)(c)).[94] It will be noted that these exemptions only operate in respect of arrangements relating to the *subject matter* of
the relevant right. Put simply, some restrictive licence conditions should be
tolerated as being necessary to allow exploitation of the subject matter.
Licensors and franchisors are expected to maintain uniform standards and
consistency in providing goods and services and to that extent quality control and technical standards may be stipulated in a contract. Licensees may
also expect some degree of protection from other licensees and territorial
restrictions may therefore be acceptable.[95] Where licence or assignment
conditions go further, however, and seek to control matters other than the
exercise of the intellectual property in question, they will be struck down.

The exemptions do not extend to the licensing of know-how, confidential information or goodwill, and nor do they override the consumer protection provisions in Pt V of the Trade Practices Act, including the
prohibition in s 52 on misleading and deceptive conduct.[96] Licensors or
franchisors must therefore resist the temptation to make extravagant claims
about product attributes or the profitability of the relevant business enterprise.[97] Also prohibited under Pt V are the publication of false or misleading
advertisements seeking persons for employment (s 53S), and the making of
false or misleading statements concerning home operated businesses or
investment opportunities requiring participants to perform work (s 59).

[22.39] **Authorisation.** The administrative body responsible for enforcing the Trade Practices Act is the Australian Consumer and Competition
Commission (ACCC, formerly the Trade Practices Commission (TPC)),
which can institute proceedings in respect of conduct which in its view
contravenes Pt IV. The ACCC also plays an important adjudicative role in

---

93. The term 'relate' should be given a broad meaning: *Transfield Pty Ltd v Arlo
     International Ltd* (1980) 144 CLR 83 at 102.
94. At the date of writing, ss 51(3)(b) and (c) had not yet been amended to
     incorporate references to the Trade Marks Act 1995. It is understood that the
     government is assuming that s 10 of the Acts Interpretation Act 1901 (Cth) will
     ensure that, pending any amendment, these provisions are interpreted to extend
     to licences granted under the 1995 Act. However, this assumption appears suspect,
     given the significant differences between the two Acts in regard to licencing
     (especially the abolition of the registered user system).
95. See eg *Re Coca Cola* [1978] ATPR 35–400; *Re Donlan Liquor Markets Pty Ltd* [1975]
     ATPR 13–900; *Re Chrysler Australia Ltd* [1976] ATPR 35–100.
96. See [16.31] ff.
97. See eg *Ducret v Colourshot Pty Ltd* (1981) 35 ALR 503.

relation to applications for authorisation (s 88) and notifications (s 93).[98] Notification provides shelter for certain conduct that would otherwise amount to exclusive dealing under s 47. The effect is that the activity may continue unless the ACCC positively decides that the anti-competitive effect of the conduct is not justified on public benefit grounds. Authorisation of certain activities with the potential to infringe Pt IV will be granted where there is some public benefit justifying the granting of an exemption from the Act. The concept of public benefit is not defined in the Act, but it has been held to include economic efficiency and progress,[99] and is to be interpreted widely so as to include anything of value to the community.[100] There is no provision for the authorisation of behaviour caught by s 46, dealing with monopolisation or the abuse of a dominant position in the marketplace, unless that activity also falls within the terms of ss 45, 45S, 47 or 50 and is excused by reason of an authorisation being in force. The sort of activity which a licensor or franchisor may get authorised includes issuing lists of recommended prices or schedules designed to help calculate retail prices,[101] joint purchasing or cooperative buying agreements,[102] and distribution networks for newspapers.[103] Standard licensing agreements for the public performance of sound recordings were also approved in *Re EMI Records (Australia) Ltd.*[104]

[22.40] Control of restrictive practices in intellectual property legislation. Beside the Trade Practices Act, there are also the various intellectual property statutes to consider. These prohibit certain restrictive trade practices, as well as imposing positive obligations in order to prevent the use of rights in a way contrary to the public benefit. An example of this is the compulsory licensing provisions of various statutes in order that the reasonable requirements of the public may be met.[105] Particular prohibitions may be found in the patents and copyright legislation. In the case of the former, tie-ins, requirements contracts, full-line forcing and third-line forcing may fall foul of the prohibition in s 144(1) of the Patents Act 1990. This catches any condition in a contract for the sale, lease or licence of a patented invention whose effect would be: (a) to prohibit or restrict the buyer, lessee or licensee from using a product or process supplied by a person other than the seller, lessor or licensor; or (b) to require the buyer (etc) to acquire from the seller (etc) products not protected by the patent. However, this prohibition is subject to s 146(d) which recognises that a licensor may impose conditions requiring the licensee to accept any new parts of a patented product needed to put or keep it in repair. The

98. See S G Corones, *Competition Law and Policy in Australia*, 1990, para 1–09.
99. *Re Westralian Farmers Co-Operative Ltd* (1979) 37 FLR 244.
100. *Re Queensland Co-operative Milling Association Ltd* (1976) 25 FLR 169.
101. See eg *Re Real Estate Institute of the ACT* [1986] ATPR 50–120.
102. See eg *Re Australian Phosphate Purchasing Association* [1982] ATPR 50–036; *Re Pharmacy Guild of Australia (Queensland Branch)* (1983) 5 TPR 45.
103. See *Re John Fairfax & Sons Ltd* [1980] ATPR 50–041; *Re Herald and Weekly Times Ltd* (1982) 17 ALR 281; *Re Queensland Newsagency System* [1985] ATPR 50–097; *Re West Australian Newspapers Ltd* [1986] ATPR 50–108.
104. [1985] ATPR 50–096. See, however, ACCC, *Draft Determination for Authorisation and Notification by APRA* (Authorisations Nos A30166 to 30173 and N30714), 16 October 1996.
105. See [7.18]–[7.24], [10.23], [13.19], [15.23].

Copyright Act provides for compulsory licensing of works and other subject matter for educational purposes[106] and for the purposes of the music industry in the use of sound recordings.[107] The conditions of such licensing arrangements are determined by legislation rather than the owner of the rights and severely restrict any scope for abusing market power. Until recently, however, the degree of market power possessed by a copyright owner in respect of parallel imports has been impressive, although this may be changing.[108]

---

106. See [7.19]–[7.21].
107. See [7.22].
108. See [8.21]–[8.23]. In *Interstate Parcel Express Co Pty Ltd v Time-Life International (Nederlands) BV* (1977) 138 CLR 534, the case in which the right of an exclusive licensee to prevent parallel importation was vindicated by the High Court, the possibility that this action constituted proscribed monopolisation was considered only in the dissenting judgment of Murphy J.

Index

References are to paragraph numbers